PENAL REFORM

Patterson Smith Reprint Series in
Criminology, Law Enforcement, and Social Problems

A listing of publications in the Series *will be found at rear of volume*

Publication No. 149: Patterson Smith Reprint Series in Criminology, Law Enforcement, and Social Problems

PENAL REFORM

A COMPARATIVE STUDY

BY

MAX GRÜNHUT

MONTCLAIR, NEW JERSEY
PATTERSON SMITH
1972

First published 1948 by the Clarendon Press, Oxford
Reprinted 1972, with permission, by
Patterson Smith Publishing Corporation
Montclair, New Jersey 07042

Library of Congress Cataloging in Publication Data

Grünhut, Max, 1893–1964.
Penal reform.
(Patterson Smith reprint series in criminology, law enforcement, and social problems, publication no. 149)
Reprint of the 1948 ed.
Includes bibliographical references.
1. Prisons. 2. Crime and criminals. I. Title

HV8982.G7 1972 365'.7 71-172568
ISBN 0-87585-149-5

This book is printed on
permanent/durable paper.

PREFACE

THIS study on Penal Reform discusses the efforts—humanitarian, educative, administrative—which have been at work to make the administration of criminal justice a rational instrument of crime prevention and social readjustment. No comparative survey can cover the whole field with anything like completeness. The scope and subjects of comparison depend on a personal selection. After the First World War I was closely associated with a band of resolute reformers who inaugurated a decade of bold experiments and remarkable achievements in German prisons. Years of research in England gave me the opportunity to re-examine the observations of the past, and to study present English penal policy and the formidable American criminological literature of the inter-war period. This threefold experience is the foundation of this book, supplemented by material concerning other European countries, so far as this was accessible in war-time England.

I am deeply indebted to the Warden and Fellows of All Souls College, Oxford, who have given me such invaluable opportunity for social and legal research. On the conclusion of this work, I therefore wish to express my sincere and lasting gratitude for their kind help and understanding.

Many subjects of this book were discussed with the Rev. R. S. Hinde, M.A., Hertford College, sometime Chaplain to H.M. Prison, Oxford. Dr. P. Berkenau, Warneford Hospital, read those sections of this book where I had to trespass on the grounds of medical psychology. Throughout the whole work the Howard League for Penal Reform was a source of constant information. I am particularly grateful to the Honorary Secretary of the Howard League, Miss Cicely M. Craven, M.A., J.P., for her generous help not only in contributing very valuable suggestions, but in devoting long hours to going through the typescript of the whole book. My grateful thanks are also due to Miss I. H. Reekie, Assistant Secretary to the Howard League, to Miss E. McCalman, of Oxford, and to Mr. Vernon Porter, Lecturer at the City Literary Institute, for expert help in the improving of the English style.

I dedicate this book to my wife in gratitude for her unfailing interest in this work and the encouragement she gave me from its beginning to its conclusion.

M. G.

OXFORD
November 1946

CONTENTS

FIRST PART

HISTORICAL EXPERIENCE

SECOND PART

GENERAL OUTLINES

THIRD PART

SPECIAL TOPICS

ABBREVIATIONS

ALR	(Prussian) *Allgemeines Landrecht*
Am. Hist. Rev.	*American Historical Review*
Am. J. Soc.	*American Journal of Sociology*
Annals	*Annals of the American Academy of Political and Social Science*
Arch. Psych.	*Archiv für Psychiatrie und Nervenkrankheiten*
BGBl.	(Austrian) *Bundesgesetzblatt*
Blackstone	W. Blackstone, *Commentaries on the Law of England*, 4th ed., Oxford, 1770
Bl. Gefg. Kd.	*Blätter für Gefängniskunde*
B.R.	*Bar Review* (Canadian, &c.)
Brit. J. Ed. Psych.	*British Journal of Educational Psychology*
Brit. J. Med. Psych.	*British Journal of Medical Psychology*
Bulletin	*Bulletin de la Commission Internationale Pénale et Pénitentiaire*
Camp.	Campbell's *Reports*
Cl. and F.	Clark and Finelly's *Reports*
Cox	Cox, *Criminal Law Cases*
Crim. App. R.	Cohen's *Criminal Appeal Reports*
Crim. Stat.	*Criminal Statistics for England and Wales*
Dig.	Justinian's *Digest*
F.F.	Foster and Finlason's *Reports*
Halsbury	Halsbury's *Laws of England*, 2nd (Hailsham) ed. 1931–42
Hansard	Parliamentary Debates, Official Report
HWB. Krim.	*Handwörterbuch der Kriminologie*
HWB. Staatsw.	*Handwörterbuch der Staatswissenschaften*
HWR	*Handwörterbuch der Rechtswissenschaft*
Internl. R. Soc. Hist.	*International Review for Social History*
J. Comp. Legisl.	*Journal of Comparative Legislation and International Law*
J. Ment. Sc.	*Journal of Mental Science*
J. Neur. Psychopath.	*Journal of Neurology and Psychopathology*
Journal	*Journal of Criminal Law and Criminology*
J. Soc. Psych.	*Journal of Abnormal and Social Psychology*
J. Stat. Soc.	*Journal of the Royal Statistical Society*
J.W.	*Juristische Wochenschrift*
K.B.	*Law Reports, King's Bench Division*
Kenny	C. S. Kenny, *Outlines of Criminal Law*, 15th ed. 1936
L.J.	*Law Journal* (Cambridge, Yale, &c.)
L.Q.R.	*Law Quarterly Review*
L.R.	*Law Review* (Harvard, Columbia, Michigan, &c.)
L.T.	*Law Times Reports*
L.T.J.	*Law Times Journal*
Mitt. Krim.-biol. Ges.	*Mitteilungen der Kriminalbiologischen Gesellschaft*
Mitt. IKV	*Mitteilungen der Internationalen Kriminalistischen Vereinigung*
MoSchrKrim.	*Monatsschrift für Kriminalpsychologie* (from 1937: *Kriminalbiologie) und Strafrechtsreform*
Q.B.	*Law Reports, Queen's Bench Division*
Recueil	*Recueil de documents en matière pénale et pénitentiaire*
Rev. droit pén.	*Revue de droit pénal et de criminologie*
R.G.	*Entscheidungen des* (German) *Reichsgerichts in Strafsachen*
RGBl.	(German) *Reichsgesetzblatt*
Schmollers Jahrb.	*Jahrbuch für Gesetzgebung, Verwaltung und Volkswirtschaft*
Schweiz. Z.	*Schweizerische Zeitschrift für Strafrecht*

Soc. Rev.	*Sociological Review*
St. Tr.	*State Trials*
T.L.R.	*Times Law Reports*
U.S. Reports	*United States Reports, Cases adjudged in the Supreme Court*
V.D.A.	*Vergleichende Darstellung des deutschen und ausländischen Strafrechts, Allgemeiner Teil*
V.D.B.	*Vergleichende Darstellung des deutschen und ausländischen Strafrechts, Besonderer Teil*
Z.	*Zeitschrift*
Zentralbl.	*Zentralblatt für Jugendrecht und Jugendwohlfahrt*
Z. Kinderforschung	*Zeitschrift für Kinderforschung*
ZStW.	*Zeitschrift für die gesamte Strafrechtswissenschaft*

BIBLIOGRAPHICAL NOTES

For general information see T. Sellin, 'A Brief Guide to Penological Literature', reprinted from 157 *Annals* (1931).

The following books are quoted by the names of their authors, unless the same author is represented by more than one book.

Purpose of Punishment

T. H. Green, *Lectures on the Principles of Political Obligation*, ed. by B. Bosanquet (1921), ss. 176 et seq., pp. 180 et seq.; A. Merkel, *Lehre von Verbrechen und Strafe*, ed. by M. Liepmann (1912); W. H. Moberly, 'Some Ambiguities in the Retributive Theory of Punishment', *Proceedings of the Aristotelian Society*, N.S., xxv, 289; A. C. Ewing, *The Morality of Punishment* (1929); H. von Hentig, *Die Strafe* (1932), English ed. *Punishment* (1937); W. Temple, 'The Ethics of Penal Action', *First Clarke Hall Lecture* (1934); M. R. Cohen, 'Moral Aspects of the Criminal Law', 49 *Yale L. J.* 987; L. Radzinowicz, J. W. Turner, A. C. Ewing, 'A Study on Punishment', *Engl. Studies in Crim. Science*, reprinted from 21 *Canadian B. R.* 91.

Penal Reform in general

H. Mannheim, *The Dilemma of Penal Reform* (1939); id., *Criminal Justice and Social Reconstruction* (1946).

Prison History

G. Ives, *A History of Penal Methods* (1914); J. F. Stephen, *History of the Criminal Law in England* (1883), i. 457–92; S. and B. Webb, *English Prisons under Local Government* (1922); L. Frede, 'Gefängnisgeschichte', *HWB. Krim.* i. 537–52; P. Klein, *Prison Methods in New York State* (1920); C. F. Lewis, *The Development of American Prisons and Prison Customs 1776–1845* (1922); H. E. Barnes, *The Repression of Crime, Studies in Historical Penology* (1926); Blake McKelvey, *American Prison, Studies in American Social History prior to 1915* (1936); G. Rusche and O. Kirchheimer, *Punishment and Social Structure* (1939).

Text-books on Penal Systems

England and Wales

E. Ruggles-Brise, *The English Prison System* (1921); L. W. Fox, *The Modern English Prison* (1934); Leo Page, *Crime and the Community* (1937); L. Radzinowicz and J. W. C. Turner (ed.), *Penal Reform in England* (1940); *Prisons and Borstals*, published for the Home Office by H.M. Stationery Office (1945).

France

A. Mossé, *Les prisons et les institutions correctives* (1929).

Switzerland

K. Hafner and E. Zürcher, *Schweizerische Gefängniskunde* (1925).

Germany

N. H. Kriegsmann, *Einführung in die Gefängniskunde* (1912); E. Bumke (ed.), *Deutsches Gefängniswesen* (1928).

United States

L. N. Robinson, *Penology in the United States* (1923); F. E. Haynes, *The American Prison System* (1939). Further the following official publications: *Report on Penal Institutions, Probation and Parole*, made by the National Commission on Law Observance and Enforcement (*Wickersham Report*) (1931); *Attorney General's Survey of Release Procedures*, esp. ii (*Probation*), iv (*Parole*), v (*Prisons*) (1939).

Latin-America

N. K. Teeters, *Penology from Panama to Cape Horn* (1946).

General Survey

N. K. Teeters, *World Penal Systems* (1944).

Criminology

Basic Criminological Research

W. Healy, *The Individual Delinquent* (1915).
W. Healy and A. Bronner, *Delinquents and Criminals, their Making and Unmaking* (1926).
W. Healy and A. Bronner, *New Light on Delinquency* (1936).
Cyril Burt, *The Young Delinquent* (1925; 3rd ed. 1938).
Sheldon and Eleanor Glueck published three series of consecutive follow-up studies:

(1) *Five Hundred Criminal Careers* (1930).
Later Criminal Careers (1937).
Criminal Careers in Retrospect (1943).
(2) *One Thousand Juvenile Delinquents* (1934).
Juvenile Delinquents grown up (1940).
(3) *Five Hundred Delinquent Women* (1934).

A summarizing report on (1) and (2): *After-conduct of Discharged Offenders* (1945).

American text-books

E. H. Sutherland, *Principles of Criminology* (1924, 2nd ed. 1934, 3rd ed. 1939); M. Parmelee, *Criminology* (1926); J. L. Gillin, *Criminology and Penology* (1927); F. E. Haynes, *Criminology* (1930, 2nd ed. 1935); R. H. Gault, *Criminology* (1932); N. Cantor, *Crime, Criminals and Criminal Justice* (1932); id., *Crime and Society, An Introduction to Criminology* (1939); J. Michael and M. Adler, *Crime, Law and Social Science* (1933); A. Morris, *Criminology* (1934); A. E. Wood and J. Barker Waite, *Crime and its Treatment* (1941); H. E. Barnes and N. K. Teeters, *New Horizons in Criminology* (1943).

Recent European Contributions

O. Kinberg, *Basic Problems of Criminology* (1935); W. A. Bonger, *Inleiding tot de Criminologie* (1932), English translation: *An Introduction to Criminology* (1936); H. Mannheim, *Social Aspects of Crime in England between the Wars* (1940); F. Exner, *Kriminalbiologie* (2nd ed. 1944).

Social Case-work

Mary Richmond, *Social Diagnosis* (1917); V. P. Robinson, *A Changing Psychology in Social Case Work* (1930); M. Karpf, *The Scientific Basis of Social Work* (1931); G. Hamilton, *Theory and Practice of Social Case Work* (1940).

European Response: Alice Salomon, *Soziale Diagnose* (2nd ed. 1927); H. Scherpner, 'Formen persönlicher Fürsorge in den Vereinigten Staaten', *Widmungen des Fürsorgeseminars der Universität Frankfurt a/M.* (n.y.); S. Clement Brown, 31 *Soc. Rev.* 177.

Periodicals

Blätter für Gefängniskunde, since 1865, ed. by the Association of German Prison Officers.
Bulletin de la Commission Internationale Pénale et Pénitentiaire. Until 1930.
Howard Journal, since 1921, published by the Howard League for Penal Reform, London.
Journal of Criminal Law and Criminology. Published (originally for the American Institute of Criminal Law and Criminology) by the Northwestern University Press, Chicago, Illinois.
Mitteilungen der Internationalen Kriminalistischen Vereinigung, 1889–1933.
Monatsschrift für Kriminalpsychologie (from 1937: *Kriminalbiologie*) *und Strafrechtsreform*, since 1904. Founded by G. Aschaffenburg.
Nordisk Tidsskrift for Strafferet, since 1878.
Recueil de documents en matière pénale et pénitentiaire. Bulletin de la Commission Internationale Pénale et Pénitentiaire, since 1931.
Revue (Belge) *de droit pénal et de criminologie*.
Revue internationale de droit pénal, since 1924, ed. by Roux a.o. for the Association internationale de droit pénal.
Revue pénitentiaire et de droit pénal. Organ of the (French) Société générale des prisons.
Revue pénitentiaire de Pologne.
Rivista di diritto penitenziario, founded by G. Novelli.
Schweizerische Zeitschrift für Strafrecht, since 1888, 1896, founded by Stooss.
Tijdschrift voor Strafrecht, since 1866.
Zeitschrift für die gesamte Strafrechtswissenschaft, since 1881, founded by von Liszt.

PENAL REFORM

CHAPTER I

INTRODUCTION

The Study of Penal Reform

IN what it has achieved penal reform belongs to history; in what it aspires to achieve it belongs to the future. As the outcome of a broad humanitarian movement it comes to demand that human rights and dignity must be respected even in the offender. But it is also good policy. It substitutes rational penal and reformative treatment for blind reaction and petrified tradition, and thus makes society better prepared to meet the threat of crime and social maladjustment. Over the last 150 years penal reform has been mainly identical with prison reform. The increasing use of imprisonment as a legal punishment at least gave some opportunity for studying empirically the personalities of offenders, for developing treatment methods, and examining and considering the prisoner's response. This experience led to the demand that penal reform, if it is to advance farther, must look beyond the prison. Where the reformative purpose was taken seriously the conclusion became inevitable that institutions designed to rehabilitate anti-social persons would be very much unlike prisons, even those of ideal conditions. For social readjustment in prison has to be effected almost in spite of punishment. 'Prisons,' said a leading American criminologist, 'are at best unnatural places . . . ', but 'so long as prisons are still necessary, we are under direct moral obligation to make them institutions for the betterment of humanity.'[1] Penal reform must, in fact, turn to new and more effective methods for the social readjustment of the law-breaker. Some examples of these new methods aimed at reducing the incidence of imprisonment in the interest of both offender and society are to be seen in the breaking up of the traditional prison type into different security grades, the rise of probation, and the growing use of parole.

Penal reform with its achievements and its aims, its progress, and even more its disappointments, has to encounter many legal, social, and psychological problems. This fact makes a concerted scientific effort desirable, a study based on experience, but advancing in the light of that experience to an assessment of what could and should be done. But though penal reform requires such

[1] L. N. Robinson, *Should Prisoners Work?* (1931), p. 299.

scientific help, and though it resorts to quantitative evaluation whenever, in dealing with certain types of personality, institution, treatment, or reaction quantity becomes significant, it is by no means a science in the strict sense of the word, by no means something which reduces every phenomenon to measured quantities and to fixed natural laws. The student of penal reform must never forget that his principal subject is men and women under penal and reformative treatment, their response and personal relationship, their lives and fate.

The Purpose of Punishment

All efforts to advance the aims of penal reform are confronted with the powerful idea of punishment. Legal punishment is a sanction against unlawful acts committed with a guilty mind. A sanction is a public reaction against the offence, to be distinguished from private compensation for damage. Punishment requires the offender's personal guilt, and thereby differs from the educative treatment of those who in view of their youth are not deemed to act with a guilty mind, or from security measures against dangerous persons who owing to mental disorder are acting without criminal responsibility. Punishment is an enforced deprivation of personal rights, life, liberty, honour, or property, but it is more than this: it is inflicted upon a man who offended against the law with a guilty mind. Taxation involves enforced payment, conscription for military or labour service is a deprivation of liberty, but they differ clearly from fines and imprisonment in their intention. The fulfilment of civil obligations is the citizen's privilege. Punishment inevitably affects the offender's social status.

Why punishment? The purpose of legal punishment has been a matter of much speculation and controversy. It implies two questions. The first one is descriptive and refers to the reasons why men have been, and are still being, punished. The answer is complicated by the fact that the idea of punishment has deep irrational roots. Psychology claims to detect unconscious motives for the demand for punishment in man's fear, in his insecurity, and even in a sense of guilt which seeks satisfaction in the vicarious suffering of the convicted criminal. The second question is speculative and asks for the reasons why men ought to be punished. This is not the metaphysical problem whether in a perfect moral order guilt should be met with punishment, but the even more disquieting question whether human judges have the right to punish their fellow men. 'More and more I come to see,' said Canon Barnett, 'that man has no call to punish man. He always fails in the attempt, and his claim destroys him. Man must educate man, but never assume the superior place of a condemner.'[1]

The unsophisticated answer to these questions is that punishment is, and ought to be, inflicted in order to check crime. This simple statement has a twofold meaning: it may mean that when one culprit is punished, other potential culprits are deterred; or it may entail a hope that the culprit himself will be prevented by his punishment from further wrong-doing. To use technical terms: the aim of legal punishment is either general or individual prevention. The infliction of punishment by human judges with their limited insight into character and motives is acceptable only in so far as it is necessary for the protection of the community and its members. This secular purpose justifies punishment, but not terror or reprisals. Legal punishment is inseparably linked with the idea of justice. Justice is an ultimate value. It is akin to the idea of truth, and closely connected with the principle of equality. It can be verified only in the judgement of a refined conscience. A just punishment is more than the overcoming of evil with force. It is also a spiritual power which may make an appeal to the moral personality of man.

The effects of punishment do not depend on the sentence and its execution alone. They are determined by the whole setting of the community. Three conditions must prevail if punishment is to act as a reasonable means of checking crime. It must first be brought home to the offender that 'crime does not pay'. For this purpose a speedy and inescapable detection and prosecution are more essential than long sentences rarely occurring. Secondly, after the expiration of his sentence the prisoner must have a fair chance for a fresh start. Thirdly, the State which claims the right of punishment must uphold superior values which the prisoner can reasonably be expected to acknowledge. In the face of general corruption, unchecked profiteering, unscrupulous abuse of power, persistent mass unemployment, and a social order grossly unjust, punishment will embitter and crush a personality, but never reform a criminal.

Punishment, by definition, is a reaction on the part of someone in authority to a wrongful act committed with a guilty mind. This implies the notion that the offender has 'deserved' his punish-

[1] *Canon Barnett, Life, Work and Friends*, by his Wife (1921), p. 588; letter to his brother, March 1906.

ment, that it is 'his due'; and, so far as this is so, punishment has been characterized as retribution. This, however, is a dangerous word. It implies not only that punishment follows crime; it implies also a demand that the punishment should be the crime's equivalent, that there should be, in other words, an approximate equation between the hardships suffered and those inflicted. In this retaliatory sense retribution has played a remarkable part in history. As the strength of the State grew, a neutral force intervened between aggressor and victim, wrested the right to vengeance from the injured party, and suppressed unrestricted clan-warfare and arbitrary private bargaining by substituting retribution according to the rules of law. At such an early stage the principle of retribution restricted society's almost unlimited demands for punishment. But when the progress of civilization allowed the State to use its punitive power more sparingly, the same principle was denounced as a pretext for excessive punishment. Equality between crime and punishment is a legal fiction. It is arbitrary to fix six weeks' or two years' imprisonment as the just equivalent for a fraudulent misappropriation by a servant of money belonging to his master, or for a brutal assault against a defenceless cripple. Members of the prison service often say that they are prepared to receive men committed to prison 'as a punishment, but not for punishment'. Retribution, then, is not a guiding principle in the choice and administration of punishment; but it has still a negative function. It is the sense of just retribution which prompts people's righteous indignation against the conviction of an innocent person, or against the execution of a dangerous but insane murderer. And it is a sense of just retribution which rules out penalties conspicuously out of proportion to the crime committed. It would be intolerable to send to prison a poor woman who took money to buy a tonic for her sick child, and to let off with a trifling fine a fraudulent attorney who abused his clients' confidence in order to indulge in extravagant gambling. In setting a limit to excessive punishment retribution does not go far beyond such obvious generalizations. It refers not so much to the proportion between an individual crime and the subsequent sentence, as between an individual sentence and the general standard of sentences associated with offences of a similar type and gravity. The practice of sentencing courts is more determined by such customary standards than by the wide statutory range of legal punishment. In English law the statutory punishment for larceny is anything up to five years' penal servitude. The Recorder of London, however, put on record that for larceny of a bicycle he would never feel justified in sentencing a man to more than twelve or fifteen months' imprisonment.[1] Courts of law cannot dispense with the principle of equality, but it remains open to question in what respect two cases must resemble each other in order to be regarded as equal: in the legal ingredients of the particular offence, the damage done to victims, the personal circumstances and motives of the offenders, or the prospects of their social readjustment? The selection of the deciding factor depends on the purpose of punishment.

Punishment materializes in three consecutive steps. According to the orthodox doctrine legislation promulgates punishments in order to prevent people from committing acts regarded as criminal; courts give sentences in conformity with relevant legal provisions; and the administration executes the judicial sentences and at the same time may do its best to work for the prisoner's reformation as far as this is compatible with the mode of punishment prescribed by law and inflicted by the court. Penal reform has reversed this traditional order and shifted the emphasis to the role of the executive. Reform programmes differ in the methods of treatment they suggest, but concur in the idea that what is to be done with the prisoner in the course of months and years must help to fit him for a place in society he can have some hope of keeping. On the basis of this idea it has been demanded that sentencing courts should give their decisions in the light of the prisoner's needs and potentialities, and that the statute book should lay down legal conditions and methods of punishment offering the best possible facilities for an adequate treatment of offenders.

This is an instance of law reform being prompted from the treatment side. The reform involved is fundamental, and it is therefore right to say that social readjustment is the principal purpose of punishment. But just as punishment is not the sole instrument for protection of society and the prevention of crime so social readjustment, though its principal purpose, is not its only one. As an unpleasant possibility, for example, punishment may act as a counterpoise to man's indulgence and negligence. It is indispensable for the enforcement of the steadily extending obligations imposed by modern legislation. And where social readjustment is not feasible, society must be protected by a long-term segregation. Punishment, moreover, does not affect the individual alone; it reacts upon the community in which he lives. The State must consider this reaction in the community, and even if an individual offender

[1] *Report of the Departmental Committee on Persistent Offenders* (1932), p. 10.

seems highly unlikely ever to relapse into crime, it cannot pass over a serious crime without proper action. Social readjustment is not the only, but the most representative purpose of legal punishment. It may apply to a minority of law-breakers only, but it gives legal punishment its ethos and dignity, and justifies the resort to security measures where efforts at rehabilitation have failed.

By the plan of this book the chapters which follow are primarily devoted to the treatment of offenders. This has meant a certain selection from the variety of single causes in which penal reform had been concerned in the course of its notable history. Not every legal punishment involves a treatment of the offender. The infliction of a fine indicates that punishment was necessary, but treatment not advisable. Capital punishment, on the other hand, makes any treatment impossible. These two penalties from the extreme ends of the scale confront penal reform with different problems.

Fines

Recent legislation and judicial practice have favoured a growing extension of the use of fines, while at the same time successful efforts have been made to reduce the number of short prison sentences. Public controls of traffic, employment, manufacture and distribution of goods, insurance, and so forth, entail the enforcement of regulations by fine. An increasing resort to fines, too, is a sign of rising social standards. The higher the average standards of employment and living, the more severe is the loss in status and amenities by committal to prison, and the greater is the probability that fines, if inflicted, will be paid. A fine involves the least possible interference with the offender's life. He is left to decide for himself what he will give up in order to pay. English law does not even prevent him from finding friends who will pay for him. If, however, the money has not been paid, a substitute punishment must be found.

The usual alternative is a short prison term. Imprisonment for non-payment of a fine is a challenge to penal reform; for obdurate debtors make for an element of fluctuation in the prison population. But the issue is ultimately a moral one. It may have been tolerable to the Middle Ages that 'he who cannot pay with his goods may pay with his blood', while 'amends' were expected and accepted from the respectable wealthy; but to-day a dual system which permits the poor to go to prison while the rich pay a fine scandalizes the sense of social justice. In most countries the law has provided for the assessment of the fine in accordance with the offender's income and resources rather than the assumed gravity of the offence, and for payment by instalments. Unfortunately the idea of discharging the money debt by voluntary work has almost everywhere proved impracticable.

Capital Punishment

The fight against capital punishment is the most dramatic aspect of penal reform, and still controversial.[1] In Europe capital punishment reached its peak at the beginning of Renaissance when medieval traditions gave way to new forms of strong centralized government. On the Continent rising State absolutism consolidated and extended numerous capital offences in newly promulgated law. Actual executions increased substantially. In the Age of Reason restriction, if not the abolition, of capital punishment was a favourite subject for reform programmes. After a wave of executions during the French Revolution, legislation in all civilized countries drastically reduced the number of capital offences, and replaced the death penalty by transportation or long-term deprivation of liberty. As a result, offences against property have everywhere been excluded from the list of capital crimes. Where capital punishment still prevails as an ordinary legal punishment in peace-time, it has been restricted to the most serious cases of treason and homicide. Some countries have removed the death penalty from ordinary civilian criminal law altogether. By the beginning of the Second World War the following European nations had abolished capital sentences as a statutory punishment: Denmark, Sweden, Norway, Latvia, Holland, Switzerland, Portugal, and Rumania. In the United States by the time of the First World War twelve states had abrogated the death penalty. It is prohibited at present in two New England States (Maine and Rhode Island), and a group of four states in the north-central part of the country (Michigan, Minnesota, North Dakota, and Wisconsin). In the middle and south of the American continent, excepting Cuba but including Argentina and Brazil, it has been abolished. And in the Pacific, Queensland and New Zealand have also abrogated capital punishment.

The rise of totalitarian dictatorships on the European continent

[1] M. Liepmann, *Todesstrafe* (1912); E. Roy Calvert, *Capital Punishment in the Twentieth Century* (1927); *Report from the Select Committee on Capital Punishment* (1930); C. W. Kirchwey, 'Capital Punishment', *Encyclopaedia of Social Sciences* (1930), iii. 192 et seq.; 'Todesstrafe', *Religion in Geschichte und Gegenwart* (2nd ed. 1931), v. 1202 et seq.; E. Kohlrausch, 'Todesstrafe' *HWB.Krim.* (1935); Sutherland, pp. 560 et seq.

was followed by a new and drastic increase in the number of death sentences. In Italy capital punishment, abrogated in 1889, was re-introduced in 1926. In Austria the Federal Constitution of 1920 banned it, but the subsequent anti-liberal period saw it re-introduced in 1934. In Germany three times there had been a fair chance of abolition: in the North German Diet of 1870; by the proposals of the—unpublished—Draft Code Radbruch of 1922; and during the deliberations of the Parliamentary Commission on the reform of criminal law in 1928. National-Socialism made abundant use of the death penalty, not only in political persecution, but also as an ordinary legal punishment. The excessive resort to it reached its climax during the war, when the statute book provided for thirty-five new civilian capital offences, when wide discretionary powers were given to sentence to death certain types of offenders even if they had committed non-capital offences, and when juveniles between fourteen and eighteen were by law liable to the death penalty.

The issue before the law-givers is not whether the State may demand the sacrifice of the individual for the sake of the community, but whether to preserve the law's authority and protect society it is necessary to take the murderer's life. The persistence of capital punishment in the modern legislation of even democratic countries is due not so much to a reasoned answer to the above question as to a deep-rooted, ultimately irrational, demand for retaliation in kind. In almost every other province of criminal law this demand has been superseded by a rational system which uses deprivation of liberty in various ways, but with the crime of murder it seems still closely associated. This is a crime which deeply affects man's feeling of security and which seems to make retaliation possible by providing a superficial parallel between the death of the victim and the execution of the murderer. Such a retaliation might be justifiable as a first step in overcoming excessive and uncontrolled forces of vengeance. Even modern civilization has not escaped the recurrence of conditions where mass executions became a weapon in political warfare and a means of exterminating individuals and groups alleged to be hostile or obnoxious. Retrograde developments of this kind throw mankind back for centuries, and make it necessary to start again where the Age of Reason began. Strict regimentation by substantive law, and legal safeguards for a fair trial even in the application of the death penalty, are essential conditions of any return to humanitarianism.

Under stable conditions like those of Western Civilization in the first quarter of the century capital punishment is not necessary. Experience in countries with different laws, but similar ethnological and social conditions, or in the same country before and after the alteration of the law, suggests that the abolition of the death penalty entails no increase in the number of offences formerly capital.

Capital punishment cannot be 'reformed'; it can only be abolished. Those who accept the death penalty as a natural or traditional weapon in the administration of justice will take no risk until they have absolute proof that the protection of human life would not be weakened by its abrogation. Conversely, those who regard the execution of the offender as substantially and fundamentally different from all other legal punishments now obtaining insist on having strong evidence to show that this drastic and irreparable measure is indeed indispensable. This amounts almost to a controversy about the burden of proof. Before the war in England about 100 cases of murder occurred every year; some thirty of the murderers committed suicide, eight or nine were executed.[1] For those reluctant to lay aside the ultimate weapon those figures seem to prove that man fears execution more than death, and that the small proportion of actual executions affects only the most vicious, dangerous, and persistently anti-social criminals. Their opponents, however, infer from the small percentage of executions that security is unimpaired even if in the overwhelming majority of cases the prescribed ultimate expiation for murder remains a legal fiction.

There is a strong case for abolition. The maintenance of capital punishment as an instrument of the ordinary legal system can only discredit the declared aim of penal reform: that the criminal's readjustment should be the supreme purpose of punishment. The State and the community ought not to answer the criminal with his own weapon, destruction; even where they have to resort to force their action should express the higher values of law and justice. For this reason they should apply a punishment which does not *per se* prevent the culprit from ever coming to a realization of ethical values, even if he may realize them only by strenuous work and the fulfilment of duties within the narrow world of a prison community.

[1] *Crim. Stat. 1938*, p. xvii.

Penal and reformative Treatment

Between the rise in the incidence of fines and the decline in the incidence of capital punishment lies the broad field of penal and reformative methods, institutional as well as non-institutional. This is the principal topic of this book. No proper name has been found for such studies within the framework of recognized academic and scientific disciplines. Criminology, though as a practical science it includes questions of treatment, is as its name indicates primarily concerned with the amount, forms, and causes of crime. Penology as a part of, or counterpart to, criminology explicitly refers to the treatment aspect. As a word penology is of international origin. It was coined by Francis Lieber when he translated Beaumont de Tocqueville's book on American prisons from French into English.[1] But this artificial compound has never been assimilated in ordinary language. Penal science at least avoids the dubious *logos* of punishment, but claims the rank of a natural science. For these reasons the title of this book refers to penal reform as the driving force of practical efforts and theoretical studies in the treatment of offenders.

[1] 'Penology', *Oxford Dictionary*.

FIRST PART
HISTORICAL EXPERIENCE

CHAPTER II
HOUSES OF CORRECTION

AT all times the law has resorted to the imprisonment of people as a means to enforce its authority. The accused has been remanded in custody. The convicted had to stay in prison to await sentence and execution. Condemnation to public works—an old form of enforced labour—pillory, and mutilation implied the culprit's captivity. Imprisonment was expected to break a debtor's obstinacy. Penal reform, in a strict sense of the word, has been primarily concerned with the prison as a typical form of legal penalty for the commission of acts made punishable under the criminal law.

The history of imprisonment as a legal punishment begins with a negative statement. The Emperor Justinian, in his *Digest* (A.D. 533), referred to a principle, coined by the Roman jurist Ulpian in the reign of Caracalla (A.D. 211–17). In this context, Ulpian dealt with the duties of provincial governors. In the Justinian tradition, Ulpian gives the following account: 'Presidents' usually sentence people to be held in prison or to be fettered. This is illegal, since such forms of punishment have been prohibited. Then he adds this principle: 'Carcer ad continendos homines, non ad puniendos haberi debet'—'Prison ought to be used for detention only, but not for punishment'. By referring to this principle in his *Digest*, the Emperor enacted it as imperial law.[1] Imprisonment, therefore, was not unheard of in the Roman Empire, but illegal as a punishment under Roman and the Civil Law.[2] This ambiguity between administrative practice and legal doctrine prevailed throughout the Middle Ages up to modern times. Canon Law tried to reconcile the Ulpian principle with a growing practice of confining members of the clergy as a measure of penitential discipline. Boniface VIII (1294–1303) enacted this statement: 'Quamvis ad reorum custodiam, non ad poenam carcer specialiter deputatus esse noscatur, nos tamen non improbamus,

[1] *Dig*. 48. 19. 8. 9.
[2] T. Mommsen, *Römisches Strafrecht* (1899), p. 963.

si subiectos tibi clericos confessos de criminibus seu convictos in perpetuum vel ad tempus, prout videris expedire, carceri mancipes ad poenitentiam peragendum.'[1]—'Although it is evident that the use of prison is authorized for the prisoner's custody and not for punishment, we have no objection if you send members of the clergy who are under your discipline, after a confession of crimes or a conviction, either for life or for a certain term, according to your discretion, to prison for the performance of penitence.' The Civil Law adopted the Ulpian principle without further comment. Many Italian statutes repeated the formula of Ferrara: 'Carcer est inventus ad custodiam, non ad poenam'—'Prison has been "invented" for custody, not for punishment'. Bracton, writing between 1250 and 1258 on English laws and customs, referred to prisons as places where men waited to be liberated or sentenced by judicial decision.[2] England, however, made more use of imprisonment as a punishment than those medieval countries which followed the Civil Law. Often imprisonment was a legal means of extortion, pressing the prisoner or his kin to pay money. The word fine is still reminiscent of this form of 'finishing' a prison term.[3] In 1275 the Statute of Westminster I provided two years' imprisonment as a legal punishment for rape. In 1576 an Elizabethan statute made one year's imprisonment 'for the further correction of such persons' the legal punishment for a culprit who was safe from the gallows by the benefit of clergy.[4] In 1595, in *Gresham* v. *Markham*, before the Star Chamber, the Lord Treasurer said this: 'Prisons are ordained for two reasons, the one for safe custody, and the other for correction'.[5] The criminal jurisdiction of the Star Chamber was supplementary to the Common Law courts, especially when servants of the Crown were concerned. In the history of criminal law, extraordinary modes of procedure often anticipated changes in the law.

On the Continent the development was more complicated than in England. Statutory provisions for imprisonment were not frequent and were of a minor and rather supplementary character. The Police Ordinance for the Reich, 1530, provided for blasphemy

[1] C. 3 in VI° *De poenis* 5. 9.

[2] Bracton, *De legibus et consuetudinibus Angliae*, Lib. III, c. 9 (ed. Woodbine, 1922), II. 346.

[3] Pollock and Maitland, *History of English Law* (2nd ed. 1898), ii. 517.

[4] 18 Eliz., c. 7, s. 3.

[5] *Les Reportes del Cases in Camera Stellata, 1593–1609*. From the original MS. of John Hawarde, ed. by W. P. Baildon (1894), p. 29. On the criminal jurisdiction of the Star Chamber: W. S. Holdsworth, *History of English Law*, iv. 273 et seq.; v. 155 et seq.

'a fortnight's tower', and for swearing and cursing tower or a fine. In 1532 the Criminal Justice Ordinance of the Emperor Charles V, the 'Carolina', twice mentioned 'eternal' prison, and provided 'incarceration for a time' as an alternative to a fine in the case of petty thieves taken red-handed (art. 158). Dealing explicitly with contemporary misuses, the same source states with express disapproval that many courts use their prisons not for detention, but for punishing prisoners and inmates (art. 218). At the same time the Ordinance has a form of indeterminate sentence: 'punishment or detention of persons who according to plain evidence are to be expected to commit unlawful acts or crimes'. They ought to be kept in prison till the court is satisfied with sufficient bail or security against any risk of their committing the unlawful act. Prevention by segregation was still associated with the idea of imprisonment as a means to enforce payment.

In principle the old rule of the Civil Law prevailed. When, under the initiative of Colbert, French inquisitorial procedure was consolidated by the Ordinance of 1670, the old phrase was re-enacted that prisons had been instituted for custody only. Meanwhile, this formula was reinterpreted in a new way. Independently of the purpose for which a man was sent to prison, the prison itself ought not to be a place for the mortification of the prisoner, but only for detaining him, even if this detention in itself was inflicted as punishment. The Carolina referring to imprisonment before trial emphasized that 'prisons have been instituted for detention and not for the prisoners' severe and dangerous torture' (art. 11). Benedict Carpcov, judge and legal scholar in Leipzig, writing in 1635, suggested that a prison should be 'locus tolerabilis, ut in eo vivere, aereque ac lumine captivus frui possit'—'a tolerable spot so that the prisoner is able to live in it and to enjoy air and light'. A modest standard indeed, and a bad testimony for prison conditions in the seventeenth century. Even in 1768, the *Constitutio Criminalis Theresiana*, the Austrian Criminal Code of the Empress Maria Theresia, said that prisons are for safety and not for punishment—except in special cases, and therefore 'prisoners should not be confined in stocks, filthily smelling dungeons, or deep and dark towers' (art. 52).

Statutory provisions with a negative content are illustrations of misuses which the law undertakes to overcome. Actually reports of old prisons reveal a gloomy and hopeless picture. Towers, gatehouses, dungeons, cellars of town halls and market-houses were used as prisons. No guarantees existed for proper administration and fair treatment. Sometimes a prison was an accessory to a court. The Star Chamber had at its disposal the Fleet Prison. But these prisons proved incapable of development into a reasonable institution of criminal justice. It was in another sphere of public life that new forms of treatment came to be initiated. The historic starting-point was the beginning of secular poor relief and public welfare work in the sixteenth century.

In all European countries the sixteenth century was a remarkable epoch in social history as well as in the development of criminal law. It was then that professional vagrants and habitual criminals became a lasting social phenomenon.[1] At the same time people became conscious of new social problems and began to discuss social defects and their reform.[2] Thomas More, in his *Utopia* (1516) dealt with the increase of thefts in England, and, for its probable causes, referred to the economic crisis as the result of the enclosures—a favourite subject of contemporary social criticism—to the numerous mercenaries discharged from the war in France, and similar factors. There was a growing public initiative in the field of criminal justice. In Tudor England, courts of royal prerogative tried to fill the gaps left by the Common Law. These courts had before them an increasing number of criminal cases prosecuted upon information. On the Continent, in the wake of the Reception of the Civil Law, the inquisitorial mode became the normal way of criminal procedure. In essence it meant that the initiative for criminal prosecutions lies with the court, and that the judge combines in himself the three functions of prosecution, defence, and decision. Finally the influence of the Reformation strengthened the authority of the secular State. Monasteries and their funds were controlled and even seized by the State. Some of their traditional tasks such as charity and poor relief had to be taken over by secular authorities. At the same time new spiritual ideas changed the attitude towards the poor. Martin Luther, in his 'Letter to the Christian Nobility', 1525, said: 'Among Christians, nobody should go begging'. Each parish ought to deal exclusively with its own poor.

About 1550 there was a successful move for a new organization

[1] T. Harman, *A Caveat for Common Cursetors, vulgarely called Vagabones* (1567); J. Awdeley, *The Fraternity of Vagabondes* (1575). Both reprinted by E. Viles and F. I. Furnivall, *The Rogues and Vagabondes of Shakespeare's Youth* (1907). *Liber vagatorum* (between 1509 and 1524), put into verses by Pamphilus Gengenbach, ed. K. Goedeke (1856). See further F. Aydelotte, *Elizabethan Rogues and Vagabonds*, Oxford Hist. and Lit. Studies, i (1913); G. Scheidegger, *Rogue und Conneycatcher* (diss. Basle (1927)).

[2] F. A. Salter, *Some Early Tracts on Poor Relief* (1926).

of London hospitals. This was the object of some Protestant clergy, Thomas Lever and Bishop Ridley, in co-operation with Sir Richard Dobbs and Sir George Barnes, Lord Mayors of London. At that time St. Thomas and St. Bartholomew were set aside for sick and infirm men, and Christ's Hospital for poor children. The new object was to provide accommodation for training and disciplining neglected children and sturdy vagrants.[1] This movement may best be illustrated by 'a very pathetical letter', written by Bishop Ridley to Sir William Cecil, the King's secretary, in order to gain royal support for the new plan.

Good Master Cecil [the Bishop wrote], I must be a suitor in our Master Christ's cause. I beseech you to be good unto Him. The matter is, Sir, that He hath been too, too long abroad, without lodgings in the streets of London, both hungry, and naked and cold. Now thanks be to Almighty God, the citizens are willing to refresh Him, and to give Him meat, drink, clothing and firing. But alas!, they lack lodging for Him, for in some one house, I dare say, they fain to lodge three families under one roof. Sir, there is a wide large empty house of the King's Majesty, called Bridewell, which would wonderfully well serve to lodge Christ in, if He might find friends at court to procure in this cause.

In 1552 Thomas Lever, as well as Bishop Ridley, made this idea the subject of sermons which they delivered before King Edward VI. As a result of these efforts the King gave Bridewell, an old royal palace in London, which in 1522 had been repaired for a visit of the Emperor Charles V, as an institution for the reception of the vagabond, idle, and dissolute. A royal charter was confirmed in 1553. Bridewell became the model and even the namegiver of Houses of Correction in England. The true aim may best be explained by the wording of the supplication which the Governors of the Poor addressed to the king—speaking on behalf of the poor themselves: '. . . that we may no longer lie in the street for lack of harbour, and that our old sore of idleness may no longer vex us nor grieve the commonweal'.[2] Accordingly Bridewells or Houses of Correction provided facilities for setting idle and disorderly people to work with the threefold purpose to make them earn their keep, to reform them by compulsory work and discipline,

[1] John Stow, *A Survey of the Cities of London and Westminster* (1598), enlarged edition by J. Strype (1720) i. 176 et seq.; A. J. Copeland, *Bridewell Royal Hospital, Past and Present* (1888), pp. 23 et seq.; E. M. Leonard, *Early History of English Poor Relief* (1900), p. 32; E. G. O'Donoghue, *Bridewell Hospital*, i. (1923); ii. (1929); Austin van der Slice, 27 *Journal* 45.

[2] Copeland, l.c., p. 39.

and to deter others from vagrancy and idleness.[1] In the London Bridewell inmates included habitual vagrants and poor boys who should be trained in craftsmanship. In the beginning, at least, work was fairly well organized. There were several departments under the supervision of governors. Some inmates were occupied with clothmaking, weaving, and spinning; others worked as ironmongers. Raw materials were given by tradesmen who collected the manufactured goods and sold them at the market. The worst men were employed at the mill or in the bakehouse—with the possibility of being removed to a better occupation. A first attempt at a Progressive Stage organization! Later on wages were paid to the inmates in return for their work. The first social reaction was a strict differentiation between the poor and beggars. The former might be cared for, the latter had to undergo institutional treatment in the Bridewells. In 1557 Orders for the Government of the Hospitals stated this: 'There is a great difference between a poor man and a beggar, as is between a true man and a thief.'[2] This policy was finally established by a statute of 1576.[3] It amended the drastic Act for the Punishment of Vagabonds of 1572[4] by provisions for the 'assignment' of Houses of Correction in every county. While the impotent poor were to be maintained by the parishes, those who refused work or were punishable as rogues should be committed to the new institutions and set to work by coercive measures.

The first results of the new development were highly satisfactory. The new industrial spirit and a resolute practice of committals to Bridewells seemed more effective in settling down or deterring the vagabond than the traditional criminal law with pillory, stocks, and gallows.[5] Coke stated, that unlike those suffering from the bad and even-deteriorating effects of the common gaol, people committed to the House of Correction or Working House 'come out better'.[6] There were, however, from the beginning, certain germs of decay. Intended as a means against new forms of destitution, local efforts fought difficulties which arose from general causes. The stream of beggars shifting to London rather increased by what, at first, seemed to them an attractive accommodation. Later on, when the first enthusiasm of the public faded away, the

[1] S. and B. Webb, p. 13.
[2] Leonard, l.c., p. 36.
[3] 18 Eliz., c. 3; *Statutes of the Realm*, iv. 610.
[4] 14 Eliz., c. 5; *Statutes of the Realm*, iv. 590.
[5] Aydelotte, l.c., p. 69.
[6] E. Coke, *Institutes of the Law of England*, ii. 734.

funds at the disposal for the maintenance of the new institutions were shrinking. Conditions of labour deteriorated, until industrial work was eventually abandoned. Coke stated that the 'excellent work' was hampered by the lack of interest among justices of the peace: as long as they 'were diligent and industrious, there was not a rogue to be seen in any part of England, but when Justices and other officers became *tepidi* and *trepidi*, rogues and so on swarmed again'.[1]

The composite of poor relief and criminal law gave rise to legal objections. According to the Royal Charter, the Governors in co-operation with special beadles had 'to search, acquire and seek out idle ruffians, tavern haunters, vagabonds, beggars, all persons of evil name and fame, and to commit them to Bridewell, to punish and to correct them as shall seem good to their discretion'. Actually, persons were committed for corporal punishment on slight and insufficient grounds.[2] In 1581 Francis Bacon opposed such administrative discretion; it had been well established by the law of the land, that to deal with criminals is the function of justices of the courts exclusively, and not of any administrative commission.[3]

There is no historical evidence that English Bridewells had any influence abroad. On the Continent Houses of Correction were erected under the influence of new model institutions in Holland.[4] In view of the striking similarity between English Bridewells and Dutch Houses of Correction, English influence is not improbable.[5] But nothing is known about links between the two systems or exchange of experience between the two countries. In 1595 the famous House of Correction at Amsterdam was erected, and in the next year there followed a Spin-House for women. The starting point for these Dutch institutions was closely connected with criminal law. In 1589 the aldermen of Amsterdam refused to send a thief of sixteen to the gallows and applied to the City Council for suitable means in order to keep such young folk in permanent

[1] Ibid., p. 729.

[2] Copeland, l.c., p. 54.

[3] Francis Bacon, 'Discourse upon the Commission of Bridewell', *Works*, ed. Spedding, vii. 505 et seq.

[4] R. v. Hippel, *Beiträge zur Geschichte der Freiheitsstrafe*, 18 *ZStW* 419–94, 608–66, separate publication, abridged, under the title: *Entstehung der modernen Freiheitsstrafe und des Erziehungsstrafvollzuges* (1931); H. v. Weber, 'Entwicklung des Zuchthauswesens in Deutschland i. 17, und 18. Jahrhundert', *Festschrift A. Zycha* (1941), pp. 427–68; T. Sellin, *Pioneering in Penology: The Amsterdam Houses of Correction in the 16th and 17th Cents.* (1944).

[5] F. D. v. Dolsperg, *Entstehung der Freiheitsstrafe* (1928).

work, and, if possible, by doing so to train them for better conduct. According to a well-established tradition this suggestion resulted in the foundation of the House of Correction at Amsterdam. It had 150 inmates, composed of four groups: first, vagrants, beggars, and idle persons; secondly, disorderly women; thirdly, thieves committed after conviction; and finally, neglected children, some admitted on application by their parents and guardians. The Spin-House, 1596, and the Separate House, 1600, took over the second and fourth group respectively. There was compulsory work. It consisted mainly of rasping logwood, and this sometimes gave these institutions the name of Rasp-House. The logwood was a raw material for dyeing industries, and had just been imported from the New World. The institution had a monopoly of this new trade, and was thereby provided with work without competing with free labour. The work was hard and monotonous. The inmates received small wages with a characteristic division, one part being at their own immediate disposal, the other saved for the day of discharge. Thus typical forms of prison life were anticipated by this early Dutch foundation. There was religious service, education in writing, reading, and arithmetic, and medical attendance. Penalties may have been severe and brutal. Whether there was actually a water-cellar, with the brutal alternative for the prisoner of either permanently pumping, or drowning, remains doubtful. John Howard 'learned on careful inquiry' that the story was a fiction.

The whole tendency of the new foundation was fundamentally opposed to contemporary criminal law. It did not involve an exclusion from society by death, mutilation, and branding with permanent degradation. The ultimate aim was to lead back the prisoner into society. As to the results, contemporary writers are full of praise. Vagrancy seemed to disappear, not least because something definite was done. Good economic results seemed to be a further recommendation. Many towns in Holland as well as in other countries adopted and imitated what they regarded as a new model institution. In 1604 the Council of Bremen sent questions to Amsterdam, and, later on, Nuremberg asked Bremen for relevant information. The Hanse towns were the first which followed the Dutch example. Houses of Correction were founded in 1613 in Lübeck, in 1622 in Hamburg, in 1629 in Danzig. At the same time, similar institutions, called *Schallenwerke*, *œuvres de sonnettes*, were erected in Switzerland: in 1614 in Berne—for vagrants, rogues, and malefactors—in 1616 in Basle, in 1617 at

Fribourg.[1] In Hamburg inmates should be kept in 'a true fear of God, good discipline, and steady work'.[2] Rasping and filing of logwood, weaving and spinning, carding of wool—the list of traditional prison occupations began with the early Houses of Correction. An inscription in Hamburg read: *Labore nutrior, labore plector*—'it is work which gives me livelihood, it is work which punishes me'—an early expression of the two conflicting purposes of prison labour. There were four types of inmates too: first, criminals, especially those convicted for petty thefts or blasphemy, and juveniles; there were, secondly, poor who were able and willing to work, came voluntarily, and received full wages after some deduction for boarding; thirdly, malicious vagrants, called 'idle flesh'; and, finally, lunatics. While in other fields of criminal justice the contact with the executioner made the prisoner an outcast—like the hangman himself—the new institution was an 'honourable house'. Those criminals, therefore, who had previously undergone criminal punishment could not be admitted. To secure the new treatment for criminals with a previous record too, special Malefactor Houses were erected. Such an institution—for instance at Danzig—received recidivist thieves and disorderly women who had been sentenced to whipping and pillory. The new form of detention thereby became a supplementary punishment. At the end of the eighteenth century there were sixty Houses of Correction in Germany. As a rule Governors had to decide on commitment and discharge of prisoners. As in England, a distrust of executive discretion gave rise to objections to interference with the administration of justice being within the exclusive competence of the judiciary. Finally, new legislation gave the courts the power to send prisoners to Houses of Correction by judicial sentences.

The historical background of the Houses of Correction was the social upheaval and spiritual movement of the Age of Reformation. In Catholic and Protestant countries alike the authorities insisted on a distinction between the decent poor who should be cared for by the parish, and the sturdy beggar and idle vagabond who was to be coerced into work. Numerous ordinances tried to suppress private almsgiving. In 1569 the Lord Mayor of London gave strict command that 'nobody give any relief, lodging, alms, or maintenance to any vagabonds, rogues, etc., or to any common or valiant beggar, but, contrarywise, to cause such beggars, rogues,

[1] Hafner-Zürcher, p. 8.
[2] Streng, *Geschichte der Gefängnisverwaltung in Hamburg* (1890).

vagabonds and masterless men to be apprehended and brought to the Ward to the end that they might be examined and punished by such as have authority in that behalf'.[1] *Vitiorum semina, otium labore exhauriendum*, read an inscription on the Rasp- and Spin-House at Groningen, 1664, 'Idleness the seed of vices to be extinguished by work'. This movement owed a strong impetus to the religious forces of the Reformation.[2] In Catholic France, the committal of beggars and vagrants to institutions, though mentioned in a royal patent of 1554, was not initiated before the establishment of the general hospital in 1656, and even then was intended as a punitive repression and inadequately performed.[3] In England Bishop Ridley, who promoted the dedication of Bridewell, died as one of the Oxford Martyrs, in 1555. Thomas Lever, who worked with him for the same cause, escaped to Switzerland. The Houses of Correction in Holland were founded during the struggle for the independence of the Protestant Netherlands from the Spanish yoke. A contemporary report, *Miracula St. Raspini*, 1612, praised the blessed results of the new treatment as miracles of a mock saint who would heal moral sins.[4] The author mentions sticks and crutches which rogues and beggars left after abandoning the misuse of their pretended deficiencies—just like gratefully dedicated tokens for a miraculous healing of bodily illness. In the light of the new estimation of secular callings and professions, hard work, even if enforced and undertaken for its own sake, seemed the true essence of moral reformation. This doctrine was more rigid than the apostolic advice which emphasized the purpose and social value of work. 'Let him that stole steal no more; but rather let him labour, working with his hands the thing which is good, that he may have to give him that needeth.'[5] In the eyes of the contemporaries the mere fact that the prisoner was forced to work justified the claim for a successful solution of a serious social and moral problem. While almost everywhere the prevailing social conditions called for new ways in dealing with the destitute and wayward, the first Houses of Correction bear the marks of a new spiritual impulse, to organize worldly affairs in accordance with Divine commandments.

In the eighteenth century, still within the period of the old

[1] J. Stow, l.c., p. 178.

[2] G. Radbruch, *Elegantiae Juris Criminalis* (1938), pp. 38–49.

[3] C. Paultre, *De la répression de la mendicité et de vagabondage en France sous l'ancien régime* (Thèse, Paris, 1906), pp. 72, 154 et seq. and *passim.*

[4] v. Hippel, *Beiträge*, l.c., p. 480.

[5] Eph. iv. 28.

Houses of Correction, but already turning to modern ideas, two particular institutions claimed special importance. The one was the *Hospice of St. Michael* in Rome—or, to be more precise, the inauguration within this old institution of special correctional quarters for boys, a work done in 1703 by the initiative of Pope Clemens XI.[1] The scheme intended by its founder has been explained by the *Motu proprio* of 14 November 1703. The place was intended for two types of juvenile delinquents. First, youths under twenty sentenced by a criminal court should be sent thither by the judge instead of being committed to the public prison where —as experience showed—'although kept separated from others, they nevertheless frequently fall into the same or worse enormities instead of coming out corrected and reformed'. Secondly, as in other similar houses, 'boys incorrigible and inobedient to their parents' were received on application by their parents or guardians. There should be an educational treatment with the double aim of religious instruction ' in all matters which should be known by all good Christians', and training in 'some mechanical arts in order that idleness may be driven away by industry, and that they may learn in fact a new mode of decent living'. Later reports show a different treatment of both groups. The juvenile offenders worked together in the central hall, occupied in spinning and knitting, chained by one foot, under a rule of silence and sometimes listening to a pious reading; they spent the night in small separate brick cells. The incorrigible boys were separated day and night. Whipping was a frequent penalty for 'past mistakes' as well as for non-performance of the daily task. As often happened in prison history, the practice may have followed less the new constructive suggestions than the traditional punitive purposes which the founder made the reason for the strict regulation for simple and modest food 'remembering that they are kept there for punishment and mortification'. The House of Correction in St. Michael had a high reputation. The classification and good order marked a favourable distinction from other contemporary institutions. The sound conception of the underlying principles was demonstrated by two famous inscriptions which deeply impressed John Howard. The visitor, entering the building, read these words over the door: 'Perditis adolescentibus corrigendis instituendisque ut qui inertes oberant instructi rei publicae serviant'—'For the correction and instruction of profligate youth, that they who when idle were injurious, when instructed might be useful to the State.' And when

[1] T. Sellin, 20 *Journal* 533.

the visitor proceeded to the central hall, he saw this inscription: 'Parum est coercere improbos nisi probos efficias disciplina'—'It is of little advantage to restrain the bad by punishment, unless you render them good by discipline.'[1] These phrases have often been repeated, and Howard himself selected the latter as a motto for his famous book.

This institution had many features in common with the *Maison de Force* at Ghent. Here, in the then Austrian province of Flanders, in 1627 a House of Correction had been erected according to the famous model of Amsterdam. In 1775, upon the initiative of Count Hippolyte Vilain XIV, the institution was thoroughly reorganized.[2] An interesting octagonal form of the building, strict separation of all prisoners at night, common work with—at first—good accommodation for industrial labour, gave this institution a prominent place in modern prison history.

[1] John Howard, *State of Prisons in England and Wales* (3rd ed. 1784), pp. 113, 114.

[2] Hippolyte Vilain, *Mémoire sur les moyens de corriger les malfaiteurs et les fainéants* (new ed. 1841); L. Stroobant-Stevens, *Le Rasphuis de Gana* (1900); Kriegsmann, p. 26; T. Sellin, 17 *Journal* 104–12, 581–602.

CHAPTER III

JOHN HOWARD AND EARLY PRISON REFORM

FROM the middle of the seventeenth century in most European countries the traditional forms of legal punishment gradually began to change. There was a tendency to make scant use of the old cruel penalties. Banishment seemed to achieve nothing but a disastrous interchange of criminals from place to place. Whipping and the pillory had a notoriously deteriorating effect upon the prisoner. These punishments were just a 'dedication to the gallows', as a contemporary slogan called them. This new tendency towards the rational and humanitarian aims in penal policy coincided with that important movement of the human mind which marks what we call the Era of Enlightenment. European enlightenment had its origin in the English empiricism of Bacon and Newton. It was based on human reason as the ultimate foundation of experience. This experience became the powerful instrument by which insight and knowledge increased. Observation and experiment brought about new discoveries by revealing the underlying laws of Nature. Not only subjects in the realm of nature, but the social facts of human life also, had to be compared and systematized, and traditional institutions were relentlessly scrutinized as to whether they were suitable means to reasonable ends. This movement involved a critical attitude which challenged customary standards and values. The Church and the constitution of the State, the law and social institutions were frankly discussed from their foundations. In the end the positive aspects of this critical attitude were religious tolerance, government by consent, and, in the field of criminal law, a movement against the abuses and the abundance of capital punishment, forfeiture, and degrading penalties as well as the use of torture. From England this new way of thinking spread to the Continent, conveyed and enthusiastically supported by progressive French publicists, especially by Voltaire, Montesquieu, and the Encyclopaedists. In the discussion of criminal law reform the outstanding figure was the Italian writer Cesare Beccaria (1738–94).[1] According to his famous *Essay*

[1] T. Bridgwater, 'Cesare Beccaria', in: J. Macdonell and E. Mauson, *Great Jurists of the World* (1913), pp. 505–16; C. Phillipson, *Three Criminal Law Reformers, Beccaria, Bentham, Romilly* (1923); M. T. Maestro, *Voltaire and Beccaria as Reformers of Criminal Law* (1942).

on Crime and Punishment, 1764,[1] the true aim and the only justification of legal punishment ought to be the principle of public utility, i.e. the safety of society by the prevention of crime. Only crimes really dangerous to society, therefore, should be defined as legal offences; and the term should not be applied to things like heresy and blasphemy, which were better regarded as sins and immoral acts. From such a rational standpoint, Beccaria and his followers fought against the use of torture and challenged capital punishment on principle. The ideas of Beccaria proved the most effective stimulus to a utilitarian approach to penal policy, which became the great cause of Jeremy Bentham.

It was a long time before the criticism of bold reformers resulted in practical improvements of the administration of criminal law. In the positive proposing of suitable substitutes for the old penalties, the enlightened writers were less imaginative. They suggested that legal punishment should fit the seriousness of the crime, that it should be meted out with a view to preventing others from committing similar offences, that penalties, in their effect, should be deterrent, and administered with a certain publicity. These considerations resulted in a growing use of deprivation of liberty as a legal punishment, and they were, thus far, in accordance with the tendency of continental criminal justice from the end of the seventeenth and the beginning of the eighteenth century. There developed various new forms of imprisonment applied as a legal punishment. At the same time the original distinction between gaols and Houses of Correction disappeared.

In England, at the end of the seventeenth century, Houses of Correction lost their avowed reformative character.[2] The treatment of vagrants by enforced work was no longer the specific aim of Bridewells. Rogues and vagrants were received for corporal punishment and discharged, or were sent to private workhouses. The fundamental Elizabethan Statute of 1597 which repealed all previous Acts had already relied on a punitive treatment of vagrancy. It reiterated the statutory list of persons who as rogues, vagabonds, and sturdy beggars should sustain 'payne and punishment'; they should be 'openly whipped', sent back to their parish 'there to put him or her self to labour as a true subject ought to do',

[1] Cesare Beccaria, *Dei delitti e delle pene*, 1st edition anonymously printed at Livorno in 1764, probably some forty Italian editions. English translations in 1767 (anonymous) with subsequent editions (see below, p. 37 n.), and in 1880 by J. A. Farrer. Bibliographical information about editions and translations in the introduction to the German translation by K. Esselborn (1905).

[2] S. and B. Webb, pp. 14 et seq.

while dangerous and incorrigible rogues should be committed to a House of Correction or county gaol till they were banned from the Realm by the next Quarter Sessions and conveyed overseas.[1] This led to a development by which Houses of Correction themselves adopted a more penal character. Under Charles I, an Order of the Privy Council of 1630 provided that Houses of Correction should be established 'adjoining to the common prison', so that prisoners 'committed for minor causes' could work there instead of living 'idly and miserably long in prison'.[2] Houses of Correction received numerous minor offenders whom the Justices of the Peace wished to save from the demoralizing effects of the common gaol. A statute of 1720 established this practice. It seemed to be 'very prejudicial and expensive' to commit criminals to no prison other than the county gaol, and, therefore, the Act authorized 'Justices of the Peace within their respective jurisdiction to commit such vagrants and other criminals, offenders, person and persons either to the common gaol or House of Correction, as they in their judgment think proper'.[3] Thus far there was no practical difference between the two institutions. Vagrants were treated as offenders and sent to the gaols, and criminals were committed to the Houses of Correction.

On the Continent minor offenders were sent to the common gaol for short and medium terms—a physical restraint rather than an attempt at correction. For serious crimes and even for capital offences prisoners were sentenced to forced public work, performed on fortifications, roads, quarries, or by drawing barges by riversides. The terms ranged to many years, and the penalty used to be aggravated by fetters or by heavy iron balls. This punishment seemed to be a revival of, and to be justified by, the Roman *damnatio ad metallum*, the commitment to mines, and was reminiscent of the use of prisoners as galley-slaves in Mediterranean countries. While the original name was 'fortification work' or 'cart penalty', regulations and reports often referred to these prisoners as slaves or galley-slaves. The third form of deprivation of liberty was a commitment to a House of Correction, which—as in England—adopted a more and more penal character, while its original aim of care for, and coercion of, vagrants and idle folk shifted to workhouses. The following suggestion by a writer of the seventeenth century is an illustration of this tendency: 'Mittantur

[1] 39 Eliz., c. 4; *Statutes of the Realm*, iv (2), 899.
[2] Text reprinted by F. E. Eden, *The State of the Poor* (1797), i. 159.
[3] 6 Geo. I, c. 19, s. 2.

igitur fures ad St. Raspinum, non ad carnificem', 'Thieves should be sent to St. Raspin, not to the hangman.'[1] This policy, however, was not at all approved of by the Houses of Correction themselves. In Lübeck, in 1667, the Provisors objected to the reception of robbers into the House of Correction, 'since this has been dedicated by Council and Corporation for sturdy beggars and disobedient children, and not for such highwaymen'!

On the Continent these various forms of imprisonment gained ground in three different ways.[2] The first was the doctrine of *poena extraordinaria*. According to this theory, the established rules of criminal law with their traditional 'ordinary' punishment exclusively applied to a presupposed normal commission of crime, so that any variation of the act itself, of the guilty mind, or even incompleteness of evidence, would enable the court to pass an 'extraordinary', i.e. a discretionary sentence. This was a remedy to avoid unreasonable penalties and to substitute for them one or other form of deprivation of liberty. The second was the prerogative of the sovereign who claimed the right either to increase or to mitigate judicial sentences. Thirdly, rather hesitatingly, legislation adopted the new forms of punishment. The Austrian Criminal Code of the enlightened Emperor Joseph II, the so-called 'Josephina', 1787, was a somewhat doctrinal attempt to replace capital punishment by the most severe and deterrent forms of imprisonment. The Prussian General Law of the Land, 1794, made imprisonment in various forms the basic method of the whole penal system. The Houses of Correction played a prominent part in this development. In the beginning of the nineteenth century, special regulations procured the transfer of 'slaves' from fortification work into Houses of Correction. Since then the German name of the latter—*Zuchthaus*—has come to stand for penal servitude. The original idea of detaining, for an indefinite period, wayward persons, who 'by their wicked tendencies may be dangerous to the common wealth', found its way into the statutory penal system too. The Bavarian Criminal Code of 1751 provided for professional thieves and notorious robbers, such as were so 'described by public charters', even if they succeeded in enduring torture, to be detained in a workhouse even for life—'since the matter is to be regarded not so much as a punishment but as good discipline'.

Such wide legal aims were in no way in accordance with the state of prisons at that time. Legislation was far ahead of the

[1] Christian Henelius, *Tractatus politicus de aerario* (1670).

[2] Kriegsmann, pp. 8 et seq.

existing penal institutions, and this discrepancy made even reasonable legislative experiments more or less complete failures. Prisons and other institutions were in no way fitted for a rational criminal justice of any sort. Since there was nowhere any centralized prison administration, conditions varied from place to place. As a whole, Houses of Correction shared the general misuses and decay of common gaols. Only in Holland and in some of the Hanse towns the original standard had been upheld. Many prisons were miniature institutions with three or five inmates. In England, in 1779, no less than 130 of the gaols and Bridewells had less than ten inmates.[1] The prisoners were a mixed company with insufficient separation between different groups. Men and women, juveniles and habitual criminals, poor debtors and witnesses, as well as lunatics and people suffering from venereal diseases, were often under the same roof, crowded together, with all the evils of uncontrolled association. An institution at Celle, Hanover, built in 1731, had this inscription: 'Puniendis facinerosis, custodiendis furiosis et mente captis publico sumpto dicata domus'—'This house has been dedicated, by public means, to the punishment of malefactors as well as for the custody of lunatics and mental defectives.' Conditions for work were quite unsatisfactory. In many gaols there was a hardly disguised idleness. The treatment alternated between brutal oppression and an indulgent compliance. In English prisons the new-comer would be greeted by the garnish, i.e. the alternative, imposed by the community of inmates, of either paying for drink, or being stripped and made to run the gauntlet.[2] In German prisons he received the official 'welcome', i.e. whipping, and often a corresponding 'farewell'. Bedding, food, standards of cleanliness were very bad. The principal cause for these defects was the undeveloped state of public administration. This proved disastrous when applied to a direct expression of public authority, i.e. the power over people under arrest. As the result of a long historical development the tasks reserved to the body politic have been gradually extended, and the costs of public activities made payable by the treasury, with one general budget covering all revenues and expenses. Formerly public administration consisted of a multitude of independent institutions and corporations, each a single self-supporting body, financially

[1] S. and B. Webb, p. 31, n. 3.

[2] The word 'garnish' is derived from the Middle English *wernen* (to warn) and has the inferred Teutonic root *warnjan* which means to become aware (*Oxford Dictionary*). Shakespeare uses garnish in the sense of decorate (French: *garnir*) in *Henry V*, II. ii. 134, and *Merchant of Venice*, II. vi. 45.

maintained by fees, income from estates, privileges and liberties, or pious endowments. General regulations were scarce, central control almost non-existent. To this rudimentary form of public administration the prison was no exception. This rather private character explains the poor conditions of the old gaol. No funds were set aside for necessary repairs. To keep the prisoners in irons was cheaper than to guarantee the safety of the prison by sufficient walls and proper locks. To avoid window tax, the keeper diminished the access of light and fresh air. Sometimes prisoners were hired out to private employers, or even sent out begging. Often a private contractor catered for the inmates, or the whole maintenance of the prison was a profit-making enterprise in private hands. The keeper, often relying on a private title, and sometimes not even resident in the gaol, required and received fees—often illegally extended and arbitrarily multiplied—for every single stage of prison life from reception to release, for all accommodation from the bare necessities of feeding and bedding up to luxurious comfort in separate 'sponging houses' for wealthy and collusive prisoners. In a rather idealized form, it might have been like the place where the hard-tempted Vicar of Wakefield found a happy release from his troubles—actually it was a source of constant bribery and extortion. Many prisons were licensed for spirits, with the tap running for the keeper's private profit. Consequently an endless incitement to drink, to revels, and to all sorts of vices was a favourite means of exploitation.

With these grave defects the old prisons were a real danger to the community. The utterly unhygienic conditions produced waves of serious epidemic diseases among prisoners as well as among the general population. Francis Bacon, in his *Natural History*, stated: 'The most pernicious infection next to the plague is the smell of a jail, when prisoners have been long and close and nastily kept. . . . Therefore it were good wisdom that in such a case the jail were aired before they be brought forth.'[1] After a first outbreak in 1414, there were repeated accounts of mass infection by prisoners brought to trial, culminating in the Black Assizes at Oxford in 1577, when, within five weeks, 500 persons died, among them the Lord Chief Baron and many jurymen and witnesses. Similar disasters occurred even in the eighteenth century. In 1750 a Lord Mayor of London, two Judges, and an Alderman were among the victims. Army and Navy were threatened by contagion from discharged prisoners. Probably the so-called gaol fever or

[1] F. Bacon, *Sylva Sylvarum or Natural History* (3rd ed. 1631), p. 238, exp. 914.

gaol distemper was mostly typhus or a malignant form of dysentery.[1] For the gaolers this risk of infection, either actual or pretended, was a welcome reason for preventing visitors from entering the prison, and so for avoiding public control and criticism. No less were the moral dangers. As to continental prisons a modern verdict called the gaols of that time 'a rubbish heap, a school of crimes, a brothel, a gambling-hell and a dram-pub,—but not at all an institution supporting criminal law in the fight against crime'.[2]

Contemporary criticism was not unaware of such calamitous conditions. The first English prison report was given in 1702 by a committee of the Society for Promoting Christian Knowledge who visited Newgate, the Marshalsea, and other prisons and disclosed the most deplorable conditions. The chairman of this committee, Dr. Bray, put the results of these investigations into the form of an *Essay towards the Reformation of Newgate and other Prisons in and about London.* Not until 1849 was this 'earliest document of any value connected with Penology in England' published.[3] The Essay makes six 'vices and immoralities' responsible for the desperate state of contemporary prison conditions: personal lewdness of the keepers, their confederacy with prisoners, the unlimited use of spirits, swearing and gaming, corruption of new-comers by old criminals, neglect of all religious worship. Certain reformative suggestions tried to meet these misuses, though not questioning the private character of prison-keeping. Instead of the disastrous promiscuity of inmates, prisoners should be kept 'in distinct cells', and, particularly, incorrigible criminals should have 'separate apartments'.

In 1729 the conditions in the Fleet Prison, where some prisoners died from brutal treatment and negligence, raised a public scandal. A parliamentary committee was set up to investigate the charges. The chairman was General Oglethorpe. The insight into pauperism and its consequences which he obtained by this inquiry had a lasting influence on his pioneer work as a colonizer of Georgia.[4] He even took with him a group of discharged debtors as his first settlers, but the wholesome development of the new colony soon demanded the influx of abler elements.[5] At home, a criminal

[1] For an historical account of the gaol distemper see W. A. Guy, *Public Health* (1870), part I, lect. vii, pp. 165–92.

[2] Krohne, *Lehrbuch der Gefängniskunde* (1889), p. 22.

[3] Hepworth Dixon, *John Howard and the Prison World of Europe* (1849), pp. 9 et seq. The second edition, 1854, does not contain the text of the *Essay*.

[4] Canon Venables, 'Oglethorpe', *Dictionary of Nat. Biography*.

[5] John S. Simon, *John Wesley and the religious Societies* (1921), pp. 106 et seq.

prosecution against the keeper and his accessories followed, but failed, either by lack and uncertainty of proofs, or by political influence.[1] In 1751, Henry Fielding, the novelist and magistrate, called the Bridewells 'schools of vice, Seminaries of idleness, common shores of nastiness and disease'.[2] In its vivid description of the neglect of magistrates and of the arbitrariness and bribery among gaolers, his *Amelia* (1752) was a worthy predecessor to Charles Dickens's immortal prison stories. Jonas Hanway, one of the early evangelical philanthropists, in 1775, spoke of Houses of Correction as of 'nurseries for thieves and prostitutes', of 'schools for instruction for iniquity'. 'The shortest and most effectual way', he said, 'of eradicating all the plants of moral rectitude which yet remain among the noxious weeds that grow in that uncultivated soil, the hearts of the common people—is to send them to Bridewell.'[3]

Apart from such sharp criticisms suggestions for new and better forms of prison discipline were scarce. As an alternative to the apparent evils of the indiscriminate community of the common gaols and Bridewells, solitary confinement, slowly and hesitatingly, demanded increasing attention. Since there was no practical experience in any reformative treatment the new idea was based upon speculative arguments. The first outspoken advocate of solitary confinement in England was Bishop Joseph Butler (1692–1752), 'this pathetic figure', as Matthew Arnold characterized him, 'with its earnestness, its strenuous rectitude, its firm faith both in religion and reason'.[4] By his philosophical efforts he undertook to harmonize faith and reason. He was an early promoter of popular education as an obligation of the community. In 1740, in his *Hospital Sermon*, he recommended what he called 'the discipline of labour and confinement', i.e. 'to exclude all sorts of revel-mirth from places where offenders are confined, to separate the young from the old, and to force them both, in

[1] *St. Tr.* xvii. 298, 310.

[2] Henry Fielding, *Enquiry into the Causes of the late Increase of Robbers* (1751), p. 63. See also B. M. Jones, *Henry Fielding, Novelist and Magistrate* (1933) and for the continuation of his work by his brother the biography by R. Leslie-Melville, *Life and Work of Sir John Fielding* (1934).

[3] Jonas Hanway, *The Defects of Police* (1775), pp. 72, 210, 53. See also J. H. Hutchins, *Jonas Hanway, 1712–1786* (1940).

[4] Joseph Butler, *The Analogy of Religion, natural and revealed, to the Constitution and Course of Nature* (1736); id., *Sermon preached before the Lord Mayor, Aldermen, Sheriffs and Governors of several Hospitals of London* (1740), pp. 23 and 20; id., *Sermon at the Annual Meeting of the Charity Children at Christ Church* (1745) (*Works*, ed. S. Halifax, ii. 258–76); Matthew Arnold, *Last Essays on Church and Religion* (1877), p. 142.

solitude with labour and low diet, to make the experiment how far their natural strength of mind can support them under guilt or shame and poverty'. In 1771 Samuel Denne published a letter to Sir Robert Ladbroke 'with an attempt to show the good effects to be expected from the confinement of criminals in separate apartments'. Jonas Hanway, too, advocated solitary imprisonment for the twofold purpose 'of chastisement and repentance',[1] and, in 1776, published a special treatise on *Solitude in imprisonment, with proper labour and spare diet, the most humane and effectual means of bringing malefactors to a right sense of their condition.*

This whole literary discussion, though interesting as an historical symptom of the time, had no practical effects. Prison reform owes its lasting stimulus to the efforts of a rare genius for social inquiry and social reform: John Howard.[2] He was born in 1726 at Clapton in the parish of Hackney. His father was a determined nonconformist, and he insisted on sending his son to a teacher who shared his own independent views on church and religion. This was not altogether an educational success. Howard never lost a feeling of self-consciousness which made him ask some friends to revise his manuscripts and to help him with the final form of his books: Richard Densham, once a fellow pupil of Howard; D. Richard Price, politician, philosopher, and divine; John Aikin, a physician and Howard's first biographer. Howard began his career as an apprentice to a wholesale grocer in the City, but he spent the greater part of his life as a landowner at Cardington, Bedfordshire. From the beginning, there were three things characteristic of him: he had a vivid interest in empirical observations, he liked travelling, and he was a man with a sincere sense of social responsibility. As a 'true lover of natural philosophy', he was elected, in 1756, to be a Fellow of the Royal Society. In the same year, after the appalling news about the earthquake at Lisbon, he wished to offer his personal help on the spot, but his

[1] Jonas Hanway, l.c., pp. 52, 66.

[2] Biographies of John Howard: John Aikin, *A View of the Character and public Services of the late John Howard* (1792); J. B. Brown, *Memoirs of John Howard* (1823); W. H. Dixon, *Howard and the Prison World* (1849; 2nd ed. 1854); John Field, *The Life of John Howard* (1850); John Field, *Correspondence of John Howard* (1855); J. Stoughton, *Howard and his Friends* (1884).

Several papers on the life and work of John Howard in *Reports and Proceedings of the 4th International Penitentiary Congress* (1891), v.

See also Leona Baumgarten, *John Howard, Hospital and Prison Reformer: A Bibliography* (1939).

The account of John Howard in the pages which follow is based upon a paper published in 6 *Howard Journal* 34. The author wishes to express his thanks to the editors for their kind permission to make extensive use of that article.

boat was captured by a French privateer, and he had to undergo the hardships of a prisoner-of-war. After his release he gave an account of his experience to the commissioners of sick and wounded seamen—the first of the famous prison reports of John Howard, but never discovered till to-day. He spent the following years performing his duties as a landowner, conscientiously dedicated to the care and protection of his tenants. He improved housing conditions, organized schools, and introduced new industries. Later generations acknowledged these progressive reforms in his estate at Cardington as 'the earliest and certainly the most complete work of physical and incidentally of moral regeneration undertaken by any English landlord'.[1] The historic turning-point was the year 1773. He was made Sheriff of Bedfordshire. In this capacity he did what none of his predecessors had tried before: he inspected the prisons of his county. He found that many prisoners, though acquitted by the court, were not released so long as they were not able to pay the gaoler's fees. He asked the Justices of the Peace for intervention, but they demanded a precedent. In search for a precedent he went out for his first prison tour. The experience which he thereby obtained immediately led to practical results. Alexander Popham, as a Chairman of the Quarter Sessions for West Somerset, became acquainted with the desperate state of the county gaol and the danger arising from an outbreak of gaol fever.[2] As an M.P. for Taunton he tried in vain to persuade the House to enact statutory regulations against the worst evils in contemporary prisons. In 1774, at Popham's request, Howard gave evidence as an expert witness before the House of Commons. His experience as well as his eloquence made the House reconsider their attitude towards prison problems. On 4 March they voted an expression of thanks to John Howard, emphasizing 'that this House is very sensible of the humanity and zeal which have led him to visit the several gaols of this Kingdom'.[3] Two Statutes were enacted, providing for the immediate release of acquitted prisoners, and some elementary sanitary measures.

Howard extended his prison investigations to Scotland and Ireland, and, in 1775, he crossed the Channel for a first inspection of continental prisons. During the next twelve years, he repeated these journeys five times, unceasingly deepening, extending, and

[1] W. Guy, 36 *J. Stat. Soc.* 1–18, 9.
[2] T. Seccombe, 'Popham', *Dictionary Nat. Biography.*
[3] *Journal of the House of Commons*, xxxiv. 535.

re-examining what he found by this unique experience. The enduring result of his observations was his classic book: *The State of Prisons in England and Wales, with preliminary Observations, and an Account of some foreign Prisons*.[1] He extended his interests farther to the state and conditions of *lazarettos* and quarantine stations, particularly in Mediterranean ports, and published his experience on this subject, together with new prison observations, in a second book in 1789.[2] In the same year he left England for the last time. He wished to make new inquiries about plague conditions and the state of sanitary measures and institutional care for sick persons and prisoners in east Europe and Asia Minor. In performing this task he died on 20 January 1790.[3] He did not refuse a patient's demand for his personal assistance, and in the end became himself a victim of the plague.

Howard's work has been embodied in his books. His *State of Prisons* is the first and the only comprehensive survey of European prison conditions, based entirely on first-hand information. Place by place, he gave all particulars: buildings and personnel, bedding and food, air and water-supply, work and religious instruction. Certain characteristics were more or less common: the lack of public responsibility and control, the lack of reasonable work and of the necessary separation between the inmates. On the other hand there were important differences, either for the better or for the worse. In Holland he found clean and well-organized institutions, and the old tradition still alive to set destitutes and criminals to work. In France he tried in vain to get entrance into the Bastille. He reports on the dirt and the lack of fireplaces in French prisons where he found numerous cases of scurvy, and where many prisoners died during the cold winter of 1775. Later on prison regulations were reasonably amended. He gives a vivid description of the Bicêtre, an institution which has been for ever connected with Pinel's pioneer work in mental treatment. When Howard saw the house, there were 1,000 inmates, less than half of them prisoners. The majority came from the poor and were as miserable as the inhabitants of an old English country workhouse. There were patients suffering from insanity and from venereal diseases. Each group was separated, criminals being kept in small rooms with a grating, mostly unglazed. In Germany

[1] First ed. Warrington 1777, 2nd ed. 1780, 3rd ed. 1784.

[2] *An Account of the principal Lazarettos in Europe* (Warrington, 1789).

[3] For the later fate of Howard's tomb at Kherson, Ukraine, see F. Kandyba, 7 *Howard Journal* 37.

he found the 'galley-slaves', and in many territories instruments for the use of torture; in Munich the torture room was 'too shocking to relate the different modes of cruelty'. In Prussia 'the present king (Frederic II) set an example in Germany of abolishing the cruel practice'. Howard further appreciated the strict and efficient police in Berlin who kept the city free from beggars. In Austria he found terrible dungeons, but good infirmaries. He was impressed by the noble institution of St. Michael's in Rome, but he did not withhold some critical suggestions with regard to the organization of the Maison de Force at Ghent, where—in his opinion—compulsory prison labour ought not to be inconsistent with political liberty. In Russia he was himself a witness to an execution with the knout. By these comparative prison studies Howard rendered a unique contribution to European social history, a valuable evidence of the inadequate state of contemporary civilization.[1] This was a striking contrast to the superficial and frivolous attitude of eighteenth-century society which Howard himself stigmatized by referring to Fénelon's words: 'The prosperous turn away their eyes from the miserable, not through insensibility, but because the sight is an interruption of their gaiety!'[2]

The same sense of social responsibility led Howard to his second object, his investigations into the *lazarettos*. This book is a valuable source for the history of medicine as well as for prison history—an early illustration of the close connexion between social reform and the advancement of medical knowledge. He asked Dr. Aikin and other friends among the medical profession to provide him with a questionnaire on the probable causes and the best treatment of the plague. He submitted this questionnaire to French, Italian, Greek, Turkish, and Jewish doctors. Afterwards English experts examined their replies. Beside many symptoms of ignorance and superstition there are some remarkable observations. The great majority of the witnesses agreed that the plague spreads by contagion. They would burn certain shrubs and herbs in the sick rooms, they would leave the clothes of infected people in the open air for a number of days; and they wondered whether infection was the sole or only the contributory cause of the illness, because they found that among people who had been exposed to the same source of contagion many were infected, but some did not fall ill at all.

[1] W. E. Lecky, *History of England* (1878–90), vi. 258.

[2] *State of Prisons* (1st ed. 1777), p. 68 n.

Such a thorough study of relevant facts and their unbiased presentation are the main characteristics of Howard's work. It was Howard who first applied to the field of social distress the empirical method of collecting and comparing personal experience. Prison by prison he described every particular in the same well-ordered way, so that all items are comparable with one another, and the reader might trace every topic through the whole amount of collected materials. The numerous repetitions of his journeys enabled him to follow up the further development of prison conditions. Valuable figures on English prison population anticipate criminal statistics. Howard's greatness lay in the modesty by which he confined himself to a mere presentation of reliable facts. 'What attention these facts deserve,' he said, 'and what measure it may be advisable to adopt in consequence of them, I leave to the determination of the proper judges.'[1] Or in even more humble words: 'I am the plodder who goes about to collect materials for men of genius to make use of.'[2] A century later a leading English statistician called Howard 'the discoverer or inventor of that modern method of dealing with social wrongs which is gradually building up for us a civilisation deserving of the name'.[3] A straight line, indeed, links Howard's prison account with modern social surveys.

Beyond these mere statements of facts, however, Howard had a definite conception on what line prison reform should go. Prison buildings, in his opinion, should afford sufficient security, spacious rooms, and satisfactory sanitary conditions. Prison officials should be reliable servants, appointed, salaried, and controlled by an independent public authority. There should be a reformative regimen of a healthy diet and of reasonable work, suitable education and religious exercises. Howard's views on prison discipline were remarkably realistic, and differed widely from the theoretical speculations of contemporary writers. Blackstone, for instance, advocating solitary confinement, could not imagine any other punishment, 'in which terror, benevolence, and reformation are more happily blended together.... Solitude will awaken reflection, confinement will banish temptation, sobriety will restore vigour, and labour will beget a habit of industry.'[4] Howard required that

[1] *Account of the principal Lazarettos* (1789), p. 2.

[2] John Aikin, *A View of the Character and Public Services of the late John Howard* (1792), p. 227.

[3] W. Guy, 38 *J. Stat. Soc.* 430–7, 436.

[4] Clitherow, Preface to Blackstone's *Report of Cases* (1781), I. xxii; Davis A. Lockmiller, *Sir William Blackstone* (1938), p. 130.

'if it is difficult to prevent criminals from being together in daytime, they should by all means be separated at night'. He would not deny that 'solitude and silence are favourable to reflection, and may probably lead to repentance'.[1] But, for Howard, all prison problems were in their substance nothing but the life and work of men in prison. It was his sincere conviction that useful labour is the essence of every sound prison discipline. Thus far he was in accordance with a well-established tradition among Quakers to provide Friends who had to go to prison with reasonable work.[2] It does, however, much credit to Howard's practical insight, that, in his opinion, prisoners could be reasonably occupied, not in isolated cells, but only in proper yards and workshops. He suggested that every prison should be provided with these facilities. He himself defined his general attitude towards solitary confinement in these words: 'The intention of this—I mean by day as well as by night—is either to reclaim the most atrocious and daring criminal, to punish the refractory for crimes committed in prison, or to make a strong impression, in a short time, upon thoughtless and irregular young persons as faulty apprentices and the like.' Solitary confinement, for a long term, however, would be 'more than human nature can bear without the hazard of distraction and despair'. It would be 'repugnant to the Act which orders all persons in Houses of Correction to work, and for want of some employment in the day . . . health is injured, and a habit of idleness and inability to labour in future is in danger of being acquired'.[3] Nothing could be more erroneous than to call Howard a doctrinaire advocate of solitary confinement. With some vestige of truth one could rather call him an early advocate of indeterminate sentences. Referring to a Dutch practice he found it 'in every case wise and beneficial' to give the prisoner longer sentences with an intention of certain deductions upon their amendment.[4]

The spiritual background of Howard's work is characterized by a combination of the progressive tendencies of the Era of Enlightenment, and of his personal attitude as a faithful Christian. More and more the misuses of traditional criminal law and its reform on rational lines became a predominant subject of enlightened writers. One year after the first publication of Beccaria's *Essay*, his ideas spread all over the Continent by the French translation

[1] State of Prisons (3rd ed. 1784), p. 22.

[2] W. C. Braithwaite, *The second Period of Quakerism* (1919), pp. 64 and 568.

[3] *Account of Lazarettos*, l.c., p. 169 n. See further for a contemporary witness: J. Aikin, l.c., p. 171.

[4] *State of Prisons* (3rd ed. 1784), p. 22.

of Morellet. In the same year, 1765, the first German translation by J. I. Butschek appeared in Prague. In 1767 an English edition, translated from the Italian, appeared in London, supplemented by a 'commentary', which Voltaire had written one year before.[1] The anonymous translator, while referring to 'the excellence of our laws and government', where 'no examples of cruelty or oppression are to be found', gave as the principal reason for his publication the prison conditions of his country: 'the confinement of debtors, the filth and horror of our prisons, the cruelty of jailors, and the extortion of the petty officers of justice, to all which may be added the melancholy reflection that the number of criminals put to death in England is much greater than in any other part of Europe'. William Eden, later first Lord Auckland, wrote a rationalistic criticism of the traditional criminal law, based not upon the authority of the law of the land as it then stood, but upon 'the unwritten law of God, imprinted in the heart of man'. He found the idea of a vindictive justice 'shocking'—'public utility is the measure of human punishment'. Banishment, though 'often beneficial to the criminal', would be 'always injurious to the community'. Capital punishment was, in his opinion, not a punishment at all, 'but merely our last melancholy resource' to exterminate those whose continuance became inconsistent with the public safety. Imprisonment 'sinks useful subjects into burdens on the community, and has always a bad effect on their morals'. The throwing together of the accused and the convicted, of innocent and guilty people, would be 'contrary to public justice and public utility'. Special statutes should protect prisoners against arbitrariness and cruelty of prison officials—'for it must be confessed that jailers are, in general, a merciless race'.[2]

Within the framework of such contemporary ideas John Howard wrote his prison accounts. He often referred to William Eden's *Principles*, and he expressed his full agreement with the 'judicious Marquess' of Beccaria. Apparently from the Appendix to the English edition of Beccaria, he picked up a phrase of Voltaire without reference to his name. When Howard discussed the beneficial Dutch tradition of prison labour as a substitute for transportation, he quoted the 'professed maxim': 'Make men diligent, and they will be honest.' In the wording of the English

[1] *An Essay on Crime and Punishment. Transld. from the Italian, with a Commentary, attributed to Mons. de Voltaire, transld. from the French* (1767), further editions 1769, 1770, 1775, 1804.

[2] *Principles of Penal Law* (1771), p. 50 and *passim*.

translator, the French author said: 'Oblige men to work, and you certainly make them honest.' According to the context, Voltaire used this sentence as an argument for the English system of transportation![1] Howard apparently felt a personal distrust for the eminent representative of French enlightenment. From Geneva, in a letter to a friend, he complained of the corrupting influence which 'the principles of one of the vilest men' had on the 'ancient purity and splendour' of Swiss morals.[2] Howard himself was one of the outstanding enlightened humanitarians, but his conscious Christian faith distinguished him from contemporary deists. His friends called him 'a moderate Calvinist'. His letters reveal a man who in every occurrence of his daily life, through all the hardships of his journeys, and during an untiring life of devotion, regarded himself as an obedient follower in the steps of his Master.

John Howard had a deep influence on his own time as well as on posterity. The conscience of mankind, once awakened by Howard, has never been set at ease. Jeremy Bentham praised Howard as the man 'who died a martyr after living an apostle'.[3] In various countries Howard found literary successors. H. B. Wagnitz, a Lutheran pastor at Halle, dedicated his *Historical Account of noteworthy Houses of Correction in Germany* 'to the spirit of John Howard and to those over whom it hovers'. Howard's merits, he said, 'should be inscribed in Heaven with golden letters'. von Arnim, an enlightened man in the Prussian Administration of Justice, anonymously published an official memorandum on the state of penal institutions.[4] These and other reports only confirmed Howard's criticism on eighteenth-century prison conditions. Conspicuous differences in building conditions and facilities for work, insufficient separation between different types of prisoners, private interests of keepers and contractors instead of a public service by an independent authority—these were the prevailing evils. The moral standards of prison life were very low. Thefts within

[1] The original text of Voltaire reads as follows: 'Forcez les hommes au travail, vous les rendrez honnêtes gens.' *Commentaire sur le livre des délits et des peines. Œuvres complètes de Voltaire* (1784), xxix. 233. First hint to the source of this famous phrase by G. Radbruch, 24 *MoSchrKrim* 92.

[2] James Brown, l.c., p. 82.

[3] J. Bentham, *Works*, ed. by Bowring, iv. 121.

[4] C. E. Wächter, *Über Zuchthäuser und Zuchthausstrafen* (1786); H. B. Wagnitz, *Historische Nachrichten über die merkwürdigsten Zuchthäuser in Deutschland* (1791–4); von Arnim, *Bruchstücke über Verbrechen und Strafen* (1801–3). First German edition of John Howard: *Über Gefängnisse und Zuchthäuser*, aus dem Englischen mit Zusätzen und Anmerkungen von G. L. W. Köster (1780).

prison walls and embezzlement of prison clothes were daily occurrences. As von Arnim said, a prison was but 'a nursery garden of temptation'. Both authors combined their accounts with reformative suggestions. Wagnitz did not refrain from advocating severe penalties in order to deter the criminal from committing further offences, and for that purpose he recommended scanty food and hard labour. On the other hand, he required, on principle, that human personality should be acknowledged even in the criminal, and he suggested moral instruction and emphasized the importance of the personnel. There should be seminaries for the training of the staff, and a reasonable after-care, instead of the traditional oath of the peace. 'After all,' he said, 'the security of the State may be the principal object of criminal law, but one ought not to forget that by reforming the criminal the security of the State would also be promoted, and other people not only warned but even confirmed in their good feelings.' von Arnim, as a practical administrator, saw reformation not so much as a moral process, but as a civil readjustment. This, however, should by no means consist of external and superficial drill. In his opinion the most effective motive for human behaviour would be hope—the only power which stimulates the moral activity of men.

The influence of this movement went even farther. Wagnitz provoked the passionate outcry of J. C. Reil against the miseries and distress of the insane and lunatic. Only too long they had, with prisoners, shared gaols and dungeons, chains and fetters, indiscriminately heaped together—'like the Digest without any system, or confused like the strange ideas of their disturbed minds'. Reil's *Rhapsodies on a Psychic Cure Method* with its strange mixture of enlightened ideas and romantic enthusiasm was one of the historic documents of the dawn of modern psychiatry.[1] Under the shadow of the French Revolution, and even suspect to ardent Republicans, P. Pinel (1745–1826) had just freed the patients of the Bicêtre from their chains and inaugurated his conservative 'wait and see method', one of the first genuine cases of the treatment, by observation, of mental disturbances.[2] At the same time William Tuke of York founded the Retreat, a fine outcome of humanitarian Quaker initiative. 'Not the slightest idea of

[1] J. C. Reil, *Rapsodien über die Anwendung der psychischen Kurmethode auf Geisteszerrüttungen* (1803). See also M. Lenz, *Geschichte der Kgl. Friedrich Wilhelm Universität zu Berlin* (1910), i. 53–60, and A. Boldt, *Stellung und Bedeutung der Rapsodien von Reil in der Geschichte der Psychiatrie* (1936).

[2] G. Zilboorg and G. W. Henry, *History of Medical Psychology* (1941), pp. 319 et seq.

a prison, but that of a big agricultural estate!'—this was the description of a Swiss visitor who drew Pinel's attention to the new foundation.[1] The same reformative tendency linked together prison reform and the new way of mental treatment. These humane methods gave, for the first time, an opportunity to study the true state of mental disturbances unaffected by the exciting and deteriorating effects of oppression and restraint. Though in the early stage even harsh devices were suggested in order to break through the stupor and the inaccessible mind of the criminal and the insane, it was the first step in replacing mechanical force by psychological insight and by an appeal to the moral personality of man.

The immediate practical results of Howard's work on English penal administration were rather small. The Popham Acts were, in Howard's own time, strictly observed in fifteen prisons out of 130.[2] The gaol fever, at least, which even in 1783 spread to parts of the general population, was almost entirely eradicated. But in general, the principal sources of evil remained almost unaltered: the private interests of keepers and gaolers, the insufficient co-operation of magistrates, and the lack of any centralized administration and control. Some few progressive followers of Howard's ideas worked for better prison conditions in their counties, like Sir George Onesiphorus Paul in Gloucestershire and Sir Thomas Beevor in Norfolk. In the towns things moved even more slowly. In 1812 nine-tenths of all prisons outside the county jurisdiction remained in a position similar to that in which they were in Howard's time.[3]

Meanwhile, however, the object of prison reform itself began to change. From the mere negative attempt to prevent contagion and deterioration among the different types of prisoners, it gradually turned into the positive task of developing reasonable methods of discipline and treatment for the readjustment of criminals. In Howard's time three-fifths of all inmates of English gaols were imprisoned for debt. Howard himself 'hearing the cry of the miserable, devoted his time to their relief . . . to this important national concern of alleviating the distresses of poor debtors and other prisoners'.[4] The American War of Independence

[1] Samuel Tuke, *Description of the Retreat* (1813); D. H. Tuke, *Chapters in the History of the Insane in the British Isles* (1882), pp. 112 et seq., 117; R. M. Jones, *Later Periods of Quakerism* (1921), i. 370.

[2] W. Guy, 38 *J. Stat. Soc.* 435.

[3] S. and B. Webb, pp. 56 and 64.

[4] *State of Prisons* (3rd ed. 1784), p. 469.

brought transportation of criminals to the New World to a standstill, and this had an effect similar to the reduction of capital offences on the Continent: it filled prisons with criminals, and confronted the administration with the new question, how to adapt imprisonment to the exigencies of a reasonable punishment and of a social rehabilitation. A first expression of these new tendencies was the Penitentiary Act of 1779, the work of Eden and Blackstone.[1] In its detailed regulations it is a strange mixture of enlightened and progressive ideas with a spirit of suspicion which for ever regards the prisoner as the desperate and rebellious inmate of the old gaols. 'Solitary confinement, accompanied by well regulated labour and religious instruction, might be the means, under Providence, not only of deterring others from the commission of the like crimes, but also of reforming of the individuals and inuring them to habits of industry.' There should be three classes of prisoners, with a gradual relaxation in confinement and labour. Visiting committees should inspect the houses every fortnight; they had to deal with serious cases of breach of discipline, and, under certain conditions, to report to the Judges at the next Assizes for shortening of sentences. On the other hand, labour should be 'of the hardest and most servile form', and of such a kind as to involve 'the least risk of being spoilt by ignorance and neglect and obstinacy, and where materials and tools are not easily stolen or embezzled'. Obviously, under such conditions, there was no variety in the kinds of work suitable. What the lawgivers suggested was treading a wheel, or drawing in a capstan, or the old rasping of logwood. Clothing should not only facilitate discovery in the case of escapes, but should also be designed to humiliate the wearer. Even the chaplain, when he—with the Governor's leave—visits the prisoners, 'shall not interfere with their stated hours of labour'.

The whole project of such a new 'penitentiary' never came into practical existence. Paul's reform work in Gloucestershire relied upon the principal suggestions of this Act. Howard himself was a member of a committee which was appointed to select a suitable site for a 'penitentiary', but after Blackstone's death he resigned. From 1787, after the discovery of Australia, a new period of transportation began, and consequently the interest in penitentiary institutions at home dwindled.

On the Continent a similar project had the same negative result. The 'Prussian General Plan for the Introduction of a

[1] 19 Geo. III, c. 74.

better Criminal Justice and for the Reform of Prisons', 1804, suggested a strict separation between remand prisoners and convicts, a classification by three classes, constructive work which would fit the prisoner for an industrious life in society, and a certain participation of laymen in prison administration.[1] But, like its English predecessor, this plan had an historical importance only. Both attempts are symptoms of a new effort towards a penal policy which hoped to turn criminals into 'good subjects and profitable members of society'. For the moment the Napoleonic Wars overshadowed every sphere of social life and hampered all reformative and progressive movements. On the Continent the prevailing French influence as well as the attempts to organize the resistance against the conqueror produced new forms of public administration. The cause of penal reform, however, needed more than merely administrative measures. It had to wait for a fresh spiritual stimulus which could not originate but from a new generation of bold and devoted pioneers.

[1] L. Frede, p. 543.

CHAPTER IV

THE TRIUMPH OF SEPARATE CONFINEMENT

AT the beginning of the nineteenth century, for the first time, the New World contributed to the cause of penal reform. The development of Pennsylvanian criminal law and penal administration raised a growing interest among European experts. Reports about the achievement of the Quaker community had a lasting influence on the theoretical discussion and the legislative and administrative development of penal policy in most European countries.

Since 1676 the Delaware district had been under the Duke of York's Laws—a Puritan conception of English seventeenth-century law.[1] Corporal punishment was frequently applied as an alternative to damages and fines. Capital offences included such sinful acts as 'denying the true God', sodomy and buggery, children smiting their parents, adultery by a married person—but not larceny. When in 1682 William Penn performed the 'Holy Experiment' and founded the Province of Pennsylvania, the Assembly enacted a new 'Great Law'. This had been drafted, in consultation with Algernon Sidney, by William Penn himself. Its foundation was the celebrated *Frame of Government*, supplemented by some 'laws agreed upon in England' with prospective emigrants.[2] 'They weakly err', said Penn in the preface, 'that think there is no other use of government than correction, which is the coarsest part of it', compared with 'the more free and mental right . . . to cherish those that do well'. The Quaker criminal law was scarcely less theocratic than the Puritan conception. 'Offences against God', such as swearing, cursing, lying, profane talking, and drunkenness, ranked as equal with murder and other felonies and should be severely punished according to further 'appointment' by the competent colonial authorities, since 'the wildness and looseness of the people provoke the indignation of God against a country'. At the same time corporal punishment was replaced by imprisonment. Prisons should be workhouses, i.e. they were to be organized according to the model of a good House of Correction. Prisons should be 'free as to fees, food and lodging'. All fines

[1] Full text in *The Colonial Laws of New York* (1894), i. 6 et seq.

[2] Full text in *Minutes of the Provincial Council of Pennsylvania* (1838), xxi–xxxiv. See also Bonamy Dobrée, *William Penn, Quaker and Pioneer* (1932).

should be moderate, saving man's 'containement'. Instead of suffering the capital penalty felons should be liable to make compensation, if necessary by their work as bondsmen in the common prison or workhouse. By this bold vision William Penn anticipated penal reform by a century.[1] The idea, that all serious crimes were to be punished by a form of imprisonment which implied occupation with useful work, went far beyond the English Order of 1630 which provided for the employment in the nearby House of Correction of minor offenders from the county gaol.[2] That Penn's new concept was due to personal impressions of Dutch Houses of Correction is a common tradition, but not supported by historical evidence.[3] Only murder, by an amendment of 1683, was made capital 'according to the law of God'. This legislative experiment, however, did not survive its author. In the year of Penn's death, 1718, Governor Keith persuaded the Assembly to reintroduce English criminal law. Numerous offences were made capital—again with the exception of larceny. Corporal punishment replaced imprisonment. This was a compromise by which in criminal proceedings the Quaker hoped to obtain the right to give a solemn affirmation instead of taking an oath.[4] There is no evidence of any complaints that an unjustifiable leniency of the original law did not provide sufficient protection of society. After 1718 the Philadelphia prisons, deprived of any reformative purpose, suffered from the same decay as gaols in Europe. Looking back, the Commissioners of 1826 stated that the alteration of the law seemed 'in practice to have restored the dominion of idleness in the interior of our prisons'. According to the concurrent testimony of all who remembered it, the provincial prison of Philadelphia was a scene of profligacy and licence, with all the evils predominant that are well known from the history of European prisons.[5]

It was not until the year of the Declaration of Independence,

[1] H. E. Barnes, *Repression of Crime* (1926), p. 43 and *passim*, also for the discussion which follows.

[2] Robinson, p. 61, presumes that the relevant clause in the Great Law was influenced by the Order of 1630.

[3] The source of the general tradition is probably George W. Smith, *Defence of the Pennsylvanian System of Solitary Confinement of Prisoners* (1829; 2nd ed. 1833), who thought a Dutch influence on William Penn 'highly probable'. This statement has been accepted by R. Vaux, *Brief Sketch of the Origin and History of the State Penitentiary at Philadelphia* (1872), p. 28. William Penn's own account of his 'Travels in Holland and Germany', undertaken in 1677 (*Selected Works* (4th ed. 1825), ii. 398–503) is exclusively concerned with personal affairs of the Friends on the Continent, and does not mention Houses of Correction.

[4] 8 Geo. I, c. 6 (1721).

[5] Barnes, l.c., pp. 95, 99.

1776, that Richard Wistar, a Quaker, organized the Philadelphia Society for Distressed Prisoners, the first prison society in the world and a model for similar agencies in other countries. After an interruption in 1783, the Society was re-established in 1786 as the Philadelphia Society for Alleviating the Miseries of Public Prisons.[1] A letter of dedication sent to John Howard in 1788 bears witness of the obligation which the Society felt to the English pioneer. There were also references to Sir Thomas Beevor, one of Howard's English followers. The Society wished that 'such degrees and modes of punishment might be discovered and suggested, as might, instead of continuing habits of vice, become the means of restoring our fellow-creatures to virtue and happiness'.[2] These efforts met with the interest and co-operation of an able jurist, William Bradford.[3] New criminal legislation was enacted, for which the original Quaker conception served as an important precedent. From 1786 to 1794, gradually all capital offences except murder were made punishable by imprisonment. Whipping-post and pillory disappeared. Prison methods were to be adapted to the new task of providing a reasonable institutional discipline for serious offenders. As to the principal remedy, the Society suggested 'solitary confinement to hard labour'.[4]

For the last decade of the eighteenth century, Caleb Lownes was in charge of the Philadelphia prison. He was a Quaker and a sincere admirer of Beccaria and John Howard.[5] In 1796 a first account of the new prison discipline appeared, written by the French author Larochefoucauld Liancourt.[6] He found in the prison in Walnut Street what he presumed would be 'Howard's practical system applied to the prisons of Philadelphia'. Self-reflection was expected to be the principal means of the prisoner's amendment. Arbitrariness and ill treatment were suppressed. Productive labour should contribute to the maintenance of the institution, overcome idleness and inaction, and provide a fund to be at hand for the prisoner's release. There were two different kinds of discipline: as a substitute for capital punishment, atrocious criminals were kept in solitary confinement for a considerable part

[1] N. K. Teeters, *They were in Prison. A History of the Philadelphia Prison Society* (1937).

[2] Barnes, l.c., pp. 95 and 99.

[3] W. Bradford, *Enquiry how far the Punishment of Death is necessary in Pennsylvania.* (Reprinted London, 1795.)

[4] Barnes, l.c., p. 126.

[5] Caleb Lownes, *An Account of the Penal Laws of Pennsylvania* (1799).

[6] *Des prisons de Philadelphie. Par un Européen* (1796); Duc de Liancourt, *A comparative View of Mild and Sanguinary Laws, and the good Effects of the former, exhibited in the present Economy of the Prison in Philadelphia* (1796). The German edition has the title *Howards praktisches System, auf die Gefängnisse von Philadelphia angewandt* (1797).

of their prison terms. This practice was intended to promote 'that calm contemplation which brings repentance', and reminded the visitor of fasting and abstinence among certain religious sects. Apparently, this group were not allowed either to work or to receive visitors. Prisoners convicted of minor offences, and felons after the expiration of the solitary stage of their confinement, worked in association, either practising their own trade, or engaged in some of the traditional prison occupations such as cutting and polishing marble stones, cutting log-wood, carding wool, beating hemp, manufacturing nails. Disciplinary punishment consisted in transferring the prisoner to solitary confinement. The author claimed excellent results for this new 'House of Amendment'; the number of recidivists seemed almost negligible. An English observer, Captain Turnbull, shared this favourable impression. He too praised the good order, decency, and fortunate results of the prison of Philadelphia.[1] This acknowledgement confirmed the Philadelphian reformers in their efforts to develop the new prison system. In 1818 they erected the Western Penitentiary at Pittsburgh, following the pattern of a celebrated prison plan of Jeremy Bentham who himself referred to Captain Turnbull's favourable report for a confirmation of his own ideas (Fig. I). In 1829 the Eastern Penitentiary at Cherry Hill was opened. It had 400 single cells with individual exercise yards. The construction of several cell wings radiating from the centre of the building was designed by John Havilland (Fig. II). He was said to have followed the English model of Ipswich Prison. In 1833 the same architect built a similar institution, the New Jersey State Prison at Trenton. In the United States it was these three prisons only which strictly maintained what has been called the Pennsylvanian system.[2]

The new prisons provided an opportunity for keeping prisoners in their cells during the whole prison term. Officials and other trustworthy persons were bound to visit prisoners—a remarkable step from solitary to separate confinement. It was meant as a separation from bad surroundings only, and presumed to make the prisoner susceptible to wholesome influence. This new system raised interest and praise among European prison experts. During the thirties many visitors went to America and collected first-hand information for the prison administrations of their countries. England sent W. Crawford; France, A. de Tocqueville, the great

[1] R. I. Turnbull, *A Visit to the Philadelphia Prison* (1797).

[2] McKelvey, p. 12.

interpreter of American democracy, G. M. de Beaumont, and F. A. Demetz, head of the model institution of Mettrai; Belgium, E. Ducpétiaux; and Germany, Dr. Julius.[1] They all reported more or less in favour of what they saw in the new Pennsylvanian cellular prisons. One visitor, however, dissented from the general enthusiasm—Charles Dickens. The celebrated historian of the distress and the scurrilous life among English debtor prisoners saw the Pennsylvanian penitentiaries in 1842. He admitted the

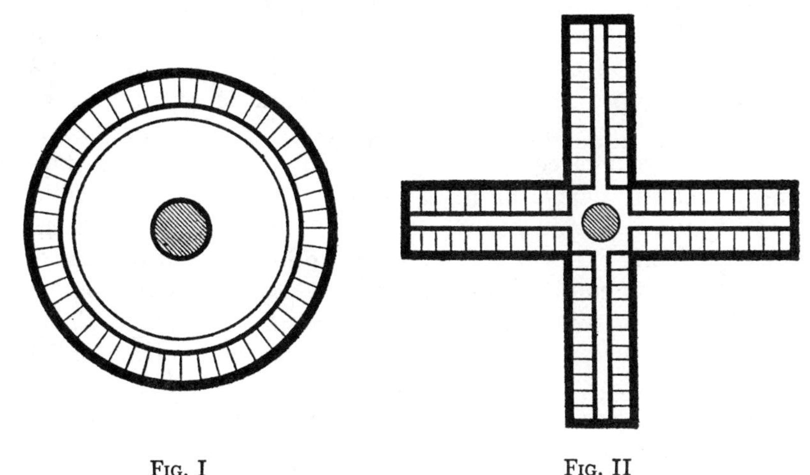

Fig. I Fig. II

Fig. I
Bentham's Panopticon.
Western Penitentiary, Pittsburgh, 1818.

Fig. II
Havilland's Ray System.
Eastern Penitentiary, Cherry Hill, 1829. Pentonville, 1842.
New Jersey State Prison, Trenton, 1833. Bruchsal, 1848.
Moabit, 1849.

humane and reformative impulse of the Friends of Philadelphia —'but they do not know what it is they are doing'.[2] He drew the attention to the disastrous effect which years of enforced solitude had on the prisoner's mind. With the imagination of a poet he developed a psychology of solitary confinement, tracing the changing stages from the first initial shock, through depression, oversensibility, and detachment from reality, up to the helpless state

[1] W. Crawford, *Report on the Penitentiaries in the United States* (1834); G. A. de Beaumont and A. de Tocqueville, *Du système pénitentiaire aux États Unis* (1833); F. A. Demetz et Blouet, *Rapport sur les pénitentiaires des États Unis* (1839); E. Ducpétiaux, *Du progrès et de l'état actuel de la réforme pénitentiaire aux États Unis, en France, en Suisse, en Angleterre et en Belgique* (1837–8); Julius, *Nordamerikas sittliche Zustände* (1840). See also G. W. Pierson, *Tocqueville and Beaumont in America* (1938), pp. 93, 206, 426, 700 et seq.

[2] Charles Dickens, *American Notes* (ed. Nelson and Sons, 1925), vii. 105–21.

of mental derangement on the final day of release. No wonder that this heresy raised angry criticism from the orthodox admirers of the cellular system.[1]

The predilection for the Pennsylvanian system was more common among European observers than among American reformers themselves. The Friends of Philadelphia did not represent the entire body of American penology. They met with a strong opposition from the Boston Prison Discipline Society which for many years was under the influence of Louis Dwight. This eminent man approached the cause of prison reform as a mission field, visiting gaols, preaching and teaching, initiating Bible reading—and providing prisoners with industrial work by contracts with private employers. This was contrary to the ideal of calm meditation in constant solitary confinement. During daytime, especially for work, prisoners had to share common workshops. After the model institution at Westerfield, Connecticut, two New York State Prisons became the historic starting-points for the new system: Auburn, opened in 1823, and Sing Sing two years later, both with hundreds of inside cells designed as single dormitories. By 1835 ten American prisons had introduced a similar scheme.[2] In Europe, however, this so-called Auburn system was discredited by the rigid discipline which Warden Lynde enforced at Auburn. The rule of silence during the hours of common work was maintained by a permanent watch and a constant threat of flogging. Preoccupied with the idea of solitary confinement, European penologists interpreted the Auburn or 'silent system' as a mere variation of the true Pennsylvanian system, with disciplinary rules substituted for cell-walls. In the United States it met with an increasing approval of prison administrators owing to the better opportunities for prison work, the lower costs of building and maintenance, and, not least, to the

[1] J. Field, *Prison Discipline and the Advantage of the Separate System of Imprisonment* (1848), i. 105 et seq., speaks of the 'shameful advantage which has been taken of the general want of information by a writer whose works have obtained a wider circulation than his veracity deserves'. Ibid., references to other contemporary critics. John Clay, prison chaplain to the Preston gaol, in a letter to Mary Carpenter, refers to Dickens and some remarks in *Hard Times*: 'He is not the only man I have met with who prefers to rely on his own theories and fancies rather than on well ascertained facts.' W. L. Clay, *The Prison Chaplain, a Memoir of the Rev. John Clay* (1861), p. 620. The judgement of modern legal history is more favourable. Sir William Holdsworth sees as Dickens's true object a description of 'the actual effects of the rules of law upon the men and women of his day', and he acknowledges that the author of the *Pickwick Papers* has portrayed the state of imprisonment of debtors 'with a vividness which is only equalled by its truth'. W. Holdsworth, *Charles Dickens as a Legal Historian* (1928), pp. 7 and 141.

[2] McKelvey, p. 18 and *passim*.

missionary zeal of Louis Dwight and his New England followers. A more appreciative judgement of the Pennsylvanian system came from without. Francis Lieber published an English translation of Beaumont and Tocqueville's Report with some commentating notes.[1] Modern American prison history, looking back at the Pennsylvanian experiment, does full justice to that 'first permanent American break with contemporary juristic savagery'.[2] 'However mistaken the Philadelphia Friends have been on some points'— a recent American text-book states—'their contribution to the welfare of prisoners was as great as that ever made by any one band of prison reformers.'[3]

During the first decades of the nineteenth century the general discussion on prison reform degenerated into a competition between different abstract systems. The time was unaware of that prudent warning which William Penn had given in his *Frame of Government*: 'Governments,' he said, 'like clocks, go from the motion men give them.' Instead, a rationalistic age was in search of a system which, once properly established, was expected to warrant satisfactory results by its mere functioning. Jeremy Bentham left his mark in the history of prison reform. The great Utilitarian always felt a sincere admiration for Beccaria. He had still more in common with him than a keen interest in a rationalized penal policy. The principle of the greatest happiness of the greatest number, the fundamental standard and aim of Utilitarian philosophy, had been anticipated by Beccaria's celebrated *Essay*. Among the abundant variety of Bentham's proposals there was also a patent solution of the prison problem. It has been said it was the 'masterpiece' which raised the optimism of its author to the extreme limit.[4] His brother Samuel designed a pattern of workshops which stimulated Jeremy to the conception of an ideal penitentiary. In 1787, by a series of letters written from Russia, he developed his scheme for 'a mill grinding rogues honest and idle men industrious'.[5] The whole treatise was published in 1791 under the title *Panopticon*.[6] This strange word expresses the gist of the new

[1] *On the Penitentiary System in the United States. Translated from the French with an Introduction, Notes and Additions*, by F. L. (1833). See also R. Harley, *Francis Lieber* (1899). [2] Barnes, l.c., p. 101. [3] Robinson, p. 76.

[4] L. Stephen, *The English Utilitarians, I, Jeremy Bentham* (1900), p. 200. See also J. W. Allan, 'Jeremy Bentham', in: F. J. C. Hearnshaw, *Social and Political Ideas of the Revolutionary Era* (1931), pp. 181–200; C. Phillipson, *Three Criminal Law Reformers* (1923). [5] Letter to Brissot, Bentham's *Works*, ed. by Bowring, x. 226.

[6] *Panopticon or the Inspection House, Works*, iv. 37 et seq. See also *Principles of Penal Law* (translated from the *Traité de Législation* by Dumont), *Works* ed. by Bowring, i. 355 et seq.

proposal: a building and a prison régime based upon the principle of an omnipresent inspection. Several storeys of cell-wings in the form of circles should run round the inspector's lodge as their centre, each cell closed to the centre by an iron grate and lighted by a window at the external wall, so that from the centre the inspector is able to look at any time into any cell he likes. In Bentham's original scheme these cells were intended for solitary confinement. Strict precautions should be taken to prevent any prisoner from seeing his fellow inmates. Later on he abandoned this rigid idea, apparently in order to reduce the enormous costs of prison buildings providing single cells for every prisoner. 'It was high time', he said, 'to inquire what the advantages were that must be so dearly paid for.'[1] He made virtue out of necessity and accepted the arguments of 'the illustrious' John Howard that permanent solitary confinement is obnoxious as a permanent régime, but might be useful as a temporary disciplinary measure.[2] It would therefore be unwise 'to expend a useful instrument of discipline in waste'. Instead Bentham suggested 'a mitigated seclusion by divisions': small groups of two, three, or four and even six inmates in every cell. He thought to make these carefully selected associations useful 'for the performance of reciprocal services, for the exercise of the affections, and the formation of habits favourable to reformation'. 'A feeling of honour might be excited even in the abode of ignominy.'[3] In his critical comments Bentham was more realistic. Like other reformers he denounced the old gaols as 'academies of crime'. Originally he was one of the supporters of Eden's Bill and the Act of 1779. Eventually, however, he objected to the principle of hard labour which, according to this Act, should aggravate the oppressive character of the punishment. 'Industry', he said, 'is a blessing—why paint it as a curse?' The prisoner should be 'taught to love labour, instead of being taught to loath it'.[4] This wise suggestion, however, was almost outweighed by a second objection, a strange consequence of his utilitarian prejudice. Public authorities, governing the prison, he thought, would result in an intolerable 'patronage'; he preferred a private contractor responsible for the prisoners and profiting by their work: such 'joining of interest with duty' seemed to him 'the strongest cement which can be found'.[5] Finally he confronted the

[1] Postscript to *Panopticon*, l.c., footnote to p. 138; see further, pp. 71 et seq.
[2] *Works*, iv. 121.
[3] Ibid. i. 499 et seq.
[4] Ibid. iv. 144.
[5] Ibid., p. 125.

prospects of his panopticon with the sinister reports on the new transportation to Australia. He met this evil in its essence, and branded it as a policy of getting rid of the responsibility which the State and the community owe to the neglected and criminal within their midst.[1] On the other hand, he found confirmation of what he expected a prison régime in a panopticon would be in the reports of Larochefoucauld Liancourt and Captain Turnbull on the peaceful order, the regular activity, and the general state of health and decency in Pennsylvanian prisons.[2]

As to immediate practical results during his lifetime, he fought in vain. With his ardent zeal, always characteristic, he repeated, deepened, and explained his arguments. He offered himself to France to become a builder and an inspector of such a model institution. In 1794 Parliament adopted his scheme, but before a prison was erected in accordance with his suggestions, after seventeen years of an unsuccessful struggle, a new committee reported against the scheme. They feared the contractual basis would lead again to the old abuses of farming out prisoners and paupers. Cell communities up to six inmates seemed incompatible with the principle of separate confinement as it was laid down in the Act of 1779. When in 1812 Millbank was definitely planned, the whole organization differed widely from Bentham's suggestions.[3]

After Bentham's death his pupils and followers initiated a new era of penal reform. The rationalizing tendency of this movement as well as many particulars bear witness to Bentham's spirit. His project of a cellular prison so constructed that even a small staff guarantees a constant and effective supervision, stimulated the development of a new prison style. The predilection of the age for the separate system is a typical expression of that trust in abstract legal institutions with which Bentham had imbued a whole generation. When by the triumph of the separate system the whole prison problem seemed to degenerate into a mere question of architecture, Bentham had certainly the main responsibility. His favourite panopticon-idea tempted him to the enthusiastic pronouncement by which he introduced as well as finished his treatise: 'Morals reformed, health preserved, industry invigorated, instruction diffused, public burdens lightened, economy seated,

[1] *Panopticon versus New South Wales. Letter written to Lord Pelham* (1802), *Works*, iv. 173 et seq. See also i. 497; F. L. W. Wood, 'Jeremy Bentham versus New South Wales', 19 *Royal Australian Historical Society, Journal and Proceedings* 329.

[2] *Works*, i. 502.

[3] 52 Geo. III, c. 44.

as it were, upon a rock, the Gordian knot of the Poor Laws not cut, but untied,—all by a simple idea in Architecture!'[1]

Bentham's panopticon was what an American author called 'one of the curiosities of prison history'. There were, however, still deeper causes for the growing appreciation of the separate system. Solitary, or at least separate, confinement meant a definite end of, and a marked contrast to, the disgusting promiscuity of the old gaols which for so long had been the unquestioned source of all evils. A calm atmosphere and a proper order and discipline seemed at once to replace the brutality as well as the revelries which had prevailed among the traditional prison community. In 1846 John Field still contrasted, as a credit to the cellular system, 'the cleanliness, order, and, above all, the moral discipline which therein prevail with the confusion, filthiness and demoralisation which in times past rendered our prisons the disgrace and the scourge of our land'.[2] The only other alternative seemed to be the unnatural rule of silence, ruthlessly enforced by a brutal discipline like that of Warden Lynde at Auburn. The solitude of the prison cell was expected to protect the first-offender against the contagious and deteriorating influence of his fellow prisoners, to lead the corrigible to a wholesome self-reflection, true repentance, and moral reformation, and at the same time, by the intensity of its seclusion, to demonstrate in an unmistakable and most impressive way the strong reaction of public authority against the criminal. The following statement of a leading German prison administrator illustrates the attitude prevailing through the nineteenth century: 'Common imprisonment means to punish the prisoner for his offence by training him, at the expense of the public, for further crimes, while solitary confinement most perfectly suits the moral foundation as well as the political purpose of legal punishment.'[3]

It was still a long way from the old gaol to the new cellular prison. On the Continent, with the rise of modern forms of public administration after the Napoleonic Wars, large central institutions were erected, mostly by converting castles or monasteries into prisons. Gradually the hygienic standards and the supply of fresh air and water improved. A semi-military routine guaranteed order, punctuality, and cleanliness. In Prussia the first of the newly organized prisons, Rawitsch (1810), was the model institu-

[1] *Works*, iv. 39 and 66.

[2] John Field, *Prison Discipline* (1846), p. 1 (2nd ed. in two vols., 1848).

[3] K. Krohne, *Lehrbuch der Gefängniskunde* (1889), p. 250.

tion for others to come. The Regulation for Rawitsch is reminiscent of the abortive 'General Plan' of 1804. It provided for two classes of prisoners. Since the staff mostly consisted of ex-servicemen, a military tone prevailed. A prison was organized like an army battalion. This involved not only good order and strict discipline, but also a certain formal justice and a suggestion of rough benevolence towards 'the men'. Prisoners continued to live day and night in community with their fellow inmates. While, undoubtedly, the new prisons were much better than the local gaols, the military routine was a mass treatment with no opportunity for any individual approach, nor even for any successful attempt to study and distinguish the various characters of the inmates. Prison officials were confined to the duty of watching and guarding the prisoner, and had no concern with his personal development and social readjustment. Even the disastrous influence of the worst elements could not be checked efficiently. In the end these partial reforms corroborated only the arguments of those who advocated the new separate system.[1]

In England, some progressive justices, followers of John Howard, had introduced a régime of solitary confinement in certain reformed prisons. The experience from these experiments, however, only confirmed Howard's insight into the incompatibility of solitary confinement and constructive work. With the introduction of handicrafts and industrial work into some of the reformed prisons, common workshops were installed where prisoners worked in association. Peel's Prison Act, 1823, bears witness to the ideas at the beginning of the Age of Reform.[2] The whole law concerning prisons was consolidated. The Act increased the responsibility of Justices of the Peace. Gaolers were made independent of fees, and set on fixed salaries. A general standard of space, cleanliness, order, and discipline was prescribed. But the law did not provide for any central administrative control, nor did it apply to prisons not under county jurisdiction. As to the underlying principle, the Act relied on classification—a flexible conception which allowed for every form of association in common workshops. This practice, however, met with increasing criticism. Numerous critics held that such a prison factory with proper workshops and an earnings scheme to stimulate the prisoner's industry was attractive rather than punitive and deterrent. This sentiment gave rise to the strange recommendation of tread-mills and other

[1] Kriegsmann, pp. 56 et seq.
[2] 4 Geo. IV, c. 64.

'labour machines'. Others complained of a relapse into the old evil prison community with its danger of contagion and mutual seduction, since taskmasters formed the groups less with regard to criminological principles than in order to organize work in a most profitable way. Finally the Industrial Revolution made an end to these early forms of profit-making prison work.[1]

Meanwhile the general development of criminal law tended to a definite solution of the prison problem. On the Continent the codification of criminal law, since the Prussian General Law of the Land, 1794, and the French *Code pénal*, 1810, resulted in a marked reduction of capital offences. Various forms of deprivation of liberty were adopted as the ordinary legal punishment for serious crimes, apart from the most dangerous assaults against personal and public safety which remained capital. In England there was still, according to the letter of the law, an appalling list of capital offences against property. Blackstone gave the number of 160 statutory capital offences, 'a melancholy truth . . . difficult to justify'. 'So dreadful a list,' he continued, 'instead of diminishing, increases the number of offenders!'[2] In the Parliamentary debates of the twenties, a figure of 200 was mentioned. During the Napoleonic era, till the dawn of the Age of Reform, all attempts to mitigate the law were doomed to failure.[3] Sir Samuel Romilly fought in vain, from his first great speech in 1808 on the frequency of capital punishment, up to his unsuccessful moves in 1810, 1811, and 1818. After his death, James Mackintosh took over his cause and raised this issue in the years between 1819 and 1822. Eventually Sir Robert Peel himself initiated new legislation, beginning with a merely permissive Act of 1823,[4] and then gradually reducing the list of capital offences. A characteristic achievement was the Act of 1832, which in the case of a number of offences against property replaced capital punishment by transportation for life.[5] The end was the Consolidation Acts of 1861 which established the law of capital punishment almost as it stands to-day with four serious violent crimes remaining capital.[6]

The actual number of executions showed not so great a difference as one might expect in view of the drastic change of the law.

[1] For the whole see S. and B. Webb, pp. 66 et seq.

[2] Blackstone, iv. 18.

[3] L. Radzinowicz, 63 *L.Q.R.* 94; Stephen, i. 472 et seq.; C. G. Oakes, *Sir Samuel Romilly* (1935); W. S. Holdsworth, 56 *L.Q.R.* 33, 208, 340, at pp. 42, 212 et seq.

[4] 4 Geo. IV, c. 48.

[5] 2 & 3 Will. IV, c. 62.

[6] 24 & 25 Vict., cc. 94–100.

Before the reform legislation executions were certainly frequent, but compared with the number of capital offences committed, they were exceptions rather than the rule. Peel himself gave the following figures: 1809–16, 4,126 persons sentenced to death, 536 executed; 1818–25, 7,770 sentenced to death, 579 executed.[1] It was less the alleged cruelty than the uncertainty, arbitrariness, and inefficiency of the traditional criminal law which was indicted by the reformers. They wished legal punishments framed in such a way that they could be expected to be applied without any hesitation and alteration. Consequently the reformed criminal statutes did not at once increase the number of convicts, but emphasized the importance of deprivation of liberty which now officially and in the letter of the law became the centre of the whole penal system. The time was in search of a true penitentiary, an institution and a régime which would combine a punitive and deterrent effect with a wholesome reformative treatment. Romilly still looked back to the Act of 1779, which was an attempt to restore criminals to the habits of industry and virtue, but 'had been a dead letter on the statute book, although it was a monument of eternal praise to those who had framed it'.[2] The reformers were very critical towards transportation. They questioned the proper management of the whole institution, 'a disgusting narrative of atrocious crimes and most severe and cruel punishments'.[3] On the other hand, they complained that it did not prove a deterrent. Fowell Buxton alleged that it 'rather offered a bounty and a temptation to crime'; he even accepted an argument of his adversary, Lord Ellenborough, who alleged that transportation was 'an easy migration by a summer's voyage from a worse situation to a better'.[4] These urgent needs led to the erection of a national penitentiary, Millbank, opened in 1821.[5] It was a costly piece of architecture, six cell-blocks in pentagon form, each adjacent to one side of a hexagon centre. This strange scheme called to mind the famous Maison de Force at Ghent. It was destined for all such transportable convicts as were not to be sent abroad or confined in the hulks. The prisoner was bound to serve

[1] *Speeches of Sir Robert Peel in the House of Commons* (1853), i. 403.

[2] Speech in the House of Commons on 9 May 1810. Cobbett's *Parliamentary Debates*, xvi. 945.

[3] Romilly in the House of Commons on 5 June 1810, Cobbett, xvii. 322; Jeremy Bentham, *Panopticon versus New South Wales* (1802), *Works*, iv. 173.

[4] F. Buxton in the House of Commons, 4 June 1822, Hansard, New Series, vii. 801.

[5] George Holford, *Thoughts on the Criminal Prisons of this Country* (1821); id., *An Account of the General Penitentiary at Millbank* (1828).

the first half of his term in solitude, and was then admitted to associated work. The number of inmates could be raised to 1,000. At the same time, there were still local prisons under the same deplorable conditions as described by John Howard. In 1810 Romilly complained of the indiscriminately mingled prison association in many a gaol and House of Correction. He spoke of the bad conditions of Newgate as of 'a monument of our disgrace and inhumanity' in close neighbourhood to the recently erected national monument of John Howard![1] Four years later, the Grand Jury of Middlesex openly represented Newgate as a public nuisance. Peel's Prison Act of 1823 did not remove the evil at once. To overcome the lack of immediate control, a new Act of 1835 created the office of prison inspectors—an important step in the direction of a national prison administration.[2] When one of the newly appointed inspectors went for his first tour to Scotland, Elizabeth Fry told him about her visit to Newgate in 1813, and sent him an account by her brother, Joseph Gurney, on *Prisons in Scotland and North England.*[3] Frederic Hill found these sixteen-year-old descriptions still a reliable guidebook to what he saw in many prisons within his venue.[4]

FIG. III
Maison de Force at Ghent, 1775.
Millbank, opened 1821.

It was this time in the thirties of the last century that the highly appreciative literature about the Pennsylvanian system appeared. These accounts met with susceptible and willing readers. Home Office officials as well as the newly appointed prison inspectors were in favour of the cellular system. Already in 1828, the Select Committee on Criminal Commitments and Convictions, under the chairmanship of Lord John Russell, made the long prison

[1] Cobbett's *Parliamentary Debates*, xvii. 324.

[2] 5 & 6 Will. IV, c. 38.

[3] J. J. Gurney, *Notes on a Visit made to some of the Prisons in Scotland and the North of England in Company with Elizabeth Fry* (1819). See also J. B. Braithwaite, *Memoirs of J. J. Gurney* (1854).

[4] Frederic Hill, *An Autobiography of Fifty Years in Time of Reform* (ed. by Constance Hill, 1894), pp. 117 et seq.

terms, administered in the traditional way, responsible for the alleged growth of the number of crimes committed. They preferred deterrent punishments to the pretence of reformation, held transportation for life 'an excellent punishment', and recommended a general application of a prison discipline similar to that developed by Sir Onesiphorus Paul in accordance with the ideas of the Act of 1779.

'Solitary confinement, without occupation, for prisoners confined for a single month; hard labour, with as little communication as possible for those imprisoned for a longer time. . . . This very simple system seems to combine all the requisites of a good prison discipline. . . . A month's solitary confinement, or six months upon the treadmill well applied, are more formidable than two years of lax imprisonment.'[1]

In 1838 William Crawford and Whitworth Russell, prison inspectors, reported highly in favour of separate confinement.[2] The mere safe seclusion of the prisoner in his cell, so different from his situation in the old prison community, would be an impressive manifestation of the strength of public authority. The prisoner had to abandon at once any idea of resistance and escape. Discipline could be maintained by a minimum of penalties. Separate confinement, however, should be distinguished from the original idea of solitary confinement. The latter really did exclude the prisoner from every human society. Even to the promoters of a separate system this seemed a mental and bodily privation, exclusively intended to inflict a punishment.

On the other hand, they recommended separate confinement as a separation of the criminal from his fellow offenders, and as a régime which paid due regard to the prisoner's bodily health, mental sanity, intellectual improvement, and moral amendment. This ideal was illustrated by references to recent reports on Pennsylvanian prisons. The inspectors still maintained the retributory idea of fixed terms of punishment, and were opposed to any indulgences or a conditional release upon supposed good behaviour. Such a policy, they thought, would weaken the deterrent effect of solitude, involve injustice to other prisoners, and tempt to a hypocritical show which could only preclude true reform. At the same time they appreciated self-determination and voluntary co-operation as necessary conditions of any lasting educational result, particularly for implanting habits of industry. Mere forced

[1] *Parliamentary Papers, 1828,* vi. 235, p. 16.
[2] Ibid. *1837–8,* xxx. 1–103, at 13, 4, 20.

labour, and treading a wheel in particular, would be 'enough to make the prisoner avoid all labour to the end of his days'. Curiously enough, this acknowledgement was a further argument for their recommendation of separate confinement: in the solitude of his cell the prisoner would long for some work as his main solace and comfort. From this experience of work, gratefully accepted as a beneficial resource from the pain of idleness, they expected a lasting effect on the prisoner's character and after-career.

In 1839 a new Prison Act repealed the classification clause of Peel's Act: 'In order to prevent contamination . . . any prisoner may be separately confined.'[1] The year 1842 saw the opening of the famous cellular prison at Pentonville. Three years later the first county gaol expressly constructed for the new system was opened at Reading. John Field, chaplain of this prison, was one of the most arduous advocates of separate confinement.[2] In concurrence with the *Report of the Prison Inspectors* of 1838, he distinguished between solitary and separate confinement as the bad and good form of seclusion. By this distinction he claimed Howard as confirming his conception of separate confinement. He was opposed to the tread-wheel and to any other form of enforced labour. Even voluntary work he admitted with a certain reluctance only. The punitive character of solitude without employment should not be diminished by the distraction of industrial occupation. The triumphant victory of the new system was finally established by the Prison Act of 1865, which provided that every prison should contain cells in a number corresponding to the highest average of prisoners housed in it.[3] The passionate struggle for and against separate confinement ought not to veil the fact that in the end in England its application was a moderate one. The solitary stage, originally admissible for two years, was at Pentonville fixed at eighteen months and later on reduced to the first nine months of the prison term, with the possibility, in the event of bad conduct and incorrigible misbehaviour, of a further six months' separation before discharge.[4]

In 1835, when British prisons were opened to an inspection by the Government, the Continent saw the victory of the cellular system.[5] In Germany the administrative reform was followed by

[1] 2 & 3 Vict., c. 56, s. 3.

[2] John Field, *Prison Discipline and the Advantage of the Separate System of Imprisonment* (2nd ed. 1848).

[3] 28 & 29 Vict., c. 126, s. 17.

[4] E. Du Cane, *Punishment and Prevention of Crime* (1885), pp. 158 and 164.

[5] For the discussion which follows see Kriegsmann, pp. 58 et seq.

a literary movement in favour of the penitentiary system. A new prison discipline, without challenging the traditional criminal law and its principle of formal retribution, was expected to lead the prisoner to legal adjustment and moral reformation. A prominent figure was Dr. Julius who at the time when Hegelian philosophy reached its climax delivered lectures on prison discipline in Berlin.[1] He began as a critic of solitary confinement, but his voyage to Philadelphia in 1834–5 converted him into an ardent follower of the new doctrine. Other eminent representatives were v. Jagemann, prison administrator in Baden, and Professor Mittermaier at Heidelberg, a pupil of the penal legislator Anselm v. Feuerbach, for years at work collecting and publishing an increasing amount of legal information from abroad. The first cellular prison institution in Germany was the prison at Dreibergen in Mecklenburg, 1839, where prisoners had to spend one year in isolated cells. Baden became the model country for the new system with the central prison of Bruchsal opened in 1851. In 1846 the first International Prison Assembly at Frankfort, with Mittermaier as president, voted for the cellular system. In 1869 the German *Juristentag* suggested that solitary confinement should legally be recognized as the ordinary form of deprivation of liberty. The German Criminal Code of 1871 regarded solitary confinement as an established practice, and provided only for its limitation: without the prisoner's consent, isolation for more than three years was made illegal.[2]

It was also in 1835 that Belgium, under the influence of Ducpétiaux, Inspector-General of Prisons, introduced the cellular system into two prisons. During the following years, the Belgian administration built numerous cellular prisons such as Tongres (1844) and Louvain (1860). In Holland there were in the forties some legislative attempts to legalize solitary confinement even for long-term convicts, but not before 1851 did the law permit isolation for six months. Subsequent legislation extended this period to two and even to five years. Tuscany introduced the new system in 1841, Denmark in 1853 and confirmed it by the Criminal Code of 1866, Norway in 1848–51, Sweden in 1846. In France, as in Holland, the legislature was in favour of long-term isolation, and the administration began with the building of cellular prisons. The Second Empire, however, resorted to transportation, and this was probably the main reason why France contributed less

[1] Julius, *Vorträge über Gefängniskunde* (1828).
[2] Sect. 22/II Criminal Code.

than other countries to the cause of prison reform. Between 1853 and 1875 the erection of new cells and, to some extent, even the use of existing cells was prohibited.

The triumphant victory of separate confinement was the dominating feature of nineteenth-century prison development in Europe, but it was neither complete nor uniform. There were prison systems, like that of Belgium, which developed the idea of isolation to its logical conclusion, with single yards for exercises, separate stalls in the chapel, masks concealing the prisoners' faces, and mere figures replacing their names. These were the requisites of a system which by a grotesque exaggeration of a pretended individualization fell back into the most unnatural mass uniformity. It resulted in a complete extinction of all personal traits which could act as reminders of the prisoner's individuality, and this made the whole scheme even more commendable to those who wished criminal law and prison discipline to be based upon a principle of strict retribution.

On the other hand, there were some remarkable attempts to deepen and to spiritualize the cellular system. In Prussia, Frederick William IV, friend and admirer of Elizabeth Fry, gave the order to build Moabit on the exact patterns of Pentonville. Against the opposition of his own administration he promoted the introduction of the cellular system. In 1842, upon the advice of Alexander v. Humboldt, he invited Francis Lieber to become Inspector of Prisons and to deliver lectures on penology at the University of Berlin, but Lieber declined.[1] In 1857 he succeeded in gaining Wichern for the Prussian prison service. Johann Hinrich Wichern (1808–81) was the founder of a celebrated industrial school, the Rauhes Haus at Horn near Hamburg, where he initiated the 'family system' of group education. With Christian tolerance, he renounced force, and relied rather upon the personal responsibility of individual boys and the sound spiritual atmosphere of the group communities. His assistants—the brethren—were trained for social service. In 1848, under the influence of the social and political unrest, he brought the German Churches to realize their social responsibility towards their distressed and neglected members, not least towards convicts and discharged prisoners. When he was entrusted with the reorganization of Moabit and the establishment of a true system of separate confinement, he introduced a new type of prison official, responsible for a personal approach to the prisoner. The brethren of the

[1] L. R. Harley, *Francis Lieber* (1899), pp. 78 and 174.

Rauhes Haus, experienced in the treatment of delinquent boys and devoted to social service, were to perform all duties which involved a personal contact with the prisoner. 'A new and purified atmosphere' replaced the old community of vices and seduction. For the first time prison reform seemed to be recognized as a personal problem, with the question of personnel as the pre-eminent issue.[1] Nevertheless the great experiment was doomed to failure. The system seemed to be compromised when, by a tragic incident, one of the new officials shot a prisoner. In distrust of a 'religious order' in a public service the Prussian Diet refused further funds, mainly under the influence of Franz v. Holtzendorff, a prominent Liberal and a keen advocate of Sir Walter Crofton's Irish system. In Baden Dr. Fuesslin made a similar attempt at Bruchsal, but he too failed. This socially minded physician recognized the primary importance of the right personnel for any wholesome purpose of penal reform. 'The success of a reformative punishment', he said, 'has as its condition not so much dead walls and partitions—though they are indispensable—as the vivid influence of prison officials based upon the right spirit.'[2] He raised the standard of prison officials and tried to make the prison service attractive for men of extraordinary gifts and devotion. Fuesslin asserted that in his institution convicts received up to six visits a day. Separation ought not to be a depressive solitude, but a natural way to gain a true insight into the prisoner's individuality, unhampered by his bad social habits. Fuesslin's practical experiment failed. He had to give way to the distrust and the obstruction of the 'old' prison officials. The deeper cause of these failures was the antagonism between the new personal approach and a rather mechanical prison routine. In the end, Wichern left the prison régime itself to the State as its own affair. He added only, from the spiritual side, a care for man's soul as a supplement to the régime. All educational efforts, however, are doomed to frustration unless they penetrate and dominate the whole prison life. After the experiments of Wichern and Fuesslin, the attempts to raise the standards for the personnel were abandoned, but the cellular system itself remained. Even in more favourable circumstances, the cellular system did not afford satisfactory conditions for a truly reformative approach. The visitor could see the

[1] Johann Hinrich Wichern, 'Zur Gefängnisreform', *Ges. Schriften*, iv (1905). See also M. Gerhardt, *Johann Hinrich Wichern* (1929–31).

[2] I. Fuesslin, *Grundbedingungen jeder Gefängnisreform* (1865), p. 94; id., *Die Einzelhaft nach fremden und sechsjährigen eigenen Erfahrungen* (1855).

prisoner in his cell and speak to him without any disturbing interference. But apart from the fact that it was impossible to afford a sufficient number of cell visits, the visitor could scarcely hope to know the true character of the prisoner who lived in an unnatural and artificial isolation. The whole idea of a personal educational link between visitors—official and voluntary—and the prisoner in the solitude of his cell had something unreal in it. Conditions of life were too different from those in the world outside to give any opportunity for observing and testing the individual's normal reactions. The most obvious shortcoming was the lack of accommodation for suitable work. Constructive work, as Howard had already observed, cannot be done in isolated cells, but requires workshops, yards, and farmland.

From an historical point of view solitary confinement was a necessary step on the way to progress. Under the exciting influence of a forceful idea the chaotic state of the old gaols was definitely removed. After the disastrous wavering between collusive negligence and brutal arbitrariness, the new order introduced a wholesome atmosphere of earnestness and dignity into prisons. Sometimes the more intense form of deprivation of liberty enabled legislation or the courts to shorten the traditional prison terms. A Dutch statute of 1851, for instance, authorized the courts to commit a prisoner to solitary confinement for half the period for which he would have been sent to prison under the previous system. Personal observation and reformation had once been suggested as the principal recommendation for the new system, but eventually found their main obstacle in the complete isolation itself. But the cellular system cannot be blamed because it failed to achieve what no previous prison system even pretended to attempt. The large cellular prisons enable England to-day to follow the wholesome practice of keeping every prisoner in a single cell at night, an indispensable condition for a sound prison discipline. In Germany the development of cell building did not go so far as to prevent entirely the use of common dormitories. In 1924 Prussia, with prison accommodation for 70,000 prisoners, had still 28,000 beds in dormitories and 3,600 cubicles.[1] In both countries some of the central institutions are still suffering from the lack of suitable workshops for which there is no room in the cell-blocks.

As long as deprivation of liberty remains a legal punishment, there will be a demand for separate confinement. It will be used for untried prisoners, for very short terms, as far as this type

[1] *Pr. Gefängnisstatistik für 1924* (1927), p. 16; Starke, in Bumke, p. 151.

remains, for a first test period, as a disciplinary or security measure, and so forth. But the day has gone when solitary confinement could be claimed to be the normal form of deprivation of liberty and the panacea for retribution, deterrence, and reformation alike.

CHAPTER V

INDIVIDUALIZATION OF TREATMENT

NEW REFORMATIVE TENDENCIES

THE triumph of separate confinement was by no means unopposed. The prevailing predilection for this panacea was in the first place an expression of a literary movement in favour of the penitentiary system. Contemporary critics of separate confinement came from the ranks of able and devoted prison practitioners. Once more, a humanitarian approach stirred man's conscience and led to a deeper understanding of the effects and possibilities of imprisonment. Throughout the whole nineteenth century there was a strong undercurrent against the prevalent trend of prison development.

A new generation took up the cause for which John Howard had fought in the eighteenth century. The prominent figure among the reformers was Elizabeth Fry, *née* Gurney (1780–1845).[1] Her principal aim was not so much to collect information and evidence, nor to begin with a thoroughgoing reform of criminal justice administration, but to offer her personal help wherever she saw any want or emergency. Her true greatness lies in the fact that she was an improviser whose work grew with the demand itself. This modest and practical approach enabled her to speak with authority as an expert in prison affairs, to communicate with reformers abroad, and to awaken a new social responsibility towards men and women in prison. The Gurneys were a Quaker family, but Elizabeth had her personal religious revival under the influence of a relative, an American Friend, William Savery, who came to England travelling in the ministry. This decisive experience immediately led her to philanthropic duties: in the laundry of her family home at Earlham she started a school for poor children. Many years later, in 1813, another American of French extraction, Stephen Grellet, told her about the deplorable conditions of the women prisoners at Newgate. She followed his suggestion and entered a world which no woman of social standing had seen before. In 1817 she began her practical work. She spoke to the women, appealed to their interest in their children, and initiated a prison school for the children whom the women prisoners

[1] *Memoirs of the Life of Elizabeth Fry*, ed. by two of her Daughters (1847); E. R. Pitman, *Elizabeth Fry* (1884); J. P. Whitney, *Elizabeth Fry, Quaker Heroine* (1937).

had with them. There were thirty children of seven and under. The next thing was to overcome their disastrous idleness by reasonable work—an old Quaker tradition. She founded a Ladies' Association for the Improvement of the Female Prisoners at Newgate. They provided the prisoners with materials for needle-work and knitting, and organized the work and its sale. The prisoners were divided into classes of twelve with monitors from their own midst. The day began and ended with a Bible reading. A mark system and small rewards stimulated industry and proper behaviour. A member of the Association, later on a permanently appointed matron, was responsible for instruction and supervision. Elizabeth Fry extended her care also to the women who were transported to Australia. When she heard of women under capital sentences, she shared with them the trying hours before execution. All this was done from the unselfish devotion of a religious personality. Wherever she helped, she did it with a directness and a strong impetus which inspired others to join her efforts. She had sincere supporters among the members of the Society for the Reformation of Prison Discipline, founded in 1816 by Samuel Hoare and Fowell Buxton,[1] her brothers-in-law. A year after the beginning of the Newgate experiment, she gave evidence as an expert witness before the House of Commons Committee.[2] For prison reform she suggested a simple programme of four points: there should be religious instruction, classification, employment, and exclusively women officials in charge of women prisoners. Her realistic outlook made her an adversary to the prevalent doctrine of solitary confinement. Under proper supervision prisoners should work together in groups, and have their meals and their recreation together, but ought to be separated at night. 'I believe it would conduce to health, both of body and mind. Their being in companies tends to the advancement of principle and industry; for it affords a stimulus.'[3] Years later, in a discussion with the French penal reformer, A. M. Bérenger, she raised the issue again. 'As man is a social being, and not designed for a life of seclusion, such a system of prison discipline should be adopted, as may be best to prepare those under its correction for re-entering active life, and all its consequent exposures and temptations.'[4]

Elizabeth Fry's practical efforts did not end at Newgate. She

[1] T. F. Buxton, *An Enquiry whether Crime and Misery are produced or prevented by our present System of Prison Discipline* (1818).

[2] *Memoirs*, i. 292 et seq.

[3] Ibid. 297.

[4] Ibid. ii. 310.

visited numerous institutions in Great Britain, stimulated reform and improvements, and initiated Committees of Visiting Ladies. In 1839 and 1840 she saw many prisons on the Continent, and enlisted the support and interest of influential personalities for the cause of penal reform. At Düsseldorf she was much impressed with the work of Pastor Theodor Fliedner. From two visits in England in 1823 and 1833, Fliedner knew Elizabeth Fry and her work, and this experience had a lasting effect on his life and work for the Home Mission.[1] In the garden of his parsonage at Kaiserswerth near Düsseldorf he established the first modest refuge for discharged women prisoners. He was the founder of a hospital with training facilities for deaconesses, i.e. nurses of a Protestant order. Ten years after Elizabeth Fry's visit, Florence Nightingale spent some time at this celebrated institution, and this proved an inspiration for her own devoted efforts for the cause of nursing the sick and wounded. The tradition that she first heard about Fliedner's work from Elizabeth Fry[2] is a legend,[3] but even so, it is symbolic of the close interrelationship between penal reform and other social causes.

The same humanitarian outlook, as an underlying motive rather than an express doctrine, was the root of some bold experiments in prison reform during the thirties of the nineteenth century. These efforts were the work of some singular pioneers, and they coincided, curiously enough, with the climax of the vogue for solitary confinement.

G. M. Obermaier, after military service during the Napoleonic Wars, was head of the Bavarian prisons at Kaiserslautern (1830–42) and Munich (1842–62). His administration led to a complete reorganization of both institutions.[4] Brutal methods and harsh treatment were banned, armed guards remained outside the prison rooms, corporal punishment and bloodhounds were abolished. Confidence, humanity, and justice were the foundation of the new régime. Industrial work, mostly manufacturing of textiles, prevailed. The work was performed under State control; no private contractor interfered with the prison administration. An earnings scheme was based on the standard of proper wages, with deduction of one-third for the prisoner's maintenance. One hour a day every prisoner had to attend the prison school, and this

[1] G. Fliedner, *Theodor Fliedner, sein Leben und Wirken* (1908–12).
[2] Still maintained by J. Whitney, l.c., pp. 295 et seq.
[3] E. Cook, *Life of Florence Nightingale* (1913), i. 62 n. 2.
[4] See for an analysis of Obermaier's work and ideas: F. Hoefer, 28 *Journal* 13.

educational work was supplemented by an attractive prison library. The whole institution and the daily routine were dominated by a true educational atmosphere, stimulated and maintained by the personality of Obermaier himself. This made it possible to appoint some of the convicts as monitors, the most controversial of Obermaier's innovations. For his adversaries it was the principal objection against the whole system. Mittermaier foresaw only 'immorality in the monitors, hypocrisy, and a spirit of revenge against the prisoners who betray their comrades'.[1] Obermaier himself regarded these monitors as assistants and helpers rather than as supervisors, and the whole atmosphere of his institution made such an attitude possible and effective.

The Bavarian Criminal Code of 1813, the work of Anselm v. Feuerbach, provided for a form of indeterminate sentence, i.e. certain frames of maximum terms of penal servitude with a minimum period after which the convict who satisfied the authorities with sufficient proofs of good behaviour and reliable amendment was eligible for the royal pardon. While similar provisions in other German Statutes failed owing to the lack of any reformative institutions, Obermaier successfully linked up his constructive treatment in the Munich prison—Kaiserslautern in the Palatinate was under the French *Code pénal*—with that anticipation of modern criminal law.

For the visible results of his work Obermaier referred to the low figures in recidivism among his ex-convicts. The unusual spirit of his institution, the quiet and pure atmosphere, and the admirable personality of the man himself, have been testified to by various foreign visitors.[2] Unlike the prevailing penitentiary systems and programmes, Obermaier's underlying ideas ran counter to the fundamental tendencies of traditional criminal law.[3] In his opinion a reasonable criminal code ought to abandon capital punishment and the lifelong 'civil death', chains and whipping

[1] Letter to John Clay, who under the impression of this description indicted Obermaier's work as a 'combination of terror and espionage'. W. L. Clay, *The Prison Chaplain, a Memoir of John Clay* (1861), p. 346.

[2] Visits by A. Baillie Cochrane, the Rev. C. Hare Townsend, and George Combe, the phrenologist, quoted from M. Davenport Hill, *Suggestions for the Repression of Crime* (1857), pp. 544, 550, and 578 respectively.

[3] G. M. Obermaier, *Anleitung zur vollkommenen Besserung der Verbrecher in den Strafanstalten* (1835), reprinted by the Hamburg Penal Institutions, with a preface by M. Liepmann (1925); id., *Die amerikanischen Pönitentiärsysteme* (1837); id., *Verhandlungen über Gefängnisreform in Frankfurt a/M, oder die Einzelhaft mit ihren Folgen* (1848). English translation under the title *Prison Discipline*. With a preface by A. Baillie Cochrane (1853).

post alike, all stigmatizing forms of punishment, and the whole 'metaphysical' discussion on retaliation. Criminal justice administration should not apply special devices to do retributory harm by fetters, tread-wheels, humiliating and harsh treatment:

'the deprivation of liberty for a shorter or longer period is the most severe punishment for everybody, and for the criminal, otherwise unrestrained, there is in the beginning and often for a long time no greater hardship than to be bound to fit into the strict order, the abstinent and compulsory regimen of my reformatory. This for the acquiescence of those who might think that without heads shaved, chains forged, and clothes striped, punishment had neither dignity nor strength!'[1]

His alternative was indeterminate sentences as a suitable legal basis for a reformative prison discipline which relies upon the personal approach and the educational effort of the right man in charge of the prisoner. 'They err', he said, 'who think that the mere construction of a prison had a beneficent influence on a man's character, that a heap of stones could break a criminal of his defects and vices, and turn the idle into an industrious man.' This implies the repudiation of solitary confinement, since 'nature herself leads man to the community, therefore he belongs to the community'.[2]

Obermaier had much in common with Colonel Manuel Montesinos, the Spanish prison reformer. The latter's attitude is characterized by the following words, ascribed to him and often repeated: 'The prison receives the man, but leaves the prisoner before the door'.[3] Like Obermaier he renounced the traditional methods of degradation and oppression. He believed in self-respect as one of the most powerful sentiments of the human mind, while ill-treatment would necessarily irritate rather than correct and reform a man. In 1835 Montesinos was appointed Director of the Prison of Valencia, and later on, he became Visitor General of Spanish Prisons. He took over the Valencia prison with a rate of recommitments of 30–5 per cent., and claimed a decrease to 2 per cent. only. As a way of implanting in his prisoners a feeling of honour, he organized a military discipline. Prisoners were divided into companies with convicts as sergeants and petty officers. Convicts were to establish workshops that their personal

[1] *Anleitung*, p. 24.

[2] Quotations by Liepmann, l.c., p. x, and Hoefer, l.c., p. 24 n. 53.

[3] Montesinos, *Reflexiones sobre la organización del presidio de Valencia* (1846), quoted from Quintiliano Saldaña, *Moderne Strafrechtsauffassungen in Spanien* (2nd ed. 1923), p. 15 n. 11.

interest in the work might be stimulated. There was a great variety of employment, particularly in the textile and wood industries. School, one hour a day, was obligatory for all inmates under twenty years of age. Montesinos's work was soon appreciated by foreign observers.[1] He resigned, however, when a new Spanish Criminal Code extended life-sentences and curtailed the discretion of prison authorities to individualize the prevailing mass treatment of prisoners.

In spite of this setback the idea of individualization made further progress. Various attempts at classification of prisoners were made, assigning each group to the most suitable treatment. By a proper combination of different modes of prison discipline, a penal establishment would provide, though not unlimited, yet sufficient opportunities for an individualizing treatment. In 1838 Aubanel introduced such a classified prison system in Geneva.[2] This Geneva system met with the warm approval of prison experts abroad. The French penologist Charles Lucas contrasted such a combined system with the unrelieved mass treatment in a uniform separate system.[3] All these ideas attained still more prominence during the next generation, when the Progressive Stage system offered anew an opportunity for reconciling the unavoidable mass treatment with the necessary individualization.

In the meantime the treatment of juvenile delinquents gave a stimulus to the development of new prison ideas. The French Judge F. A. Demetz turned from his judicial experience to direct care for the neglected and delinquent youth. He became the founder, and for many years the head, of the agricultural colony at Mettrai, near Tours, erected in 1839.[4] This establishment had accommodation for 500–700 young offenders who were admitted when under sixteen, many of them between seven and eight years of age. Like Wichern at the Rauhes Haus near Hamburg, Demetz introduced a family system. The institution consisted of various houses, each the home of a family of forty inmates, divided into two sections. Demetz too recognized the importance of a new

[1] G. H. Hoskins, *Spain as it is* (1851); S. T. Wallis, *Glimpses of Spain* (1850), quoted from M. D. Hill, l.c., pp. 532 and 539.

[2] M. C. Aubanel, *Mémoire sur le système pénitentiaire* (1837).

[3] J. M. C. Lucas, *Système pénitentiaire en Europe et aux États Unis* (1828–30); id., *De la réforme des prisons ou de la théorie de l'emprisonnement* (1836–8). See also Kriegsmann, pp. 62 and 69.

[4] Contemporary reports by M. D. Hill, l.c., pp. 118 et seq. (the author visited Mettrai in 1848 and 1855), and by J. L. Tellkampf, *Essays on Law Reform* (1859), pp. 237 et seq.

type of personnel as a prerequisite for constructive work. For the post of house fathers, he appointed teachers who were specially trained for educational and social work. Sisters were in charge of kitchen and infirmary. The agricultural work gave ample opportunity for healthy employment. It was an educational system, based on moral suasion rather than on force, with the object of making the juvenile capable of self-control and self-support. Discharged boys were placed under the supervision of a *patron*. Often the institution remained in touch with the boy's employer.

These were some eminent figures of a first heroic generation of prison pioneers. Certainly they had a genius for exercising personal influence. They tried and performed the impossible, they broke through the walls of horror and suspicion which for so long had isolated the prisoner, and recognized him as a fellow man. It was a discovery of a new field of the human soul. They relied on the moral authority of example, persuasion, and atmosphere rather than on force, deterrence, and penalties. There is no reason to doubt that the contemporary reports on their successes are true, that the standard of their institutions rose, and that even the number of recidivists decreased. The dawn of a new relation to the destitute and depraved inspired the moral strength and the optimistic self-confidence of bold reformers. 'When the whole system is founded on humanity,' said Obermaier, 'loyalty to the general good speedily becomes the object of all, gross excesses, scandalous behaviour and brutality are no longer to be apprehended, they are no longer possible, and become exceptions very rarely occurring.'[1]

Less fortunate, however, were these prison reformers in convincing the leading authorities in penal policy. On the Continent, the era of comprehensive codifications and administrative centralization preferred a well-regulated system, equally applicable by every average official, rather than the outstanding work of a few eminent personalities. A phrase, uttered at the International Assembly for Prison Reform at Frankfort, 1846, has often been repeated: 'The system of Mr. Obermaier is Mr. Obermaier himself!' On the one hand, these words frankly acknowledged the outstanding personal efforts of the man, on the other hand, they rejected what apparently could not be framed into regulations of a well-balanced system. The predilection for a rational penitentiary system, more or less on the basis of solitary confinement, remained almost un-

[1] Quoted from M. D. Hill, l.c., p. 582.

shaken. The time was not yet ripe for the general recognition that the legal and administrative foundation of prison discipline ought to be a framework only which must be filled by personal efforts for the prisoner's readjustment and rehabilitation.

An important factor for the final acknowledgement of those ideas was the support by a new group of realistic educational and social reformers which rose in England about the middle of the century. Mary Carpenter at Bristol dedicated her efforts to the education of wayward youth. Matthew Davenport Hill, the Recorder of Birmingham, again and again addressed the Grand Jury on questions of law reform. His younger brother, Frederic Hill, was the first prison inspector of Scotland. John Clay, prison chaplain of the Preston gaol, was still influenced by experience of the old prison community which frustrated any pastoral work and personal approach, and therefore in favour of a moderate use of separate confinement for reflection and self-examination. For reformative efforts he desired reasonable individualization, and this attitude brought him into contact with Mary Carpenter and M. D. Hill. His son, Walter Lowe Clay, had still more in common with that group of reformers.[1] Like Howard this whole group was keen in collecting information from institutions at home and abroad, not so much, however, about the prison conditions in general, but about experiments with new reformative schemes and the experience obtained in constructive attempts. They felt themselves confirmed and inspired by a true fellowship with those who shared similar ideas in other countries. Penal reform became a matter of international aspect. From the manifold observations and criticism which they collected and interchanged, they came to a new insight into the possible means and true ends of prison discipline. The issue was no longer mere remedies for 'alleviating the miseries of public prisons', but the promotion of reformation, or prevention of criminal deeds. A realistic approach to these questions seemed incompatible with the over-emphasis on the value of solitary confinement, the official panacea of the age. Under the influence of Crawford's Reports on Pennsylvanian Prisons and of the apparent superiority of Glasgow Bridewell,

[1] Mary Carpenter, *Juvenile Delinquents, their Conditions and Treatment* (1853); id., *Our Convicts* (1864); id., *Reformatory Prison Discipline* (1872); M. D. Hill, *Suggestions for the Repression of Crime* (1857); R. and F. Hill, *The Recorder of Birmingham. A Memoir of Matthew Davenport Hill* (1878); Frederic Hill, *Crime: its Amount, Causes, and Remedies* (1853); id., *An Autobiography of Fifty Years in Time of Reform*, ed. by C. Hill (1894); W. L. Clay, *The Prison Chaplain. A Memoir of the Rev. John Clay* (1861); id., *Our Convict System* (1862).

Frederic Hill began as an advocate of the separate system. Subsequent observations and reflections, however, convinced him that Crawford's reports had been too favourable, and the wholesome prison discipline at Glasgow was not necessarily bound up with the principle of separation. A uniform system of separation, he realized, was insufficient to train the offender in self-control and to prepare him for life in society; it restricted facilities for reasonable employment, weakened the spirit of labour, and—if carried to excess—would enfeeble mental and physical powers and foster habits of deception.[1] The underlying idea of such a critical attitude was that a term of imprisonment was not, and ought not to be, a given state of certain conditions regulated in one way or another, but a dynamic process in human life.

This attitude was a first recognition of the fact that, taking the long view, moral strength is more effective than enforced suppression, that the promotion of self-respect requires confidence, and that the training of will-power and self-restraint is impossible without the prisoner's active co-operation. 'The prisoner', said Matthew Davenport Hill, 'instead of dragging him through a dull routine of duties where he starts every morning at the same point and finds himself at the same exact spot every evening,—should be exposed to the stimulus of an onward course.'[2] Instead of leaving the prisoner to solitary contemplation, one should try 'to elevate the prisoner's mind by rational encouragement'.[3] Prison discipline should therefore clearly expose certain aims which the prisoner would be able to attain, so that even in prison man's ultimate fate rests upon his own hand. Consequently, these mid-century reformers advocated a progressive structure of prison discipline, as it had been successfully worked out by two British prison pioneers: Alexander Maconochie and Sir Walter Crofton.

THE LESSON OF TRANSPORTATION

The idea of a progressive form of prison discipline is the lasting contribution of the English transportation system.[4] This is the

[1] F. Hill, *Crime*, pp. 234 et seq.

[2] M. D. Hill, l.c., p. 252.

[3] G. L. Chesterton (Governor of the House of Correction of Cold Bath Field), *Revelations of Prison Life* (1856), i. 53.

[4] There is no complete survey of transportation covering the whole period from 1787 to 1867. Studies on particular phases are: Eris O'Brien, *The Foundation of Australia (1786–1800). A Study in English Criminal Practice and Penal Colonisation in the Eighteenth Century* (1937); M. Barnard Eldershaw, *Phillip of Australia. An Account of the Settlement at Sidney Cove 1788–92* (1938); W. Douglas Forsyth, *Governor Arthur's Convict System. Van*

positive side of a policy which unfortunately diverted attention from, and weakened the responsibility for, the true aims of penal policy. For decades, transportation was the characteristic feature of the English penal system. It was in practice a denial of the spiritual forces of reconstruction, yet in the end even this strange and costly experiment presented, in an indirect way, new ideas on social readjustment.

The tendency to get criminals out of sight goes back to primitive stages of criminal law. Among towns and principalities of the Continent, banishment of criminals, vagrants, and obnoxious lunatics was in its effect nothing but a senseless interchange of antisocial elements. In England many a prisoner was saved from the gallows by abjuring the realm. Transportation has never been a punishment under the common law. 'No power on earth', said Blackstone, 'except the authority of Parliament, can send any subject of England out of the land against his will; no, not even a criminal.'[1] In many cases transportation was granted by the Crown as a conditional pardon, an alternative to execution, and it was thus far inflicted by the choice of the criminal himself. During the seventeenth century not only prisoners-of-war and political offenders, but also felons from English gaols were sent to the plantations in America.[2] In 1717 a special statutory provision initiated a systematic transportation to the New World. The preamble complained that so far 'many offenders to whom royal mercy has been extended, upon condition of transporting themselves to the West Indies, have often neglected to perform the said condition, but returned to their former wickedness, and been at last for new crimes brought to a shameful and ignominious death'. An apparent want of servants, 'who by their labour and industry might be the means of improving and making the said colonies and plantations more useful to this nation', was another motive for the lawgivers. According to this Statute, prisoners, by an order of court, were made over to the use of private contractors who shipped them to the colonies.[3] After arrival the contractor sold—by a nice legal distinction—not the man, but his service to an employer. Prisoners who had private means or wealthy friends and could procure the price of sale may have gained their liberty at once.

Diemen's Land 1824–36. A Study in Colonisation (1935). For short accounts see 'Transportation', 'Convicts', *Australian Encyclopaedia* (1927); H. E. Barnes, 'Transportation of Criminals', *Encyclopaedia of the Social Sciences*.

[1] Blackstone, i. 137.

[2] J. D. Butler, 2 *Am. Hist. Rev.* 12; A. E. Smith, 39 *Am. Hist. Rev.* 232.

[3] 4 Geo. I, c. 11, s. 1.

This practice came to an end by the American Declaration of Independence in 1776. At the close of the period, about 1,000 British subjects a year were sent abroad. Public opinion in England was very favourable to this system, and almost unanimously regretted that the loss of the American colonies brought to an end so easy an opportunity for disposing of criminals.[1]

In 1776, as a first preliminary measure, the hulks were established for the reception of prisoners who, in other circumstances, would have been sent overseas. A contractor of the last convict-transports was in charge of these floating gaols. As to definite policy, the penitentiary project of the Act of 1779, that first attempt to resume responsibility for the criminals in the country, was superseded by transportation to Australia. The legal basis was an Act of 1784 which left it to the Crown and the Privy Council to determine the place to which offenders should be transported 'either within his Majesty's dominions or elsewhere. . . .'[2] Three years later Arthur Phillip sailed with the first fleet, founded Sydney, and became the first Governor of New South Wales. This was the beginning of an extraordinary social experiment, the attempt to reconcile penal policy with a colonial purpose. During the eighty years' history of Australian transportation, 160,000 convicts were sent from Great Britain and Ireland. Contrary to the previous transportation to America, the Government itself had an immediate responsibility for the convicts. There was no free population ready to absorb an infiltration by English prisoners. Convicts, sailors, and marines formed the population of Phillip's settlement. For the British government, the principal object of this transportation policy was to meet an urgent demand of the administration of criminal justice. English prisons would be relieved of their disastrous state of overcrowding, and a punitive measure would be applied which was expected to combine security for the mother country, deterrence, and even reformation under changed conditions somewhere far away. Colonial purposes prevailed more in the public mind, and seemed to recommend a scheme 'combining moral and commercial interests', if one could 'export vices and receive hereafter an ample equivalent in bales of goods'.[3]

Phillip, the first Governor (1788–92), laid out the system which

[1] O'Brien, l.c., pp. 120 and 128.

[2] 24 Geo. III, c. 56, s. 1. This Act has been repealed by 55 Geo. III, c. 156 (1815) and 5 Geo. IV, c. 84 (1824).

[3] *Edinburgh Review*, ii. 32. Quoted from F. L. W. Wood, *R. Australian Historical Society, Journal and Proceedings*, xix. 334.

prevailed for the following decades.[1] The Government, though minutely regulating the transports, left the Governor ample discretion with regard to convict management. From the arrival in the colony, the ownership of the services of the convict was vested in the Governor.[2] He employed the prisoners in public works such as bush clearing, road building, in various craftmanships, and as messengers and clerks in public offices. With the development of agriculture, convicts were assigned as unpaid servants to free settlers or emancipated convicts, often fed and clothed from public stores. An Act of 1790 enabled the Crown to authorize the Governor to remit or shorten terms of transportation.[3] The first Governors made scanty use of this authorization. A few exceptional remissions were granted as rewards for extraordinary public services in fighting bushrangers or suppressing a mutiny. Arthur Phillip was a just man with a sense of responsibility for the men and convicts entrusted to him. He performed the first voyage to the unknown country with extraordinary skill and success. He made strong representations when, under the appalling conditions of the second fleet, the death roll of those dying during the voyage and immediately after arrival amounted to 40 per cent. of the convicts.[4] For the prosperous development of the young colony, he urgently demanded provisions, tools, and clothes, asked for a temporary suspension of new transports of convicts, and insisted on the sending out of free settlers, selected farmers, and artisans. If the colony were to become self-supporting, he said, industry must be carried out by free men: fifty farmers would do more than a thousand convicts.[5] In vain he pleaded for patience and special regard for the colony, before any relief for English prisons and hulks could fairly be expected. The lack of supplies led to years of distress and famine, with rations strictly limited and the hours of work drastically reduced—a most unfavourable background for the readjustment of criminals. Discipline among convicts and soldiers was strict and severe. Criminal procedure in this military penal establishment had the forms of a court martial, with a Judge Advocate presiding over a court of military officers. Breaches of discipline, idleness, and disobedience as well as petty offences of

[1] Besides O'Brien and Eldeshaw see also G. D. Milford, *Governor Phillip and the early Settlement of New South Wales* (1935).

[2] 5 Geo. IV, c. 84, s. 8.

[3] 30 Geo. III, c. 47.

[4] *Account and Papers relating to Convicts on Board the Hulks and those transported to New South Wales* (1792), pp. 38 and 61.

[5] O'Brien, l.c., p. 228.

convicts were dealt with summarily by magistrates. Flogging was in excessive use. Serious offences led to retransportation to Norfolk Island, if not to execution.

After the end of Phillip's term, under a military oligarchy, an illicit liquor trade among a rising class of rich settlers, traders, and officers was a new source of crime and destitution. This epoch, though it raised the general economic standard of the colony, proved disastrous for order and discipline among convicts and free men. To overcome the spirit of mutiny and desperation, and to re-establish public authority, Governor Lachlan Macquarie (1810–21) initiated a drastic change of the prevailing system.[1] As a reaction against the unscrupulous selfishness of the ruling group his rule was favourable to the ex-convicts. In his opinion the penalty should consist in the mere transportation—the new life in the colony being a fresh start toward rehabilitation. Ex-convicts, therefore, were to be regarded as on equal footing with every free citizen. He wished to build the colony on 'an aristocracy of merit among the convicts', and he raised some of them to the status of public officials, attorneys, and even magistrates. This policy provoked considerable opposition which resulted in the commission by the Government of John Thomas Bigge for special investigation on the spot. The complaints did not allege that the emancipation policy of the Governor was not to the benefit of the colony. Rather was he criticized for putting its economic and social development before what was regarded as the principal aim of the Government: a receptacle for British offenders, a severe punishment, and a terror for the criminal class in England.

The most prominent representative of this policy was Sir George Arthur, first independent Lieutenant-Governor of Van Diemen's Land (1824–36).[2] He regarded the colony as a British penal institution, and he felt himself responsible for the effective administration of British criminal justice. In his opinion free settlers were necessary for the management of the penal establishment, voluntary gaolers who would provide convicts with employment and who would submit to a strict control themselves. Arthur developed the administrative machinery to the highest possible degree of efficiency. A permanent vigilance and supervision and a strict centralization subjected convicts, officials, and settlers to a constant and thoroughgoing discipline. Forty per cent. of the rapidly increasing population were transported

[1] Arthur Jose, 'Lachlan Macquarie', *Builders and Pioneers of Australia* (1928), pp. 3–35.

[2] W. D. Forsyth, op. cit.

offenders, and more than one half of the convicts worked in the service of settlers, either as assignees or as paid ticket-of-leave men. Enforced labour was the essence of the penal treatment, and the reformative tendency was based upon stimulation and deterrence. Exemplary behaviour or an outstanding act of public service might shorten the assigned servitude, be rewarded by a post as constable or in the field police, or even lead to a partial remission of the sentence, while a system of gradually increasing penalties awaited the idle, obstinate, and criminal convict in chain-gangs or in special penal settlements. These penal institutions were much feared for the hard labour, the rigid surveillance, and their isolated position which frustrated any desperate attempt to escape. Such colonial penalties—in Arthur's own words—'as severe as they could be afflicted on a man', reached the ultimate limit of human suffering. For many a prisoner in the penal settlements death appeared the only desirable escape. Even capital offences were committed as a desperate attempt to be relieved from an intolerable existence. One quarter of the convicts avoided any further punishment at all, and one half out of these were said to be of exemplary behaviour. On the other hand many emancipated convicts yielded anew to temptation, even if they had been 'good prisoners' before.

With the highly efficient administration of Governor Arthur, British transportation reached its climax. In 1837 a select committee was appointed to inquire into the system of transportation. Sir Walter Molesworth, the philosophical radical, closely connected with James and John Stuart Mill, was chairman, Lord John Russell and Sir Robert Peel were among the members. In vain Arthur himself pleaded in defence of the prevailing system. The Report of 1838 was a peremptory verdict against the principle no less than the practice of transportation. 'The two main characteristics of transportation as a punishment', the Report reads, 'are inefficiency in deterring from crime, and remarkable efficiency not in reforming, but in still further corrupting those who undergo the punishment—and these qualities are inherent in the system, which therefore is not susceptible of any satisfactory improvement.'[1] The committee recommended abolition of transportation and its substitution by a penitentiary system, consisting of confinement and hard labour, either at home or abroad. Due attention was also given to some suggestions of Captain Alexander Maconochie, Colonial Secretary in Van Diemen's Land, who

[1] *Report from the Select Committee on Transportation* (1838), p. xli.

proposed that—in accordance with express regulations—the lengths of prison terms should depend on the behaviour of the prisoners themselves.

In 1840 Molesworth, in an impressive speech before the House of Commons, delivered a vivid extract from that Report.[1] He described transportation as 'unequal, uncertain, productive of more pain than terror, cruel, tyrannical and disgraceful, . . . and still worse as a means of colonisation'. He moved for its definite substitution by a 'penitentiary system' at home. Lord Russell, on the other hand, proposed still to maintain a certain less obnoxious portion of the prevailing system. In the end the bold effort resulted in partial success. The assignment system was abolished and transportation to New South Wales abandoned. Van Diemen's Land, so far, remained a penal colony. There convicts worked together in probation gangs, before they were allowed to seek private employment—sometimes a difficult enterprise when cheap labour far exceeded the demand. In the same year, 1840, Maconochie was given an opportunity for a realization of his reformative ideas, when he was appointed Superintendent of Norfolk Island.[2]

On principle Maconochie was not against transportation which he even preferred to the 'delusion' of solitary confinement, but he saw its main defect in the incompatibility of harsh coercion with the professed reformative purposes. 'The evil', he said, 'is due to the union of direct punishment from which physical coercion is inseparable, with training and probation of which moral influence undoubtedly ought to be an ingredient.'[3] He was a convinced opponent of the assignment system, and recommended a clear separation between punishment for the past and training for the future. The first should consist of enforced labour, supplemented by instruction, and performed exclusively under the Government's responsibility, the latter of a probation stage where parties of six were to be employed in public works. The whole discipline should be based upon four principles:[4] the duration of sentences should be measured not by a definite time to be served, but by a certain amount of labour to be performed, so that the prisoner's liberation would 'depend on the consequent conduct and character evinced by him rather than on the quality

[1] *Speech of Sir William Molesworth on Transportation* (1840). The sentence quoted above at p. 45. Also 53 *Hansard* 1236.

[2] 'Convicts', 'Maconochie', *Australian Encyclopaedia.*

[3] A. Maconochie, *Thoughts on Convict Management* (1838), p. 10.

[4] A. Maconochie, *Norfolk Island* (1847), p. 3.

of his original offence'. The progress of his performance should be made evident by a mark system as an impressive way 'to place the prisoner's fate in his own hands'. These checks and stimulants should obtain not for the individual prisoner, but for a working group of six men in order to 'create an *esprit de corps* in all towards good'. And, finally, all this should be worked out with as little direct force as possible. By such a system Maconochie intended 'to mix persuasion with punishment, and to make their effect improving, yet their operation severe'.[1]

Such were the ideas of the man who became responsible for Norfolk Island. There he found 1,400 of the worst prisoners, removed thither from New South Wales and Van Diemen's Land for further punishment. The military guard was insufficient, and there were no provisions for religious service and instruction. The experiment of the mark system could be initiated only with the 'new hands' who came from England without any additional 'colonial' punishment, and even with these it did not work in accordance with the idea of its inventor, as the marks had no fixed value toward liberation. Many a prisoner earned more marks than he was expected to do, but conditions in Van Diemen's Land did not permit his reception on conditional release. In these circumstances Maconochie had to rely on spiritual strength and on the power of moral influence and a wholesome atmosphere—one more example of that first generation of bold prison reformers who set personal devotion against the routine of suspicion and deterrence.

> 'I sought generally by every means to recover the men's self-respect, to gain his own will toward his reform, to visit moral offences severely, but to reduce the number of those that were purely contraventional, to mitigate the penalties attached to those, and then gradually to awaken better and more enlightened feelings among both officers and men.'[2]

In doing so he was convinced that this was to 'work with nature' rather than against it as other prison systems did. He built churches, introduced instruction, distributed books, gave every prisoner a small garden, and 'went everywhere alone and unattended, showing confidence and winning it in return'. The whole enterprise ended after four years. The underlying principle of flexible sentences was inapplicable under the criminal law of the time, for which prison terms, definitely fixed by the sentencing court were the ordinary form of legal punishment for non-capital

[1] Sub-title of a treatise on *Crime and Punishment* (1846).

[2] Maconochie, *Norfolk Island*, p. 6.

crimes. After his return to England in 1844 Maconochie, under the auspices of Matthew Davenport Hill, was for a short time in charge of the prison at Birmingham. Under the prevailing criminal law Maconochie's scheme was never put to a fair test. He was much interested in similar attempts abroad and gave the work of Montesinos at Valencia a wide publicity in England.

In the meantime the burden of carrying out sentences shifted from the colonies to the mother country. In vain in 1847 a Select Committee of the House of Lords, with the approval of High Court judges, reported that transportation could not safely be abandoned, 'since it has terror for offenders generally which no other penalties short of death possess', and it spares the mother country the danger of a high proportion of liberated convicts! The same Report, however, admitted 'that those who have actual intercourse with convicts feel the least sanguine as to the deterring and exemplary effect of penal infliction' and are rather inclined to look for reformative methods of treatment.[1] From the same year, 1847, the whole term of prison confinement and the subsequent stage of public works were to be served in England. Ticket-of-leave men only were sent to Australia. Some years later transportation came to a definite end. 'By reason of the difficulty of transporting offenders' an Act of 1853 prescribed sentences of penal servitude for all crimes punishable by transportation for less than fourteen years. Four years of penal servitude should be equal to seven years of transportation.[2] A further Act of 1857 prohibited any sentence of transportation at all.[3] In 1864 the ordinary terms of penal servitude were extended to five, and for recidivists to seven years.[4] Until 1867 sentences of penal servitude were partly carried out in Western Australia with a view to facilitating emigration into this undeveloped colony. Strangely enough, toward the end of this period, English opinion about transportation seemed to be less critical. Looking back at his own colonial policy under Lord John Russell's administration, Earl Grey summed up the history of that penal experiment by these words: 'If the scheme of sending convicts to Port Jackson has worked much evil, it has worked still greater good.' The proportion of ex-convicts who did not live honestly would have been, he argued, much greater

[1] *First Report from the Select Committee of the House of Lords appointed to inquire into the Execution of Criminal Law, especially Juvenile Offenders and Transportation* (1847) (Reports from Committees, in 10 vols.) vii. (3), 3 and 7.

[2] 16 & 17 Vict., c. 99, ss. 1 and 4.

[3] 20 & 21 Vict., c. 3, s. 2.

[4] 27 & 28 Vict., c. 47, s. 2.

if they had remained in the mother country.[1] Such optimistic views could not overcome the violent opposition to transportation which arose in the colonies themselves.

The ultimate judgement of history confirms the verdict by the Select Committee of 1837. To the modern historian transportation of criminals appears as a 'most futile, wasteful and harmful' experiment in colonial policy, and from a purely penal point of view equally a failure.[2] Judged by standards of its own time transportation corresponded to the public works which on the Continent by a similar system of commutation of sentences and statutory provisions were substituted for the execution of the *poena ordinaria*, i.e. capital punishment. It remains an open question whether the treatment of transported convicts exceeded the harsh and deterrent discipline of continental public works. The hardship of being sent away many thousand miles overseas was felt more by English countryfolk than by the inhabitants of the London slums who might have found their conditions changed for the better. Transportation had a selective rather than a reformative effect: those who could stand that unusual strain and temptation had, in the end, an opportunity of 'turning over a new leaf'. During the first years transport facilities and the means for maintaining the convicts in the colony were desperately insufficient. Mass transport of prisoners by private contractors, sent to an empty and undeveloped country, must necessarily entail an appalling amount of human misery. Notwithstanding, contemporary criticism complained at the lack of deterrent effect. In vain Governor Arthur argued that even the better living conditions and ample food of the assigned servants were outweighed by the rigidity of discipline. The want of a realistic insight into the conditions of convict life in a remote and unknown country, and boastful accounts in personal letters from convicts themselves, explain the illusion that the colony was attractive rather than deterrent. Human suffering has always been silent. The personal destiny of the convict depended on whether he was assigned to a good or a bad employer. 'The lottery of assignment' frustrated the equality of sentences, quite contrary to the prevalent principle of just retribution. The empty land with a high percentage of convicts among its population was not a proper background for social adjustment. It was a source of new temptations with its constant opportunities for mutual contamination, adventurous enterprises,

[1] Earl Grey, *The Colonial Policy of Lord John Russell's Administration* (2nd ed. 1853), ii. 76.

[2] O'Brien, l.c., p. 362.

and escape from orderly ways of life and work. The inequality of sexes made things even worse, particularly for the small number of women convicts among a predominantly male population. The deeper root of the failure, and an essential evil in itself, was the forsaking of responsibility by the mother country. Transportation had been initiated in order to get rid of undesirable antisocial elements, and to clear over-crowded gaols and hulks at home. No constructive social policy can be pursued with the purpose of simply putting out of sight the symptoms of evil. Bentham, with his usual lucidity, ironically characterized that fatal attitude: 'I rid myself of the sight of you, the ship that bears you away saves me from witnessing your sufferings,—I shall give myself no more trouble about you. . . .'[1] And it was likewise this attitude of discounting a responsibility and shifting it out of sight which raised opposition in the colonies. In 1850 the newly founded New South Wales Association, in a petition to Queen Victoria said, 'that the inundating of feeble and dependent colonies with the criminals of the parent state is opposed to the arrangement of Providence, by which the virtue of each community is destined to combat its own vice'.[2]

The socio-biological aspect of transportation and its result on the trend of general population was less important than one might have expected. The question is what effects, if any, had the eradication from the English stream of propagation of certain anti-social elements, and their infiltration, in an unnatural proportion, into a growing population of a young nation? For an unbiased examination the first difficulty arises from the fact that it is impossible to ascertain to what degree the transportees were actually antisocial elements. On their way to Australia they did not take with them any records of their previous criminal careers. The great majority served sentences of seven years, only a minority had fourteen years or life sentences. Judging from the standards of contemporary criminal law a seven years' sentence would correspond to a minor offence against property, but in so far as these terms of transportation were the result of commutation of more severe sentences, serious crimes would have been concerned. In England the loss of these elements has been more than balanced by the fact that the main transportation period coincided with the unprecedented increase in population between 1780 and 1820.[3]

[1] *Works*, ed. by Bowring, i. 497.
[2] Mary Carpenter, *Our Convicts*, i. 227.
[3] G. T. Griffith, *Population Problems in the Age of Malthus* (1926), p. 254.

In Australia the influence of the convict element was, in the end, comparatively negligible. The free population abstained from marriage with convicts. In New South Wales, owing to the scarcity of women convicts, less than 10 per cent. of the convicts married at all. The rapid inflow of free immigrants after the discovery of gold turned the balance even more against convicts. One generation after the cessation of transportation, the descendants of convicts numbered no more than 1·5 per cent. of the whole population.[1] The social influence of this declining group has been further minimized by the attitude of the native-born children who set themselves with the vigour of a young generation against the corrupting influence of convictism, drunkenness, and the abuses of state-controlled settlements.[2] Even in 1895, in *R.* v. *Dean*—an Australian *cause célèbre*—the defence tried to discredit the main witness for the prosecution by alleging that more than forty years ago she had been transported and married a ticket-of-leave man.[3]

THE PROGRESSIVE STAGE SYSTEM

As a punitive measure, transportation had a graduated pattern. The convict was expected to pass one stage after the other: confinement in English prisons or hulks, transportation to the colony, work in public employment or assignment to a private master, ticket-of-leave, conditional pardon—with chain-gang, penal settlement, and re-transportation on the negative side. In order to turn the punitive stages into a constructive treatment, a re-orientation was indispensable. The progressive readjustment of the prisoner himself had to be made the principal purpose of the whole prison discipline, and the gradual progress from strict coercion to liberty under supervision had to be regulated by clear and simple principles so that the aim should be understandable as well as attainable for the average prisoner. This was the lasting importance of the work done by Captain Maconochie and Sir Walter Crofton. The mark system was a mere instrument to make the progress visible and to direct will-power and competition to practical ends within a comprehensive reformative scheme.

The Act of 1853 which turned British penal policy from transportation to the administration of penal servitude at home, was also the foundation of a new convict system in Ireland. This Irish system was developed by Sir Walter Crofton, 1854–62,

[1] T. A. Coghlan, *Labour and Industry in Australia* (1918), i. 562.

[2] O'Brien, l.c., p. 364.

[3] C. K. Allan, 57 *L.Q.R.* (1941) 85, 92.

Chairman of the Board of Directors of Convict Prisons for Ireland.[1] This particular form of prison discipline consisted of four stages. The initial or probationary stage was regularly nine months of solitary confinement at Mountjoy near Dublin. A monotonous atmosphere and the oppressive work of picking oakum emphasized the punitive character; otherwise, it was thought, the prisoner would 'fail to acknowledge the benefit of a true industrial labour'. He would, however, even at Mountjoy, proceed to some simple handicrafts. There was also provision for education and religious instruction. The second stage consisted of public works at Spike Island in the Cove of Cork. Here, by an elaborate system of marks and figures, the prisoner rose through five classes with the chance that by good behaviour and exemplary zeal and industry he could shorten the specific terms for the particular classes. The various classes did not differ in the sort of work to be done, but in the prisoner's clothes and the amount of the award—the main stimulus being the shortening of the whole prison term by a speedy progression. Then came the intermediate stage at Lusk and Smithfield. This 'filter between prison and the community' was the main characteristic of the Irish system. The idea was that employment of convicts 'under circumstances of exposure to the ordinary temptations and trials of the world where the reality and sincerity of their reformation may be fairly and publicly tested, will present the most favourable chances for their gradual absorption into the body of the community'.[2] Therefore prisoners worked without supervision or went to work unattended. There were no disciplinary measures, but the possibility of recommitment to a former stage. The work was similar to what the prisoner would probably do at large: agricultural work, carpentry, &c. There was a special technical education. Crofton had the advantage of a close co-operation with an able teacher, James P. Organ. He combined in himself the duties of a teacher with the task of a social worker: care and protection for discharged prisoners, constant contact with employers, finding out suitable posts for ex-convicts, personal visits to former convicts in Dublin once a fortnight. Through this personal link the penal institution itself remained responsible for the after-care of former inmates. This fact and the test-character of the intermediate prison were

[1] W. Crofton, *A Few Remarks on the Convict Question* (1857); id., *Convict System and Transportation* (1863); Mary Carpenter, *Reformatory Prison Discipline* (1872).

[2] *Second Report of the Directors of Convict Prisons for Ireland*, p. 23, quoted from the treatise mentioned in p. 85 n. 1.

expected to win the confidence of employers and the goodwill of the general public. The last stage was a conditional release, under the supervision of Organ or the police, with strict regulations for good behaviour, which might be enforced by a recommitment to prison. Such was this carefully designed Progressive Stage system, rising from deterrent and oppressive forms of confinement to almost unrestricted probation stages. The whole machinery was permeated by the personal energy and educational devotion of its promoter.

Crofton's bold experiment raised passionate opposition as well as enthusiastic admiration. In England a favourable report of four visiting justices of the West Riding prison at Wakefield[1] was followed by angry criticism, which denied the alleged favourable results in criminal statistics, maintained that the gist of the pretended 'Irish system' was simply the old 'colonial practice', or, if anything was virtually new such as the intermediate and supervisory stages, it was not applicable in England.[2] Sir Joshua Jebb, the influential Surveyor General of English prisons, lent his authority to the adversaries of the Irish innovations. On the other hand, Matthew Davenport Hill, Mary Carpenter, and the younger Clay published valuable material in order to explain and propagate the underlying ideas.[3] These reformers saw in the efforts of Maconochie and Crofton a new educational principle at work. Prison discipline was a training of will-power and a strengthening of self-control. For this end the prison régime was to be adapted to the inner development of the inmate, and converted into a gradual progress toward self-responsibility and liberty. But even the advocates of such elastic and dynamic principles were not free from the temptation to over-estimate the mere form of prison organization. There remained still a predilection for mechanical devices in the recommendation of labour sentences as a substitute for the traditional fixed time sentences. 'Under the influence of time sentences', Maconochie said, 'the will is now active for evil,—under task sentences it would be drawn to good.'[4]

These principles seemed to be supported by utterances from men whose penal doctrines differed from the reformative optimism

[1] *Observations on the Treatment of Convicts in Ireland*, by four visiting justices of the West Riding prison at Wakefield (1863).

[2] *Irish Fallacies and English Facts*, by Scrutator (1863); John T. Burt, *Irish Facts and Wakefield Figures* (1863); *Convict Discipline in Ireland* (London, without year).

[3] M. D. Hill, *Suggestions for the Repression of Crime* (1857), pp. 585 et seq.; Mary Carpenter, *Our Convicts* (1864), ii. 1–20; W. L. Clay, *Our Convict System* (1862).

[4] Quoted from M. D. Hill, op. cit., p. 264.

of M. D. Hill and his friends. The idea of labour sentences goes back to William Paley (1743–1805), Utilitarian author of popular text-books on moral philosophy and natural theology.[1] Archbishop Richard Whately justified legal punishment only as a means to 'the prevention of crime by the terror of example or of threat',[2] and at the same time was an ardent adversary of transportation and a prominent advocate of labour sentences. Although he found the treadmill 'less eligible' for prison work, he would apply the wholesome principle of labour sentences to every sort of hard labour: 'Every step', he said, 'a man took in the tread-wheel, he should be walking out of the prison, every stroke of the spade would be cutting a passage for restoration to society.'[3] Such a mechanical device could scarcely be expected—as the author hoped—not merely to enforce industry and steady work, but 'to form some agreeable association with the idea of labour'. The labour sentences, recommended also by Herbert Spencer,[4] were an acknowledgement of the sound principle that the prisoner's fate should be put into his own hands; but the whole idea was discredited by the doctrinal conception of its advocates.

The value of a Progressive Stage system depends on the type of prison discipline within the different stages. The elder Clay foresaw the dangers of material rewards as an incitement to industry: this would be an appeal to lower and selfish motives. He insisted on a first period of reflection and self-examination in separate confinement—after which a mark system would be advisable for the rest of the prison term. His son held the Irish system 'the best and most complete in the world', a gradual rise in liberty, not in material gains. He thought if his father and Maconochie could have combined their experiences, the result would have been similar to Sir Walter Crofton's scheme![5]

The administration of penal servitude in England, by its historical connexion with transportation, never entirely lost its progressive form. The initial period of nine months in strictly separate confinement and the first three months in associated work belonged to the probation class. Then the convict rose

[1] T. Sellin, 22 *Journal* 264.

[2] R. Whateley, *Introductory Lectures on Political Economy* (4th ed. 1855), Appendix E, p. 227.

[3] R. Whately in an article published in the *London Review*, 1829, reprinted as Appendix I to the author's *Thoughts on Secondary Punishment, in a Letter to Earl Grey* (1832).

[4] Herbert Spencer, 'Prison Ethics', *Essays Scientific, Political, Speculative* (1868), ii. 210–50.

[5] W. L. Clay, *The Prison Chaplain* (1861), pp. 252, 397, 418.

through three further classes, with the chance of promotion to the special class. Marks were earned for exemplary industry and could be forfeited by bad conduct. The stimulating rewards of the higher classes were certain privileges with regard to visits, letters, exercise, and a gratuity of money paid on discharge, and finally, a remission, by conditional release up to one-fourth of the associated stage, under the supervision of the police. Thus far English penal servitude also claimed that it made the prisoner 'perfectly to see and feel that his fate is in his own hands, and that he has something more to work and to hope for than the mere avoidance of punishment'.[1] It differed, however, from the ideas of Crofton in something more than the absence of any intermediate stage. The progression was a mere lessening of pressure, certainly a sound and effective means of discipline, but not an increasing process of testing and burdening with responsibilities, nor was it a gradual way to social readjustment.

On the Continent the Irish system met with great interest and warm appreciation. Even Mittermaier, for so long the influential advocate of separate confinement, welcomed the apparent success of the new form of prison discipline in Ireland.[2] von Holtzendorff, the adversary of Wichern's experiment with a deeply personal separate treatment at Moabit, after a careful analysis of Crofton's system, contrasted this healthy 'moral duress', this 'enforced work of the human mind', with the 'close atmosphere' of solitary confinement.[3] Further followers of Crofton were van der Brugghen in Holland,[4] Bonneville de Marsangy in France,[5] and Beltrani-Scalia in Italy.[6] The new method of treatment facilitated the idea of combining various forms of prison discipline upon the basis of a classification of criminals. Hence the maxim 'reformation by individualization', coined by Eugen d'Alinge, who for thirty-six years was Director of Osterstein Castle at Zwickau in Saxony.[7] He divided the prisoners into three progressive 'disciplinary classes'.

[1] E. Du Cane, *Punishment and Prevention of Crime* (1885), pp. 152–92, especially 169.

[2] C. I. A. Mittermaier, *Der gegenwärtige Zustand der Gefängnisfrage* (1860), pp. 122 et seq.

[3] F. von Holtzendorff, *Das Irische Gefängnissystem* (1859), English translation: *The Irish Convict System* (1860); id., *Kritische Untersuchungen über die Grundsätze und Ergebnisse des irischen Strafvollzuges* (1865).

[4] J. J. L. van der Brugghen, *Études sur le système pénitentiaire irlandais*, from the Dutch, edited by F. von Holtzendorff (1865).

[5] Bonneville de Marsangy, *De l'amélioration de la loi criminelle* (1864).

[6] Beltrani-Scalia, *La riforma penitenziaria in Italia* (1879).

[7] E. d'Alinge, *Besserung auf dem Wege der Individualisierung* (1865). See also Glauning, 23 *MoSchrKrim.* 722.

A 'psychological quarantine' i.e. an initial period of observation, and 'the institute of special advisers'—anticipating the personal approach of a social worker—were recommended as instruments of an individualizing treatment.

Such practical attempts coincided with a new theoretical principle of individualization of punishment.[1] Individualization, however, is a relative conception. In its extreme, it would imply an almost unlimited discretion, incompatible with the general rules and standards of any legal system at all. In the light of practical experience, a reasonable and sufficiently flexible Progressive Stage system facilitates that degree of individualization which is possible and desirable for the treatment of some 500 prisoners in an average penal institution.

The first German text-book on prison discipline had the Irish system as its foundation.[2] As to the practical response to the new idea, the result remained considerably behind the appreciative literary response. The Swiss prison at Lenzburg in the Canton of Zürich claimed to be the first Continental penal institution which accepted the Irish pattern.[3] In Germany, apart from d'Alinge's individualizing policy, there were local experiments with a progressive form of prison discipline,[4] e.g. at Untermassfeld in Saxony-Meiningen according to a Regulation of 1834, and at Vechta in Oldenburg under the initiative of Hoyer. In Hungary Emil Tauffer introduced the new system at Lipotvar and Lapoplava.[5] The Danish and Norwegian prison regulations too were influenced by the idea of progressive stages in prison. On the whole, Continental prison systems developed in their traditional way with the prevalent trend in favour of fixed sentences and separate confinement. This inheritance from the past proved still the main obstacle when, for the Continent, the Progressive Stage idea was to be rediscovered by penologists of the twentieth century.[6] In the meantime the whole idea went through a new period of trials and transformation when it was amalgamated with a fresh reformative move in the New World.

[1] Wahlberg, *Individualisierung in der Strafrechtspflege* (1869); R. Saleilles, *L'Individualisation de la peine* (1898), English translation by R. S. Jastrow (Mod. Crim. Science Series, No. 4) (1911).

[2] Haenell, *System der Gefängniskunde* (1866). For further German literary followers of the Progressive Stage idea see R. Plischke, 19 *MoSchrKrim.* 417.

[3] M. Laurent Mathéron, 'Lenzbourg', *Études sur pénitenciers suisses et allemands*, i. (1868); Hafner–Zürcher, pp. 300 et seq.

[4] L. Frede, p. 546.

[5] E. Tauffer, *Die Erfolge des progressiven Strafvollzugssystems* (1883); Langer, *Der progressive Strafvollzug in Ungarn, Kroatien und Bosnien* (1904).

[6] H. Kriegsmann, *Das progressive Strafensystem* (1913).

THE AMERICAN REFORMATORY

Much more than any European country, the United States was prepared to accept and develop the new ideas of individualization of treatment and a progressive form of prison discipline. Not that the Americans just imitated the Irish system, but the bold experiments of Maconochie and Crofton and the theoretical considerations of M. D. Hill and his followers proved an inspiration for a reform movement of great impulse and vigour.[1] From the forties, among the young generation, something more was aimed at than merely a settlement of the obsolete rivalries between the solitary and silent systems. Some of the states introduced so-called good-time laws which were expected to improve prison discipline by the stimulus of a shortened prison term. Quaker reformers organized after-care for discharged prisoners. Under the inspiring leadership of Dorothea Lynde Dix, asylums for mental defectives were founded.[2] And most important of all, the rapidly growing cities erected reform schools for neglected children and delinquent juveniles. The new educational outlook of these institutions extended to the treatment of adolescents and adults. For American reformers—as for M. D. Hill and Mary Carpenter—the experience gained in these juvenile institutions became a valuable basis for a reorientation of prison discipline in general.

After the end of the Civil War there began a new era for American prison reform. The tasks of reconstruction aroused and deepened the sense of social responsibility. An enthusiastic interest in an active and conscious penal policy spread over the United States. Francis Lieber was still alive, a link between the old and the new generation of reformers. Enoch Cobb Wines, secretary of the New York Prison Association, and Theodore W. Dwight, the first head of Columbia Law School, were the 'heralds' of the new movement. All seemed to agree upon the ultimate aim, i.e. to make the utmost efforts, by appealing to the positive side of the prisoner's character, to reclaim the criminal for useful membership in society. With such an avowedly reformative attitude, the American reformers had much in common with the European promoters of differentiated and graded forms of prison discipline. E. C. Wines had a deep admiration for the work done by Obermaier and Montesinos. G. B. Hubbell and F. B. Sanborn were

[1] McKelvey, p. 61 and *passim*.

[2] F. Tiffany, *Life of Dorothea Lynde Dix* (1891); H. Marshall, *Dorothea Dix, forgotten Samaritan* (1937).

ardent advocates of the Irish system. E. C. Wines and T. W. Dwight, in a report of 1867, advised the Legislature of New York to pursue the ultimate aim of penal policy, i.e. the reformation of the criminal, 'by placing the prisoner's fate, as far as possible, in his own hand, by enabling him, through industry and good conduct to raise himself, step by step, to a position of less restraint; while idleness and bad conduct, on the other hand, keep him in a state of coercion and restraint.'[1] From the beginning such a scheme was inseparably linked with the introduction of indeterminate sentences. The latter should be a means rather than an end in themselves. F. H. Wines, the son, regarded them as 'merely a tool, a dead thing', and contrasted them with the true forces of reformation: labour, education, and religion.[2] This programme was in full harmony with the ideas of M. D. Hill and his friends. The daily practice, however, did not reflect the same ideal standards. When, in 1873, Mary Carpenter visited the United States, she frankly censured the prevailing defects of American prisons: overcrowding, idleness, insufficient separation, and an unsuitable supervision of women prisoners.[3]

The peak of that movement was the celebrated First National Prison Congress at Cincinnati in 1870.[4] Sir Walter Crofton and M. D. Hill submitted valuable papers. The outstanding event was an address given by Z. R. Brockway, at that time an experienced prison superintendent at Detroit. His paper on the 'Ideal of a true Prison System for a State', read long before the dawn of Lombrosionism and the new social school of criminal law, anticipated the programme of modern penology.[5] Punishment, in his opinion, should not be the aim but merely an instrument of penal policy. The true object ought to be the protection of society, and the means to this end: the prevention of crime and reformation of the criminal. Reformation, in this context, was understood as turning the obnoxious and troublesome into tolerable, acceptable, and, if possible, useful citizens. Brockway's practical suggestions were: an independent board of guardians controlling the new reformative institutions, primary and reform schools for children and juveniles, a graduated system of reformatories for adults, i.e. a house of reception, an industrial reformatory, and an intermediate reformatory. The latter, like Crofton's intermediate prison, 'an

[1] Quoted from F. H. Wines, *Punishment and Reformation* (1895), p. 196.

[2] Ibid., p. 208.

[3] McKelvey, p. 83.

[4] *Transactions of the National Congress on Penitentiary and Reformatory Discipline at Cincinnati, 1870* (1871).

[5] Op. cit., pp. 38 et seq.

outpost on the brink of society', should be established as a co-operative settlement. Indeterminate sentences should commit the prisoner to the care and custody of the board of guardians. The Congress approved of most of these suggestions and promulgated a celebrated *Declaration of Principles*. These *Principles* emphasized the urgent importance of a professional prison service under State control, and required indeterminate sentences and a progressive form of prison discipline. They are a solemn recognition of the spiritual forces upon which such a programme ought to rely: suppression and degradation are contrary to the lessons of practical experience as well as to Christian principles, but hope is a more powerful motive than fear, and the best way to reformation would be to gain the will of the prisoner himself.

'In prison administration, moral forces should be relied upon, with as little admixture of physical force as possible, and organized persuasion be made to take the place of coercive restraint, the object being to make upright and industrious freemen rather than orderly and obedient prisoners; moral training alone will make good citizens. To the latter of these ends, the living soul must be won; to the former, only the inert and obedient body.'

For many decades this *Declaration* had an inspiring influence on the cause of prison reform. In 1930 it was published again in a slightly revised form.

The Congress was the precursor of that important international forum for penological discussions, the International Penal and Penitentiary Congress, which even survived the First World War. Due to the initiative and the unceasing efforts of E. C. Wines the first International Prison Congress was held in London in 1872. The practical outcome of the Cincinnati Congress, however, was the creation of a new type of penal institution: the reformatory. After years of legislative and administrative preparations, in 1877 the New York State Reformatory at Elmira was ready to be opened. Z. R. Brockway became the first superintendent of the new institution, and he held this post until 1899—growing in authority and reputation as an international authority in the educational treatment of prisoners.[1]

The reformatory system is a special form of prison discipline for adolescents and young adults between sixteen and thirty who have been committed, under indeterminate sentences, for terms

[1] McKelvey, p. 144; Z. R. Brockway, *Fifty Years of Prison Service* (1912).

varying between a certain minimum and maximum.[1] A minutely regulated progression is designed to stimulate the inmate to gain his liberty by work and good behaviour. Much had been done to exclude the traditional prison atmosphere: there was no intentional degradation, no over-emphasis on the past, but a fresh start for the duties of to-day and the tasks of to-morrow. School, library, and a prison paper offered further educational opportunities. The institution felt also a responsibility for the after-care of discharged prisoners.

On the other hand, from its beginning, the new system suffered serious set-backs. The first blow was a growing tendency of American legislation to curtail, if not to eradicate, industrial prison labour. Brockway himself tried to compensate for this disastrous restriction by the introduction of sport and military drill. Even from the model reformatory, the nightmare of over-crowding could not be banned. Elmira had been built with some 500 cells. In 1892 there were 1,296, in 1899 as many as 1,500 inmates. The movement for the erection of reformatories rapidly spread over the United States. The benefit of reformative sentences was more and more extended to other groups of offenders. At the same time, what had begun as a bold experiment lost the inspiring impulse of its first promoters, and became routine work and mass treatment. The spirit of Cincinnati died with the first generation of humanitarian reformers. Once more prison walls proved stronger than theoretical principles and ideal programmes.

Even so, the reformatory system remains a lasting American contribution to penal reform. After all unavoidable deductions, a definite standard had been established which could never be entirely abandoned. Once the fathers of Elmira had been impressed by European ideas—now the American example inspired a new reformative impulse in the Old World. Under the influence of those new institutions indeterminate sentences, a specialized treatment of young offenders, and even a general reformative and educational reorientation of prison discipline became not only favourite subjects of theoretical discussion and controversy, but also a growing concern of criminal legislation and penal administration in Europe. History seemed to repeat itself. Once again a pilgrimage of experts to the New World began. They praised the newly discovered reformative system and recommended indeterminate sentences as its indispensable complement. These reports

[1] A. Winter, *The New York State Reformatory Elmira* (1891); F. H. Wines, *Punishment and Reformation* (1895; 3rd ed. 1919).

for the most part described the new institutions in the light of the intentions of their founders, and they sometimes seemed to identify Elmira and Brockway's ideas with *the* American penal policy. On the other hand, some critical observers, from an avowedly European standpoint, suggested that the progression from stage to stage was too much a mechanical one, and that the breathless strain and competition which pervaded the whole life was exclusively directed towards the selection of the successful.[1]

Recent judgements on Elmira and the reformatory system differ widely. Nathaniel F. Cantor appreciated the historic importance of the reformatory experiment and attributed to Elmira 'a good educational programme'.[2] On the other hand, E. R. Cass of the American Prison Association denounced the reformatory system as 'weak, often trivial, and even wretchedly automatic'. In 1927, after an American prison tour, a German penologist described the following weak spots of Elmira: inappropriate building conditions with inside cells, lack of productive work, absence of full-time prison teachers, and the long lock-up from six to six.[3] For a just assessment of American reformatories it is only fair to consider the change in the composition of their inmates. The growing use of probation saved many a hopeful first-offender from prison, but at the same time lowered the standard of the average prison population. Roughly speaking, the same types who thirty years ago had to undergo reformative training are nowadays eligible for probation. Consequently, comparative statistics of alleged successes and failures of ex-prisoners are no reliable indication for the true merits of an institution. In 1888 Elmira claimed 78·5 per cent. of its former inmates living self-supporting and orderly lives. In 1912 the Ohio State Reformatory made the following classification: 65 per cent. of the former inmates were regarded as above the average standard of their particular class and circumstances in their successful conduct of life and their usefulness as citizens; 25 per cent. were of low value, and 15 per cent. committed new crimes.[4] Recent criminological studies carefully following up every individual's after-career revealed the startling fact that out of 500 ex-prisoners of the Massachusetts Reformatory some 80 per

[1] These observations found their literary expression in a number of German reports; noteworthy instances are J. M. Baernreither, *Jugendfürsorge und Strafrecht in den Vereinigten Staaten von Amerika* (1905); P. Herr, *Das moderne amerikanische Besserungs-system* (1907); B. Freudenthal, *Amerikanische Kriminalpolitik* (1907); id., 27 *ZStW* 121.

[2] N. Cantor, *Crime and Society* (1939), p. 145.

[3] M. Liepmann, *American Prisons and Reformatory Institutions* (1928), pp. 18, 21 et seqq.

[4] L. N. Robinson, p. 149.

cent. continued their criminal behaviour during a five-year test period, beginning at the end of their parole terms.[1] Once more a new generation faces the old penological problem and discovers new perplexities.

[1] S. and E. Glueck, *Five Hundred Criminal Careers* (1930), p. 191 and *passim*.

CHAPTER VI

NEW SOCIAL AND LEGAL ASPECTS OF PUNISHMENT

THE CHANGE-OVER TO INDIVIDUAL PREVENTION

WITH the beginning of the twentieth century European penal policy turned to a new era of reform. The example of the American reformatory inspired not only literary discussion, but led also to the erection of new types of institutions in various European countries. In 1902 England made the first experiment with a reformative training of 'juvenile adults' between sixteen and twenty-one, consolidated as the Borstal system by the Prevention of Crime Act of 1908.[1] Sir Evelyn Ruggles-Brise inaugurated the new scheme, impressed by what he had seen of the American efforts.[2] The Borstal System is the outstanding English contribution to one of the principal objects of penal reform, i.e. the constructive treatment of young offenders. It gained a high reputation among experts abroad, not least because it recognized a non-punitive treatment within the penal system. 'To be sent to Borstal', according to a leading English authority, 'is a punishment, but to stay there is to have a chance to learn the right way of life.'[3] In Germany the American example succeeded where the academic advocates of the Irish system had failed; it overcame the prevailing resistance to the Progressive Stage idea. In 1912 Krohne himself, the leading German authority in favour of the classical separate confinement, opened the Prussian prison for young offenders at Wittlich. This special institution for adolescents between eighteen and twenty-one was the first modern experiment in Germany with a Progressive Stage system. Only prisoners of the third stage were eligible for conditional release, and a full-time social worker was employed who was also responsible for a well-planned system of after-care.[4]

Such practical achievements were part and parcel of a fundamental reorientation of penal policy in Europe. In England the historic turning-point was the *Report of the Gladstone Committee* in 1895.[5]

[1] 8 Edw. VII, c. 59, s. 1.

[2] Ruggles-Brise, p. 91; Shane Leslie, *Sir Evelyn Ruggles-Brise. A Memoir of the Founder of Borstal* (1938), pp. 122 et seq.

[3] A. Paterson, Introduction to S. Barman, *The English Borstal System* (1934).

[4] W. Bleidt, in Bumke, pp. 371 et seqq.

[5] *Report of the Departmental Committee on Prisons* (1895).

In 1877 the prison administration had been transferred to the Prison Commissioners,[1] and a centralized and rationalized system of prison management introduced. A Progressive Stage system prevailed, but without Crofton's intermediate institution, and with more emphasis upon the rigours of the earlier stages than the privileges of the later ones. Prison labour was developing from hard and monotonous tasks to useful work but was hampered by the prevalence of separate confinement. Now a careful investigation challenged the whole so-called 'Du Cane régime' on principle. 'While much attention has been given to organisation, finance, order and health of the prisoners, and prison statistics'—the *Report* reads—'the prisoners have been treated too much as hopeless and worthless members of the community, and the moral as well as the legal responsibility of the prison authorities has been held to cease when they pass outside the prison gates.' Fundamental changes were necessary.

'The system should be made more elastic, more capable of being adapted to the special cases of individual prisoners. Prison discipline and treatment should be more effectually designed to maintain, stimulate or awaken the higher susceptibilities of prisoners, and to develop their moral instincts, to train them in orderly and industrial habits and, whenever possible, to turn them out of prison better men and women, both physically and morally, than when they came in.'[2]

Adequate provisions for productive labour should be made. In conformity with the enlightened opinion of Howard, the *Report* prefers reasonable labour conditions to the principle of strict separation. Separate confinement may be advisable as a deterrent, or as a safeguard against contamination—but not as an opportunity for meditating on misdeeds. Relying on the experience at a model workship at Wandsworth, the *Report* expected no harm from association for industrial labour under proper conditions. From such a realistic point of view the final verdict on the tread-wheel was given: 'It keeps the prisoner in a state of mental vacuity, and this we regard as a most undesirable result.' Aid and after-care for the discharged prisoner ought to be initiated before the date of release. For the Committee, the key to crime prevention was the treatment of young prisoners. They recommended that 'the court should have the power to commit to penal reformatories offenders under the age of twenty-three for periods of not less than

[1] 40 & 41 Vict., c. 21.
[2] *Report*, pp. 7 and 8.

one year and up to three years, with a system of licences graduated according to sentence which should be freely exercised'. There should be 'a half-way house between a prison and a reformatory'. Such a suggestion was a step in a new direction, contrary to the prevailing doctrine of just retribution. It was unacceptable to the Du Cane school. Reformation, they argued, may be the object of charity organizations, but not of a State institution. With the repudiation of this traditional attitude, the new social conception of the relation between State and individual extended to penal policy. Apart from young offenders, habitual criminals required special attention. To punish them for the particular offence which they happened to commit seemed useless. 'A new form of sentence should be placed at the disposal of the judges, by which the offenders might be segregated for long periods of detention, during which they would not be treated with the severity of first-class hard labour, but forced to work under less onerous conditions.'

The first practical outcome of the *Gladstone Report* was the Prison Act of 1898, still the legal foundation of the English prison system.[1] But the true significance of those suggestions went even farther. They anticipated modern reform programmes, and were a well-considered formulation of their principal aims: rehabilitation of the prisoner, individualization of treatment, productive work, planned after-care, educational training of young offenders, and long-term detention of habitual criminals. These proposals indicated a marked change in the conception of penal reform. Early reformers had been content to overcome the notorious defects of the prevailing prison system, while the criminal law itself and the legal conditions under which the courts sent offenders to prison were more or less accepted as a given fact. Now, prison reform affected the wider field of law reform. The experience gained by careful observation of prisoners for months and years, during and after their prison terms, proved an important factor for a new critical attitude towards criminal law and its administration. The emphasis shifted from 'general prevention', i.e. the prohibition and deterrence from wrong-doing of people in general to 'individual prevention', i.e. the responsibility for the individual criminal, in the dock and in prison, and the obligation to make every possible attempt to prevent him, by reformation or segregation, from any further relapse into crime. The interest in criminal law turned from a purely juristic analysis of a self-contained legal system to a critical examination of a means to the end of preventing

[1] 61 & 62 Vict., c. 41.

the culprit from further sinking into destitution and waywardness. This new outlook resulted in a socialization of the treatment of the criminal. Criminal law was now seen to be only one means for crime prevention and was to be co-ordinated with other elements of social reform. The execution of legal sanctions should aim at the repression of the prisoner's anti-social tendencies for which the particular offence committed was only a symptom. Penal administration was expected to come into its own, and to get a more prominent place in a rational system of criminal law. At the same time, prison discipline was to be 'legalized'. New forms of legal guarantees were to be developed in order to establish the rule of law within the administration of punishments and other sanctions. Even at present, penal reform is still aiming at a compromise between social and legal tendencies which often go parallel, but are sometimes divergent.

THE RISE OF CRIMINOLOGY

The change in penal policy had its roots in a new outlook on crime. The history of penal reform testifies to the lasting influence of spiritual forces. The religious motive was evident in the foundation of the first Houses of Correction. It strengthened the efforts of John Howard and Elizabeth Fry to alleviate the fate of their fellow men in prison. A humanitarian impulse made M. D. Hill and his friends fight for constructive methods of penal and correctional treatment in the face of early Victorian *laissez-faire*. Now the process of secularization went farther. Science took over the part in the past played by religion and humanitarianism. A new positivism extended the scope of scientific investigations to man himself, and the laws and actions prevailing within human society. A new science, criminology, studied the causes and forms of crime with a view to its repression and prevention. The term itself is of Italian origin. Since in 1885 R. Garofalo published his *Criminologia*,[1] the word 'criminology' has been generally accepted for empirical investigations on crime and criminals. Such studies had been undertaken even before they were labelled as criminology. There were two starting-points for criminological research: the social and the biological approach.

The social approach to the problem of criminality implies the conception of crime as a phenomenon in social life, something that

[1] French translation, 4th ed. 1895, English translation by R. W. Millar, *Criminology* (Mod. Crim. Science Series, 1914).

occurs within a nation, a group, a family. Crimino-sociology tries to explain the amount and form of crime by revealing its social causes, i.e. the social background of individual life, relations between members of a social group, economic conditions which in themselves are regarded as determined by social factors.[1] This attitude goes back to Adolphe Quetelet (1796–1874), Belgian astronomer and mathematician.[2] He was a promoter of 'the era of statistical enthusiasm', when in the thirties he succeeded in widening the international scope of statistics and in improving methods by mathematical acuteness. With the French lawyer A. M. Guerry[3] he competed in establishing scientific criminal statistics, then a branch of moral statistics covering such human actions as marriages, suicides, and crimes.

Since Quetelet and Guerry, criminal statistics have proved an indispensable instrument for any scientific attempt to approach crime as a mass phenomenon in human society. Quetelet himself went even farther and drew definite conclusions from his statistical observations. By tracing the amount of crime through a number of years he determined a regularity in illegal reactions. For the scientific observer, chance—'that mysterious veil for our ignorance' —seemed to be replaced by insight into the newly discovered natural laws in human society. Quetelet regarded 'the part of prisons, of irons, and of the Scaffold fixed for humanity as much as the revenue of the State'.[4] Hence the idea of 'social physics' based on factors calculable like the facts in the realm of nature. From his mass figures he determined the average probability of committing a crime for each specific age-group, and identified this average standard with an alleged unalterable proclivity to crime. A 'brazen budget' seemed to dominate the legal and moral behaviour of mankind. For the explanation of this sombre result he relied on a simple logical conclusion. Constant results indicate permanent causes, and for the latter he substituted social condi-

[1] W. A. Bonger, *Criminalité et conditions économiques* (1905), English translation: *Crime and Economic Conditions* (1916); id., *Introduction to Criminology*, translated from the Dutch (1932), by E. van Loo (1936); T. Sellin, 'Crime', *Encyclopaedia of Social Sciences*; F. Exner, 'Kriminalsoziologie', *HWBKrim.*

[2] A. Quetelet, *Penchant au crime* (1831); id., *Sur l'homme, ou essay de physique sociale* (1836). See also Frank H. Hankins, *A. Quetelet as Statistician* (1908); I. Lottin, 'Quetelet, son système sociologique', *Université de Louvain, Annales de l'Institut Supérieur de Philosophie* (1912), i. 99–172; R. Wassermann, *Entwicklungsphasen der kriminalstatistischen Forschung* (1927), pp. 10 et seq.; H. Westergaard, *Contribution to the History of Statistics* (1932), pp. 136 et seq.

[3] A. M. Guerry, *Statistique comparée de l'état de l'instruction et de nombres de crimes* (1829); id., *Statistique morale de l'Angleterre comparée avec la statistique de la France* (1864).

[4] (1826), quoted from Westergaard, l.c., p. 55.

tions. 'Society prepares the crime,' he said, 'and the guilty is only the instrument, an expiatory victim for society, his crime the result of the circumstances in which he finds himself, and the severity of his punishment is perhaps another result of it.'[1] This assumption anticipated the doctrine of an exclusive social determination of crime for which the so-called Lyons school coined the celebrated phrase: 'Society has the criminals whom it deserves.'[2]

By these provocative ideas Quetelet initiated a century of research in criminal statistics, steadily widening its scope and refining its methods. In the course of these studies the interest turned from static observations to a dynamic approach. Subsequent investigations traced through given periods the trend of crime figures, described the character and probable cause of the deviation from its previous level, and established correlations to the trend of other social factors and occurrences. Business cycles, war, economic crises, were like large-scale experiments to demonstrate the influence of social factors on the trend of criminality. Man within his changing surroundings became the true subject of sociology. Criminality seemed to be only one possible reaction beside others. At the same time the widened field of modern statistics found its necessary supplement in new social studies, based on direct observation. In England an empirical school produced valuable reports on the social conditions prevailing at the bottom of industrial society. Buchanan and Henry Mayhew, worthy successors of John Howard, described what they saw of the social background of crime, destitution, and the effects of punishment.[3] Their accounts are the immediate precursors of present-day social surveys.[4]

This social outlook had a lasting influence on the attitude towards the criminal. If crime was primarily a consequence of certain social conditions, moralizing judgements were discredited. Uncontrolled emotions gave way to a recognition of the responsibility of the community. To prevent crime by improving social conditions seemed preferable to repressive punishment. Slum-clearing, extension of school age, prohibition of child labour,

[1] 'Sur l'homme', quoted from Westergaard, l.c., p. 88.

[2] Lacassagne, 'Marche de la criminalité en France 1825–1880', *La revue scientifique* (1882).

[3] Buchanan, *Remarks on Juvenile Crime in the Metropolis* (1846); H. Mayhem, *London Labour and the London Poor* (1851); id., *Criminal Prisons of London* (1862). See also Y. Levin and A. Lindesmith, 'English Ecology and Criminology in the past Century', 27 *Journal* 801.

[4] For the development of this important branch of literature see A. F. Wells, *The Local Survey in Great Britain* (1935).

effective steps against alcoholism, and a general raising of the standard of life—all these measures were certainly justified in themselves, but also important factors for the prevention of crime. Penal policy was to be relieved of its dependence upon a retributory criminal law. The reformative tasks of prison discipline were to be co-ordinated with the constructive forces of social service and welfare work.

No system of crime-prevention could dispense with the necessity of dealing with individual offenders. Even a complete insight into the social implications of crime offers no guidance for the actual treatment of wayward and criminal personalities. A one-sided sociological approach suffers from an undue generalization. It cannot explain why, as experience shows, men react in different ways to an economic crisis, or why, even under an accumulation of unfavourable conditions, most people withstand criminality. Mass observation, while emphasizing the general causes of crime, loses sight of the individual criminal. Quetelet knew only the average man, a fictitious being who is supposed to react in accordance with laws derived from the analysis of vast numbers—a phenomenon closely akin to 'the reasonable man' of the classical school of political economy. Criminology, therefore, had to rediscover the criminal.

The new biological approach began with a startling statement, in its one-sided acuteness no less provocative than Quetelet's thesis one generation before. Cesare Lombroso (1835–1909), Italian psychiatrist, developed the doctrine of inborn criminality.[1] According to him approximately one-third out of the total prison population, including especially the serious persistent offenders, belong to an anomalous biological type. Lombroso claimed to distinguish this type by bodily marks and mental characteristics similar to certain traits found with children and savages and

[1] Cesare Lombroso, *L'uomo delinquente*. First published as a series of papers in *Atti dell' Instituto Lombardo*, 1871–6. Book edition 1878; 5th ed., vols. i–iii, 1896–7. German translation by Fränkel, *Der Verbrecher in anthropologischer, ärztlicher und juristischer Beziehung* (1887). French translation, *L'Homme criminel* (vol. ii, 1888; 2nd ed., vols. i–ii, 1895). Abridged English translation by Gina Lombroso-Ferrero, *Criminal Man* (1911). Id., *Le Crime, causes et remèdes* (1899, 2nd ed. 1906), German translation by Kurella and Jentsch, *Ursachen und Bekämpfung des Verbrechens* (1902), English translation by Henry P. Horton, *Crime, its Causes and Remedies*. With an Introduction by Maurice Parmelee (1911). See also K. G. Kurella, *Cesare Lombroso als Mensch und Forscher* (1911), English translation by Eden Paul, *C. Lombroso, Modern Man of Science* (1911). Gina Lombroso-Ferrero, *Cesare Lombroso, storia della vita e delle opere, narrata dalla figlia* (1915); C. Kenny, 'The Italian Theory of Crime: Cesare Lombroso', Radzinowicz-Turner (ed.), *Modern Approach to Criminal Law* (1945), pp. 1–11; also 10 *Journal Comp. Leg.* 220; H. Mannheim, 28 *Soc. Rev.* 31.

diagnosed as stigmata of degeneration. Consequently he explained criminality as an atavism, a pathological relapse into an earlier stage of human development—a counterpart of psychosis and epilepsy. From such a proposition followed the elimination of moral responsibility, and strong measures for the protection of society up to a lifelong segregation of the incurable enemies of the community. These legislative consequences have been developed by Enrico Ferri[1] and Raffaele Garofalo, who supplemented Lombroso's anthropological doctrine by legal and social considerations.

The revolutionary conception of the inborn criminal was a challenge to medical observation and anthropological research. The English prison doctor Charles Goring, Baer in Germany, Olaf Kinberg in Sweden, and many others re-examined—and finally rejected—the extreme Lombrosian thesis.[2] Investigations of vast numbers of prisoners compared with corresponding data of non-criminal control groups led to the conclusion that there is no definite mental or bodily criminological type. There are only differences of degree between prisoners and the general population. The Lombrosian idea that a certain configuration of the body inevitably indicated an inward criminal disposition was denounced as 'superstition and confusion masked under the scientific name of Criminology'.[3] But the refutation of that doctrine was no futile digression. Careful examinations, for the first time, led to a well-established knowledge, though not of *the* criminal, but of those human types who frequently lapse into crime and determine the composition of the prison population. The impression prevailed that criminals are the result of a negative selection. A comparatively high proportion of them are people in body and mind less fitted for the performance of their social obligations than the average law-abiding citizen. 'In every class and occupation of life', said Goring, 'it is the feeble mind, the inferior forms of physique, the less mentally and physically able persons, which tend to be selected for a criminal career.'[4]

[1] E. Ferri, *I nuovi orizzonti del diritto e della procedura penale* (1881), 3rd ed. under the title *Sociologia Criminale*. English translation: *Criminal Sociology* (1895), German translation by Kurella, 1896. See also G. Nicotri, 20 *Journal* 179.

[2] C. Goring, *The English Convict* (1913), Abridged 1915, New edition by K. Pearson, 1919, German comment by A. Wegner, 44 *ZStW* 593, and Brack, *Giessen Diss.* (1930); Baer, *Das Verbrechen in anthropologischer Beziehung* (1893); G. Aschaffenburg, *Das Verbrechen und seine Bekämpfung* (1902, 3rd ed. 1923), English translation: *Crime and its Repression* (1913); O. Kinberg, *Basic Problems of Criminology* (1935).

[3] Goring, op. cit., p. 9.

[4] Goring, op. cit., p. 182.

Lombroso's theory of the inborn criminal was an attempt to give an answer to the eternal question of an interdependence between physique, character, and destiny. Experience seems to confirm that certain traits and reactions of man are fixed and unalterable like body-types or psychoses. Modern biological research does not rely on single bodily marks but on a comprehensive view of man's constitution and personality type, and from such a broad basis tries to establish certain correlations between physique and character.[1] From a criminological point of view[2] such constitution types do not differ markedly with regard to respective crime risks, but have some significance for the motives and circumstances of criminal behaviour. Recently, the case of Lombroso won the support of fresh crimino-anthropological research at Harvard.[3] Ernest A. Hooton's investigations throw light on the specific criminality of the divers ethnological groups among the American white population. The final conclusion, that 'criminals present a united front of biological inferiority',[4] is not convincing, owing to insufficient comparison with representative non-criminal control groups and to the inevitable subjective judgement in assessing morphological differences as symptoms of biological inferiority.[5]

In their practical results, Lombroso's and Hooton's anthropological predestination and Goring's negative selection differ less. Both doctrines explain the prevalence among criminals of a significant proportion of persons unfit for the struggle and the temptations of the world at large. In the end the rising current of crimino-biological studies influenced criminal law itself. The abstract 'doer' of particular offences had to give way to a variety of criminological types. As a symptom of an offender's antisocial tendencies the same theft or arson has an entirely different significance, if committed by a juvenile, a mental defective, or an habitual criminal. Different ways of treatment should be adapted to the specific susceptibility of the individual criminal, and made applicable by a flexible system of legal sanctions. This was the programme of a new continental school of criminal law represented

[1] E. Kretschmer, *Körperbau und Charakter* (1921, 10th ed. 1931). English translation: *Physique and Character* (1925).

[2] K. Böhmer, 19 *MoSchrKrim.* 192; W. A. Willemse, *Constitution Types in Delinquency* (1932).

[3] E. A. Hooton, *The American Criminal* (1939); id., *Crime and the Man* (1939).

[4] Id., *The American Criminal* (1939), p. 300.

[5] Critical comment by R. K. Merton and M. F. Ashley Montagu, 42 *American Anthropologist* (1940), p. 384; M. F. Ashley Montagu, 217 *Annals* 49; H. Mannheim, 57 *L.Q.R.* 435.

by Franz von Liszt,[1] van Hamel,[2] and Adolphe Prins.[3] As a sociological school they repudiated the one-sided Lombrosian anthropological outlook and emphasized the significance of the environmental factor, but, for the social needs of the community, they advocated a system of individualization based upon a scientific classification of criminals. von Liszt's celebrated '*trias*': deterrence of incidental criminals, reformation of persistent but corrigible criminals, and segregation of incorrigible habitual criminals, was only a rough formula for the new principle of differentiation. Various schemes of classification were suggested, mostly based upon a combination of social and biological factors. For the practical purposes of legislation, modern criminology has been mainly concerned with the following groups: juveniles, mental defectives, drunkards and drug-addicts, vagrants and disorderly people, and habitual criminals.

EUROPEAN CRIMINAL LAW REFORM

The challenge of criminology met with a vigorous legislative response. As in the Era of Enlightenment, a new epoch of criminal law reform dawned over Europe. A Swiss Draft Code of 1893–4, the celebrated work of Carl Stooss, inaugurated this period of legislative activity. Again the Swiss Criminal Code of 1937,[4] in force from 1942, as a representative achievement, marked the end of the recent reform movement.

In accordance with the continental tradition of codified law in most countries the reform movement aimed at replacing the prevailing retributive law by new comprehensive codes framed in conformity with the objects of reformation and prevention. Codification, however, is a slow and tedious process. In many countries numerous consecutive draft codes and counter-proposals raised a lively academic discussion; in some countries they led to the promulgation of new criminal codes. Norway enacted a criminal code in 1902, after various amendments published in a new wording in 1929. Denmark, after producing drafts from 1912

[1] F. von Liszt, 'Der Zweckgedanke im Strafrecht' (1882); 'Kriminalpolitische Aufgaben' (1889–92), reprinted in *Aufsätze und Vorträge* (1905). See also G. Radbruch, 'F. von Liszt, Anlage und Umwelt', *Elegantiae Juris Criminalis* (1938), pp. 72–94.

[2] van Hamel, *Inleiding tot de Studie van het Nederlandsche Strafrecht* (3rd ed. 1913).

[3] Adolphe Prins, *Criminalité et répression* (1886); id., *Science pénale et droit positif* (1899); id., 'La défense sociale et les transformations de droit pénal', *Travaux de l'Institut Solvay. Actualités sociales*, No. 15 (1910); L. Wodon et J. Servais, *L'Œuvre d'Adolphe Prins* (1934).

[4] English translation, Supplement to 30 *Journal* (1939) No. 1.

onwards, enacted a new code in 1930. Italy entered the reform period with a comparatively new code of 1889. The Draft Code of 1921, the work of Enrico Ferri, was an outstanding legislative expression of criminological positivism.[1] After the rise of Fascism it was superseded by the Draft Rocco of 1927, which reverted to stern retribution, but retained certain of the proposed reforms of prison discipline.[2] This draft was the foundation of the Criminal Code of 1930.[3] Switzerland took more than forty years to replace the variety of cantonal laws by the uniform modern Federal Criminal Code of 1937. After the First World War some of the new independent states passed criminal codes which were more or less influenced by the legislative preparations in other European countries: Estonia in 1928, Jugoslavia in 1929, Latvia in 1930, Poland in 1932.

Other continental countries, after subsequent draft codes, anticipated parts of the intended reform by statutory amendments. In Sweden, Johan Thyrén published *Preliminary Considerations* in 1910, which, from 1916, were followed by formulated partial draft codes, leading to an official draft of 1923. In 1927 and 1930 special statutes provided for the detention of recidivists and of offenders with limited responsibility. Germany produced eight draft codes between 1909 and 1930, but the imminent political storm made it impossible to finish the long-delayed reform by the enactment of a new code. Juvenile Courts had been established by an Act passed in 1923. When National-Socialism came into power a Statute against Dangerous Habitual Criminals and on Measures of Security and Reformation, passed in 1933, made ample use of the proposals embodied in the preceding draft codes. Austria published a draft code in 1906. After the First World War she accommodated her legislative reform programme to the German drafts; the Austrian Draft Code of 1927 was almost a duplicate of the German proposals. In the meantime Austria passed Statutes on Conditional Sentences in 1920 and on the Treatment of Young Offenders in 1928. Czechoslovakia published a first draft of a general part of a criminal code in 1921 and a preliminary draft

[1] *Relazione sul progetto preliminare di Codice penale italiano*, vol. i (1921), with official French, English, and German translations. See also S. Glueck, 41 *Harvard L.R.* 453; H. Kantorowicz, *Festschrift für Otto Lenel* (1923), pp. 21–51.

[2] W. T. S. Stallybrass, 'Comparison of the General Principles of Criminal Law in England with Progetto Rocco', in Radzinowicz-Turner (ed.), *Modern Approach to Criminal Law* (1945), pp. 390–466, also *Journ. Comp. Legisl.* xiii. 203; xiv. 45, 223; xv. 77, 232.

[3] English translation: *Penal Code of the Kingdom of Italy*, published by the British Foreign Office (1931), German translation by K. Bunge (1933).

code in 1926. In 1919 she enacted a statute on Conditional Sentences and Conditional Release. Finland published a draft code of 1921–2 and enacted a Statute on Dangerous Recidivists in 1932. France published a preliminary draft of the general part of a criminal code in 1932.

England, with her traditional system of non-codified law, has been spared the cumbersome way of total reform. Instead, substantial innovations were introduced by special statutes. In 1907 the Probation of Offenders Act[1] established the prevailing probation system. In 1908 the Prevention of Crime Act[2] introduced Borstal sentences and preventive detention. In the same year the Children's Act established juvenile courts, further developed by the Children and Young Persons Act of 1933.[3] On the eve of the Second World War the Criminal Justice Bill of 1938[4] proposed new measures of institutional and semi-institutional treatment. Even some of the continental countries, though under a system of codified law, preferred this way of reform by special statutes. Holland amended her Criminal Code of 1881 by an Act of Reform of the Penal System, Prison Discipline, and Detention of Habitual Criminals of 1929. Belgium, still under the modified French *Code pénal*, passed an Act for Social Defence against Abnormal and Habitual Criminals in 1930.

A comparative survey of these legislative precedents discloses different legal solutions of similar social problems. All these recent enactments, while differing in technique and in their immediate objects, had a common tendency. They aimed at prevention of crime by a differential treatment of criminals. To achieve this purpose the systems of legal punishments at the disposal of the courts had to be made more flexible. Due regard to preventive aims required judicial discretion. If sentences should be means to reasonable ends, the statutory limits of legal punishments ought to be more elastic. From the French *Code pénal* most continental codes accepted the method of supplementing the ordinary statutory range of legal punishment for the particular offences by a reduced alternative scale, applicable if certain specified extenuating circumstances obtain. The recent Danish and Swiss codes and the former German draft codes gave the court the power to mitigate the sentence even below these excep-

[1] 7 Edw. VII, c. 17.
[2] 8 Edw. VII, c. 59.
[3] 8 Edw. VII, c. 67 (1908); 23 Geo. V, c. 12 (1933).
[4] 2 Geo. VI, Bill 4.

tional statutory minima, but restricted this possibility to certain types of offences. With the exception of capital punishment for murder, England abolished statutory minima altogether and thereby granted judges a unique discretionary power of remitting punishments.[1]

The recognition by recent legislation of conditional suspension of punishments was an even more significant step towards a flexible penal system. The Anglo-American system of probation relies on the positive side of guidance and supervision of the probationer. On the European continent law-givers contented themselves with merely suspending sentences or even with suspending only the execution of the punishment. The lead was given by a Belgian Statute of 1888 and the French 'loi Bérenger' of 1891.

Greater elasticity of the lower statutory limit of legal punishments, an increased use of fines, and suspension of punishment, have resulted in a more sparing application of the punitive power of the State. The statutory law, which finally established these judicial powers *in mitius*, often consolidated existing customs of administrative discretion or acts of pardon. It was a more formidable task to secure the opposite object and to give criminal courts the authority to go beyond the standardized retributive punishments when prevention of crime by reformation or segregation made longer or special sentences necessary. A lenient treatment of trivial offences still seemed compatible with the principle of just retribution. Crime prevention, however, involves a treatment of the offender not in accordance with what he has done, but with a view to his dangerous propensities. Mitigation of statutory punishments could be left to judicial discretion. The Bill of Rights, prohibiting the infliction of 'cruel and unusual punishments' and the rule *nulla poena sine lege* were a bar to the creation of new penalties save by an Act of the Legislature.

In most countries the statutory range of legal punishment was, according to the letter of the law, wide enough to allow for long sentences for preventive purposes. Many legal systems provided for an increasing scale of punishments for recidivists. But in Germany and Austria this applied to few particular offences only, in Holland and Norway it was more extended, and in England it obtained for all felonies.[2] The *Code pénal* had a general clause

[1] Kenny, p. 581.

[2] 7 & 8 Geo. IV, c. 28, s. 11 (1827). For the further development of statutory law see J. F. Stephen, *Digest of Criminal Law* (7th ed. 1926), p. 17, n. 3.

aggravating the punishment for the repetition of criminal offences.[1] Almost everywhere, however, the judges, educated in the tradition of just retribution, refrained from giving sentences near to the legal maximum. Criminal law had apparently no concern with a dangerous persistent offender who left the prison gates after the expiation of what had been regarded as the just equivalent of a single illegal act. Nor had it any remedy for the mentally subnormal offender, who in spite of his dangerous propensities successfully pleaded for leniency, or for the army of 'ins and outs', the vast number of low-grade people who sink into vagrancy and destitution. For these social aspects of crime and punishment the administration of criminal justice wanted a lead from progressive legislation.

The Norwegian Criminal Code of 1902 provided for a prolongation of penal servitude for preventive purposes, but the new version of the Code of 1929 repealed this provision. Most statutory enactments retained the traditional system of retributive punishment, but supplemented it by new reformative and protective sanctions which were to be applied when the orthodox methods fell short of the aim of crime prevention. The *Gladstone Report* recommended a 'half-way house between a prison and a reformatory' and 'a new form of sentence' for the segregation of habitual criminals. The theoretical foundation of this new departure was developed in Switzerland. Carl Stooss, the author of the Swiss draft codes, proposed a system of new legal sanctions apart from punishment, and called them *mesures de sûreté*, *sichernde Massnahmen*, measures of public security.[2] According to this conception a dualistic criminal law should comprise two types of sanctions: penalties meted out according to the amount of personal guilt, and measures applied with a view to the degree of social dangerousness. Legal punishment might still be administered by fixed sentences; but measures of public security should, on principle, last as long as they were necessary in view of the prisoner's dangerousness. In Stooss's opinion the two sanctions were substantially different: punishment looking back at the single illegal act committed, and measures intended to alter a certain psychological and social state. Only expediency required that they should both be placed at the disposal of the criminal court. Such a dual system seemed to reconcile the classical doctrine with

[1] *Code pénal*, art. 56–8. Comparative survey by G. Radbruch, in *VDA*, iii. 204 et seq.

[2] C. Stooss, 8 *MoSchrKrim.* 367; E. Hafter, *Lehrbuch des Schweizerischen Strafrechts. Allg. Tl.* (1926), pp. 237 et seq.; H. Pfander, 6 *Howard Journal* 216.

criminological requirements. Theoretical followers of the classical school were prepared to concede to 'mere measures' what they emphatically refused to true penalties. It was expected that judges could more easily be persuaded to make adequate use of the new more intense ways of treatment if the latter were markedly different from what had been traditionally regarded as just punishment.

The new continental drafts and codes supplemented the system of legal punishments by a comprehensive list of measures of public security. The Swiss Criminal Code introduced detention of habitual criminals, industrial training of idle and disorderly persons, and inebriates' asylums, with further non-punitive measures for mental defectives and juveniles. The Danish code provides for similar measures against mental defectives, inebriates, habitual criminals, and idle persons. The Czechoslovak draft proposed five measures: workhouse, commitment to an institution for sick prisoners, preventive detention, prohibition of visits to public-houses, and confiscation. The German draft codes suggested six measures of reformation and public security, i.e. mental hospital, inebriates' asylum, workhouse, preventive detention, protective supervision, and deportation of aliens. Apart from deportation, which became the subject of a special statute, and protective supervision, that system became law by the Statute of 1933—with two additions: castration of sexual offenders, and exclusion from a specific trade or profession. The Italian Criminal Code provided for commitment to an agricultural colony or workhouse, detention in a mental hospital, in a forensic asylum, or in a reformatory. The Polish Criminal Code introduced segregation in an enclosed institution for mentally diseased persons, compulsory treatment of inebriates, workhouse, and an institution for incorrigible prisoners.

The dualism of punishment and measures of public security led to the question of the relation between the two forms of legal sanctions. Should the new measure be applied in addition to the punishment deserved, or should the court have the alternative of either punishing the prisoner for his offence or committing him to one of the new institutions for the sake of public security? The English Prevention of Crime Act with regard to preventive detention, the Polish and Italian Criminal Codes, the majority of German draft codes, and the German Statute of 1933 adopted the cumulative method. According to this 'double-track system' a prisoner has to undergo punishment plus a further measure of public security, usually in this order. The Danish and Swiss codes, the Swedish Act on the Internment of Recidivists, and the English Criminal Justice Bill of 1938 in accordance with the existing law regarding Borstal sentences have an alternative clause, enabling the court to resort to a measure of public security in lieu of an ordinary punishment.

The alternative solution is a first step in the direction of superseding the doctrinal differentiation between punishment and measures of public security. The dual system was typical of a transitional period which still preserved the retributive conception of punishment, but would not deny the criminal court wider powers for reformative and preventive purposes. The ideal preventive system has still to be found. On the one hand, the 'hospitalization' of vagrants and disorderly people may be divorced from criminal law altogether and find its place in a comprehensive social administration. On the other hand, the segregation of habitual criminals should be effected by long-term, if not indeterminate, punishments. There is no substantial difference between safe custody as punishment and as a measure of public security. 'A prison is a prison,' said Du Cane before the Gladstone Committee, 'you must lock up a prisoner in a prison and in a farm.' In Italy, where the Government spent millions in building a double system of prisons for punishment and institutions for detention, an American observer did not detect any substantial differences in the programmes of either prisons or preventive institutions. He called this expensive experiment 'a superficial attempt to reconcile the irreconcilable'.[1] A theoretical distinction between 'genuine' punishments and 'mere' measures deprives the prisoner, when exposed to the most severe sanctions, of the full weight of the legal guarantees which have traditionally been attributed to legal punishment. The rule of *nulla poena sine lege* literally applies to punishments, not to measures. But the constitutional guarantees of a due process of law must not be limited to what a particular doctrine would call a legal punishment, but ought to apply to any curtailment of the prisoner's life, liberty, status, or property, inflicted for a crime committed and a criminal tendency manifested by the offence.

A satisfactory solution of the problem of punishment and measures of public security becomes difficult when the antisocial tendencies are due to the offender's mental abnormality. By definition punishment is a legal sanction against criminal offences committed with a guilty mind. Punishment implies criminal

[1] N. Cantor, *Crime and Society* (1939), p. 218.

responsibility and thereby recognizes the offender as a personality. This distinction would be levelled by a solution which reacts against the responsible and the insane law-breaker alike with the same preventive measure. This was the object of the abortive Italian Draft Ferri of 1921, which substituted for the traditional terms of guilt and punishment the conceptions of dangerousness and sanctions. In principle the proposals made no difference between the defence of society against, on the one hand, a serious offence committed with conscious criminal intention on the part of the offender, and on the other hand against the outburst of a lunatic incapable of self-control. The Mexican Criminal Code of 1929 also supplanted the ethical concept of punishment by the indifferent term of sanction.[1] By referring to the different reasons for personal dangerousness, and even more, by retaining an exclusive list of particular statutory offences, the Italian proposals and the Mexican code are still criminal law. The change of terminology suggests a resolute turning away from punitive to preventive aspects, which the Mexican law further emphasized by substituting for the jury an expert council for diagnosis and for advice on treatment. There is, however, a limit to these tendencies towards the complete abandoning of even a sublimated conception of punishment. Law must appeal to the moral personality of man. For this reason, the recognition of personal responsibility ought not to be sacrificed to theoretical demands for a monistic conception of preventive sanctions.

In the end the recent trend of criminal legislation will result in a few types of punishment adapted to the needs of certain groups of criminals, and of measures of public security for law-breakers with antisocial tendencies, acting without criminal responsibility. At the same time traditional differentiations made with the object of ensuring just retribution for single illegal acts are on the wane. The statutory system of legal punishment is faced with a drastic simplification. The abandonment of oppressive and degrading punitive elements makes distinctions between different forms of deprivation of liberty, save as to the length of time, illusory. In a rational penal system there is no room for a qualitative differentiation between imprisonment and penal servitude. Popular feeling regards the prospect of penal servitude as a spectacular threat, supposed to impress those who remain untouched by prison sentences. Practical experience, however, indicates that there is no difference between the two penalties save in the length of time.

[1] S. Mendoza, 21 *Journal* 15.

As early as 1885 Du Cane said: 'The distinction made by the use of the terms imprisonment and penal servitude no longer has any significance, now that they are both carried out in the United Kingdom. . . . The only point to be kept in view is that the treatment should be adapted to the length of sentence.'[1] Nearly fifty years later the Departmental Committee on Persistent Offenders called the reasons for that distinction 'purely historical'; the abolition of the term penal servitude would have 'the advantage of making clear that a sentence of five years differs from a sentence of one year in length only or in such minor features as are incidental to length'.[2] In accordance with this suggestion the Criminal Justice Bill of 1938 proposed to eliminate the term penal servitude.

The idea of one 'uniform punishment' instead of the two forms of deprivation of liberty has been much discussed in Switzerland.[3] The Criminal Code of 1937, however, followed the dual system of penal servitude and imprisonment with certain insignificant differences. In Germany some theoretical considerations had been advanced in favour of the substitution of short and long imprisonment for the obsolete differentiation between detention, imprisonment, and penal servitude,[4] but, of the numerous draft codes, only the unpublished Draft Radbruch of 1922 proposed such a clear breach with tradition. The Danish Criminal Code provides detention for short, and imprisonment for long sentences. The Finnish draft code proposed only one form of deprivation of liberty, but in the case of long terms called it *tukthus*, i.e. house of correction, corresponding to the German word for penal servitude.

The English Criminal Justice Bill of 1938 went even farther in the purification of the traditional criminal law. It proposed to abolish corporal punishment, except as the ultimate disciplinary penalty in prison, the misleading conception of 'hard labour' and the power of the court to assign the prisoner to a certain prison 'division', and so to remove from the statute book what the Home Secretary of the day, Sir Samuel Hoare (now Lord Templewood), called 'the stage properties of the Victorian melodrama'.[5]

The substitution of preventive methods for retributive standards

[1] E. Du Cane, *Punishment and Prevention of Crime* (1885), p. 159.

[2] *Report of the Departmental Committee on Persistent Offenders* (1932), p. 51.

[3] References by E. Hafter, op. cit., p. 282, n. 2.

[4] H. Seuffert, *Ein neues Strafgesetzbuch für Deutschland* (1902), p. 63; M. Liepmann, *Reform des deutschen Strafrechts* (1921), p. 131.

[5] Sir Samuel Hoare (now Lord Templewood) in the House of Commons, 29 Nov. 1938, 342 *Hansard* 269.

affects the function of the sentencing court. As long as the judge is concerned with the question of what the prisoner deserves for the particular offence he has committed, the court resorts to shorter or longer fixed sentences. Once the court has regard to the prospects of the prisoner's readjustment or the protection of society, the judge can only give general directives and authorization to be implemented by those responsible for the administration of punishments. These tendencies have strengthened the case for indeterminate sentences.

A *Report of the New York Prison Association*, published in 1847, reads: 'You ask me, for how long a time he should be sentenced to such confinement? Obviously, it seems to me, until the evil disposition is removed from his heart, until disqualification to go at large no longer exists; that is, until he is a reformed man.'[1] No psychological refinement of the art of sentencing can determine in advance what time would be sufficient and necessary for such a purpose. The court may prescribe a range between a certain minimum and maximum, but the final determination with due regard to the personal conditions of the individual prisoner can only be achieved by observation and experience.

Indeterminate sentences have been developed as an element of the American reformatory system. In Brockway's programme and in his scheme for Elmira they served the purpose of reforming the corrigible. The prospect of shortening the sentence imposed was expected to stimulate the prisoner's zeal, industry, and self-control. Whilst this might actually be achieved by conditional release, indeterminate sentences give the judge an opportunity to consider the prospects of the prisoner's treatment, and make the prisoner realize that the sentence puts his fate into his own hands. Influenced by American experience the Austrian Federal Act of 1928 on the Treatment of Young Offenders introduced indeterminate sentences. Two years later a German draft made a similar proposal with regard to juveniles and adolescents up to twenty-one years of age.[2] Subsequent German statutes of 1941 and 1943 adopted this institution as a corrective sentence for juvenile offenders.

In the course of the theoretical discussion of European penal reform not only were short minima recognized as reformative incentives, but long maxima were recommended also as a safeguard of society against the irreclaimable. Advocates of a preventive penal policy recommended indeterminate sentences as a

[1] Reprinted in 25 *Journal* 130.

[2] Art. 72, No. 9, Draft Introductory Law to the Criminal Code, 1930.

protection against dangerous persistent criminals.[1] In the field of legislation, however, the dualistic doctrine obtained which accepted flexible sentences for measures of public security only.

In 1900 the Sixth International Prison Congress in Brussels stated: 'As to legal punishments, the system of indeterminate sentences is inadmissible.' Ten years later the Washington Congress 'approved of the principle of sentencing to indefinite terms', but confined its application to the detention of morally or mentally abnormal personalities, and a reformative system, mainly for juveniles. The turning-point was the London Congress in 1925. Although the Home Secretary of the day, Sir William Joynson-Hicks, warned the assembly that indeterminate sentences were not in favour in this country, the Congress carried the following resolution (i. 3): 'Indeterminate sentences are the necessary consequence of individualization of punishment and one of the most effective means for the social defence against criminality.' This historic resolution was followed up by a renewed theoretical discussion in some of the countries.[2] In the meantime the United States made an attempt to check the crime-wave in the wake of the failure of prohibition by new statutory provisions like the Baumes laws in New York which made life-sentences for felony mandatory after a certain number of previous convictions. The disappointing result of this rigid policy seemed to suggest that society would be better protected against habitual criminals by an appropriate application of indeterminate sentence laws.[3] Thus far the indeterminate sentence as a method of preventive punishment has been a goal rather than an achievement of criminal reform.

The simplification of the traditional system of legal punishments, the idea of a preventive punishment, and the recommendation of indeterminate sentences—all this tends in the same direction. The variety of judicial sentences shall be restricted in order to facilitate individualization of treatment at the executive stage. Differentiation shifts from the judicial to the administrative sphere. A new technique is expected to classify prisoners for their

[1] van Hamel, *Mitt. IKV.* i. 102; iii. 305; iv. 305; Enrico Ferri, *Criminal Sociology* (1895), pp. 207 et seqq.; von Liszt, *Aufsätze und Vorträge* (1905), i. 195; ii. 309; E. Kräpelin, *Abschaffung des Strafmasses* (1880).

[2] E. Kohlrausch, 44 *ZStW.* 21; Graf zu Dohna, 51 *ZStW.* 449; E. Schmidt, 25 *Schweiz. Z.* 200; E. Hafter, op. cit., p. 343; K. Glöersen, in K. Schluyter, *Extrait de l'Annuaire des Associations de criminalistes nordiques* (1938), pp. xvi et seq.; L. Radzinowicz, 7 *Cambridge L.J.* 68.

[3] G. K. Brown, 23 *Canadian B.R.* 630, 672.

specific treatment. The point is not so much the particular motives and causes which explain a criminal career, but the prisoner's response to a certain treatment. Behaviour types shall be replaced by treatment groups. Under such a scheme judicial sentences become less definite, and assume within certain limits a preliminary and permissive character. The final redistribution of powers between judicature and administration will be one of the main issues of post-war penal reform.

The changeover, in recent criminal legislation, to individual prevention strengthened the power of society against the criminal. This calls for safeguards for the individual's rights and liberty. If social investigations and institutional experience rather than ingredients of particular statutory offences and legal conclusions determine the prisoner's fate, new guarantees are necessary against arbitrariness and abuse of discretion, whether actual or suspected.[1] Constitutional limits of socialization are indispensable in order to uphold the supremacy of law. The rule of law must obtain within prison discipline itself. No ideal pattern has been discovered so far for 'the relation between rule and discretion' in penal administration. Certain general tendencies, however, are becoming prevalent in recent criminal jurisprudence and legislation.

Continental legal thinking distinguishes between private and public law, stressing the authoritative character of the latter and, at the same time, strengthening the legal position of the citizen by specific remedies supplied by public law.[2] This process of placing administrative law between constitutional limits affected even the extreme subjection to public authority which a commitment to prison involves.[3] The executive has to comply with certain particular rules as well as with the established purpose of legal punishment. Thus far the binding authority of the law determines the prisoner's legal position. Even in his restricted sphere certain personal rights must be respected and legal remedies be accessible. This concept of imprisonment is the basis for the interpretation of the existing law as well as for future legislative policy. The changing legal character of the prisoner's earnings is a relevant illustration. The Italian and the Swiss Criminal Codes

[1] S. Glueck, 41 *Harvard L.R.* 453; N. Cantor, l.c., p. 265.

[2] Otto Mayer, *Deutsches Verwaltungsrecht* (3rd ed. 1924); F. Fleiner, *Institutionen des Verwaltungsrechts* (6–7th ed. 1922); W. A. Robson, *Justice and Administrative Law* (1928).

[3] B. Freudenthal, *Die staatsrechtliche Stellung des Gefangenen* (Frankfurter Rektoratsrede 1910); id., *ZStW.* xxxii. 222; xxxv. 917; xxxix. 493; M. Grünhut, in Frede–Grünhut, *Reform des Strafvollzuges* (1925), pp. 17–30; L. Jacobi, 50 *ZStW.* 376.

and the proposals formulated in the German Draft Penal Code of 1927 replaced the conception of a mere gratuity by a provision entitling the prisoner to the earnings as his property, though under special conditions laid down by public law.[1] This theory was always accepted under French law, where the *pécule* comprises the prisoner's earnings as well as his former property under the same legal conditions. Other provisions which influence the prisoner's fate still more concern disciplinary penalties, measures of protection and safety, promotion and degradation within a Progressive Stage system, and conditional release. As in constitutional law, safeguards for the individual depend on a reasonable distribution of powers. The head of a penal institution must be entrusted with personal responsibility for immediate disciplinary action, but, in serious cases, the ultimate decision should not rest exclusively with those who represent the case of the institution against the prisoner. This consideration makes the intervention of an independent body advisable as a guarantee against error, favouritism, and real or suspected abuse of power. Comparative law indicates different solutions to this problem. England relied on the tradition of visiting justices, the United States entrusted boards of laymen with the decision on the distribution and conditional release of prisoners, Italy—in conformity with Ferri's proposals—provided for a supervisory judge. Thus far, this branch of the law has not yet been sufficiently developed. The need for independent judicial functions in the executive sphere prevails not only with regard to the award or revision of disciplinary penalties, but also to measures of protection and safety, to degradation and promotion within a Progressive Stage system, and to decisions granting or revoking conditional release. What is of equal importance for the prisoner's personal fate ought not to be separated by artificial conceptions which exclude one or the other group of 'measures' from the rule of law.

Social and legal aspects of prison discipline supplement and limit each other. Under a prison system which makes his adjustment and rehabilitation the principal aim, the prisoner would cease to be a mere subject of a minutely regulated régime and become a person with duties and rights. Training for self-determination and responsibility can never be enforced by the administration of indulgences and penalties, but must rely on a gradual extension and strengthening of the prisoner's legal position, and

[1] Art. 145, Italian Criminal Code; art. 376, Swiss Criminal Code; sects. 91, 98, German Draft Penal Code, 1927 (II).

entrust and burden him with personal rights and obligations. There will come a point at which a personal approach and the 'educational atmosphere' of good will and co-operation would be frustrated, if prisoner and official regarded their mutual relationship only from the strict legal point of view. In present circumstances, however, this consideration should not be allowed to impede the tendency to supplement the growing responsibility of the executive by specific legal guarantees. An unlimited administrative discretion will fail even in its efforts at reformation. Subject though he may be to discipline man has a deep and genuine longing for formal justice.

Such then has been the trend of recent European criminal law reform. The purpose of individual prevention has been generally recognized. New penal and correctional methods have been assigned to the courts. At the same time, the variety of judicial punishments and measures of public security underwent a continuous process of simplification, with the resort to indeterminate sentences as the final aim. The growing importance of the executive stage made the provision of new legal guarantees imperative. All this proved a challenge to the administration of penal and reformative institutions. The outcome of the whole movement still depends on the crucial question, whether appropriate methods of treatment are available to fulfil the expectations raised by the policies embodied in recent statutory reforms.

PRISON DISCIPLINE BETWEEN THE WARS

In the light of political events the inter-war period seems to have been dominated by the aftermath of the First and the imminent threat of the Second World War. It should not be forgotten that the years between the wars were also filled with efforts for social reform in many walks of life. With marked differences, due to historical rather than rational causes, the trend of prison administration in many countries was towards constructive methods of penal and correctional treatment.[1] Various factors favoured this tendency. On the Continent, in belligerent and neutral countries alike, the First World War and the post-war crisis with its unprecedented rise in offences against property made the urgency of preventive penal policy obvious. After years of destruction and frustration the pendulum seemed to swing

[1] T. Sellin, 21 *Journal* 485; J. L. Gillin, *Taming the Criminal* (1931); 'Prisons of To-morrow', 157 *Annals* (1931); 'Les Systèmes pénitentiaires en vigueur dans divers pays', *Recueil*, vols. spéc. iv (1935), vi (1937); N. K. Teeters, *World Penal Systems* (1944).

from reliance on force to faith in constructive methods. A new educational movement extended its sphere beyond home and school to youth movements, vocational training, and adult education. It inspired social services of every description and did not halt before the prison gates. Under the impact of the war men and women with no criminal record or tendencies were sentenced for breach of defence regulations, as conscientious objectors, for conflicts with a foreign occupation army, or as members of a resistance movement. This personal experience brought the grim reality of imprisonment home to respectable and influential citizens,[1] who in turn became ardent advocates of penal reform.[2]

England

In England prison discipline continued to develop on the lines laid down by the *Gladstone Report*. A drastic reduction in the number of small local prisons and a considerable fall in the prison population facilitated a rise in the general standards of prison administration. All prisoners, except in some Borstal institutions, were separated at night. The percentage of prisoners punished for breaches of discipline sank from the pre-war figure of twelve to four. For some time the aim of an uninterrupted eight-hour working day in association could be maintained. English prisons were in a position to keep their inmates in full employment with a high proportion engaged in productive work, though the manufacture of mail-bags was the staple employment. The idea of a remuneration for the prisoners' work made slow progress; after certain experiments made in 1929 a general earnings scheme was gradually introduced in all prisons from 1933. While the aid for discharged prisoners has not been developed into a service of personal after-care comparable to probation, England solved the problem of linking the prisoner with the positive forces of the world outside by the organized service of voluntary teachers and prison visitors. From 1921 the Howard League for Penal Reform, a voluntary association of men and women devoted to the improvement of prison conditions on humanitarian and scientific lines, did much towards exposing unsatisfactory conditions,

[1] S. Hobhouse, *An English Prison from within* (1919); E. D. Morel, *Thoughts on the War; the Peace and—Prison* (1920), pp. 50–70; K. Liebknecht, *Briefe aus dem Felde, der Untersuchungshaft und dem Zuchthaus* (1920); Oberbürgermeister Holler, *Sechs Monate Gefängnis, Erinnerungen aus der Franzosenzeit 1923–24* (Offenburg, Baden).

[2] The outstanding example of critical suggestions based on personal experience in the First World War is S. Hobhouse and F. Brockway, *English Prisons to-day* (1922).

stimulating progress, sponsoring new experiments, and enlightening public opinion.

When the International Penal and Penitentiary Congress met in London in 1925 visitors from abroad were impressed by what they saw, and reported favourably on the English prison system.[1]

The two pre-war innovations of the Prevention of Crime Act of 1908 developed in different ways. The Borstal system has generally been regarded as the principal asset of the administration of criminal law in England. For the boys the inter-war period brought new types of 'open Borstals' with a minimum of supervision and a due emphasis on trust and self-discipline. Only the girls, owing to the smaller number of convicted offenders, had to content themselves with one walled institution at Aylesbury. Administrative practice extended the Borstal idea to higher age groups. The Wakefield scheme[2] provided a constructive training for a selected number of prisoners under twenty-six with individualized group work, association for meals and recreation, educational activities, and a discipline based on trust and the prisoners' self-control. One group worked at New Hall Camp, several miles from the prison, with neither bars, locks, walls, nor even barbed wire, but only white marks on trees to show where lay the boundary of the camp. The model institution at Wakefield was used as an Imperial Training Centre for prison officers. Another experiment was initiated at Chelmsford, where persistent offenders between twenty-one and thirty were kept under a modified scheme combining firm control with intense physical training and systematic evening education.

The other measure introduced by the Prevention of Crime Act, preventive detention of habitual criminals, proved less successful. Courts made insufficient use of this new type of sentence, partly owing to the cumulative system of penal servitude plus detention, by which the lawgivers had hoped to meet judicial objections. The decrease in sentences of penal servitude made fewer recidivists eligible for preventive detention. Terms of sentence seldom reached the statutory maximum. A high rate of reconviction seemed to confirm the assumption that the régime failed to make good citizens and that the periods of detention were too short to protect society.

In 1932 the Departmental Committee on Persistent Offenders

[1] E. Ferri, *Rev. droit pénal* (1925), pp. 1136 and 1153; L. Verwaeck, ibid. 1926, p. 5; M. Liepmann, 47 *ZStW* 292; A. Starke, ibid. 332.

[2] *Report Prison Commissioners 1923–4* and *1935*; Page, pp. 220–4.

examined the results of the prevailing penal system. This *Report* is an outstanding document of a constructive penal policy which met with appreciation by experts abroad.[1] While the Gladstone Committee and the Prevention of Crime Act approached the subject of crime prevention from the two extreme ends of the scale, viz. Borstal training for young offenders and preventive detention for habitual criminals, the new *Report* tried to come to grips with the intermediate group and suggested new measures to check the criminal careers of adults on their way to persistent criminality. The Criminal Justice Bill of 1938 was the outcome of these considerations. It was indeed 'the magistrates' hope'. It proposed to simplify the legal conditions for Borstal sentences, to introduce two new alternatives for prison sentences, viz. corrective training on the lines of the Wakefield scheme, and preventive detention in two forms for offenders whose persistence was established or beginning to be so, as a substitute for the obsolete cumulative sentence of the existing law. The Bill supplemented the provisions for probation to facilitate psychological treatment, and made two bold proposals for new methods of semi- and non-institutional treatment in order to fill the gap between probation on the one hand, and deprivation of liberty on the other. The proposed measures were Howard houses for residential control and Attendance Centres for spare-time training. The Bill reached the Committee stage in the summer of 1939 but was shelved after the outbreak of war.

In the wake of the war, penal reform suffered inevitable setbacks.[2] Evacuation, overcrowding, reduced staffs, and a scarcity of commodities put a heavy burden on prison administration. Borstal institutions had an unduly long waiting list. The eight-hour working day in association could not be maintained, the services of voluntary teachers and prison visitors were cancelled. There were, however, certain gains too. Industrial war-work for Borstal girls proved a success. War necessities led to experiments with the employment of inmates outside prison walls. By 1943 parties of a total of 1,000 prisoners with scarcely any supervision went out to work on farms and timber-yards. Women prisoners did cleaning in hospitals. The hostels for difficult evacuated children were a successful experiment in the preventive treatment of juvenile delinquency.[3] They were small units of a family

[1] R. Sieverts, 53 *ZStW*. 676.

[2] A. Paterson, 6 *Howard Journal* 13; L. W. Fox, 36 *Journal* 184; *Report Prison Commissioners 1939–41*, pp. 5–14.

[3] *Hostels for 'Difficult' Children* (A Survey issued by the Ministry of Health, 1944).

character with the close co-operation of psychiatric social workers and child guidance clinics. The imminent post-war reform will profit by this war-time experience.

Holland

In Holland[1] the Criminal Code of 1881, in force from 1886, provided for one type of deprivation of liberty only and laid down that prison sentences up to five years were to be served in isolation. During the First World War this rigid principle had to be modified. Since the rise in offences of dishonesty and smuggling threatened Dutch prisons with overcrowding, 1,000 selected prisoners were transferred to Veenhuizen, a central work-colony for vagrants. Here prisoners were divided into four classes and worked in association in the fields and workshops. Prisoners who after the five-year solitary period pass into the association stage were transferred to the special prison at Leeuwarden. In 1925 a Progressive Stage system was introduced for this group. An Act of 1929 provided for the erection of juvenile prisons in accordance with the English pattern of Borstal institutions. Unfortunately the Dutch law tried to combine the cumulative and the alternative principles. Young prisoners between sixteen and twenty-three or twenty-five had first to serve one year of their term in separate confinement in an ordinary prison, and were then transferred to a special institution where they were gradually brought into association with other prisoners and from which they could be conditionally released.

Belgium

For half a century Belgium has been the model country of a rigid solitary system. A special law of 1870 and supplementary regulations prescribed separate yards, stalls, masks, and other requisites of enforced isolation. In the convict prison of Louvain, even as late as 1924, men had to live ten years in isolation. After such an excessive period of enforced solitude, five out of six chose to stay in solitary confinement rather than be transferred to an association prison under the strict rule of silence.[2] The experience of the First World War, when many educated Belgian citizens were imprisoned, brought about a change in the traditional prison discipline.

[1] A. Paterson, *Belgian and Dutch Prisons* (1924); M. H. MacColl, 2 *Howard Journal* 242; J. W. Eysten, 22 *MoSchrKrim.* 310.

[2] A. Paterson, l.c., p. 28.

Since 1920 a scientific penal policy, sponsored by E. Vandervelde as Minister of Justice, has gradually superseded the mechanical routine of the cellular system.[1] A Royal Decree initiated the Crimino-anthropological Service. Under the inspiring leadership of L. Verwaeck a central laboratory at Forêt and eight regional laboratories attached to the main prisons of the country examined and classified all first offenders with more than a three-month sentence, all prisoners under twenty-one years, and all recidivists. These investigations were the basis for the commitment of the individual prisoner to the institution where he was expected to find the appropriate treatment. The first object of this scheme was to assign normal criminals, abnormal criminals, and physically sick persons to different types of institutions. A long-term programme anticipated a further differentiation within each group. For normal criminals there should be a prison school for adolescents between sixteen and twenty-one, reformatories for adults, a prison factory for convicts amenable to reform, a prison for hardened recidivists, and a preventive detention institution for incorrigible recidivists. As for abnormal prisoners the scheme provided special institutions for the criminal insane, psychopathic personalities, epileptics, and sexual offenders. Invalids were to be sent to a prison hospital, a prison sanatorium for tuberculosis, or an inebriates' asylum. The Law on Social Defence against Abnormal and Habitual Criminals of 1930[2] was a further step in the direction of prevention and classification. It introduced a long-term detention of insane, mentally disturbed, and defective criminals as well as of recidivists and habitual criminals. In the first case, the court orders a detention of five, ten, or fifteen years, dependent on the severity of the sentence otherwise deserved. A committee consisting of a judge, a lawyer, and a medical officer assigns the prisoner to the special institution and has the power to discharge him conditionally or unconditionally. As to recidivists and habitual criminals, the court refers the prisoner for ten years after the expiration of his punishment to the discretion of the administration. A notable Belgian reform was the agricultural prison school at Merxplas under A. Delierneux. This institution for some fifty boys of seventeen and over was adjacent to three other special prisons for tubercular, epileptic, and feeble-minded offenders,

[1] Héger-Gilbert, *Rev. droit pénal* (1921), p. 3; L. Bélym, ibid. 1926, p. 702; W. Petrzilka, *Persönlichkeitsforschung und Differenzierung im Strafvollzug* (1930), pp. 62–85; L. Verwaeck, 20 *Journal* 198.

[2] *Moniteur Belge* (1930), No. 131, p. 2447; 1 *Recueil* 16.

established on the grounds of a pre-war agricultural colony for vagrants. The cottage system facilitated an individualized group life. After careful classification during an observation period of two to three weeks, the rise to higher grades of a system of progressive stages began where marks were to be earned by personal efforts in readjustment, success during lessons, use of spare time, self-respect and self-control, economy, order, and cleanliness. In the corresponding industrial reformatory at Ghent, even in 1924, an English visitor found the silence rule strictly observed.[1] Both institutions were claiming good results, but complained that often short sentences did not allow lasting reformative efforts. New legislative proposals, drafted in connexion with the Law on Social Defence, were designed to replace the traditional prison terms by a judicial commitment to a prison school for no less than a year with the possibility of extension till the young prisoner reaches the age of twenty-three. For wayward and delinquent juveniles Belgium established a model observation house at Moll.

France

In France the statutory distinction among legal offences, between crimes, delicts, and contraventions, has its counterpart in a corresponding threefold system of specific legal punishments for each group of offences. The Administration, however, simplified the plurality of statutory punishments by a twofold system of penal establishments for terms up to one year and those for the execution of longer sentences.[2] Prisons for short sentences have been attached to every court in the country. Sometimes they are miniature institutions, often with no organized prison work. Some are cellular, others not. Reform projects in the twenties proposed to reduce the number of small local prisons and to use larger interdepartmental institutions instead, where prisoners might be kept in isolation. Sentences exceeding one year are served in central prisons and convict prisons. With the exception of a women's prison at Rennes, none of these twelve central institutions has been built for its present purpose. Prisoners live and work in association. Isolation in cells at night is the exception rather than the rule.

The French penal régime has been overshadowed by transportation. From a legal point of view French law used transportation for the execution of three different penalties, namely, deportation, enforced labour, and relegation.[3] Deportation is a special life

[1] A. Paterson, l.c., p. 26.

[2] Mossé, *passim*.

[3] J. Goldschmidt, in *VDA* iv. 124 et seqq.; Mossé, pp. 201 et seq.

sentence for political offenders, administered as an internment in New Caledonia or at one of the *îles de salut* near Cayenne. Enforced labour, the most serious penalty short of death, with far-reaching civil disqualifications even after the abolition of 'civil death', has been executed by the transportation of men to the penal colonies Guiana and New Caledonia. Relegation after the expiration of an ordinary sentence is a security measure against recidivists, and leads to lifelong detention in Guiana or New Caledonia for the purpose of 'eliminating from the mother country an individual who has shown himself undesirable'.[1] On the eve of the Second World War a Statute of 1938 prohibited the transportation to Guiana of men sentenced to enforced labour. The war brought French transportation to a standstill, if not a final end. A statute of 4 July 1942 prescribed a régime in French penal establishments for those under sentence of relegation 'temporarily maintained in France'.[2] If the new France abstains from resuming transportation, this will give her an opportunity for a fresh departure in penal reform.

Germany

In Germany the years from the end of the First World War to the beginning of the depression witnessed a resolute reorientation of penal discipline. A band of progressive theorists and social workers under the inspiring leadership of M. Liepmann[3] gave this movement its impetus, whilst a doubtful Administration followed rather hesitatingly. For the reformers retributive elements were to give way to a new educational approach, the old precepts of breaking the vicious will and suppressing personal self-expression to be abandoned for constructive methods of 'setting free and building anew' and for raising self-respect and a feeling of responsibility. For this purpose enforced obedience should give way to an 'educational atmosphere' of personal guidance and mutual confidence. The legislative trend seemed to favour these aims. In 1923 the inter-state agreement of 1897 was replaced by new Principles of Prison Discipline.[4] Beyond a co-ordination of administrative practice, the new Principles were an authoritative statement of a reformative penal policy. 'The prisoner', they said, 'shall be accustomed to order and work, and morally strengthened

[1] Mossé, p. 15.

[2] Information by Professor Bouzat, University of Rennes, given to the Howard League for Penal Reform. See also 'loi No. 46–931 du 10 Mai 1946'.

[3] M. Liepmann, 22 *Mitt. IKV.* No. 4, 22 et seq.; id., 'Strafvollzug', *HWBR.* (1928) v. 788–96.

[4] *RGBl.* ii. 263, reprinted by Bumke, p. 511.

in order that he shall not relapse into crime again.' This was the object of relevant provisions for work and recreation, education, and communication with the world outside, welfare and after-care, and a recommendation for a system of progressive stages, which made the prisoner's personal fate and rehabilitation the central issue of the prison régime. In the wake of the criminal law reform movement, two consecutive draft penal codes of 1927 seemed to secure those principles a final place in the statute book.[1]

The fact that the administration of justice was left to the particular German *Länder* or 'states' encouraged competition and experiments. Thuringia had a reformative system of progressive stages with the service of trained social workers, educational activities of a high standard, and a gradual method of entrusting prisoners with responsibility and self-government.[2] Saxony developed her traditional classification system by the appointment of trained social workers within penal institutions and for the welfare work among discharged prisoners. Bavaria introduced a crimino-biological service similar to Verwaeck's Belgian system.[3] Hamburg added to the prison service a social department, and at the dawn of the whole movement initiated a new prison discipline for youths. Two young penologists were made responsible for some thirty juvenile prisoners and helped them to a personal experience of moral standards and higher values by a personal approach in the spirit of the youth movement.[4] Prussia, with more than half the total German prison population and a vast administrative machinery of some 7,000 prison officers, followed only slowly the bold experiments carried out in some of the smaller *Länder*. A Regulation concerning the System of Progressive Stages of 1929 was a radical attempt to replace the traditional routine by a classification of institutions with an open intermediate institution at the last stage.[5] All this, however, remained a mere programme, which never had a chance to be put into practice.

These manifold reformative efforts took the form of a belated introduction into German penal law of a system of progressive stages. This coincidence explains why the German reforms like

[1] L. Frede and M. Grünhut, *Reform des Strafvollzuges* (1927).

[2] *Gefängnisse in Thüringen* (Weimar, 1930); L. Frede, 46 *ZStW* 233; *SchwZ* (1930), pp. 209 and 305; 16 *Mental Hygiene* 610.

[3] *Der Stufenstrafvollzug und die kriminalbiologischen Untersuchungen der Gefangenen in den Bayerischen Strafanstalten*, i–iii (1926–9).

[4] W. Herrmann, *Das Hamburgische Jugendgefängnis Hahnöfersand* (2nd ed. 1926).

[5] *Verordnung über den Strafvollzug in Stufen v. 7. 6. 1929* (gedruckt in der Strafanstalt Berlin-Tegel); report by W. Gentz, 1 *Recueil* 253.

others overestimated that external organization which seemed to identify the prisoner's progress to higher privileges with his moral progress.[1] The final blow, however, came from outside. When in the early thirties the growing social and economic insecurity prepared the ground for the coming political storm, it became increasingly difficult to maintain adequate standards of prison discipline. The 'principle of less eligibility', which demands lower standards of living for the prisoner than for the honest unemployed, once more proved the true 'dilemma of penal reform' (H. Mannheim) and forced the reform movement on to the defensive. With the rise of National-Socialism the battle for penal reform was lost.[2]

The authoritarian doctrine that punishment should be a spectacular manifestation of the supremacy of the community over the individual was a convenient disguise for the misuse of criminal law as a political weapon. In legislative promulgations the reformative purpose had to give way to a new emphasis on retribution. In 1934 a revision of the Principles of 1923 provided that imprisonment should be 'a serious hardship' supposed to produce 'lasting inhibitions against temptations'.[3] The Prison Discipline Regulations of the Reich of 1940,[4] though less outspoken, betrayed a similar tendency. Even the training of young prisoners should primarily rely on 'just severity' and 'firm discipline', so that the young offender learns 'to become hard towards himself'.[5] Administrators and social workers of the preceding system were dismissed, social work in prisons drastically reduced, experiments in self-government prohibited, and discharged prisoners' aid left exclusively to the party welfare organization.[6] The Progressive Stage idea was perverted and a severe initial stage put before the ordinary prison routine. Even young offenders—'in order to produce a deeper impression'—should spend the first three months in solitary, or at least, separate confinement. Constructive efforts were spared for those who could be expected to become valuable members of the national community. Special institutions were set aside for offenders supposed to have only 'stumbled' (*Gestrau-*

[1] See M. Liepmann's discussion of the 'problem' of the Progressive Stage system in *MoSchrKrim.* (1926), Beiheft i, pp. 56 et seq.

[2] N. Cantor, 25 *Journal* 84 and 721.

[3] *RGBl.* i. 383, reprinted by E. Kohlrausch, *Strafgesetzbuch* (34th ed. 1938), p. 669.

[4] 'Strafvollzugsordnung v. 22. 7. 1940', *Amtl. Sonderveröffentlichung der Deutschen Justiz*, No. 21, semi-official report in 9 *Recueil* (1941) 221.

[5] 'Jugendstrafvollzugsverordnung v. 22. 1. 1937', *Dtsch. Justiz* (1937), p. 97; reprinted by Kohlrausch, l.c., p. 709; subsequent amendments.

[6] C. Leiser, 29 *Journal* 345; O. Kirchheimer, ibid., p. 362; F. Hoefer, 35 *Journal* 385, and 36 *Journal* 30.

chelte) and for the administration of indeterminate sentences for juveniles susceptible to such methods; others were to be handed over to the police for indefinite detention. German criminal law was debased by the 'dual system'[1] which undermined the authority of the law courts by assigning almost unlimited powers to the secret state police even more than by increasing severity in the selection and administration of sentences. Neither acquittal by the courts nor expiration of sentence gave any security against detention in a concentration camp where not even a pretence was made to restrict arbitrariness and brutality by legal rules. Penal reform in Germany has to re-start from the conditions prevailing before 1933—or even earlier—and first to re-establish the rule of law by restoring formal justice.

Italy

In Italy, too, prison discipline has been affected by the authoritarian political doctrine.[2] Enrico Ferri's positivism, which had not been regarded as representative of contemporary Italian criminology, was superseded by Rocco's 'principle of chastisement'. The penal system of the Criminal Code of 1930 was characterized by a rigid retribution and a strict distinction between fixed punishment matching the gravity of the offence and additional measures of public security corresponding to the prisoner's dangerousness. Legal penalties were severe, especially with regard to offences against the State and the foundations of its powers. At the same time Rocco's Code owed some of its characteristic provisions for prison discipline to the proposals of the abortive Draft Ferri. This applies to the organization of prison labour, the prisoner's right to certain earnings, a judicial control of classification and prison administration in general, and municipal welfare councils for the after-care of the prisoners. Owing to these institutions the Italian prison régime of the Fascist period retained certain assets for a future resumption of penal reform.

Switzerland

In Switzerland, even after the enactment of the Criminal Code of 1937, the administration of penal institutions has rested with the Cantons.[3] The new federal law prescribes the outlines of prison

[1] E. Fränkel, *The Dual State* (1941).

[2] A. Paterson, *Italian Prisons* (1923); G. Novelli, 2 *Recueil* 9; G. Dybwad, *Theorie und Praxis des fascistischen Strafvollzugs* (1934).

[3] Hafner-Zürcher, op. cit.; E. Delaquis, 43 *SchwZ* 265; *Jahresberichte der Strafanstalt Witzwil*.

discipline in order to guarantee uniformity in the execution of sentences imposed under the unified criminal law. These regulations provide for a differentiation between the various methods, either punitive or preventive, of deprivation of liberty, and lay down certain common principles: separation between men and women, prohibition of alcohol, certain rudiments of a Progressive Stage system, an earnings scheme, and the interruption of imprisonment for urgent reasons, whilst detention in a mental hospital counts as equivalent to the same period of the prison term. For obvious reasons the Cantons objected to a system which necessitated a variety of special institutions. They tried to comply with the requirement of classification by creating combined prison colonies for the execution of different punishments and preventive measures. The model institution of this type is the agricultural Colony Witzwil in the Canton of Berne with accommodation and work for various types of offenders and different age groups. It is still an open question how far this experiment might be translated into general practice. Whilst the Draft Code of 1918 proposed that the Federal Council might grant exemptions from statutory rules in order to facilitate the establishment of new agricultural colonies, the Federal Parliament dropped this Witzwil proviso.

United States

Nowhere would generalization be more misleading than with regard to prison discipline in the United States. The legal system consists of the independent legislations and jurisdictions of the forty-eight states plus the District of Columbia and the Federal Administration. This makes even a brief discussion of American legal and social institutions a study in comparative law.[1] There are striking differences in history, cultural background, ethnological composition, and social structure between the New England states and the south, between the Pacific coast and the Middle West. What the United States lacks in uniformity it has gained in a variety of experience and in opportunity for competition in new ideas and experiments. For a European observer, accustomed to the rule of abstract principles, almost every American institution seems to have its own penal philosophy.

It is impossible for a student of penal reform to give a fair picture of recent American developments without first-hand knowledge. All that the following discussion can do is to offer

[1] S. B. Warner and H. B. Cabot, 50 *Harvard L. R.* 583.

some comments on reports made by foreign visitors and American experts. Throughout history such reports have influenced European legislation. The cellular system, the reformatory, probation, and the Juvenile Courts have subsequently been taken over from the New World. The more these institutions were adapted to the needs of each country and developed in the course of fresh experience, the more European observers became self-assured and critical.[1] Unlike former generations which had made pilgrimages to Cherry Hill or Elmira they kept progress and setbacks fairly balanced.

The magnitude of the American prison problem is due to the great number of prisoners. Crime is more formidable in the New World than in the Old. The ratio of homicide is ten times the corresponding figure in Great Britain. While the total of victims of murder and manslaughter per 10,000 living persons is 0·1 in Great Britain, it is 1 in the United States.[2] Sentences are longer in the United States than in England. Between 1923 and 1940 the yearly average prison population of the 150 state and federal institutions rose from 84,761 to 191,776.[3] There were also approximately 4,000 local gaols with a daily average population of some 50,000, but a turnover of more than 600,000 receptions a year.[4] American publications present ample information about prison conditions. An independent service secures a fair investigation of individual penal and correctional institutions.[5] In 1931 the *Wickersham Report* examined the general situation in the light of progressive principles and indicated the American prison system as 'traditional, antiquated, unintelligent, and frequently cruel and inhuman'.[6] George W. Kirchwey even alleged that this verdict

[1] *England*: A. Paterson, *The Prison Problem of America.* (H.M.C. Prison, Maidstone); Margery Fry, 6 *Howard Journal* 162.

Holland: Eugenia Lekkerkerker, *Reformatories for Women in the U.S.A.* (1931).

Germany: M. Liepmann, *Amerikanische Gefängnisse und Erziehungsanstalten* (1927), English translation by C. O. Fiertz, *American Prisons and Reformatory Institutions* (1928); F. Exner, *Kriminalistischer Bericht über eine Reise nach Amerika* (1935); reprinted from 54 *ZStW* 345, 512.

Czechoslovakia: E. M. Foltin, *Amerikanisches Gefängniswesen* (1930).

Switzerland: H. Kellerhals, in *Jahresbericht der Strafanstalt Witzwil, 1922.*

Norway: Arne Omsted, *Traek av Strafferetspleien i de Forenede Stater i Nordamerika* (1922).

[2] E. Roesner, 28 *MoSchrKrim.* 46.

[3] *Prison Labor in the United States 1940* (U.S. Department of Labor, 1941), p. 8; *Statistical Abstract of the U.S. 1942*, p. 98, table 76.

[4] L. N. Robinson, *Jails* (1944), pp. 1–6.

[5] *Handbook of American Prisons and Reformatories*, published by the National Society for Penal Information since 1925; *Handbook of American Institutions for Juvenile Delinquents*, published by the Osborne Society since 1938.

[6] *Wickersham Report*, ix. 171.

'erred by moderation rather than by excess of condemnation'.[1] In 1939 a comprehensive survey submitted by the Attorney General presented the results of thorough quantitative investigations on the prevailing methods of penal and correctional treatment. According to this official source, out of a total of 137,000 male prisoners 40,000 lived in over-crowded quarters, 55,000 had no work, and 100,000 were not enrolled in training courses of any kind.[2]

It would be unfair to compare the results of such sincere self-criticism with favourable reports from other countries which are less frank in the admission of failures and setbacks. Overcrowding and idleness and the preservation of the local gaol were the main defects of American prison discipline between the wars. Against these odds must be set the remarkable achievements in progressive institutions, the spirit of educational optimism, and the readiness to give new and unorthodox methods a fair trial. Foreign visitors have been much impressed with institutions for juveniles and adolescents such as the Children's Village at Dobbs Ferry (N.Y.), the Whittier State School at Los Angeles, or the Sleighton Farm at Philadelphia. The work of such model institutions seemed to be based upon a constructive approach of understanding and confidence to boys and girls 'in conflict', a resolute breach of the prejudice of 'less eligibility', and a wise magnanimity which deliberately made a life of higher standards and true values accessible to the pupils. The beginning of this period has been marked by the classic experiment by Thomas Mott Osborne in prisoners' self-government, which for him was symptomatic of a common-sense solution of the prison problem. From the United States came the idea of breaking the uniform routine of safe seclusion behind walls, bars, and locks by custodial differentiation into maximum, medium, and minimum security institutions. This principle was bound to stimulate a new prison architecture. The Federal Prison Administration under the influence of Sanford Bates and James V. Bennet has recently given the country a proper lead by raising the standards of prison personnel and the inauguration of reforms with regard to the organization of prison labour, prison libraries, and an effective parole system. The rise of social science raised high expectations of a methodical classification as the basis of differentiation of treatment. A social branch has been recognized as an element of prison administration with influence

[1] *Prisons of To-morrow*, l.c., p. 20.
[2] *Attorney General's Survey*, v. 61.

not only on welfare matters but also on the daily routine of prison life and parole decisions. The Massachusetts State Colony, Norfolk Prison, at one time celebrated as a 'community prison', was the best example of these progressive tendencies. The outstanding achievement of recent American penal policy has been a new type of reformatory for women.

Canada

The penal system of Canada was surveyed by a Royal Commission in 1938.[1] In the inter-war period Canada maintained a high rate of men and women in prison, with more than one-half of all convictions for indictable offences followed by a non-suspended prison sentence.[2] Among the proposals made by the *Report* of 1938 are a strong centralized administration by a Prison Commission and the introduction of a probation service conformable with English patterns.

India, Burma

In India an official *Report* of 1919–20[3] initiated a period of reforms which have been reflected in recent relevant literary publications.[4] As a result of special investigations a British expert has discussed the penal questions which arise in Burma.[5]

CONCLUSIONS

At first sight the historical experience seems not very encouraging. Prison history is a history of 'ideals and errors'. System after system has been advocated by enthusiastic supporters and opposed by no less passionate adversaries. Many a bold prison pioneer has had to give way to administrative difficulties and general prejudices. Prison discipline seems to be in a permanent state of reform. A continual rise of fresh reformative impulses alone can hope to overcome the inevitable human inertia, resentment, and misuse of power. It is a general experience of social and legal history that every institutional form has its specific manner of decay. Whilst strict regulations degenerate into legalistic formalism, flexibility tempts to weakness and inefficiency. Unrestricted discretion as

[1] *Report of the Royal Commission to Investigate the Penal System of Canada* (1938). See also H. G. Wyatt, *Crime in Canada and the War* (1944).

[2] Margery Fry, 6 *Howard Journal* 176.

[3] *Report of the Indian Jails Committee* (1921).

[4] P. K. Sarapore, *Prison Reform in India* (1936); F. A. Barker, *The Modern Prison System of India* (1944).

[5] A. Paterson, *Prevention of Crime and the Treatment of the Criminal in Burma* (1927).

well as petrified routine will be felt as arbitrariness. This makes a periodical swinging of the pendulum almost inevitable. In the endless stream of changing programmes the same ideas seem to repeat themselves. The prisoner should be kept in safe custody, he ought not to leave the prison worse than when he entered it, but should be trained rather for an honest life in society; work should be useful and instructive; a gradual transition to life at large and an efficient after-care should help the ex-prisoner to fit in with the community of law-abiding citizens.

Even in the face of such modest progress prison history shows one remarkable result. In little more than one century mankind made the extraordinary step from considering imprisonment as a mere substitute for the death penalty and a mortification closely allied to other forms of bodily punishment to considering it as something which, by its underlying principles, is an appeal to the moral personality of the prisoner.[1]

Social reformers cannot be expected to exhibit the objectivity of unbiased historians. They work hard to overcome prevailing evils which they ascribe to the deficiencies and omissions of the past, whilst they often owe their advanced standards to the ill-rewarded achievements of the former generation. Capital punishment had to be drastically reduced before a major problem of imprisonment could arise. The period of transportation had to be closed before the mother country felt full responsibility for the readjustment of criminals. Separate confinement offered the first opportunity for studying the prisoner's personality, but not before further unnatural and oppressive elements of prison discipline had been removed could such observation lead to an understanding of the prisoner's mind. It was one thing to acknowledge reformative principles of prison discipline and another to provide special facilities for pursuing this object and to try to develop appropriate methods of treatment. Each new task became necessary—and possible—by the preceding stage of reform.

In the pursuit of these aims humanitarian impulses and rational crime prevention went a long way together. To acknowledge the personality of the prisoner and to win his co-operation will eventually prove the only way to the social readjustment of the prisoner. 'De-stigmatization' of legal punishment is sound preventive policy. In the end, however, no social work can be undertaken from utilitarian motives only. It must be carried on even in the face of disappointments and, for this reason, based, apart from any

[1] Robinson, pp. 309 et seq.

regard to visible success, on a genuine devotion to the task of helping the weak and erring, supported by the conviction of the indefeasible value of every human soul.

The study of prison history offers a threefold lesson. First, it makes it clear that it is fallacious to rely upon the automatic efficiency of a more or less ideal organization. Separate confinement, the Progressive Stages idea, the reformatory—each 'system' was hailed as a panacea and subsequently rejected as a disappointing failure. Penal reform suffered from the rationalistic prejudice that an ideal form of prison discipline would produce—by its functioning alone—the expected results of reformation and prevention. Sound principles are necessary, but they are at their best merely an opportunity in that they direct and facilitate the indispensable efforts of man. This experience applies to every legal and social institution. Trial by jury and a parliamentary régime do not of themselves necessarily realize justice and democracy, but they are instruments valuable for legal and political administration, capable of use and misuse. A great pioneer of the League of Nations summarized the twenty years' experience in the following observation: 'No machinery can do more than facilitate the action of the peoples. Unless they and their governments really put the enforcement of the law and the maintenance of peace as the first and greatest of national interests, no confederation or federation can compel them to do so.'[1]

Secondly, there is not, and cannot be, any universal scheme for the indiscriminate treatment of all prisoners. The conception of *the* prisoner is an abstract generalization. We have to deal with men and women, with juveniles, adolescents, and adults who are in prison, and who have—under various circumstances and from different motives—committed acts punishable by law. Principles of prison discipline which were suitable for a certain type of offender have been compromised by an indiscriminate application to all prisoners. Differentiation of treatment is a condition of, and at the same time a task for, a successful penal policy.

Finally, all efforts for penal reform are doomed to failure if hostile tendencies within the administration or among the general public are allowed to take root. Public opinion needs enlightenment and guidance. In a long historical process law has neutralized the destructive forms of uncontrolled emotions and retaliatory feeling. But these primitive reactions are always alive and it needs constant vigilance to prevent legal punishment from being misused

[1] Viscount Cecil, *A Great Experiment* (1941), p. 351.

by a deliberate infliction of suffering. To subject prisoners—beyond the enforced deprivation of liberty—to further hardship for the sake of retribution and deterrence deprives prison discipline of its dignity.

Such then are the lessons of history. Penal reform will have its expectations fulfilled only when it can rely on personal reformative efforts, differentiation of treatment, and the support by an enlightened public conscience. These conclusions transcend the conception of prison. The history of penal reform, as it has been outlined in the preceding chapters, seemed to culminate, after the First World War, in the dawn of a 'new penology'. Men like Thomas Mott Osborne and M. Liepmann were convinced that it ought to be possible to make the prison a house of education, differing from other educational institutions, by degree and method rather than in substance, and permeated by the rising tide of a powerful universal educational movement. Seen from the present post-war period, imprisonment as a legal punishment as well as an expedient for social education has reached its climax. The rise of probation, not yet complete, was a first step in the direction of legal sanctions and social treatment of a non-institutional character. Prisons, though less numerous, will probably remain indispensable for the enforcement of the law and for the protection of society. As to their qualification as instruments for the rehabilitation of the criminal, serious doubts arise. Even under ideal conditions, the enforced deprivation of liberty, the atmosphere of constant surveillance and suspicion, the monotony of a minutely regulated routine too often frustrate any educative efforts. If an institution is to be designed for the rehabilitation of the antisocial, it should certainly be very unlike a prison. Social readjustment as the primary aim of legal punishment has shifted the emphasis from prison to supplementary and alternative methods of extra-mural treatment.[1]

These tendencies are a challenge to the student of penal reform. On the one hand, their acceptance might sabotage sincere efforts to reorganize prisons on constructive lines, before the new prison education has had a fair chance. No exclusive alternative to imprisonment has been suggested. As long as men have to go to prison and, in due course, return from there into the community, every effort must be made to enable them to join the ranks of law-abiding citizens. On the other hand, the insight into the process

[1] G. W. Kirchwey, 157 *Annals* 15; Sanford Bates, *Prisons and Beyond* (1936), pp. 295 et seq.; Haynes, pp. 335 et seq.; H. E. Barnes and N. K. Teeters, op. cit.

of social readjustment gives new forms of semi- and non-institutional treatment a proper place in a rational penal policy. The principle of custodial differentiation may result in a flexibility of prison sentences with opportunities for reformative efforts unhampered by locks and bars. Observations made in prisons with regard to work, educational activities, methods of discipline, and personal approach represent an experience on human reactions and relationships which is relevant not only inside prison walls. It is the purpose of the following chapters to draw from this experience for a discussion of outlines of institutional and non-institutional penal and reformative treatment.

SECOND PART

GENERAL OUTLINES

CHAPTER VII

CRIMINOLOGICAL FOUNDATION

A STUDY of crime and criminals is the appropriate starting-point for a scientific approach to the questions of penal and reformative treatment. Prison administrators and social workers expect from criminology an insight into their task and suggestions for performing it. In the nineteenth century, when penal reform was dominated by competitive rival systems, criminology seemed to exhaust itself in a contest between the social and the anthropological schools of thought. After the First World War these theoretical controversies gave way to a search for relevant facts as the necessary pre-condition of a new evaluation and synthesis.[1] In the inter-war period America took the lead in criminology.[2] Comprehensive research work was undertaken with a view to approaching the dynamics of criminal behaviour by new methods. William Healy and Augusta Bronner of Boston inaugurated steadily extended investigations on the individual criminal with special regard to his personal relationships within his natural environment. Such horizontal studies were supplemented by a vertical approach. Sheldon and Eleanor Glueck of Harvard examined and re-examined by consecutive follow-up studies the behaviour of former offenders throughout many years. The rise of criminological research has been reflected in a formidable array of recent American text-books.

THE IMPACT OF SOCIAL AND BIOLOGICAL FACTORS

Criminology is an aetiological science. Its primary aim is to explain criminal behaviour and to disclose the causes of crime. Innumerable individual and mass observations with endless data, figures, and correlations have been scattered in blue books, reports,

[1] W. C. Reckless, *The Etiology of Delinquent and Criminal Behaviour* (Soc. Sc. Research Council, 1943), p. 1 and *passim*.

[2] See Bibliographical Notes, p. xiv. For a survey on current American Criminology see J. P. Shalloo (ed.), 'Crime in the United States', 217 *Annals* (Sept. 1941); H. Mannheim, 34 *Soc. Rev.* 222.

and monographs. For the clarification of treatment problems the following criminological conclusions are submitted.

The question of causes of crime, like the conception of crime itself, has a twofold meaning. Crime is a social mass phenomenon. Why in England before the Second World War were there 70,000 persons found guilty of indictable offences? Why out of 100,000 boys of thirteen no less than 1,315 committed criminal offences? An understanding of crime as a social phenomenon has an indirect bearing on reformative treatment. It shows the general perspectives of an individual case as only one among many others, and makes the field-worker aware of the wider implications of his own limited approach. But crime is also an occurrence in the life of an individual. Even the most perfect interpretation of crime in general does not suffice to explain why a particular individual embezzled money, or forcibly entered a dwelling-house, or lived among vagrants and disorderly persons. The criminology of the nineteenth century had neglected this question until, at the time of the First World War, W. Healy initiated new research into the behaviour problems of 'the individual delinquent'.

Crime, like many other human reactions, has many causes. As a social science criminology explains a certain behaviour as the individual's response to the challenge of his environment. This implies a threefold object of criminological research, viz. to disclose the effect of certain environmental conditions, to recognize the individual's inclinations and susceptibility, and to study the nature of the individual's reaction to the stimulus from without.

Repeated mass observations have confirmed the proposition that crime as a social phenomenon follows the fluctuations of a nation's economic life. A hundred years ago, under the less complicated economic conditions then prevailing, the rise of corn prices in Bavaria was followed by a rise in theft, mendicancy, and emigration.[1] The complex structure of the present economic and social system makes it difficult to isolate those factors which are indicative of probable economic factors of crime. Up to the First World War German observation allowed a positive correlation between the price-wage ratio and the frequency of thefts.[2] When from 1888–9 to 1891–2 the working time necessary to earn the equivalent of 100 kg. bread rose from 8·9 to 10·6 working days, the rate of thefts increased from 202 to 226; when in 1895–6 the necessary

[1] G. v. Mayr, 'Statistik der gerichtlichen Polizei im Kgr. Bayern und anderen Ländern', *Beiträge zur Statistik des Kgr. Bayern* (1867).

[2] H. Schwarz, 3 *Internl. R. Soc. Hist.* 334.

working time fell to 7·5 working days the theft rate sank to 188.[1] An investigation based on English data from 1826 to 1913 on the social aspects of business cycles revealed a tendency of offences against property with violence such as robbery, house- and shop-breaking to increase in bad times and to decrease in good times.[2]

The First World War demonstrated beyond any reasonable doubt the economic character of war criminality. The number of offences against property rose in the same proportion as the countries were affected by the consequences of economic warfare, blockade, scarcity of raw materials and food, and opportunities for black-market activities. From 1914 to 1918 England had no increase in the total number of crimes against property known to the police, but an increase in shop-breaking and larceny by servants, and a rise by almost 50 per cent. in the number of juveniles tried for indictable offences. This was far surpassed by an unprecedented rise in offences against property on the Continent, in belligerent and neutral countries alike. In Germany first and second convictions for theft among juveniles, women, and old men not eligible for military service increased by 141 per cent. Likewise in neutral Holland, simple thefts rose by 135 per cent., and in Sweden petty thefts even by 218 per cent. At the same time Canada, while at war, but far away from the economic stranglehold of the European theatre of war, had no increase in crime.[3] The subsequent post-war experience in Germany confirmed the economic character of the inflated war criminality. When in 1923 the collapse of the currency led to a complete breakdown of the economic system and an upheaval of the whole social structure, the economic catastrophe was accompanied by a new peak of offences against property. The rate of offences against property, per 100,000 of the age of criminal responsibility, which had been 522 in 1913, reached the record figure of 1,220 in 1923, and sank to 546 with the recovery in 1926.

Like a grotesque experiment, this shows how an economic

[1] G. Aschaffenburg, *Das Verbrechen und seine Bekämpfung* (3rd ed. 1923), p. 124.

[2] Dorothy S. Thomas, 'Social Aspects of Business Cycles' (London Thesis, 1925); Summaries of relevant studies on the relation between economic conditions and crime by E. Roesner, *Einfluss von Wirtschaftslage, Alkohol und Jahreszeit auf die Kriminalität* (Strafgefängnis Berlin-Tegel, 1931); T. Sellin, *Research Memorandum on Crime in the Depression* (1937). Recent studies on economic conditions of crime by L. Radzinowicz, 31 *Soc. Rev.* 1 and 139.

[3] Figures computed from *Crim. Stat. 1923*, p. 28; H. Mannheim, *War and Crime* (1941), pp. 92 and 94; M. Liepmann, *Krieg und Kriminalität in Deutschland* (Carnegie publication, 1930), p. 58; F. Zahn, 47 *Schmollers Jahrb.* 243, 262 (Holland); O. Grönlund, 16 *MoSchrKrim.* 331 (Sweden); *The Canada Yearbook* (1919), p. 618.

catastrophe involves a mass outburst of dishonesty which affects vast groups of the population with no previous criminal tendencies, but it does not mean that every crisis has the same criminal consequences, or even leads to any rising criminality at all. An analysis of relevant statistics in Boston showed that 73 per cent. of the years under observation had a simultaneous fluctuating rise and fall of prosecutions for property crimes and unemployment in manufacturing establishments.[1] Even so, it came as a surprise that the worldwide depression of 1932 did not coincide with the same spectacular rise in mass criminality as the preceding war and post-war crises.[2] In England unemployment of more than 2¼ million people, or 22 per cent., coincided with a general increase in offences against property. The rate of burglaries known to the police rose from 55·66 in 100,000 in 1928 to 99·64 in 1932, but continued to rise when unemployment receded. In 1937 the rate of unemployment was 10·6, slightly below the level of 1928, but the rate of burglaries had reached 110, i.e. almost twice the figure of 1928. At the same time the rate of simple and minor larcenies climbed from 120·3 in 1928 to 306·7 in 1932 and to 412 in 1937.[3] In Germany the depression led to a steeper rise in burglaries than in simple thefts. During the prosperity year 1928 the conviction rates were 29·8 for burglary and 145·3 for simple theft. When in 1932 the unemployment figures reached the peak of more than 5½ million or 31·1 per cent., the burglary rate was 54·2 and the rate for simple thefts 170.[4] The rise in thefts of goods from dwelling-houses, warehouses, and in transit was reflected in growing insurance risks. The ratio of damages claimed per 1,000 insurance contracts rose from 10·6 during the prosperity to 17·2 in the depression, and receded again with full employment and the industrial boom before the war.[5] As a mass phenomenon the increase in crime during the depression was less conspicuous than during the post-war currency crisis. Throughout the years 1919 to 1934 there was a constant correlation of −0·825 between the output of coal and the number of simple thefts, but the theft curve reacted to the crisis of 1923 with the steep jump of 300 per

[1] S. B. Warner, *Crime and Criminal Statistics in Boston* (1934), pp. 34 et seq.

[2] G. B. Vold, 40 *Am. J. Soc.* 803; A. H. McCormick in *Yearbook of the National Probation Association* (1936), p. 368.

[3] *The Ministry of Labour Gazette*, 1938, p. 2; *Crim. Stat., passim.*

[4] *Annuaire statistique de la Société des Nations*, 1937–8, p. 65; 'Entwicklung der Kriminalität im In- und Ausland nach dem Kriege', *Vorabdruck zu Kriminalstatistik 1933* (1935), p. 7.

[5] E. Roesner, 'Wirtschaftslage und Straffälligkeit', *HWBKrim.*; id., 28 *MoSchrKrim.* 487.

cent. and to the mass unemployment of 1932 with the moderate rise of 17 per cent.[1] The United States had the highest unemployment figure of 12·7 million or 24·3 per cent. in 1933. Compared with the state of affairs two years previously there was a slight increase in the rates of offences known to the police, i.e. with regard to burglaries, from 192 to 214·11, and with regard to simple larcenies, from 424 to 453.[2]

While an analysis of general criminal statistics indicates no conspicuous mass criminality due to the depression, other observations suggest a connexion between unemployment and juvenile delinquency. The onset of the depression hit the industrial north of England more severely than the rural south. At the same time the increase in offences of dishonesty in the north exceeded the rise of the same offences in the less affected south by more than 100 per cent. Boys under sixteen were involved at a rate of 25 per cent. in the higher criminality due to depression in the north as compared with their share of 18·1 per cent. in the moderately increased criminality of the south.[3] Comparisons between young offenders and corresponding non-delinquent control groups show a markedly higher percentage of unemployed among the offenders. This applies not only to times with a normal employment standard, when, in 1924, 70 per cent. of prisoners under eighteen at Wandsworth had been unemployed against 10·3 of their contemporaries at large, but also to times under the impact of the depression when, in 1934, 69 per cent. of offenders between fourteen and sixteen in Liverpool were unemployed, whilst only 9·8 per cent. of insured young men between sixteen and seventeen were out of work. Likewise 61 per cent. of young prisoners in Massachusetts penal institutions had been unemployed when only 15 per cent. of young workers in the building trade were out of work.[4] Where an increase in crime coincides with sinking employment figures, a causal connexion is probable.[5] Unemployment, though not always a cause of, is a contributory factor to frequent perpetration of crimes.

So far, the criminological aspects of the Second World War can only be traced with regard to juveniles. In England the outbreak

[1] H. Schwarz, l.c., p. 379.

[2] *Annuaire statistique*, l.c.; G. B. Vold, in W. F. Ogburn, *Social Changes during Depression* (1935), p. 803 and *passim*.

[3] *Crim. Stat. 1929*, p. vii.

[4] H. Mannheim, *Social Aspects of Crime in England* (1940), p. 132; J. H. Bagot, *Juvenile Delinquency* (1941), p. 56; F. E. Haynes, *Criminology* (2nd ed. 1935), p. 183.

[5] H. Mannheim, l.c., p. 151 and *passim*, with a careful analysis of local variations.

of the war occurred after a continuous rise in juvenile delinquency which had doubled the rate of the 'peak age', i.e. boys under fourteen found guilty of indictable offences, from 592 per 100,000 in 1932 to 1,183 in 1938. From this level the war set in with a new jump in juvenile delinquency.[1] The annual number of juveniles under seventeen found guilty of indictable offences rose from the 1939 level of 30,543 by 37 per cent. in 1940—the maximum percentage increase during the First World War in the record year 1917—it reached an increase of 42 per cent. over the pre-war level in 1941, dropped to 25 per cent. in 1943, with a flattening of the curve near this level in the later years of the war.[2] The increase of the first year varied locally between 28 per cent. in London and 80 per cent. at Manchester. The rising tide affected children under fourteen more than young persons between fourteen and seventeen. Compared with the corresponding time in 1939, during the first four months of 1940 the number of children found guilty of indictable offences increased by 3,316 or 62 per cent., the number of young persons by 1,811 or 41 per cent.

Social events not only affect the rise and fall of criminality but also its qualitative variations. Crime, like other forms of social behaviour, adapts itself to changing conditions. During the First World War the high tide of offences against property in belligerent and neutral countries coincided with a fall in juvenile suicides. Apparently in the feverish atmosphere of the war, the alluring thrill of acquisitive crime left 'no time for suicide'. Conversely in the depression, with no comparable mass criminality, the number of suicides rose markedly. Switzerland, after the lowest annual total of 701 suicides in 1917, reached the unprecedented peak of 1,218 in 1932. In the same year the United States had a rate of 17·4 suicides per 100,000, the highest figure since the previous record of 1910.[3] These variations reflect the difference between the ill-founded war and post-war boom and the desperate apathy of the depression. In Germany the mass criminality in the wake of the currency crisis was a 'flight into goods'. The number of thefts climbed to two and a half the pre-war standard, cases of receiving stolen property reached even six times the previous

[1] For the following see: *Juvenile Offences*, Home Office Circular 807 624/Board of Education 1554 (June 1941); *The Times Educational Supplement*, 12 Apr. 1941; H. Mannheim, 217 *Annals* 128.

[2] Mr. Oliver, Under-Secretary of State for the Home Department, in the House of Commons, 2 Nov. 1945, 415 *Hansard* 836.

[3] H. Gruhle, 27 *MoSchrKrim.* 129; *Statistisches Jahrbuch der Schweiz* (1934), p. 95; *Statistical Abstract of the United States* (1936), p. 82.

figure, while frauds rose but slowly, and arson—often an expedient to get money from the insurance company—sank to one-third its previous amount. After the stabilization the year 1924 brought an unprecedented number of cases of counterfeited currency, and in 1927 frauds outnumbered five times the cases of receiving. Money had again become the most coveted object of crime.[1]

Besides such temporary fluctuations there are certain continuous trends of crime. The history of criminal law in England reflects an increasing sophistication in acts of dishonesty from cattle-lifting to new forms of misappropriation which developed with the growing trade and traffic. They led to the recognition of larceny by a servant or a bailee, or committed by a trick, and to the statutory offences of embezzlement and false pretences.[2] This process of intellectualization of crime is still going on. With a further growing mobility of money and credit or the substitution of less visible methods of keeping goods for personal physical possession, frauds are gaining ground at the expense of crude taking. Criminal statistics are misleading, since Continental countries with the principle of mandatory public prosecution limited the prosecution of simple thefts. This, however, is in itself an indication that public opinion no longer regards every petty theft as a significant offence. In the years between the First World War and the general depression Denmark, Holland, France, Italy, and Austria had a fall in thefts and a rise in frauds. Sweden had a slight increase in thefts, whilst frauds trebled. Poland had an increase in petty thefts by almost two-thirds, a decrease of burglaries, whilst embezzlement and fraud reached three times their previous levels. In Belgium, during the decade 1920–30, thefts decreased by 55 per cent., frauds by 45·1 per cent., and forgeries rose. In Germany thefts were markedly below the pre-war level in 1927, but frauds reached the record rate of 112 per 100,000.[3] In 1936 the total of thefts had decreased even more, but the sinking figures for fraud were still slightly above the pre-war level. In England, where the years after the First World War witnessed a rise in burglaries and house-breaking known to the police, which surpassed in 1933 the pre-war rate by 185 per cent., frauds at the same time increased by nearly 200 per cent. That the difference between the two curves is less conspicuous in England than in

[1] *Kriminalstatistik 1927*, pp. 56 and *passim*. Similar observations with regard to the Swiss Canton Aargau by Thut, 24 *MoSchrKrim.* 129.

[2] J. Hall, *Theft, Law, and Society* (1935).

[3] Computed from figures given in *Entwicklung der Kriminalität*, l.c., *passim*.

other European countries is due to the fact that the figures for theft known to the police are not affected by a lessening energy in prosecuting, and that in English criminal law certain types of fraudulent acts are classified as larceny by a trick, and therefore not recorded as frauds. These facts are sufficient evidence of the prevailing trend towards the more sophisticated forms of offences against property. Fraudulent misrepresentations are becoming more significant as methods of gainful crime. This tendency is not a mere question of legal qualification. Sophisticated crime is more closely associated with a persistent criminal career. According to American observations, boys between sixteen and seventeen guilty of fraud and false pretences had the highest reconviction rate, viz. 48·8 per cent. against the general ratio of 29·6 per cent. for all crimes of the same age-group.[1]

These illustrations suffice to show, in the light of recent experience, the close relationship between environmental conditions and crime. A similar association between man's natural endowment and his criminal conduct has been demonstrated by crimino-biological investigations, especially by studies on the behaviour patterns of twins. Twins are supposed to live under the same environmental influence of home, family, upbringing, school, economic level, and so on. If they differ in their behaviour it cannot be due to external causes. They offer therefore an ideal observation field for the effect of internal factors, isolated from the surroundings which are in both cases equal. Biology distinguishes between fraternal and identical twins, the former not being nearer to each other from a biological point of view than other brothers and sisters, while the latter, true doubles, are supposed to have developed from one and the same ovum. The first investigations of thirty twins with at least one criminal brother or sister had the startling result that among the 17 fraternal twins, in 2 cases only, or 12 per cent., were both twins criminal, whilst among the 13 identical twins, 10 cases, or 77 per cent. showed crime in both twins.[2] This seemed to be impressive evidence that behaviour patterns are determined by internal factors. As a rule, identical biological endowment leads to the same social behaviour. Further investigations of greater numbers of twins and material of a less pathological character than that of the first study have reduced the difference between the proportions of comrades in

[1] T. Sellin, *The Criminality of Youth* (American Law Institute, 1940), p. 115.

[2] J. Lange, *Verbrechen als Schicksal* (1929), English translation: *Crime as Destiny*, ed. by Professor Haldane (1929).

crime among the two biological groups to 33 per cent. among the fraternal and 67 per cent. among the identical twins.[1] Even these less spectacular figures indicate a higher probability that identical twins in so far as they have criminal tendencies have them in approximately the same degree, thus lending support to the evidence that anti-social behaviour depends on biological conditions.

Such instances of social and biological crime factors can easily be supplemented by further illustrations. It is a question of final evaluation to sort out a few factors of special frequency and weight as the typical causes of crime. As a result of his experience in a London metropolitan police-court, Claud Mullins has come to the conclusion that crime is mainly due to inheritance, lack of parental love, broken homes, and illegitimacy.[2]

The close relation existing between social and biological factors and crime gives the impression that criminal behaviour is determined by facts beyond the individual's control. The criminal seems to be in the inescapable grip of destiny. Such one-sided interpretation, however, overlooks essential aspects of criminological experience.

A high degree of correlation between social and biological factors on the one hand, and a typical anti-social behaviour on the other, suggests the direction for further aetiological research, but it is not in itself a conclusive proof that those factors are the causes of crime. Goring had already warned of 'the misuse of the term "cause" for the mere co-existence of associated phenomena'.[3] Where certain conditions, according to statistical evidence, imply a high probability of crime, it is advisable to speak of a crime risk rather than of a cause of crime.[4] Poverty is a crime risk. In Liverpool 85 per cent. of the juvenile delinquents came from homes below the poverty line, according to the Rowntree standard, as against 30 per cent. of representative working-class families.[5] In London every second juvenile delinquent came from a poor home as against 30 per cent. of all London children.[6] Even so, the majority of children from poor homes are not delinquents, whilst

[1] M. F. Ashley Montagu, 217 *Annals* 46, co-ordinating the results of Lange, Legras, Kranz, Stumpfl, Rosanoff. For a similar summary see Popenoe, 27 *Journal of Heredity* 388.

[2] Claud Mullins, *Why Crime?* (1945).

[3] C. Goring, *The English Convict*, new ed. by K. Pearson (1919), p. 185.

[4] W. C. Reckless, *Criminal Behaviour* (1940), pp. 2 et seq.

[5] J. H. Bagot, *Juvenile Delinquency* (1941), p. 61.

[6] Cyril Burt, *The Young Delinquent* (3rd ed. 1938), p. 69.

40 per cent. of London juvenile delinquents came from comfortable surroundings. For the determination of causes of crime, statistical evidence must be supplemented by the study of individual cases of a sufficient number and of a representative character. This applies to social and biological factors alike. Not every adverse biological symptom is an inherited cause of crime. According to an early study on pupils of an industrial school in Baden, fifty out of a hundred delinquent boys were mentally abnormal; the anti-social conduct of twenty-two could be explained by the abnormal mentality; in the case of only eleven the unsatisfactory mental equipment, which was the cause of the boy's trouble, was due to parental drunkenness and abnormality.[1]

The close association of crime with adverse environmental conditions and natural endowment may be due to causation or to selection. Are instability of work and habitual bad work causes of crime or are criminals unreliable and bad workers? Are parental desertion and neglect causes of juvenile delinquency or do they frequently occur in low-grade families which have a socially maladjusted offspring? Are the high re-conviction rates of juveniles guilty of frauds indicative of the formative influence of early sophisticated crime, or do young offenders with persistent criminal tendencies resort to frauds? In many cases it works both ways. Low-grade people coming from broken homes, living in bad surroundings, are severely hit by unemployment and are thus exposed to strain and temptations which they are less able to resist than their more fortunate contemporaries.

A cause of crime is a fact or event which, in the light of frequent experience, explains a subsequent piece of anti-social behaviour by the way of conclusion. But the same cause may explain similar reactions as the result of different motives.[2] An economic crisis may be a cause of a coinciding rise in offences of dishonesty, committed by men who act with different purposes. Whereas some might be misled by their own or their family's distress, others are incited by the prospect of exploiting their fellow creatures' difficulties, or give way to the alluring opportunity of achieving riches easily gained in the exciting boom of an unusual situation. An abnormal demand for commodities facilitates trading in stolen goods. When inhibitions to buy from a possible receiver of stolen goods weaken, theft flourishes. To *become* penniless or to *lose* work is an even more significant crime risk than to be poor or

[1] H. Gruhle, *Die Ursachen der jugendlichen Verwahrlosung und Kriminalität* (1912).

[2] Id., 27 *MoSchrKrim.* 113; 51 *ZStW* 469; 22 *Journal* 506.

unemployed.[1] Lack of the will or of the ability to accommodate oneself to a lower standard of living, to give up the little things which matter much in life, involves a serious strain. With the loss of status, the traditional moral standards of the former social position seem to lose their authority and to be no longer worth any sacrifice.[2] When the father and the natural breadwinner loses his work his self-respect and authority are threatened and the family is put to a hard test.[3] During the depression family life weathered the storm, on the whole, better than sceptical observers had expected. Mass unemployment is apt to level the loss of status or to compensate by a new solidarity of interests. Not only a deterioration in a man's economic position, but also a rise in the social ladder, involves characteristic crime risks. The newcomer will bring with him the specific antisocial patterns of his former group, or else break with the moral standards of his past too abruptly before he has fully adapted himself to the style of life of his new environment. This observation applies to the criminality of immigrants and explains the notoriously high crime rate of American-born sons of foreign-born parents.[4] 'Social capillarity' implies a typical crime risk, which is often the expression of an inherent 'culture conflict'.[5]

These manifold motives under the surface of identical causes of crime are further complicated by selective processes. Adverse events first hit those who are less prepared for defence. At the first onset of unemployment, the loss of work by juvenile delinquents seemed due to laziness or low mental abilities or otherwise to be personally conditioned.[6] Likewise, the outbreak of the war made potential delinquents stumble first and foremost, viz. typical 'court children' from broken homes or unhappy families.[7] In the wake of severe bombing, however, looting of quasi-derelict property which seemed to have lost any visible link with a personal owner, was a typical offence of the non-criminal juvenile. The over-

[1] H. Mannheim, *War and Crime* (1941), p. 39; id., *Social Aspects*, l.c., pp. 111 and 124.

[2] For the psychological effects of unemployment see *Men without Work* (A Report made to the Pilgrim Trust, 1938); E. Wight Bakke, *Citizens without Work* (1940); Zawadski, Bohan, and Lazarsfeld, 6 *J. Soc. Psych.* 224.

[3] R. S. Caven and K. H. Ranck, *The Family and the Depression* (1938).

[4] C. C. van Vechten, 32 *Journal* 139; E. H. Stofflet, 217 *Annals* 84.

[5] 'Social capillarity' used by E. Hacker, 28 *MoSchrKrim.* 353, referring to A. Dumont, *Dépopulation et civilisation* (1890). See also T. Sellin, 44 *Am. J. Soc.* 97, and 'Crime and Culture Conflict', *Soc. Science Research Council Bulletin* (1938).

[6] W. Villinger, 4 *Mitt.Krim.-biol.Ges.* 147; Schürer von Waldheim, 45 *Z.f.Kinderforschung* 1.

[7] Eileen Younghusband, 6 *Howard Journal* 19.

whelming majority of these delinquents were without any previous criminal records, and in every second case the goods looted worth less than £5.[1] Observations made in the slums of Chicago and other big American cities have shown that these marked delinquency areas are inhabited by a high proportion of transitory population. In the deteriorating and declining residential districts impoverished immigrants found cheap quarters and expected little resentment in regard to their coming; in the past Germans and Irishmen, then Italians and Poles, and recently coloured people from the south. Whilst many such slum-dwellers succeeded, by dint of strenuous efforts, in working their passage out of these breeding places of vice and delinquency, their less capable contemporaries stayed on or were even kept by what an old criminal called 'the telepathy that is from one derelict to another'.[2]

Selective processes are at work even where antisocial behaviour seems due to biological deficiencies. Instability of character or subnormal intelligence let a man find only casual and low-grade work with a minimum of remuneration and no personal satisfaction, and this situation exposes him to a considerable crime risk. Likewise the great probability that the identical twin of a criminal exhibits the same antisocial tendencies may be due to the fact that this close companionship leads them to socially similar environments where they both fall victims to the same crime-producing conditions.[3]

THE PSYCHOLOGICAL APPROACH

The analysis of causative and selective processes throws some light on the interdependence of environmental and personal factors. Human behaviour is determined less by isolated motives than by man's impressionability, his temperament, his emotional qualities, and manner of response, shaped by a lifelong experience since the formative events of early childhood. As a result of such observations the naturalistic, if not purely economic, conception of social factors is to be supplemented by the recognition of the psychological aspects of environment. The economic standard, social status, complete or incomplete families, determine the wider limit of the individual's external surroundings. Within these limits the

[1] H. Mannheim, 217 *Annals* 134; Report on the Work of the Metropolitan Police Force, according to *Sunday Times* of 11 May 1941.

[2] C. Shaw, *Delinquency Areas* (1929); *Wickersham Report* XIII (Report on Causes of Crime, ii, 1931), pp. 23–188.

[3] H. H. Newman, *Multiple Human Births* (1940).

individual's behaviour is influenced by his personal situation. It is his ordinal position among brothers and sisters, the fact whether a boy or girl is the only, the beloved, or the unwanted child, success or failure at school, play, or work, the lack of personal contacts or abundance of affection, recognition or repudiation by his fellow citizens, friendships and enmities, which shape man's life in society. The crime risk of a child from a 'broken home' depends on the reason for the breach in the family unit. The father's death is less momentous in regard to a child's delinquency than the desertion of the mother, with the father living with an unmarried woman. Not the external event, but what it means to the individual, determines human behaviour. This 'stimulus value' is relative and depends on the person himself. Environmental influences are selected and interpreted by the individual. Economic distress and social strain depend in their effects on whether people can accept and master them, surrender, or try to escape. The personal attitude of one's fellow men, an essential factor of the personal situation, is often the reflection of a man's own hypersensibility or overpowering self-confidence, of his suspiciousness or blind credulity. But the surrounding world is not mute or lacking in impressions. Individuals not only conceive similar outward surroundings in a different way, but by their own attitude and reaction help to create the personal atmosphere in which they live. The causation of social behaviour is a dynamic process. Man undergoes a process of development within changing surroundings. By a 'circular response' (Healy) the human self is constantly being shaped by the influences around it and is at the same time ceaselessly at work trying to modify its environment.[1] Men do not only make history, they also influence their daily surroundings by a psychological process of 'milieu provocation' (H. Hoffmann).[2]

The emphasis on the individual's personal contribution to the factors which mould his destiny ought not to minimize the limits set to human beings. There are men and women with such unfavourable physical and mental equipment that they are doomed to failure under whatever conditions they live. Likewise there are situations of such extreme gravity that only an heroic resistance can hope to overcome them. The strenuous efforts of a few do not relieve society of the responsibility for its weaker and less successful members. A right combination of firmness and kindness, healthy affective links between the members of the family, and

[1] W. Healy, *Personality in Formation and Action* (1938).

[2] H. Hoffmann, *Charakter und Umwelt* (1928).

encouragement of constructive spare-time activities are more essential for a child's upbringing than social status and economic level, but those psychological conditions cannot fairly be expected to flourish in an overcrowded dilapidated house, among inhabitants haunted by utter insecurity, with the father frequently without employment and the mother overworked by household cares and the additional burden of being the principal breadwinner.

Without losing sight of these limitations criminology is in search of the personal 'something' without which sociological and biological explanations of crime remain unsatisfactory. Even if a marked proportion of criminals come from poor surroundings and 'broken homes' and are intellectually dull or of an unstable character, there is still an even greater number of dull or unstable persons who are not criminal in the face of adverse environmental conditions, whilst others resort to crime in spite of a good home background, comfortable economic conditions, and a normal mental state. It is the final object of criminology to find out the reasons for 'the differential response' (W. C. Reckless) to the same crime risks.[1] Why, under adverse conditions, do some people revert to crime while others do not? In order to understand the criminal, one has to turn one's attention to the non-criminal. From this point of view a classic study by W. Healy and A. Bronner has indeed thrown 'new light on delinquency'.[2]

This investigation tried to disclose why among brothers and sisters, living within the same surroundings and burdened by the same heritage, individuals develop in a different way. Among 111 families, living under adverse conditions, 45 per cent. of the children were delinquent, but the others were not. When searching for the reason why these children kept straight, the investigation shifted the emphasis to the emotional implications of personal relationships. By far the greatest difference between the delinquents and the non-delinquents lay in the balance of emotions and affection; 91 per cent. of the delinquents were under an emotional stress. They were unhappy and discontented, they felt excluded, inferior, or envious. Juvenile delinquency seems to have its roots in an emotional maladjustment. This disturbance in the balance of feelings, affections, and emotions in respect of the individual's personal relationships is the decisive factor which turns a notorious crime risk into a virtual cause of juvenile delinquency. Even this profound study does not completely close the gap. 9 per cent. of

[1] W. C. Reckless, *Etiology*, l.c., p. 52.

[2] W. Healy and A. Bronner, *New Light on Delinquency* (1936).

the delinquents had no emotional disturbance, whilst 13 per cent. of the non-delinquents had. Whereas the latter were fortunate enough to find an innocuous outlet for gaining satisfaction, the nine emotionally adjusted delinquents had to face serious odds of poverty, bad companions, or lack of supervision. Even scientific perfection will not rule out the chance of a man sometimes doing the unexpected, but the progress of research consists in a constant narrowing down of the unexplainable margin.

These results are apt to bridge the gap between diagnosis and treatment. The emphasis on personal relationships and their effects on the individual's emotions and reactions turns criminological considerations in the direction of the social worker's endeavours at readjustment. Insight into the social and biological factors of crime and delinquency makes him aware of the limits of his efforts, when he has to expect succour from social reform, full employment, slum clearance, marriage law reform, a legal solution of the problem of illegitimacy,[1] and the measures requisite for the care of the subnormal and for finding him an appropriate place in work and life. The psychological approach to the cause of crime and the dynamics of delinquency enables the student of criminology to see the needs and opportunities for preventive and corrective treatment. This applies to child guidance, institutional and non-institutional methods, psychological treatment, welfare, and pastoral work. While all these differ in methods and degrees, they imply an approach to the individual in his relationship to his personal surroundings.

SOCIAL CASE-STUDIES

Every theoretical outlook has its specific method of investigation. The social approach to the questions of crime and delinquency was based upon statistical mass observation, the biological approach relied upon anthropological examination, and the psychological approach has been associated with the development of social case-work.[2] Social case-studies are life histories of individuals, based upon inquiries into personal circumstances and the social background of a person. This form of social and psychological investigation originated in the United States. Through the pioneer work of Mary Richmond and William Healy it became an invaluable instrument not only for criminology, but also for other branches of social science, welfare work, and psychiatric treatment. Mary

[1] C. Mullins, l.c., *passim*.

[2] See Bibliographical Notes, p. xiv.

Richmond's conception of social diagnosis, borrowed from medical science, implies the observation of a living individual, the study of human character, reactions and behaviour with a tendency towards a certain treatment. It is not only the necessary condition but often also the first part of the cure and the beginning of a conscious process of adjusting an individual to his social environment. A German translation interpreted social diagnosis as a method of understanding and dealing with personal destiny.[1] Whilst it is never undertaken for information only it opens up a valuable source of knowledge. Like witnesses in legal procedure, investigators are bound to distinguish between objective facts and subjective impressions. They are expected not to withhold their personal views, but they must make clear from which factual data they are drawing their conclusions. When they convey an experience from hearsay they must ascertain the reliability of their source. In a social record, that which seems to be mere hearsay may be direct evidence in itself. The neighbour's opinion, the attitude of 'the street', reflect a person's 'circular response'. In its application to various spheres of life, social case-work has drawn the general attention to the psychological aspects of environment. A comparison between early and recent case-studies reveals a tendency to turn from external surroundings to the personal situation.[2] Most case-records drawn up in 1924 pointed to general types of behaviour and material conditions. Ten years later they emphasized the specific aspects of the persons concerned and the nature of their family relationships. The experience that personal reactions and social relationships are more significant than outward habits and physical surroundings has affected the concept of environment itself. As a result of social case-work, sociology concentrates its interest on 'the person's social world' (W. C. Reckless), i.e. those individuals, groups, and objects which appeal to a person and stimulate his response.[3] It is the aim of social case-studies to reflect and follow up the dynamics of human life. Personal situations change, human attitudes and reactions alter, and the individual's character is being re-shaped and linked with the changing world by mutual response. Case-studies often require corroboration by supplementary reports; the social worker, the psychologist, the medical officer, the vocational expert, have

[1] K. Mende, 17 *Zentr.Bl.* 60.

[2] S. Clement Brown, 'Methods of Social Case Workers', in F. C. Bartlett and others, *The Study of Society* (1939), pp. 379–401.

[3] W. C. Reckless, l.c., p. 21, and 217 *Annals* 77.

to give their views. The individual, however, is not the total of his parts, but an organic entity, which calls for more than a cumulation of different observations, or a superficial compromise by way of generalization. Investigators must work as members of a team, frankly exchange their views, and mutually control and limit their divergent outlooks. The result will often be a tentative assessment only, to be reconsidered in the light of further inquiries and fresh experience. Only such flexible methods are apt to pay due regard to the time factor. Human life and social conditions are constantly moving. The juvenile grows up, makes new contacts, meets with acknowledgement or loses sympathy and affections; conditions of work and earnings improve or deteriorate. A record on a person's social background refers to observations of the past and suggests a certain procedure for the time to come. The mere expression in words seems to transform a fluid process into static facts. Realism in social observation requires a certain relativity. Definite statements obtain within strict limits only, and they must be checked by supplementary considerations from other viewpoints. Adequate provisions are necessary for a subsequent re-testing and amending of the suggestions made in the original report. A flexible system of observation and treatment should allow for a certain amount of trial and error and adequate alterations of the original plan. By adopting such a course, practical case-work adapts itself to the 'dynamic aspects of social diagnosis'.[1]

Diagnosis is knowledge for the sake of prognosis and therapy. Within the orbit of penal reform, social case-studies serve various constructive purposes.[2] Sentencing courts or other agencies competent for the disposal of convicted persons need accounts of the individual's character, life, and social background as a basis for their decision. For the legal conditions of probation, of special methods of reformative training, or of measures of public security, recent legislation does not refer to the circumstances of a single act, but to the typical behaviour, personal inclinations, and further prospects of the individual offender. English law explicitly provides for a relevant social report, if the court makes a probation order or gives a Borstal sentence. For the actual treatment within the frame laid down by the probation order or sentence, case-studies are a proper foundation for the treatment plan for the probationer and for the assignment of the prisoner to a particular institution

[1] Clara Maria Liepmann, *MoSchrKrim.* 1930, Beiheft 3, pp. 152–61; I. Arlt, 2 *Dtsch. Z. für Wohlfahrtspflege* 169.

[2] W. J. Ellis, 32 *Journal* 72.

or treatment group, and for the selection of the appropriate kind of work. Conditional release in its different forms requires a reliable estimate of the social risks involved in the prisoner's return to the community before the expiration of his sentence. Institutional experience alone would be based too much on the man's reaction to the artificial prison situation to allow for conclusions with regard to ordinary social life. After-care as a post-institutional treatment requires much individualization and depends on personal help and an appeal to the ex-prisoner's self-control. It needs a fair knowledge of the manner in which the person responds to guidance and trust, but also of his reaction to the pressure and temptations of his environment. Under ideal conditions, these consecutive functions of case-studies should be co-ordinated or even carried out as a continuous contribution of one thoroughgoing service of social information. The original report would be the foundation for subsequent social and psychological considerations during the whole penal and reformative process. Such a continuity burdens the social case-work with a tremendous responsibility for human destiny. While judicial decisions are bound by strict constitutional guarantees, the value of social reports depends on a free observation of manifold facts and an intuitive understanding of human personalities. Such personal experience leaves little room for verification by legal evidence and judicial review. A comprehensive, consecutive use of social case-studies calls for flexibility, lest first impressions harden into misleading prejudices.

Provision for social investigation and personal assessment is the indispensable condition for any differentiation of treatment. A penal and reformative régime, based upon consecutive social case-work, has sometimes been characterized as a classification system. This expression had better be avoided. History is a warning against over-estimation of a single aspect of penal treatment and its identification with the whole complex organization of rehabilitative and protective processes. Classification suggests a definitely fixed order rather than a constant resort to fresh experience for a flexible treatment within the framework of a legal sentence.

From a theoretical point of view, the psychological efforts, by means of social case-studies, to disclose the personal roots of crime and delinquency have revealed the final limits of causative explanation. No rational penal policy is feasible on the assumption that crime is only the effect of the free will of sinful man. But a one-sided emphasis on causes of crime is no less misleading. In the past, criminology, by analogy to certain branches of medicine, gave the impression that if only the causes of anti-social conduct were detected, the problems of prevention and treatment would be solved. True progress with regard to a social prognosis and treatment plans is only possible if the interest turns from isolated causal factors to man's personal reactions and behaviour patterns.[1] By this development, criminology seems to lose something of its character as a science with clear-cut conceptions and specific technical methods. Recent research centres on the human personality and its behaviour, and recognizes that a true understanding of man cannot be isolated from responsibility for his destiny. The case-study method, though apt to be refined and controlled, cannot dispense with untechnical personal experience and intuitive judgement. This implies a certain amount of subjectivity, but at the same time, by a frank admission of this limitation, its results may come nearer to truth than an alleged accuracy which tries to compute the immeasurable.

[1] W. C. Reckless, *Etiology*, l.c., p. 2; id., 217 *Annals* 82.

CHAPTER VIII
MEN IN PRISON

THE COMPOSITION OF THE PRISON POPULATION

Legal Distinctions

IMPRISONMENT is the traditional and most characteristic method of penal treatment, but it is not the only one, nor does it exclusively serve reformative purposes. Men and women are committed to prison for other reasons: unconvicted prisoners in custody awaiting trial, debtors, and the vast number of those serving short prison terms. At the same time, present penal policy tends to supplement, if not to supplant, institutional treatment by extra-mural methods of social rehabilitation, particularly by probation and parole. Imprisonment and reformative treatment are not identical, but overlapping conceptions.

Year by year, penal and correctional institutions receive a great number of men and women. Prisoners come and go according to their respective length of terms. The number of inmates at a particular date differs therefore from the total of yearly commitments. Up to the present there has been no international prison inquiry, nor are there any uniform prison statistics which allow a fair comparison between different countries. In 1935 the International Penal and Penitentiary Commission collected relevant data from twenty-two countries.[1] This material, supplemented by official information, was the basis of a survey of the prison population of the world submitted to the League of Nations by the Howard League for Penal Reform in 1936.[2]

In the last pre-war year, i.e. in 1938, there were 50,060 admissions into English prisons. The average daily prison population was 11,086.[3] In Germany, during the recovery between the inflation crisis and the general depression, the total of yearly admissions was probably near to 400,000.[4] On the 1 July 1927 there was a prison population of 62,080.[5] Seven years later, in July 1934, in the second year of the National-Socialist régime, the

[1] *Aperçus des systèmes pénitentiaires* (1935).

[2] *The Prison Population of the World* (Sept. 1936).

[3] *Report Prison Commissioners, 1938.*

[4] Available reception figure for Prussia in 1927: 280,000. *Strafvollzug in Preussen*, ed. by Preuss. Justizministerium (1928), p. v.

[5] 'Statistik des Gefängniswesens im Deutschen Reich', *Reichstag*, iv, 1928, No. 814, p. 2.

prison population had risen to 102,349—apart from the unknown number of prisoners in concentration camps.[1] In the United States the total of persons committed to state and federal prisons, county and city gaols, and institutions for juvenile delinquents during the year 1933 was approximately 693,988 and the prison population on 1 January 1933 was about 233,631.[2]

These three instances illustrate characteristic differences. The number of yearly receptions reflects the rise and fall in crime, the frequency of arrests, and the statutory or traditional standards for the selection of sentences. The average daily prison population depends on the number of commitments, the terms of remand in custody, and the length of sentences. Germany, with a reception figure more than six times the daily prison population, has apparently frequent arrests and numerous short sentences. The United States, where the prison population reaches one-third of the yearly reception figure, seems to resort to longer sentences. For comparative purposes, the total of prisoners—like the number of criminals—must be brought into relation to the population of the particular countries. On a single day, out of 100,000 of the general population in England and Wales (1934) 29·9, in Germany (1934)—apart from concentration camps—156·9, and in the United States (1933)—convicted prisoners only—158 were in prison. In Europe the average daily prison attendance rate varied between a minimum of 19·4 for Eire (1934) and a maximum of 275·2 for Estonia (1935).[3] When in the United States in 1940 the total of persons under sentence in state and federal prisons rose to 191,776, it was estimated that one in every 500 of the total population of sixteen years and over served a sentence in a state or federal institution.[4]

The reception figure and the average daily prison population correspond to two different aspects of prison life. The daily population reflects the impression of a visitor who sees the institution on a single day. It is the basis for the daily routine of the prison service. In many institutions, however, work and education are hampered by the restless atmosphere created by considerable numbers of prisoners constantly streaming in and out of prison. Thus far, taking the prison service as a whole or a particular institution, the total of yearly receptions affects the

[1] *Prison Population*, l.c., Appendix.

[2] *Prisoners in State and Federal Prisons and Reformatories, 1933* (U.S. Dept. of Commerce, Bureau of Census, 1935), p. 1.

[3] *Prison Population*, l.c.

[4] *Prison Labor in the United States, 1940* (U.S. Dept. of Labor, 1941), p. 6.

administrative work and educational programmes. Not every prisoner is susceptible to treatment or in need of social re-adjustment. A high proportion of men received in prison are unconvicted, either on remand or awaiting trial or pending an appeal. Civil debtors are another transitory and non-criminal group. Among convicted prisoners numerous offenders with short sentences present an administrative rather than a treatment problem. A rational penal policy will aim at reducing, if not altogether abolishing, these three types of imprisonment where there is neither need felt nor provision made for attempts at the prisoners' social rehabilitation.

In 1938, out of 50,060 prisoners who entered prisons in England and Wales, 9,506 were on remand or awaited trial without receiving a subsequent prison sentence, 8,205 were unconvicted and committed for non-payment of money, and 23,338 were sentenced to less than three months imprisonment. This threefold group amounted to 41,049, or something more than four-fifths of the receptions of that year. Owing to the transitory character of these commitments, the daily average attendance of unconvicted prisoners and those serving sentences of no more than three months reached only 2,223, or approximately one-fifth of the daily prison population.[1] Among the 280,000 receptions into Prussian prisons in 1927, presumably 83,000 or 29·6 per cent. were committed before trial, and 107,000 or 38·2 per cent. sentenced to imprisonment of less than three months. The difference in the number of unconvicted prisoners before trial in England and Prussia is partly due to a different statistical approach: the Prussian figures cover every prisoner received before trial, the English only those who did not receive a subsequent prison sentence. Even apart from this artificial difference, prison commitments before trial are more frequent in Germany than in England. On 1 July 1927 there were 10,353 unconvicted prisoners in German prisons awaiting trial, or 16·7 per cent. of the prison population,[2] whereas the corresponding average figures for England and Wales in 1938 were 677 or 6·1 per cent.

The present incidence of these undesirable methods of imprisonment is only a fraction of what it was in the recent past. This illustrates the negative function of penal reform, i.e. the efforts to avoid measures which are unjust, unnecessary, or unsatisfactory. In England the number of persons received on remand or before

[1] *Report Prison Commissioners, 1938.*

[2] *Statistik des Gefängniswesens,* l.c.

trial without a subsequent prison sentence dropped from 15,402, the annual average in 1913–14, to 9,506 in 1938. Compared with the total of persons tried for indictable offences, this was a decrease from 23·6 per cent. to 11·3 per cent. Relevant legislation resulted in a drastic fall of committals to prison for non-payment of money. When the Criminal Justice Administration Act, 1914,[1] required time to be given for payment of fines, the total of imprisonments in default sank from an average for the years 1909–13 of 83,187 to an average of 13,433 for the years 1926–30. The Money Payments (Justices Procedure) Act, 1935, which provided for inquiries as to the offender's means and for his personal supervision before his committal to prison is considered, resulted in a further reduction of imprisonments in default from 11,214, the yearly average 1931–5, to 7,022 in 1936.[2] At the same time, the number of offenders fined increased, partly owing to the extension of social legislation, traffic regulation, and administrative by-laws. Even after the growing use of fines, fewer people had to go to prison in default of payment. Whilst the number of offenders fined by Courts of Summary Jurisdiction rose from 433,137 in 1923 to 633,929 in 1938, the number of those who had to go to prison in default of payment sank from 15,551 or 3·6 per cent. to 7,936 or 1·25 per cent.[3] The effects of the Probation of Offenders Act, 1907, further contributed to a more sparing use of short prison terms. In the end, the appalling total of 128,182 prison sentences for not more than three months in 1913 had been reduced to 23,338 in 1938.

In other countries, fines were used as a substitute for short prison terms. In Germany, during the late twenties, two-thirds of the cases which, forty-five years previously, would have been punished by a short prison sentence were fined. In 1882, out of 100 sentences inflicted for crimes and delicts against the laws of the Reich, 60·8 amounted to imprisonment of less than three months, and 22·2 to fines. In 1928 there remained eighteen short prison sentences as against 69·2 fines. Out of the eighteen short prison sentences at least five were remitted and one remission was revoked. Ten per cent. of the fines were commuted into prison terms for non-payment—a much higher percentage than in England! The

[1] 4 & 5 Geo. V, c. 58, ss. 1–6.

[2] 25 & 26 Geo. V, c. 46; W. Thoday, *Imprisonment for Non-payment of Money* (1936); Figures from *Report Prison Commissioners, 1939–41*, p. 23.

[3] *Crim. Stat. 1923*, p. 77; *1938*, pp. xix and 68; *Report Prison Commissioners, 1938*, pp. 9 and 14; *Report of the Departmental Committee on Imprisonment in Default of Payment of Fines* (1934), p. 95.

final proportion for 1928 was therefore approximately twenty-one short prison committals to sixty-two fines paid.[1]

The criminological aspects of the prison population change in the course of time. The numbers of persons received into prison for begging and sleeping out fell from 15,871 in 1913 to 1,341 in 1938, the number of drunken women and prostitutes from 23,179 to 1,715. This was the result of a change in penal policy, which facilitated the payment of fines, or tried to deal with the underlying social evils by non-punitive measures. At the same time, the number of thieves sent to prison fell from 17,290 to 8,248, while burglars rose from 1,956 to 2,498, and those sentenced for obtaining money by false pretences and other frauds remained almost constant at 1,429 and 1,408. These figures reflect rather the growing reluctance of the courts to impose prison sentences than the development of criminality. In all these groups the number of crimes known to the police rose: larceny from 68,247 annual average 1910–14 to 197,424 in 1938, house and shopbreaking from 10,898 to 39,499, and false pretences and frauds from 4,982 to 15,976. Only burglary—its incidence almost quadrupled—resulted in a moderate rise of imprisonments! The number of prisoners sentenced for assault fell from 8,622 in 1913 to 1,762 in 1938, and those guilty of cruelty to children from 1,819 to 301. This development corresponds to a decline in the numbers of persons tried for these particular offences. Before Courts of Summary Jurisdiction the total of persons tried for assault dropped from 43,032, the annual average 1910–14, to 18,537 in 1938, and of those tried for cruelty from 3,440 to 1,058. With regard to this group of offenders against the person, the decrease in the number of prisoners is in conformity with a falling trend in criminality and/or in the frequency of prosecution.[2]

Similar fluctuations have been observed abroad. In the penal institutions of Württemberg, among the prison population before and after the First World War, the number of those convicted for assault dropped rapidly, that of thieves showed a considerable decrease, while the number of those guilty of frauds increased in accordance with the rise of sophisticated forms of crimes of dishonesty on the Continent.[3]

The growing resort to fines for the enforcement of social

[1] *Kriminalstatistik, 1928,* p. 65; K. Schäfer, 52 *ZStW* 246, 249; Ministerialrat Schaefer, in *Reichstag* iii, 1924–7, 32 Ausschuss (*RStGB*), 26 Sitzung, 5. 11. 1927.

[2] *Report Prison Commissioners, 1938,* pp. 11 et seq.; *Crim. Stat. 1938,* pp. 14 and 16.

[3] J. Griesmeier, 'Statistik über die Württembergischen Landesstrafanstalten 1926 und 1927', *Württemb. Jahrb. f. Statistik und Landeskunde,* Jahrg. 1929, pp. 167–208, 172.

legislation and administrative regulations and the sparing use of prison sentences indicate a tendency by which, if developed, the prison would become reserved for those serious criminals who need institutional seclusion either as an indispensable stage of an elaborate treatment and training, or for security reasons. Before the war, out of a total of 800,000 persons found guilty by English criminal courts, less than 10 per cent. were convicted for indictable offences. Of the 45,000 adolescent and adult offenders over seventeen guilty of thefts and other indictable offences, one-third received prison sentences. Beyond this moderate immediate application, the threat of imprisonment remains in the background for the enforcement of a probation order or a fine.[1]

Social Structure

The prison population is a cross-section of society with its manifold social classes and occupational groups. Prison sociology tries to find out how far the composition of the prison population differs from the social structure of the community. The following observations have been drawn from the census for England and Wales, 1931. Unlike the general English population with its surplus of women, increasing in the higher age-groups, the prison population has only a small minority of women. There are no more than 9·9 young women between twenty and twenty-four among every 1,000 prisoners, compared with 59 young women among 1,000 members of the general population of fourteen years and over, and only 6·8 women between twenty-five and twenty-nine among prisoners compared with 56·8 women of this age in an equal group of the general population. The disparity of sexes affects the distribution of social classes and occupations. While among 1,000 members of the general population of fourteen years and over the largest group is 348·1 not gainfully occupied women, viz. the vast number of housewives, among 1,000 prisoners the largest group is 261·5 not gainfully occupied men, viz. vagrants, professional criminals, and those who prefer not to disclose their former occupations. Personal service, the traditional unskilled occupation of women, is represented by 62·1 women among 1,000 persons of the general population and by 26·2 women among 1,000 prisoners.

Prison administration to-day is mainly concerned with younger

[1] A. Maxwell, 'Treatment of Crime', *Sidney Ball Lecture, 1937* (Barnett House Papers 21, 1938), p. 6 et seq.; Sir Samuel Hoare (now Lord Templewood), House of Commons, 29 Nov. 1938; 342 *Hansard* 267, 270.

men from industrial occupations. In order to eliminate the artificial disparity of sexes, the Table shows the vocational distribution of men only. As a result of a twofold selection with regard to age-groups and lack of social adaptation, there are in prison fewer men from commerce, from the professions, fewer men from extractive occupations—fewer miners and agricultural workers, for example—fewer clerks, warehousemen, and engine attendants, almost an equal proportion of transport workers and men from public administration, more general labourers, men employed in entertainments, and servants, and almost three times

Distribution of Occupations among Men Fourteen Years and over among Prisoners and in the General Population

	I	II	III	IV	V	VI	VII
Prisoners . . .	209·0	86·2	114·5	108·3	81·7	19·1	10·4
General Population .	290·3	144·2	99·0	107·0	100·2	19·8	24·4
	VIII	**IX**	**X**	**XI**	**XII**	**XIII**	***Total***
Prisoners . . .	12·1	42·5	19·9	4·9	4·6	286·8	1,000
General Population .	6·3	31·6	54·4	17·4	10·7	94·7	1,000

I. Manufacturers; II. Extractive industries; III. General labourers; IV. Transport; V. Commerce; VI. Administration; VII. Professions; VIII. Entertainments; IX. Personal service; X. Clerks; XI. Warehousemen; XII. Engine attendants; XIII. Not gainfully occupied.

more men without any known gainful occupation, than in the general male population.

American experience confirms most of these observations, although the wide variety of the American population in origin, social structure, and urban and rural character makes it difficult to compute representative figures for comparative purposes. In trying to verify the Lombrosian doctrine, recent crimino-anthropological studies gave relevant social data about more than 4,000 American white prisoners of native parentage.[1] As in England, among convicted men prisoners there was a higher proportion of servants and general labourers and a smaller proportion of men from trades, professions, and clerical occupations than in the general population. Unlike the English figures, extractive occupations among prisoners exceeded the proportion among the general population, since in the United States this group has a high crime rate for homicide and offences against public welfare.

With the fluctuations in the occupational status as well as the

[1] E. A. Hooton, *The American Criminal* (1939), i. 224 and 301, Appendix Tables ii–30, xii–7.

variations in crime and punishment, the social composition of the prison population is changing. In the seven years between the last census and the outbreak of the war, the number of convicted persons received into prison in England and Wales fell from 37,417 in 1931 to 32,225 in 1938, i.e. at a rate of almost 14 per cent. At the same time, the group of shopkeepers, tradesmen, and land workers in prison decreased at a rate of nearly 18 per cent. and domestic servants by 56 per cent. In spite of the decreasing total, however, the numbers of vagrants and prostitutes among prisoners increased, although there were fewer convictions for prostitution. The small number of professional people rose from 96 to 195.[1] These recent fluctuations run counter to the trend of occupations among the general population, as has been revealed by previous censuses. From 1921 to 1931, the total of tradesmen and domestic servants rose both absolutely and proportionately; the number for the professions, though rising absolutely, decreased proportionately.[2] Under the assumption that this trend has been continuing, the recent changes in the social structure of the prison population do not reflect the development in the general population, but are due to variations in the groups participating in crime and/or to modifications in the practice of sentencing courts.

Similar fluctuations have been observed abroad. As in England, there was in Württemberg a marked increase among the prison population in the proportion of casual workers and men without a known occupation. When the total of prisoners rose after the First World War, the percentage of domestic servants fell and the small number of members of the professions increased. Unlike England, Württemberg had a rising proportion of shopkeepers and commercial employees imprisoned.[3]

Distribution of Mental Abilities

Within the particular occupations, the question repeats itself whether the prison groups of tradesmen, labourers, servants, &c., are random samples from the corresponding classes at large, or whether they have a specific composition. Before the First World War, Charles Goring found that English convicts, compared with some of the occupational groups at large, were a negative selection with regard to physical forms and abilities.[4] From this observation

[1] *Report Prison Commissioners, 1931*, p. 77, and *1938*, p. 108.

[2] A. M. Carr Saunders and D. Caradog Jones, *Survey of the Social Structure of England and Wales* (2nd ed. 1937), p. 48.

[3] J. Griesmeier, l.c., p. 172.

[4] C. Goring, *The English Convict*, new ed. by K. Pearson (1919), p. 182 and *passim*.

he concluded that the mental equipment of the convicts was inferior to the standards ruling in the particular social groups. The use of standardized intelligence tests is supposed to reduce the investigator's personal equation to a minimum and to allow comparisons between the prison population and corresponding control groups outside prison walls. The results of such investigations differ widely. This is partly due to the use of different mental tests, the application of different standards for the assessment of higher or lower grades of intelligence, and the selection of representative control groups. It may also indicate actual differences in the mental distribution of sexes, ages, and social groups among the general prison population. One is left with the impression that the intellectual equipment of prisoners differs less from the distribution of mental abilities in the general population than was originally presumed.[1] A pessimistic outlook seems supported by Sheldon and Eleanor Glueck's examination of 466 former inmates of Concord Reformatory, Massachusetts,[2] 67 per cent. of whom had an inferior intelligence with an I. Q. of less than 90, and the ratings of 3,000 male offenders in New Jersey State Prison[3] with 62 per cent. below the average level. This evidence, however, must be related to the ethnological, cultural, and social composition of the prison group under observation. Among the 3,000 New Jersey offenders, only 57·4 per cent. were native-born whites. In a similar investigation in the Western Penitentiary, Pittsburgh,[4] the proportion of prisoners with inferior intelligence was reduced from 57·4 to 38·2, when the group was restricted to native-born whites. Parallel examination of prisoners and control groups of army drafts supported the conclusion that, on the whole, the mental distribution of the prison population is representative of the particular community from which the prisoners were drawn.[5] With regard to feeble-minded persons among prisoners and the general population, a critical analysis of relevant investigations which eliminated inequality in standards and control groups

[1] R. K. Merton and M. F. Ashley Montagu, 32 *American Anthropologist* 384, 401.

[2] S. and E. Glueck, *Five Hundred Criminal Careers* (1930), p. 156.

[3] *Osborne Association News Bulletin*, August 1935, vi, No. 4, p. 11, quoted from J. S. Roucek, 31 *Journal Soc. Psych.* 375, 378.

[4] W. T. Root, *A Psych. and Soc. Study of 1,916 Prisoners in the Western Penitentiary*, quoted from A. M. MacCormick, *Education of Adult Prisoners* (1931), p. 24.

[5] H. M. Adler and M. R. Worthington, 'The Scope of the Problem of Delinquency and Crime as related to Mental Deficiency', *Journal of Psycho-Asthenics* (1925); quoted from MacCormick, l.c., p. 23; C. Murchison, *Criminal Intelligence* (1926); S. H. Tulchin, *Intelligence and Crime* (1939).

suggests a slight mental inferiority among offenders.[1] For every adult man with a mental age below eleven there were 1·3 offenders, for every woman, 2·8 offenders. By a further conclusion, the same study assumed for every adult man with a mental age below eight 3·2 offenders, for every woman 5·9.

If these observations are correct, the more favourable assessment in recent investigations of the prisoners' mental distribution may be due to a change of policy with regard to subnormal offenders. Mental defectives and borderline cases are more easily recognized and better cared for by welfare agencies. If prosecuted for a criminal offence they are more frequently exonerated. With the modern classification of prisoners, inmates of low intelligence are collected in special institutions. As a result the average intellectual standard of the 'normal' prison population is rising.

PSYCHOLOGY OF IMPRISONMENT

As an application of a psychology of abnormal situations, the psychology of imprisonment offers particular difficulties. As an ex-prisoner once said: 'So many prison reformers know everything about prisons except what it feels like to be inside. That knowledge is the most essential part of a reformer's equipment.'[2] This frank statement contains the nucleus of the problem, viz. the lack of a realistic insight into the psychological effects of imprisonment.

While the prison population, as a group, has a characteristic composition with regard to sexes and ages, occupational status, health and mental equipment, the individual prisoners are men and women with the same demands and urges, hopes and fears as their fellow men at large. The understanding of prisoners, no less than a treatment of mental patients, requires the abandoning of the prejudice that criminals and lunatics are substantially different from 'normal' human beings. The description of a mental asylum in the words attributed to Esquirol, one of the founders of modern psychiatry, obtains equally for the prison population: '. . . the same ideas, the same errors, the same passions, the same misfortunes; it is the same world, but in such a house, the traits are stronger, the colours more vivid, the shadows more marked. . . .'[3] Like everybody else prisoners are dependent on recognition and confirmation, they want affection and excitement, they need

[1] L. D. Zeleny, 38 *Am. J. Soc.* 564.

[2] Page, p. 86, from Anon., *Five Years for Fraud* (1936)

[3] According to a reference by H. Maudsley, *Responsibility in Mental Disease* (1874), p. 2.

security and the feeling of belonging to someone.[1] They all have to undergo the same experience of a complete deprivation of liberty in an enclosed institution. Prison life is an illustration of an overwhelming environmental factor, levelling the variety of individual reactions. Like a heavy blanket, the loss of self-determination, the compulsory institutional life, the regulations framed to include the most minute details, and constantly interfering with man's whole existence, seem to extinguish all personal characteristics and to result in the artificial grey product: the prisoner. Materials from three sources have been presented as a possible foundation of relevant considerations.

The first method relies upon the manifold reports, memoirs, and other private and official publications written by prison officers and social workers and administrators. Their responsibility, not only for the prisoners' safe custody but also for their personal reactions in the strange circumstance of imprisonment, does not impair, but rather facilitates the understanding of what is going on in the prisoner's mind. Human understanding depends on personal relationship. Devoted efforts of help and forbearance are often rewarded by an unexpected insight into the hidden traits of an individual life, which remain veiled to the professed objectivity of a detached observer. The humane approach of a prison doctor, pastoral work, or—in favourable circumstances—a casual meeting in connexion with routine duties may open the prisoner's mind. Bishop Berggrav's considerations on 'the prisoner's soul and our own', based upon his experience as prison chaplain in Oslo, is an outstanding contribution, not least by its combination of sober realism and sincere devotion, which bears witness to the 'hardness of love', but also to its final triumph.[2] There are, however, limits to an understanding of the prisoner's feelings. In assessing the possible effects of a strange situation, the observer is easily misled by a false analogy. Imprisonment does not differ by degrees only from other forms of subordination and dependence. It is more than deprivation of liberty aggravated by a retrogression to primitive standards of living, it coincides with a 'collapse of the whole life' (Berggav). Only situations which similarly involve isolation and outlawry and the breakdown of man's social existence, like unemployment, bankruptcy, and exile, allow parallels to the psychology of imprisonment. It requires an unusual power of

[1] *Wickersham Report, XIII*, ii. 250, with regard to juvenile delinquents.

[2] Eivind Berggrav, *The Prisoner's Soul and our own*, translated by Laura Gravely (1932).

self-criticism to overcome the personal bias which separates the prison official from the prisoner. It is not so much the contrast between the respectable and the sinner, as that between the free and the powerless, the man with access to the stimulating news and amenities of the world and the man dependent on censored communications and rationed food, which creates a class antagonism and thereby makes it very difficult to pierce through the surface behaviour to the deeper layers of the human mind.

A second approach to the psychological effects of imprisonment would be first-hand information through personal experience. Before Thomas Mott Osborne entered the New York Prison Administration he spent a voluntary prison term at Sing Sing.[1] The time he spent behind bars and locks helped him to accomplish his celebrated experiment in prison self-government. Such personal experience is an opportunity to see for oneself prison life from within and to judge fairly the working hours, food, recreation facilities, the attitude of prison officers, and the communication between prisoners. If he gains his fellow prisoners' confidence, the imprisoned student of penal discipline may hear something about the psychological effects of imprisonment. He ought to be careful, however, not to identify his own reactions with what is going on in the prisoner's mind. While he is sharing with his fellow inmates the depressing experience of being locked up, he never loses sight of the sham character of the unpleasant situation, he is free from self-reproach or accusations against others, and not for a single moment does he feel that his social status and the peaceful refuge of his home are in jeopardy.

These limitations justify the resort to a third source, the prisoners' self-expression.[2] The use of prison memoirs meets with the objection that they are even more biased than observations of the staff, if not deliberately perverted as expressions of resentment and propaganda. The prisoners' own statements, however, are not used merely as objective descriptions of actual prison conditions, but as evidence of their reactions towards prison life. Their bias is significant for the study of the psychological effects of imprisonment. The limitation of this source is due to the selection of ex-prisoners who are able and willing to write a book. Prison memoirs reflect the experience of the educated or

[1] T. M. Osborne, *Within Prison Walls* (1914).

[2] G. Radbruch, 32 *ZStW* 339; R. Sieverts, *Die Wirkungen der Freiheitsstrafe und Untersuchungshaft auf die Psyche des Gefangenen* (1929), also for the discussion which follows.

intellectual. They have often been written by political offenders. Imaginative understanding and expression are the privilege of the artist. If a great poet has to undergo the ordeal of imprisonment, his narrative may transcend the mere historical events and reveal something of the inner truth of human destiny behind prison walls. The actual story of Dostoievski's *House of the Dead* is of historical interest only, with the life in the old fortress, the forging of fetters, the brutal corporal punishment, and so forth. Beyond all these features of former Russian prison life it remains an ingenuous revelation of man in prison, of the tragic loneliness of the educated in the community of his proletarian fellow prisoners. Oscar Wilde's *Epistola ex carcere et vinculis* is a passionate outcry of human weakness, a pitiless self-revelation even when it accuses the disloyal friend.[1]

A study of prison memoirs presents much evidence of the effects of imprisonment on the prisoner's mind and the manner in which his experience is reflected in his own conscious self-expression.[2] Refined psychological methods would not only draw from literary sources but would also interpret the prisoners' unconscious self-expression as shown by handwriting, drawings, and sculptures.[3]

Prison life begins with the prisoner's reception into an institution.[4] He may be convicted or unconvicted, and this alternative makes a significant difference. A man taken into custody before trial as a rule suffers mainly from shock. Suddenly, and often unexpectedly, he has been taken away from his family and his business. Personal links and social connexions have been severed. The immediate results of this enforced change vary. The reaction of some prisoners is primarily stupor and complete passivity, but then they recover a natural form of adaptation. Others, mastering the first blow with rigid self-restraint, gradually relax and

[1] The complete text has been published in the German edition only: Oscar Wilde, *Epistola ex carcere et vinculis*, German translation by M. Meyerfeld (1925). The English edition by Robert Ross contains a selection from the original manuscript under the title *De profundis* (New York, 1926).

[2] Further prison 'classics': Silvio Pellico, *Le Mie Prigioni* (Italia, 1832); numerous English editions up to *Prison Memoirs* by Silvio Pellico (The Scotch Library 133, 1915); Paul Verlaine, *Mes Prisons* (1893). Some recent prison memoirs: W. F. R. Macartney, *Walls have Mouths* (1936); R. Harvey, *Prison from within* (1937); Mark Benney, *Low Company* (1936); Jim Phelan, *Jail Journey* (1940); Kate R. O. Hare, *In Prison* (1923); Victor Nelson, *Prison Days and Nights* (1933); Karl Hau, *Lebenslänglich* (1925); K. Plättner, *Eros im Zuchthaus* (1929).

[3] H. Prinzhorn, *Bildnerei der Gefangenen* (1925).

[4] For psychological studies on prison life see further: H. E. Field, 157 *Annals* 150; id., 12 *Brit. J. Med. Psych.* 241; Haynes and Ash, 4 *Am. Soc. Rev.* 362; Hargan, 30 *J. Soc. Psych.* 361; Roucek, 31 *J. Soc. Psych.* 375; Klemmer, 29 *Journal* 861; Weinberg, 27 *Am. J. Soc.* 717.

suffer from weakening powers of resistance. More and more the prisoner's entire interest and all his ideas centre upon his trial and defence. In the isolation of his cell he feels helpless against the overwhelming superiority of the prosecution. Fear and hope keep his mind alert. He is in a fighting frame of mind and suspicious towards everyone from the opposing side. He may, however, try to regain self-control and enable himself to stand his hearings and his trial as best he can. These efforts, dictated by mere self-preservation, often have a wholesome influence on his bearing and self-discipline.

After this enormous strain the reception into a penal institution following conviction and sentence mean first of all rest. A deep rift separates the prisoner's present life from his previous existence and the tension and struggle of his trial. A strict regularity determines the daily routine. He knows his destiny, in a most accurate sense under a system of strictly determinate sentences. The change from a social individual, who had his private sphere of life, however small, to the artificial status of a prisoner has become unalterable, but at least it has been decided definitely. In a twofold sense, prison life seems to be the reverse of the life at large. Where the free man could follow his own mood and convenience in his daily life and habits, the prisoner has been subjected to a dull and uniform routine which regulates almost every hour in the lives of hundreds of men. But where his existence at large was linked with his fellow men, with his family, work, and recreation, he has been pushed back into the isolation of his cell. In his private existence the prisoner has been socialized and as a social being he has been isolated. The new environment with its minute regulations dominates his existence for weeks, months, and even years. His inward life, however, is free to alternate through various phases. Firstly, the prisoner has to learn to adapt himself to the strange new world to which he now belongs, with its specific rules—many written and others unwritten—with the officers and fellow inmates and their demands, expectations, and attitude. This process of adaptation occupies his mind. The prisoner may feel that, after all, things might have been even worse than they actually are. Suddenly, sometimes as a consequence of a trifling incident, but often from no visible cause at all, he falls into sheer desperation. He feels completely lost to the whole world and unable to stand the strain of his present life. And then comes the third phase, a more or less final assimilation of the artificial circumstances of prison life. He is now a prisoner indeed, a wheel like others in the vast machinery. Even then, however, his mind may still swing in cyclical phases under cover of the unchangeable monotony of his daily life.

Men in prison are inclined to excessive day-dreaming, and prison life favours its weakening effects upon the inmate's character. There are practically no social links and responsibilities, the healthy counterpoise of the life at large. The prisoner, addicted to his imaginary world, fails in personal 'directness' when confronted with the real demand of a new situation. His judgement loses all sense of proportion. He suffers from a dwindling memory.

The undisturbed 'windless' atmosphere of prison has in itself certain psychological effects. The scarcity of new impressions, the absence of any stimuli, produce an increased sensibility and an almost abnormal differentiation of feelings. A slight alteration in the daily routine, a new face among fellow prisoners or the staff are important events. Many prisoners, particularly those in solitary confinement, are extremely sensitive to even a slight noise or a low sound. A bird on the sill, a brightly coloured leaf in the prison yard, are deeply felt. But even so the external perceptions are insufficient. Most prisoners are suffering from a 'mental vacuity'.[1] Unhealthy tendencies are only too apt to compensate for the want of reasonable thoughts and aims. Imagination and the alluring objects of wishful thinking dominate the inmate's ideas more and more. His power of associating ideas becomes accelerated and distorted, a 'film-like thinking' with one picture rapidly following the other, automatically demonstrating itself rather than deliberately produced by his own will.[2] Names and data, facts and events, the whole world of the pre-prison life sink into oblivion, at least so far as these things have no connexion with his present interests. The prisoner's inward life alternates between a state of intensified intellectual apperception and a sudden and often apparently motiveless fall into dull passivity.

All this involves a fatal separation from reality. The artificial character of institutional life protects the prisoner against the strain and competition, the temptations and dangers, of the world outside. 'The stamp of the cell' is nothing but the utmost degree of being institutionalized, the final result of 'desocialization' (Berggrav). The permanent supervision and the constant subjection to regulations favour many ways of achieving an inward

[1] W. Healy, *The Individual Delinquent* (1915), p. 170.

[2] E. Kretschmer, *Medizinische Psychologie* (3rd ed. 1926), pp. 114 et seq.; R. Sieverts, l.c., pp. 90 et seq.

escapism. The prisoner's own mind seems to alienate him even more from a true social life. He lives in the past, not in the true past, and not with the whole past: it is an arbitrarily selected and coloured reflection of his former life. Often his ideas about the past are the results of his 'elaboration of failure reactions'. Certain specific events are permanently in his mind, and he has before his inward eye the entire situation with an overstressed, unnatural exactness, repeating every word of a conversation, recalling the faces and gestures of the persons concerned and even the timbre of their voices—whilst numerous other events and persons fade away entirely. Sometimes the death of a once-beloved person means less to him than the loss of a bird or of a tame mouse which ate the crumbs from the prisoner's plate. Furthermore, he lives in the future, when he will have to start a new life, and then all the sunny sides of life are again open to him. But the present, his life in prison, does not count. Prison life is timeless. The seasons involve some regular alterations in the daily routine, and the sun travels a shorter or wider way around the window of the prison cell. For the prisoner the present is almost entirely suppressed, an unpleasant interruption, an unfortunate state he has to endure up to the very moment when life, the true life, will begin once more, starting just where it had been cut, or beginning anew under better conditions. But meanwhile his strange existence is not life itself, making him older, stamping permanent marks upon his mind, forming his character through years, amid a changing world. He does not realize that outside the prison walls people continue to grow and become older, that the world is changing and a new generation is filling the vacant places. Once more this unrealistic outlook and the tendency to over-simplify things, making them either black or white, so to speak, swing between the extreme poles of 'ill-founded optimism or gloomy despair'.[1] He either sees no obstacles and difficulties whatsoever, or he sees so many that he cannot find any way out of them. This is often so because many prisoners, particularly offenders against property, put their demands on life too high. They think they have a fair claim to standards they pretend they were accustomed to, and consequently, either they under-estimate the difficulties involved in attaining them in the face of strong competition on the labour market, or they relapse into disappointment or cynicism.

When entering the prison atmosphere the prisoner soon joins

[1] H. E. Field, 157 *Annals* 150.

a community of interests. This prison community has been the subject of endless discussions since the day of early penal reform. It differs in degrees according to the organization of the prison system; its shape depends on whether there is an association of prisoners by day and night, or association in work and recreation but separation by night, or single-handed work in cells with common exercises and services, or strict isolation by day and night. The specific feeling of solidarity, i.e. all the men forming one body within the walls, prevails in every prison as a psychological fact. Prisoners are people, driven into a primitive form of human existence, challenged to defend themselves against the inconvenience and hardships of this artificial life and they are very ingenious in inventing means to this end. This leads to an equalization of standards and to a uniformity of behaviour.[1] There is a group loyalty with unwritten rules, there is gregariousness and leadership on the one hand, and jealousy and rivalry on the other. Here, too, a psychology of contrasts becomes evident. The individual, suppressed by the uniformity of group feeling, rebels against the fact that he has been submerged in a completely isolated community. It is these outbursts of unsocial resentments against one another which make life in an enforced community intolerable, particularly when men are troubled about the uncertainty of their personal destinies. A peculiar expression in a neighbour's face or bad manners at the dinner-table may give rise to an unexpected outburst of long-repressed irritation.

These observations illustrate the strange duality of prison life. It has its official side, the prisoner's relations to officials and visitors, his behaviour during common work and recreation, and his attitude and feelings as they express themselves on these occasions. Beneath this surface, however, there lingers a second life, a desperate attempt to preserve and regain a certain privacy, distorted and often feverishly enhanced by resentment. This duality makes it difficult to give a fair judgement about the part which sexuality plays in the life of prisoners. It would be equally wrong, either to rule out the whole problem as non-existent, and to maintain that the problem's importance is exaggerated and concessions to sex an unnecessary indulgence, or to over-emphasize the sexual aspect as the only and necessarily dominating factor. Official utterances are sometimes inclined to take the first view, while a certain type of prison memoirs tend to the latter. One has to admit that in this, as in any other, question prison conditions

[1] Ibid., p. 163.

cannot fairly be compared with other forms of life. It is not only the separation of sexes with all the problems arising whenever such an unnatural state of social conditions occurs. It is the fact that this separation from the other sex takes place within the prison atmosphere, i.e. an atmosphere of a deeply felt compulsory character, with a scarcity of stimuli, little or no opportunities for acquiring higher interests, and an insufficient outlet for physical energies. During longer prison terms these difficulties vary, since, at least for certain periods, the fact of imprisonment seems to weaken physical functions. There is not, and cannot be, a definite solution of this intricate problem. The prevention of normal sexual relations is an inevitable consequence of the deprivation of liberty, and this will be so as long as imprisonment remains a legal punishment. Leave and visits are neither practicable nor even beneficial solutions. A healthy influence can be expected from indirect measures. Here, too, the importance of a more personal approach and a sound re-socialization of prison life become evident. All efforts to change and at the same time to cleanse the prison atmosphere, to overcome the attitude of passive endurance by constructive activities and interests help to diminish, at least, these difficulties, which are inseparable from every form of longer confinement. In individual cases the prison doctor may help, who, by his care for the patient's bodily needs, meets the prisoner on neutral ground.

Even the hardened criminal develops a strong sensibility for formal justice. In a state of constraint, formal justice is the last remedy which makes life tolerable in the face of adverse and desperate circumstances. The prisoner, however, in the process of his self-justification, exaggerates this sentiment. He has done wrong, or at least he has failed to adjust himself to the prevailing social conditions, he has been sentenced and is serving his prison term. But what about the others? The prison officials who watch over his doings day and night, the chaplain who preaches the Commandments and the Gospel, the Governor, the judge, the prosecutor, the injured party—all these people with their spectacular respectability, and, after all, the world in general? He under-estimates his own case and overstresses all possible extenuating circumstances. With regard to crime, prisoners are ardent adherents of positivism, always ready to substitute heritage and environment for personal responsibility. With regard to punishment, they represent the classical school of orthodox believers in retribution. They may challenge their sentence as arbitrary and unjust, but with the expiration of their term they have expiated whatever guilt might have been found in them, they are quit with society, if not entitled to special consideration in view of what they have suffered. In his relation to his fellow men and particularly to members of the staff, a prisoner is always suspicious and often a Pharisee, intolerant towards the slightest irregularity. His judgement on men is either black or white. On the one hand, as far as his feelings are honest, he has, at the bottom of his heart, a genuine longing for people with a pure and unselfish character. He does not like the weak, but the strong, i.e. the steadfast and fundamentally just Governor, the chaplain, who 'actually lives according to what he says', the officer, who with a kindly uprightness works with them man to man. There are many reports of a true allegiance of prisoners and ex-prisoners to 'their' officers. Even in prison, fairness and an appeal to mutual loyalty and co-operation seldom fail. On the other hand the prisoner uses every alleged fault of one of the other side, i.e. the official world, as an excuse for himself and a satisfaction of his need for self-justification, and this gives him a feeling of power and triumph.[1] This perversion of legal conscience, a strange testimony of the innermost demand for justice, is 'an opiate to every reconstructive effort'.[2] It is connected with the escape from reality and it affects the prisoner's personal attitude to his own past. Many long-term prisoners pass through a time when they are convinced that they have been wrongly sentenced. First they argue that a flaw in legal proceedings or a gap in the evidence for the prosecution should have impeded the conviction, and finally they make themselves believe that they have not been guilty.

The psychological effects of prison life do not end with the prison term itself.[3] A weakened faculty of concentration, a strange obliviousness, the tendency to illusions and self-deception, a lack of will-power—all this contributes towards creating a serious handicap when the discharged man has to struggle once more with the hardships of life, hampered by the odds against him, caused mainly by the prejudices with which society meets the ex-prisoner. The day of release, so longed for every instant through months and years, is in itself a severe crisis. The sudden change from the institutional life where, after all, the inmate was well cared for, to the social reality with its claims and responsibilities,

[1] Weinberg, l.c.
[2] Field, l.c.
[3] Sieverts, l.c., pp. 173 et seq.

tasks and obstacles, fills him with fears and hesitations. 'In a very real sense, punishment begins only when a man enters the world again and joins in the struggle for a living.' These bitter words of an ex-prisoner reflect the feeling of anxiety and inferiority in the anticipation of the stormy weather awaiting him outside the prison walls, where he was 'sheltered from contempt and pity'.[1] Facing the realities of life comes as a shock. 'You lost every sense of reality to such an extent', another ex-prisoner said, 'that you feel like holding out your arms to your fellow men whom you missed so long, as if they were prepared to make good for something, but with a few exceptions one has to realize that one is an outcast.'[2] In his hopes and thoughts the prisoner had looked forward with longing to the final hour of his discharge, anticipating all that he would do. When at last it strikes he walks like a dreamer through a strange world.

These observations do not take into consideration any deliberate oppression or the results of active educational efforts. They merely reflect the traditional penal discipline with its impersonal routine, regular order, and formal justice. Similar psychological considerations obtain under changing prison conditions. Even a progressive prison discipline, educational activities, and recreation facilities are still applied to men and women under the strain of imprisonment. Constructive measures are intended as a counterpoise to the detrimental effects of confinement. Healthy interests and stimulating pursuits are intended to dispel mental lethargy; new responsibilities strengthen the prisoner's weakened will-power, overcome his self-centredness, and enable him to face squarely the reality of life. Such a course, however, is not free from new psychological difficulties. A Progressive Stage system or indeterminate sentences, designed to spur the prisoner to greater efforts, often entail a restless atmosphere, full of tension and nervousness. Decisions on promotion are based on administrative discretion. This involves an additional strain of expectation and speculation for the prisoners, as well as a feeling of inequality, which arouses suspicion and resentment. Promotion and release should not depend upon the inmate's prison conduct but on his personality and those antecedents and circumstances which, according to criminological experience, allow the conclusion that promotion to a higher grade or conditional discharge has a fair chance of success. From the prisoner's point of view, to be kept in prison

[1] R. Harvey, *Prison from within* (1937), pp. 285 and 276.

[2] Dr. X, 18 *MoSchrKrim.* 698.

for security reasons is much more brutal and unacceptable than stern retribution.[1] These psychological difficulties explain why administrative practice tends to standardize the application of discretionary measures even at the expense of otherwise desirable flexibility. Promotion to a higher stage is often granted if a certain number of marks has been earned, or even after the expiration of a minimum period without overt breaches of discipline. Indeterminate sentences, originally recommended as commitments to prison for an unlimited or only relatively fixed time, are sometimes judicial blank sentences to be filled in by a final disposition as the result of a first observation stage of penal and reformative treatment. A rational penal policy would defeat its own purpose if it lost sight of the psychological effects of its methods.

Even under the overwhelming influence of the prison atmosphere there are differences in the individual reaction to the enforced deprivation of liberty. The preceding outlines of a psychology of imprisonment must be supplemented by a differential psychology of prisoners. There is the exceptional situation of the innocent in prison. It is regrettable, but sometimes unavoidable, for defendants who in the end are acquitted to be in custody awaiting trial. In 1925, 1,981 prisoners awaiting trial in Prussian prisons, or 9·4 per cent. of the total of unconvicted prisoners were not found guilty. In 1938, 1,684 prisoners committed to English prisons, or 17·7 per cent. of the total of remand and trial prisoners not sentenced to imprisonment, were not found guilty.[2] A miscarriage of justice may even lead to the conviction of the innocent. The German Code of Criminal Procedure provides, even beyond ordinary appeals, for a fresh trial under certain exceptional statutory conditions. Before the First World War, approximately 800 sentences a year were reversed for the defendants.[3] Many prisoners honestly believe, at least for a certain time during a long prison term, that they are innocent. In a Thuringian convict prison 10 per cent. of the inmates applied for a new trial.[4] Prisoners who are, or believe themselves to be, innocent are in a position to fight, and this determines their attitude towards prison life. Political and other 'conscientious' offenders are in a similar position. In normal times their number is very small. In 1927 they were supposed to amount to 0·2 per cent. of the German

[1] Berggrav, l.c., p. 41.

[2] E. J. Gumbel, 5 *Justiz* 744. *Report of Prison Commissioners, 1939–41*, p. 29.

[3] H. v. Hentig, *Wiederaufnahmerecht* (1930), p. 261. For relevant cases see Sello, *Die Irrtümer der Strafjustiz* (1911); E. M. Borchard, *Convicting the Innocent* (1932).

[4] v. Hentig, l.c., p. 92.

prison population. In time of war or political unrest they present a serious problem. They are regarded as fanatics who might be taught by punishment that it is senseless to propagate their ideas by force; they might even be brought to admit that the opposing side is at least fair and just, but they are not expected to abandon their convictions under the pressure of force. They accept imprisonment as a martyrdom, a holy war for a better cause. This is the testimony of a conscientious objector from the First World War: 'We were more or less powerfully sustained in our endurance by a faith in the righteousness, and, in many cases, the supremely Christian character of the cause for which we conceived ourselves to be suffering loss of liberty and a measure of persecution.'[1]

Such men have little in common with either repentant or hardened criminals. Their devotion and steadfastness make them dangerous whenever they proceed to acts of violence and aggression. Formal justice, as well as due regard for the preservation of the peace, make it impossible to give exceptions to common offenders who acted from political motives. If, however, a mere conscientious objection or civil disobedience necessitates legal punishment, prison discipline should be confined to the minimum necessities of an enforced deprivation of liberty.[2]

The vast majority of prisoners are not affected by such scruples. According to American observations they might be broadly divided into three general types.[3] One-half of the total represents what one might call 'the regular fellow'. These are men from poor cultural surroundings, with weak and unhealthy social attachments, mostly convicted for crimes of dishonesty. One-half of this group consists of men who were under thirty years of age on their last admission. There is a group of sex offenders, amounting to 20 per cent. of the prison population, mostly of a low intellectual standard. There are finally 16 per cent. 'life men' who, apart from some periods of discouragement and depression, form the best group in the institution. An English investigation of 200 Dartmoor convicts[4] distinguishes a subnormal group of some 48 per cent. of all inmates, the professional criminals of 41 per cent., and an abnormal group. Among the subnormal group, offences by violence and sex offences are represented by equal numbers. These men are constitutionally inferior and they show

[1] S. Hobhouse, *An English Prison from within* (1919), p. 14.

[2] G. Radbruch, 44 *ZStW* 34, pleads for a privileged treatment of all conscientious offenders.

[3] Field, l.c. Similar observations by A. Morris, 217 *Annals* 138.

[4] Landers, 84 *Journal Ment. Sc.* 960.

a passive indifference towards the prison. They are known to prison practitioners as 'the quiet old lags'. Among the professional criminals there are more violent types and only very few sex offenders. They all successfully adapt themselves to prison conditions. Among the abnormal group there were no convictions for acts of violence or for sex offences. These men started early with their criminal careers and had more convictions per head than their subnormal and professional fellow inmates. They are restless, conceited, 'touchy', and their attitude towards the prison is 'a mild hostility'.

These observations are supplemented by relevant conclusions which Sheldon and Eleanor Glueck have drawn from their consecutive follow-up studies on juvenile delinquents. They confirm that the intense restraint and permanent control of prison life is a strong levelling factor which leaves little opportunity for individual reactions. Adaptation to institutional life seems to be facilitated if the date of the first arrest was early and so cut a criminal career at its beginning; and a further helpful condition is that general adaptability which is shown by those juvenile offenders who committed their offences in the company of other boys.[1] Less fitted for institutional treatment are lonely offenders, the boys who keep to themselves, and this is even more so if they are less burdened by handicaps due to their personality. This type would probably respond better to probation.

The experience of prisoners-of-war is apt to throw further light on the psychology of imprisonment.[2] At first sight, war captivity, like a large-scale experiment, seems to throw the mere fact of deprivation of liberty into isolation without other implications due to personal guilt or social outlawry. The Geneva Convention of 1929 provides legal guarantees for certain standards of treatment and thereby gives the prisoner-of-war a proper status. In spite of these essential differences in the personal situations of convicts and prisoners-of-war, the psychological effects of a long captivity resemble those observed in penal institutions. Life in prison camps is determined by a typical mentality. During the First World War this psychological reaction was characterized, not only metaphorically, as a barbed-wire disease;[3] in the Second World War it was appropriately interpreted as a specific mental

[1] S. and E. Glueck, *Juvenile Delinquents grown up* (1940), pp. 180 et seq.

[2] R. Guerlain, *Prisonnier de guerre* (1944); T. C. F. Prittie and W. E. Edwards, *South to Freedom* (1946); E. Ward, *Give me Air* (1946).

[3] A. L. Vischer, *Barbed Wire Disease* (1919).

attitude due to extraordinary inner and outward conditions.[1] Like the arrested and convicted prisoner the prisoner-of-war has to undergo consecutive stages of a psychological process. The shock and disappointment of being captured give rise to depression, gloomy pessimism, and a hypercritical attitude towards those deemed responsible for defeat and captivity, still further aggravated by the enforced adaptation to primitive conditions in transit camps. After the settlement in permanent quarters a 'convalescence' sets in, an adaptation to the routine of the camp with its armed guards, barbed wire, and roll-calls. Morale improves, countenance and appearance show increasing self-discipline. In the end, a certain *modus vivendi* has been reached, which has to sustain the prisoner through months and years of boredom and uncertainty. War captivity is aggravated by its indeterminate duration. While the ranks are under an obligation to work, officers are left to occupy themselves. Learning and teaching, which developed in many cases into flourishing 'Camp Universities', proved a valuable antidote; often these were supported by international agencies. Every activity was helpful which gave the life in the camp tangible targets in the pursuit of an ultimate goal. Prisoners-of-war are haunted by the fear of becoming 'forgotten men' who will be ousted from fresh experiences, vocational prospects, friendship and love, to see one fine day their places taken by younger men at home. Regular Red Cross parcels, beyond their immediate value in providing better nourishment, are bound to testify to the unbroken link with the home country. Like the discharged prisoner the repatriated prisoner-of-war faces a crisis. He has been detached from the reality of the day, and the final liberation has raised his hopes and expectations to a pitch, while his mind is still occupied with the daily occurrences and personal contacts in the camp for which he meets with little interest in his new surroundings at home. In the end it is the forbearance, sympathy, and understanding of his people at home which alleviate his re-adaptation to the old, though in many respects new, civilian life.

These observations suggest that every enforced deprivation of liberty implies an unreal life of mental vacuity, lack of purpose, and the cutting-off of personal relationships. Imprisonment as a legal punishment facilitates the origin and persistence of psychological reactions which, though not unknown in war captivity,

[1] P. H. Newman, *Brit. Med. Journal* (1944) (I), p. 8, also for the statements which follow.

are typical consequences of a culprit's imprisonment after trial and sentence.

CLASSIFICATION OF PRISONERS

Horizontal Classification

The influence of social factors and personal traits on the prisoner's attitude and reactions suggests a policy of deliberate classification. Classification means a method of assigning certain types of prisoners to different forms of custody and treatment. If such differences obtain from the beginning throughout the whole prison term, one may speak of a horizontal classification of the prison population. If they are to rationalize prison discipline, subdivisions of prisoners must be based upon their susceptibility to the various forms of training and treatment available. For this purpose the legal conceptions of the particular offences are of no avail. The psychological approach levels legal distinctions. An offence against property may be committed by a fugitive as a consequence of an escape, a libel may, by its motive, be an attempt to elicit money from the intimidated victim. Careful plans are often more revealing than overt acts. Crimino-psychology therefore substitutes certain types of criminal personalities for the legal conceptions of particular offences. The leading principle of most classifications is a distinction between offenders committing crimes from strong motives or the lack of counter-motives, and those whose offences seem an almost inevitable expression of deep-rooted anti-social tendencies. The first group may be further divided into casual, emotional, and deliberate or negligent offenders, while the second comprises habitual and professional criminals.[1] None of these subdivisions is exclusive. There may be a persistent carelessness, and there is a large group of low-grade personalities and weak characters who almost habitually fall victims to every alluring opportunity. Even with the necessary amendments, division into such psychological types is the result of abstract generalization. It is more useful for the outlines of penal policy than for a differentiation of treatment. A classification based upon such types presumes rather than indicates different penal methods, supposed to meet the special needs of each group. Classification must rely upon observation and experiment. This explains why the function of classifying prisoners has shifted from the sentencing court to the penal administration. In England the Prison Act of 1898

[1] G. Aschaffenburg, *Das Verbrechen und seine Bekämpfung* (3rd ed. 1923), p. 231.

established the divisional system, which meant that the sentencing court (having regard to the nature of the offence and antecedents of the offender) directs whether the prisoner shall serve his term in the first, second, or third division.[1] The first division was intended as a privileged form of detention for those guilty of seditious libel or other political offenders, a concession to the principle of a privileged treatment of conscientious offenders. The second division comprises those who in the opinion of the sentencing court are not depraved or of criminal habits. If no direction is given by the court, the prisoner serves his term in the third division, though the court had discretion to lay down that his punishment should be aggravated by 'hard labour'—a reminiscence of the 'labour of the hardest and most servile kind' of the Act of 1779.[2] This system of judicial classification had little practical effect. The hard-labour clause had no influence on the actual assignment to work; the last remnant of a more severe treatment, viz. deprivation of the mattress for the first fortnight, was abolished in 1945. There was no other difference between the second and third divisions, while the first division has almost been in abeyance. Practical prison experience superseded doctrinal differentiations. The Criminal Justice Bill of 1938 finally proposed to abolish the divisional system together with other legal institutions of a penal policy which belongs to the past.

In the meantime English prison administration built up a new classification consisting of four groups: star class, comprising prisoners of good character, with no serious previous convictions, who are not habitual criminals or of depraved habits; special class of prisoners between twenty-one and twenty-six years of age with previous convictions, out of the third division and hard-labour group; ordinary class; all young prisoners under twenty-one. The present English prison régime compromises between the judicial and the administrative classifications. In 1938 out of 5,673 men and 435 women serving terms of imprisonment, none was in the first division, 238 men and 44 women were in the second division, 1,448 men and 64 women in the star class, 631 men and 6 women were specials, 285 men and 18 women young prisoners, and 3,071 men and 303 women ranked as ordinaries.

Since prison discipline is dominated by the demand for security, classification should begin with the consideration whether every prisoner needs the same amount of safe custody in order to prevent

[1] 61 & 62 Vict., c. 41, s. 6.
[2] 19 Geo. III, c. 74, s. 32.

assaults and escapes. The idea of custodial differentiation originated in the United States. The overcrowding of the old prisons made it advisable to look for new methods of accommodation for the growing influx of prisoners. This led to a classification into security groups, i.e. prisoners requiring custody with maximum, medium, or minimum security. So far no general standards of security grades have been established, nor is there any recognized normal proportion between the three groups within a sample group of prisoners. Maximum security corresponds to the traditional walled prison with locked cells and omnipresent supervision. A minimum security régime resorts to trust and responsibility rather than mechanical restraint. It takes the form of honour camps, agricultural annexes, or open colonies. Suggestions vary with regard to the possible application of the different methods of custody. A New York estimate puts 25 per cent. of all prisoners into the minimum security and a further 34 per cent. into a temporarily restricted group.[1] A more optimistic estimate assigns 30 per cent. to 40 per cent. of the prisoners to the minimum security group, and considers an even higher proportion possible with a lengthening distance from metropolitan areas.[2] Taking a state with an average prison population of 2,500, a recent proposal suggests the following distribution: reception and classification centre 250 inmates; maximum security institution 500; two minimum security institutions with a total of 750 inmates.[3] In 1930 a test investigation of 353 male prisoners of a Thuringian prison with no convicts resulted in the following estimate: 30·8 per cent. requiring confinement in an enclosed institution, 46·7 per cent. suitable for a medium, and 22·5 per cent. for an open institution.[4]

Practical experiments with custodial classification have either set apart single institutions for particular security grades or differentiated within a composite penal establishment. In 1938 custodial classification was applied in some of the federal institutions in the United States. The island penitentiary Alcatraz, Ca., with a population of some 300 prisoners, has been reserved for maximum security. Two reformatories with more than 500 inmates each and four prison camps with a total complement of 676 prisoners offered minimum security only. Three penitentiaries and a reformatory with a total of 8,907 prisoners provided different security grades within the same institutions. They applied the

[1] *Wickersham Report*, ix, p. 77. [2] J. D. Sears, 23 *Journal* 261.

[3] J. Callender, 61 *The Survey* 305, quoted from Haynes, p. 35.

[4] Brandstätter, quoted from von Hentig, 21 *MoSchrKrim.* 289.

term maximum security for those requiring more than the traditional close supervision. In these four institutions 0·7 per cent. were kept under maximum security, 34 per cent. in close custody, 44·6 per cent. under medium and 14 per cent. under minimum security, while 6·7 per cent. were unclassified. All institutions mentioned in this brief survey housed more than two-thirds of the federal prison population of 14,815 persons.[1]

Custodial differentiation is more than an expedient for occupying groups of prisoners outside prison walls. The use of prisoners for outdoor work, especially land reclamation, was started by Austria in 1886 and by Prussia in 1895.[2] The change from cell and workshop to marsh and field alone does not necessarily imply a lessening of enforced custody and a resort to trust and responsibility. The concept of imprisonment remains unaltered, as long as permanent armed supervision is substituted for bars and locks. Work in the open may be performed by enforced labour gangs or by selected honour parties. Only the latter is recognized as a method of minimum security imprisonment.

Custodial differentiation does not merely imply certain exceptions in an otherwise unaltered uniform prison routine. It breaks up the traditional concept of prison. This is a question of economy in means. It seems unreasonable to provide for the whole prison population the maximum of physical restraint by solid buildings throughout and omnipresent guards, which are indispensable for the safe custody of a minority only. Nor ought those who require a less rigid supervision to be deprived of better opportunities for constructive efforts in work and recreation merely because such privileges might be abused by less reliable prisoners. Custodial differentiation is the basis, though not the only principle, of a classification of prisoners.

Classification is a means to an end. Its success depends on the variety of treatment methods available. At present there is still a gap between a refined technique of analysing personal factors and social background of individual offenders, and only slight variations of a uniform prison routine. American experts admit that progress in individualized treatment has been 'more apparent than real',[3] and they are still looking ahead for the development of differentiated treatment methods.[4] An American manual for

[1] Computed from *Federal Offenders, 1938* (U.S. Dept. of Justice, 1939).

[2] Kriegsmann, p. 219.

[3] *Handbook of American Prisons and Reformatories* (1933), p. xlviii.

[4] J. D. Sears, 23 *Journal* 248, also for the discussion which follows.

the classification of prisoners recommends the ascertaining of the individual's character and temperament with a view to deciding on the method of supervision, his attitude, aptitudes, and disabilities as indications of his possible self-discipline and work, his original or acquired capabilities with regard to learning and adjustment, and finally his physical and mental condition in general.[1] Such a comprehensive diagnosis is intended as a basis of a simple fourfold classification which does not differ much from traditional administrative practice, viz. a differentiation into first offenders, recidivists, mentally abnormal, and physically defective prisoners.[2] The New Jersey scheme distinguishes seven classes. They are the difficult class of constitutional defectives, recidivists, drug addicts, and alcoholics; the better class with the three sub-groups of those serving long terms, those not serving long terms, and young and intelligent prisoners not serving long terms; the feeble-minded class; the senile and incapacitated class; those suffering from some psychosis or epilepsy; the defective delinquent group; and the insane. A study of 2,000 commitments during the years 1928 to 1930 assigned more than half of all prisoners to the better class, more than one-third to the difficult class, including psychopathic personalities, while the rest was divided into 10·5 per cent. feeble-minded, 1·7 per cent. incapacitated, and 1·4 per cent. psychotic and epileptic.[3] This is apparently not more than a preliminary sorting out of the most conspicuous differences. Differentiation of treatment begins within those wider groups. The same applies to the suggestion that accommodation should be provided for the insane, feeble-minded, tubercular prisoner, for venereal cases, for the sex pervert, the drug addict, the aged and crippled, and that, after the removal of these misfits from the ordinary routine, the remaining 'normal' prison population should be divided into the three main security grades.[4] On the basis of such preliminary classification, a programme for the individual or the small group with regard to housing, custody, work, education, exercises, social services, release procedure, and so on should be designed in accordance with the information gained in the course of classification.[5]

[1] E. A. Doll, *Handbook of Case Work and Classification Methods* (Am. Prison Association, n.y.), p. 6.

[2] Ibid., p. 26.

[3] L. N. Robinson, *Should Prisoners Work?* (1931), p. 148.

[4] *Wickersham Report*, ix. 63 et seq.; *Handbook of American Prisons and Reformatories* (1933), p. li.

[5] E. R. East, 35 *Journal* 93 with regard to Camp Hill Industrial School, Pa.

The assignment of lads between sixteen and twenty-three to English Borstal institutions illustrates a classification into treatment groups. It is an unacademic scheme, developed by trial and error. Before the Second World War, the boys were assigned—after careful observation—to one of the following seven groups:[1] mature adolescents with an average age of twenty-one, nearly a third of the group married and most of them with several previous convictions and even former prison experience; a similar type, but slightly younger and less mature; a still younger group, more amenable to discipline, but requiring certain restrictions as a check on an impulsiveness which may lead to attempted escapes; better educated and more intelligent boys who despite previous convictions are profiting by a considerable freedom from detailed supervision and control; boys with difficult medical and educational problems; boys likely to respond to training accompanied by a large measure of trust; selected boys thought likely to respond to comparatively short training and to require little or no provision for security. This scheme substitutes treatment groups for criminological conceptions. Borstal training offers a unique opportunity for a treatment classification. Adolescents regarded by the court as susceptible to such instruction and discipline show more differences in general development, attitude, and reactions than the common adult prison population. The elastic framework of Borstal training facilitates a wider variation of treatment than does ordinary prison routine. Even so, further sectors of the traditional prison system will, as often before, benefit from the example given in model institutions for juvenile or adolescent offenders. There is, however, a final limitation to the application of these principles. A rigid classification would result in grouping together the same types only and thereby place the prisoner in an unnatural community of equals. Training for citizenship means enabling a man to live with his neighbour and fellow workers. It is a test of social adjustment whether a man can stand the frictions of daily life which result from the disparity of human personalities. An ideal classification system ought to operate with flexible units, and aim at an optimum of differentiation between the two extremes of an unhealthy prison promiscuity on the one hand, and a frustration of any community feeling by an artificial accumulation of identical types on the other hand.

Whilst aiming at a relative differentiation of treatment, the principle of classification demands a method of diagnosis which

[1] *Report Prison Commissioners, 1938,* pp. 22 et seq.

makes it possible to distinguish which prisoners are best fitted for the respective treatment groups. The means to that end are investigation and observation. The former comprises technical and non-technical examinations of the man, physically and mentally, of his past career, and social background; the latter puts on record his development and reaction in the course of a certain period. Observation, however, ought not to be isolated from treatment. Both are different functions of prison discipline, but they should not be separated by consecutive stages of the prison term. This does not rule out a short initial reception and observation stage up to four weeks' separate confinement, when the prisoner adapts himself to his new surroundings, and examinations can take place without interfering with the hours of associated work and educational services. Isolation does not facilitate personal observation. A human personality can only be 'observed' when a man is exposed to situations which provoke his response. Since this is the nucleus of a constructive penal treatment, the sooner active treatment begins the better are the prospects for a reliable observation.

Investigations for penal classification rely mainly on social case-studies with due regard to the 'dynamic aspects' of case work by a multiple approach from different angles and regular reconsideration of former statements in the light of fresh experience. Investigations for the complex questions of the appropriate placement, work, educational prospects, physical needs, social assistance, both in view of the prisoner's readjustment and public security, require the co-operation of a team of experts. But the duplication of inquiries has its limits. In some American institutions the prisoner has to be interviewed by eight or nine specialists. One may fairly ask whether such abundance of experts does not eventually defeat its own ends. If a man has to tell his story and answer similar questions put by the physician, the identification officer, disciplinary officer, psychiatrist, psychologist, chaplain, director of education, director of industries and training, and field social investigator, his replies and reactions become more and more conventionalized and less and less spontaneous. The fallacy involved makes it imperative to verify the results of the initial investigations in the light of further experience during the treatment itself.

In some countries the diagnostic methods for the classification of prisoners have been influenced by the recent development of genetics. Belgium led in the establishment of a crimino-anthropological service. Bavaria followed with even more emphasis on the genetic aspects.[1] Under the National-Socialist régime these principles were extended in principle to the whole German prison system.[2] This was not so much a belated vindication of Lombroso as the outcome of a new interest in biological characteristics and personal traits which link the individual with his forbears. Criminological research found that persistent offenders had more psychopathic individuals, drunkards, and criminals among their forbears than adjustable offenders had.[3] It seemed therefore justifiable to study the prisoner's ancestry with regard to constitutional traits and social achievements for an assessment of his personality and future prospects.

On the basis of such considerations, Bavaria started in 1923 collecting genetic data in connexion with anthropological investigations and social inquiries. This system met with opposition from critics who uttered warnings against disregard for the social aspects of crime and punishment.[4] At the beginning the Bavarian experiment suffered from a discrepancy between means and ends. Investigations relied too much upon the prisoners' own statements. In the official introduction of these crimino-biological examinations it was said that the 'first cardinal task' should be to distinguish between the corrigible offender, eligible for a reformative Progressive Stage system, and the incorrigible criminal doomed to be subjected to a repressive retributory penal discipline.[5] Two years later one of the promotors of the scheme gave warning against premature expectations, since the stage at which genetics then was made outright conclusions with regard to corrigibility or incorrigibility too risky.[6] This is indeed the crucial question. Frequency of deficiencies among forbears is not tantamount to inborn incorrigibility. If social conditions and personal relationships contribute equally, their investigation should not be restricted by the genetic bias. The one-sided biological outlook, however, was an expression of the widely accepted doctrine, that 'the

[1] *Der Stufenstrafvollzug und die kriminalbiologische Untersuchung der Gefangenen in den Bayerischen Strafanstalten*, i–iii (1926–9); W. Petrzilka, *Persönlichkeitsforschung und Differenzierung im Strafvollzug* (1930), with references to Belgium and Bavaria; T. Viernstein, 23 *Journal* 269. Critical survey of relevant methods: F. von Rohden, 'Methoden der Kriminalbiologie' in E. Abderhalden, *Handbuch der biologischen Arbeitsmethoden*, iv. 12, 1/1 (1938), pp. 581–829.

[2] E. Schäfer and F. von Neureiter, 7 *Recueil* 151.

[3] F. Stumpfl, *Erbanlage und Verbrechen* (1935).

[4] M. Liepmann, *MoSchrKrim.* 1926, Beiheft 1, p. 66; W. Petrzilka, l.c.; R. Sieverts, *MoSchrKrim.* xxiii. 588; xxiv. 107.

[5] *Stufenstrafvollzug*, i. 73 and 15.

[6] R. Degen, in Bumke, p. 314.

individual is only a single link in the chain of his forbears, descendants and laterals who must be attributed to him by the blood'.[1] This attitude met with the support of National-Socialist tendencies which recognized the individual personality exclusively as a representative of the biological group into which he has been born.

Now that these ideological claims have been repudiated, practical experience may reduce the contrast between social case-studies and genetic investigations to a difference in emphasis. But the right emphasis is decisive for the theoretical conception as well as for the functioning of a classification scheme. It would be wrong to deny the significance of biological and social conditions among men's forbears. Inherited endowment and family background are factors among others which determine man's reactions to his personal surroundings. Only a comprehensive view allows a reliable assessment of an offender's needs and prospects.

Scientific classification of prisoners is still too much in its initial phase to claim spectacular success. Rather can the need of an early diagnosis and appropriate treatment be demonstrated by the after-careers of criminals, whose previous anti-social activities had been met with the traditional retributory punishment. In the early thirties Germany seemed to be hit by a wave of sexual mass murders, and this experience influenced the swing of the pendulum against the abolition of capital punishment. All these mass murderers had been in prison before.[2] They were men with no positive feelings towards other persons, with no friends, no care for relatives. All exhibited strong, and sometimes abnormal, impulses at an early age. All had one parent a drunkard, sexual pervert, or anti-social, three at least also had sexually pervert brothers and sisters. Grossmann began with larcenies and physical attacks; Schumann, when only eighteen, as a robber; Haarmann by ill treatment of his grandfather; Kürten by embezzlement, larceny, and four cases of arson; Seefeld by physical assault and vagabondage; Böttcher as a thief and highwayman. These facts are a challenge to scientific methods of social diagnosis and crime prediction. The question suggests itself, whether by applying the present methods of classification a progressive penal system would make it possible to recognize in time the extreme dangerousness of such men when they were committed for less serious offences,

[1] T. Viernstein, quoted from K. Wilmanns, *Verminderte Zurechnungsfähigkeit* (1927), p. 159.

[2] F. Leppmann, 32 *Journal* 366.

and whether adequate methods of treatment or segregation are available to deal with such potential mass murderers according to the insight gained.

Vertical Classification

The horizontal classification of prisoners into a number of treatment groups has its counterpart in a vertical differentiation of the prison term into a number of consecutive stages through which the prisoner is expected to proceed from reception to release. The long account of the Progressive Stage system in Part I might be referred to. The Progressive Stage system is an organization of prison discipline which enables the prisoner to rise from the initial form of imprisonment to further stages when coercive elements are gradually replaced by an appeal to self-control and a sense of responsibility right up to supervised forms of liberty. As an instrument of social readjustment it puts before the prisoner stimulating targets, tries to win his co-operation, to strengthen and test his will-power, and finally to place his destiny in his own hands.[1] This definition indicates the possible aims and the limits of the Progressive Stage idea. The gradual proceeding from coercion to liberty must be marked by inner obligations and responsibilities rather than by alleviations and privileges. Work and recreation, educational activities, meals and leisure hours in association with fellow prisoners offer opportunities for an appeal to the prisoner's power of self-discipline and test his responsiveness. In the words of an American prison administrator, prison should not mean for the prisoner 'an easy, aimless existence', but 'a hard road', though one 'with a possibility of success at the end, if he has the element of success in him'.[2] It would, however, be unrealistic to overlook the fact that less pressure and a greater opportunity for personal initiative are in themselves an important step towards a better way of living. The implications of these principles go even farther. Self-respect and a feeling of privacy require a curtailment of omnipresent supervision, of the rigid austerity of orthodox prison life. Men with months and years ahead of them, living under the rule of silence, in the monotony of four bare grey cell walls, with an unvarying minimum of books, letters, and visits, the same food without any stimulants, the same unnaturally early hours of lights off, cannot be expected to prepare

[1] Formulation of the German Draft Penal Code, 1927 (II), s. 163; Prussian Regulation on a Progressive Stage System, 1929, I/3.

[2] J. D. Sears, 23 *Journal* 268.

themselves for a fresh start, to embark on new educational activities, to work in, or even lead, honour parties entrusted with particular tasks, or to be responsible for good order and decency within a group of fellow prisoners. Education begins by associating the pupil's well-being with his right behaviour—if only it does not end there! If it is wrong to indulge in privileges which are not balanced by responsibilities, it would equally be unjust to condemn the Progressive Stage idea because it gradually alleviates the prisoner's lot. John Clay regarded such a system as 'fundamentally wrong', since it appeals to lower selfish motives.[1] K. Krohne gave a similar verdict: 'A system which distinguishes several stages by granting material privileges—tobacco, meat, bacon, higher earnings—would only strengthen instead of repressing the materialistic lust, the main source of crime.'[2] This criticism is unjust if it meets the Progressive Stage idea on principle, but it is a sound warning against a substitution of a mere graduated scale of privileges for true progress. Even a well-balanced system of privileges and liabilities is open to objections. In sheer self-defence prisoners exhibit a shrewd adaptation to the prevailing conditions, which makes them comply even with cumbersome obligations as a means of alleviating their position regardless of any loyalty to the principles they profess. Hypocrisy is the inherent danger of a Progressive Stage system—but it is not confined to this particular method of prison discipline. It is unavoidable whenever men have to live in a state of utter dependence, and it is by no means excluded under a solitary or separate system. Adolphe Prins, who spoke with the authority of practical experience in the Belgian Prison Administration with its model solitary system, testified that it is difficult to detect hypocrisy in a cell, where the prisoner has only to exhibit subservience to the prison guard, while it is easier to study a man who is passing through consecutive stages of a true social life.[3] A sober judgement on the merits and faults of a Progressive Stage system has to avoid fallacious extremes. Like other human beings, prisoners cannot be expected to follow a categorical imperative only and to despise utilitarian motives. At the same time, temporary habits, whether enforced or assumed for tactical reasons, are not in themselves an educational success.

In order to be effective, a properly administered system must make the progression understandable and attainable for the average

[1] W. L. Clay, *The Prison Chaplain: A Memoir of John Clay* (1861), p. 397.

[2] K. Krohne, *Lehrbuch der Gefängniskunde* (1889), p. 258.

[3] *L'Œuvre d'Adolphe Prins*, ed. by L. Wodon and J. Servais (1934), p. 348.

prisoner to whom it applies.[1] This calls for a middle way between arbitrary discretion and pedantic regimentation. Certain rules must obtain with regard to the conditions of promotion and retardation and the main characteristics of each stage. Such general standards put before the prisoner certain well-defined forms of behaviour as targets at which he must aim and for which he can hope. Most systems have three consecutive stages. Certain minimum periods or portions of the sentence must have expired before promotion can be considered. Maconochie's invention of a marks system was an expedient to make the prisoner constantly aware of his position and his prospects. The marks are either credits with a view to prospective promotion or negative assessments entailing retardation or degradation. Conditions of promotion should require strenuous efforts, but they must be adequate to the particular type of prisoner and the specific method of prison routine. A Progressive Stage system remains a dead letter, if in exceptional cases only a few selected prisoners are admitted to the uppermost or third stage. In 1924 in Bavaria only 3 per cent. of the convicts, 2 per cent. of the common prisoners, and none of the adolescents belonged to the third stage. In a large Prussian prison the third stage consisted of three men. A sound proportion would mean that out of those eligible for a Progressive Stage routine 20–5 per cent. belong to the first, some 60 per cent. to the second, and 10–15 per cent. to the third stage. This corresponds to the experience in Thuringia where the convict prison of Untermassfeld with some 240 prisoners had a third stage of 22–45 men, and 37 per cent. of all inmates reached this target.[2] Even so, the promotion to the third stage had a selective function. It applied to a prison aristocracy of skilled workers and older first offenders with a high proportion of men convicted of perjury or sexual offences, but not of recidivist thieves.[3] This group responded well to the extended library facilities, educational activities, and communal life.

The distinguishing patterns of the different stages vary with the prevailing prison system. As long as prison discipline emphasized the repressive character of punishment by separate confinement, hard work, curtailment of privacy, and unattractive forms of exercises and formal education, a gradual mitigation of coercion suggested itself for the distinction of the higher stages. But one

[1] M. Liepmann, l.c., p. 67.

[2] E. Holler, 5 *Erziehung* 612.

[3] A. Krebs, 19 *MoSchrKrim.* 152; F. Rösch, in *Gefängnisse in Thüringen* (1930), p. 108.

cannot instigate a man's co-operative efforts by the mechanical effects of standardized punitive elements. Educational activities, books, regular letters, healthy links with the outside world, useful and instructive work, are not so much privileges and amenities as instruments of a reformative treatment. It would be unwise to delay their application for the sake of a visible distinction between different stages. Not the sort of work or the amount of earnings, but the prisoner's power of free disposal of his money, the time he is allowed to use for his own purposes, the initiative he may show in his work, a greater choice with regard to educational activities, the private character he is permitted to give to his cell, and finally some responsibility as a foreman or leader of a work party or in other forms of self-government—these are essential differentiations in a progression worth the name. Such a scheme justifies a provision that only those who successfully stand the test of the third stage are eligible for conditional release.

Under such conditions as these a Progressive Stage system is an adequate form for a rehabilitative prison régime. Its value depends on the particular prison discipline which has been organized as a vertical progression of consecutive stages. The immediate effect of such an organization is a negative one. It works as an antidote to the enervating influence of prison monotony. Discipline improves and has less resort to enforced punishments. This reduces bitterness and obstinacy and promotes a quiet atmosphere. The progression fits the prisoner anew into a sound rhythm of life, and finally gives the critical day of release its proper place within a planned and gradual transition from the upper stages of prison discipline to a preliminary form of supervised liberty.

The Progressive Stage idea is no panacea indiscriminately applicable to prisoners of every description. A policy of classification, both horizontal and vertical, offers ample opportunity for various methods of penal and reformative treatment according to the needs and prospects of different types of prisoners. Prison discipline would thereby assume that degree of flexibility which is desirable and possible as an optimum of differentiation within the mass treatment practised by the prevailing penal system.

Classification and Prison Architecture

Important ideas concerning prison discipline find their visible expression in prison architecture. Throughout most civilized countries the triumph of solitary confinement left large and solid cellular buildings as a lasting mark of a movement of the past.

Strange witnesses of bygone days, they seem to represent primarily the principles of security and deterrence. Solid structure and technical devices are used to guarantee safe custody and permanent supervision of all prisoners alike. Walls, turrets, and pinnacles emphasize the Bastille character of penal establishments, as a spectacular demonstration of the superiority of criminal justice which quells at its source any outbreak of violence and insurrection. Changing methods of penal treatment create new demands on prison architecture.[1] The division into sub-groups of the vast impersonal mass of prisoners will be reflected in the breaking up of the huge cell-blocks into organic groups of smaller separate buildings. Continental hospital planning with its preference for the 'pavilion style' may serve as a model for future prison architecture. The ultimate form of the new prison type depends on whether classification leads to a variety of different institutions or to a differentiation within the single particular prison. The Belgian reform of 1920 envisaged a great number of specialized institutions and the Prussian proposals of 1929 even suggested that prisoners should serve each stage of the Progressive Stage system in a different prison. Practical experience will probably suggest a mixture of institutional and departmental differentiation. Juveniles and persistent offenders will always be housed in special institutions. Ordinary prisoners should serve the three stages of a progressive system in the same prison. This not only facilitates a prompt and flexible administration of promotion and degradation but also puts the stimulating target of the higher stages before the prisoner's eyes. Most prisons will have some horizontal differentiations as well as a certain form of progression. The figures do not represent any existing prison building, but they illustrate the underlying principle. They try to transform by two different designs a horizontal and vertical classification into the language of a builder's blueprint. Figure IV develops recommendations made by K. Wilmanns, whose suggestions have been influenced by the layout of a modern mental institution.[2] According to this design, from a reception centre prisoners are assigned to three different forms of imprisonment. An enclosed house with three panoptic cell wings and a fourth workshop wing offers

[1] H. H. Hart, *Plans and Illustrations of Prisons and Reformatories* (1922); A. Hopkins, *Prisons and Prison Buildings* (1930); R. L. Davison, 'Prison Architecture', *Architectural Record*, January 1930 (Natl. Committee on Prisons and Prison Labour, New York); id., 157 *Annals* 33; von Hentig, 21 *MoSchrKrim.* 281; L. Frede and A. Perret, 22 *MoSchrKrim.* 10.

[2] Wilmanns, l.c., p. 352.

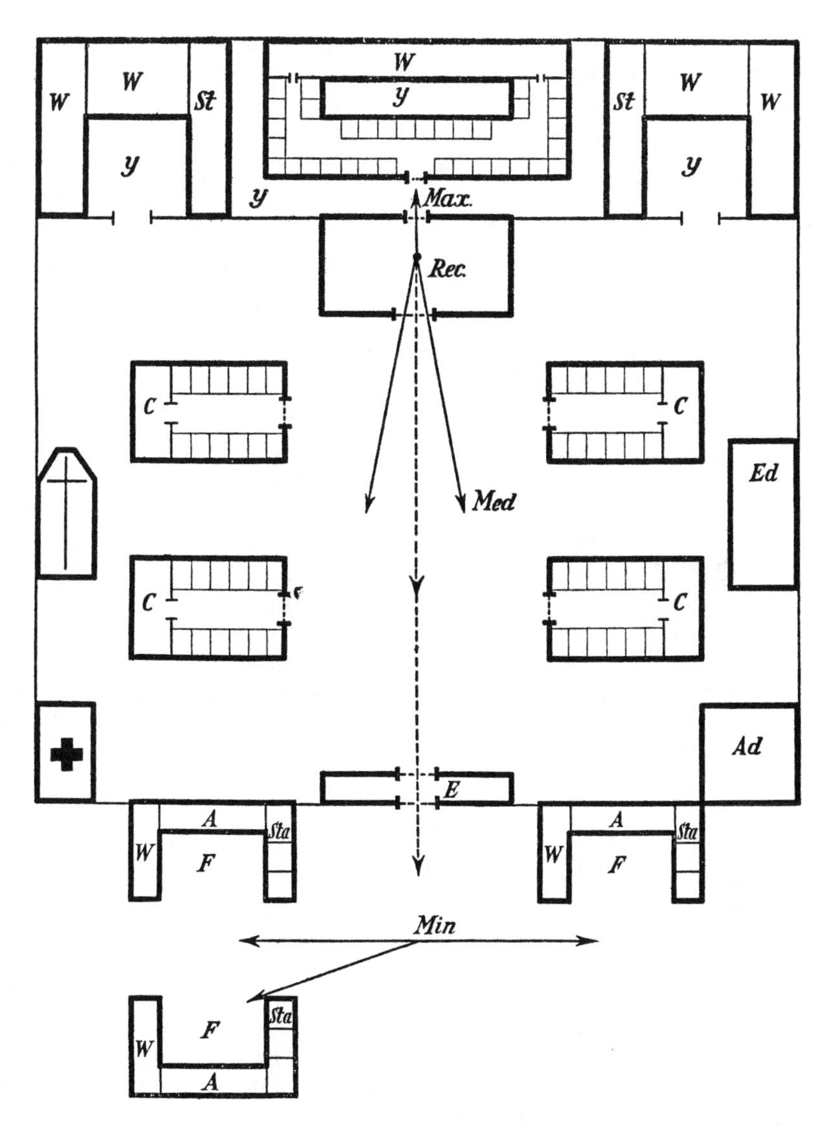

FIG. IV. Horizontal classification: rough sketch of a mixed prison with three security groups.

A	Accommodation for agricultural labourers	Med	Medium security
Ad	Administration	Min	Minimum security
C	Common Room	Rec	Reception and distribution centre
E	Entrance	St	Store
Ed	Educational Department	Sta	Stable
F	Farm	W	Workshop
Max	Maximum security	Y	Yard

maximum security. The medium security men have smaller houses and separate workshops within the outer yard. Outside the walls are farms for those who need the least amount of physical restraint. Figure V is a rough illustration of a plan designed by the architect Alfred Perret.[1] It envisages a Progres-

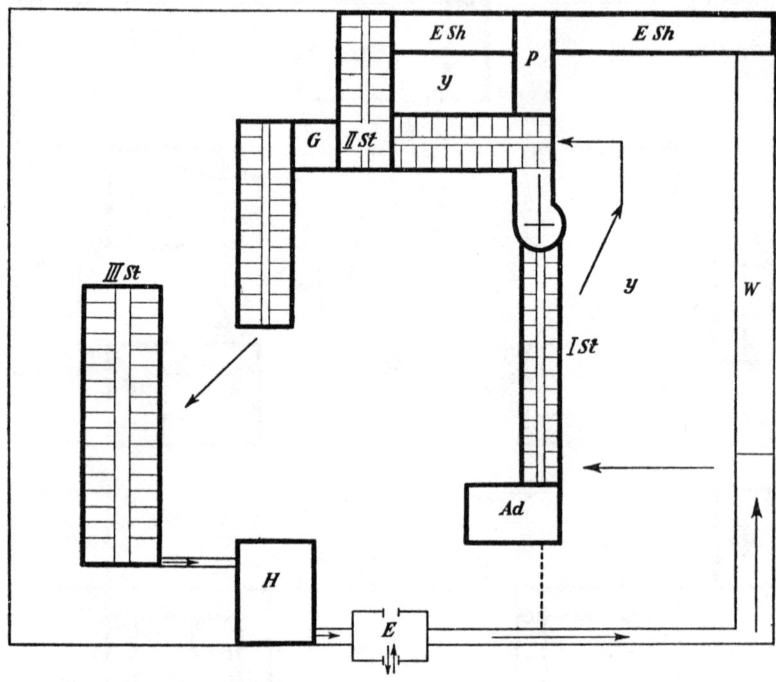

FIG. V. Vertical classification: Perret's plan of a Progressive Stage prison.

Ad	Administration	P	Power-station
E	Entrance	St	Stage
E Sh	Engineering shop	W	Workshop
G	Gymnasium	Y	Yard
H	Hall		

sive Stage system, where the prisoner enters the institution at the gate-building, begins his term in the panoptic wing of the first stage and will be transferred to the second stage; later he may cross the marked gap to the building of the third stage which leads back to the entrance for release. A gymnasium is connected with the wing of the second, a lecture hall with the house of the third stage.

The demands of prison administration will produce variations and combinations of such pure types. Some new American insti-

[1] Frede and Perret, l.c.

tutions have begun to replace the old uniformity by a variety of housing facilities corresponding to the needs of classification. The North Eastern Federal Penitentiary at Lewisburg, Pa., has a small inside block for hardened criminals, strong outside rooms for those not presumed to be constantly planning an escape, dormitories for those who live peacefully with their fellows, smaller dormitories subdivided into wards for those who show improvement of character, and for the most advanced prisoners honour rooms similar to living quarters of normal persons. Norfolk State Prison Colony, Mass., has a receiving building with 105 outside cells constructed as a maximum security institution. It has furthermore two dormitories with quarters for 150 inmates each, divided into units of 50; both are minimum security buildings, but the one, with facilities for restricting freedom of movement within the unit, can easily be converted into a medium security building. There is a farm colony outside the prison wall with accommodation for the inmates.[1] The needs for differentiation within a single prison depends on the size of the institution and the number of its population. Up to now the United States has been the country of excessively large prisons. By the end of 1933 four state prisons had more than 5,000 inmates each. European prison administrations prefer medium institutions of 500 prisoners. This standard has been accepted by the International Penal and Penitentiary Congress in London in 1925. Recently American expert opinion accepted the view that the right number lies between a minimum of 250 and a maximum of 1,200, with 500 as the ideal size.[2] English prison history shows how a central administration succeeded in overcoming prison abuses by closing down small local gaols. Monster institutions are no less obstacles for a progressive penal policy. It is the mission of prison architecture to design appropriate buildings which facilitate an optimum of individualization within the limits of a modified mass treatment.

[1] Haynes, pp. 41 and 53.
[2] Ibid., pp. 34 and 40.

CHAPTER IX

PRISON LABOUR

CHANGING ASPECTS OF PRISON LABOUR

PRISON labour is the essence of prison discipline.[1] Throughout history the rise and fall of penal systems coincided with changing conditions of prison work. In the early Bridewells and Houses of Correction the element of useful labour was added to enforced custody. It was the first inroad of a moral force into a prison atmosphere of physical hardship and mortification. With the decline of work the institutions frustrated the enlightened intentions of their founders. John Howard's version of the Voltairian maxim, 'Make men diligent and they will be honest', became the classic formulation of the labour principle. The words show its truth and its fallacy. Useful work is indispensable for any reformative programme, but enforced labour is not an infallible method of achieving a lasting social readjustment. In the United States proper regard for good working conditions had the effect that the Auburn system was preferred to solitary confinement, until even the rule of silence had to give way to more natural forms of common industrial work. Thus industrial policy did much to shape the nineteenth-century patterns of American prisons.[2] At the same time in many of the larger European institutions a doctrinal adherence to the cellular system resulted in a lack of appropriate workshops and other facilities for industrial or agricultural work. Between the wars, however, the American depression closed the market for prison-made goods and hit overcrowded prisons with the curse of unemployment. For some of the less advanced penal institutions, the impending idleness between prison walls proved a challenge which made it possible to subject them to a thorough overhauling of their traditional management and routine.

The attitude towards prison labour reflects the prevailing opinions about man and work in general. The traditional social and ethical standards pre-suppose sufficient work for every willing hand. Regular work is everybody's duty and the price for

[1] L. N. Robinson, *Should Prisoners Work?* (1931); id., 'Prison Labor', *Encyclopaedia of the Social Sciences*, xii. 415; 'Gefangenenarbeit', *HWB. Staatswiss.* (4th ed. 1926); *Report of the Departmental Committee on the Employment of Prisoners*, Part I (1933); *Prison Labor in the United States, 1940* (U.S. Department of Labor, Bureau of Labor Statistics, Bulletin 698, 1941); McKelvey, 25 *Journal* 254; Borchers, 54 *Bl.GefgKd.* 1–146.

[2] H. B. Gill, 157 *Annals* 83.

social status and economic security. Vice and poverty are regarded as the outcome of idleness. It seems therefore right that the criminal should work hard for his rehabilitation. But the mass-unemployment of the inter-war years changed all this and made it necessary to distribute and even ration work like other necessities of life. Labour, so long regarded as a 'damned duty', claims a high rank in the Bill of Rights. This experience affected a whole generation's outlook on life and extended its influence even to the remote sphere of penal policy.

Under the impact of this experience the attempt has been made to interpret the whole history of criminal law from an economic point of view. According to such attempts, the particular forms of legal punishment are not the outcome of social and legal doctrines, but almost inevitable repercussions of conditions on the labour market and the general attitude resulting therefrom.[1] A growing demand for labour facilitates lenient penalties which preserve and utilize the prisoner's working capacity, while shortage of work and the ensuing feeling of insecurity lead to the mortification and extinction of criminals. Such motives have been effective, but they are by no means the only historical factors. Recent history offers sufficient instances when, for good or for evil, powerful ideas crossed and even superseded rational and economic considerations. The new ethical principles of the Reformation, the rationalist theories of the Era of Enlightenment no less than the widespread feeling of insecurity in recent times, are paramount movements with deeper causes than the social and economic conditions which sometimes determine their shape and extension.[2] Prison history is no exception. Like other institutions, legal punishment bears the impress of human ideas and material conditions both, which sometimes support, but often impede, each other. In the face of actual or impending unemployment, individuals and groups are inclined to deny the prisoner what they themselves fear to lose. When honest men have to live on the dole, why should prisoners work and ex-prisoners find employment? There is a twofold answer to this objection. Lack of work frustrates any attempt at achieving social readjustment. But the issue is ultimately an ethical one. Whatever the State's responsibility might be with regard to full employment for everybody, it would forfeit the right to inflict punishment in the name of justice if it were to take a man from his place in society to enforced idleness within prison

[1] G. Rusche and O. Kirchheimer, *Punishment and Social Structure* (1939).

[2] D. Riesman, 40 *Columbia L.R.* 1297.

walls. It is a fundamental principle, independent of changing penal systems, that 'the prisoner, as a human being, has a right to work. It is immoral to refuse it permanently and to condemn him to a long period of idleness.'[1] Prison labour, in spite of many shortcomings and abuses, justifies the use of deprivation of liberty as a legal punishment.

There is a paradox with regard to prison labour. On the one hand, enforced labour has long been regarded as a mere hardship, deliberately inflicted as a punishment proper. The English Act of 1779 was a classic expression of this idea. The statutory conceptions of 'penal servitude' and 'hard labour' are reminiscent of the obsolete association of ideas between enforced work and punishment. The same attitude suggests the device of marking several stages of prison discipline or different types of punishment by work of a more or less oppressive character. A Prussian Regulation for Rawicz of 1835 provided that prisoners of the second class and recidivists should be employed for 'the most unpleasant and dirtiest work', while 'remunerative work' should be the privilege of the first class. Continental countries sometimes resorted to similar distinctions for the difference between penal servitude and imprisonment. France allocated to convicts harder work,[2] Italy lower earnings,[3] Germany longer working hours and lower earnings. Whenever the principle of retribution dominates the administration of legal punishments, the demand for a qualitative differentiation between single penalties arises and this leads to the device of making the prisoners' work differ in its degrees of oppressiveness.

On the other hand, work is a much-coveted remedy which helps men to endure the unnatural state of captivity: 'No greater cruelty can possibly be inflicted than enforced idleness.'[4] Prison labour is a benefit, and to forfeit it is a severe blow to the prisoner. In many an 'old prison' with no organized recreation and insufficient educational facilities, the idle Sunday was much dreaded, and permission to continue work granted as a privilege. Deprivation of work in connexion with solitary confinement is a severe disciplinary punishment. Enforced labour may be oppressive, but to withhold it would mean even more hardship to the prisoner.

[1] K. Krohne, *Lehrbuch der Gefängniskunde* (1889).

[2] Art. 15, *Code pénal.*

[3] G. Dybwad, *Theorie und Praxis des fascistischen Strafvollzugs* (1934), pp. 23 and 45.

[4] E. R. Carr at a National Conference on the Reduction of Crime, 1927, quoted from L. N. Robinson, *Should Prisoners Work?* (1931), p. 2.

ECONOMIC PATTERNS

Scope of Employment

Prison labour, though performed in the seclusion of penal institutions, is part and parcel of the general economic system. Depression and mass unemployment in the world at large force prisoners, too, into idleness. The boom of war production increased the demand even for prison labour. At the same time the employment of prisoners involves its own problems owing to the conditions of prison life and the purpose of penal policy. More than any other aspect of prison discipline the work reveals the possibilities and limitations of a rational penal system.

The amount and economic significance of prison labour cannot be described in terms of a simple formula or a short statistical abstract. Conditions vary from country to country, and often differ between single institutions under the same administration. The Table offers a preliminary illustration only. The figures have been computed from official sources.[1] Some exchanges of items under different headings were necessary in order to make the figures comparable.

Average Numbers of Prisoners employed

	England and Wales 1938		*Scotland 1938*		*U.S.A. State and Federal prisoners 1940*	
	daily average	per cent.	daily average	per cent.	daily average	per cent.
Making or repairing mailbags	2,358	21·1	114·6	7·2	..	..
Teasing	..	..	86·1	5·4	..	..
Manufacturing other products	3,773	33·8	443·1	28·0	..	..
Total manufacturing	6,131	54·9	643·8	40·6	33,640	17·5
Building	1,584	14·2	178·4	11·2	24,337	12·7
Farming and land-development	569	5·1	103·4	6·5	21,664	11·3
Mining and quarrying	..	..	..	..	3,874	2·0
Total productively employed	8,284	74·2	925·6	58·3	83,515	43·5
Maintenance and other domestic work	1,879	16·8	429·3	27·0	68,894	36·0
Non-effectives	1,005	9·0	233·2	14·7	16,519	8·6
Attending school	..	..	..	..	11,868	6·2
Idle	..	..	..	..	10,980	5·7
GRAND TOTAL	11,168	100·0	1,588·1	100·0	191,776	100·0

[1] England and Wales, *Report of the Prison Commissioners, 1938*, Appendix 6, pp. 93 et seq.; *Annual Report of the Prison Department for Scotland, 1938*; *Prison Labor in the United States, 1940* (U.S. Department of Labor, Bureau of Labor Statistics, 1941).

At first sight this Table suggests that full employment with productive work is by no means a universal feature of prison discipline. The percentage of prisoners productively employed varies between 74·2 in England and Wales and 43·5 in the United States, where one-fifth of all prisoners have no work at all. It is the overwhelming problem of prison management to provide penal institutions constantly with useful work. The *Report on the Employment of Prisoners* of 1933 stated that 'the root of all evil is the definite shortage of work'. According to a German prison practitioner existing work has to be stretched 'like bread in a besieged fortress'.

Every free economic enterprise makes its appointments in the light of the work to be done. A prison, however, has to find work for men who have been committed for reasons quite other than the demand for suitable craftsmen. Prison authorities obviously lack the versatility of private enterprises. Sometimes the administration would establish special agencies which explore and divert demands and distribute orders to the several institutions. The Thuringian Prison Regulation of 1924 assigned this task to a Thüringische Gesellschaft für Werkarbeit m. b. H. Since 1935 industrial work in U.S. federal penal institutions has been directed by the Federal Prison Industries, Inc.

Even under favourable conditions not all prisoners will be at work all the time. There will always be some who are invalids or sick, under disciplinary punishment, on transport, or involved in reception or release routine. England, with a pre-war ratio of less than 10 per cent. of prisoners without work, comes very near to the optimum of full employment. Even among prisoners assigned to jobs, there is a number of 'invisible' unemployed. This applies to institutions with an unduly high proportion of inmates assigned to maintenance and other domestic work. American experts suggest 12½ per cent. as a reasonable ratio for such work in a well-run institution.[1] A recent official statement regards even 25 per cent. as still normal.[2] Again the English figure of 16·8 per cent. compares favourably with the American 36 per cent. or even the corresponding figure for prisoners in U.S. federal institutions, viz. 47 per cent. The good record of English prisons not only testifies to successful labour management, but is also one of the beneficial results of the centralization of administration, the reduction of local gaols, and the small number of remand prisoners.

[1] L. N. Robinson, l.c., p. 169.

[2] *Prison Labor in the U.S., 1940*, p. 10.

In Germany most of the large prisons used to have a fair standard of occupation. Before the First World War, however, the high proportion of short prison sentences was a serious obstacle to full employment. Prussian prison regulations of 1902 provided that, as a rule, prisoners serving terms of less than a fortnight should be left without work. Up to the Second World War remand prisoners were not under a legal obligation to work. In 1927, among convicted prisoners, the ratio of unemployment was 10 per cent. and among remand prisoners 43·9 per cent.[1] A great number of remand prisoners was kept in small court gaols, where a rational working scheme was not feasible. In 1927 17 per cent. of all occupied prisoners were engaged in maintenance work.

These figures show that for the years preceding the Second World War the proportion of unemployed prisoners and mere maintenance workers was higher in the United States than in England, Scotland, and Germany. Observers on the spot corroborate this conclusion. In 1940 an American expert called northern prisons 'for the most part idle houses'. In one of the largest prisons of the United States he found 1,000 totally idle prisoners.[2] Another observer indicted the pre-war industrial programme as 'the weakest item in a generally retarded system of prison administration'. He asserted that 'a feeling of inertia and hopelessness' pervaded the whole administration.[3]

Such criticism calls for a closer investigation of labour conditions in American penal institutions. In 1928, among twenty-seven penal institutions with a total of 36,798 prisoners, two had 50 per cent. of their population in idleness, three between 30 per cent. and 50 per cent., and six between 20 per cent. and 30 per cent. In the same year the New York State Prison Commission reported that out of 9,980 prisoners more than 2,500 were kept without employment.[4] While in 1940 the absolute number of prisoners productively employed was slightly higher than in 1932, they produced goods of only three-quarters the value of what their predecessors had done eight years before.[5] Apparently labour has been stretched in order to check the growing number of idle prisoners. This observation justifies the suggestion, made in the *Attorney General's Survey* of 1939, that not merely the official assign-

[1] 'Statistik des Gefängniswesens im Deutschen Reich', *Reichstag*, iv, 1926, No. 814, 1 March 1929.

[2] A. H. MacCormick, 53 *Harvard L.R.* 1216.

[3] W. H. Burke, 35 *Journal* 78.

[4] *Wickersham Report*, ix. 14.

[5] *Prison Labor in the U.S., 1940*, pp. 2 and 22.

ment sheet should be taken into account but also the virtual amount of idleness. For this purpose the *Survey* divided the total estimated value of the products gained or manufactured by a standard value for a single job.[1] Allowing for the fact that a prisoner might fairly be expected to produce one-fifth as much as a free worker and that 25 per cent. of the inmates would be assigned to maintenance and other domestic work, the conclusions reveal an appalling amount of manifest and 'invisible' unemployment. In 1935–6, among 106,818 inmates of 85 prisons, more than every second one, viz. 55,822, were idle. In 47 out of these 85 prisons more than 50 per cent. of the prisoners were idle. These 47 prisons belong to 24 states, including New York, Pennsylvania, Illinois, California, and the District of Columbia. Only 6 out of the 85 prisons under investigation had no idleness among their inmates. This applies to state prisons only. Conditions are even worse in the numerous municipal and county gaols, where unconvicted prisoners are remanded and misdemeanants serve short sentences. An inquiry based on figures from 1923 estimates that at least 75 per cent. of all prisoners, sentenced and unconvicted, in institutions for misdemeanants are idle. While these prisoners are exposed to this enforced idleness for a comparatively short time only, the number of persons affected is by no means negligible. More than 85 per cent. of all prison commitments apply to persons sent to local gaols and workhouses.[2]

Labour Systems

In the course of continuous efforts to ensure constant work in the face of the fluctuations and deficiencies of the prison population, several systems of employing prisoners have been developed. The prisoners' work may be done either under private or public control. The most primitive way of contracting out the prisoners' work is the Lease system. It originated in the United States after the Civil War, when many prisons had been destroyed and reconstruction increased the demand for labour. Under this system prisoners would be 'lent' to a private entrepreneur much as deported prisoners were assigned to a settler or prisoners-of-war to a farmer. An improved form of private control is the Contract system, on the Continent called *Entreprise*. Instead of prisoners going out to a private employer, the entrepreneur moves his workshop into the prison. There he installs machinery, tools,

[1] *Attorney General's Survey*, v. 50 et seq.

[2] L. N. Robinson, l.c., pp. 42 et seq.

stores, and sometimes even electric light and power. He sends his foremen who train the prisoners and supervise their work. Under this system workshops have been established for the manufacture of shirts, baskets, wooden yardsticks, and rulers, &c. The Contract system relieves the Administration of the strain of continuously providing the inmates with work, but at the price of admitting a strange element of private economic interest to an influential position within the prison. The Piece-price system, sometimes called Accord system, tries to uphold the advantages of the Contract system without conceding influence to forces outside the penal administration. The institution collects orders from private firms. The firm provides the raw materials and pays a fixed price per piece of the manufactured goods. The prison administration alone organizes the workshops and supervises the work.

Public control or the *régie* system, too, has been developed in three different ways. The counterpart to the private contract or Piece-price system is the Public Account system. The State itself undertakes to manufacture goods by prison labour and to sell the products on the open market. This applies to industries like those performed by private contractors, tailoring and other forms of textile industry, manufacture of carpets and mats, brooms and brushes, cane-work. In order to exclude the State as a competitor to private manufacturers the State Use system restricts the manufacture of prison-made goods to products exclusively used for state purposes, e.g. stationery for government offices, mailbags for the postal service, and furniture and other utensils for public institutions. The most characteristic application of this principle is the Public Works system, i.e. the employment of prisoners on enterprises of road-building and land reclamation or on state farms.

The enumeration of these six systems of employing prisoners reveals a characteristic tendency for prison labour to pass from private to public control. The preference of public control is due to both criminological and economic considerations. For a rational penal policy interference by private profit-seeking interests is incompatible with the social and rehabilitative function of public punishment. In 1888 von Jagemann, an international authority on prison administration, held the opinion that the Contract system was doomed from the point of view of penal science. In 1890 the International Prison Congress in St. Petersburg voted in favour of State-controlled systems, though still allowing for the difficulties of countries where it seemed 'understandable' that the administration should resort to private enterprise. At the same time complaints against the alleged unfair competition of industries 'benefited' by cheap prison labour influenced public opinion against Contract and Piece-price systems. By 1923 the Lease system had practically disappeared. In 1931 it was still retained in law but not in practice in Louisiana, North Carolina, and Arkansas.[1] Up to recent times the Contract system played a considerable part in Germany, where prisoners were employed for private enterprise as well as for public account or state use. In 1927, in Prussia and Saxony, approximately one-half of the total of prisoners employed worked for private contractors, while in Württemberg, in 1925, more than half was employed under the State Account system. A similar mixed system of private enterprise and public *régie* prevails in France and Scotland. In the United States the rise of the Contract system coincided with the development and growing industrialization of the Auburn régime by the middle of the nineteenth century. In recent times legislation and administrative practice have excluded private contractors from American prisons. In 1885 40 per cent. of the prisoners productively employed worked for private contractors and 26 per cent. under the Lease system. By 1923 there were still 12 per cent. working for contractors, but none under the Lease system. In 1940 none worked under either system. At the same time the percentage of prisoners working under public control rose from 26 per cent. in 1885 to 81 per cent. in 1923 and 100 per cent. of all prisoners productively employed in 1940.[2] In Europe England, Switzerland, Holland, and Belgium have been the stronghold of an exclusive State Use system.

Experience shows that the installation of no one system as such is a solution of prison labour problems.[3] In Great Britain England and Wales with their exclusive State Use system have a higher ratio of industrial employment of prisoners than Scotland with her mixed system of working for the government and the open market. In the United States the drastic curtailment of the production of prison-made goods for the market coincided with a considerable fall in the numbers of prisoners engaged in industrial occupations. From 1923 to 1940 the amount of goods produced for the open market was reduced from an annual output worth

[1] *Wickersham Report*, ix. 83.
[2] *Prison Labor in the U.S., 1940*, p. 5.
[3] L. N. Robinson, l.c., p. 122.

forty-seven million dollars to little more than nine million. At the same time the percentage of prisoners productively employed sank from 61 per cent. to 44 per cent.[1] The unemployment among American prisoners before the war must therefore be explained as the crisis of an enforced abrupt adaptation to an exclusive State Use system, doubly difficult under the impact of the economic depression. New York state prisons have an average population of 14,390, but the pre-war demands for goods for exclusive state use allowed only the employment of some 2,000 prisoners working at one-fifth the efficiency of free workers.[2]

Types of Production

The prisoner himself is obviously less concerned with the prevailing system of employment than with the work he is obliged to perform. As a matter of expediency, certain industries are preferred to others in prison workshops. Such are boot-making and repairs, tailoring and other textile industries including weaving and the manufacture of bags, mats, and brooms, cane and willow-work, carpentry, and simple forms of printing and stationery. The running of the institution itself provides ample opportunity for kitchen work, bakery, and laundry. Beside such work, prisons must often resort to odd jobs in order to fill gaps in the inmates' employment. Among such obsolete, but still surviving, prison jobs are the sorting of peas and lentils, picking of oakum, untwisting and teasing of ropes and wool, sticking of envelopes and paper bags. Colloquial language uses some of the old-fashioned forms of convict-labour—e.g. 'sticking paper bags'—as synonyms for prison. Sorting of salvage and cutting fire-wood are further typical prison occupations.

The term industrial work covers a variety of occupational status from skilled handicraft to attending machines and simple manual processes. In Germany, between the wars, approximately 18 per cent. of prisoners were occupied as bootmakers, tailors, locksmiths, carpenters, bricklayers, bakers, and weavers. In 1927, among 1,473 prisoners in Württemberg, 123 were employed as bootmakers, 90 as tailors, 61 as carpenters, 36 as smiths and locksmiths; at the same time 361 were making mats. In England and Wales the manufacturing and repair of mail-bags is the staple prison industry. Out of a total of 6,000 to 7,000 prisoners occupied in industrial work between 1924 and 1929 about 45·2 per cent.,

[1] *Prison Labor in the U.S., 1940*, p. 6.
[2] *Attorney General's Survey*, v. 188.

and in 1938–9 about 38·4 per cent., were sewing mail-bags. It has been put on record that a longer occupation with this sort of work makes prisoners 'soft'. Governors therefore give prisoners for the last weeks of their terms a job in the garden or coalhouse 'to tune them up'.[1] It is by this staple occupation, the manufacture of mail-bags, that England maintains the high rate of 74·2 per cent. of the prisoners productively employed. In 1938–9 approximately 10 per cent. were employed as tailors and shoemakers. In the United States many a well-equipped prison foundry or furniture factory was seriously affected by the dwindling demand for prison-made goods. In several institutions stone-cutting still persists, though sometimes developed into the manufacture of cement and concrete products and the establishment of brick plants. The most favoured American prison article is auto-licence tags. As early as in 1936 thirty-nine prisons provided three-quarters of all licence plates used. In total value of goods produced, binder twine comes out as a close second. At a considerable distance there follow whole milk, cotton-yarn goods, shoes, canned fruits and vegetables—which offer seasonable employment only—and cotton.[2] Alabama made an experiment with a 'vertical concentration' of textile industry. Prisoners raise the cotton seed, grow the cotton, gin, spin, and weave it, and make garments.[3] New York prisons specialize in producing a variety of 40–50 different garments for state hospitals. In the federal prisons the manufacture of cotton ducks for postal mail-bags and of canvas specialities takes the first place in the prisoners' industrial occupation.

The foregoing instances illustrate the types of industrial work performed in penal institutions. Not all prisoners can be employed with industrial occupations in cells or common workshops. The difficulties in extending productive work in the prison and even maintaining a sufficient amount of it make a strong case for open-air work in garden and fields, roads and forests. At present such suggestions and experiments coincide with the policy of differentiating penal establishments into maximum, medium, and minimum security institutions. Prisoners eligible for minimum security camps and farms would mostly work outside prison walls. Open-air work, however, has been performed under the most varying conditions, ranging from strict custody to liberty restricted by

[1] *Report of the Departmental Committee on Persistent Offenders* (1932), pp. 34 and 82.
[2] *Prison Labor in the U.S., 1940*, p. 38.
[3] *Attorney General's Survey*, v. 190.

bonds of trust and honour only. The prison camps in the southern states of the United States are an illustration of open-air work with a 'purely custodial programme'.[1] In 1937 there were 25,660 state prisoners in 221 road camps and 63 farm camps in nine southern states. As a rule primitive accommodation and elementary discipline prevailed. It was not unusual for prisoners to be locked up in wooden huts with three-deck bunks, chained at night, or even kept in portable cages on wheels. Lash and stripes were used.

Three states had armed inmate guards. Education, organized recreation, and sometimes even religious services were non-existent. In Louisiana no less than 450 prisoners with life sentences underwent this form of prison discipline. Under such a régime the social and rehabilitative functions of legal punishment are ignored. It is equally unsatisfactory from the point of view of prison labour. Eyewitnesses report that these squads of twenty to thirty men with at least two armed guards, working with pick and shovel, present the appearance of a poorly organized and directed group of labourers.[2] The administrations claim financial success with low costs of maintenance and a surplus of the value of the products over the total of expenditure. Since this balance depends on a somewhat arbitrary estimation of the 'value' of roads built and maintained, it is open to question whether unskilled convicts, working under the eyes of armed guards, can economically compete with honour groups and the use of road machinery. In 1943 Georgia prohibited the further use of leg irons and chains and established a Department of Correction with a view to abolishing the prevailing system of road camps.[3]

These observations on road and farm work by 'chain gangs' corroborate the criminological considerations that open-air work as a form of penal discipline has a chance of success only as a régime for minimum security prisoners with fully developed educational services and recreation facilities. Road, forestry, and farm camps in the northern states of the United States are chiefly comprised of 'trusties', many of them working in 'honour camps' without armed guards.[4] In 1937 1,500 prisoners worked in seventeen road and forestry camps and 2,979 prisoners in forty-eight farm camps.

An expedient way of combining facilities for open-air work with

[1] Ibid., p. 41; J. F. Steiner and Roy Brown, *North Carolina Chain Gang* (1927).
[2] Steiner and Brown, l.c., p. 53.
[3] J. V. Bennet, in *American Yearbook, 1944*, p. 610.
[4] *Attorney General's Survey*, v. 46.

the constructive efforts of an appropriate prison routine is the assignment of prison inmates to work on the grounds belonging to the institution or nearby farmland and moors, forests, and roads. Selected groups of prisoners may be transferred to agricultural prison annexes. In practice many variations and combinations of such systems are feasible. In Germany, after the First World War, 6–8 per cent. of all prisoners worked outside prison walls. In 1935 5,500 prisoners in six camps were assigned to the reclamation of the Emsland Moors, an area of 124 million acres, where the men worked under a strict semi-military discipline. In the United States, in 1937, approximately 5,400 state prisoners, living in or at major institutions, were engaged in farm work. Forty-one state prisons maintain separate farm colonies under the supervision of the prison warden, forty institutions send out inmates daily for farm work.[1] In England and Wales agricultural work has been slowly but steadily extended in the wake of experiments with minimum security facilities. Before the war 5 per cent. of the prisoners employed were occupied with farming. Some Borstal institutions have farms of their own. In connexion with the Wakefield scheme 100 selected men of the combined treatment group of first offenders plus a proportion of selected 'specials' with previous convictions worked in a camp, some living in huts, some going out to work from the prison. This tradition has been upheld when, during the war, recidivists were transferred from Leeds prison to Wakefield.[2] As a further outcome of the war, by 1943 English prisons were sending out daily some 1,000 prisoners to work on farms, timber-yards, and elsewhere.[3] Likewise American experience during the war led to the conclusion that more prisoners can be trusted outside the wall than was previously thought possible.[4]

The agricultural prison colony may be illustrated by Witzwil, Canton of Berne, Switzerland. A mixed prison population of some 500 convicts, vagrants, juveniles, idle persons, military and remand prisoners has been organized into an agricultural working community with the usual ancillary industries plus sorting out of salvage. Most of the inmates are accommodated in non-panoptic cell-blocks at night and work together in daytime. Some discharged prisoners stay for voluntary employment at an annex of

[1] *Attorney General's Survey*, pp. 47 and 200.
[2] A. Paterson, 6 *Howard Journal* 13.
[3] 6 *Howard Journal* 136.
[4] W. H. Burke, 35 *Journal* 83.

the institution. Witzwil is a self-supporting establishment. The individual's share in the common effort binds the different elements together to a homogeneous treatment group.[1]

CRIMINOLOGICAL CONSIDERATIONS

Criminological principles, no less than economic considerations, determine the patterns of prison labour. The German *Principles of Prison Discipline* of 1923 prescribed the following aims for the administration of prison labour. 'Regular work is the foundation of a proper prison system. Every prisoner should be permanently occupied with useful work. At work, prisoners should be gradually accustomed to independence and responsibility.'

This formula not only emphasizes the need for the prisoners' full employment, but also explicitly rejects the prejudice that beneficial results might be expected from enforced labour without any regard to its purpose. This fallacy did once support the introduction into English prisons of the treadmill and the capstan, as if there were no difference whether, by treading a wheel or turning a handle, the prisoner acted as a substitute for horse-, water-, or steam-power, or whether he trod empty air as an end in itself. The prisoner is much aware of the profound psychological difference between real work and mere fatigue. Real work is a blessing, but useless occupation is felt as a provocation, an embittering 'torture and most cruel revenge' (Dostoievski). Social readjustment implies a positive attitude towards work, even if performed by hard and monotonous manual labour. This can only be achieved if the prisoner is made to understand by experience the useful purpose of even the humblest work as a necessary contribution to a common effort.

Training for Work

The object of prison labour in a rehabilitative programme is twofold: training for work and training by work.[2] In a properly administered institution training for it should not be too difficult. The organized life with its meticulous regimentation and daily routine takes firm hold of the prisoner. Often he accepts work as a relief from boredom and frustration, even as a stimulus or at least an antidote against the deadly monotony of endless days and

[1] *Jahresbericht der Strafanstalt Witzwil pro 1940* (1941).

[2] W. Herrmann, *Das Hamburgische Jugendgefängnis Hanöfersand* (1923), pp. 37 et seq.; C. Bondy, *Pädagogische Probleme im Jugendstrafvollzug* (1925), p. 67.

weeks until the far-off day of release. Satisfactory work-habits in prison promote good discipline and are indispensable for creating an atmosphere in which personal trust and the prisoner's co-operation in educational activities are possible. But standards of craftsmanship with the average prisoner are low and the skill and ability essential to results of the better quality are exceptional.

Working Hours

Various means have been devised in order to make training for work successful. Experience in industrial psychology shows that the worker's efficiency depends on the right assessment of the time he is obliged to work. Under the influence of retributory and deterrent tendencies, long working hours have been the rule in penal institutions, especially in convict prisons. In practice, however, these long working hours rather led to a slackening in work-habits. Other routine matters, like reports to the Governor, to the doctor, and so forth, caused endless interruptions and resulted in an atmosphere of restlessness, with prisoners, escorted by guards, constantly coming and going. It was therefore a great achievement when enlightened administrations introduced an eight-hour day exclusively devoted to work, while all other routine affairs, including educational activities, had their proper place during spare time. Such a scheme requires a considerable staff for supervising eight hours of work in association plus further hours of routine outside working-hours. In England and Wales, after the First World War, the eight-hour day was introduced for work in association. When in 1931, owing to the economic depression, the prison staff was reduced, this system broke down except in Borstal institutions. Group work in large prisons sometimes fell to approximately twenty-five hours a week with a corresponding increase of cellular work.[1] By 1937–8 the eight hours of associated work were re-established, but again broke down under the impact of the war. In Scotland the time for associated work never fell below 7½ hours. A similar system prevailed in Thuringia during the reform period after the First World War. The advantages of such a system are obvious. The concentration on uninterrupted work for an optimum of time not only increases production, but also emphasizes the dignity of work. It introduces into the artificial prison atmosphere a sound rhythm of work, leisure, and spare-time activities, corresponding to the world at large.

[1] *Report of the Departmental Committee on the Employment of Prisoners, I* (1933), p. 66, s. 156.

Tasks

Training for work may be facilitated by an appropriate system of incentives. Mere working for time has a deadly effect on morale, but a target stimulates interest and energy. It is an old tradition in prisons to assess in terms of time a certain task (*Pensum, Tagewerk*) which the prisoner, or a team of prisoners, is required to perform. This can be an oppressive device if the task has been assessed without allowing for the individual prisoner's abilities, if its performance in the prescribed time is enforced by disciplinary punishment, and the prisoner is under the obligation to work on without any reward after its performance. Tasks must be assessed not with regard to the abilities of an average worker, but of an average prisoner. In a Prussian prison the task assessed for shoe manufacturing was 75 per cent. of the work output of an average home-worker; even then 25 per cent. of the prisoners failed to attain it. A properly assessed task, sufficiently flexible to allow for differences in age, training, and fitness, and further enticements for surplus work makes for more successful training.

Compensation

The payment of wages to prisoners has long been controversial. Since prison labour is an essential part of the legal punishments which imply a deprivation of liberty, it is by law forced labour and is, as a rule, work assigned rather than voluntarily undertaken. From this presupposition the conclusion was drawn, with some American precedents, that the produce of the work undertaken by prisoners is entirely the property of the State.[1] This, however, should not rule out the practice, if only for the sake of improving conditions for profitable work, of granting prisoners a remuneration out of the produce of the work performed. Every honest piece of work is worth its reward. Obviously no legal obligation can be derived from a natural right to a just reward. From a psychological point of view, however, it is strange to expect, in a world of paid labour, that a prisoner should show unselfish devotion to enforced unpaid work. It would be hypocritical to condemn as vile materialism the common human experience, that adequate earnings are a stimulus to work and a visible expression of its successful performance. Other suggestions propose that wages should enable prisoners to maintain their families and to compensate the victim of their crime.

[1] References by L. N. Robinson, l.c., p. 199, nn. 1–3.

Such far-reaching plans depend on the amount of earnings feasible under prison conditions. Unlike England, most countries divide the sum allocated to the prisoner into house-money and a savings account. The former, subject to certain restrictions, is at the prisoner's disposal. He may buy utensils and additional food from the canteen, postage stamps and note-paper, books and magazines—with special permission—or send money to his relatives. The savings account is kept for him for his release. Sometimes the ex-prisoner receives it in instalments through the local office of a discharged prisoners' aid agency. The legal character of this remuneration is rather complicated.[1] In the world at large, the claim for wages is a legal element of the employer's obligations arising from the labour contract. The prisoner's obligation to work has been imposed by public law. Legal provisions for his compensation, if any, have their place in administrative regulations which the officers are legally bound to apply. If they fail to do so the prisoner may be entitled to a complaint under administrative law, but could not sue for his alleged wage-bill. German prison regulations provide that the prisoner has no legal claim to his earnings and savings account. Such a proviso is not founded merely on an unjustifiable reluctance to concede rights to the prisoner, but is intended also to prevent creditors, including the treasury, from defraying the costs of proceedings and detainment by distraining the prisoner's earnings. France and Switzerland too, contrary to certain obsolete precedents, except the prisoner's earnings from assets open to the creditor's seizure. Austria gave the heirs of a deceased prisoner a right to the accrued amount of his earnings, France at least to the disposable part of the prisoner's accounts. Recent legislation in Italy and Switzerland and corresponding proposals in Germany have recognized the prisoner's right to his earnings with qualifications as to his protection against creditors and the exclusion of a civil lawsuit.[2] Certain Swiss Cantons provided the deprivation of earnings as a disciplinary measure, while in Germany only restrictions on the prisoner's disposal of his earnings were permissible.

In England the Gladstone Report of 1895 recommended an extension of the tradition that prisoners should receive a gratuity up to 10*s.* which could be earned in six months. From 1913 gratuities were discontinued. Only remand prisoners working

[1] Guggenheim, *Zur Frage des Arbeitsertrages im Straf- und Sicherungsvollzug* (1923).

[2] Art. 145 Italian Criminal Code; art. 376 et seq. Swiss Criminal Code; ss. 91, 98 German Draft Penal Code, 1927 (II).

voluntarily received 6*d*. a day. A fresh start was made in 1929, when the Wakefield plan included an experimental earnings scheme made possible by the co-operation of the Howard League for Penal Reform. When the prisoner, after his first twelve weeks, was promoted to the second stage, he received 3*d*. a week for his task plus extra-payment for surplus work. Kitchen and laundry workers, stokers, &c., received 3*d*. to 5*d*. and in certain cases 6*d*. to 7*d*. The Departmental Committee of 1933 was impressed with the results of this experiment.[1] Upon their express recommendation, the earnings scheme has been extended to all English prisons. During the war the earnings varied between 3*d*. and 1*s*. a week, with an average for piece-work of about 7*d*.[2] In Germany, before the First World War, the admissible maximum was 30 Pf. a day for prisoners and 20 Pf. for convicts, though the usual payments were far below this standard, e.g. 7 Pf. in Bavaria or 2 Pf. for a recidivist convict in Prussia. After the First World War Hamburg had a tariff, ranging from 10 Pf. for a juvenile in the lower stage to 45 Pf. for a special worker at the top stage. In 1929, 220 out of a daily population of 240 convicts at Untermassfeld, Thuringia, earned an average sum of 100 RM. for their savings account and an additional 50 RM. at their immediate disposal; one-third of the men forwarded up to 50 RM. to their families.[3] During the Second World War, in the wake of an almost unlimited demand for industrial labour, German prison earnings were fixed at 10 to 50 Pf. a day for prisoners, and 5 to 40 Pf. for convicts. A further reward, up to 10 RM. a month, was provided for additional work.[4]

In the United States conditions with regard to prisoners' compensations vary. In 1931 fifty-eight institutions in thirty-six states and two out of the five federal institutions paid money wages. Three further institutions in two additional states compensated the inmates either in 'good time', i.e. remission of sentence, or by an allowance. More than 47,305 prisoners, or 46 per cent. of all inmates employed, were paid in one way or another. Ten c. a day was a common wage bill. Twenty-five c. to 1 dollar seemed rather generous.[5] In 1940 only thirty states and the District of Columbia were reported to be paying financial rewards to prisoners. In the

[1] *Report on Employment of Prisoners*, i, l.c., pp. 34 and 70.

[2] *Prisons and Borstals*, p. 16.

[3] A. Krebs, in *Gefängnisse in Thüringen* (1930), pp. 75 et seq.

[4] Strafvollzugsordnung, 22 July 1940; *Amtl. Sonderveröffentlichung der Dtsch. Justiz*, No. 21; Semi-official report in 9 *Recueil* 221.

[5] L. N. Robinson, l.c., pp. 208, 203, 211.

majority of cases payment ranged between 1 and 25 c. per working day. At Auburn Prison the average pay in any one shop did not exceed 20 c., while for farm workers an average of 5 c. and a maximum of 10 c. prevailed. In Sing-Sing prisoners in the industries, paid on a piece-work basis, earned approximately 22 c. per working day, while in state shops prisoners were paid from 2 to 30 c. per day. Federal institutions are said to have a more established wage-payment policy than state prisons. Practically all prisoners employed in shops run by Federal Prison Industries, Inc., are receiving compensation. This is based either upon group piece-work or an hourly rate ranging from 3½ to 10 c. However, only a small proportion of the total of inmates are benefited by this scheme. In 1940 the federal institutions had an average population of 18,492 prisoners under sentence. Out of these only 2,938 were paid workers with an average annual earnings of 94·65 dollars per man.[1] The merits of the prevailing practice are open to question. Critics maintain that the expectations attached to such a policy and the complicated reckoning are out of proportion to the trifling amounts of money paid.[2] The application of an earnings scheme to maintenance workers offers further difficulties. Unless they are unjustly treated, adequate rates must be assessed for the remuneration of their work. Since earnings are usually paid out of the produce of the prisoners' industrial work, high payments for maintenance work curtail the funds available for the compensation of those employed in industrial occupation. With these implications an earnings scheme seems to emphasize rather than to counterbalance the artificial character of institutional life. These objections, however, affect the prevailing application rather than the principle itself. They overlook the particular function of an earnings scheme within a rational system of penal discipline, which bears no comparison with the part played by the wage bill in the life of a free worker. Even what seems negligible as a sum of money may be a target worth while striving for, an opportunity for personal choice and decision, or simply a means of access to some amenities of life which turn the scales against the strain of a life deprived of liberty. Like many other factors in prison life an earnings scheme has primarily a negative function, counteracting the disadvantages of prison life. After the recent introduction of an earnings scheme in English penal institutions, reports were appreciative of the good effect it has on the prisoners' increased interest and industry, the tempo of their work, and the

[1] *Prison Labor in the U.S., 1940*, pp. 32 et seq.

[2] Kriegsmann, p. 224.

morale in the workshops. As an incentive to speedy and accurate work an earnings scheme affects the atmosphere of an institution, helps to maintain discipline without repressive measures, and thereby creates and upholds conditions which make constructive efforts possible. At the same time, the opportunity for gaining and disposing of money or money-value is an antidote to the passive indolence of men obliged to live under unnatural restrictions. The possibility of reverting to non-earning gives something like the outside worker's liability to 'the sack' if he is worthless to the employer.

Training by Work

Uninterrupted working-time, an assessment of adequate tasks, and an earnings scheme are elements of industrial policy in penal institutions. By a well-considered use of these inducements a prison has good prospects of training the inmates *for* work. This observation primarily applies to the prisoner's work during his term. It is open to question whether a man with a good work record in prison will continue to work honestly and steadily in the world at large. With this problem, the wider issue of training *by* work suggests itself. At first sight it seems an obvious conclusion that the habit of regular work acquired in prison will persist even under changed conditions in the community. Experience, however, shows only a slight relation between good institutional work records and successful after-careers. Among ex-prisoners of the Massachusetts Reformatory, those who had been good workers in prison had a rate of 24·4 per cent. successes and of 62·2 per cent. total failures with regard to post-parole conduct, against 21·4 per cent. successes and 67·2 per cent. total failures on the part of the bad workers.[1] Most of the disappointments experienced are due to the fact that a man did not live up to the expectations which his good work record seemed to justify. This is only one illustration of the general over-estimation of enforced habits. Patterns of human behaviour are dependent on underlying motives, either conscious or unconscious. Enforced habits slacken as soon as the situation from which they arose no longer exists: when there is no power to compel their observance, a power which was doubly felt in the absence of emotional escapes and diversions. Habits acquired in unusual circumstances have a chance of persisting only if they are supported by strong motives which apply also to normal situations. The *Third Report of the Prison Inspectors* of 1838

[1] S. and E. Glueck, *Five Hundred Criminal Careers* (1930), p. 258.

testifies that the prisoner's own attitude is an essential factor: 'While enforced habits are useless, only the will operated upon by the judgement can produce an active attitude even for the post-prison time.' Regular performance of useful work certainly produces valuable educational factors: the acquisition of skill and abilities, the habit of exactness and regularity, the experience of the beneficial rhythm of work and leisure, and the satisfaction that a job has been properly done. Experience with occupational therapy in mental hospitals corroborates the observation that the ability 'to accomplish something' awakens and strengthens a person's self-esteem. This opens up an approach even to difficult patients, hastens the cure by stimulating natural interests and activities, and sustains the patient besides raising him to a higher level.[1] But the ultimate aim of a 'will operated upon by judgement' can only be achieved when those beneficial forces are deliberately linked up with the conscious effort of a constructive treatment and personal approach, with educational activities, and with planning for the future. Even when such ideal methods fall short of the desired success, they at least allow a deeper understanding of the prisoner's attitude and the obstacles impeding a successful education by work. After the First World War a social worker summed up his experience in a German prison for juveniles by emphasizing the negative attitude of the young prisoners; work appeared to them as the inevitable alternative to unbearable hardship in prison, and to want and indigence in the community.[2] Likewise an American expert said: 'The greatest lesson any man can learn is that, if he would eat, he must work, if he would enjoy the good things of life, he must earn them by honest labours, by the sweat of his brow if necessary.'[3] An English ex-prisoner with a considerable criminal career gave this verdict about training by work: 'It can hardly be said, that the Borstal system fitted lads for industrial life; but this can be said for it, that it removed the superstition, common among thieves, that hard work is something to be ashamed of.'[4]

For their right valuation such statements must be interpreted with reference to the general relationship existing between man and work in present-day society. The majority of prison inmates belong to the working class. Like many of their contemporaries

[1] D. K. Henderson, 71 *J. Ment. Sc.* 64; A. G. Thomson, ibid., p. 73.
[2] W. Herrmann, l.c., p. 38.
[3] Warden Oscar Lee of Wisconsin, quoted from L. N. Robinson, l.c., p. 160.
[4] Mark Benney, *Low Company* (1936), p. 240.

they have great mobility with frequent changes of job. Inside and outside prison much dull and monotonous work must be done. Hard and dirty manual work is indispensable even in a machine age. Rationalization of production makes work even more impersonal. While, to the few, the machine offers the fascinating experience of controlling its ingeniously developed technical potentialities, it sets the pace for the vast army of unskilled operatives. It is useless to expect from the prisoner a loyalty to, and an affection for, his work. For these would scarcely be found in the world at large among subordinate machine-hands and stevedores, refuse-collectors and street sweepers, or girls washing dishes in canteens or restaurants. The unsatisfactory relation between man and work not only sets a limit to lasting results of rehabilitation efforts: it is a much wider issue of the industrial age. Training by work in prison must therefore allow for the experience of modern industrial psychology.

A deeper insight into the psychological aspects of work shows that the forms of industrial occupations produce results surprisingly similar to the effects of imprisonment.[1] The curse of monotonous manual work is boredom rather than toilsomeness. Like the prisoner, the repetition worker resorts to day-dreaming, and this endangers his reliability and feeling of security. He, too, is exposed to mental fatigue. The work for which the majority of prisoners are eligible seems to strengthen rather than overcome the effects of prison life. The remedies for maintaining personal initiative and contentment are the same, whether healthy emotions are suppressed by dull work or by loss of liberty. Both adverse situations must be counteracted by 'a long-range interest and purpose'.[2] In the long run fear and want are insufficient motives for work, as they are unable to prevent the criminal from further wrong-doing. Much has been gained if emotional incentives arise from the work itself. It may be that its technical ingenuity appeals to the operator's mind, that he sees his way 'to make a good job of it', is satisfied by the personal responsibility involved, or is interested in the outcome. These observations make a strong case for variety in prison occupations and a method of assigning work so thought out as to enable many prisoners to be raised above the level of primitive mass production. Furthermore they provide useful hints about work and its economic function in prison education. Reports

[1] The discussion which follows is based on A. Barratt Brown, *The Machine and the Worker* (1934), chapters VIII–X; M. G. Dickson, 28 *Soc. Rev.* 295.

[2] A. Barratt Brown, l.c., p. 81.

on how prisoners co-operated in making toys for children, or responded to increased requests for the war effort, show that it is possible to arouse positive interest in spite of repetition and enforced labour. In favourable circumstances the prisoners' co-operation has even been won by enlisting their aid in maintaining the high standards of a model institution which might influence the cause of penal reform. Thus, 'social motives'[1] might be created by linking the worker's interest with the purpose and final destination of his products and promoting a healthy group loyalty. However, inside and outside prisons the dull and monotonous character of the work will often frustrate such efforts. Other forces must therefore counterbalance the detrimental effects of boring routine work. Such antidotes are an outlet for creative activities and are provided by hobbies and spare-time occupations directed at 'doing things', and the stabilizing effect of a fair prospect of 'social security'. The same applies to the prisoner. As early as 1883 Lady Meath founded the Brabazon Employment Society to provide workhouses and infirmaries with materials, tools, and instructors for artistic handicrafts such as cross-stitch, fine art embroidery, Smyrna rugs, and so on. In 1901 Glasgow prison was the first penal institution in Great Britain to enlist the co-operation of Brabazon visitors. By the time of the First World War much valuable work had been done, not only among women, but also among epileptic Borstal boys and weak-minded young prisoners. In the experience of the Society nowhere was the power to produce something beautiful a greater help than in the midst of prison monotony with its suppression of self.[2] Prisons have their 'artists' producing drawings, plastics, and woodwork. Such leisure activities are supposed to benefit the performance of ordinary task work.

When the prisoner knows that his family is being kept safe from want and disruption, and if he sees before him a fair chance of a fresh start after his release, it will be easier for him to settle down with his work in prison. Welfare work has a particular function during the prison term. These psychological observations show that, once the rehabilitation of the prisoner has been adopted as the guiding principle, all the factors of prison life are interrelated. Even a technical subject like prison labour cannot be isolated from spare-time activities, prison education, and welfare service.

[1] A. Barratt Brown, l.c., pp. 127 et seq.

[2] Kind information from Miss Jean Alexander, Hon. Secretary Brabazon Employment Society.

In view of the underlying purpose of prison discipline the industrial policy of penal institutions must be subordinated to the twofold object of training for work and training by work. This principle applies to the selection of the sort of work suitable for prisoners. Since they are not essentially different from ordinary men and women the best prison work is that which corresponds to the work done outside. Prison workshops are training centres, and should therefore be model plants, not only in order to reach efficient working methods, but also to demonstrate the dignity of work. Instead, prison shops frequently retain obsolete manual methods for tasks which, in the world at large, have long been taken over by the machine. In most countries the introduction of technical equipment, especially in State-use workshops, has been unduly delayed. The reasons have been lack of funds and the fear that machinery might deprive even more 'prison hands' of full employment. These objections against modernization have been strengthened by a theoretical prejudice. The observation that an increasing number of criminals seemed to be recruited from growing industrial centres was taken as an argument that prisoners at least should be spared the curse of impersonal machine work. Nothing could be more unreal. Incompetent and antiquated work breeds contempt and makes the prisoner still less capable of competing with his contemporaries in the community. Before the Second World War experts observed that, with full allowance for exceptions like Wormwood Scrubs and Maidstone, workshops in English prisons were still too ill-equipped for a successful vocational training and for making a man fit to earn his livelihood in a world of relentless competition.[1] Prisons have to train men for the world as it is. For a great number of prisoners, regular employment in factory work would mean maintaining, if not improving, their economic and social status. An expert before the New York State Crime Commission maintained that many ex-prisoners had to go back to work at machines; 'to acquire the habit of industrial work', to become 'machine-minded' should therefore be the proper aim for some 40 per cent. of the prisoners.[2] In view of the poor abilities and unsatisfactory work habits of a considerable proportion of prisoners, tending a machine implies a good training in alertness and perseverance.

The assignment of the individual prisoner to the particular

[1] L. Page, *passim*; *Report on Employment of Prisoners*, i, l.c., p. 64, s. 150, and p. 72, ss. 173 et seq.

[2] H. B. Gill, quoted from L. N. Robinson, l.c., p. 161.

job is an important question of classification. Due allowance for his abilities and prospects in conjunction with considerations of safe custody may determine the committal to a particular institution—agricultural or industrial institutions or establishments with opportunity for building and construction. Within an institution of 500 and more prisoners the variety of jobs with different demands on skill, reliability, and independence offers further possibilities of individualization. Vocational guidance is a valuable element of a classification service. Its present methods arrive at much the same conclusions as common-sense experience, but they help the examiner and adviser to detect probable impediments and prospects. In a Borstal Institution 69 per cent. of the boys allocated to jobs after a psychological examination of their abilities and characteristics of temperament proved to be good workers, as against 45·6 per cent. of a control group assigned to work by routine methods.[1] A wrong selection of work can contribute to initial or persisting criminality. It is less frequent, but not impossible for the right assignment to a particular trade to be the main cause of the prisoner's readjustment; e.g. a prisoner with a good family background, after a change of his environment, may be kept straight by a persistent ambition to enter the engraving trade, which originated in the vocational experience at a reformatory.[2] Such instances emphasize the need for vocational training as an essential part of a reconstructive programme. This has often been suggested with regard to reformative schemes for juveniles and adolescents. Owing to the composition of the average prison population a small proportion of inmates only will be fit to learn a fully skilled trade. For these men no opportunity should be lost to make and keep them fit for the qualified job they are able to perform. For certain other types, too, to understand one particular job thoroughly may be an educational success in itself and prove beneficial, even if they have to earn their livelihood by doing unskilled or mere machine work.

For the last sixty years open-air work has been recommended in theoretical discussion. It is beneficial to the prisoner's health and superior to the monotony and artificial seclusion between prison walls or the solitary work in a cell. There is, however, an unrealistic bent in the slogan 'reclaiming man by reclaiming the soil'. Such romanticism idealizes something which is hard and

[1] A. Rodger, *A Borstal Experiment in Vocational Guidance* (1937), p. 21.

[2] Case of Antonio, from S. and E. Glueck, *Criminal Careers in Retrospect* (1943), pp. 65 et seq.

often dull work. A comparison of southern chain gangs with the honour camps of the north states of the Union shows that even from the point of view of prison labour a resort to trust and responsibility is indispensable. Since the labour problem cannot be isolated, educational and recreational facilities must be provided for the men working at farm annexes, in road gangs, quarries, marshes, and so on. The *Wickersham Report* of 1931 made detailed suggestions for the co-ordination of road work with a regular educational programme. 'The maintenance of a properly staffed library, the provision of entertainment in the form of a radio set, an occasional educational movie, deliberate cultivation through correspondence courses, and regular visits of the educational director would give such work an educational objective.' In such circumstances farm work, road-building, land reclamation, and afforestation with the change in environment and interests and the almost unlimited amount of work available would be the best and most feasible means of employing many of the considerable proportion of minimum security prisoners.[1]

This observation points to the close connexion between prison labour and educational activities. As in other sectors of adult education, lessons and discussion in prison should be related to practical work experience. Their first aim should be to develop the prisoner's special abilities and to make him feel that he is an expert in carpentry, gardening, or even domestic work. From such vocational training teaching may proceed to general education, taking the work, the materials, and the economic functions of the products as the first objective, thus building the world anew around the prisoner's work.[2] There is a gradual, rather than substantial, difference between vocational and general education. In a deeper sense the latter, too, is a contributory factor in training for work. What has been observed in the community at large is equally true with regard to prison education, viz. 'the result of an all-round liberal education is not only a good citizen, but a good workman, observant and adaptable to new methods and alternative jobs'.[3]

The success of such efforts depends on the co-ordination of labour management and educational services. Practical experience as well as psychological observation have shown that it is futile to expect lasting results from enforced work alone. The

[1] *Wickersham Report*, ix. 103.
[2] A. H. MacCormick, *Education of Adult Prisoners* (1931).
[3] George Cadbury, *Education in Industry* (1938), p. 6.

same is true of a vocational education which is not supported by the experience of real work done for a useful purpose. Under the pressure of unemployment some American prison administrations tried to fill the empty time with education as a substitute for employment. As the experience in prisoner-of-war camps shows, cultural activities and academic courses overcome frustration and emptiness if they are directed to definite attainable targets. Isolated instruction defeats its own ends. To erect, for purposes of training, a brick wall which will afterwards be destroyed can only evoke the same cynicism and bitterness as did treadmill and crank in bygone days.

Within a Progressive Stage system the question suggests itself whether type, duration, and remuneration of work should be affected by the prisoner's grade. A gradual improvement in the prisoner's job and pay seemed to recommend itself as an impressive way of marking his progress from lower to higher stages. Sir Walter Crofton let the prisoner proceed from irksome work and drudgery at the initial stage to higher forms of industrial occupation. Otherwise, he felt, 'the prisoner would fail to acknowledge the benefit of a true industrial labour'. In Borstal Institutions the rule prevails that new-comers are occupied for the first two to three months with house cleaning and other domestic work; then for six months they are assigned to a labour party; and only then, if suitable, are they sent to a workshop. The Departmental Committee of 1933 raised the objection that this system shortens the time for industrial training and delays its beginning. In 1933, out of 2,000 Borstal boys, only 300 were occupied in workshops.[1] If prison labour is meant to train the inmate for a useful life in the community, work should be allocated exclusively on the ground that it fits the worker. Whatever his place in the classification system, a man should be required to do his best in the job supposed to fit his abilities. At the same time it is a sound reflection of the life in the community that a master earns more than an apprentice. Progress on the scale to higher grades should find its expression in a growing individual responsibility and independence with regard to the performance of work and in a higher proportion of the money earned left at the prisoner's own disposal. Such a scheme demonstrates the dignity of work and emphasizes with its progressive stages not so much a lessening of pressure and hardship as a putting the prisoner's character to the test by temptations and responsibilities.

[1] *Report on Employment of Prisoners*, i, l.c., p. 45, ss. 98 et seq.

Promotion may be used as an inducement to do good work. In several institutions in the western states of the Union prisoners are paid for their work in 'good time'.[1] For a certain number of satisfactory days' work one day is commuted from the sentence. Such a scheme prevails either as a substitute for money payments or as a supplementary reward. The latter applies to prison industries in federal institutions where prisoners occupied with industrial work are paid wages plus two to five days' 'industrial good time'.[2] It has been said, in support of such methods, that prisoners faced with the alternative of money or remission invariably 'want out'. However, the granting of credit marks for the performance of the ordinary task tends to become rather automatic, while money payments can more easily be made flexible with due allowance for output and quality of work. A money-earnings scheme is therefore preferable. This does not mean that no consideration should be given to the prisoner's work within a graduated system of penal discipline. Under a scheme of negative marks, bad work-habits together with other unsatisfactory behaviour may delay or even rule out parole, while under a positive system the assessment of the prisoner's adjustment, as a condition for his promotion or release on parole, takes his work record into account.

OBSTACLES TO A RATIONAL SOLUTION OF THE LABOUR PROBLEM

Individualization in the allocation of work, appropriate incentives, co-ordination of labour management and educational service, and Progressive Stage methods which do not interfere with the needs of industrial policy are the instruments of a constructive programme of training for work and training by work. The realization of such plans has to face considerable obstacles from within and without. Prison industries are running against heavy odds. With the exception of institutions where convicts are serving long sentences prison workshops are hampered by the constant change of men coming and going for terms of different length. The most serious difficulty is the low working-ability of the average prison population. Prisoners, though not different from people at large, are a negative selection with regard to ability and inclination for regular work. According to an English

[1] L. N. Robinson, l.c., p. 207.

[2] *Attorney General's Survey*, v. 360; *Prison Labor in the U.S., 1940*, p. 37.

observer 69 per cent. of the prisoners seem fit for any form of hard labour in the community, 18 per cent. for intermediate and light labour, 11 per cent. for light labour only, and 2 per cent. unfit for labour at all. As to the quality of work which these men are expected to perform, some 30 per cent. of the first offenders might be retained by a private employer in the competitive world at large, while only a few of the recidivists would escape dismissal if a private employer were going to reduce his staff.[1] A corresponding investigation in New York assessed 40 per cent. as capable of a productive re-education, though half of them were below average intelligence, but above feeble-mindedness; a further 40 per cent. capable of productive work by tending machines which fix the standard of production; and the remaining 20 per cent. as totally unfit to meet the ordinary requirements of modern society.[2] Even in a shoe shop at Massachusetts State Prison, which evidently represents a positive selection among prisoners, 56 out of 146 inmate workers proved incompetent, indifferent, and unco-operative.[3]

These adverse personal conditions explain the low output of prison industries. Obsolete working methods have sometimes contributed to the same result. Working with inefficient machinery is not only uneconomic, but frustrates training by work. It is difficult to assess the produce of prison labour qualitatively and to compare it with the output of corresponding work in the community. Estimates have sometimes been based upon the crude assumption that the *per capita* value of prison labour could be computed by totalling the compensation paid by contractors, the returns of public-account industries, the sums either paid or assessed for public-use goods and maintenance work, and dividing this sum by the number of the prisoners employed or even by the total of all prisoners. Before the First World War a German long-term prisoner in large institutions was expected to earn for the State one-third to one-fourth, a short-term prisoner one-fifth to one-tenth or less, the wage of a free worker (Krohne). In the United States, in 1885, the efficiency of the work of some 50,000 prisoners had been assessed at 78 per cent. of the corresponding number of free labour, and in 1905 at 64 per cent.[4] In 1929 prison shops in Massachusetts were estimated to work at about

[1] N. East, in *Report on Employment of Prisoners*, i, l.c., pp. 14 et seq.
[2] *New York Prison Survey Committee, 1920*, quoted from H. B. Gill, 157 *Annals* 166.
[3] H. E. Field and R. S. Winslow, 23 *Journal* 205.
[4] H. B. Gill, 157 *Annals* 99, with reference to *Convict Labor, 1886*, p. 291; *1905*, p. 312.

one-third the full efficiency.[1] In the same year the *per capita* work output of New York prisoners was one-tenth the produce of corresponding free labour.[2] A critical English investigation credits one-sixth of the value of prison-made goods for labour, and consequently assesses the total value of the work of 6,700 prisoners engaged in manufacture and farming at £46,400 a year, or approximately £7 *per capita* as against the official estimation of £36. 12*s*. 0*d*.[3] None of these divergent estimates is free from more or less arbitrary assumptions. Even so, they present sufficient corroborating evidence of the prevailing low standards of efficiency in the usual prison industries.

Even in the face of such poor results, almost throughout its whole history prison labour has been denounced by trade and free labour as unfair competition. This is a much-contested issue between prison reformers on the one hand, and pressure groups from industry and labour on the other. While the average prisoner is markedly below the normal output of free labour, the total of prisoners engaged in industrial work is a negligible proportion of the labour operative in the same field. In 1923 American prison-made goods reached the volume of 0·12 per cent. of all goods manufactured in establishments doing business of 5,000 dollars and more.[4] Compared with the corresponding branches of free industries, in 1940 American prison workshops produced goods of the total value of 0·38 per cent. the output of the same trades in the community during the preceding year.[5] Even with such a negligible percentage of production, prison industries can prove harmful to private business if they concentrate on a few selected articles or dominate local markets and thereby develop a monopoly. By the end of the last century skilled coopers are said to have almost been driven out of Chicago by a monopoly on the part of the prisons.[6] Recently a considerable proportion of American shirt production has been done in prisons. On the other hand, certain primitive methods of manufacturing baskets, brooms, and brushes have long shifted away from private enterprise and become traditional occupations for prisoners and inmates of other institutions without much attraction for free labour. Even in such

[1] H. B. Gill before the New York State Crime Commission, quoted from L. N. Robinson, l.c., p. 234.

[2] L. N. Robinson, l.c., p. 60.

[3] *Report on Employment of Prisoners*, i, l.c., p. 39, s. 83.

[4] L. N. Robinson, l.c., p. 53.

[5] *Prison Labor in the U.S., 1940*, p. 24.

[6] L. N. Robinson, l.c., p. 62.

special institutional trades, prisoners are still a minority of the workers employed. Before the First World War the number of Prussian prisoners engaged in carpentry under the Contract system corresponded to 0·32 per cent. of carpenters in the community, the number of prisoners working in shoeshops for contractors to 0·44 per cent. of shoemakers, while the corresponding figure for the manufacture of brushes was 16 per cent. In 1940 ninety-seven different industries were operative in American state and federal prisons. In no more than eight of these did the output exceed 1 per cent. the value of goods produced by the same trade in the community. This list was headed by cordage and twine with 6·4 per cent., and stamped and pressed metal products with 2·2 per cent.[1]

In view of the qualitative conditions of prison industries it has been asserted that prison workshops rely on tax revenues for capital investment and compensation of economic losses, are independent of labour disputes, or may even 'sell' prison labour for far less than its economic value. Against this must be set the low output of prison labour and in many cases the restrictive clauses of prison contracts, by which prison administrations accommodate private enterprise to the exigencies of prison routine. Difficulties arising from the selection and organization of prison work may be overcome by co-operation between the administration and the representatives of trade and labour. In principle, however, the case against prison competition is untenable. The administration of criminal justice is a public function of the State. The economic loss through crime is considerable, and far surpasses the alleged detrimental effects of prison labour on private enterprise. What is indispensable for social readjustment must be accepted. But apart from rational weighing-up, men and women in prison are members of a wider community. Neither crime nor punishment would justify forfeiture of the right to work.

In spite of a strong case for prison labour, administrations have again and again been exposed to the pressure of social and political forces. Fierce opposition came from craftsmen's guilds in Germany and organized labour in the United States. As long as economic pressure groups fought the Contract system they seemed to join hands with prison reformers. When they attacked the Public-account system they seriously threatened the employment of prisoners in countries with a high ratio of prisoners and a less developed State-use system. But even the latter system has

[1] *Prison Labor in the U.S., 1940*, p. 24.

been denounced by the organizations of trade and enterprises as an encroachment of state socialism on competitive economy. In 1928 a leading representative of German craftsmen protested against a resolution of the Prussian Diet, which demanded, for training purposes, rationalization of prison labour and the use of suitable machines.[1] The most hostile attitude towards prison labour prevails in the United States. Even an official *Report of the Department of Labor* alleged that 'no matter which system is used, prison labour competes with free labour to some extent, in the final analysis, to the detriment of the labour of free men'.[2] Organized labour in the United States was mainly responsible for recent legislation which excluded prison-made goods almost entirely from the open market. Since previous attempts at labelling and restricting prison-made goods by state legislation were held to be unconstitutional, Congress enacted in 1929 the Hawes-Cooper Act which divested prison-made goods of their inter-state character and made it possible to subject the products of prison industries of another state to the same restrictions which apply to goods manufactured in the state where they shall be sold. This Act came into force in 1934.[3] Its enforcement was tightened up by the Ashurst-Sumners Act of 1935 which forbids transport companies to accept prison goods for delivery to districts where they have been excluded from the market by state legislation.[4] Since these two Federal Acts are merely 'enabling', their effect depends on the response of the member states to this opportunity for banning from the home market not only goods made in their own prisons, but also products manufactured by prisoners of other states in the Union. In 1931 it was expected that the effects of the Hawes-Cooper Act, while enforcing certain adjustments and a considerable shifting from a few big contractors to a number of small business men, would not fatally check the employment of prisoners.[5] Under the impact of the depression, however, state legislation freed industry from the odious competition of imported prison-goods more thoroughly than had been anticipated. While in 1929 only four states confined their prison industry to an exclusive State-use

[1] K. Lubert, President of the Chamber of Craftsmen in Berlin, in *Strafvollzug in Preussen* (1928), p. 231.

[2] 'Laws relating to Prison Labor', *Bulletin 596 of the U.S. Bureau of Labor Statistics* (1933), p. 1.

[3] *U.S. Code of Laws*, Supplement 1925–32, Title 49, Ch. 2 A, s. 65.—'Laws relating to Prison Labor' (1933), p. 134.

[4] *Attorney General's Survey*, v. 34, n. 123.

[5] H. B. Gill, 157 *Annals* 91.

system, up to 1933 twenty-nine further states passed legislation excluding prison-made goods from the market.[1] As a result of the Hawes-Cooper and Ashurst-Sumners Acts, the legislation of a state with an insignificant prison industry could cripple the production under administrations with large prison industries. In 1933 three-fifths of prison-made goods in the United States were sold in states other than that of their origin.[2] In certain branches the ratio of inter-state export was higher, e.g. for shoes 86 per cent. and garments 81 per cent.[3] The drastic curtailment of these industries is mainly responsible for the unemployment in state and federal prisons. According to the *Attorney General's Survey* 'with the passage of those laws, the industrial prison was eliminated. In 1935, for the great majority of prisoners, the penitentiary system had again reverted to its original status: punishment and custody.'[4] In 1940, when the total value of goods manufactured in prison for the open market had decreased by 80 per cent. as compared with 1923, one-fourth of this reduced output, or goods worth some 2¼ million dollars, were still sold outside the state of their origin.[5] In the same year, however, Congress passed a further Act, which, with certain exceptions, prohibits the export of prison-made goods from one state into another.[6]

The war changed American prison labour. While the number of committals declined, the demand for labour did not halt before prison gates. The population of state and federal prisons and reformatories fell from the record figure of more than 190,000 in 1940 to less than 120,000 in 1943. In the same year American prisoners produced war materials worth 10 million dollars. Ninety-eight per cent. of the federal prison industries were engaged in war-work. Twenty-five thousand state prisoners worked in agriculture, 10 per cent. more than in 1942.[7] It remains to be seen how American prisons will adjust themselves to post-war conditions. By an appropriate accommodation for minimum security prisoners, they will be able to shift a considerable proportion to agricultural, road, and other constructive work. Is it too much to hope that in the era of reconstruction a general policy of full employment will accept and even demand the industrial occupation of men and women serving sentences in penal institutions?

[1] *Attorney General's Survey*, v. 32.

[2] 'Laws relating to Prison Labor', l.c., p. 1.

[3] H. B. Gill, l.c., p. 92.

[4] *Attorney General's Survey*, v. 34.

[5] *Prison Labor in the U.S., 1940*, p. 27.

[6] Ibid., p. 1.

[7] J. V. Bennet, in *American Yearbook, 1943*, p. 584.

CHAPTER X

THE PERSONAL APPROACH

PENAL and reformative treatment has a twofold aspect. Prison labour is the essence and ultimate justification of imprisonment as a legal punishment. But even in prison man is more than a machine-hand. After the prescribed working hours, outside shops, stables, and kitchen, there is need and opportunity for education, the provision of books, spare-time activities, organized recreation, welfare work, and religious services. These all imply a personal approach to the prisoner, a direct working from man to man, and an appeal to the whole personality rather than an enforced compliance with certain rules of behaviour and standards of work.

The personal approach to the prisoner is an indispensable element in the process of social readjustment. It helps him to face squarely his true position, to understand the reasons for what he is required to do, and to substitute positive motives for mere obedience to orders. But it has even deeper effects as an opportunity for the prisoner to experience, by personal contact, the reality of higher values. Truth, honesty, loyalty, unselfishness, and a striving for knowledge and inspiration even under austere living conditions can only be taught if the prisoner meets men whose lives are testifying to the reality of these values. Prisoners are often cynics. Their past and their environment seldom foster confidence in man's moral qualities and spiritual values. Many a prisoner may well say what a man wrote to one of the early pioneers of the Danish Folk High School: 'We have no childhood, we are never young, and we have no soul in our homes.'[1] The prison might be the first and perhaps the last opportunity of meeting men whose intentions are pure and whose attempts to fulfil them sincere. Preaching abstract ethical doctrines is of no avail. The adoption of moral standards and spiritual aims is not an intellectual process. There must be an inner experience, overwhelming and convincing, supported by personal links of affection and sympathy. A man will try hard not to disappoint someone he has learnt to trust and respect, 'his' Governor or prison visitor. He will not do what he knows is wrong as long as he feels himself bound not to fail the chaplain or welfare officer who once helped and trusted him. Such personal links are invaluable if moral standards and a new

[1] John C. Møller and Katherine Watson, *Education in Democracy* (1944), p. 41.

pattern of life are to be inculcated, but although more effective than enforced habits, they are a first step only. Ultimately the inner obligation must be transferred from personal dependence to wider objectives: to family and country, calling and profession, a good cause, and the general values of ethics and religion.

The personal approach as the substance of reformative treatment outside working hours applies to the proper use of leisure. In the world at large leisure is not a mere absence of work, but something positive, an occupation complementary to work, intended to satisfy those demands of an individual which remain unfulfilled by his work alone.[1] Leisure presupposes work and should alternate with it in a healthy rhythm. Unemployment is not leisure—hence the difficulty of overcoming its effects inside and outside prison walls by spare-time activities. Leisure is a challenge as well as an opportunity. It implies a new task: 'education for leisure'.[2]

If the aim of legal punishment is adaptation to the community, the prisoners need the wholesome experience of a full working day, but also of a sound rhythm between work and leisure. Even more than in the world at large, under the artificial conditions of prison life monotonous work needs an outlet for imaginative thinking and creative activities. 'Education for leisure' is an important factor of crime prevention. Many offences are committed owing to the temptations of an existence without any personal satisfaction, of a life of dull work and drudgery which is easily thrown away for a criminal career. Whatever brings joy and inspiration into a humble way of living helps to make life worth while and strengthens the barriers against the incitements of illicit gains.

Sincere efforts to make a personal approach and teach prisoners how to use their spare time constructively affect the whole atmosphere of an institution. When the staff is united in the purpose of rehabilitation, every officer will feel the result as a help in the performance of his particular duties. Social worker, teacher, prison visitor, and chaplain have a special obligation to their fellow officers. Their effort and example having more favourable conditions than the daily routine in hall and workshop are a counter-balance to the enervating monotony of prison life for prison officers as well as prisoners.

[1] E. Barker, *Use of Leisure* (London, n.y.); H. Durant, *The Problem of Leisure* (1938).

[2] K. Hahn, *Education for Leisure* (1938).

EDUCATION

As a recognized aim of penal policy, education has a twofold meaning. In a wider sense it comprises all constructive efforts for the prisoner's social readjustment and rehabilitation. Thus far, it is almost identical with the object of a progressive penal administration. In a narrower sense, education means organized teaching by lessons, lectures, discussion, or tutorial courses. In the following section education will be discussed in the second, technical meaning of the word.[1]

In a rudimentary form, prison education originated with the rise of imprisonment as an ordinary legal punishment. The establishment of the Dutch Houses of Correction provided for a 'predikant and schoolmaster' who should exercise a pastoral influence and teach the juveniles writing and reading.[2] Howard found that in Holland 'great care is taken to give the prisoners moral and religious instruction and reform their manners, for their own and the public good'.[3] When Sir Walter Crofton inaugurated the Progressive Stage system in Ireland he gave the prison teacher comprehensive tasks in vocational training and personal after-care work. As early as 1847, in the penal institutions of New York, the law provided for the appointment of instructors whose duty it was 'with and under the supervision of the chaplain to give instruction in the useful branches of an English education to a selected number of convicts'.[4]

As a rule, the prison school of the nineteenth century was a modest undertaking with regard to its aims and achievements. In England the prison administration claimed the role of the Educational Authority to make up for the defects or absence of ordinary elementary school education. Up to the eighties, when compulsory school attendance—operative from 1870—made itself gradually felt with the new generation, every third prisoner was illiterate. In order to teach these illiterates reading and writing, 'capable and intelligent warders' acted as schoolmasters under the chaplain's supervision.[5] Originally, lessons were given to individual prisoners in their cells. A Departmental Committee of 1896 recommended an increase of the usual lessons from fifteen minutes twice a week to twenty minutes three times a week. Classes

[1] L. Frede, in Bumke, pp. 294–309; Austin H. MacCormick, *The Education of Adult Prisoners* (1931); Walter M. Wallack, Glenn M. Kendall, Howard L. Briggs, *Education within Prison Walls* (1939).

[2] v. Hippel, 18 *ZStW* 462 et seq.

[3] John Howard, *State of Prisons* (3rd ed. 1784), p. 45.

[4] W. M. Wallack, G. M. Kendall, H. L. Briggs, l.c., p. 4.

[5] Ruggles-Brise, p. 126.

seemed inexpedient, even for juveniles, since 'in prisons in large towns mischievous, idle and badly-disposed boys' would make the association baneful. Only in convict prisons were classes held, since convicts worked in association in any case.[1]

After the First World War conspicuous efforts were made to work out an educational policy for English prisons. Local Educational Authorities were asked to lend certified teachers for elementary and continuation classes in institutions for young prisoners. Lectures, which the Departmental Committee of 1896 had tentatively recommended for the benefit of a few prisoners,[2] were arranged on the initiative of the chaplains. In larger prisons the men were assembled, under the presidency of the chaplain, for debates and discussions. An important departure occurred in 1923, when, under the auspices of the Board of Education, the Adult Education Scheme was put into operation. Before the Second World War 400 men and women volunteered as teachers for evening classes after the hours of associated work. The subjects were educational in a wide sense of the word, including academic topics such as history, mathematics, and languages, vocational subjects such as shorthand, book-keeping, and needlework, and general subjects such as play-reading, music, and Bible study. In 1936–7 more than 10,000 prisoners were reached by this scheme. Local educational advisers co-operated with the Governors in enlisting voluntary teachers and arranging classes. From time to time the teachers were invited to general conferences at the Home Office.[3] Unfortunately the war put a temporary end to this scheme.

In Germany the Principles of 1897 provided that in institutions for juveniles the prisoners should have lessons 'in the subjects taught in elementary schools'. Adult prisoners under thirty with terms exceeding three months were eligible 'as far as they were still in need of the same instruction'. As a rule the prison school consisted of a lower and higher course, followed by a continuation school. Equipment and methods were those used in elementary schools. Before the First World War wider aims were ruled out, owing to the view that lessons for adults were psychologically objectionable and lectures incompatible with prison discipline.[4] The post-war reforms affected the scope and aims of prison education. According to the Prussian Prison Regulations of 1923 the

[1] *Report of the Departmental Committee on the Education and Moral Instruction of Prisoners in Local and Convict Prisons* (1896), pp. 1, 23, 41.

[2] Ibid., p. 69.

[3] Fox, pp. 99 et seq.; J. A. F. Watson, *Meet the Prisoner* (1939), pp. 127 et seq.

[4] Kriegsmann, pp. 235 et seq.

object of the prison school was to 'lift the prisoners morally, stimulate them mentally, and fill the gaps of their knowledge'. The teaching of young prisoners should be adapted to the curricula of continuation and vocational schools. A Prison School Order of 1924[1] gave warning against the constant alternation of question and answer in the teaching of new subjects and the repeating of old ones, and recommended discussions, debates, and papers as means of a directed self-instruction. The principal subjects were: personal and civil life, German, arithmetic, industrial, commercial, or agricultural vocational courses, domestic science and needlework, drawing, hygiene, gymnastics, and singing. Special courses of one to two hours a week up to six months could be offered to qualified prisoners. The realization of such schemes suffered from the small number of teachers available. As a rule, during the twenties, there was one teacher for every 100 to 150 prisoners. Prisoners used to have about two hours a week. Progressive reformers wished to extend this to an hour a day.[2] Most regulations emphasized the importance of this service by the provision that the time for lessons should be set aside from ordinary working hours. Only Thuringia and Brunswick followed the English pattern in that they instituted an evening school after a full uninterrupted working day.

In the United States, with her vast number of prisoners and the twin curse of overcrowding and unemployment, there still seems much space for the extension of educational facilities. In 1936–7, among the male prisoners of state prisons, less than 35,000 were enrolled in educational activities, while in camps and cellular prisons 100,000 did not take part in a training course of any kind.[3] Fourteen state prisons had no educational programme at all; in ten prisons, classes, mostly for illiterates, but also on commercial subjects, were held several evenings a week; in forty-five prisons there were regular prison day schools. Contrary to English practice, in America the prison evening school is a 'relic of the past', with little or no significance for constructive treatment.[4] On the positive side, the *Attorney General's Survey* of 1939 lists twenty-four state prisons as the vanguard of a new educational policy. The initiative has often been due to a newly appointed full-time director who would make use of social case-work and enlist inmate

[1] Klein-Wackermann-Wutzdorff, *Vorschriften über Verwaltung und Vollzug in den Gefangenenanstalten der Preuss. Justizverwaltung* (1924), p. 680.

[2] L. Frede, l.c., p. 300.

[3] *Attorney General's Survey*, v. 61.

[4] Ibid., p. 238, and *passim* for the discussion which follows.

teachers for individualized instruction. In St. Quentin, Ca., the educational director worked with a staff of one hundred inmate helpers, all of them with practical and theoretical qualifications in education. In Wisconsin the change came with the provision of reading courses by the public library. Pennsylvania and New York benefited by the central direction of state bureaux or boards of correction. These and similar further schemes worked by day school courses, vocational training related to shop practice, and correspondence courses up to university extension work. There is a tendency to replace classes by individual tuition.

These instances from different countries illustrate the trend of the recent development. From a substitute for ineffective elementary education the prison school becomes a branch of adult education. Like prison labour, education in prison cannot be isolated from the corresponding problems in the world at large, of which it is a fragment. In the recent past vocational training has steadily extended its scope, and this process has by no means come to an end. The revolutionary development, however, is the rise of adult education. Varying in historical origin and principal outlook, similar movements in several countries have contributed towards a great adventure of the human mind. Denmark looks back to a hundred years' tradition of her Folk High Schools. They are rural residential institutions with a strong communal life and a curriculum of cultural subjects related to the country and its history. Under the influence of this example a similar movement developed in Sweden, where the idea of people's colleges was adapted to the needs of urban industrial workers.[1] About the turn of the century, in England, the university extension movement and educational forces from the co-operative adult school movement brought about the Workers' Educational Association. Its characteristic feature is tutorial classes for the study of present-day social and economic problems and their historical background, though classes are not limited to these subjects.[2] Furthermore there are in England and Wales ten residential adult colleges, more of Scandinavian pattern, which affect some 300 pupils.[3] After the First World War German adult education developed on three different lines, viz. rural residential schools with an ideological or religious bias, outwardly modelled on the Danish pattern; 'neutral' evening schools (Thuringia) appealing to the young

[1] Møller and Watson, l.c.; F. M. Foster, *School for Life* (1943).

[2] A. Mansbridge, *An Adventure in Working-Class Education* (1920).

[3] F. M. Foster, l.c., pp. 90 and 92.

generation of workers interested in social studies, geography, and modern languages, and resembling the English W.E.A.; and finally, educational instruments for the political emancipation of the working class. Nearly all of them adopted forms of communal life from the German youth movement. When, in the teeth of the general depression and mass unemployment, the American National Youth Administration established small centres for educational activities and the occupation of young people, Danish models provided valuable suggestions.[1]

Adult education is a universal spiritual movement in our time.[2] It has created new demands and unforeseen possibilities. Grundtvig, the 'father' of the Danish Folk High School, believed that only barbarians and tyrants could imagine that 'the root and kernel of the people . . . does not need any more enlightenment than can be obtained behind the plough, in the workshop, on the ship and behind the counter.'[3] There is indeed a genuine desire to strive hard for 'the means for life rather than for sheer livelihood.'[4] New methods of instruction have been developed. Grundtvig propagated the 'living word', an unorthodox, vivid, and comprehensive presentation of the subject. England developed the tutorial class, Germany the *Rundgespräch* and *Arbeitsgemeinschaft*. No longer do pupils exhaust their energies in answering the teachers' questions, but teacher and student unite in a common effort to find out the truth in a gradual progress by mutual contributions. Since school attainments in the past were often insufficient as a basis for further studies, ways and means had to be found to build upon the student's practical experience.

This experience applies to prison education no less than to any other field of adult education. In prison, as elsewhere, no greater educational mistake could be made than to under-estimate the students' capacity and demands, if only the subjects are presented in the appropriate manner.[5] Even if the target is elementary knowledge of the three R's, approach, text-book, and tuition ought not to be those applied to children. The educational effect of the atmosphere should not be overlooked. Lessons should be free of repressive elements, apt to elicit the students' self-confidence, to encourage their co-operation, and thus express something of the

[1] D. C. Fisher, *Our Young Folks* (1943).
[2] R. Livingstone, *Future in Education* (1941).
[3] Motto to Møller–Watson, l.c.
[4] Frequent quotation; probable source a French thesis by Camille Riboud, referred to by Mansbridge, l.c., p. 58.
[5] For an illustration see E. Roellenbleck, 113 *Bl. GefgKd.* 284.

dignity of knowledge and learning. Teaching prisoners 'through the bars' is degrading for teacher and pupil alike.

Adult education depends on the students' own interests and initiative. A prison school, therefore, is well advised to link its subjects as closely as possible with what concerns the inmates in their own sphere of life. Such links between the individual and the wider issues of the community are in themselves an educational achievement. This may be illustrated by the following 'social studies units', worked out for New York state institutions: 'To work and not to work', 'How do people depend on each other in modern life?', 'Social Security—for whom?', 'Personality—can I do anything about mine?'[1] At the same time the prison school —more than other adult education—aims at vocational training. The free worker seeks further knowledge even if he enjoys a fully satisfactory status in his work and calling. The prisoner should be made fit to earn his livelihood as a law-abiding citizen. Teaching the prisoner a trade which he will be able to exercise in the community has long been the ideal aim of prison education. The mobility of labour to-day, and especially of men of the types found in prison, makes it improbable that an ex-prisoner will find employment in the trade for which he has been trained in prison. This makes the demand for vocational training somewhat unreal. If the prisoner has any reasons to suspect that there will be no prospect of a job in the trade which he is learning, he loses interest and grudges any further effort. Educational policy must allow for this difficulty. Vocational training may be modest in its scope, but should concentrate intensely on specialized subjects. An apprenticeship for a skilled trade will in any case be the exception. But special accomplishments could be taught which would benefit a man or woman in many ways. Specific techniques in plumbing, electrical engineering, carpentry, gardening, fruit preservation, and so forth are suitable subjects for vocational instruction, as they are related to the actual work done in prison, and at the same time possible starting-points for the discussion of wider issues in the social and economic field. Such related vocational training gives prison labour, including the maintenance work, its proper place in a constructive treatment scheme. Casual routine directions during the performance of the work itself are not enough, even if labelled as vocational training. Instruction sheets, progress reports, and tests are technical means for instruction related to industrial or maintenance work, although good

[1] W. M. Wallack, G. M. Kendall, H. L. Briggs, l.c., p. 39.

teaching will not invariably depend on such standardization. In view of the fluctuating prison population, it is advisable to split subjects into small units, in order to give an inmate the chance to begin on a course which he has a fair prospect of completing. Experience with cultural activities among prisoners-of-war shows how essential it is to stimulate interest and energy by providing targets which can be reached by strenuous efforts, such as competitions, examinations, and so on. Nothing is more deadly than attending classes which go on independently of one's own presence or absence, progress or lack of progress. Separate short courses, following each other on a graduated scale, should give the prisoner the reassuring feeling that, by his own efforts, he has achieved a basis for further progress.

The foregoing considerations strengthen the case for correspondence courses for prisoners. American prisons make much use of them. They vary in their quality and standards; sometimes university extension courses are offered and attended. This method makes individualized tuition possible. Every student starts where his needs begin, and goes on according to his personal progress. There is a comprehensible and recognized target, to be reached step by step. Against this must be set the lack of personal contact between teacher and student. To the devoted teacher the written word alone is a poor substitute for oral discussion. In English prisons correspondence courses were first undertaken by tutors of the National Adult School Union, and continued in war-time by the Howard League for Penal Reform in co-operation with Ruskin College, Oxford. This experience showed that much can be done, if the prison staff and the tutor outside are working closely together, sharing their observations, and exchanging suggestions with regard to the individual prisoner.[1]

While vocational training plays a larger part in prison than in free adult education, it will never be the exclusive aim. Practical knowledge is the beginning rather than the end of the studies. It breaks the ice, gives a new self-confidence, and makes the instruction start with the students' own experience. In the old days of English workers' education, when a Carters' and Lorrymen's Union was approached, a man said: 'We're always behind the horse, we don't know much about him, let us have a class on the horse.' And a class on the horse they got with 120 students for two consecutive winters.[2] Under a good teacher the view will soon widen from technique and raw materials to the economic

[1] F. M. McNeille, 6 *Howard Journal* 197.

[2] Mansbridge, l.c., p. 24.

function of the work in hand, its social aspects and vocational prospects, whether related to tailoring and carpentry, to baking or laundry work, to feeding pigs or milking cows. What has been confirmed by generations of adult students is not impossible in prison. Students will forget a good deal of the instruction, and yet they leave the school different people, having learnt to hear, to see, and to think with new powers. Or, as another adult student described his experience: 'A stream of life was racing through the world . . . it was necessary to get into that stream, to be borne by it . . . and to help to strengthen its flow. . . .'[1] Something of this feeling of awakening and fellowship should be the ideal, whenever teacher and students meet in the right spirit outside or inside prison walls.

With the proclamation of such ideals the question suggests itself whether prison education does not lose sight of its primary object of readjusting offenders to a law-abiding life in the community. If the instruction were to be related to the prisoner's work and personal experience, to his higher demands which may be hidden or repressed, then in the first place it ought to be 'related' to the reduction of criminality.[2] There is no major contrast between striving for a wider outlook and a conscious life on the one hand, and prevention of crime on the other. Treatment of human personalities is not a magic cure, but an attempt to make effective those forces of mind and spirit in man which raise human life above weakness, disappointment, and frustration. Canon Barnett's words obtain: 'A mind is kept clean, not by being swept and garnished, but by being kept full of thought about things which are lovely, virtuous and of good report.'[3]

This is a justification for the presentation of genuine art to prisoners. Imprisonment throws man back to a primitive stage of existence. In their situation prisoners are often open to, and greatly impressed by, all that is human and sublime in poetry and music. Prison choirs sometimes tend to sentimentality, to dreamy, brooding music rather than to music which invigorates the soul and stimulates the mind. They should be encouraged to practise fresh and natural singing. Whoever has heard Schubert or Beethoven played by and for prisoners will have been impressed by the strength and purity of emotion among players and audience. Experienced observers maintain that in penal and correctional

[1] Quoted from Møller and Watson, l.c., pp. 66 and 70.
[2] *Attorney General's Survey*, v. 282.
[3] *Canon Barnett, His Life, Work and Friends*, by his Wife (1921), p. 284.

institutions music relieves the repressed emotions and thus removes a great obstacle to direct educational efforts.[1] It is said that the rhythm in itself provides 'a bracing tonic' for the weary and despairing.[2] Whether it is by manual work or by music and dramatics, the experience of creating something of beauty has a wholesome psychological effect. Actors who read plays and other poetry to prisoners testify to the genuine response. With the sensibility of the artist, these actors never fail to discern differences in response they receive from their audience. In their experience, it is sincere works of art only which, far from being 'high-brow', will reach the deeper layers in the listeners' souls and 'call out in them the most worthy aspects of their common humanity'.[3]

The conclusions drawn from these observations support the elaborate proposals presented in a study of present-day prison education by Austin H. MacCormick. They form an ideal scheme, to be aimed at rather than to be copied from precedents. They have been based upon practical experience in American institutions and on a considered judgement of what is desirable and possible. In substance the scheme undertakes to offer every prisoner, as far as time and ability permit, whatever he requires of the following 'educational foundations': fundamental academic education, providing the intellectual tools for everyday life; vocational training for a suitable occupation; health education with the fundamentals of personal and communal hygiene; cultural education for intellectual and aesthetic satisfaction; social education to which all other branches should contribute so as to integrate the individual's understanding and will-power into the social community.[4]

The qualified performance of industrial work and the achievements of organized education have similar limits, due to the composition of the prison population and the psychological effects of imprisonment. Since the repudiation of the Lombrosian doctrine of inborn criminal types, the prison population is usually regarded as a negative selection out of the total community. This observation obtains for social status, economic standards, vocational skill, and physique. For mental equipment, the evidence is far from being conclusive. Even the assumption that, on the whole, the

[1] M. Liepmann, *American Prisons and Reformatory Institutions* (1928), pp. 50 et seq., with reference to William van de Wall, *The Utilization of Music in Prisons* (1924); also *Proceedings 53. Annual Congress Am. Prison Association* (1924).

[2] J. A. F. Watson, *Meet the Prisoner* (1939), p. 139.

[3] R. H. Ward, 6 *Howard Journal* 210.

[4] A. H. MacCormick, *The Education of Adult Prisoners* (1931), pp. 7 and 12.

distribution of intellectual abilities among the general prison population differs only slightly from corresponding groups in the free population does not rule out an accumulation of dull and feeble-minded inmates in particular institutions. The handicaps of prisoners are not only due to inadequate intellectual abilities. Success in work and school depends on an adequate mental equipment plus perseverance and reliability, alertness and energy. Investigations of English women prisoners showed an intellectual standard in almost reverse proportion to the development of the women's emotional power. While 64 out of 100 had normal intelligence, 61 had only rudimentary emotions.[1]

Even with an almost normal intelligence, adolescents and adults, because of an incomplete or unsuccessful school education, have often to fight against serious odds. Investigations in the Western Penitentiary, Pittsburgh, showed, by a co-ordination of the results of intelligence tests and achievement tests, that 58 per cent. of the group studied had less education than they were able to attain according to their mental rating; 61·9 per cent. of the white natives and 91·4 per cent. of the negroes were rated sixth grade or lower.[2] According to observations made during the First World War, a vast group of American white native prisoners compared favourably in their intelligence scores with a control group of army recruits. And yet 47·3 per cent. of the prisoners had not been able to have a school education of seven to eight years, as against only 28·2 per cent. of the army group.[3] Among the juvenile delinquents followed up by Sheldon and Eleanor Glueck's investigations, over four-fifths were retarded as against one-third of the Boston schoolboy population in general. Among adolescent criminals, only one in ten had entered the ninth grade, while over 50 per cent. of the Boston school-children had.[4] Among the patients of the London Child Guidance Clinic, Wm. Moodie found no difference in general intelligence between delinquents and non-delinquents, but the delinquents were six times more backward in schoolwork than their non-delinquent contemporaries.[5] There is still a considerable amount of illiteracy in

[1] G. W. Pailthorpe, *Studies in the Psychology of Delinquency* (Med. Research Council, 1932), pp. 16 et seq.

[2] The scale applied consists of Illiteracy, Grades 1–8, High School, College. Root, quoted from MacCormick, l.c., p. 25.

[3] C. Murchison, *Criminal Intelligence* (1928), pp. 43, 98.

[4] S. and E. Glueck, *After-conduct of discharged Offenders* (1945), p. 15.

[5] Quoted from E. A. Hammond, 'A Study in Juvenile Delinquency' (Unprinted Oxford Barnett House Thesis, 1938).

present-day prisons. In 1938 the small proportion of 2·9 per cent. illiterates in English prisons still amounted to 794 men and 153 women. To them must be added a further 1,672 prisoners who could read and write only imperfectly. In the same year approximately 9·5 per cent. of some 12,500 inmates of New York state prisons were illiterate; if prisoners in special institutions for mental defectives were omitted, the ratio was still 6 per cent.[1] The discrepancy between intelligence and achievements is due to psychological as well as social factors. Unfavourable qualities of temperament impair the use of man's mental abilities. Social conditions in home, school, neighbourhood, and wider community are further causes of retardation and backwardness.

An analysis of educational activities in New York state prisons showed little correlation between standards of mental capacity and achievement of prisoners on the one hand, and their enrolment in courses on the other.[2] If this observation can be generalized, it means a challenge for educational services in prison. It strengthens the case for individualization lest the more capable students be unduly retarded, if the pace is set by the dull lower average. As vocational guidance aims at a sensible assignment to work, so intelligence and achievement tests should be used in order to direct students to the most profitable instruction. Under a rational classification system, social case-work would equally support custodial differentiation, work assignment, educational activities, health services, and parole decisions.

In addition to the composition of the student body itself, the prison situation and the psychological effects of imprisonment involve impediments to educational achievements. The prison population fluctuates as the discharged depart and new arrivals come. This applies particularly to institutions with a high proportion of short-term prisoners. Moreover, in the case of long-term prisoners, the psychological effects of imprisonment are apt to thwart the efforts of prison education.[3] Deprivation of liberty and the minutely regulated compulsory routine seem to negate freedom of choice and initiative, which are indispensable for successful studies. An educational approach will often meet with suspicion, a rejection of all that savours of 'preaching', a resentment against what seems like the whitewashing of those 'on the other side'. Even if a certain enthusiasm has been kindled, perseverance

[1] Wallack, Kendall, Briggs, l.c., p. 111.

[2] Ibid., 103 and 112.

[3] J. S. Roucek, 31 *J. Soc. Psych.* 375; H. E. Field, 157 *Annals* 150.

and patience soon give way to apathy and indifference. The community of interests which unites all those under the same strain strengthens a group-feeling unfavourable to individual efforts at self-improvement. And yet the same psychological reactions make it even more necessary to break the spell of embitterment and repression and to mobilize the crippled forces of mind and spirit. This is the only way to help to restore the prisoner's sense of proportion, a medium course between the two extremes, of a Pharasaic self-righteousness adopted in self-defence on the one hand, and a paralysing sense of frustration and failure on the other. Prisoners with their hypersensibility to formal justice are constantly suspecting hypocrisy. They assess a teacher or lecturer according to his personal qualities. In the long run, a man whose devotion is sincere and pursuit of truth uncompromising will never fail to impress his pupils, within prison walls or in the world.

LIBRARY

A library service with a regular provision of suitable books is indispensable to prison education. Lessons, discussions, play-reading, and other activities are confined to the appointed hour and the assigned place. The book follows the prisoner into his cell. It is his own experience. In a world whose community is artificial because imposed, reading at least is a sanctuary of privacy. By excluding almost every other diversion and stimulus, the book has a strong influence, a monopoly. This entails a risk as well as an opportunity. Prison libraries have been established in almost every modern penal institution. The assortment of books varies. For a long time prison libraries were stocked by voluntary gifts alone. They contained a high proportion of religious and other edifying books, some fiction, including numerous odd volumes of old-fashioned magazines, a sprinkling of travel and adventure books, and non-fiction including elementary science and other text-books. The rise of the modern public library as a supplement to adult education has brought benefits even to the remote seclusion of prison cells. Scientific methods have been developed to assess the reading demands of a given group of the community, to direct readers to the right books, thereby improving their taste and judgement and their reading capacity. The prison library offers a wide field for such efforts. Men read more in prison. It has been estimated that the average prisoner in American penal institutions reads five to ten times as many books as the average citizen using public libraries. In 1937–8 the number of volumes issued *per capita* of prisoners was 41·4. Approximately three-quarters were readers and the average reader had 70 books during the year. Alcatraz, Ca., scored the record with 93 per cent. of the population using the library and a circulation of 102 books per reader. Almost one-third of the books read in federal prisons was of the non-fiction class. In institutions with trained full-time librarians the proportion of non-fiction exceeds the average, up to 45 per cent. The admission of readers to the open shelves proved a great success.[1]

Experience in other countries confirm the prisoners' demand for good books. In English prisons books most in demand were travel books, biographies, books dealing with present-day problems, short stories, books by Edgar Wallace, but also works by Conrad, Masefield, Galsworthy, modern verse, and plays. As to the reading of poetry and drama aloud, after many experiments, Shakespeare and Shaw proved most successful. In one institution Drinkwater's *Abraham Lincoln* was very popular.[2] In Thuringian prisons during the reform period of the twenties, only 16 per cent. of the inmates showed no interest at all in reading. The majority of those who liked reading included 122 prisoners, or 18 per cent. of the total, with no previous reading experience.[3] The selection of books resembled the taste of workers at large. Goethe, Tolstoy, and Gustav Freytag were favourite writers. There was a constant demand for books on technical subjects and on science. In a convict prison, a popular science handbook, *Kosmos*, scored the record of 94 readers in one year.

It is difficult to over-estimate the influence of good books. Jean Paul asserted in a much-quoted sentence that even 'if books do not make a man good or bad, they do make him better or worse'. Such possibilities cannot be left to the hazards of charitable book collections and salvage drives. In England between 1923 and 1929, due to the generosity of the Carnegie Trustees, a special Prison Education Library of several thousands of volumes was established, supplementing the work of the voluntary teachers. In Thuringia, from 1924 the revenue from fines imposed in connexion with the remission of prison terms was set aside by the Ministry of Justice for prisoners' welfare, including purchases for prison libraries.

[1] *Attorney General's Survey*, v. 367; *Federal Offenders, 1938*, p. 11.
[2] *Report Prison Commissioners, 1929*, pp. 44 and 46.
[3] L. Frede, in Bumke, p. 302.

NEWSPAPERS

From the time of the First World War almost every country has faced the question of how to make the prisoner participate in current events. With few exceptions, all prisoners are expected to return to the community. Re-adaptation will be more difficult if the prisoner is out of touch with the present and the experience through which his contemporaries have gone. At the same time access to the news seems almost a natural right, which is not forfeited by a prison sentence.[1]

After the political upheaval of 1918 Prussia recognized the prisoners' right to order and read a newspaper. This caused many inconveniences throughout the restless post-war period. The German Principles of 1923 had a permissive clause; the prisoner may be allowed to order a newspaper at his own expense, unless the paper were banned as inciting to sedition or lawlessness. In England, Zurich, and Thuringia newspapers have sometimes been provided for the prisoners' common rooms; such privileges have usually been granted in the course of the prisoner's promotion in a Progressive Stage system. Many administrations publish news-sheets or prison journals. From the prisoner's point of view, however, no substitute can compete with the 'real thing'. The ethical standard of present-day newsprint is not always very high, and the sensational presentation of the content and the prominence of crime stories do not recommend themselves for reformative efforts. Prisoners, however, cannot be educated for a better world than the existing one. Provision should be made for the entry of provincial and local papers to maintain the links between the prisoner and his home surroundings. Prison journals can be useful as an expression of communal life within an institution. They offer an opportunity for introducing lectures to come and musical performances, new books in the library, sporting events, and so forth. A section may be used for civil advice and legal information.

News-sheets and prison papers appear in prisons of almost every country. They vary from general news surveys to educative periodicals. They differ in the way they resort to regular co-operation of prisoners. The pioneer paper was *The Summary*, published at Elmira in 1883, the achievement of an inmate with an Oxford education. During the First World War, a Belgian prison paper started as a successful model, *L'Effort vers le bien*. In 1885, at the

[1] For the discussion which follows see L. Frede, l.c., pp. 305 et seq.; J. M. Paz Anchorena, 9 *Recueil* 361.

International Prison Congress in Rome, the Spanish delegate Concepción Arenal suggested that an international prison weekly should be created, *Le Dimanche*.

PRISON WELFARE WORK

In a community with a social conscience, the prisoner's welfare does not cease to be an object of concern. Once he is confined in an institution the State undertakes to house, feed, and clothe him. He has a right to medical attendance. Accident or illness caused by his work may bring up the question of workmen's compensation. A German statute of 1900 made the law of public insurance applicable to industrial accidents in prison workshops. An even more important question concerns those needs which have been revealed or caused by the punishment itself. From a legal point of view imprisonment is deprivation of liberty in an enclosed institution, minutely regulated and strictly limited to years, months, weeks, or days. Any additional hardship for the prisoner's family or his future career is without legal foundation and ought to be prevented or removed. From a social point of view imprisonment is not a forfeiture of a man's position in life, but an opportunity for adapting him to the community of law-abiding citizens. This cannot be achieved by individual persuasion alone. Much has to be done to disentangle difficult family and other personal relationships, to protect legitimate economic interests, and to prepare the ground for a fresh start. All this is the responsibility of the social services in penal institutions.[1]

Social welfare work in prison comprises all that is done, not so much with as for the prisoner.[2] Taken literally, this applies to measures which the prisoner himself welcomes as personal advantages, whether they merely help to alleviate his lot or give him greater access to the amenities of life. Measures susceptible only of such an interpretation would be a perversion of social work. True help will procure what is best for the prisoner: what he himself, in so far as he is reasonable, will see is best for him even though he may fail to recognize it as such for the time being. But if the first, subjective definition is too narrow, the second, objective one, exceeds any limits at all. With the prisoner's social rehabilitation as the aim of penal and reformative treatment, criminal law and welfare work seem to share the same final object. This far-reaching

[1] 'Gefangenenfürsorge', *HWB Staatswiss.* (4th ed. 1926); H. Ottenheimer, *Sozialpädagogik im Strafvollzug* (1931).

[2] Wallack, Kendall, Briggs, l.c., p. 1.

conclusion found expression in the statement of an ardent social servant: 'True punishment is social welfare work.'[1]

Even where criminal law and penal administration have been thoroughly socialized, punishment and welfare work differ in their characteristic approach and emphasis. Administration of criminal justice primarily implies the application of public power, even though this be not mere repression but the mobilization of constructive efforts towards regaining the prisoner for a useful life in the community. Social welfare work, although compulsion may not be entirely absent, begins and ends with the recognition of the individual, of the whole man within his natural environment. The client of social welfare work is anything but a mere object of benevolent activities. Like education, social work strives to make itself superfluous. It offers 'help to self-help'. These observations explain the common aims as well as the divergent features of punishment and social welfare work. Punishments are not inflicted exclusively for the sake of the individual's rehabilitation. Nor does an enforced imprisonment offer favourable conditions for remoulding a broken existence. And yet it calls for co-operative efforts on the part of the social servant, lest it fall short of one of its declared objects. There is an inherent tension between punishment and social work as between force and an appeal to personal devotion. This is the root of the difficulties of an educative conception of punishment and a challenge to the supporters of penal reform.

Penal discipline and prisoners' welfare work developed under the twofold influence of State and society. As in other fields of legal and social history, there was a characteristic division of functions between statutory authorities and voluntary agencies. With the rise of a State prison system as a necessity for the administration of justice, the imprisonment of convicted criminals in addition to remand prisoners and civil debtors has been accepted as the State's prerogative and obligation. But social conscience and religious convictions felt bound to relieve their fellow men in distress. John Howard, 'hearing the cry of the miserable', devoted his time to their relief and succeeded in 'exciting the attention of my countrymen to this important national concern of alleviating the distress of poor debtors and other prisoners . . .'.[2] Likewise, when in 1776 Richard Whistar founded the first Philadelphia Prison Society, it was called a Society for Distressed Prisoners. These

[1] M. Sommer, *Die Fürsorge im Strafrecht* (1925), p. 33.
[2] John Howard, *State of Prisons*, l.c., Conclusions.

early reformers could not possibly content themselves with bringing personal relief to individual prisoners. Howard did not withhold his memorable suggestions for the improvement of penal administration. The Philadelphia Society, when re-constituted in 1787 under the influence of Dr. Rush, was styled the Society for alleviating the Miseries of Public Prisons. The preamble of its constitution described as one of its objects that 'such degrees and modes of punishment may be discovered and suggested, as may, instead of continuing habits of vice, become the means of restoring our fellow creatures to virtue and happiness'.[1] In England the foundation of similar associations was due to the social consciousness of devoted Quakers. In 1814 Peter Bedford and Wm. Crawford started a Society for investigating the Causes of the alarming Increase of Juvenile Delinquency in the Metropolis, which society undertook to visit the prisoners and their homes.[2] One outcome of this undertaking was the re-establishment in 1816 of a Society for the Improvement of Prison Discipline.[3] In 1818 Fowell Buxton, one of its most influential members, published the results of his systematic inquiries.[4] When, in 1813, Elizabeth Fry visited Newgate, her main concern was the moral and spiritual welfare of the women prisoners. The helpers whom she inspired formed a Ladies' Association for the Improvement of the Female Prisoners at Newgate (1817). This movement spread to the Continent. The Society of the Netherlands for the Moral Amelioration of Prisoners was founded in 1823. One year later two English Quakers came from Petrograd to Berlin and tried to found a prison society. In 1827 a second attempt by Major von Rudloff led to the establishment of the Berlin Association for the Improvement of Convicted Prisoners. One year before, in Düsseldorf, T. Fliedner, inspired by Elizabeth Fry's work, inaugurated the Rhenish-Westphalian Prison Society, not only for the betterment of housing and the treatment of the prisoners, but also for their moral reformation as a personal service of religious devotion. Dr. Julius of Hamburg worked for prison reform as a concern of

[1] N. K. Teeters, 28 *Journal* 374; for the history of Prison Societies see further: H. E. Barnes, *Repression of Crime* (1926); N. K. Teeters, *They were in Prison. A History of the Philadelphia Prison Society* (1937); v. Rohden, *Geschichte der Rhein.-Westfäl. Gefängnisgesellschaft* (1901); Rosenfeld, *Geschichte des Berliner Vereins zur Besserung der Strafgefangenen* (1901); id., *Zweihundert Jahre Fürsorge der Preuss. Staatsregierung für die entlassenen Gefangenen* (1905).

[2] W. Tallack, *Peter Bedford, the Spitalfields Philanthropist* (1865).

[3] S. and B. Webb, p. 72, n. 1.

[4] T. Fowell Buxton, *Inquiry whether Crime and Misery are produced or prevented by our present System of Prison Discipline* (1818).

Roman Catholic charity, while Joh. H. Wichern enlisted the Evangelical Home Mission to help the distressed souls of prisoners. This development illustrates the liberal conception of the mid-century: formal retribution by the State, but reformative and educative efforts by the voluntary work of church and charitable organizations. When, in 1895, the Gladstone Committee inaugurated a new era in English penal policy, the Du Cane School contested the State's right and obligation to procure the prisoner's reformation. Similarly K. Krohne (1889) declared that the giving of sentences and their execution fell to the State and its authorities, but that it was the task of society to lead the prisoner back to a decent social life. Accordingly, in Berlin the first social workers for juvenile and women prisoners were appointed by voluntary associations.

When the State began to take a wider view of its obligations, it claimed to incorporate into a progressive discipline those aims which had previously been confined to the voluntary efforts of pioneers. The work of voluntary associations was thus re-directed to a special function outside prison administration, viz. after-care of the discharged. Even in 1801 a Prussian Cabinet Order admitted that a perfect criminal law would attain its aim only unsatisfactorily, 'unless pains have been taken beforehand to ensure that criminals released from prison find opportunity and means for gaining an honest livelihood'. After several abortive attempts the foundation of local associations was recommended as the best policy for the reformation and occupation of discharged prisoners. This division, with the State authorities exclusively responsible within prison walls and voluntary forces called upon to co-operate once the prisoner was released, found its expression in local organizations all over the country, co-ordinated in a national framework. Such are the English county prisoners' aid societies, since 1918 co-ordinated in the Central Discharged Prisoners' Aid Society, and the German local Gefängnisgesellschaften combined in 1892 into the Verband deutscher Schutzvereine, from 1926 into the Reichsverband für Gerichtshilfe, Gefangenen- und Entlassenenfürsorge.

This was not the final solution. Mere aid for discharged prisoners is not enough to reintegrate men and women into the social world at large. Instead, thorough after-care work must be developed in connexion with a parole system of conditional release as a form of post-institutional treatment. Aid to discharged prisoners will often be too late if it starts only with the day of release.

While the prisoner is serving his term, ways and means should be considered of finding him lodging and employment for the time of his release. 'For this purpose', said the German Principles of Prison Discipline of 1923, 'in due course after the reception of the prisoner his circumstances are to be investigated; if necessary, communication should be resumed with his relatives, former employers and other suitable persons.' The help may consist in material assistance. An opening has to be secured, tools provided, or information collected about possibilities of emigration. A technical book may be necessary for vocational preparation. The prisoner's family must be maintained; his children need education; family conflicts may call for reconciliation, or the prisoner may need legal aid in a divorce suit. Arrangements must be made with any creditors which will enable the man to make a fresh start on an honest basis. All these measures, too, help him to live his prison life. Family worries and worries about his future livelihood irritate the prisoner in the many lonely hours in his cell and are often the deeper causes of depression, unruly behaviour, and even serious breaches of discipline. If his difficulties can be settled he will be much more receptive to educational efforts and more successful in his work.

In the face of distress and insecurity, material assistance is an essential part of welfare work. But it does not end there. Experience shows a much greater need for personal sympathy and advice than one might expect. Mathilde Wrede, the Finnish pioneer of prison welfare, when asked what she told the prisoners, replied: 'So many people talk to them; what they want is someone who listens to what they are saying.' A social servant's first duty is to listen with patience and sympathy to a fellow man's difficulties and to take a sincere interest in them. This is especially true in prison with its lack of ordinary human intercourse. No wonder that the prisoner, thrown back on himself in the isolation of his cell and in the depressing prison atmosphere, talks first and foremost about himself. This is his constant theme, whether he begins with wife and children, with his past experience and future prospects, men who have disappointed, exploited, and misled him, the injustice of the world, or more directly his own case. Visitors are rightly warned that it is tactless and offensive to open the conversation with a direct allusion to the prisoner's offence, or even to ask moralizing questions such as: 'You know why you are here?' But the talk of prisoners shows that it is natural for them to tell their story. In many cases such interviews are more than a psychological relief. Mutual affections may begin which will prove to have a deep influence on a man's attitude and behaviour. The discussion of personal difficulties or a piece of advice proffered can be the turning-point for a fresh start. It is wrong to imagine the prisoner as always the habitual criminal with a steady record of dishonesty, and to fit all measures to this pre-conceived picture. Life is the greatest inventor of human destinies. Abnormal times with social upheavals and growing insecurity throw people into crime in circumstances which call for much wisdom and forbearance. The right personal intervention may get a life straight again which would otherwise end in habitual crime alternating with steadily increasing prison terms.

There is a field for the social worker, too, among prisoners awaiting trial who concentrate on the issue ahead and are often troubled by the sudden interruption to their private affairs. Two difficulties arise. The prisoner may accept his position as a temporary misfortune only and therefore repudiate a stranger's intervention. And only an experienced social worker will be safe against the risk of being exploited as an unsuspecting agent of collusion.

Who then should render such services and make these approaches? The work began historically with voluntary initiative from outside. The devoted efforts of people, not officially concerned but prompted by religious and humanitarian motives, bear witness that even in prison the obligations of man to man still exist. This is the lasting renown of the early Quakers, of the founders of the Home Mission, of enlightened associates of prison societies, who approached the distressed human soul while the official machinery was exclusively concerned with the prosecution of crime and the execution of sentences. With the beginning of a socialization of prison discipline those services were to be integrated into the administration itself. It was often the chaplain who undertook welfare work as part of his pastoral duties. Sometimes educational instruction and welfare work were in the same hands. Experience has justified such personal union of two constructive functions. A teacher who has an opportunity of knowing the prisoner and winning his confidence will often be the right person to advise and help him. At the same time, responsibility for social work with the pupils gives prison education a background of reality, an opportunity to adapt instruction to actual needs and experience. The Prussian Prison Regulations of 1923, referring to the obligations of prison teachers, mention 'co-operation in welfare work for the prisoners' families and for prisoners awaiting release'. Other

German administrations appointed social workers who often undertook educational activities too. The Saxon Welfare Law of 1925 declared the helping of discharged prisoners to be a function of statutory welfare work. With an average prison population of some 5,000 persons, Saxony had twenty-six welfare workers—only one a woman—some of them attached to the institutions, others like parole officers in the districts which were a public prosecutor's venue.

Official welfare work in prison is supposed to be more efficient than charitable efforts from without. Much depends on the social worker's position within the institutional administration. Even devoted efforts are doomed to frustration if they are only reluctantly tolerated in a penal régime dominated by custodial and repressive principles. Social work can only get recognition, if the social servant is a member of the staff and has the same rights as officers and foremen of workshops. Even in an ideal institution with a perfect 'socialization' of penal discipline, the co-operation of neutral forces outside is still desirable. This is the lesson of the English prison visitors.[1] The idea goes back to Elizabeth Fry. She inaugurated the institution of lady visitors for women's prisons: but the practice fell into disuse afterwards and was not resumed before the last decade of the century. The Gladstone Committee of 1895 recommended 'outside helpers' who should 'supplement the work of the prison staff'. All this referred to the work with women prisoners. In 1900 a Governor reported to the Prison Commissioners that the admission of men visitors to male prisons 'would exert a great influence for good . . .'. But not before 1922 was this permitted. The innovation proved a success. It included the visiting of boy prisoners by women. Prison visitors are voluntary workers. They are invited to visit for one year by the Prison Commissioners on the Governor's recommendation. They are expected to visit the prison once a week and to see those prisoners allocated to them by the Governor. They receive keys to the cells and move freely. They are not permitted to communicate with the prisoner's family without the Governor's consent. Suggestions entered in a visitor's book are always welcome.

The prison visitor should offer the prisoner an opportunity for social conversation, 'essential to most men as an ingredient of ordinary life', the personal friendship and sympathy of a man with good sense and experience, and information on current

[1] G. Gardiner, *Notes of a Prison Visitor* (1938); J. A. F. Watson, *Meet the Prisoner* (1939).

topics.[1] At first sight this seems an unreal undertaking. The doctor, teacher, and chaplain have a professional basis for their approach. They come to see the prisoner for a purpose obvious to both sides. The prison visitor, however, has no intention other than that of making personal contact. It is difficult to establish a personal relationship for its own sake. Everything depends on the right first approach. Hard-and-fast rules are useless. A visitor may start with the place from which the prisoner comes, with his work, his reading, or he may even resort to a talk about the weather. The main thing is a natural, sympathetic, and unspectacular attitude. Fortunately, for the right man the meeting itself is less difficult than its anticipation. The prison visitor must be a man with a sincere liking for his fellow men even if they come from less attractive spheres of life. Only then will he succeed in gaining access to the prisoner's mind, will he be able to relieve mental distress, encourage new impulses, and direct and assist a reasonable planning for the future, and thus, in consecutive visits over a longer period, enter the prisoner's thoughts and life as a friend. Such efforts prepare the ground for after-care work. They are, like the work of voluntary teachers, the English public's great contribution to the prison service. In 1931 557 men and 85 women visited prisoners in English penal institutions. These visitors have been incorporated into a National Association of Prison Visitors and an Association of Visitors to Women's Prisons.

In the United States prison visiting has the noble precedent of the Quakers of Pennsylvania, who regarded regular conversations with a kind and interested visiting friend the indispensable supplement to solitary confinement.[2] The professional character of American social work has left little room for voluntary service by laymen from without. The Pennsylvanian Prison Society which still upholds the old tradition employs trained social workers for this purpose.[3] Only recently attention has been drawn to the English example of linking together the prisoner in his seclusion with the beneficial forces of the community.[4]

RELIGIOUS WORK

Inasmuch as educational activities and welfare work demand a personal approach to the prisoner they are allied to pastoral work

[1] 'Regulations and Advice for Voluntary Workers', Fox, Appendix F, pp. 249 et seq.
[2] N. K. Teeters, 28 *Journal* 378.
[3] Id., *World Penal Systems* (1944), p. 198.
[4] M. May, 32 *Journal* 35.

undertaken from a religious basis.[1] Secular and spiritual efforts have much in common: the appeal to the whole personality, the work from man to man, and even the resorting to forces beyond the individual life. Where the secular method tries hard and falls short, religion still seems to offer a way to a lasting reformation from within.

Religious experience, however, is not merely the perfecting of what teaching and social work have left undone. It differs in kind rather than degree from secular achievements. It means complete surrender, transformation of life, and its influence is not confined to a single province of the human mind. Man with his craving for knowledge and his demand for personal sympathy and mutual affection is capable of responding to an even higher call. Spiritual fellowship is something which will not be attained by an action of man's will only, nor can it be explained by human nature alone.

Throughout history the better part of what has been done for prisoners beyond the maintenance of a marginal existence and the provision of work originated in pastoral work. Education and welfare work in prison—even more than in the world at large—are a secularization of tasks undertaken originally by the Church and her ministers. The prison chaplain's original importance was that he was the one neutral force in an otherwise impersonal and repressive régime. An early beginning of such beneficial influence is marked by John and Charles Wesley's visit to Oxford prison in 1730. They went to the prison twice a week, read and discussed edifying books, and, with the Bishop's consent and 'good wishes', delivered a sermon once a month. Charles Wesley continued such work at Newgate and accompanied those under death sentence to their execution at Tyburn.[2] Generations of ministers have met the prisoner as their fellow man in need of mental and spiritual help. Even at present the chaplain is often 'the man of all jobs' (Robinson). In England he arranges lectures and debates, has contact with the prison visitors, and is often responsible for the library. American prison chaplains undergo a special training in social case-work. Practical help facilitates the minister's approach. A sympathetic understanding of the prisoner's needs and a readiness to lend a hand when personal difficulties are to be adjusted are

[1] E. Berggrav, *The Prisoner's Soul and our own*, translated by L. Gravely (1932); C. Meyer, 'Seelsorge an katholischen Gefangenen', in Bumke, pp. 270–93; T. E. Harvey, 'The Christian Church and the Prisoner in English Experience', *The Beckly Lecture, 1941* (1942).

[2] John S. Simon, *John Wesley and the Religious Societies* (1921), pp. 91 and 215.

more convincing than words alone. In the religious sphere an unbiased study of the man and his personal environment is the condition for a lasting influence. Even more than teachers and social workers, the minister of religion will try hard to enable the prisoner to face the realities of life. Analytical psychology has shown the healing power of an interview which brings a man's true difficulties into the open. In the same way the minister will help a prisoner to attain to that ruthless honesty towards himself which alone makes him ready for a genuine religious experience. Pastoral work has always gone hand in hand with a brotherly care for the troubles of others. By means of his connexion with the Church Army, with parishes, and congregations, the chaplain can reach the prisoner's family and employer, and refer him to people who are willing to help him after his discharge. The devoted work of prison chaplains left its mark on the development of prison discipline as a whole. Some of them became leading figures in modern prison history, as for instance, Louis Dwight in the United States, John Clay in England, and Karl Krohne in Germany.

With the socialization of penal discipline a new situation has emerged. It is no longer the duty of the State merely to apply the rigidity of the law regardless of the prisoner's welfare and inner progress. Even in prison, educational and social services are developed with a secular philosophy of their own. This produces a rivalry of secular and spiritual forces, the Church being referred more and more to the religious sphere. The process varies from country to country. In spite of some ground lost to secular forces, the Church has gained by an intensification of her effort. Energy is no longer wasted in wresting concessions from a repressive régime. Pastoral work fits better into an institution with a good educational programme and proper social case-work. Library service, discussion groups, adult education, organized spare-time activities give welcome opportunities for finding contacts, for getting to know a man, studying his habits, his response, whereas a merely custodial routine often makes the inmate sullen and suspicious.

The service of organized religion for prisons has been provided for two reasons. The teaching of religion has always been regarded as the most powerful factor in bringing about the prisoner's reformation.[1] For many it is a 'bulwark against anti-social behaviour', for others merely 'an emotional stabilizer'.[2] A lasting

[1] Watson, l.c., p. 157.

[2] *Attorney General's Survey*, v. 177.

influence on the prisoner's life requires more than the teaching of certain doctrines and commandments. It can only result from a sincere religious experience with the recognition of high standards and the acceptance of help in living up to them. But religion is not a means to an end. It is the inalienable right and obligation of the Church to bring her message to every man, whether in prison or not. This obtains even if the State pursues no reformative object. It applies to prisoners under death sentences as well as to prisoners-of-war. Religious work within prison walls is no less important for the Church herself than for the prison. In the prisoner and his destiny the minister of religion is faced with stern reality. Ultimate questions of individual conscience and collective guilt, of the purpose of life and the prospect of death, demand an immediate and unequivocal answer. Men with pastoral experience in prison rose to the occasion when the whole cause of Church and religion was at stake. Pastor Jacobi, who began his ministry with prisoners' after-care work, became a prominent member of the Confessional Church in Germany. Bishop Berggrav, sometime prison chaplain in Oslo, made a gallant stand for the Norwegian Church against the foreign invader. On the losing side, the prison chaplain misses a congregation that has grown up from generation to generation, the support of experienced lay members, and the life within a parish with a natural distribution of families, of youth, adults, and old people, and of various social groups.

There has been much controversy as to whether the State should merely grant the clergy access to the prisoners for the performance of their ministry under the sole responsibility of the Church, or whether it should appoint chaplains as members of the prison service. In Germany, after the last war and the disestablishment of the Church, Saxony, Thuringia, and Hamburg dispensed with appointed chaplains, once social workers had been appointed, and contented themselves with the admission of ministers. In England, chaplains of the Established Church are appointed, at present, for a period of five years, in larger institutions on a full-time basis. Ministers of other denominations are appointed or called according to particular demands. In the United States, out of eighty-two prisons under review in 1936–7, seventy-five had appointed chaplains and the rest ministers provided by the Churches.[1] The policy of dispensing with appointed chaplains may be due either to a secularizing tendency which wants to keep

[1] Ibid., p. 176.

public administration aloof from denominational influence, or, conversely, to the reluctance of the Church to share responsibility for and to yield to the control of the secular State. Experience shows that the advantages of a contribution to the routine life of a prison outweigh the risk of conflicting loyalties.

There is no particular 'theology for prisoners'. Nor should a secular penal science discuss how the Christian message should be preached to prisoners. But since, as George Fox said, a minister should speak 'to the conditions of man', certain observations on the mental and spiritual situation typical of prisoners may clear the way for the right approach. The first impression gained by an inquirer of the prisoner's mind is that of a mental vacuum and an ignorance of even the elementary facts and conceptions of the Christian faith. Prison ministry is missionary work. But introduction to the stories of the Bible and fundamental doctrines should only be instrumental towards effecting a reorientation of life, a surrender to a living force beyond man and human institutions. With this ultimate aim the minister will approach his fellow man in prison as a sinful man also, but one who knows a way out. This approach implies comfort, personal recognition, and new demands. In prison pastoral work and sermons must be 'tuned to souls in distress'.[1] The prisoner will accept this consolation if he witnesses in the minister a sincere religious experience. Like St. Paul, the minister should be 'able to comfort them which are in any trouble, by the comfort wherewith we ourselves are comforted of God' (2. Cor. i. 4). In the community of men, sinful but eligible for grace, lies the final recognition of equality before God, of humility as well as of human dignity. And again, when the minister tries to encourage the prisoner to strive hard for a pure life and higher standards, he will speak 'not as though I had already attained, either were already perfect: but I follow after, if that I may apprehend that for which also I am apprehended . . .' (Phil. iii. 12).

The instruments of this message are pastoral interview and divine service. They are supplementary to each other. Pastoral visits to prisoners require much tact and patience. The minister must be 'a good listener'.[2] An experienced prison chaplain gave the advice that the prisoner should always talk more than the minister.[3] Experience and judgement are necessary, not only in order to detect truth and lies, but also to hear the unspoken 'yes'

[1] C. Meyer, in Bumke, p. 282.
[2] Watson, l.c., p. 155.
[3] D. Klatt, in Bumke, p. 265.

behind the defiant 'no'. Services in the prison chapel should bear witness to the dignity of true worship and present religion not as a wearisome routine duty, but as 'a real living necessity for daily life'.[1] Most prisons have dispensed with individual 'stalls' for the separation of prisoners in chapel, or with supervising officers facing the prison congregation from high seats, not to speak of a guard with a lighted torch beside a loaded cannon, who is said to have protected the first American prison preacher in Walnut Street Prison in Philadelphia in 1790. Whether concealed outlets for tear and nauseating gas are a better device may be open to question.[2] Before the Second World War much was done in English prisons by repainting chapel walls in bright colours, introducing comfortable seating, and providing pipe organs, with the result that—in the words of an official Report—'the prison chapel of to-day can be compared favourably with the parish church . . .'.[3]

Experienced prison preachers say that sermon subjects should not be too specific. Outspoken 'judgement sermons' are out of place. Bishop Berggrav puts forgiveness *before* repentance. This seems paradoxical, but it testifies to a deep understanding of the prisoner's soul. For a lonely, repressed, and often perverted personality, the assurance of love and grace, the belonging to a spiritual fellowship must come first, before repentance and dedication can fairly be expected. This pastoral experience with prisoners confirms the wisdom of the Calvinist authors of the Heidelberg Catechism of 1563, who taught the doctrine of man's distress and his redemption first and then the commandments as duties required by thankfulness. The prison situation is an illustration of the unique character of the Christian way of redemption. It tries to recognize every human soul, and at the same time to subdue it by allegiance to higher goals beyond the individual self.

Spiritual influence cannot be assessed by testing and measuring. A man may have responded well to religious instruction in prison and yet succumb to the first temptation. Another may have passed almost unnoticed through the prison congregation and still, years later, remember in a difficult situation a generous act of trust on the part of his prison chaplain, or even in his last hour think of a word spoken from the prison pulpit. Certain factors, however, can be discussed in a consideration of the possibilities and limitations of pastoral work in prison.

[1] *Report Prison Commissioners, 1938*, p. 31.
[2] *Attorney General's Survey*, v. 182.
[3] *Report Prison Commissioners, 1938*, p. 31.

Many prisoners show hostility and suspicion towards organized religion. They are on the losing side, the under-privileged, hopelessly outfought by the State, society, vested interests, and so on. To them the Church seems to take the part of the respectable 'haves' against the rebellious 'have-nots'. In countries with no traditional Dissenters outside the Established Church, this is more difficult to repudiate. If the arguments are sincere, the minister will take them seriously and even go a long way in sharing the criticism of prevailing evils in the social order and economic distribution. The prisoner has been punished by the State in accordance with the law of the land. The deeper justification of his destiny is an object for pastoral work. The idea of retribution is deeply rooted in man's natural feelings. It is not too difficult to make a prisoner realize that it is just, that 'everybody gets what his deeds are worth'. But, as Bishop Berggrav shows, it is a desperate undertaking to explain to a prisoner that the protection of society demands his detention. While retribution recognizes the human personality, social protection as a reason for punishment needs to be justified by the value of the society which sacrifices the individual for its security. A minister of religion will not hesitate to include himself in the collective guilt of sinful men. He must, however, avoid pharasaic self-righteousness as well as a professed levelling of standards which must appear equally dishonest to the prisoner. Before God, the murderer or thief and the law-abiding citizen are sinners alike. But a deliberate waiving of every difference provokes the indignant question, why then has the one to pay with his life, liberty, and social status, while the other enjoys respectability and the security of civil life. A legal offence is not in all circumstances an act of moral depravity, but it is in the overwhelming majority of cases the evidence of something having gone wrong in that particular life.

In prison the Church has almost a monopoly in offering mental and spiritual stimulation. This was unchallenged until the rise of secular education and welfare work. Nowadays, even with the competition of these new forces, the supply lags behind the demand. Many prisoners may attend church services and Bible study classes because they lack other diversions. This monopoly is an opportunity as well as a danger. Compulsory attendance at divine service has been abolished in most countries, often with the approval of the ministers themselves. But if attendance is made entirely a matter of choice those who go have to be protected against the terrorism of those who do not. And so church attendance as the rule, with exceptions granted for 'conscientious objectors', has proved an expedient solution. For many a prisoner, the time spent in the penal institution may be the one opportunity to consider, under careful guidance, a new way of life drawn from springs long buried or never known before. Experienced ministers are sceptical with regard to dramatic conversions. For pastoral work in prison Luther's words obtain: 'The believer's whole life should be penitence.'

It is a common objection that religious work in prison breeds hypocrisy. Whenever men, living under strained conditions, are constantly dependent on others, hypocrisy, in the hope of alleviating pressure and deprivation, becomes inevitable. It is more serious, however, if it affects the prisoner's attitude toward religion.

All available evidence supports the opinion that pastoral work and divine service meet with a sincere response from the prison congregation. Good attendance at the chapel services, earnest hymn-singing, loyal co-operation of prisoner vergers or organists, lively interest in the sermon and religious discussions, numerous serious talks in the cell—all this has been recorded and confirmed by many prison chaplains. An official English report even asserts that prisoners show more interest during the service than the congregation of an ordinary parish church.[1] In spite of this there is a constant number of recidivists. Approximately every second adolescent received into an English prison during the formative years under twenty-one comes back again.[2] Progressive criminologists doubt whether imprisonment even under ideal conditions can be claimed as a method of social readjustment. These contradictory observations suggest the question: Are the prisoners sincerely affected by that contact with religious influences, or do they still cling to a life of least resistance and personal indulgence? The answer is: *both*, and this attempt to reconcile the incompatible is the cause of their failure. The average prisoner is susceptible to fairness and trust, he appreciates justice and kindliness, he has a craving for mental stimulation, and he may often—behind a screen of cynicism—long for a pure life and participation in a spiritual fellowship rather than a partnership of selfish interests. All this is certainly sincere; only many will not forsake the easy and exciting way of illicit gains for the toilsome task of starting anew and persevering in spite of the handicap of a prison record. Here the Christian message must be unmistakable. There can be no

[1] *Report Prison Commissioners, 1938*, p. 31.
[2] Ibid., p. 130.

'and' between God and mammon. Swift detection and prompt trial must teach the lesson that crime does not pay—according to an external balance of gain and loss. Reviewing his life in the light of religion, the prisoner may realize that in a deeper sense, as a man capable of being a vessel of spiritual powers, he cannot live in defiance of the fundamental standards of truth, reliability, and self-discipline. This simple statement is the nucleus of the contribution which the Christian message may make to the rehabilitation of offenders.

CONCLUSIONS

Prison education, welfare work of the social worker, and religious work of the minister are the principal examples of a personal approach to the prisoner. More than anything else in prison life these personal efforts defy the regimentation of a uniform system. Together with prison labour they constitute the substance of prison discipline, but results are less tangible than the organization and performance of work. Even under a classification scheme, work demands some standardization. It sets the pace, and the prisoner has to adapt himself, as does the worker in the world at large. Education, welfare work, and religious work are highly individualized. They recognize and even look for the individual soul and its needs and they express the personalities of teacher, social worker, and minister in their response to their fellow men's demands. Therefore these services are far from being uniform, nor do they even pretend to reach equally every single prisoner. But they do make inroads into the dull mass-treatment. They are worth while, if successful with the few, provided only they do not content themselves with satisfying a prison aristocracy, but act in accordance with the experience of adult education, that to know something means to achieve more.

The results of educational, social, and spiritual activities depends on whether these are integrated into the prevailing discipline as a whole. Ideal programmes and devoted efforts are doomed to frustration if they are regarded as intruders, and reluctantly accepted as extra luxuries like tobacco and biscuits. The first educational target is to convince the prison staff itself. The different functions, whether custodial or educational, must be performed in the spirit of teamwork. This means that teachers, social workers, and chaplains must share the responsibility for decisions which are vital for the prisoner's destiny. Where social case-work is the foundation of penal treatment, assignment to work and to the particular custodial régime, disciplinary punishment, parole decisions, and, in a Progressive Stage system, promotion or degradation are all based on the prisoner's progress reports and consequently on the judgement of teacher, social worker, and chaplain. Anything else would fall short of the conception of a reformative process which affects and demands the whole man. Such a policy has to face a conflict in the minister or social servant himself. They are bound to win and to justify the prisoner's confidence, but this function differs from the obligation of a counsel for the defence not to assert anything in disfavour of his client. If a prisoner tells a social worker or minister something which amounts to the admission of an offence, he will often accept their advice and clear his conscience by informing the authorities concerned. But, if he cannot be persuaded to do so, or if it were unfair to try to persuade him? Confidence ultimately depends on the assurance that without a man's consent his secrets will not be divulged by his confessor. In tragic circumstances this may lead to a conflict between due respect to the confidential source of a certain piece of information and the legal obligation of a witness to tell 'the whole truth'. English law recognizes the right and obligation to refuse to disclose facts confided to a person as far as legal counsels and solicitors are concerned.[1] Unrestricted communication between client and legal adviser has been deemed a necessary element in a due process of law. With a strictness which has sometimes been questioned,[2] similar privileges have been denied to the clergy and the medical profession.[3] As a rule, counsels and judges would refrain from forcing the issue,[4] but in 1860 a priest had to go to prison for contempt of court, as he refused to disclose the name of a repentant thief on whose behalf he restored a watch.[5] In America, by 1905, as a result of relevant legislation during the last quarter of the century, two jurisdictions of Canada and more than half of all the jurisdictions of the United States had recognized clergymen as privileged witnesses.[6] In 1942, the Draft Model Act of Evidence, promulgated by the American Law Institute, made allowance for the priest-penitent privilege and proposed a privilege for the

[1] *R.* v. *Withers* (1811), 2 *Camp* 578.

[2] Pitt Taylor, *Treatise on the Law of Evidence* (12th ed. 1931), i. 577, s. 916.

[3] *Normanshaw* v. *Normanshaw and Measham* (1893), 69 *L.T.* 468; *Garner* v. *Garner* (1920), *T.L.R.* 196.

[4] *R.* v. *Griffin* (1853), 6 *Cox* 219.

[5] *R.* v. *Hay* (1860), 2 *F.F.* 4.

[6] J. H. Wigmore, *Treatise on the System of Evidence* (1905), iv. 3363, s. 2395, n. 1.

physician restricted to the prosecution of misdemeanours.[1] In Germany, clergymen have a statutory right to refuse evidence on facts 'confided to them in the discharge of their pastoral work'.[2] After the rise of social services in connexion with the administration of criminal law it was even discussed whether a similar privilege could be recognized for social workers.[3]

The law, as it stands, does not relieve the conscience of all scruples. In disciplinary matters and release decisions social worker and prison chaplain need much tact in order to reconcile the obligations of personal adviser and confessor with the duties of a social case-worker and prison administrator. They are called to give judgement on what is best for the prisoner and the community and yet they are bound not to betray his personal confidence. In dramatic circumstances, failing to get the culprit's consent, social worker and minister must decide for themselves whether their conscience demands of them to defy the law and to accept the consequences.

[1] *Model Act of Evidence*, promulgated by the American Law Institute (1942), Rules 219, 220–3.

[2] Section 53, no. 1, Code of Criminal Procedure; s. 383, no. 4, Code of Civil Procedure.

[3] *Mitt. IKV*, N.F. 4 (1930), p. 19.

CHAPTER XI

DISCIPLINE

IN the State the maintenance of law and order is the basis of civilization and morality. Likewise in penal institutions, discipline is the condition of education and rehabilitation. Good discipline may be aimed at in the process of correction, and though it should not be identified with educational success, it is essential to success. Breaches of discipline are fatal for any progressive régime. They discourage the pioneers of reform and discredit their cause.

The word and conception of discipline suffer from an ambiguity. John Howard made immortal the 'admirable sentence' inscribed at the boys' prison of San Michele: 'Parum est coercere improbos poena nisi probos efficias disciplina.' 'It is of little advantage to restrain the bad by punishment, unless you render them good by discipline.' Thus, for him, discipline meant constructive as opposed to punitive treatment. This is the original meaning of the word: instruction imparted to disciples and scholars.[1] A chronicler of 1548 reports that Edward IV founded 'the solemn school at Eton' for 'his own young scholars to attain to discipline'. In 1813, however, Wellington complained that 'if discipline means obedience to orders as well as military instructions, we have but little of it in the army'. Here the meaning is shifting from the instruction to its result, viz. the pupils' or soldiers' conduct, or, in a narrower sense, the order observed by people under control. Likewise, prison discipline in a wider sense is 'a way of living' contrived for the purpose of punishment and reformation,[2] and is thus far identical with the whole subject of penal science. It also refers, however, to the formal order among prisoners, their obedience to orders and rules, and even the means by which this order is enforced. This Chapter discusses discipline in the second sense. But the history of the word shows that the conception of discipline does not necessarily imply chastisement.

Discipline as the order and conduct enforced on prisoners under the prevailing law has three objects. It is expected to prevent escapes, to maintain a decent institutional life, and to train the inmates in good habits. Whatever definition of prison discipline may be accepted, its typical feature is due to the fact that it has to uphold an enforced deprivation of liberty. This entails not only

[1] 'Discipline', *Oxford Dictionary*.

[2] *Attorney General's Survey*, v. 109.

seclusion in an enclosed institution, but also subjection to a daily routine which permeates the entire personal life. Compliance with these requirements is compulsory.

Custodial security ranks first. Walls, bars and locks, an almost omnipresent supervision, and numerous regulations are intended to prevent escapes. The danger of these is the great obstacle to a reformative personal approach. It breeds suspicion and bars a natural relationship between officers and inmates. Cases of escape and breach of prison, including attempts at them, conspiracy and preparatory acts, are severely punished. Other rules are not unlike those which prevail in any institution where numerous people are living together. They enforce certain standards of decency, cleanliness, and self-discipline which are necessary for the protection of the individual and a healthy communal life. Finally, social adjustment, while never attained by mere prohibitions, requires a ban on anti-social behaviour, like smuggling of narcotics, acts of dishonesty, wilful slackness, and obstruction.

Disciplinary law and criminal law are separated by a fluid line with a certain overlapping. Breaches of discipline may amount to thefts, forgeries, or assaults. Unless such acts are serious they will not be prosecuted before the courts, but dealt with by disciplinary measures. The administrative authorities, thereby deputizing for criminal courts, sometimes have their own standards. They take a most serious view of acts imperilling the security of the institution and its officers. Even on the Continent, in spite of the prevailing principle of mandatory public prosecution, the administrative authorities content themselves with the disciplinary punishment of typical prison offences, without referring them to the public prosecutor. In the absence of definite legal principles, conflicts may arise between the administration which claims a right to settle what it regards as a matter of discipline, and the public prosecutor who is bound to take action whenever there is suspicion of a criminal offence committed.[1]

With regard to escapes and breaches of prison by the prisoner, legal systems vary. The Civil Law declared an escape punishable by law, but a mere flight without the use of force or violence has probably never been prosecuted. Feuerbach pleaded that 'legislative wisdom should strike a mere escape from the list of crimes'.[2]

[1] Such a conflict was the basis of allegations and prosecution against the American prison reformer Thomas Mott Osborne. F. Tannenbaum, *Osborne of Sing Sing* (1933), pp. 203 et seq.

[2] A. v. Feuerbach, *Lehrbuch des peinlichen Rechts* (13th ed. 1840), s. 197 n. a.

Continental legislation of the nineteenth century followed the same line. The French *Code pénal* penalized prison breaking, but not escape (art. 245); the Austrian Criminal Code does not punish the escaping prisoner at all (ss. 217 and 307); the German Criminal Code only if a breach of prison has been committed by the combined efforts of several prisoners (s. 122). English law, however, has preserved breach of prison and escape by the prisoner himself as common law felonies and misdemeanours,[1] whereby—according to a medieval statute—a felony is confined to the breach of prison by a prisoner arrested for a capital crime.[2] Prosecutions have been rare. In 1762 Wm. Hawkins observed that with regard to escapes 'there is little remarkable in the books'.[3] In the United States[4] a forcible departure from custody is punishable under the common law as prison breach. Under the weight of a 'humane jurisprudence' an unresisted escape of an unguarded man is no longer regarded as an indictable offence. In some legislations, like those of California, Kansas, and North Carolina, escape from work outside prison walls has been made a statutory offence. So far as escapes and breaches of prison are punishable, the prison administration is bound to report all cases to the district attorney. American prisoners are frequently prosecuted for such offences before the courts.[5]

It is open to question where legislation should draw the line between criminal and disciplinary punishment. Logical considerations would assign prison breaches and escapes to the jurisdiction of the courts rather than refer them to disciplinary action. This would relieve the administrations from the irksome burden of punishing the fugitive who has fooled and outwitted them. Staff–inmate relationships would be improved if disciplinary action were confined to acts against the communal life and good order within the institution itself. Practical experience, however, prefers the discretionary sanctions of discipline to the cumbersome mode of court procedure. Many of the prison regulations are intended to facilitate control and to prevent escapes. Infractions of these rules are disciplinary offences, and so are preparatory and conspiratory acts aiming at escape. It is therefore natural to treat

[1] Halsbury, ix. 361 and 359; W. O. Russell, *Crime* (9th ed. 1936), i. 254 and 262.

[2] 'De fragentibus prisonam', 23 Edw. I (1295), sometimes cited 1 Edw. II (1307).

[3] W. Hawkins, *Pleas of the Crown* (1762), book II, ch. 17, s. 5.

[4] F. Wharton and I. C. Ruppenthal, *Criminal Law* (12th ed. 1932), ii, s. 2019, p. 2332, and s. 2025, p. 2337, n. 8.

[5] *Attorney General's Survey*, v. 115.

actual and attempted escapes alike, and in principle to leave them to disciplinary punishment. Different views apply to minimum security institutions and honour camps. Here the custodial régime relies on trust rather than on enforced control and supervision. It seems only fair that if by a 'breach of trust' a man forfeits his privileged position, he should return to ordinary prison discipline or even face a trial before a law court.

Three ways are open to prison authorities for the maintenance of good discipline. First, they may and often will use repressive methods, viz. punishment and restraints. Secondly, they may resort to incentives, e.g. to an earnings scheme or a grading system. Thirdly, they may rely on constructive methods and appeal to the prisoners' self-respect and co-responsibility by the recognition of inmate participation and self-government. No prison régime will succeed by adopting one exclusive pattern of discipline. It is only reasonable to use every means at its proper place. Progress from repressive to constructive methods should be the aim for every good institution. As Schleiermacher said: 'Punishment should be a waning factor in education.'

PUNISHMENTS

Disciplinary punishment differs from common criminal law by its flexibility. It substitutes for an exclusive list of legal offences the principle that any behaviour at variance with obedience and institutional order is punishable, and for the statutory tariff of punishments a general punitive power. The latter has its limits determined by law, while its application has been left to the disciplinarian's discretion. Recent legislation has had a tendency to soften this contrast. Even in countries with codified law the discretion of criminal courts has been considerably extended. At the same time legal safeguards have been established for a rational and equal application of disciplinary punishment.

Disciplinary Offences

The discretionary conception of a behaviour incompatible with obedience and order covers a variety of acts from assault and theft to mere insolence, fooling, and forbidden talking. For security reasons prisoners are punishable for possessing tools or civilian clothes, passing notes, or smuggling out letters. In the interest of the common life in the institution other rules require personal cleanliness, keeping of clothes in good order, a quiet behaviour in the cell. Prisoners may be punished for lying, using foul language, loitering, quarrelling. In some prisons inmates are forbidden to stare at visitors, or, if they meet them in passing, are required to stop and stand facing the wall. Up to recent times there have been remnants of the enforced rule of silence of the Auburn system. In 1925 a Regulation of Basle forbade prisoners to talk with one another and provided that 'they must never be left without supervision as soon as two or more are gathered together . . .'.[1] Obviously, imprisonment with its many strange and unknown demands is for most entrants a drastic change of environment. Fairness requires that the prisoner shall know what he is expected to do and not to do. Usually a copy of the house regulations is put in every cell. Sometimes such rule-books contain lists of the principal offences which involve disciplinary punishment. In Idaho such a black list contained forty items,[2] in Massachusetts more than sixty plus 'any other improper conduct or breach of discipline'.[3] In other institutions it was felt that such a 'barbed wire' of prohibitions would only add to the entrant's bewilderment. Turning a blind eye to lesser infractions would make things worse. It may even lead to arbitrariness, since it leaves an ill-tempered prison officer the opportunity of making a case against a man whenever he likes. Instead, it may be better to tell the prisoner positively what he is expected to do if he wants to earn privileges, promotion to higher grades, and remission of a part of his sentence. Appeals are therefore made to him in order to win his co-operation and to fit him into the rhythm of life in the institution. After the First World War posters in Hamburg prison cells began by saying 'You are in need. This house will help you. . . .' The printed advice given to new-comers to an American county workhouse explains the purpose and routine of the institution, offers educational and recreational facilities, and says rather positively when and where talking, reading, and smoking, burning of light, and so on are permitted. Michigan state institutions offer suggestions 'to face yourself honestly in the light of your present difficulty' and 'to use your present confinement as an opportunity . . .', in connexion with a long list of prison rules. In Norfolk, Massachusetts, prisoners are instructed in the institutional programme and in two fundamental rules: no escapes and no contraband; beyond this they are required to act like reasonable men.[4] Such an approach tries to

[1] Text given by Hafner-Zürcher, p. 137.

[2] *Attorney General's Survey*, v. 110.

[3] *Wickersham Report*, ix. 26 et seq.

[4] Ibid., 39; *Attorney General's Survey*, v. 118 and 113.

substitute incentives and co-operation for prohibition and repression. This is not contradictory to the conception of disciplinary punishment. It ought to be the aim to make the culprit recognize by his own will that the measure imposed upon him was just and necessary.

Sanctions

Disciplinary punishments are administered to persons while they are undergoing the penalty to which they have been sentenced by the court. They are 'the ultimate limit of hardship which can be lawfully inflicted short of capital punishment'.[1] In minor cases the general discretionary power of the prison administration provides ample opportunities for informal adjustment. Disbanding of a work party, moving a prisoner to other living quarters, change in the assignment of work, or merely an altered attitude in personal communication have often the desired psychological result. Deprivation of privileges is more punitive, e.g. the forfeiture of the right to buy in the canteen, to attend a concert, to smoke, or restrictions in correspondence, visits, use of the library, and so forth. Punishments proper are the imposition of harder living conditions for a certain time, e.g. by restricted diet, deprivation of the mattress, or exclusion from exercises in the open. The typical severe penalty is punitive detention, i.e. an intensified deprivation of liberty by solitary confinement, which might be aggravated by hard bed, bread and water, and a darkened cell for certain days. It has been questioned whether this is enough to make disciplinary punishments deterrent and to mark the difference between normal prison routine and punitive treatment. Where the answer is in the negative, prison discipline resorts to the infliction of physical hardship and pain by fetters and corporal punishment.

Legal and administrative systems differ in the measures and hardship which they deem necessary for the enforcement of discipline in penal institutions. In England and Wales the usual disciplinary punishments beyond loss of privileges and of remission marks are restriction of diet, forfeiture of associated work, deprivation of the mattress for men, and cellular confinement, in the more serious cases up to a maximum of twenty-eight days, but without darkening.[2] The Prison Act of 1898 admits corporal punishment, but restricts its application to cases of mutiny or gross personal violence to an officer or servant of the prison.[3] In Scotland

[1] Kriegsmann, p. 169. [2] Fox, p. 83. [3] 61 & 62 Vict., c. 41, s. 5.

corporal punishment is admissible for inmates of the convict prison, Peterhead, as the ultimate penalty for mutiny, personal violence, and other acts of gross misconduct or insubordination.[1]

In the United States disciplinary measures are loss of privileges or of 'good time' (remission), solitary confinement, and corporal punishment. In 1928, 10 out of 68 prisons and 2 out of 19 reformatories used dark cells.[2] In 1937 corporal punishment persisted in 26 prisons, mostly in western and southern states. In 14 prisons inmates may be cuffed to the bar or shackled, especially for attempted escapes. Two institutions apply cold baths and one gagging.[3] In France, according to art. 614, *Code d'instruction criminelle*, prisoners may be put into 'irons' in cases of serious outbursts of violence or threats. From 1876 institutions for those serving long sentences have a punitive ward (*salle de discipline*), where prisoners under constant supervision are kept marching for three-quarters of an hour with a rest of one-quarter of an hour.[4]

In Switzerland corporal punishment has been banned by the Federal Constitution. The Criminal Code of 1937 repealed cantonal provisions which gave the court power to make a sentence of penal servitude more severe by a dark cell or chains. In 1925 several cantons still applied as ultimate disciplinary punishments the dark cell (Basle, Regensdorf), the straitjacket (Baselland, Uri), chains (Basle, Lugano), or shackles (Lucerne).[5] In Germany the Principles of 1897 permitted detention in dark cells and refrained from interfering with the traditional practice of corporal punishment (Prussia, Saxony, &c.) and narrow or 'laths arrest' administered in cells where the prisoner could not stand up or had to lie on the top of sharpened laths (Saxony). Although denounced by prison administrators,[6] corporal punishment was not abolished until the end of the First World War. The Principles of 1923 provided as the utmost penalty punitive detention up to four weeks with hard bed, restricted diet, and no outdoor exercises except

[1] Peterhead Harbour of Refuge Act, 1886, 49 & 50 Vict., c. 49, s. 23, referring to the powers of the Director of English Convict Prisons, defined by prison rules; rules 5–13, Part III of the Prisons (Scotland) Rules.

[2] *Wickersham Report*, ix. 31.

[3] *Attorney General's Survey*, v. 122.

[4] Mossé, p. 141.

[5] E. Hafter, *Lehrbuch des Schweizerischen Strafrechts. Allg. Tl.* (1926), pp. 265 et seq.; Hafner-Zürcher, pp. 139 et seq.

[6] K. Krohne, *Lehrbuch der Gefängniskunde* (1889), pp. 354 et seq.; P. Pollitz, *Strafe und Verbrechen* (1910), pp. 100 et seq. See also Kriegsmann, pp. 171 et seq.

every third day. No darkening of the cell was permitted. The Draft Penal Codes of 1927 followed this precedent with a further tendency to restrict drastic punishments. No detrimental effects on discipline were encountered. It was put on record that 'nobody thinks of fetching back from the prison museum the penalties of a past civilization-era'.[1] The National-Socialist régime, however, fell back upon sterner measures. The re-drafted Principles of 1934 cancelled for convicts under punitive detention the intermittent 'good days', and the Regulation of 1940 reintroduced the darkening of the cell for certain days, but not corporal punishment. The conception of the 'dual State' prevailed. While unlimited arbitrariness of the police executive resulted in the cruelties and tortures of concentration camps, within the restricted field of the administration of justice corporal punishment remained illegal. Similar observations apply to Italy, where the penal administration under the Ministry of Justice emphatically rejected corporal punishment as 'incompatible with the standards of a civilized man of our time'.[2]

These illustrations show the common features as well as the divergences of disciplinary systems. Certain differences may be explained by national temperament and standards. More probably they are due to the hazards of historical development. These factors make it difficult to define the limit of disciplinary powers which should rightly be conceded to prison authorities. Controversy is most acute over the question of inflicting physical hardship, especially corporal punishment.

Corporal punishment brutalizes the prisoner and executioner alike. It breeds hatred and bitterness, uproots personal dignity, and frustrates any attempt at social readjustment. At the same time it arouses among fellow prisoners a community of interests against the prison régime and a sympathy with its victims. In 1847 Lord Henry Thomas Cockburn, a Scottish Judge of the Court of Sessions, gave this opinion to a Select Committee of the House of Lords: 'Whipping, I have no doubt, would often be salutary, but it is attended with two risks which it is difficult to avoid; one is the danger, especially in obscure places, of undetected cruelty, the other, that where the infliction fails to amend, it makes the culprit a greater blackguard than he was.'[3] Twelve years before, when harsh

[1] E. Starke in Frede–Grünhut, *Reform des Strafvollzuges* (1927), p. 178.

[2] G. Dybwad, *Theorie und Praxis des fascistischen Strafvollzuges* (1934), p. 21.

[3] 'Report from the Select Committee of the House of Lords appointed to inquire into the Execution of Criminal Law, especially Juvenile Offenders and Transportation' 1847 (*Reports from Committees in 10 vols.*, vii. 3), Appendix, p. 93.

treatment was a common device for the maintenance of discipline, Obermaier had declared: 'One cannot reform a prisoner by beating him, since thereby one will not imbue a man with confidence. By such brutal punishment, men will become only more shrewd, surreptitious and malicious.'[1] This observation is corroborated by an English prison official, who asserted that in his long experience he 'never knew of a single case in which the "cat" did not brutalize a man', nor did he know 'one of its victims who was not a worse man in every sense afterwards than he was before'.[2]

In spite of such disastrous effects on the individual prisoner concerned, the threat of corporal punishment as a deterrent of others might be thought indispensable for discipline. The experience of continental countries and a number of American states where corporal punishment is illegal repudiates this assumption. Whether it might be better to substitute dark cells and shackling for corporal punishment may be open to question. It is idle to argue their relative merits, though flogging probably degrades more and is a more lasting obstacle to rehabilitation. When in 1929 the International Penal and Penitentiary Commission drafted Standard Minimum Rules for the Treatment of Prisoners, allowance was made in sections 36 and 37 for States which felt bound to retain corporal punishment or dark cells.[3] The final text, accepted for recommendation by the Fifteenth Assembly of the League of Nations in 1934,[4] at least declared it 'desirable' to reach a stage where corporal punishment and dark cells are no longer disciplinary punishments. In England, the *Report of the Departmental Committee on Corporal Punishment* of 1938,[5] after a careful weighing of abundant evidence, concluded that corporal punishment as a court penalty should be abolished for juvenile offenders as well as for adults, but should be retained, under certain safeguards, as the ultimate disciplinary punishment for prisoners other than the inmates of Borstal institutions. The abortive Criminal Justice Bill of 1938 followed these suggestions.

The Report of 1938 held only a 'moderate view' on deterrence with regard to the culprit himself. According to the evidence, corporal punishment never brought an improvement, but 'in all

[1] G. M. Obermaier, *Anleitung zur vollkommenen Besserung der Verbrecher in den Strafanstalten* (1835), reprinted Hamburg, 1925, s. 19, p. 64.

[2] 'Warden', *His Majesty's Guests*, quoted from G. Benson and E. Glover, *Corporal Punishment* (1931), p. 14.

[3] *Bulletin*, N.S., No. 5, Oct. 1929.

[4] For the revised text, 3 *Recueil* 156.

[5] H.M. Stationery Office, Cmd. 5684; for statistical evaluation see E. Lewis-Faning, 102 *J. Stat. Soc.* 565.

but a few cases' seemed 'effective in deterring the individual punished from committing another serious assault on an officer which might merit a second flogging'.[1] With regard to the effect on others, 'the evidence of all witnesses was definite and unanimous', that the fear of 'the cat' does in fact deter violent prisoners from committing serious assaults on officers.[2] It is hard to contest this statement by theoretical considerations, which have been denounced as 'charity at the expense of a third party', a claim of ethical perfection at the expense of those who are exposed to the daily strain of professional prison service. Only if they are sure of an effective personal protection can they fairly be expected to perform their duties with patience and forbearance.

With regard to these two sides of the problem, experience in general varies. Like Lord Cockburn, continental experts have maintained that a regimentation of flogging does not work, and that the only way of eradicating the evils of an unauthorized beating is to outlaw corporal punishment altogether. 'Where the laws permit the flogging of prisoners', said Obermaier, 'beating soon becomes general, since then every officer can and will punish, because nobody is any longer very particular.'[3] This statement has been confirmed by recent experience.[4] Conversely, English expert opinion maintains that it cannot fairly be insisted that prison officers restrain themselves to the utmost and refrain from the use of physical force, unless they can depend on the probable infliction of a penalty which they firmly believe to be an effective deterrent.[5] It is by their confidence in this deterrent that in England prison officers are able to go unarmed except for a short wooden stave. Only parties of convicts working outside prison walls are accompanied by guards with fire-arms. In Prussia, after the abolition of corporal punishment, all officers still carried side-arms, and those on night duty, and all who had to control prisoners in the open, or larger gatherings of prisoners, carried fire-arms.[6] One way or another the threat of physical force is inseparable from punishment by deprivation of liberty. The English solution typifies the English tendency not to part with traditional institutions unless the necessity is urgent, and to trust that a high standard of administration will be a sufficient safeguard against any misuse.

Corporal punishment is a question of principle rather than a

[1] *Report on Corporal Punishment*, l.c., p. 108.

[2] Ibid., p. 109.

[3] Obermaier, l.c., p. 65.

[4] C. Bondy, *Pädagogische Probleme im Jugendstrafvollzug* (1925), p. 80.

[5] *Report on Corporal Punishment*, l.c., p. 112.

[6] Section 44, Prussian Prison Regulation of 1 Aug. 1923.

regular occurrence of ordinary prison routine. The incidence of its infliction in English local and convict prisons for the last six pre-war years 1933–8 was 6, 3, 0, 5, 2, 5. For inmates of male convict prisons alone, with a yearly total of approximately 1,600 men, the figures are 1, 1, 0, 2, 2, 1.[1] In Prussia, before the First World War, the ratio of convicts flogged was even smaller. Out of a yearly total of approximately 17,000 male convicts, the incidence for the years 1905–9 was 5, 2, 6, 0, 6.[2] After due consideration of the evidence, the fact remains that corporal punishment is alien to a prison régime which pursues the social readjustment of prisoners and their rehabilitation in a free society. Its preservation belies the reformative purposes of the prevailing penal policy, and strengthens the cynicism which denounces the social and educational objects of penal reform as wanton self-deception.

Present-day criminal law provides two different sanctions: punishments for criminal offences committed with a guilty mind, and measures of public security against dangerous criminals. The same duality applies to disciplinary law in penal institutions. Here, too, punishments have been supplemented by preventive measures. Such security measures are deprivation of articles which may be used for obnoxious purposes, isolation in special observation-cells, mechanical restraint by shackling or straitjacket. In criminal law and disciplinary law alike, the distinction between both measures is more easily drawn in theory than in practice. Punishment looks back to the offence committed; a security measure looks forward to the infraction which it tries to prevent. For the prisoner himself, however, it makes little difference whether he has to go to the isolation cell as a punishment for his attempted escape, or as a preventive measure in order to hinder him from trying it again. This flexibility has its dangers. To meet an immediate or imminent danger, security measures are applicable with a minimum of formalities and a maximum of discretion. This involves the risk that a serious penalty may be inflicted as a 'mere' security measure without the legal safeguards which the law requires for even a minor punishment. Therefore, with the exceptions necessary for handling emergencies, security measures should be inflicted by the same procedure and a similar graduation of jurisdiction as disciplinary punishments. In England a Governor's power is limited to the punishment of a prisoner with cellular confinement up to three days and to place him under restraint up to twenty-four hours.

[1] *Report Prison Commissioners, 1938*, p. 26.

[2] E. Pollitz, l.c., p. 102; Kriegsmann, p. 171, n. 2.

Two other preventive measures are further to be distinguished from disciplinary punishment as well as from security measures. They are use of arms and measures taken under doctor's orders. The use of arms is lawful if it complies with the administrative rules and regulations on the application of force. In Germany the Principles of 1923 as well as the Draft Penal Codes of 1927 referred to the relevant administrative law of the particular German *Länder*. The Prussian Prison Regulation of 1923, section 44, permitted the use of arms for the suppression of a mutiny, the prevention of an attempted escape, defence against assault, and overpowering resistance. Measures taken under the prison doctor's orders are determined by the medical purposes and the professional responsibility of the physician.

Modes of Procedure

In the infliction of disciplinary punishment there are two salient principles: the head of the institution is responsible, and certain legal safeguards must be observed. These two principles are antagonistic and limit each other. If the head's prerogative is unrestricted, directorial dictatorship results; while excessive attention to constitutional niceties impede proper administration. Penal institutions must find the right balance between the two views. Like the commanding officer of a military unit, the head of a penal establishment bears the responsibility for good order and discipline. He must therefore have the means to maintain and enforce them. In every penal system, at least certain disciplinary powers are entrusted to him, but many countries do not assign the infliction of serious punishments to him alone. The legal guarantees for the prisoner are concerned with ensuring that the facts are fully ascertained, including those constituting *mens rea*, that the hearing is fair and the judgement unbiased, and that a proper record is kept of both facts and proceedings, which makes a later review possible. These requirements are best met by supplementing, if not supplanting, the orders of the head of the institution by decisions of a bench of several members. Such a system ensures a full presentation of the case, since the head of the institution, if he is a member of the disciplinary board himself, has to convince his colleagues, or, if he is not a member, has to state his case before the tribunal. Members from outside the prison service will dissipate the suspicion of administrative bias. The legal safeguards will even be strengthened by the inclusion of judicial or quasi-judicial members on the disciplinary board. Prevailing prison systems show numerous variations of such a scheme.

The traditional features of prison discipline in Prussia reserved the punitive power exclusively to the administration, but limited the authority of the Director acting alone. Before the First World War, when stern measures were still admissible, the Director had the power to inflict medium punitive detention up to four weeks, and severe punitive detention and shackling up to two weeks. More serious punishments required the approval of the supervisory administrative authority. From 1869 corporal punishment and 'laths arrest' could not be inflicted against the veto of a committee of prison officers (*Beamtenkonferenz*) unless the supervisory authority decided otherwise.[1] An abortive German Draft Penal Code of 1879 proposed to consolidate the last-mentioned provision as the law of the Reich. The German Principles of 1923 provided for a Prison Officers' Committee as a consultative body beside the Director. Prussia, in section 46 (1, a) of the Prison Regulations of 1923 assigned to this Committee the task of discussing serious infractions of order and discipline and the infliction of severe punishments. Short of this vague provision for consultation, the Director alone had the full punitive power up to the permissible maximum of four weeks' 'severe detention'. In Hamburg the Prison Regulations of 1924 confirmed the disciplinary authority of the Director of Penal Institutions, but provided that the latter should delegate the power to inflict punishments to Institutional committees (*Anstaltsausschuss*), consisting of the head of the particular institution and two other officers, appointed by the Director. Likewise in French institutions for long-term prisoners, the Director presides over a tribunal of prison officers (*prétoire disciplinaire*), which hears inmates reported for disciplinary offences, suggests the punishment, and accepts complaints from prisoners.[2] In France and Germany further provisions for Supervisory Commissions, composed of men from outside the prison administration (*Gefängniskommission, Commission de surveillance*) remained almost a dead letter.[3] In the United States, among state prisons under review in 1937, seventy-five entrusted the handling of disciplinary matters exclusively to single officers, usually the Deputy Wardens. Only five institutions had prison courts of three to five officers for

[1] Kriegsmann, p. 173, nn. 1 and 2.

[2] Mossé, p. 142.

[3] Kriegsmann, p. 158, n. 6; Mossé, p. 103; Hugueney, *Actes du Congrès Pénal et Pénitentiaire International de Berlin* (1935), ii. 36.

adjudication of offences. In one of the latter prisons, Jackson, Michigan, the prison court refers a prisoner who pleads not guilty to a special behaviour clinic for consideration. The federal administration avoids one-man decisions in matters of discipline and has established disciplinary courts of prison officials in most of its institutions.[1]

England is the classic country for the judicial control of prison discipline. As long as English prisons were under Local Government, they were 'owned' and administered by the Justices in Quarter Sessions. When the Prison Act of 1877 transferred all prisons in the country to the centralized State administration of the Prison Commissioners, justices were empowered to form visiting committees with the right to inspect prisons and to co-operate in matters of discipline.[2] For convict prisons boards of visitors were established. With these the influence of the State authority is stronger. Members are appointed by the Secretary of State; only a certain proportion of them must be magistrates. The same applies to visiting committees attached to Borstal institutions. The punitive power of an English prison governor has been limited to three days' cellular confinement. More severe punishments are under the jurisdiction of the committee or board. Corporal punishment may only be inflicted if a tribunal, consisting of no less than three members of the committee or board, two being justices of the peace, or one a stipendiary magistrate, has held an inquiry on oath and has submitted the order to the Secretary of State for confirmation.[3]

This English tradition of judicial control met with much admiration abroad.[4] In France and Prussia it left its mark in the legislation rather than in the practice of prison administration. In Baden the English model was instrumental in the establishment of joint local prison advisory councils (*Beiräte*). They consisted of prison officers and a number of laymen, with a professional lawyer as chairman. The latter, or the President of the District Court, hears appeals of prisoners against disciplinary punishment.[5] The Judge of Surveillance in contemporary Italian law is a further recognition of the rule of law in penal administration, but he has only such disciplinary powers as involve the prisoner's assignment

[1] *Attorney General's Survey*, v. 120 and 332.
[2] 40 & 41 Vict., c. 21, s. 13.
[3] Prison Act 1898, 61 & 62 Vict., c. 41, ss. 3 and 5; Fox, pp. 46, 57 et seq., 84.
[4] P. F. Aschrott, *Strafensystem und Gefängniswesen in England* (1887), pp. 157 et seq.; J. Goldschmidt, in *VDA*. iv. 105 and 395.
[5] Kriegsmann, p. 159; *Badische Dienst- und Vollzugsordnung* (1925), s. 260.

to a special prison régime or his removal to another institution.[1] Critics have asserted that these functions are so vague that they are a source of endless conflicts.[2] Far-reaching proposals for the judicial control of prison discipline have been made by the Czechoslovak Draft Codes. They provide for a supervisory council consisting of a public prosecutor as commissioner, a judge, an attorney, two social workers, and four other members. The judge and two other members of the council form a prison court. This tribunal has a twofold jurisdiction. First, it has the power to inflict disciplinary punishment in cases for which the maximum permissible to superintendent and commissioner seems insufficient, i.e. solitary confinement of more than a fortnight. Secondly, it is the trial court for prisoners accused of common criminal offences punishable with not more than eight months' imprisonment.[3] With these proposals the Czechoslovak lawgivers intended to give to prisoners the legal guarantees of a due process of law, and at the same time to entrust the decisions to a bench with first-hand knowledge of the inside life of a penal institution.

A consultative administrative committee of the Prussian and French type gave the opportunity for an experiment in Thuringia, where prisoners were admitted to the disciplinary board. After encouraging experience in one institution this innovation was extended to the whole Thuringian prison administration in 1929.[4] This institutional tribunal (*Anstaltsgericht*) consisted of the Director as chairman, two representatives of the staff, and two prisoners, elected, with the Director's consent, by and from members of the third stage. Other prisoners might act as counsel for the defence. After examination and trial the Director asked the prisoners and official assessors for their proposals. The final decision rested with the Director. This procedure applied the principle of inmate participation to the administration of disciplinary punishments. After six years' experience the Director who initiated this experiment testified that the innovation proved a full success. In many cases he concurred with the most lenient suggestion, not infrequently his decision was even less severe.[5] These tribunals contri-

[1] Italian Criminal Code, 1930, art. 144; Code of Criminal Procedure, 1930, art. 585; Prison Regulation, 1931, art. 4; G. Novelli, 55 *ZStW* 201.

[2] Jiménez de Asúa, *Actes du Congrès Pénal et Pénitentiaire International de Berlin* (1935), ii. 56.

[3] Ss. 92–4, 105, Czechoslovak Draft Criminal Code, General Part, 1921; ss. 96, 104–6, Draft Criminal Code, 1926.

[4] Revised Thuringian Prison Regulation of 24 Sept. 1929, ss. 165–72.

[5] M. Vollrath, in *Gefängnisse in Thüringen* (1930), p. 14.

buted to an atmosphere of mutual trust and respect. Complaints to the Ministry on allegedly unjust punishments decreased markedly.[1]

The foregoing comparative notes suggest a certain relation between prison discipline and general political tendencies. The question naturally arises whether the monocratic administration of prison discipline corresponds to authoritarian, and the establishment of collegiate boards and judicial control to a democratic and liberal structure of the body politic. Apart from such wider issues, prison discipline itself benefits from constitutional institutions. They secure the rule of law in the remote seclusion of prison life. A trial before a bench brings the underlying facts of a case into the open, and thereby prevents suspicion and resentment. Prisoners who despise a single disciplinarian as a personal enemy are less truculent before a tribunal. The head of the institution is relieved from the precarious obligation of trying single-handed cases which affect his own authority nearly as much as if he were a party himself.

Legal remedies against disciplinary decisions depend on the particular form of jurisdiction. Where, as in Prussia, the entire disciplinary power has been vested in the administration, the prisoner has an administrative 'complaint' to the higher authority. Where, as in England, judicial committees and boards have been established outside the prison machinery, they are an impartial body to hear the prisoners' complaints and applications. Under the particular conditions of prison discipline it will often be necessary to execute the punishment at once, even pending an appeal. At the same time it should be possible for the prisoner afterwards to apply for 'a new trial' and revocation of a punishment which he underwent undeservedly. Promotion to higher stages and remission of parts of the sentence depend on the prisoner's institutional record. He therefore has a right to a clean sheet, if indeed he has been punished unjustly.

Incidence of Offences and Punishments

It is almost impossible to present comparative figures of the incidence of disciplinary offences and punishments. To refer the total of incidents during a year to the average daily prison population would result in an unduly high ratio, since many more prisoners are passing through the institution throughout the year

[1] L. Frede, 'Reform des Strafvollzugs in Thüringen', offprint from *Schw. Z.* (1930), p. 36.

who might be concerned with breaches of discipline. The total of inmates admitted during a year does not allow for the fact that some of them are for longer, and others for shorter, time exposed to the temptation of breaking the prison rules. The proper basis for assessing a ratio of disciplinary offence and punishment would be the product of the number of prisoners housed and the days they spent in prison. Since such figures are not available, the following discussion has to content itself with a few sketchy illustrations.

There is no more striking difference between the 'old' prison discipline and the recent development than the amount of disciplinary punishments. In Prussia the percentage of male convicts punished sank from 42·8 in 1894 to 20·4 in 1907. At the same time the average number of infractions per head of punished inmates decreased from 2·6 to 1·6.[1] The same trend continued for the following decades in England. Here, the percentage of male convicts punished sank from 37·4 for an average of the years 1903–7 to 14·4 in 1938, with the ratio of offences per head of prisoners punished decreasing from 2·6 to 1·9. In local prisons the percentage of all prisoners punished for the last two years before the outbreak of the Second World War kept almost stable at 4·3.[2] Observers agree that outbreaks of violence are less frequent than formerly. In England cases of violence against persons and property in relation to the total of inmates of male convict prisons sank from 15·9 per cent. as the yearly average 1903–7 to 9 per cent. in 1938. Within this falling trend there was a peak of 13 per cent. for the average for the years 1927–30. In local prisons, with a much smaller ratio of violent offences, conditions remained almost stable for the last ten years before the outbreak of the Second World War. The curve slowed down from 1·16 per cent. in 1929 to 0·95 per cent. in 1938.[3] There are various reasons for the calming down of the prison atmosphere. It may be a reflection of a general change in criminality, and of the social strata from which criminals emerge, especially of the rise of frauds and other sophisticated offences against property and of 'white-collar' crimes. Whether new forms of armed hold-up and auto-robbery will increase the number of tough prisoners remains to be seen. It is more likely that the change in the prisoners' reactions is due to the methods of treatment. Experience in mental institu-

[1] Computed from figures given by Pollitz, l.c., p. 102.

[2] Computed from figures given by *Report Prison Commissioners, 1938*, p. 26.

[3] Ibid., pp. 25 et seq.

tions has shown that, with the abandonment of harsh treatment, most of the violent symptoms disappeared. Likewise in prison, the decrease in violence goes hand in hand with a steady reduction of repressive coercion. In 1894 Prussia had almost 22,000 male convicts, and corporal punishment was inflicted ninety-six times; in 1907 there were still almost 18,000 male convicts, but only six cases of corporal punishment. In English local and convict prisons the yearly average number of corporal punishments was forty-four for the years 1898–1902, and three for 1934–8.[1] The sinking curve of corporal punishments markedly outruns the fall in the total number of prisoners. The good effect of a less brutal discipline is strengthened if supplemented by positive means such as a reasonable routine, satisfactory work, proper diet, sufficient exercise, and mental activities. A comparison of prison discipline past and present must further allow for the fact that with the reduction of the total number of convicted prisoners in European countries the smaller residue becomes a negative selection. Compared with the last generation, by an increased application of fines and probation, a considerable proportion of the most amenable offenders have been spared prison experience. This observation gives even greater significance to the achievement of a calmer prison atmosphere maintained with less rigorous punishments.

Apart from this general historical trend, the incidence of disciplinary offences varies considerably. According to an American investigation of the records of 14 state prisons, the ratio of reported offences to the prison population varied from 5·65 per cent. for San Quentin, Ca., to 411·77 per cent. for Mansfield, Ohio. Even apart from such extreme cases the majority of the prisons under review showed a ratio ranging between 27 per cent. and 66 per cent.[2] For the interpretation of these figures it must be remembered that a reference to the prison population of a single or an average day does not allow for the fact that some prisons have a more fluctuating population and therefore a higher number of possible offenders than other institutions of the same capacity. Even with this reservation the figures suggest that the causes of prison offences are as multiple as the causes of crime. In both cases similar psychological factors are relevant. They are the prisoner's ability and willingness to fit himself into the order of institutional routine, the loss of personal status and security, real and imaginary family troubles, anxiety for the future, and all this

[1] Pollitz, l.c.; *Report Prison Commissioners, 1938*, l.c.
[2] *Attorney General's Survey*, v. 121.

accentuated by the psychological effects of long imprisonment with its alternating phases of indifference and irritability. Unexpected acts of violence and many stupid attempts to escape are often 'short circuit acts', dictated by a sudden overwhelming impulse without consideration even for the immediate consequences. Increasing truculence and obstruction by long-term prisoners are sometimes initial symptoms of a mental disturbance. At the same time the common destiny of imprisonment conceals an immense variety of environmental factors. Prison discipline depends greatly on the scope and type of the institution. In most institutions discipline easily assumes impersonal and repressive features. The predilection of nineteenth-century reformers for separate confinement was not least due to its good influence on discipline. While the supervision of the old prison association alternated between indulgence and repression, the cellular structure seemed to guarantee quietness and order almost without disciplinary intervention. Conversely, the silent system could only be upheld by a rigid discipline enforcing the unnatural prohibition of harmless human intercourse. In 1836, Coldbath Fields Prison, where the silent system had been brought to the highest perfection in England, reported 5,138 punishments for 'talking and swearing' in addition to 6,794 punishments for other offences.[1] Classification has a favourable influence on discipline. By separating drug addicts and psychopathic personalities from the rest of the prisoners, it removes potential trouble-makers. At the same time they can receive the individual treatment they need, which in the general prison would be resented as unjust indulgence towards the main sinners. There may be more disciplinary incidents in an institution with a frequent coming and going of inmates, and fewer, but more serious ones, in a prison where 'old lags' are serving long sentences. Much depends on the number and training of the staff, on the wisdom of the prevailing rules, and on incentives and constructive methods which require a man's whole strength to reach targets worthy of the effort. Of all these factors, none has such a marked relation to the rise and fall of disciplinary punishments as the personal influence of the head of the institution. This is the result of an investigation, based on the disciplinary records of twenty-four Prussian prisons before the First World War.[2] In three-quarters of the institutions a change

[1] 'II. Report of the Inspectors of Prisons of Great Britain' (1837) (*Reports from Commissioners, vol. 32*), p. 2.

[2] von Koblinski, 12 *N.F. Schmollers Jahrb.* 217.

in the directorship coincided with a change in the curve of disciplinary punishments, the classification of the offences, or the selection of measures applied. In two-thirds of institutions with a new Director the number of disciplinary punishments either rose or sank markedly. This effect of the 'personal equation' is not merely a question of severity or leniency. Rather is it a question of the head's personal influence on the spirit of the institution. Much depends on the way the officers respond to the new chief's intentions, whether they regard it as their right that a man they report should be punished, or are willing and capable of an informal adjustment of minor difficulties without misusing such discretion by unauthorized punishments and fatigues. Numbers alone are fallacious. One disciplinarian punishes slightly but frequently, another regards close confinement as the only effective penalty, but spares it for serious cases. The British reports for 1938 reveal some of these differences in disciplinary policy. In England and Wales the punishment ratio in local prisons is 4·8 per cent. as compared with 14·4 per cent in male convict prisons, but the proportion of close confinement is slightly higher among the less numerous punishments in the local prisons, viz. 27·6 per cent. of all punishments inflicted against 23·1 per cent. in male convict prisons. Conversely, in Scotland, solitary confinement has been exclusively inflicted at Peterhead Convict Prison, where out of a total of 216 convicts twenty-eight men were reported for sixty-one offences and got forty-five punishments, one-third of them being solitary confinement.[1]

The maintenance of discipline is a test of skill in handling men. Even more than the sentencing function of criminal courts the administration of disciplinary powers defies any hard-and-fast rules. Disciplinary law is more flexible than common criminal law. A wide discretion will enable the disciplinarian to allow for the prisoner's personality and to assess his will and inclinations rather than the act committed. Disciplinary action should fit into the man's treatment. There are, however, certain limits to the individualization of disciplinary justice. In view of the sense of justice of other prisoners and in the prison community as a whole it is often impossible to inflict divergent sanctions for what at its face value seems to be the same act of obstruction or illicit communication. This leads to the observance of certain traditional standards of punishment for a number of typical prison offences.

[1] *Report Prison Commissioners, 1938*, p. 90; *Annual Report of the Prison Department for Scotland for 1938*, p. 33.

Less than any other behaviour problem is discipline the concern of a single individual who is to be checked or adjusted. It is the attitude and behaviour of men as members of a group. The dangers of prison life are not the insolence and disobedience of individual prisoners, but the irritability and truculence of a mass, which might grow into a tense and electrified atmosphere, where a single spark of discontent suffices for a dramatic explosion.[1] In such circumstances it is extremely difficult to steer the right course, and neither to lose authority by compromise, nor to jeopardize it by stubbornness. In matters of discipline the prison administrator must not only check and deter the unruly, but also strengthen the good-will and influence of the rest, so that the group mind is not against but behind the administration.[2] Disciplinary actions must be just, in a formal meaning of the word, and administered in such a way that the majority of prisoners can fairly be expected to accept and understand them.[3] Where punishment has had to be inflicted and accepted without arguing, no trouble should be spared to explain the reasons for the steps taken to the man concerned and his fellow prisoners.

INCENTIVES

It is commonly recognized that the strongest antidote to the temptations of crime is a status and security in civil life too much prized for them to be risked on the chances of illicit gains. Conversely, if little seems to be lost by abandoning the standards of a decent life, even the threat of heavy punishments will prove ineffective. Applied to prison conditions this means that, for the sake of good discipline, there must be targets the prisoner can hope to reach and which are worth the effort required, stakes which he has a strong interest in not losing. This is the foundation of a more or less elaborate system of privileges, granted or forfeited according to conduct. An earnings scheme contributes much to good discipline. More than anything else it helps to overcome the apathy of a monotonous prison routine and thus removes the roots of many troubles. Money earned and at the prisoner's disposal gives him not only access to certain modest amenities, but a sense of privacy and self-respect, jealously guarded against forfeiture by his own fault. By far the most important target is the prisoner's restoration

[1] *Wickersham Report*, ix. 35; Weinberg, 47 *Am. J. Soc.* 717; H. du Parcq, *Report on the Circumstances connected with the recent Disorder at Dartmoor Convict Prison* (1932).

[2] Field and Winslow, 23 *Journal* 205.

[3] Field, 157 *Annals* 158.

to liberty. Therefore the most powerful incentive is to put the advancement of the day of release into his own hands.

In England the earning or forfeiture of remission marks has long been regarded as 'the root of convict discipline'.[1] The scheme was introduced in the convict prisons in 1864 and extended to local prisons on the recommendation of the Gladstone Committee by the Prison Act of 1898. A prisoner has to earn six marks a day. If his total of marks amounts to five times the number of days of his sentence, he will be free. He thereby earns the remission of one-sixth of his sentence. The development of industrial work in association makes it almost impossible to grant or withhold remission marks according to the prisoner's progress at work. Instead, he normally earns his marks, but risks losing a number of them for bad conduct or idleness. A vertical classification, i.e. a Progressive Stage system with additional privileges and increased responsibilities, multiplies the targets. In England the Du Cane system of the last quarter of the nineteenth century was more differentiated by the rigid character of the lower stages than by trust and privileges at the higher. Since 1934 prisoners remain three months in the first, six months in the second, and then proceed to the third stage. The stages differ in the eligibility for concerts and lectures, the number of library books available, the duration of visits, and recreation in cells. The progress from stage to stage is almost automatic by the earning of stage marks. Their forfeiture delays promotion and is mostly used as an additional sanction, supplementing disciplinary punishment.[2]

In the United States all legislations have enacted so-called good-time laws, which enable the prisoner, as a reward for good conduct and industry, to earn a shortening of his sentence.[3] As in England, the practice reversed the original conception. Good time is automatically granted as of right, but may be forfeited for disciplinary offences. The same is true of grading systems which by 1937 had been introduced in twenty-two prisons. It requires much hardihood and fortitude in the prison administrator to maintain a system where, by a discretionary or quasi-judicial decision, every prisoner is to be promoted according to his merits. Instead, prisoners proceed to the higher stages after the expiration of certain minimum periods, but may be degraded as a disciplinary sanction. Some states combine the good-time privilege with the grading

[1] E. Ruggles-Brise, p. 35.

[2] Fox, pp. 80 et seq.

[3] *Attorney General's Survey*, v. 123 et seq.

system, and grant members of the upper stages a higher proportion of the sentence remitted. In 1920 an elaborate so-called Progressive Merit system was introduced in Illinois. The prisoner enters the institution at a medium stage which involves neither loss nor gain in respect of his sentence. After three weeks he is eligible for promotion to higher stages with five or even ten days good time per month. He may be degraded to lower stages which imply a delay of his release for five or ten days per month served in these grades. Again, this scheme has been administered negatively rather than positively, i.e. prisoners have been promoted automatically, if there were no charges of bad conduct, and degraded for misconduct.[1]

In Germany partial remission of sentences has been used in a discretionary way. The relevant section 23 of the Criminal Code provides for a 'preliminary', i.e. conditional, release for good conduct if three-quarters of the sentence with a minimum of one year has expired. Practice, however, preferred the more flexible way of a pardon on the recommendation of the head of the institution. The prospect of such a recommendation was expected to be an effective motive for good conduct and industry. The influence of a grading system on the maintenance of discipline was first discussed in connexion with reports on the American reformatories.[2] When in 1912 Prussia established the first Youth prison at Wittlich, with accommodation for 169 young men between eighteen and twenty-one, the administration accepted the Progressive Stage system together with other features of Elmira. The young prisoner proceeded after four months of 'good conduct' from the first to the second, and after a further four months to the third stage. Only members of the third stage were eligible for conditional release before complete expiration of the sentence.[3] In the reform period after the First World War, the Progressive Stage system pursued even more ambitious ends and was almost identified with an educational prison discipline. Attempts were made to replace the negative by a positive grading scheme, and to promote prisoners only after a full assessment of the individual case and its merits. In Thuringia the promotion from the observation to the treatment stage was granted after a certain period, but could be either delayed or advanced by the Director in consultation with an institutional council, consisting of the Deputy Director,

[1] Ibid., p. 130.
[2] Herr, in *VDA* (1908), iv. 483 et seq.
[3] Appendix to Institutional Rules, s. 1. For the text see W. Bleidt, in Bumke, p. 372.

social worker, and other appointed officers. Promotion from the treatment to the probation stage required not only the expiration of half the remaining sentence, but also a positive decision that educational treatment could be expected to prove successful. To reach this decision the Director had to hear the institutional council and the spokesmen of the prisoners of the third (upper) stage. Only prisoners of the third, probation, stage were eligible for conditional release.[1] Under this system within three years the number of disciplinary punishments sank by two-thirds. Within four years only nineteen out of 234 third-stage prisoners had to be degraded.[2] Hamburg Prison Regulations provided for automatic promotion to the medium stage, while promotion to the upper and to the so-called free group required an explicit decision.[3] The Prussian Regulation on a Progressive Stage system of 1929 required a positive decision for every promotion from a lower to a higher stage, but this scheme remained a dead letter.[4]

These manifold features of remission schemes, good-time laws, and grading systems have one thing in common. They act as incentives to good conduct and industry. Almost everywhere experience confirms that they have a marked influence on good discipline, and help produce a healthy atmosphere in penal institutions. The loss of advantages and improvements in the prisoner's position, or even of a fair chance of getting them, acts as a stronger deterrent than increasing the severity of his punishment. The incentive policy, however, has to face the question, whether bribing into good behaviour is morally sounder than deterring by punishment from bad conduct. Thomas Mott Osborne held both methods equally doomed to failure. 'So far as the ultimate effect on the prisoner is concerned', he said, 'there is little to choose. Both systems leave altogether out of sight the fact that when the man leaves the shelter of the prison walls, there will be no one either to punish or to reward.'[5] This verdict is right in so far as it asserts that discipline does not of itself change the docile prisoner into the law-abiding citizen of a free community. But whatever methods may be most appropriate to the ultimate educational purpose of social readjustment, good discipline is indispensable as a precondition and as a preliminary step. If, in maintaining

[1] Revised Thuringian Prison Regulation of 24 Sept. 1929, ss. 41 et seq.

[2] E. Holler, 5 *Erziehung* 618, 614.

[3] 'Hamb. Dienst- und Vollzugsordnung', 24 Oct. 1924 (*Hamb. Gesetz- und VO-Blatt*, 635), ss. 74, 80, 81.

[4] 'Pr. VO über den Strafvollzug in Stufen', 7 June 1929, art. iv. 1; ix. 1.

[5] Thomas Mott Osborne, *Society and Prisons* (1916), 216.

discipline, the authorities prefer a system of incentives to one of punishments, the atmosphere will be more favourable to a personal approach to the prisoner and to educational efforts.

INMATE PARTICIPATION

There seems only one possible way of integrating the maintenance of discipline into the process of social readjustment itself. This is to appeal to the prisoners' own sense of responsibility and to rely on an organized inmate participation.[1] From a theoretical point of view such an attempt alone satisfies higher ethical standards. Whatever has been enforced from without, undertaken on the line of least resistance or from motives of material advantage, is of inferior moral value and likely to have only a temporary effect. Only what a man accepts of his own will and for its intrinsic merits is incorporated into his character and builds up his personality.[2] The application of these theoretical principles to the reality of prison life is a delicate task. It requires self-determination within the bondage of an enforced deprivation of liberty.

From the very beginning the idea of inmate participation has been beset with controversy and misconceptions. They are partly due to terminology. The term self-government which has often been used suggests an analogy with politics. This may be helpful in winning the prisoners' interest and directing their demands for self-expression and activity into healthy channels. The drawing up of a constitution, elections, and the 'swearing in' of new deputies can be used as educational means for a higher communal life. In democratic countries to be trained in political self-expression is a recognized object of education for citizenship. But the political analogy is fallacious if it is taken to indicate an original right on the part of the prisoners or an unalterable civil liberty to be respected at all costs, for such self-government as is introduced should be introduced only for the sake of the prisoners' adjustment to a higher communal life within the institution, and finally to life within the community at large. As the highest form of institutional discipline, self-government means the inmate's co-operation, by his activity and responsibility, in his own rehabilitation.[3]

By this conception inmate participation is clearly distinguished from such travesties as the so-called Kangaroo Courts in American

[1] C. M. Liepmann, *Die Selbstverwaltung der Gefangenen* (1928).
[2] W. D. Wills, 6 *Howard Journal* 154.
[3] C. M. Liepmann, l.c., p. 185.

local gaols. These are an excuse for the warden to relinquish his duties, rather than an opportunity for responsible co-operation, and are often misused to frighten the new-comer into accepting the rule of the old lags. They are one of the notorious defects of obsolete penal institutions.[1] Rightly understood, the idea of prisoners' self-government is a general principle which permits several variations. The granting of certain privileges or the assignment to an honour group are an expression of the trust put in selected prisoners. Thus inmate participation should be an exceptional feature, open to the few who seem to deserve it and to benefit from it. The opposite view would be to organize and acknowledge the social responsibility of the whole group, and thereby to bridge the antagonism between inmates and staff. Inmate participation may be conceived of as an educational aim, e.g. as the crowning summit of the last stage of a grading system; and it may be applied as an instrument to help obtain a useful communal life and good discipline throughout the whole institution.

Much can be learnt about the participation of inmates in the life of the prison from experience gained elsewhere. Internment camps and prisoner-of-war camps leave much of the inner administration to the inmates themselves. Administrative expediency and the men's need for responsibility in their own affairs make such a course advisable. In many schools some form of self-government is an educational tradition. For it is realized that advanced pupils often have a talent for leading their fellows which requires recognition and opportunity; and by relieving the teacher of the onus of discipline such a system clears the atmosphere of resentments and obstinacy and makes for good relations between teacher and pupil. In conformity with this tradition, experiments in inmate participation in connexion with punitive and reformative treatment were mainly made in institutions for juvenile delinquents, intended to be schools rather than penal establishments. In the Swiss poor school at Hofwyle, Canton Aargau, established in 1810 by E. v. Fellenberg and F. Wehrli under the impulse of Pestalozzi's educational ideas, elected 'elders' had a responsible share in authority and helped to overcome a crisis which threatened the continuation of the whole work. In J. H. Wichern's 'family system' at the institution 'Rauhes Haus' near Hamburg,

[1] L. N. Robinson, *Jails* (1944), p. 21. The American colloquialism Kangaroo Court was originally used to designate irregular tribunals jumping from place to place in frontier districts. Another explanation takes 'kangaroo' as referring to Australian wild animals for the characterization of something below proper civilized standards; by kind information from Dr. F. Hoefer, Arlington, Va.

'Children of the peace' played a responsible part in the educational scheme. In the Boston House of Reformation E. M. P. Wells built up a grading system which relied on the common judgement of the whole group and the services of elected monitors. The George Junior Republic at Freeville, New York, established under the principle 'Nothing without work' is an educational settlement with the most complete imitation of political patterns of a free commonwealth.

In applying these precedents to prisoners, certain differences ought not to be overlooked. More consideration and judgement may be expected from adults than from juveniles in need of guidance and instruction. At the same time, life in an adult group will often be affected by party spirit and power politics. In educational institutions the loss of liberty serves the sole purpose of securing continuous educational influence. Therefore, educational considerations alone draw the line between dependence and self-determination. Prisoners, on the other hand, are deprived of their liberty as a legal punishment. Their participation in the institutional rule and discipline is limited by the consideration that the purpose of the law must not be reversed. The limit of what is admissible depends on what restrictions beyond mere confinement are essential to the legal conception of imprisonment.

In England no one prisoner is set over another. Honour parties, working without supervision, are sometimes directed by a leader from among themselves. He marches them to and from work and may use his personal persuasion, but he has no disciplinary powers.[1] It is only a small step to extend such honour groups to prisoners' departments, responsible for certain sections of institutional life. Numerous American prisons have organized activities undertaken by prisoners, in co-operation with the staff, such as the editing of a prison magazine, the library service, the prison school, and even the administration of certain funds like canteen profits, the sports fund, or the fund for the aid of families in distress.[2] The 'community prison' of Norfolk, Mass., began as a combination of the family or house systems with a recognized inmate participation. Each housing unit of fifty prisoners elected two delegates for the Inmate council. The council and the prison staff worked together and appointed joint committees on numerous prison activities such as work, maintenance, entertainment, sport, education. Neither the council nor the joint committees were directly

[1] Fox, p. 93.
[2] *Attorney General's Survey*, v. 131.

concerned with discipline. This is not self-government, but rather—in the words of Superintendent Howard B. Gill—'a supervised community within a wall'.[1] Similar principles apply to Annandale, N.J., where the eight cottages are component parts of an organized communal life with regular joint meetings of cottage delegates and staff members.[2]

All these attempts, although deliberately barred from any direct influence on the administration of discipline, affect the whole atmosphere of the institution. As far as they are successful, they are positive contributions to good order and discipline. By winning the prisoners' interest for good purposes they prevent offences. The question suggests itself whether, in all circumstances, this must be the ultimate limit, or whether the principle might even be extended to direct responsibility for matters of discipline. Such a far-reaching proposal has to face two objections. First, it may be argued that direct participation by inmates in the administration of discipline would be only a new label for the organized use of informants from the prisoners' midst. It is difficult to say how far a prison administration should accept information from inmates, and whether it should even encourage the giving of information or enforce it as a disciplinary obligation. Practical administrators sometimes give warning that it would be too hazardous to eliminate informing altogether.[3] Information, however, given away by 'stool pigeons' often stiffens the hostility of the prison community and provokes acts of terrorism. According to observations by the New York Crime Commission, any leakage is soon known to the entire prison population, and may even result in the death of the informer during or after his prison term. Such gang loyalty is a powerful obstacle to social readjustment. The group feeling is so strong that even men with a moral sense might refrain from betraying their comrades, while the ready informer is not always the best character. In the community at large, criminal law is reluctant to enforce an obligation to communicate to the authorities information about the commission of offences. In England the common law misdemeanour of misprision of felony consists in concealing the fact that a felonious act has been committed. The vague conception of 'concealing'[4] seems to cover the mere failure to communicate information to the authorities,[5] even if

[1] Haynes, p. 59.
[2] *Attorney General's Survey*, v. 134.
[3] H. E. Field, 157 *Annals* 159.
[4] J. F. Stephen, *Digest of the Criminal Law* (7th ed. 1926), p. 455.
[5] Kenny, p. 320.

the alleged felon only intended, but never tried, to commit a crime. This extensive interpretation has sometimes been recommended as an expedient to avoid the otherwise more severe punishment of the defendant of an accessory before the fact,[1] while J. F. Stephen maintained that the mere knowledge of an intended crime is not enough to make a person an accessory.[2] The whole controversy is academic, since prosecutions are practically unknown.[3] In certain continental countries criminal provisions enforce the obligation to assist the authorities by 'preventing a crime'[4] or by rendering information about the imminent commission of certain serious crimes.[5] As far as such legal obligations go they do not exclude prisoners, and they may by analogy be applied to disciplinary law too. With regard to administrative discretion the reference to criminal law suggests a middle course. It would be detrimental to the authority and dignity of an administration to insist on information about every occurrence and even to enforce it by an organized spying system, but prisoners should be expected to lend a hand in preventing acts which endanger the security of the institution and of individual lives, and to do so, where other means fail, even by informing the administration of impending offences. This, however, is not inmate participation in the maintenance of discipline, as long as there is antagonism between the majority of prisoners and the staff. Conversely, where the bulk of the prison population, in an organized way, willingly co-operates with the administration, stolen property or smuggled narcotics may be recovered, escapes prevented, and even hints to the staff about infractions of discipline lose the stigma of moral ambiguity.

The second objection against inmate participation in the maintenance of discipline concerns the doubtful proposition that a man sent to prison for a criminal offence should have a say in the application of disciplinary power over other prisoners. This view was emphasized by the prison inspectors in their *Report* for 1837.

> Is a culprit [they asked], probably the greatest delinquent in the prison walls, probably the most ingenious villain, the most finished hypocrite, certainly one of the most guilty of the law,—is this man to be released from the condition of a criminal suffering for his offences and placed in a situation which invests him with authority which is every moment felt over his fellow prisoners, every one of whom is perhaps less stained with moral turpitude than himself?[6]

[1] Hawkins, l.c., c. 29, s. 23; Russell, l.c., ii. 1481.
[2] Stephen, l.c., p. 46.
[3] Kenny, p. 321, n. 1.
[4] Austrian Criminal Code, s. 212.
[5] German Criminal Code, s. 139.
[6] II. Report of Inspectors of Prisons, l.c., p. 4.

This indictment denounces the use of monitors to help enforce the Silent system. It remains true of any repressive system which relies on picked prisoners to help administer disciplinary punishment.

In the face of these objections the co-operation of prisoners in the administration of discipline is feasible only where it can be developed as a natural consequence of an inmate participation which embraces the entire prison routine. The following outstanding examples illustrate two different ways of realizing this idea. One aims at an entirely new conception of prison discipline as a whole; the other establishes a target within an elaborate Progressive Stage system.

The first example is Thomas Mott Osborne's inauguration of a Mutual Welfare League in the New York State Prisons, Auburn and Sing Sing, and the U.S. Naval Prison, Portsmouth, in the years 1913–20.[1] This League was the visible expression of the prisoners' self-determination and co-operation in all matters concerned with the life of the institution. In principle every prisoner was expected to be a member of the League. It was the instrument which was to transform a repressive, monotonous, and unimaginative routine into an enlightened practice with educational and recreational facilities, a liberal handling of letters and visits, and a healthy communal life. These improvements, so essential for the prisoner's life, were privileges granted to members of the League. The League acted and co-operated through its elected delegates. The election was essential, since it excluded any suspicion of 'stool pigeons'. The elected officers of the League marched prisoners to and from work, took over supervision of workshops, dining-hall, and chapel, and administered discipline. A prisoners' court of delegates of the League took over the disciplinary adjudication, in Auburn of minor cases, in Sing Sing of all offences against discipline. Its punitive power consisted in a suspension for a stated period from any or all privileges of the League. The culprit fell back to his former status of a convict under the old routine, who was marched to and from work by a guard, excluded from communal activities and all constitutional rights, and stigmatized by a mark on his arm. This solution brought home to the prisoner the mutual dependence of privileges and responsibility. But the privileges were granted to the League which maintained the standards of behaviour required for the preservation of those benefits. There was no opportunity for a partisan feeling against the administra-

[1] Thomas Mott Osborne, *Society and Prisons* (1916); id., *Prisons and Common Sense* (1924); F. Tannenbaum, *Osborne of Sing Sing* (1933).

tion since the latter was no longer the primary source of disciplinary punishment. The Warden's authority was secured by an official observer at the League's court who, like the prisoner himself, was entitled to appeal to the Warden's court, consisting of the Warden himself, the Principal Keeper, and the prison doctor. Under the inspiring influence of Thomas Mott Osborne's personality, this bold experiment met with a full success. The old drastic disciplinary punishments were almost in abeyance. The number of escapes, prisoners referred to mental institutions, or treated for injuries due to fights decreased markedly, while within five years the output of the shoe shop almost doubled.[1] Twenty years later the League survived merely as an elected 'grievance committee' between the Warden and the inmate body.[2] The bold idea of corporate responsibility had become history.

In Thuringia, for ten years from 1923, a recognized self-government was the outstanding feature of the third, so-called probation, stage.[3] Members of this stage formed a group of 10–16 per cent. of the prison population, i.e. twenty-five men in the convict prison and thirty-five men in the central prison. These men lived in a special wing with unlocked cells, free access to the yard, and a common-room. No guards entered their quarters. They administered the community life outside working hours on their own responsibility. As with the Mutual Welfare League, the constitution of the group said in its first article: 'Privileges imply an obligation.' The group elected a foreman and an executive committee of three. As a self-contained group the prisoners at this privileged stage enjoyed a somewhat esoteric life; but they undertook certain responsibilities also for the institution as a whole. Delegates of the third stage co-operated in the arrangement of the canteen, acted as assessors with consultative votes in the disciplinary court, and were consulted and entitled to make suggestions for the promotion of prisoners to the probation stage. All these privileges were given and administered with a conscious educational intention. A social worker was attached to the group. Like an 'elder statesman', he gave advice which was willingly accepted. The result of such an experiment can hardly be assessed by statistics. The ratio of recidivists among ex-convicts of the third stage was 15 per cent. This is not an unfavourable result. In Prussia, out of the total of offenders

[1] Thomas Mott Osborne, *Society and Prisons*, pp. 208 et seq.

[2] *Attorney General's Survey*, v. 134.

[3] Revised Thuringian Prison Regulation of 24 Sept. 1929, s. 115; A. Krebs, 19 *MoSchrKrim.* 152; E. Holler, 5 *Erziehung* 608; F. Rösch, in *Gefängnisse in Thüringen*, Weimar (1930), pp. 105 et seq.

who were granted conditional remission of their sentences, some 20 per cent. saw the remission revoked.[1] Success does not depend solely on having a small ratio of relapses. It is even more decisive if those who keep straight are better prepared for the new trials which await them in the community at large.

These two examples illustrate the possibilities as well as the limitations of self-government as a principle of discipline. More than any other feature of prison life it requires constant efforts from the head and staff and the prisoners. It is a truism that only strong personalities are capable of governing without a minimum of physical force. Two conditions are essential: unreserved sincerity and rigid self-control. For the rank and file of prison officers it is difficult to change from an authoritarian to a constitutional system. All depends on their willing co-operation. In Sing Sing the guards themselves welcomed Thomas Mott Osborne's efforts to overcome the 'disheartening and revolting' conditions of the old routine,[2] and the foremen of the workshops felt benefited by the new régime. With regard to the prison population, a responsible share in the administration of discipline requires that it should be homogeneous. This does not mean a classification by offences, nor should there be too strict a separation between first offenders and recidivists. The empiric method of forming treatment groups for the different Borstal institutions and under the Wakefield scheme will also lead to the selection of appropriate self-governing groups. In Sing Sing the difficulties that arose were due to a conflict between the 'highbrows', i.e. educated 'white-collar' criminals, and the ordinary 'roughnecks'. While the former had secured most of the privileges as casual 'trusties' under the old less organized system, the elections under the Mutual Welfare League shifted the main influence to the second group. In the Thuringian convict prison promotion to the self-governing probation group resulted in a positive selection. Almost all first offenders, and nearly all skilled workers, succeeded as members of the third stage, while few of the recidivist burglars could reach the standards required. The superior life of this prison aristocracy was not the privilege of a particular social class. Peasants and industrial workers were the nucleus, with a few members of the professions according to the criminality in Thuringia at that time.

Everything in prison life contributes to the standard of discipline. Housing, work, education, recreation, sport, personal approach,

[1] K. Schäfer, 52 *ZStW* 249.

[2] F. Tannenbaum, l.c., pp. 116 and 213.

and general atmosphere, all affect the order within the institution and the behaviour and attitudes of the inmates. Direct means for the maintenance of discipline are punishment, rewards, and the organization of the inmates' co-responsibility. The word-order of these three disciplinary elements implies a progress from force to self-restraint, from direct to indirect rule. Such a progress helps the mass of the prisoners in a negative way by eliminating probable causes of resentment and obstruction. For the few who take an active share of responsibility as foremen or committee members, and in a lesser degree even for members of a self-governing group or of an electorate, this is a test and training for a responsible life in the community. A Borstal Governor has said that in order to teach punctuality you must give the opportunity of being late; and, similarly, Thomas Mott Osborne maintained that liberty alone fits men for liberty. Such a method will overcome the discrepancy between prison discipline and the requirements of life in the community, and thereby serve the society and help protect it. Only then the 'good prisoners' will not mainly be the habitual 'gaol birds' who profit from repeated prison experience and shrewd adaptability. A system which relies on the prisoner's self-determination and responsibility is as far as it is possible to go towards transforming a punishment of which loss of liberty is an integral feature into an education for liberty. One step farther leads to a rehabilitative treatment within the patterns and framework of the community itself.

CHAPTER XII

NON-INSTITUTIONAL TREATMENT

AT the heart of the various aspects of imprisonment, whether they concern work or education, or are social, spiritual, or disciplinary, there is always the problem of the human personality. It is man himself in his relation to work, in his craving for higher knowledge, his need for guidance and help, his ultimate dependence on forces beyond the secular sphere, and his response to either trust or threats. At this level only, social adjustment is feasible, a process intended to result in the formation of attitudes, the acceptance of an aim in life, and to lead to the moulding of a character. At the same time, the limits of such reformative efforts are obvious. As a work team the prison population is a shiftless and ill-selected group. The work available, jealously guarded, is often insufficient, and neither attractive nor instructive. Where a prescribed task is performed under the threat of force the daily work will scarcely yield full satisfaction. The loss of liberty increases the demand for mental and spiritual stimulation, but suspicion and a misplaced defensiveness create new inhibitions. All prison activities are curtailed by the implied proviso that nothing should impede the constant vigilance against possible escapes. As long as prisoners are held by force their attempts to evade custody, though a serious breach of discipline, are not an abuse of trust and therefore in themselves not morally disreputable. An understanding of prison problems gives a deeper insight into the forces which shape character and behaviour; but unfortunately this happens in a situation utterly unfavourable to social adjustment and rehabilitation. Wherever strenuous efforts and unselfish devotion have been rewarded by a lasting success, it has been achieved not because, but in spite, of the man's imprisonment. As long as the imprisonment of criminals is accepted as a necessity, rehabilitative efforts must be made even in the face of the inherent difficulties. But if social readjustment is recognized as the primary aim and the best means of promoting justice and protecting society, then the question is inevitable: Why prison at all?

Before this startling question can be answered, the discussion must turn to the possible alternatives. Present-day penal policy has developed certain methods of extra-mural treatment. They are far from being consolidated in a comprehensive system. So far there are only isolated routes of approach, some fully developed and generally accepted, others vaguely considered and tried as an experiment. But all of them are turning away from the idea that enforced confinement in an enclosed institution is the only and obvious legal sanction, and has precedence over any other correctional treatment. They are probation, parole, psychological treatment, camps, and other types of treatment in a controlled but relatively free environment.

PROBATION

History

The rise of probation is the most remarkable feature of the recent history of criminal law. Within the lifetime of the present generation it has profoundly changed the prevailing penal policy. Since the usual probation period is longer than an average prison term, states with a well-functioning probation system have more probationers than prisoners. In New York, from 1917, the yearly totals of probationers have surpassed those of prisoners.[1] In 1932 California had 7,520 prisoners and 8,739 probationers, New York 18,418 prisoners and 22,370 probationers, and Massachusetts 6,032 prisoners and 22,444 probationers.[2] From 1931 to 1941 the annual average total of federal probationers rose from 8,139 to 29,303, while the federal prison population slightly sank from 24,192 to 23,666.[3]

For comparative purposes probation may be defined as a combination of two equally essential elements: suspension of punishment plus personal supervision. The manner in which punishment is suspended differs with the prevailing system of criminal procedure.[4] By the Norwegian, Danish, and Dutch procedure against juveniles and by the proposals of the German Draft Introductory Act to the projected Criminal Code of 1930, prosecution may be suspended before trial begins.[5] English Courts of Summary Juris-

[1] *Wickersham Report*, ix. 162.

[2] J. R. Moore, 23 *Journal* 639.

[3] W. Hurwitz and B. Mead, in W. C. Reckless, *Etiology of Delinquent and Criminal Behaviour* (Soc. Science Research Council, 1943), p. 126.

[4] v. Liszt, in *VDA*, iii. 1 et seq.; H. F. Pfenninger, 'Bedingte Verurteilung oder Bedingte Begnadigung im Schweizerischen Strafrecht' (offprint from *Festgabe zum Schweizerischen Juristentag, 1928*) (1928); F. Hoefer, 'Bewährungsfrist vor dem Urteil', *Abhdl.Krim.Inst. Berlin.* IV. Folge, ii. 3 (1931).

[5] Sections 85, 87, 91, Norwegian Code of Criminal Procedure in the wording of 25 July 1919; s. 30, Danish Criminal Code, 1930; s. 488, Dutch Code of Criminal Procedure, 1931; Hoefer, l.c., pp. 9, 11, 12; German Draft Introductory Law to the

diction may discharge the offender conditionally, if they think that the charge has been proved, 'without proceeding to conviction'.[1] The distinction between recognition by the court that the defendant is guilty and a formal conviction is technical, though it has a certain psychological importance for the probation officer's approach to an 'unconvicted' probationer.[2] English higher courts, most American courts, and, on the Continent, Austrian Juvenile Courts suspend sentences after conviction. The majority of continental legal systems do not distinguish between conviction and sentence as separate elements of the final judgement. They therefore provide only for a suspension of the execution of a sentence and have different attitudes towards the legal situation which arises at the end of a successful probation period. Belgium, France, Switzerland, and Czechoslovakia presume the preceding 'conditional condemnation' (*sursis*) as non-existent (*non avenu*),[3] while Germany and Austrian criminal law for adults merely give the probationer the chance of a final remission of his punishment.[4] These manifold legal provisions have this in common, that they enable the court to suspend the prisoner's punishment. This, however, is only one aspect of probation. The other, no less important, element is an organized supervision of the individual probationer. It is this particular social service which distinguishes probation from a mere conditional sentence.

The idea of combining the two elements of suspension of punishment and of personal care and supervision owes its origin less to legal doctrines than to social needs emerging from practical experience. In England an established tradition permitted the court to bind over a man in his recognizance to keep the peace, either as an act of preventive justice by the magistrates, if there were grounds for apprehending future misbehaviour,[5] or in criminal

Criminal Code, 1930, art. 70, No. 88, with reference to s. 153/III, Code of Criminal Procedure.

[1] Summary Jurisdiction Act, 1879, 42 & 43 Vict., c. 49, s. 16 (1); Probation of Offenders Act, 1907, 7 Edw. VII, c. 17, s. 1 (1).

[2] *Conviction and Probation*, Pamphlet 1, English Studies in Criminal Science, reprint from 19 *Canadian B.R.* 500.

[3] Belgian 'loi établissant la libération conditionnelle et les condamnations conditionnelles dans le système pénal', 31 May 1888, art. 9; French 'loi (Bérenger) du sursis', 26 Mar. 1891, *Journ. Off.* No. 85; v. Liszt, l.c., pp. 22 and 26; Czechoslovak Act No. 562, 1919, s. 1/II; Swiss Criminal Code, 1937, art. 41.

[4] Regulations of German Länder, first issued in 1895 and 1896, repealed by s. 20 *Gnadenordnung* of 6 Feb. 1935 (*Dtsch. Justiz*, p. 203); ss. 40 et seq. German Draft Criminal Code, 1930; ss. 1 et seq. Austrian Law of 23 July 1920.

[5] Blackstone, iv, c. 18, p. 251; *Lansbury* v. *Riley* [1914], 3 *KB* 229; *R.* v. *Sandback*, ex parte *Williams* (1935), 153 *T.L.R.* 63.

cases in addition to a prison committal on a sentence for a misdemeanour.[1] Common law recognized a suspension of punishment for temporary purposes only, e.g. for a review of the case by a superior court, or an application for pardon,[2] but it did not enable the court 'permanently to refuse to enforce the law'.[3] Nevertheless, progressive Benches anticipated modern legislation by measures which were forerunners of probation. Matthew Davenport Hill, about 1820 as a counsel at the Midland Circuit, witnessed the practice of the Warwickshire Quarter Sessions of consigning young offenders to the care of the prosecuting party, if the latter consented to receive back a dishonest servant or apprentice. Twenty years later, as Recorder of Birmingham, he handed over juvenile offenders with a reasonable prospect of reformation to the care of selected guardians. In twelve years, out of 417 offenders 80 were reconvicted; but 94 had come to be known as reputable citizens.[4] Edward W. Cox, Recorder of Portsmouth, used recognizances to come up for judgement as an alternative for prison terms and, with growing experience, was even more inclined to follow this course.[5] In the United States similar experiments led to the consolidation of this practice by legislation. This movement originated from 'human rescue work', voluntarily undertaken by devoted pioneers.[6] In 1841 John Augustus, a cobbler in Boston, first offered bail for a prisoner and undertook, after further investigation, to take care of him for a certain period. Rufus R. Cook, chaplain to the county gaol, volunteered for the same service. In 1878 Massachusetts enacted the first Probation Act, which provided for the appointment of a paid probation officer in Boston. Subsequent Acts of 1880, 1891, and 1898 made a probation service available at every court of the state. In the following decades probation spread to the other states of the Union, supported by the Juvenile Court movement. In 1933 all but two states provided probation for juveniles, and thirty-four states, the District of Columbia, and the federal administration had a probation system for adults.[7] The number of probation officers in the United States rose from 200 in 1912 to 4,000 in 1933.[8]

[1] *Reg.* v. *Dunn* (1848), 12 *QB* 1026, 1041; *R.* v. *Trueman* [1913], 3 *KB* 164. The Consolidating Acts of 1861 permitted such recognizances also in lieu of imprisonment; e.g. 24 & 25 Vict., c. 96, s. 117.

[2] Blackstone, iv, c. 31, p. 387.

[3] Chief Justice White in ex parte *U.S.*, 242 *U.S. Reports* 27, at p. 44 (1916).

[4] M. D. Hill, *Suggestions for the Repression of Crime* (1857), pp. 117 and 351.

[5] E. W. Cox, *Principles of Punishment* (1877), p. 163.

[6] C. L. Chute, in S. Glueck (ed.), *Probation and Criminal Justice* (1933), p. 228.

[7] Ibid., p. 232.

[8] C. E. Hughes, 23 *Journal* 915.

In England statutory recognition of probation followed the American precedent. The development testifies to the necessity of combining suspension of punishment and personal supervision. The Summary Jurisdiction Act of 1879 entitled Courts of Summary Jurisdiction to dismiss trifling cases altogether, or to order the convicted offender to give security.[1] The Probation of First Offenders Act of 1887 provided that an offender might be released on entering into recognizance to come up for judgement.[2] Since the Act made no provisions for the probationer's guidance and supervision, the courts made use of police-court missionaries, appointed by the Church of England Temperance Society. Finally, the Probation of Offenders Act, 1907, consolidated and extended this practice.[3] Lord Samuel introduced the relevant Bill which, however, attracted little attention and passed both Houses of Parliament almost without discussion.[4] Its effects were far-reaching. The Act established a probation service of appointed and salaried welfare officers of the courts. It gave the courts threefold powers: to dismiss a defendant unconditionally, to bind him over without supervision to appear for conviction and sentence, or to bind him over with supervision. For the latter function the courts have at their disposal the services of probation officers. These are professional social workers, locally appointed, paid and supervised by the Probation Committees of the Petty Sessional Courts acting singly or in combined areas, though under the general direction of the Home Office. For the Metropolitan area the Secretary of State, on the advice of a London probation committee, appoints the probation officers, who serve under the supervision of the metropolitan magistrates or chairmen of juvenile courts and are attached to their Benches. The Criminal Justice Act, 1925, made the appointment of probation officers mandatory in all Courts of Summary Jurisdiction.[5] In 1934 there were 503 men and 328 women appointed, one-third of them as full-time officers.[6] By the end of the Second World War there were 595 full-time and 451 part-time probation officers.[7]

[1] 42 & 43 Vict., c. 49, s. 16. [2] 50 & 51 Vict., c. 25, s. 1.

[3] 7 Edw. VII, c. 17, s. 1; amended by Criminal Justice Act, 1925, 15 & 16 Geo. V, c. 86, ss. 1–7, and Criminal Justice (Amendment) Act, 1926, 16 & 17 Geo. V, c. 13.

[4] Viscount Samuel, *Memoirs* (1945), p. 54. [5] 15 & 16 Geo. V, c. 86, s. 1.

[6] L. le Mesurier (ed.), *Handbook of Probation* (1935), pp. 31–9; *Report of the Departmental Committee on the Social Services in Courts of Summary Jurisdiction* (1936), pp. 90 et seq. For a short orientation on the English probation system see S. W. Harris, 'Probation and other Social Work of the Courts', *Clarke Hall Fellowship* (1937); *The Probation Service* (H.M. Stationery Office, 1938).

[7] Information by the Home Office, quoted from Viscount Samuel, l.c.

On the Continent a growing interest in the American and English probation systems led to numerous legislative enactments which enabled the courts to suspend punishment for a certain probation period. At the same time law-givers were reluctant to create an official service for the probationer's care and guidance. Such an official control of men at large seemed reminiscent of the obsolete police surveillance of ex-prisoners, once an implement of the 'Police State', but recently denounced as detrimental to the social objects of penal policy. This institution had first been introduced in the Austrian Criminal Code of 1787, further developed in article 44 of the French *Code pénal* of 1810, whence it was adopted in Belgium, Germany, and elsewhere. Imposed as part of the sentence, this surveillance implies not only registration and regular reports, like the control over licensed convicts in England, but also a discretionary restriction in the choice of residence. Adverse experience with this repressive measure seemed an objection even to a constructive supervision by State officials. A social service under the direction of the court was further presumed to be incompatible with the prevailing separation between judicial and executive functions.[1] In the face of these objections the Belgian and French model laws of 1888 and 1891 contented themselves with a suspension of punishment pure and simple. By this conception continental 'conditional condemnation' was to serve a negative as well as a positive purpose. It has been a welcome substitute for short prison terms which have all the disadvantages and none of the potential opportunities of a rational legal punishment. And the probationer is expected to be persuaded towards law-abiding behaviour by the prospect of having his sentence annulled, or under the less perfect German system, its execution finally remitted. Like the prisoner under a Progressive Stage system or under good-time laws, the probationer is left alone to 'work his passage' and to earn the status of a free citizen.

It was experience rather than arguments from legal theory that favoured personal care and guidance. The complete theory of probation got its main support from the Juvenile Court movement. Before relevant statutory provisions were enacted, juveniles were handed over to the care of voluntary helpers or representatives of educational or youth welfare authorities and their committal to a correctional or penal institution suspended. In 1920 a German Juvenile Court judge summed up the experience in the observa-

[1] See Thomas Eliot's (Belgian) objections to any scheme confounding welfare and justice, referred to by S. Glueck (ed.), l.c., p. 311.

tion that it was a 'merely intellectual conception' to expect the prospect of remission to act as a motive when the fact that the offence had been committed at all showed that intellectual controls were ineffective. 'The true meaning of a probation period is, that it offers a legal framework for educational treatment.'[1] As the result of such considerations, 'protective supervision' (*liberté surveillée*, *Schutzaufsicht*) has been accepted as an educational measure in every Juvenile Court system.

In Belgium the Child Protection Law of 1912 introduced Juvenile Courts and provided that the judge may ask helpers to make inquiries and to supervise probationers. Apart from a few full-time officers, these officers are voluntary social workers.[2] In France an Act of 1912 provided[3] that young offenders between twelve and eighteen might be placed under probation, with or without a controlled residence, with an approved person or at an institution. The court appoints the person appropriate for the particular case, mainly from among members of charitable organizations, legal defence committees, and other approved agencies. Poland, according to Ordinances of 1919 and 1928, commits delinquent children up to thirteen to the care of a probation officer. The service is rendered by full-time social workers and voluntary helpers.[4] In Norway investigation and supervision of probationers under twenty-five have been rendered by private agencies, merged into a central Norwegian Welfare Association.[5] In Denmark juveniles between fourteen and eighteen, whose prosecution has been suspended, are committed to the educational care of an honorary Protective Council (*Vägeraad*), elected by the Local Government.[6] In Germany 'protective supervision' (*Schutzaufsicht*) grew up with the first Juvenile Courts before the First World War. The Youth Welfare Act of 1922 and the Juvenile Court Act of 1923 consolidated and extended it. Protective supervision may be ordered by the Guardianship Court as a preventive educational measure, or by the Juvenile Court, mainly in connexion with the suspension of punishment. The service is rendered either by a social worker of the Municipal Youth Welfare Board, or by a voluntary helper, usually a member of a charitable

[1] W. Hoffmann, *Verhandlungen d. 5. dtsch. Jugendgerichtstages 1920* (1922), p. 24, quoted from Hoefer, l.c., p. 36.

[2] Cornil, in Glueck (ed.), l.c., p. 310.

[3] Loi sur les tribunaux pour enfants et adolescents et sur la liberté surveillée, art. 20 et seq.

[4] By kind information from the Howard League for Penal Reform.

[5] F. Hoefer, l.c., pp. 22 et seq.

[6] F. Lucas, 19 *MoSchrKrim.* 587.

organization. The social report and personal care and supervision are the principal functions of a comprehensive Juvenile Court Aid (*Jugendgerichtshilfe*).[1] The Austrian law of 1928 follows similar lines.

In many respects the law relating to juvenile delinquents, intended to meet the particular needs of youth, proved a forerunner of a progressive criminal law for adults. This applies to personal supervision as a positive supplement to the negative suspension of punishment. Under the German system of conditional pardoning, the voluntary acceptance of supervision may be made a condition of the suspension of punishment.[2] Certain Swiss cantons[3] and the Austrian law of 1920[4] give the court discretionary power to order supervision in connexion with a conditional remission of sentence. The same course was adopted by the abortive German and Austrian Draft Codes and the Swiss Criminal Code of 1937. Practice, however, lagged behind these legislative intentions. Distrusting official supervisors, continental countries had to resort to voluntary organizations, especially those concerned with aid and after-care for discharged prisoners. In 1885 France did away with police surveillance of discharged prisoners and committed them instead to the care of *Sociétés et institutions de patronage*.[5] This course was generally accepted as a substitute for a probation service of the English and American patterns. German law assigns this function to a colourless 'agency' (*Vertrauensstelle*) as exemplified by welfare committees, municipal welfare departments, youth welfare boards, or temperance committees. The Austrian law mentions 'persons, departments, institutions and associations, engaged in the care of orphans, juveniles and discharged prisoners'. The German Draft Codes referred to similar welfare agencies, but allowed also for the employment of special officials (*Schutzaufsichtsbeamte*).[6] There had been no provisions suggested for an official service.

In its results the continental system of supervision by charitable agencies and voluntary helpers varies according to whether juveniles or adults are in question. For juveniles a probation service has been developed and satisfactory results achieved. In many

[1] H. Haeckel, *Jugendgerichtshilfe* (1927), esp. pp. 74 et seq.

[2] Section 22, German *Gnadenordnung* of 6 Feb. 1935.

[3] e.g. Zürich, Berne, St. Gallen, Lucerne. See E. Hafter, *Lehrbuch des Schweizerischen Strafrechts, Allg. Tl.* (1926), p. 340.

[4] Section 2/II, Austrian Law of 23 July 1920.

[5] J. Goldschmidt, *VDA* iv. 440.

[6] German Draft Penal Code, 1927, (I), s. 293; (II), s. 317.

countries the law favours a flexible system of co-operation between statutory youth welfare authorities and charitable agencies, relying on full-time social workers and voluntary helpers. Continental Juvenile Court Acts give the Juvenile Court Aid a strong position throughout the whole course of proceedings. It is not too difficult to enlist suitable men and women to take responsibilities for maladjusted youth. But this does not apply to the care for adult criminals. Societies for the aid of discharged prisoners, nowadays mostly confined to the distribution of modest financial assistance and some support in the struggle for work, cannot be expected to supply adequate resources and staff for the new and difficult task. French observers complain of the lack of suitable persons. In 1925, out of 300 Paris *délégués*, only twenty were said to work satisfactorily, and in the provinces there was sometimes no one available at all.[1] In 1933 the Belgian Minister of Justice observed that efficient *Comités de Patronage* were the exception, and that in many places their work was inefficient.[2] In the Swiss Cantons which preceded the unified Federal Criminal Code in introducing conditional sentences with discretionary personal supervision, the supervision was ordered and provided in exceptional cases only.[3]

To sum up: the rise of probation in the United States and England encouraged continental countries to introduce conditional sentences. In one way or another the countries concerned followed the lead of the Belgian law of 1888. Practical experience in social work, especially in the treatment of delinquent youth, led people to recognize that protective supervision was a necessary positive supplement to mere suspension of punishment. While continental countries developed well-organized social services at the disposal of Juvenile Courts, no satisfactory solution has been found of the difficulty caused by relying on charitable agencies and voluntary workers for adult offenders. Suspension of punishment must be accompanied by personal supervision, but this must be the function of a specialized trained full-time service. This makes a strong case for the Anglo-American form of probation.

Probation Methods

The method of suspending punishment depends on the particular criminal procedure; and this varies with the legal system. The

[1] Kenny, p. 604, n. 4; Hoefer, l.c., p. 84, n. 182, with reference to French sources.

[2] Cornil, in Glueck (ed.), l.c., p. 308.

[3] Hafter, l.c., p. 340; G. Sterk, *Ausgestaltung und Resultate des bedingten Straferlasses im Kanton St. Gallen* (1931), p. 100.

performance of the probation service itself, the establishment of a personal relationship between probationer and officer, and the principles involved are based upon human experience which prevails everywhere.[1] The probation officer has a threefold task: investigation, report, and treatment, although this should not be a clear-cut partition. A personal approach for the purpose of investigation is also the foundation, if not the beginning, of the treatment. The report, in explaining life-history and background, should emphasize those facts and considerations which point to the appropriate treatment. And finally, observation and evaluation should never cease during the treatment.

With these three stages probation is the most advanced application of social case-work in the field of criminal justice. Like social case-work in general it resorts to individual case-studies, the 'prognostic orientation' (Healy) in the collection and interpretation of facts, and it tries to get beyond dispassionate observations in order to establish a personal relationship. The subject of the investigation is the man himself within his environment. This latter comprises external surroundings and the personal situation. The external surroundings include economic and social status, home and neighbourhood, employment, and the use of spare time. The personal situation is a man's position among his fellows, in the family, among friends and companions: the state of his affections, abundant or lacking; of his status in the eyes of himself and others, superior or inferior; his popularity or unpopularity; his emotional condition, jealous, indifferent, or repressed, with or without proper outlets and compensations. The main source of information is the man's own story and his reactions to the social worker's approach, together with the impressions the worker gets from home visits and talks with members of the family. The distinction between the offender himself and the others around him ought not to be unduly stressed. In many cases the family or group to which he belongs should be investigated as a unit. In assessing the results of personal interviews two things must be clearly faced: the facts, verified by further observations, and the personal bias of the offender, an important fact in itself. The probation officer must understand his client's version, honest or concocted, even if he feels bound to reject it. Other social agencies should be consulted and their relevant experience used, subject

[1] For the discussion which follows: E. J. Cooley, *Probation and Delinquency* (1927); S. Glueck (ed.), *Probation and Criminal Justice* (1927); L. le Mesurier (ed.), *Handbook of Probation* (1935); P. V. Young, *Social Treatment in Probation and Delinquency* (1937).

to the probation officer's obligation to see for himself. A probation officer is well advised not to trespass into the field of psychological and psychiatric investigation; but he should know enough to be able to suggest when it is advisable to call in a psychological or psychiatric expert. Cases may occur where, even more than the offender himself, his wife or neighbour needs an examination and special 'care and protection'.[1] It depends on the attitude of the general public how far interference with an individual's private affairs is acceptable. The American suggestion that in cases of alcoholics, psychopathics, and sex-deviants the offender's wife should be physically and psychiatrically examined,[2] is not unreasonable. But it has little prospect of being accepted in England, where it seems incompatible with the individual's liberty and feeling of security, that he should be liable to such interference. Comprehensive investigations take a considerable time. While endless requests and interviews annoy the man and his family, especially if they themselves are trying hard to find a way out of the difficulties revealed or created by the offence committed, hurried and superficial investigations are worse than none. Legal considerations decide at which stage of the proceedings the probation officer may begin his inquiries. As a social worker he will be inclined to do so as early as possible. Social situations are never static: personal relationships, sympathies, and antipathies, and a man's reaction to his surroundings, change quickly. Where the law of criminal procedure allows suspension of punishment, or informal adjustment, to be considered early, as is the practice of American Juvenile Courts, social investigations will start almost simultaneously with police inquiries about the offence and its circumstances. On the other hand, where the presumption of innocence until guilt has been established by due process of law is so strong as in England, objections have been raised against inquiries into the prisoner's past and his personal circumstances before he has been proved guilty.[3] From this point of view, an interval between the finding of guilt and the final decision is the appropriate stage to undertake social investigations. In England, even, this has been opposed as unduly delaying the final disposition of the case, especially in rural districts where the prisoner is unlikely to come before the same bench again and special arrangements must be made for at least two of the justices of the trial

[1] Claud Mullins, *Crime and Psychology* (1943), pp. 138 and 163 et seq.
[2] R. H. Ferris, in Glueck (ed.), l.c., p. 148.
[3] C. Mullins, l.c., pp. 144 et seq.

court to be present at the second hearing. In some ways, post-trial inquiries facilitate the probation officer's approach. The fight is over, and the offender and his family can be expected to co-operate in a fresh start.

The results of the investigations have to be laid down in a report submitted to the court. This report must contain the investigator's interpretation and conclusions: he must point out the factors, personal and environmental, which explain the offender's career and conduct, the circumstances which make his adjustment likely or unlikely, and suggest what is the best course to be adopted. Such a diagnosis is more than a more or less complete summary of facts. It requires the judgement to select and evaluate the single facts, and to see a man's life-patterns as an organic whole rather than a sum total of single data. The probation officer ought not to be afraid of a personal view, so long as he makes sure that it is based on experience. As a safeguard against subjective predilections and prejudices the final interpretation and suggestions should not be isolated from the underlying facts. Rather should the judge, by studying the report, be in a position to draw for himself the conclusions from the material presented, and in doing so either concur or disagree. Like a good witness, the probation officer should refer to his sources and leave no doubt about what is his own experience, what is hearsay, and what is inference.

Such reports will exert a strong influence on the judge's decision. The question therefore arises: at which stage of the proceedings the report should be made accessible to the court. The answer is less controversial than in the corresponding problem of the proper time to begin the investigations. Where something similar to a probation order is feasible before or during the trial, or an informal adjustment is admissible, the judge or referee must have early access to the report. For delinquent juveniles, especially under a flexible system of guardianship and criminal jurisdiction, such a practice has proved useful. Where adults appear before a criminal court the principle of English law is the only acceptable one, that the report must not be submitted before the prisoner has been found guilty. Attempts on the Continent to introduce a social court aid similar to probation failed mainly because it proved incompatible with the law of evidence to render a confidential report to the trial judge. The only possible solution of this dilemma is for Continental law to adopt the English and American partition of the judgement into conviction and sentence with an interval between as the proper stage for social considerations.

For the third and final stage, the treatment proper, the usual term 'supervision' is nothing but an expedient abbreviation. There is certainly a supervision, with the law and the threat of an impending sentence behind it. But the probation officer's task is much wider. It is a treatment, consciously undertaken as professional social work, and at the same time depending for its success on a personal relationship of trust and guidance. The probation officer shall 'advise, assist and befriend' the probationer.[1] The primary aim will be to help him to face his situation and to win his co-operation in the planning of his rehabilitation. The first of these tasks begins with a frank explanation of the probationer's position and the conditions of the probation order; the second, with the reminder that probation, although an alternative to imprisonment, nevertheless has been voluntarily accepted. In developing and pursuing the plan, the officer needs much tact and experience to combine firmness and flexibility, to know when to insist on perseverance and patience, and at the same time, never to forget that human affairs can only be mastered by trial and error. In such co-operative efforts the question before the probation officer's mind is this: can the probationer fairly be expected to overcome this adverse situation? If so, he will encourage him, strengthen and stimulate his will-power, and help him to conquer the difficulties. If, on the other hand, he decided that the situation requires more than the probationer is able to bear and afford, he will try to adjust the situation. For this purpose he may talk to members of the family, to the teacher or employer, approve of a change of employment, help the family to settle down in another district, find a club or organized spare-time activities for the probationer, and so forth. Probation is highly individualized treatment, and as multiple in its features as human affairs usually are.

Probation orders differ in the particular conditions imposed. There may be 'plain probation', a blank to be filled by the personal relations between the probation officer and his client. In other cases the probationer may be required to accept psychological treatment,[2] to stay for a prescribed term in an institution or hostel, or to submit to other forms of residential control. Or he may be made liable to pay damages or render other forms of compensation.

The methods of probation are essentially the same as those used

[1] 7 Edw. VII, c. 17, s. 4 (d).

[2] C. Mullins, l.c., Chs. II and III, pp. 38 et seq.

in other fields of social case-work. Its characteristic feature is that it has behind it the force of the law. It has been rightly said that this support involves an inherent weakness. The fact that the probationer can be brought before the court may slow down personal efforts and impede prospects of winning and keeping his real co-operation.[1] Obviously the use of power will frustrate whatever good will has been built up by patient work between individual and individual. A probation officer who squarely faces this dilemma will do his utmost to leave the law in the background and try again and again to establish a relationship based on trust, encouragement, and persuasion.

Incidence and Success

Criminal statistics show a high incidence of probation among the sanctions imposed by criminal courts. In 1938 English Courts of Summary Jurisdiction found 75,402 persons guilty of indictable offences. Out of these 23,655 or 31·1 per cent. were put on probation. In the same year English prisons received 15,145 persons sentenced for indictable offences.[2] Fifty-one per cent. of all offenders appearing before Juvenile Courts are put on probation.[3] Adults have been placed on probation by Courts of Summary Jurisdiction at a rate of 30 per cent., by Quarter Sessions and the Central Criminal Court at a rate of 16 per cent., and by Assizes at a rate of 4 per cent. Practice varies in different places. Adults before Courts of Summary Jurisdiction are put on probation in the Metropolitan Police District at a rate of 24 per cent., in Birmingham at a rate of 9 per cent., in Liverpool at 3 per cent.

Similar conditions prevail in the United States.[4] Before the outbreak of the Second World War approximately one-third of the persons found guilty by criminal courts were sent to prison, and another third put on probation. According to figures collected from twenty-five states in 1939, out of a total of 54,929 convicted persons, 18,328 or 33·4 per cent. were put on probation. There are striking local variations in America too, between the extremes of 60·3 per cent. in Rhode Island and 14 per cent. in North Dakota and Montana, with the classical probation state Massachusetts steering a medium course of 32·8 per cent. In 1940, before

[1] H. Weiss, in Glueck (ed.), l.c., p. 185.

[2] *Crim. Stat. 1938*, pp. 8 and 122; *Report Prison Commissioners, 1938*, p. 100.

[3] For the discussion which follows: C. D. Rackham, 'Probation System', in Radzinowicz and Turner (ed.), *Penal Reform in England* (1940), p. 116.

[4] Figures from H. E. Barnes and N. K. Teeters, *New Horizons in Criminology* (1943), p. 384.

federal courts, 36·2 per cent. of offenders found guilty were put on probation.[1]

The results of probation are difficult to assess by statistical evidence. Even in England and the United States there are conspicuous differences from court to court, both in the selection of cases presumed suitable for probation and method of supervision. No generally accepted standards for the evaluation of success or failure are available. From a social and educational point of view, success is more than the absence of a reconviction, and a failure is not merely a revocation of the order. A reasonable standard would regard as success a fairly stable social adjustment in the post-treatment period. But results in some such sense as this can be determined only on the basis of methodically collected and critically analysed individual follow-up studies of a representative group.[2]

The generally assumed ratio of success is 70 per cent. This figure corresponds to observations from selected probation areas in England[3] and certain probation departments in the United States.[4] Such general assumptions need further elucidation. In 1935–6 the American federal probation service reported only 3·3 per cent. of violators of the probation orders, while probation officers themselves classified as strikingly improved 26·8 per cent. and as moderately improved 34·7 per cent. of the probationers.[5] According to an American survey of almost 20,000 probation cases, two-fifths of the probationers violated the conditions of the probation order, but less than one-fifth had it revoked. The incidence of revocations differs with the type of offenders. It is 32 per cent. for recidivists and 14 per cent. for first-offenders.[6]

A final assessment of the results must compare the after-effects of this treatment with those of other penal sanctions. An English investigation computed the reconviction rates during a five-year period for male first-offenders found guilty in 1932 for finger-printable offences. These reconviction rates are higher in the lower than in the upper age-groups. But in all age-groups, those put on probation have a higher reconviction rate than those treated by other sanctions. For example, of the young men of

[1] L. N. Robinson, *Jails* (1944), p. 77, with reference to *Federal Offenders, 1940*, p. 292.

[2] B. Mead, 23 *Journal* 631; id., in 'Coping with Crime', *Yearbook of the National Probation Association* (1937), pp. 130 et seq.

[3] C. D. Rackham, l.c., p. 120.

[4] *Wickersham Report*, ix. 160 et seq.

[5] B. Mead, *Yearbook*, l.c., p. 132.

[6] Barnes and Teeters, l.c., p. 389, with reference to the *Attorney General's Survey*.

sixteen and seventeen, 21·7 per cent. of those fined, 24·7 per cent. of those sent to prison, 26·3 per cent. of those dismissed and bound over without supervision, and 35·5 per cent. of those put under probation were reconvicted.[1] At first sight these figures look like a black record for probation. But the offenders sent to prison, fined, or dismissed are not proper control groups. They are not offenders of the same type but treated in a different way: they were selected for the specific treatment applied to them. Therefore, their lower reconviction rates may be due to their personal conditions and antecedents no less than to the treatment, whereas it is quite possible that those put on probation might have produced the same or even a higher rate of reconviction if they had not been put on probation.

An examination of the six-year period 1927–32 shows that with an increasing criminality and growing use of probation the general reconviction rates tend to decline. While the number of persons tried summarily for indictable offences rose in that period from 56,275 to 62,103, and probation orders increased absolutely and relatively from 12,385 or 22 per cent. to 14,971 or 24·1 per cent., the reconviction rates decreased in all age-groups, e.g. for male first-offenders of sixteen to twenty from 30·3 to 27·6 per cent.[2] Likewise in Massachusetts a marked increase in the use of probation was accompanied by a rise of the ratio of success, and at the same time a reduction in the number of serious crimes against the person and property. While for a period of twenty years the number of persons placed on probation was tripled and the percentage of court cases dealt with by a probation order rose from 9·4 to 22·4 per cent., the ratio of successes rose from 70 to 85 per cent.[3] Even if probation did not diminish the number of relapses, something would be gained for the community if its security could be maintained on a tolerable level with less resort to degrading penalties. And such penalties probation does help to avoid: for it is a superior method of treatment which does not disrupt a man's life, but pursues its object by preserving, if not rebuilding, his social relations within his personal environment.

The use and scope of probation may still be extended.[4] The selection of cases could be improved by more thorough investigations and the use of scientific prediction methods based upon

[1] *Crim. Stat. 1938*, pp. xxi and xxvi.
[2] *Crim. Stat. 1927*, p. 76; *1932*, p. 64; *1938*, p. xxi.
[3] *Wickersham Report*, ix. 164.
[4] Sanford Bates, 32 *Journal* 324.

factors frequently observed in other cases.[1] Trained probation officers in sufficient numbers must be at the disposal of the courts. Mass treatment inevitably frustrates even well-intended personal efforts. It is usually taken that an officer can give personal supervision to 50 cases in urban areas, and to fewer still in rural areas, while a voluntary helper can deal only with 2 or 3. If the number of officers were increased there would be a difference, too, in the quality of treatment; personal supervision would be combined with specialized forms of clinical treatment, vocational training, part-time attendance at special centres, or residential control. In the end, probation may become a common denominator for a variety of treatments, a legal basis for manifold ways of dealing with offenders within the community itself.

With these far-reaching aims probation has conspicuously influenced present penal policy. The presentation of social reports and the offer of an alternative to prison terms awarded on traditional retributory standards has had certain effects on the outlook of the courts. More than any theory, probation brought near to them the social aspects of crime and punishment. It is no longer a 'handmaid of the prison system' (Sir Evelyn Ruggles-Brise); it is a partner, and marks a new stage of development in penal policy. Whether it is a punishment may still be a moot point. According to the wording of prevailing Probation Laws and unanalysed feeling, it is an alternative to punishment. This is correct as long as punishment implies hardship deliberately inflicted for guilt. With the increasing use of probation and other constructive methods, a wider conception of punishment can be envisaged, comprising all corrective and preventive sanctions. In such a wider sense probation would be a punishment. But even more important than definitions remains the fact that probation has been the forerunner of extra-mural treatment of offenders and its most significant example.

PAROLE

Conditional Release

Parole is the counterpart to probation. Both combine suspension of punishment with personal supervision. Probation is an attempt to make the penalty superfluous; for this purpose punishment is suspended altogether. Parole applies when the prisoner has served part of his sentence. Then the rest may be suspended

[1] E. D. Monachesi, *Prediction Factors in Probation* (1932).

under certain conditions which the prisoner accepts on his 'word of honour'. It was because of this latter element that in 1847 Samuel G. Howe of Boston, champion of Greek liberty and the abolition of slavery, suggested the word 'parole'.[1] From a legal point of view punishment is suspended by conditional condemnation in the case of probation, and by conditional release in the case of parole. This, however, is only one side of these measures. No less important is the personal supervision during the period of suspense.

The history of probation and parole shows parallels in their origin and development. Both are contributions which England and America rendered to penal reform. From them Continental legislation accepted the idea of shortening prison terms by conditional release before the expiration of the sentence. The demand for personal supervision and help arose from the experience of practical social work. The development of parole still lags behind that of probation. In many countries the legal institution of conditional release and the social object of a personal supervision of discharged prisoners are still not integrated into a consistent parole service. So far, only modest beginnings have been made. They call for a resolute reform programme in the immediate future.

Conditional release serves a twofold purpose.[2] As long as the prisoner is serving his sentence the prospect of an early release is a target for his efforts and an incentive to discipline. Once he is discharged the pending threat of re-committal to prison is supposed to strengthen his inhibitions against crime.

Conditional release originated in connexion with the transportation of convicts from England to Australia, and was applied to convicts in the motherland in 1853[3] and 1857.[4] In connexion with residence in an intermediate institution it was an element of Sir Walter Crofton's Irish prison discipline. As a disciplinary instrument the present system of earning a remission of a fraction of the sentence goes back to the Penal Servitude Act of 1864 and the Prison Act of 1898. Convicts, prisoners undergoing preventive detention, and Borstal trainees are released on licence. In the United States conditional release as part of a Progressive Stage system originated from the reformatory movement. A New York

[1] Eugenia Lekkerkerker, *American Reformatories for Women* (1931), p. 540.

[2] For the comparative notes: W. Mittermaier, in *VDA*, iv. 506 et seq.; E. Umhauer, in Bumke, pp. 392 et seq.

[3] 16 & 17 Vict., c. 99.

[4] 20 & 21 Vict., c. 3.

law of 1877 preceded Brockway's experiment at Elmira and marked the statutory beginning of parole. The American conception of indeterminate sentences emphasizes the flexible character of prison committals, and implies special machinery to deal with prisoners who are eligible for release after the expiration of a minimum term determined by the sentencing court. By 1910 twenty states had passed legislation providing for release on parole.[1] In 1939, with the exception of two, all states, the District of Columbia, and the federal administration had statutory provisions for releasing prisoners on parole.[2] In 1942 everywhere throughout the United States a system of parole prevailed in one way or another.[3]

As in the case of conditional sentence, Continental legislation is far from being uniform with regard to the extent and legal foundation of conditional release. In most countries the release decision has been assigned to the executive, either as a rationalized act of pardon, or as a special administrative discretionary power based upon and restricted by explicit statutory provisions. The reform movement of the Era of Enlightenment produced some forerunners of the prevailing forms of conditional release. In Austria a Patent of Joseph II of 1788 promised prisoners, whose conduct was good and who showed a prospect of lasting improvement, a discharge after the expiration of one-half of the sentence.[4] The Bavarian Criminal Code of 1813, the work of Anselm v. Feuerbach, had a provision for indeterminate sentences. Convicts who had given 'clear proofs of an improved mood' and had served a certain statutory minimum of their sentences, or sixteen years of a life-sentence, should be eligible for pardon.[5] In more recent times Saxony took the lead. Under the influence of reports on contemporary English penal policy and the suggestions of Schwarze, Public Prosecutor General, Regulations of 1862 introduced 'leave on good behaviour' as an act of pardon for long-term convicts. In 1864 Brunswick followed the Saxon precedent. This latter was also the model for a provision of the German Criminal Code of 1871 which empowered the administration to grant conditional release after the expiration of three-quarters of a prison term.[6] Practice, however, preferred the

[1] W. D. Lane, 24 *Journal* 91. [2] *Attorney General's Survey*, v. 284.

[3] C. H. White, 32 *Journal* 600.

[4] W. H. Hirschberg, 'Neue Aufgaben der Gefangenenfürsorge', supplement to *Bericht der Zentralstelle für Gefangenenfürsorgewesen Brandenburg, 1926*, p. 20.

[5] Bavarian Criminal Code of 1 Oct. 1813, arts. 11 et seq.

[6] German Criminal Code, ss. 23 et seq.

flexible form of a conditional pardon, which had the further advantage that the probation period could be extended beyond the expiration of the sentence. In 1920 Baden granted conditional release according to the Criminal Code to eighty-one prisoners, or 17·23 per cent. of those eligible, while 488 prisoners, or 52·55 per cent. of those eligible, were pardoned.[1] For outstanding parts of a term with no more than six months to serve, German law enables the public prosecutor and, in the case of minor punishments up to one month imprisonment, the municipal judge, to discharge the prisoner conditionally.[2] In Germany conditional sentence as well as conditional release still have their legal foundation in the prerogative of mercy. The abortive draft codes proposed to assign both to the trial court as a judicial function.[3]

In France and Belgium conditional release is a statutory power of the administration. For many years French criminologists like Charles Lucas, Bonneville de Marsangy, and A. M. Bérenger, and the Belgian Ducpétiaux had propagated the idea of conditional release.[4] The institution of *Libération conditionnelle* was introduced in France by a law of 1885 and in Belgium by a similar statute of 1888. Conditional release has become an implement of almost every recent criminal enactment, e.g. of the Czechoslovak statute of 1919, the Italian Criminal Code of 1930, and the Swiss Criminal Code of 1937 in conformity with the former law of the majority of the Swiss Cantons. In Austria, according to a law of 1920, the decision rests with a committee, consisting of the president of the court in the venue of which the sentence is served, the public prosecutor, and the head of the penal institution.[5]

With the exception of the present German law the trend of European legislation has changed the legal basis of conditional release and substituted for vague powers of pardon a limited statutory discretion on the part of the administration. In the Austrian law and the German draft codes a new tendency arises to recognize the quasi-judicial character of a release decision. In its psychological effects a conditional release gives the prisoner a chance to try to find a way back to law-abiding conduct, under

[1] Umhauer, l.c., pp. 409 and 428.

[2] Section 20/I *Gnadenordnung* of 6 Feb. 1935; *Dtsch. Justiz*, 203.

[3] Draft Criminal Code, 1930, s. 40; Draft Penal Code, 1927 (II), s. 231.

[4] M. Bonneville de Marsangy, *Traité des diverses institutions complémentaires du régime pénitentiaire* (1847); Bérenger, *De la répression pénale* (1852); E. Ducpétiaux, *De libérations conditionnelles en Angleterre* (1855); id., *Des conditions d'application du système de l'emprisonnement séparé ou cellulaire* (Mémoires couronnés de l'Académie Royale, vii, Bruxelles, 1859), pp. 91 et seq.

[5] H. Streicher, *Bedingte Entlassung in Oesterreich* (1923).

the impending threat of re-committal. As a release procedure such a stage of suspense is superior to an abrupt change from prison to liberty. Experience, however, shows that the threat of an impending re-committal alone is not strong enough to procure the desired rehabilitative result. As with probation, the suspension of punishment needs a positive supplement: personal care and supervision. This demand is a challenge to organized after-care work for discharged prisoners. Such welfare work has long been recognized as a supplement to, if not an essential element of, penal and correctional treatment; but, for the better part of their history, conditional release and prisoners' after-care have not been integrated into a comprehensive system of extra-mural treatment.

Prisoners' After-care: Organization

As in the case of probation, the human side of the work for ex-prisoners should mean more than 'supervision'. Nor should it mean only economic help. The true object of the prisoners' after-care is an individualized treatment of the offender during the critical period of his return to the community. An English *Report* of 1935 complains that 'there is in general a tendency to concentrate on relief payments to prisoners on the day of discharge, and, generally speaking, too little is at present done either by way of finding employment on discharge, or of assistance of wives and families of men in prison, or in maintaining personal contact with prisoners after release'.[1] At the same time the personal services of prison visitors extended to an intensified after-care work. It was observed that prisoners resent supervision by an aid society, while a prison visitor who has succeeded in establishing a friendly relationship with a prisoner can often keep in touch with him. In one case a visitor with eight years' experience found employment for about one hundred men, and with very rare exceptions they have made good.[2]

Prisoners' after-care is inseparable from welfare-work during imprisonment. One without the other is unreal and ineffective. Welfare-work in prison must be done with a view to the man's eventual discharge and try to lay the foundation for his after-care. The same forces, official and voluntary, have been active in both fields and have found common features in the work at both stages.

[1] *Report of the Departmental Committee on the Employment of Prisoners.* ii. *Employment on Discharge* (1935), p. 15, s. 15.

[2] *Report Prison Commissioners, 1929*, pp. 27 and 42.

After some early attempts to enlist public administration for the ex-prisoner's adjustment, after-care became a charity until it was finally recognized as a public responsibility.[1] In pre-constitutional Prussia, from 1710 to 1824, successive Royal Patents and Regulations insisted on the obligation of the authorities to find work for discharged prisoners.[2] In England Peel's Gaol Act of 1823 provided that visiting justices should report to the justices in session prisoners of 'extraordinary diligence or merits' for recommendation to Royal Mercy. If pardoned they should receive, together with the necessary clothing, the sum of 5 to 20 shillings from county rates.[3] The nineteenth century saw the rise of prison societies. These charitable agencies had strong support from religious forces. The Society of Friends, the Church Home Mission, and denominational groups founded the first and most important of them. When the State took over the cause of prison reform their interest concentrated on aid for discharged prisoners. At the middle of the century experts of all European countries agreed that, subject to stimulation and benevolent assistance by the public administration, care for ex-prisoners should be left to the free charity of individuals and voluntary associations.[4] Up to the present day European associations have maintained their local character, the local society attached to the local prison, with a certain adjustment to the recent centralization of penal administration. In England, even after the reduction of local prisons to twenty-six, there are still forty-eight local prison societies.[5] They have been co-ordinated by the Central Discharged Prisoners' Aid Society. In its *Report* of 1935, the Departmental Committee found that not enough had been done in guiding and stimulating the work of the various local societies, but nevertheless the time seemed not yet ripe for replacing the old pluralism by one central national organization. For convicts and Borstal inmates semi-official central organizations are operating: the Central Association for the Aid of Discharged Convicts, the Aylesbury After-care Association (for women), and the Borstal Association, presided over by government officials. All these organizations are represented by the National Association of Discharged Prisoners' Aid Societies. In the United States, beside some thirty-seven private agencies, mostly operating

[1] B. Freudenthal, 46 *ZStW* 403.

[2] Muntau, in *Strafvollzug in Preussen* (1928), p. 264.

[3] 4 Geo. IV, c. 64, s. 16.

[4] E. Ducpétiaux, *Du patronage des condamnés libérés* (Mémoires couronnés de l'Académie Royale, viii, 1859), p. 55, with references to contemporary writers.

[5] *Report on Employment of Prisoners*, ii, l.c.

on a state-wide basis, the most widespread activities are undertaken by the Salvation Army in connexion with their general welfare and rescue work for the homeless and destitute. In New York City alone, during one year, some 10,000 ex-prisoners are handled by the Salvation Army.[1]

Germany, too, inherited a great number of local societies from the past, mostly co-ordinated in a common provincial organization. It has long been difficult to ascertain how many of the local agencies were alive for any real work. In Prussia central provincial offices were established in connexion with some of the renowned prison societies for Berlin, Saxony–Anhalt, Rhineland and Westphalia, and Silesia. The old substructure had been kept in order to enlist local interest and support. Everywhere State influence has been growing, either by direct financial assistance, or indirectly by handing over the prisoner's earnings to the society to be used for his benefit. Financial assistance implies administrative control. In England there is a 'partnership' between State control, operative in the central organizations, and voluntary local effort.[2] Likewise in Germany the legislative proposals of the Draft Penal Codes of 1927 recognized the after-care for discharged prisoners as 'a common object of State and society'.[3] Voluntary efforts have further been limited by the growing need for professional work. Experience in Switzerland confirmed the advantage of the employment of trained social workers in this field.[4] In 1925 Saxony assigned care for discharged prisoners as a statutory obligation to public welfare authorities, to be performed by prison welfare officers and the general district welfare authorities.[5] The Italian Criminal Code of 1930 established a council of patronage (*Consiglio di patronato*) at every district court for the assistance of the families of prisoners and the after-care of ex-prisoners.[6] These councils draw on funds provided by incoming fines.[7]

The trend from private charity to public responsibility corresponds to a change in the underlying theoretical conceptions. As long as the principle of retribution dominated the administration

[1] L. N. Robinson, *Jails* (1944), pp. 234 et seq.

[2] Fox, p. 130.

[3] German Draft Penal Code, 1927 (I), s. 232; German Draft Penal Code, 1927 (II), s. 240.

[4] E. Delaquis and D. Widmer, *Grundlagen, Grenzen und praktische Durchführung der Entlassenenfürsorge* (1925), pp. 6 and 23.

[5] *Sächs. Wohlfahrtspflegegesetz* of 28 Mar. 1925, s. 2, No. 12; *Ausführungs VO zum Wohlfahrtspflegegesetz*, 20 Mar. 1926, s. 72.

[6] Italian Criminal Code, 1930, art. 149.

[7] N. Cantor, 24 *Journal* 768.

of criminal justice, the State contented itself with executing the penalty in accordance with the law. With the expiration of a prison term, however, the social effects of punishment were by no means extinct. It was left to society to help the ex-prisoner with shelter, work, and bare necessities of life, and thereby to compensate for any additional hardship beyond the limits of legal punishment proper. With the recognition of social adjustment as a primary object of penal policy, the negative intention of avoiding undesirable after-effects became a positive aim and an essential stage in the rehabilitative process.

Practice

The practical work of prisoners' after-care is as manifold as the needs of men discharged from prison. Shelter must be provided for men who have nowhere to go. Charitable efforts founded homes for discharged prisoners in Germany, from Fliedner's Refuge for women prisoners in 1833, to the *Sachsenhof* near Halle and Hedwig Wangel's 'Gate of Hope' in 1925. Most of them served useful purposes, but almost all had to close because of difficulties of finance and management. The method itself has been controversial. In 1885 the International Prison Congress in Rome rejected the idea of refuge homes for prisoners. It was feared that the salutary effects of separate confinement would be undone by a subsequent community of ex-prisoners. On the other hand, there is a strong case for an intermediate home between prison and full liberty. Such a transitional stage might be either the last phase in a Progressive Stage system like Sir Walter Crofton's Intermediate Prison at Lusk and the proposals of section 103, Czechoslovak Draft Criminal Code of 1921, and the Prussian grading system of 1929,[1] or it might be the first step in controlled liberty as in Hesse, where a policy was under consideration for making residence and work at a particular agricultural estate a condition of preliminary release.[2]

Homeless ex-prisoners are often received in public asylums or charitable hostels. Whether such spreading of prisoners among thriftless and destitute people is preferable is still open to question. To mix ordinary prisoners with vagrants and beggars has proved a failure. As an ideal solution it has been recommended that shelter should be found for homeless ex-prisoners in private foster-

[1] *Preuss. VO über den Strafvollzug in Stufen* of 7 June 1929, ss. x–xii (*Ausgangsanstalt*).
[2] Dapper, in *Fürsorge für Gefangene*, ed. by *Vereinigung für gerichtliche Psychologie und Psychiatrie in Hessen*, p. 33.

families. Personal association with people of respectable life would, if feasible, certainly be the best help which society could render to the readjustment of offenders.[1]

The most urgent task of after-care is the placing of the prisoner in appropriate employment. Obviously, the success of social adjustment depends on the prisoner's immediate resumption of work. First to take a 'holiday' before starting life and work anew has often proved disastrous. Again, alleged and real disappointments in the competition for a job are easily taken as an excuse for complacency and relaxing and a fresh turn to illicit gains. The difficulties of finding suitable work are manifold. In an age cursed by the threat of mass unemployment the man with a prison stamp finds himself at the bottom of the queue. State service and public corporations and numerous other callings are almost closed to him. Even if a master would not object, fellow workers might. Prison labour seldom makes men fit for qualified work. And even with all credit to the willingness of the prisoners, they are not, taken in general, alert, painstaking, and persevering workers. According to German experience, 5 to 10 per cent. of ex-prisoners rejected jobs which had been found for them.[2] Only elaborate individual follow-up studies could show how many kept the same job for a reasonable time. Among 500 ex-prisoners of the Massachusetts Reformatory, 59 either left their first job at once, or held it for a period of less than a month.[3] Before the establishment of public labour exchanges the directing of ex-prisoners to vacancies was a primary function of the prison societies. Nowadays it has been mostly taken over by the general labour authorities, although there is still room for additional efforts to compensate for the handicaps and obstacles which beset the prisoner's after-career. According to an investigation of the Regional Labour Office, Weimar, out of a total of 1,425 prisoners discharged during the years 1922–5, 338 got work by the Labour Exchange and 312 by other channels.[4] In England the Borstal Association succeeded, even at a time of widespread unemployment, in finding work for 93·7 per cent. of former Borstal boys.[5] Social adjustment implies the placing of a man in a job with union wages, if only to relieve

[1] A. Starke, in Frede–Grünhut, *Reform des Strafvollzuges* (1927), p 228.

[2] M. Sommer, *Fürsorge im Strafrecht* (1925), p. 107, with reference to v. Baehr, *Zuchthaus und Gefängnis*, p. 146.

[3] S. and E. Glueck, *After-conduct of Discharged Offenders* (1945), p. 57.

[4] Lüttgens, in *42. Jahrbuch der Gefängnisgesellschaft für die Provinz Sachsen und Anhalt* 1926), p. 53.

[5] *Report on Employment of Prisoners*, ii. 35.

him from the feeling of being under-privileged, which is often the psychological root of a criminal career. During the depression many workers had to join communal emergency squads. Some societies found it expedient, for a trial period, to supervise men enlisted in such emergency work before they were expected to stand the competition of the labour market.

Many ex-prisoners need economic assistance with regard to the bare necessities of life. Not infrequently the ordinary social services are not available before a certain minimum of continuous contributions which has fallen into abeyance during the prison term. It requires much wisdom and tact to know when to give the help in kind and when in cash. To pay the rent, buy tools, and retrieve belongings from the pawnbroker is the safer way, but gives the man the feeling of being under tutelage.

Besides shelter, work, and financial assistance, there is the task of helping the prisoner readapt himself psychologically to a free community. Experienced observers concur in the verdict: the true punishment starts with release. Even prisoners-of-war need not only a hearty welcome at home, but also much patient understanding till they overcome a feeling of frustration, of being behind the times, and outrun by their more fortunate contemporaries. This is even more so if a man comes back after a long confinement in a penal institution. He looks in vain for his old surroundings, so cherished in prison day-dreams. When an old man, after a converted life-sentence, was discharged in Hamburg after the social upheaval and the collapse of the currency in the early twenties, a welfare officer could only bring him to an asylum. A man released in London after years of penal servitude for espionage was frightened by wireless and automatic telephones.[1] Educational activities, opportunities for debating, and an appeal to the prisoner's initiative and will-power during his imprisonment can do much to ease his return to the community. Even an ideal prison régime cannot spare the man the prison stamp. Many a prisoner, not least those with moral resources, has to start life anew from a broken existence. It is not only the worst for whom life has long lost any sense at all. The prisoner's over-sensitiveness to formal justice persists even after his release, often distorted to pharisaic self-righteousness. As in prison, work must be supplemented by constructive spare-time activities. It is sometimes advisable to procure the man's admittance to a lending library, a sports club, or to encourage a healthy hobby.

[1] W. F. R. Macartney, *Walls have Mouths* (1936).

Successful after-care work needs much education of the general public.[1] Distrust and resentment against the man who has been in prison has always proved an obstacle to the work of welfare agencies as well as to the honest efforts of the former prisoner himself. At this critical moment he finds himself an outcast, excluded from the workshop and the companionship of respectable contemporaries. In the early thirties, at the close of the reform period in Germany, in Berlin many ex-prisoners lost their posts three or four times in spite of satisfactory records, merely because something had leaked out about their former careers. Man cannot live in self-contained isolation. Rejected from decent society, he falls back to the community of those he has met in prison. Berlin had 'Ring-Associations' of ex-prisoners, which provided economic self-help, legal aid, and social intercourse. The root of society's uncompromising attitude is fear of a man who committed a criminal offence, and a reluctance to share the responsibility of working and living together with a convict.[2] The present prison system cannot be recognized as a successful institution of reformation which rules out any risk with regard to men released from custody. But the negative attitude of society is even more contradictory to the idea of retribution which it professes. Even if it were justifiable to shun the criminal, it is unpardonable to ignore the fact that a man has expiated his guilt by the punishment inflicted on him as a just retribution.

After-care work, if thoroughly pursued, is individualized treatment. As an instrument of social readjustment it is a corrective measure in the framework of penal policy. This has been further emphasized by the tendency to substitute protective supervision by prisoners' welfare agencies for the less effective resort to mere repression and control. In Germany police surveillance of released prisoners and a committal of discharged vagrants to a workhouse used to be suspended if the prisoner accepted the protective supervision of a prison society.

Such are the demands for, and potentialities of, aid and after-care for discharged prisoners. It is almost impossible to add to the description of what it can and should do an account of what it has done. Apart from a few non-converted life-sentences, every prisoner is bound to be released into the community. Not all of them need care and assistance. A group of fortunate men with

[1] D. Klatt, *Das Los der Vorbestraften* (1926).

[2] H. Muthesius, 'Straffälligenfürsorge als sozialpädagogisches Problem', *Berliner Gefangenenfürsorge*, *1928*, p. 32.

stable home conditions, unbroken family ties, and work available, will take up the struggle alone and sever as soon as possible any link with prison. Other men, inclined to persist in unlawful activities and to exploit charities for pecuniary advantages, must be dealt with by preventive measures against habitual criminals. Between these two extremes there is the great majority of those who in one way or another need care and assistance. So far, in spite of much valuable work, the supply lags behind the demand. In 1916 10 per cent. of the prisoners released from Prussian penal institutions received aid in one form or another.[1] In 1930, in Berlin, out of approximately 56,000 prisoners, 24,420 applied to the Prisoners' Welfare Agency. Among them 1,468 were cases of protective supervision.[2]

The Parole Idea

In their historical development, European release procedures followed two separate lines. Under English and American influence, Continental legislation provided for the shortening of prison terms by conditional release. Practical social work, grown up from voluntary religious and humanitarian efforts, opened new ways of supervision and care for discharged prisoners. A solution which integrates both methods and combines conditional release with personal care and supervision is the essence of the parole idea.[3] The parallel with probation is evident.

In England the Commissioners of 1863, called to report on transportation and penal servitude, complained of 'the want of any proper means for the supervision of convicts released on a ticket of leave and of any adequate arrangements of placing them, when their punishment is over, in a situation in which they will not be likely to return to a criminal life . . .'. They denounced this defect as a contributory factor of the rising recidivism. While in their opinion the police should abstain from this task, they recommended that licence holders should be under the supervision of an officer of the convict department with assistants, appointed for the duties discharged in Dublin by Mr. Organ, the social worker of Sir Walter Crofton's Progressive Stage régime.[4] This recommendation anticipated the parole idea. In the course of the German criminal law reform movement, protective supervision was recog-

[1] M. Sommer, l.c., 116.

[2] Muthesius, l.c., p. 34; *Berliner Gefangenenfürsorge, Tätigkeitsbericht 1930–1*, p. 21.

[3] W. la Roe, *Parole with Honour* (1939).

[4] 'Report of Commissioners appointed to inquire into Transportation and Penal Servitude', 1863, *Parliamentary Papers*, xxi, *Reports from Commissioners*, ix. 23 and 32.

nized as the essential element of conditional release.[1] It was suggested that, as a rule, every prisoner should be released under conditions only, one being that he submitted himself to protective supervision.[2] American experts, too, wish parole, i.e. conditional discharge under continued supervision, exclusively applied as the appropriate release procedure. If properly administered they regard it as the best method of prevention, with its negative functions of watching the ex-prisoner and enforcing certain conditions supplemented by a positive process of social rehabilitation.[3]

Legislation and administration have not yet fully realized these principles. Actual progress is difficult to assess, since there are no general standards for what is recognized as a proper parole system. In the United States parole is a typical release procedure. In 1927, 49 per cent., and in 1936, 46 per cent. of all prisoners released from state and federal penal and correctional institutions were paroled.[4] States differ in their application of parole. In one-half of all states 51–94 per cent. of all prisoners discharged are paroled, in the other half 1–49 per cent. are paroled.[5] In 1927 Illinois, New York, Massachusetts, Indiana, and Washington had a ratio of more than 80 per cent. of all prisoners released on parole.[6] In these general statements parole covers every form of conditional release before the expiration of the sentence. In the true meaning of the word, parole—like probation—implies two things, viz. a social report based on expert investigations as the basis for the parole decision and effective supervision by trained social workers. In accordance with such standards, only 30 state prisons have been listed, which provide pre-parole reports referring to the results of social investigations, to special examinations, institutional progress, and future plans.[7] Only 8 states and the Federal Government have an adequate field-service with a substantial number of parole officers working under central supervision.[8] Even here the case-load of a single parole officer is too high. While 50–75 parolees per officer has been regarded as acceptable, in some of the advanced parole services the average is 243.[9] States with a high reputation both with regard to social investigations and organized supervision

[1] W. Mittermaier, l.c., p. 573.
[2] Umhauer, l.c., p. 431.
[3] *Wickersham Report*, ix. 130 et seq.
[4] Ibid., p. 127; W. la Roe, l.c., p. 179.
[5] *Attorney General's Survey*, v. 284.
[6] *Wickersham Report*, ix. 127.
[7] *Attorney General's Survey*, v. 287.
[8] *Wickersham Report*, ix. 136; W. la Roe, l.c., p. 65.
[9] Ibid., p. 78.

are Illinois, Massachusetts, New Jersey, New York, and Pennsylvania.[1] These diversities of incidence and method make it impossible to assess the success of parole by a general statement. As a result of the differences in parole administration, the ratio of violations of parole orders varies from 5 to 35 per cent.[2] In 1936, 31,131 prisoners were paroled from state and federal institutions, or 46 per cent. of all prisoners discharged. Out of these, 4,575, or 14·7 per cent., were recalled for violation of their parole orders.[3] In 1938, 2,834 parole cases from federal institutions were terminated; out of these, 174, or 6·1 per cent., ended with the issue of a warrant for violation.[4] A study of nearly 10,000 prisoners released from Californian prisons during the ten-year period 1925–35 showed a ratio of successful adjustment of 58 per cent. of those discharged without parole and of 74 per cent. of those under parole.[5] These figures do not reveal how far the better prospects of parolees are due to the selection of those eligible for parole, or to the treatment they underwent during the parole period. In the after-studies of some 500 young men paroled between 1911 and 1922 from Massachusetts Reformatory, Sheldon and Eleanor Glueck assessed a total failure rate of 56·1 per cent. for the parole period and 62·1 per cent. for a five-year post-parole space. At the same time they found that over half the number of parolees were not seen by the parole agent on his own initiative, and, with a few exceptions, the others were visited and seen less than once a month.[6] Even with such short-comings, the contribution of parolees to serious criminalty is less significant than generally presumed. Out of 771 prisoners convicted for felonies in 1938 in the Districy of Columbia, only 4 were parolees.[7]

In England, prisoners serving sentences of imprisonment are released unconditionally. Convicts, serving sentences of penal servitude or preventive detention, and Borstal trainees are discharged on licence. The licence of a convict discharged from penal servitude has a merely negative character. He is permitted to live at large provided he abstains from crime and reports to the police as required.[8] The Central Association for the Aid of Discharged Convicts may help him to find work and lodgings and assist him with maintenance, clothing, and tools. The licence of a prisoner from preventive detention is a positive one. The licence-holder is

[1] *Attorney General's Survey*, v. 287; W. la Roe, l.c., 67.

[2] C. H. White, 32 *Journal* 600.

[3] W. la Roe, l.c., p. 179.

[4] *Federal Offenders, 1938* (1939), p. 26.

[5] W. la Roe, l.c., p. 181.

[6] S. and E. Glueck, *After-conduct of Discharged Offenders* (1945), pp. 22 and 60.

[7] W. la Roe, l.c., p. 174.

[8] Fox, p. 172 and *passim*.

bound to work and live under the direction of a society or person under whose authority he has been placed. This supervision is undertaken by the Central Association. The *Report on Persistent Offenders* of 1932 testifies that, in spite of widespread unemployment, the Association was remarkably successful in finding employment. At the same time the *Report* emphasizes the need for a personal service of individual attention and friendship, and the establishment of personal relations as an incentive and moral support for men who easily take the view that it is useless to renounce the past.[1] The after-care undertaken by the Borstal Association is an equivalent to a parole system. Lads discharged from a Borstal institution are placed under the care of the Borstal Association for the rest of their sentence plus an additional year. The official *Principles of the Borstal System* regard institutional custody and freedom under supervision as two almost equal parts of one comprehensive training scheme.[2] The Association has some 1,000 paid and unpaid associates all over the country for an equal number of boys discharged every year from Borstal institutions. The associate to whom a lad has been assigned must supervise and befriend him, help him to find and keep employment, and advise him on useful spare-time activities. Change of lodgings or employment needs the associate's consent. Every month the associate is expected to forward a progress report to the Association.

On the Continent recent legislation has combined conditional release with protective supervision. The relevant laws of Czechoslovakia of 1919 and of Austria of 1920, the Swiss Criminal Code of 1937, and the German Draft Penal Code of 1927 and the Regulation on Pardon of 1935 provide that the prisoner's submitting to protective supervision may be made a condition of the release granted. The effectiveness of this measure depends less on legal provisions than on the appropriate forces available for this service. As a rule, the legislation relied on protective supervision as an institution grown up from voluntary social work. For an effective preventive and correctional treatment within the framework of the administration of criminal justice, a resort to charitable organizations proved insufficient. During the twenties Saxony established a consistent public service of welfare workers within penal institutions and in the main reception areas, responsible for social work with prisoners and after-care and supervision of those under conditional release. In 1927–8 Saxony had an average

[1] *Report of the Departmental Committee on Persistent Offenders* (1932), pp. 59 and 33.

[2] *The Borstal System: Principles* (1926), p. 28.

daily prison population of 5,000 prisoners and twenty-six full-time social workers.[1]

Co-ordination of Probation and Parole

In a rational penal system probation and parole should be co-ordinated. Sanford Bates, for years the head of the American Federal Prison Administration, envisages a development by which probation, prison, and parole together will constitute one protective penal process.[2] Such a co-ordination would mean that if a man who has been on probation before has to go to prison the probation officer's experience should be at the disposal of the prison authorities and provide the foundation for an individualized treatment programme. Likewise, where the prisoner's parole is considered—and this should be the normal release procedure—institutional progress reports and any former probation experience should be submitted to the parole board and forwarded to the parole officer. Such a scheme applies a thorough-going case-study method to penal and corrective treatment. In the practical administration of such planned treatment full allowance must be made for the flexibility of the assessments which accompany the prisoner's progress. The findings on record must be constantly verified in the light of new insight and fresh experience.

The need for co-ordinating probation and parole has been confirmed by practical experience. In 1932, in England and Wales probation officers undertook the after-care of 219 pupils discharged from approved schools, 435 ex-Borstal inmates, and 1,891 discharged convicts and prisoners.[3] It has been the official view of the Home Office that 'after-care in its general technique bears a close resemblance to the functions which a probation officer discharges in supervising a person placed on probation', and therefore his experience and aptitude 'may render him especially suitable for helping in this all-important work'.[4] With regard to pupils from approved schools, the association with offenders under probation or conditionally discharged from penal institutions is objectionable. Recently the Home Office has therefore assigned the after-care of boys licensed from approved schools to special welfare officers, appointed for this particular function to areas about county size.[5]

1 Starke, in Frede–Grünhut, l.c., p. 223, n. 23.
2 Sanford Bates, 32 *Journal* 324, 327.
3 L. le Mesurier, *Handbook of Probation* (1935), p. 151.
4 *Home Office Circular*, 21 Oct. 1932; le Mesurier, l.c., pp. 341 and 344.
5 *Making Citizens* (H.M. Stationery Office, 1945), p. 59.

In Germany some of the prison societies undertook 'social court aid' by submitting reports and undertaking personal supervision in connexion with the conditional remission of punishment. Halle was renowned for such a practice. Here social workers of the prison society, from their previous investigations, knew most of the ex-prisoners placed under their care and supervision. Thus, after-care was transformed into a consecutive welfare work.[1] The U.S. Federal Government has amalgamated the functions of probation and parole into one comprehensive service. Federal probation officers are the field parole officers of the federal institutions. The administration expects from this measure a close co-operation between institutional staff and field-workers, and a mutual exchange of experience with regard to men committed to penal institutions and placed under supervision and non-institutional treatment.[2]

There are good reasons for such an amalgamation. The technique of probation and parole supervision is essentially the same. The English Probation Rules of 1926 and 1930 prescribe that the probation officer shall 'advise, assist and befriend the probationer'. In very similar terms the *Wickersham Report* characterizes parole supervision as 'a continuous process of helpfulness, guidance, and friendly assistance'.[3] Both services require the same type of social worker. Against this may be said that a mixing of probationers with men recently discharged from prison is inadvisable. If probation were confounded with parole it would lose its appeal as a treatment of unconvicted, or at least not sentenced, men. In rural districts, however, a duplication of services is impossible, and parole supervision by the probation officer the only way of enlisting a trained social worker for after-care work.

The rise of probation and the potentialities of parole illustrate the shifting of emphasis from institutional to non-institutional treatment. The parole stage is decisive for success or failure in the prisoner's social readjustment.[4] This view has been stressed by the U.S. *Attorney General's Survey* of 1939.[5] Prisons are regarded as institutions for protection and segregation and, in favourable

[1] G. Jacobi, in *41. Jahrbuch der Gefängnisgesellschaft für die Provinz Sachsen und Anhalt* (1925), p. 17.

[2] J. Bennet, in 'Coping with Crime', *Yearbook of the Natl. Probation Association* (1937), pp. 122 et seq.

[3] *Wickersham Report*, ix. 131.

[4] B. Freudenthal, 'Wie sorgt die Allgemeinheit in Amerika und England für Gefangene und Entlassene?' Offprint from *Monatsblätter des Reichszusammenschlusses für Gerichtshilfe* (1928), p. 8, with reference to an official statement of the Prussian Ministry of Justice. Starke, in Frede–Grünhut, l.c., p. 206; Muthesius, l.c., p. 34.

[5] *Attorney General's Survey*, v. 292 et seq.

circumstances, for diagnosis and preparation, while rehabilitation is the chief function of parole. Social readjustment is a process of two phases, a preparatory institutional and a final non-institutional treatment. The prison will justify its existence by the degree to which it accepts this function of playing a part in a wider scheme, and helps, by observation and preparatory training, to lay the ground for educative treatment in the community itself.

PSYCHOLOGICAL TREATMENT

The depreciation of imprisonment as a correctional treatment of criminals is further due to the hopes attached to the psychological treatment of offenders. This idea originated from the recent developments in psychology for which the Viennese analytic school and the Zurich school of individual psychology are mainly responsible, and of which Healy's approach to the individual delinquent within his particular human relationships has been the most fruitful application to practical criminology.[1] These fresh developments in doctrine and method have made possible deeper insight into the causes of crime and the dynamics of criminal behaviour. No longer does explanation stop at innate intellectual capacities and temperament, or at given facts of environment. Life itself, with its unceasing stream of events and changing relations, is a permanent process of 'circular response' (Healy), initiated by man and yet moulding his character and behaviour. Impressions and occurrences in early childhood, successes and failures, affection or the lack of it, approval or disapproval, independence or fear of insecurity, these are some of the roots of human behaviour, criminal as well as non-criminal. This approach which considers the complex of a man's personal reactions rather than isolated static causes of crime, not only enriches criminological understanding, but also opens new prospects in criminal treatment. It shows at least the layer of human life where therapeutic efforts must be brought to bear.

Psychological treatment is a technique of medical psychology. Penal science can discuss only some of its general implications in order to determine its proper place within a system of correction and crime prevention. By the definition of psycho-therapy suggested by the Mental Health Committee of the British Medical

[1] S. Freud, *Introductory Lectures on Psycho-analysis* (1922); II (1933); C. G. Jung, *Contributions to Analytical Psychology* (1928); A. Adler, *Social Interest: A Challenge to Mankind* (1938); W. Healy, *The Individual Delinquent* (1915); W. Healy and A. Bronner, *New Light on Delinquency* (1936).

Association, psychological treatment can be described as a treatment by mental analysis, suggestion, persuasion, or re-education.[1] In this sense, psychological treatment does not mean a cure for psychoses or a treatment of marked mental deficiencies. As a diagnostic as well as a curative instrument it extends its effects into the unconscious life and, in doing so, deals with the irregularities and conflicts of what, by ordinary standards of illness and health, is to be regarded as a normal mind.

The starting-point and significant characteristic of psychological treatment is that it should reveal the hidden roots of man's thoughts, wishes, omissions, and acts. This is also what psychoanalysis purports to do. Such a claim may provoke the comment that in psycho-therapy—as in criminology—diagnosis is still far ahead of a successful curative treatment. Yet the experience of religious confession confirms that the mere fact of unburdening oneself of the inhibitions and accusations of one's own past is a relief. The deeper the probe advances into the unconscious, the less the patient is able to recognize the true significance of what to him seem remote and irrelevant facts. Here the psychologist undertakes to offer an explanation and to make the unknown relationship between the deeper root and the pattern of thought and conduct understandable. The twilight of shunned and repressed feelings and their disturbing effects is to be replaced by a brave facing of even the undesirable factors in one's life. Only a conscious order instead of the vain attempt to escape from chaos will enable man to master his wishes and emotional reactions; and these ultimately determine whether his deeds will be good or bad.

The wisdom of this approach is confirmed by experience in education or pastoral work. Critical consideration indicates the limitations of such methods. Extreme care must be taken to ensure that the psychologist's presentation reveals to the patient the true working of his conscious and unconscious motives, and that it avoids an explanation which reveals the investigator rather than the patient. The danger zone begins when a symbolic meaning is given to dreams, pictures, and other unconscious expressions of the mind, and that meaning is interpreted. To interpret involves attributing a meaning to something which of itself has none, or only an insignificant one. This entails the risk that something alien to the patient is suggested to him—result which would be in flagrant contrast to the declared aims of psycho-

[1] *Report of the Feversham Committee on Voluntary Mental Health Services* (1939), p. 14. See also B. Hart, *Psychopathology* (2nd ed. 1929), p. 125, n. 2.

analysis. Where this danger has not been avoided, the symptoms will be aggravated rather than relieved.

Psychological treatment is more than an intellectual process of making a patient understand his own motives. Where the difficulties have been traced back to a certain conflict, a similar conflict situation may be repeated under controlled conditions. All these direct and indirect efforts are based upon the underlying principle of reality. Facing the facts, recognizing even the undesirable traits in one's own character, substituting honesty for self-pity and indulgence, are some of the ethical elements of psychological treatment. This means a challenge to man himself, an appeal to rely on his own strength for the lifelong process which has been described by an English psychiatrist as 'psycho-biological adaptation'. 'Psychiatry', he said, 'will help people to meet the actual difficulties in their lives' and 'enable the individual to come to a better understanding of himself, so that he can adapt more easily to his changing circumstances as they affect either himself or his environment'.[1] To this aim the analytical achievements are often an indispensable first step. Once the ground has been cleared of inhibited desires and perverted tendencies, a re-evaluation of life is to begin. Personal experience is the only convincing proof of ethical values. Fairness, truth and loyalty, self-sacrifice, and devotion to higher objects must be seen in action to be believed and accepted as patterns of character worth a lifelong effort. The desire to have affectionate links with personalities of understanding and goodness is the secret of human influence in the family, in every field of education, in social welfare and religious pastoral work. As a Governor of a Borstal institution observed: 'Lads have no use for virtue in abstract. They will love and follow virtue when they see it exemplified in someone they admire and respect.'[2] Psychological treatment needs not only the patient's active co-operation, but also his confidence and affection. Only when higher values have been experienced as realities rather than presented as abstract virtues is the last step possible, i.e. the formation of a new emotional disposition, the moulding of a social character.[3]

There is, however, a limit to the aim of re-arming the patient for the struggle. Personal difficulties are often due to a disproportion between the individual's abilities and the social demands which confront him. In many cases this disproportion may be adjusted

[1] D. K. Henderson, 85 *J. Ment. Sc.* 1–21.
[2] *Report Prison Commissioners, 1937*, p. 61.
[3] R. G. Gordon, 11 *J. Neur. Psychopath.* 239.

by strengthening the individual's forces and relieving hidden energies which had been repressed. In other cases it cannot be fairly expected that an individual of certain abilities and potentialities should master an adverse situation which for him proves an unnatural obstacle. It requires much wisdom and experience to decide in each case where to insist on a categorical imperative, and where to ease the way and to allow for human weakness. If the patient cannot be enabled to stand the strain of his environment it must be adapted to his limited strength. Parents may be persuaded to change their attitude towards a child, a child may be removed from a bad home, a man be transferred to a more suitable employment. Psychological treatment demands supplementary social work.

Presented in such broad outlines, the principles of psychological treatment differ in degree rather than in kind from other ways of personal guidance and influence. They have a twofold significance. On the one hand they reveal the ultimate personal factor by which educative treatment, institutional or non-institutional, is distinguished from mere drill and the enforcement of habits. On the other hand, they are the foundation for a specialized clinical treatment in the hands of expert medical psychologists.

As a psychology of educative treatment, the foregoing observations seem rather trivial and obvious. It is, however, no objection to their validity, but a test of good psychology, that they confirm and make explicit what occurs daily to parents, teachers, and youth-leaders. In their application to penal and reformative treatment, moreover, these observations emphasize the unconscious educational factors, the small things in the daily routine and surroundings, the key to which the whole life has been tuned, the things that go to make up the educational atmosphere. They make it clear that education can only work by 'challenge and response'. It is not an arcanum, given in a prescribed dose; it requires the pupil's co-operation no less than the teacher's direction. This makes a strong case for a dynamic process of treatment, for an organized progress from lower to higher stages with succeeding objectives to be won by increasing efforts up to the final test of a probationary period among the adversities and temptations of the world at large. To be more specific, psychological treatment provides an argument against separate confinement and fixed prison terms; and an argument for vertical classification and gradual inmate participation, no less than for probation and parole.

As regards clinical treatment proper, these psychological outlines suggest a comprehensive approach to the patient's problems. This has been practised by the child-guidance clinics which developed in England after the stimulating example of Wm. Healy's work in Boston. Child guidance is team-work, the co-ordinated effort of a psychiatrist, a psychologist, and a psychiatric social worker.[1] In dealing with behaviour problems and personal difficulties, they contribute to the prevention of juvenile delinquency. Similar methods have been applied by organizations specializing in the treatment of young offenders. The Institute for the Scientific Treatment of Delinquency in London handles between 100 and 120 cases a year, the majority of them being sent from courts and probation officers.[2] One-half of the cases dealt with are cases of theft. The clinic provides a diagnosis done by a team consisting of a psychiatric social worker, medical psychologist, educational psychologist, and organic physician, and, if necessary, psychiatrist; it gives a recommendation for the disposition of the case; and it provides psychological treatment where this seems advisable. While originally the psycho-neurotic types of delinquents were presumed susceptible to psychological treatment and character types refractory, more recently treatment is recommended according to the quality of the personality, the strength of will-recovery, and the potential rapport with the therapist. Follow-up inquiries showed that before the war more than one-quarter of those referred to the Institute accepted treatment, and of these every second was cured or improved. Allowing for interruptions and short-comings due to the war and for the possibility of a spontaneous remission of psychological difficulties, the Institute reckons with a success ratio of 40 per cent.

This raises the question whether such treatment should not have a place within the prevailing penal system.[3] In 1932 the Departmental Committee on Persistent Offenders recommended that a medical psychologist should be attached to one or more penal establishments, and with the assistance of social workers apply psychological treatment to selected prisoners.[4] Accordingly, in

[1] G. S. Stevenson and G. Smith, *Child Guidance Clinics* (1934); D. K. Hardcastle, 18 *Brit. J. Med. Psych.* 328 (America); D. R. MacCalman, 85 *J. Ment. Sc.* 505 (Great Britain); W. M. Burbury, E. M. Balint, B. J. Yapp, *Introduction to Child Guidance* (1945).

[2] E. Glover, 'Diagnosis and Treatment of Delinquency', in Radzinowicz–Turner (ed.), *Mental Abnormalities and Crime* (1944), pp. 269 et seq.

[3] In England, first advocated by M. Hamblin Smith, *Psychology of the Criminal* (1922; 2nd ed. 1933).

[4] *Report of the Departmental Committee on Persistent Offenders* (1932), pp. 48 and 67.

the years 1934–8, 214 prisoners over seventeen underwent treatment for the purpose of an investigation on the value and prospects of such a course.[1] They consisted of a group of 124 sexual offenders and 90 other criminals, 72 of whom were early recidivists. The numbers were too small and the time was too short to assess success and failure. While 20 of 124 sexual offenders and 36 of the 90 other criminals were re-convicted after having received at least partial treatment, the investigators reject the conclusion that the former type will always respond better than the latter to a therapeutic approach. The therapy applied was either 'psychotherapy', or 'psychiatric treatment', or 'psychiatric supervision'. The official report comes to the conclusion that psychological treatment beside general psychiatric methods is an effective means of reducing the risk of further criminality, if properly applied to suitable prisoners. For this purpose it has been recommended that special institutions should be established where selected prisoners would serve their sentences and at the same time undergo medical examination and treatment. Such special prisons have been envisaged as a clinical hospital and training institution.[2]

Prison routine, with its insufficient stimulants to initiative and will-power and, often enough, an atmosphere of dullness and repression, does not offer the right conditions for treatment which aims at encouraging the patient to face the facts squarely and to use his own energy. Such attempts demand a comparatively free life in a controlled environment. In England the idea of Q camps, tested by four years' practical experience, is an example of communal life under responsible educational guidance in the free environment of an improvised camp. While a flexible daily routine could easily be adapted to changing conditions in work and personal life, allowance was made for individualization and psychological treatment.[3] During the war new experience has been gained in military rehabilitation centres which offered special modes of camp routine with opportunity for psychological group treatment.[4] These are valuable precedents for new methods of semi-institutional treatment of offenders amenable to psychotherapy while living in a controlled community.

A further step to treatment within normal surroundings is the

[1] W. N. East and W. H. de B. Hubert, *The Psychological Treatment of Crime* (1939).

[2] Ibid., p. 159; *Report Prison Commissioners, 1938*, pp. 49 et seq.

[3] W. D. Wills, *The Hawkspur Experiment* (1941); M. E. Franklin (ed.), *Q Camp* (1943). Similar methods applied to children with behaviour problems have been described by W. D. Wills, *The Barns Experiment* (1945).

[4] J. Abrahams and L. W. McCorkle, 101 *Am. J. Soc.* 455.

combination of psychological treatment with probation. The *Report on Persistent Offenders* of 1932 suggested that in suitable cases psychological treatment should be made a condition of a probation order. By this arrangement the necessary control and pressure are provided to make a man persevere in attendance: for offenders who have been discharged on the mere undertaking to submit to a prescribed therapy too often evade it by failing to attend the clinic. Since probation, though given as an alternative to an otherwise unavoidable sentence, needs the offender's consent, a probationer will be more ready to co-operate than a prisoner. Recent experience in a London magistrate's court indicates the prospects and limitations of such a procedure.[1] Out of ten cases reported, seven can fairly be claimed successful. Six out of the seven successful cases concern sexual offenders, three of them with previous sentences. Though the experiment proves nothing for the overwhelming number of crimes of dishonesty, it applies to a type of offender whose treatment by repeated prison sentences has proved futile and discouraging. It has been estimated that every year about 500 offenders against women and girls, 400 exhibitionists, and 200 homosexual offenders are sent to English prisons.[2] In an extreme case, elsewhere reported, a man had, within thirty years, sixteen convictions for indecent assaults on young girls.[3] In the special group under observation, out of three cases where offences of dishonesty against property were treated, two were unsuccessful, both with a very bad home background. The third, an 'obsessional neurotic' with persistent dishonesty from his eleventh or twelfth year to his eighteenth seemed to go straight when he joined one of the fighting services. This brief analysis shows that psychological treatment gives good promise of success in some cases which would benefit neither from plain probation nor from a traditional prison term. In the light of these results, the Criminal Justice Bill of 1938 proposed to lay down certain legal conditions for the insertion in probation orders of provisions for clinical or residential mental treatment of not certifiable offenders (clause 19).

Psychological treatment is not a general alternative to prison. It is a method, subject to further development, overcoming certain deep-rooted difficulties which lead to crime and bar a satisfactory social adjustment. It requires the patient's confidence

[1] Claud Mullins, *Crime and Psychology* (1943), pp. 38 et seq., esp. 69–98.
[2] East and de Hubert, l.c., p. 152.
[3] *Report of the Departmental Committee on Persistent Offenders* (1932), p. 4, n. †.

and co-operation and thereby strengthens the case for preferring to repressive and punitive sanctions a controlled life in smaller and wider communities: special institutions for prisoners under treatment, life in a camp community, probation. This fits in with penal policy's general tendency to substitute personal requirements for outward compulsion. According to this tendency capital punishment is less and less resorted to, long prison terms have become shorter and involve less personal hardship than one or two generations previously; short prison terms are less often inflicted. At the same time society expects that the personal surroundings and private affairs of the individual should be investigated by a social worker, that the hidden secrets of his unconscious mind should be probed by a psychologist, and his life, work, spare time, and social intercourse should be adapted to conform with recommendations which have behind them the power of the law. The reformative process may be more and more transferred from the prison cell to the community at large, but it demands no less a sacrifice of personal liberty.

CAMP LIFE AND OTHER METHODS OF EXTRA-MURAL TREATMENT

The rise of probation, the growing potentialities of a parole system, and the demands for psychological treatment, are instances of a new departure in non-institutional treatment. This is the positive side of the classification of prisoners according to different degrees of security. Minimum security prisons have been recommended not only in order to avoid the notorious disadvantages and heavy costs of a fortress prison for all, but to act also as a challenge for the development of new methods of penal and reformative treatment in a supervised community.

In considering these objectives it is interesting to note that camping has become a temporary way of living for growing sections of the present generation. This is a reaction against urban and industrial civilization. Scouts and other organized youth groups spend some of the summer weeks in camps. The inter-war period witnessed the rise of labour camps. The idea had forerunners in England, where Ruskin persuaded Oxford undergraduates to volunteer for work on the roads. After the First World War labour camps began in Bulgaria and Switzerland as an attempt to give unemployed and destitute youth the opportunity of a period of useful work and active community life and to help them to overcome indifference and apathy, to regain self-confidence, and to profit by new skills. Almost everywhere university students undertook responsibilities in running the camps. In Great Britain undergraduates shared vacation camps with unemployed miners and steelworkers from depressed areas. In Germany voluntary labour camps grew up as the last stand of a young generation threatened by frustration and mass unemployment, till National-Socialism perverted the original conception and replaced the voluntary service by general conscription. In 1933 the United States established the Civil Conservation Corps, an army of 350,000 civilian volunteers between seventeen and twenty-eight living in work camps of some 200 men under military command.[1] During the war young men and women of all nations have lived in military or industrial or agricultural training and labour camps. At the same time, on the Continent, the camp-idea has been utterly discredited by the sombre memory of concentration camps. As in many other fields of education and youth welfare work, new constructive forces have to strive hard to overcome the shadows of the recent past.

These facts are closely related to penal reform. While it would be a mistake to resort forthwith to labour camps as a substitute for prison, there is every reason to study the social and educational effects of camp life, and to find out what can be learnt from them for the treatment of offenders.[2] Like prison, the camp separates the individual from his environment, but not by removing him to the unnatural seclusion of a cell or an association of prisoners, but to an intensified life with fresh stimuli and challenges. The camp is what the prison only pretends to be: a perfect opportunity for observation. Camp life is a test of social qualities and the best school where they can be learned and developed. Campers have to live closely with one another; there is competition in work and play, and much opportunity for self-discipline after a hard day's work, when self-indulgence makes life in the group intolerable. Campers, however, should not be left to themselves and to the formative influence of group life. Educational and social workers—the 'counsellors' of the American camps—who share the life of a group and are responsible for a certain number of campers, find ample opportunity for individualization, personal guidance, and conscious and deliberate treatment. American C.C.C. camps have developed a five-point programme for the guidance of campers

[1] C. H. Taylor, in *Yearbook of the National Probation Association* (1937), pp. 325–40; K. Holland and F. E. Hill, *Youth in the CCC* (1942); D. C. Fisher, *Our Young Folks* (1943), pp. 117 and *passim.*

[2] For the discussion which follows: L. J. Carr, M. A. Valentine, M. H. Levy, *Integrating the Camp, the Community and Social Work* (1939).

which is reminiscent of the vertical classification of prisoners: orientation, counselling, assignment to an appropriate place in work and play, evaluation of the immediate effects of camp life, placement and following-up in the community at large. An essential factor of the educational value of camps is the cultural standard. Living conditions may be austere, the work hard and toilsome, but there should be full opportunity for stimulating lessons, debates, excursions, dramatics, and music.

Experiments have already been made in the use of camps as training and adjustment centres for juvenile delinquents. From 1930, in Ohio, a short-time summer camp has been conducted for boy probationers.[1] It proved effective for offenders whose behaviour problems were mainly due to environmental factors, but two or three weeks was too short a time for any lasting success. In 1931 the Probation Department and the Juvenile Court of Los Angeles County established the first forest camp.[2] It caters for boys whose committal to an industrial school has been suspended, and it gives them a chance of a four months' training period. The boys are bound to an eight hours' day of paid work with pick and shovel, and there are games and discipline by organized inmate participation. A counsellor is responsible for every ten boys. The camp claims a ratio of no more than 20 per cent. parole violators which does not compare badly with the results of a good institution. In 1935 there were six forestry camps in the northern and western states.[3] While any artificial hardship would be resented as deliberate drudgery, these camps are necessary for the preservation of the forests and the prevention of fires. The campers do useful work which they know must in any case be done under similar conditions. America is fortunate in providing natural conditions which make possible a pioneer life which would be unreal in a densely populated area a stone-throw from the amenities of urban life. Los Angeles County further maintains eight road camps for selected adult misdemeanants sentenced to the county gaol for a term of ninety days or more. In these honour camps the men are never locked up, but free to come and go within a certain radius of the camp. There is some form of self-government through elected dormitory and camp judges. Escapes are prosecuted as a felony and occur at a ratio of less than one-half of 1 per cent.[4]

[1] I. A. Wagner, in S. and E. Glueck, *Preventing Crime, a Symposium* (1936), pp. 231 et seq.; id., in *Yearbook of the National Probation Association* (1937), pp. 341 et seq.

[2] H. G. Stark, ibid. (1937), pp. 357 et seq.

[3] *Attorney General's Survey*, v. 46.

[4] L. N. Robinson, *Jails* (1944), pp. 138 et seq.

In Germany limited experiments were made to enable difficult adolescents from educational institutions to join voluntary labour camps.[1] Though not advisable for offenders with active criminal tendencies, this proved successful for certain types with passive psychopathic traits and a lack of will-power and steadfastness, often with a long history of escapes from institutions and trade masters. After an appropriate preparation by institutional treatment, the voluntarily accepted discipline and the comradeship with equals—many of them after long unemployment likewise in need of special care—seemed a better solution than either prolonged institutional confinement or free employment.

In England the so-called Q-camp methods not only provide the appropriate milieu for psychological therapy, but are also in themselves a good example of non-institutional treatment for young men under twenty-five, mainly relying on the experience of pioneering and self-government.[2] For the four years before the war a camp for twenty members received selected adolescents, delinquents as well as non-delinquents, who volunteered for camp membership. Communal life of staff and members in simple surroundings, shared responsibility between staff and members, an atmosphere of mutual affection and tolerance, but equally of reality and sincerity, and a constant psychological supervision with facilities for individual attention and therapeutic treatment, are the main principles of Q camps. Members stayed for some months. Most of them seemed to profit from community education in a free environment, although, it should be added, these methods do not seem suitable for psychotics, or for men whose symptoms spring from deeply rooted causes, or whose long and repeated prison experience has profoundly marked them.

In 1935 a new Borstal institution was established as a North Sea camp on the shore of the Wash, north of Boston.[3] Before the war 120 lads lived in huts, mainly built by inmate labour, with a housemaster for every 15 boys. It was an open camp without continuous supervision by house officers. Boys were selected who could be expected to respond to trust and were not in need of special vocational training. After selection by a selection board it was left to the boy to choose whether he would go and give the pledge: 'Because of the trust put in me, I promise on my honour to do my best to keep up the good name of the North Sea Camp.'

[1] W. Gerson, 25 *Zentralbl.* 117.

[2] W. D. Wills, *The Hawkspur Experiment* (1941); M. E. Franklin (ed.), *Q Camp* (1943).

[3] W. W. Llewellin, 4 *Howard Journal* 252.

The camp was engaged in the hard work of reclaiming an area of salt marshes for agriculture. On five days a week there were two hours' evening classes. There were organized games and systematic physical training. Contact with the community was encouraged. Campers attended evening classes and church services in a nearby place, or met other teams at sporting matches. Half the camp joined the Sea Scouts.

Camp life is not the only possible form of communal life in a free environment under educational control. The group life may assume more permanent forms without the patterns of an institution. This applies to a youth settlement, for which W. R. George's Junior Republic at Freeville is a remote, but still classic, example.[1] Or there may be attempts to reach, by correctional and preventive efforts, youngsters even within their natural surroundings. In wartime England local experiments were made with youth squads undertaking useful work in emergencies. The proposals of the Criminal Justice Bill of 1938 were a bold step in this direction. In accordance with a suggestion made in the *Report on Corporal Punishment* of the same year they provided for juvenile attendance centres for the age-group of twelve to sixteen and attendance centres for the age-group of seventeen to twenty-one, where, by order of the court, juveniles were to attend up to three hours a day for a maximum of six months. Here they would find constructive occupation and suitable instruction without interference with their ordinary school and working hours.[2] Likewise, the Bill envisaged Howard houses for adolescents between sixteen and twenty-one, i.e. hostels where the residents live under disciplinary conditions for a period not exceeding six months, while in the daytime they leave the house for employment outside.[3]

Great expectations of new alternatives to imprisonment have been aroused by reports on experiments in Russia. The almost unlimited space of open country with its unexhausted possibilities of economic development offers ample opportunity for employing prisoners in useful work under a minimum of restraint. The revolutionary spirit of the new Russia fostered an unorthodox approach to the prevention and repression of crime. Accessible material, however, is scarce, and does not permit a fair judgement of the Russian penal system as a whole. Russia has a twofold

[1] W. R. George, *The Junior Republic, its History and Ideals* (1910); W. R. George and L. B. Stowe, *Citizens made and remade* (1913); D. T. Urquhart, in S. and E. Glueck, *Preventing Crime*, l.c., pp. 291 et seq.

[2] Criminal Justice Bill, 1938, cls. 12, 13, 29.

[3] Ibid., clause 13.

penal policy. Progressive methods on record applying to 'ordinary' criminals do not prevail as far as political offenders and persons deemed dangerous to the State and social order are concerned. With regard to the first group, certain bold experiments in open penal and correctional establishments call for careful study and consideration.[1]

The Commissariat of Justice maintains two types of penal establishments, viz. prisons and minimum security camps. It appears that the prison population mainly consists of homicides, burglars and robbers, with a high proportion of persistent criminals, while in some of the camps the largest group consisted of men convicted of neglect of duty in office and non-payment of tax duties. The camps have no walls and a small staff only—in one instance one supervisor for every 300 prisoners. Escapes are so treated as to put no obstacles in the way of the prisoner's return. A first escape, for example, does not count at all, if the prisoner returns within twenty-four hours; and the first 'real' escape may be punished with deduction of a day's earnings, the second by a short term of isolation. Re-committal to an enclosed prison is the most severe punishment. Treatment relies on the stimulating effect of productive work. The rising current of an impetuous industrialization of the whole country does not halt before prison gates. The five-year plan assigned prison workshops to their proper targets. Penal and correctional establishments seemed to be permeated by the bracing atmosphere of a great common effort. Work competitions with factories, and 'shock brigades' who pushed forward and tried even to surpass the target, were impressive features of penal treatment. 'Use a book as a tool for your work' is a slogan written on the wall of a dormitory. At the same time, prisons take part in the struggle against illiteracy. The paramount claim for work efficiency gives Russian penal policy its strongest impulses. It implies full opportunity for productive work and appropriate instruction. It fosters an active inmate participation, with a 'Comrades Court' for violations of discipline, especially in connexion with work, and a wall newspaper to express criticism of unsatisfactory conditions and pillory men suspected of lagging behind the standard. The over-riding interest in rising production

[1] Lenka von Koerber, *Soviet Russia fights Crime* (1934); Sanford Bates, *Prison and Beyond* (1936), pp. 295 et seq. Anton Makarenko, *Road to Life* (1936) describes the emergence of the Gorki Colony for boys near Kharkov from the troublesome aftermath of the Civil War. The present writer is much indebted to the Howard League for Penal Reform for kind permission to use unpublished reports written by British visitors to Russia.

solves the problem of after-care. An abundance of work keeps labour in high demand. A man's productive ability, not his past criminal career, determines his status in the community, and a successful ex-prisoner regains full citizenship. This background made feasible a large-scale experiment with open colonies which are work and training centres in the wider framework of a paramount productive effort.

Outside the jurisdiction of the Commissariat of Justice, the O.G.P.U. administers the Bolshevo Colony near Moscow, which became a model for other similar establishments. It was founded in 1924 as an educational camp for wayward youth after the Civil War, and owes its progressive features to Felix Dzorzhinsky. Bolshevo Colony is an open industrial settlement with a large factory for various articles of sporting equipment, surrounded by dwelling blocks and dormitories, a canteen, a co-operative store, and a radio receiving station. The more than 2,000 colonists are mostly young men between sixteen and twenty-four with three previous convictions for offences against property. They are picked up from ordinary prisons by a selecting committee consisting of colonists themselves. The committee declares who in the opinion of its members might profit from the life in the colony. The average 'cure' for a colonist requires residence for two to three years. A considerable number of colonists have their wives with them. Many former colonists stay as free citizens. There is a small staff of five technicians and educationists. The Colony has complete self-government. The administration is in the hands of an executive committee, which is responsible to the 'Collective', i.e. the general assembly of colonists. Colonists have to have the consent of the Collective for marriage, get their pay in special colony coinage, and have a curfew at 11 p.m. Otherwise they are free, even to leave the colony. But if they do go before being honorably discharged, they have no chance of being readmitted, no prospect of regaining citizenship, and, if part of their original prison term is unexpired, they face a recommittal to prison. Eighteen per cent. of the total of colonists leave the Colony without being properly discharged. This has been regarded as the failure rate of this experiment.

A recent suggestion from the United States elaborates the idea of a youth village as a new educational departure which would take into account the unprecedented amount of waywardness that has followed the war.[1] Such a youth village is envisaged as a composite

[1] C. Bondy, 'The Youth Village', MS.

settlement with every sort of schooling and training facilities, with a right balance of freedom and authority, with useful work and high cultural activities, and a youthful community life permeating the whole atmosphere and shared by the members of the educational staff and their families. This settlement would cater for displaced and normal youth of every description, and be so secure in its educational determination that it could absorb a considerable proportion of wayward juveniles. It does not lead to a new method of treatment for maladjusted juveniles as a separate class, but approaches the problems in an indirect way, i.e. by a comprehensive character-forming educational activity which is expected to reach youth in general at a highly critical moment, and thereby to affect causes as well as symptoms of waywardness and delinquency.

The manifold methods of extra-mural treatment, though scattered and unco-ordinated, form a characteristic trend of present-day penal reform. As often in the past, the new tendency is more obvious with regard to juvenile delinquents. Considerable inroads have been made into the traditional domain of prison sentences, and more and more groups of offenders have been claimed susceptible to new modes of a constructive treatment interfering less with the individual's life within the community. A continuous widening of this sphere shows that the pendulum is swinging from institutional to non-institutional treatment. This might not lead to a final overthrow of the prison, but it will affect its function. The prison of the future will probably abandon something of its claim to be a self-contained reformative institution, and will instead serve as a first stage of observation, resettlement, and preparation within a wider composite treatment scheme, and as a means of security detention for the protection of society against the irreclaimable.

THIRD PART

SPECIAL TOPICS

CHAPTER XIII

JUVENILES AND ADOLESCENTS

THE treatment of young offenders confronts penal reform with a conspicuous problem. Its solution affects a considerable section of the younger generation. Their future careers and the contribution which, as the citizens of to-morrow, they will be able to render to the community, depend on a successful handling of early maladjustment. But the care of juvenile delinquents has an even wider bearing. It sets an example for the treatment of adult offenders. Time and again new methods, introduced to deal with delinquent youth, have come to be applied to higher age-groups also, thus superseding policies which were deterrent or repressive.

THE CRIMINOLOGICAL SITUATION

It is almost impossible to assess the amount of juvenile delinquency in a way which allows a fair comparison between different countries. The difficulties begin with the conception of delinquency itself. This term may be either restricted to the commission of legal offences, or even confined to those which are returned by criminal statistics. While the common offences of dishonesty and personal assault are punishable in every country, national laws are far from being uniform with regard to the age-groups presumed to act with criminal responsibility. And sometimes delinquency is understood in a wider sense, comprising waywardness and maladjustment in general. There are, moreover, no common standards of undesirable behaviour by means of which the experience of different countries could be reduced to statistical terms. The following observations are only some illustrations of the amount and characteristics of juvenile delinquency.

English criminal statistics offer an insight into delinquency among very early age-groups. English criminal law is unique in fixing the lower limit of criminal responsibility at the early age of eight years. In other countries, too, schoolboys pilfer and commit acts of destruction, but only those belonging to the higher age-groups are regarded as legal offenders who appear in the columns of criminal statistics. Before the war, out of 3 million English boys between eight and seventeen, some 24,000 a year were found guilty, mostly of dishonesty.[1] More than 35 per cent. of all indictable offences are committed by children and young persons under seventeen. In 1938, when the crime rate for males of all ages over ten was 407 per 100,000, the peak group consisted of boys of thirteen with a crime rate of 1,315 per 100,000.[2] This record figure was the climax of a steady increase in juvenile delinquency before the war, with a steeper rise among the lower age-groups. From 1931 to 1938 the crime ratio for lads between sixteen and twenty rose from 647 to 841, but those for boys between eight and thirteen from 540 to 1,183.[3] The inevitable increase of juvenile delinquency after the outbreak of the war, which followed the previous rising trend, again manifested itself more markedly at the beginning of the youth period. The first four months of 1940 compared with the corresponding months of 1939 showed, among adolescents of seventeen and under twenty-one, an increase by 16 per cent. in convictions for indictable offences, among the young persons of fourteen and under seventeen an increase by 41 per cent., and among the largest group of children under fourteen by 62 per cent.[4]

In Germany, too, the years before the war coincided with a rise in delinquency among juveniles of very early age-groups. In Hamburg the specific crime rate of school-children of fourteen—i.e. their share in the total of criminality of juveniles between the ages of fourteen and eighteen—rose from 6·3 per cent. in 1931 to 17·4 per cent. in 1936, in Munich from 9·6 per cent. in 1932 to 21·2 per cent. in 1935.[5] In the United States the delinquency rate of 1934 per 100,000 was 1,480—1,510 for boys and 250–80 for girls of juvenile court age.[6] These American figures cover delinquency in a wider sense than English criminal statistics which record persons found guilty of legal offences. The typical symptoms of delinquency in the wider meaning of the word are stealing, acts of carelessness or mischief for boys, and being ungovernable, running

[1] *Fifth Report of the Children's Branch* (1938), p. 9.

[2] *Crim. Stat. 1938*, Appendix II (A), p. xxxiii; T. Sellin, *Criminality of Youth* (1940), p. 59.

[3] *Crim. Stat. 1938*, Appendix I, p. xxix; Sellin, l.c., p. 58.

[4] *Home Office Circular 807 624 / Board of Education Circular 1554*, June 1941; H. Mannheim, 217 *Annals* 128, 137.

[5] O. Kirchheimer, 29 *Journal* 362, 366, quoting from Kruse, 28 *MoSchrKrim.* 499, and from Seibert, *Jugendkriminalität Münchens* (1937).

[6] *Juvenile Court Statistics, 1934* (U.S. Department of Labor, Children's Bureau, 1937), p. 7.

away, and sex offences for girls.[1] In the United States, too, the outbreak of the war coincided with a rising trend in juvenile delinquency. While between 1929 and 1936 the totals of juvenile delinquents fell in spite of an increase in the number of delinquent coloured boys,[2] the amount of juvenile delinquency in 1941 was already 7½ per cent. higher than in 1940, and increased under the impact of the war by a further 8½ per cent. in 1942 as compared with 1941. The rate of increase was more than four times greater among girls than among boys.[3]

The criminality of adolescents shows even more homogeneous features. The peak group roughly coincides with the threshold of civil maturity and gradually recedes with the higher adult groups. In the age-groups over juvenile court age in England and Wales, Czechoslovakia, Denmark, and Sweden, the older minors are those with the highest crime rates, while Germany, Switzerland, Italy, and Norway have the highest crime rates among those in the early twenties.[4] American investigations show that even with these record crime rates the group of young offenders exhibits no excessive participation in the total of legal offences committed. Their contribution, however, is abnormally high in offences against property. In the United States one-fourth of those arrested or committed for robbery, and an even larger proportion of those concerned in burglary or auto-theft, are under twenty years of age. Among male offenders almost every second auto-thief is under twenty, and so is nearly every fourth arrested for rape.[5]

Juvenile delinquency, much more than adult criminality, is an expression of group life. In England over 70 per cent. of juvenile offenders,[6] in the United States 70–90 per cent. of boys committed to correctional institutions, acted in association.[7] Since gangs consist of few leaders and many followers, among the totals of delinquent associates there is a considerable proportion without persistent criminal tendencies. Among juvenile delinquents in Liverpool, 57·7 per cent. of socially readjusted former first-offenders, but only 43·5 per cent. of recidivists with several reconvictions were members of a gang.[8] Among delinquents before Juvenile

[1] *Juvenile Court Statistics, 1936* (1939), p. 15.

[2] Ibid., pp. 7, 8, 12.

[3] J. V. Bennet, in *American Yearbook, 1943*, p. 585.

[4] T. Sellin, l.c., p. 65, Table xxix, with reference to E. Hacker, 'Statistique comparée de la criminalité', 1937 (reprint from *Revue internationale de droit pénal*, 1936).

[5] Sellin, l.c., pp. 67 and 30 et seq.

[6] Carr-Saunders, Mannheim, Rhodes, *Young Offenders* (1942), p. 110.

[7] N. Fenton, *The Delinquent Boy and the Correctional School* (1935), p. 79.

[8] J. H. Bagot, *Punitive Detention* (1944), p. 41.

Courts more than one-fifth had previously appeared before the court, viz. 22·9 per cent. in London, 29·7 per cent. in English provincial towns,[1] and 23 per cent. of the boys and 13 per cent. of the girls before American Juvenile Courts.[2]

The causes of juvenile delinquency do not differ from those of criminality in general: and theories which hold good for crime in general may often be based on juvenile delinquents; for their lives and background are more accessible to penetrating investigation than those of adults. The outstanding fact in juvenile delinquency is its 'multiple causation', whether we are considering it as a social phenomenon within a smaller or larger community, or considering the criminal career of an individual.[3] According to Sir Cyril Burt's classical study the following four causes account for more than 50 per cent. of juvenile delinquency: mental dullness, temperamental instability, conditions of the family life, and the influence of friends outside the house. Among the environmental factors the home stands first. Institutions for delinquent juveniles report that more than one in two of their pupils come from a broken home.[4] This calls for further elaboration. There is a closer correlation between a broken home and children being ungovernable, running away and playing truant, than there is between a broken home and offences against property, traffic violations, and misdemeanours.[5] The crime risk depends on the reason why the home has been broken; it is smaller for semi-orphans, higher when one parent deserts the family. The emotional atmosphere in the family is more important than its completeness or incompleteness. A recent English investigation confirmed that 80 per cent. of non-delinquents against 68 per cent. of delinquents come from a normal complete family with father, mother, and at least one brother and sister. If, however, incompleteness is eliminated and delinquents and non-delinquents from outwardly normal and complete families are compared, only 55 per cent. of the delinquents against 84 per cent. of the non-delinquents come from homes where the parents' attitude is satisfactory, i.e. neither over-strict, nor over-indulgent. A child from a normal family with a good home

[1] Carr-Saunders, Mannheim, Rhodes, l.c., p. 99.

[2] *Juvenile Court Statistics, 1936*, p. 53.

[3] Cyril Burt, *The Young Delinquent* (2nd ed. 1931), p. 607 and *passim*; id., *The Subnormal Mind* (2nd ed. 1937 and 1944), pp. 161 et seq.; S. and E. Glueck, *After-conduct of Discharged Offenders* (1945), p. 76.

[4] *Fifth Report of the Children's Branch* (1938), p. 44.

[5] H. A. Weeks, 5 *Am. Soc. Rev.* 601, quoted from W. C. Reckless, *Etiology of Delinquent and Criminal Behaviour* (1943), p. 24.

atmosphere may, of course, for some reason become delinquent; but a child from a family which, though of normal structure, does not provide the right attitude of parents towards children will have three to four reasons to the other one.[1] This result corroborates the criminological observations of Wm. Healy and others in the United States, that the personal situation with its emotional and affectional elements is more decisive than outward conditions, favourable or adverse.[2] The experience of youth-leaders confirms the opinion that psychological reactions to human relationships are at the root of many acts of delinquency and much maladjustment: a feeling of insecurity, a desire for independence, the frustration of fundamental needs for affection and recognition.[3]

A rational policy must aim at preventing juvenile maladjustment from developing into a lasting criminal career. The earlier the first misbehaviour, the higher is the risk of a serious criminality in later years. American investigations show that the percentage incidence of serious criminality during a fifteen-year span following treatment by a Juvenile Court is 16·1 for those with the first misbehaviour between thirteen and sixteen, 28·9 for those between nine and twelve, and 35·3 for those under nine.[4] Before the First World War 39 per cent. of English convicts had their first punishment between the ages of fifteen and twenty, 14·3 per cent. when under fifteen.[5] According to more recent observations in Germany 45 per cent. of those under preventive detention and 69 per cent. of long-term prisoners, had had their first sentence when they were under eighteen years.[6] In 1936, out of 15,000 ex-Borstal men living in England, 688 were serving sentences, which is equivalent to 8·1 per cent. of the total male prison population.[7]

This contribution of former juvenile offenders to adult criminality is a challenge to educational and penal policy. But the task of reducing that contribution is not impossible. Since crime rates recede with every age-group after the peak of adolescent crime, a substantial part of the large group of young offenders evidently does not reappear in the ranks of older criminals. In England the extraordinary rise in juvenile delinquency during the First World War was not followed by a corresponding peak in adult criminality

[1] Carr-Saunders, Mannheim, Rhodes, l.c., pp. 68 and 149 et seq.
[2] W. Healy and A. Bronner, *New Light on Delinquency* (1936).
[3] J. Macalister Brew, *In the Service of Youth* (1943), p. 210.
[4] S. and E. Glueck, *Juvenile Delinquents grown up* (1940), p. 139.
[5] Computed from Goring, *The English Convict* (new ed. 1919), p. 123.
[6] H. Kruse, 28 *MoSchrKrim.* 497.
[7] Healy and Alper, *Criminal Youth and the Borstal System* (1941), p. 214.

during the next decade.[1] Likewise in Germany, the record crime rate of 1,082 per 100,000 juveniles during the currency crisis of 1923 was followed six years later by a crime rate of 1,843 for adolescents which was below the pre-war level of 2,007.[2] While the fluctuations of the crime curve are due to a coincidence of various factors, these figures suggest that the treatment of the unusual juvenile delinquency of the war and post-war crisis did—to say the least—not prevent the final readjustment of a substantial proportion of young offenders.

The links between juvenile delinquency and adult criminality cannot be ignored by penal reform. The fact that now and again prisons receive men and women who as boys and girls had been before courts and in correctional and penal institutions, calls for the concerted efforts of all the forces which contribute to the social education of youth. As a result of the development of the last 150 years, the concern of the State for the maladjusted juvenile has undergone a characteristic change. On the one hand, children and juveniles have been released from the clutches of the criminal law. On the other hand, legislation has steadily extended the responsibility of the community for a wholesome upbringing of the younger generation. English common law has adopted the classical rules of the civil law,[3] by which children under seven are excluded from criminal liability, and offenders between seven and fourteen are presumed to be incapable of a guilty mind as long as there is no evidence that 'malice supplies age' and that the juvenile acted with a guilty knowledge that he was doing wrong.[4]

Continental legislation has gradually modified its application of criminal law with regard to juveniles.[5] The French *Codes pénals* of 1791 and 1810 replaced both the absolute age limit of seven and the legal presumption with regard to the age-group of seven to fourteen by the rule that a defendant under eighteen is punishable only if he acted with *discernement*, i.e. if he was capable of knowing that he was doing wrong. Belgium and Prussia followed the French example. In this way the law recognized that an offender over

[1] W. Elkin, *English Juvenile Courts* (1938), p. 287. See also T. Sellin, l.c., p. 96.

[2] Computed from figures given by Roesner, 'Altersaufbau', *HWB-Krim*, and in *Kriminalstatistik, 1927*, p. 33, and *1928*, p. 27.

[3] *Dig*. 47. 2. 23; *Dig*. 47. 10. 3; *Dig*. 47. 19. 8. 2. Corresponding rule of Canon Law: c. 1 (inc.) X *de delictis puerorum* 5. 23.

[4] Matthew Hale, *History of the Pleas of the Crown*, i, ch. 3, ed. S. Emlyn and G. Wilson (1778), pp. 16 et seq., esp. 24 et seq.; Kenny, p. 56; Russell, *Crime* (9th ed. 1936), i. 13 et seq.

[5] For a comparative survey of nineteenth-century legislation see K. v. Lilienthal, *VDA*, v. 104 et seq.

fourteen could have the mind of a juvenile; at the same time it dropped the absolute barrier protecting children under seven. Other criminal codes preserved a legal limit for the criminal liability of children and gradually raised the statutory age up to thirteen in Poland; fourteen in Austria, Czechoslovakia, Germany, Italy, Norway, Switzerland; fifteen in Denmark and Sweden. Only for juveniles above these statutory limits some continental laws adopted the French formula of *discernement*, until recent legislation supplemented this one-sided intellectual requirement by provisions which allow also for the development of the juvenile's will-power. In the meantime, in 1912, after considerable criticism from her jurists, France introduced a statutory lower age limit of thirteen, and in 1933 England raised the traditional age of seven to the present statutory limit of eight. American legislation solved the problem of age-groups by substituting for the legal punishment of those deemed capable of a criminal intent an educative treatment of all delinquent children up to sixteen or seventeen.

This regress in punitive competence was accompanied by an extension of the State's administrative and educative powers. Most criminal laws provided that children and juveniles committing acts which, but for their lack of criminal responsibility, would be legal offences, might be committed to appropriate institutions for education. The same course was applied to wayward children and juveniles who had not committed acts punishable by law, and even became an alternative treatment for young offenders on whom the law permits the infliction of a legal punishment. An increasing number of penal provisions against adults were enacted to protect children against neglect and cruelty. Even parental rights have had to give way to the demands of the community in the interest of the child. Parents may be formally deprived of care and the right of custody if they exercise their rights in a way impeding the child's claim to an education which develops him to physical and mental fitness and enables him to play his part as a useful member of society.

These social and educational tendencies eventually affected criminal law. No longer was the purpose of the reform movement a negative one—to spare defendants of tender years the rigour of punitive sanctions. It became positive: to provide for a flexible variety of measures which would meet the needs and possibilities of youth. The aim was not lenient treatment, but the appropriate one. The law had to part with its makeshift policy of treating children and juveniles as 'small-size adults'. G. S. Hall's classic treatise on adolescence and numerous subsequent studies made it clear that youth is not a state of immature adulthood, but has its own conflicts, its own mode of living, its own method of development and making contact with a world of established values, which at the same time every young generation wants to build anew.[1] As the law accepted this new approach to the needs of youth, the contrast between penal sanctions for legal offences and treatment of social maladjustment began to disappear. By contemporary theories the offence of a juvenile is less significant as an unlawful act than as a symptom of the delinquent's personal condition; and it may even be a good opportunity for finding out his particular difficulties of adjustment. The modern Juvenile Court is a characteristic expression of these tendencies. From the beginning of the present century a steadily growing movement spread through all civilized countries. Together with the rise of probation, the increasing jurisdiction of Juvenile Courts affected almost every penal system and paved the way for a new social conception of crime and punishment.

THE LEGAL MACHINERY

Juvenile Courts

The rise of Juvenile Courts is a common feature of the recent social and legal history of most civilized countries. It was the principal aim of this movement to divorce the treatment of juvenile delinquents from the administration of criminal law prevailing for adults. Not every tribunal, however, with jurisdiction over certain groups of minors is a Juvenile Court. For comparative purposes, and beyond historical and national differences, three characteristics are essential for the conception of a Juvenile Court: a separate hearing of juveniles, a flexible system of preventive and educative measures at the discretion of the court, and access to expert advice and experience. No less important than these questions of organization is the spirit in which the Court exercises its jurisdiction. A Juvenile Court must be ready to act with flexibility, encouraging experiments and the modification of treatment according to fresh experience, like a 'clinic and laboratory of human behaviour' (Miriam van Waters) rather than a traditional court of law with final legal decisions. The juvenile's welfare, his

[1] G. S. Hall, *Adolescence* (1908); W. Hoffmann, *Die Reifezeit* (1920, 3rd ed. 1930); E. Spranger, *Psychologie des Jugendalters* (1924, 3rd ed. 1925); Charlotte Bühler, *Das Seelenleben der Jugendlichen* (2nd ed. 1923); id., *From Birth to Maturity* (1935); Claparède, *Psychologie de l'enfant* (1920).

education and social adjustment, must be the court's primary concern. In the words of the English Act of 1933, the court must have regard to 'the welfare of the child or the young person', and shall in a proper case 'take steps for removing him from undesirable surroundings and for securing his education and training'.

United States

While many tribunals fall short of these ideal standards, the underlying ideas have been generally accepted.[1] The movement began in the United States, where in 1899 the first Juvenile Courts were established in Chicago (Ill.) and Denver (Col.).[2] The legal foundation of the American Juvenile Courts is statutory law which adopted the equity principle, that the sovereign, represented by a Chancery Court, exerts guardianship over minors.[3] This implies the duty of the State to act as the legitimate guardian and protector of children, when the parents' care or other guardianship fails to do so. By a liberal interpretation this rule served as a constitutional justification for a comprehensive jurisdiction over neglected, destitute, and delinquent children. Equity has a less formal law of evidence and a greater variety of legal remedies. In conformity with the idea of chancery jurisdiction children were brought to the new Juvenile Courts, not on particular criminal charges, but for delinquency. In this context 'delinquents' are children who have committed offences against the law, or are falling into bad habits, or seem to be incorrigible,[4] i.e. juveniles whose general behaviour is socially undesirable. The conception of delinquency is a statutory one and sometimes includes disobedience, bad associations, wandering, using indecent language, truancy. The classification of children as delinquent, neglected, and dependent is elastic. In a broad sense, delinquent juveniles are all those who 'deport themselves in such a way as to injure or endanger the morals and health of themselves or others'.[5] Besides this comprehensive jurisdiction over delinquent juveniles, American Juvenile Courts deal also

[1] Comparative surveys: B. Flexner and R. N. Baldwin, *Juvenile Courts and Probation* (1914); 'Enquête sur les tribunaux pour enfants', *Bulletin*, N.S., No. 3, Dec. 1927; 'Organisation of Juvenile Courts', *League of Nations, Child Welfare Committee*, IV Soc. 1931 iv/13 (1932); 'Organisation of the Juvenile Courts and the Results attained hitherto', publ. by the League of Nations and International Penal and Penitentiary Commission, L.o.N. Publ. 1935 iv/5; 'Principles applicable to the Functioning of Juvenile Courts', L.o.N. iv, Soc. 1937, iv/9.

[2] H. H. Lou, *Juvenile Courts in the United States* (1927); K. L. Lenroot and E. O. Lundberg, *Juvenile Courts at Work* (U.S. Department of Labor, Children's Bureau, 1925).

[3] J. W. Mack, 23 *Harvard L. R.* 104.

[4] Wharton–Ruppenthal, *Criminal Law*, i. 479, s. 365.

[5] H. H. Lou, l.c., p. 54.

with non-delinquent cases of juvenile dependency and neglect. The latter amount to approximately one-third of the total number of cases. The chancery idea emphasizes the purpose of help and protection. It gives the hearing an informal character without a charge being read to the child, without pleas of guilty or not guilty, with witnesses only exceptionally sworn in, and the possibility of assigning the hearing to referees who may even talk with the juvenile or his parents in confidence. This is the origin and legal foundation of the American Juvenile Courts which, since the pioneer work at the beginning of the century, are to-day a common feature everywhere in the United States. It should be added, however, that social services are in general found to work more satisfactorily in urban areas than in rural districts. In 1925 American cities with a population of 100,000 and over were all well served by Juvenile Courts, while in rural communities courts with special equipment for dealing with children were available to only 16 per cent. of the population. In half of the forty-eight states less than a fourth of the population was within the reach of Juvenile Courts which complied with higher standards.[1]

American Juvenile Courts have the choice of two alternatives. One leads to a formal hearing of the young delinquents before the court, which may then order probation, commit the juvenile to a correctional institution, inflict a fine or—for higher age-groups—give a sentence to be served in a reformatory. The other alternative aims at an informal adjustment. The judge or a referee, who may be the probation officer, holds an informal and sometimes confidential conference with child and parents and tries to come to a solution of the difficulties by moral suasion. This may result in supervision as a substitute for probation, reparation of damage, or reference to an educational or welfare agency. If an agreement has been reached and approved by the judge, the case will not be brought before the court. In the large cities almost one-half of all relevant cases are informally adjusted. This applies especially to the younger age-groups of fourteen and fifteen, to cases of malicious mischief, disorderly conduct, vagrancy and escapades, and gambling. Theft and sexual offences are usually brought before the court.

The court has at its disposal a report of the probation officer or social case-worker on the juvenile's social background and personal relationships; and very often it has, too, the results of psychological and psychiatric examinations. Contrary to English law, the report

[1] K. Lenroot and E. Lundberg, l.c., p. 1.

is submitted before the judicial hearing of the juvenile, in order to enable the judge to plan the appropriate procedure. The social report and the results of preliminary informal investigations are the basis for his decision whether to try an informal adjustment or to authorize the prosecutor to file a petition with a subsequent summons for formal hearing.

In 1936 twenty-eight American Juvenile Courts under observation handled 22,630 delinquent boys and 4,143 girls. 46 per cent. of the boys and 35 per cent. of the girls were dismissed or informally adjusted, 32 per cent. of the boys and 28 per cent. of the girls put on probation, 11 per cent. of the boys and 19 per cent. of the girls committed or referred to institutions. In the same year twenty-seven of these courts dealt with 11,490 cases of juvenile dependency and neglect. Out of these, 30 per cent. were dismissed or informally adjusted, 29 per cent. committed or referred to an agency or individual, 23 per cent. supervised by a probation officer, and 16 per cent. committed or referred to an institution.[1]

England

In England Juvenile Courts were first established by the Children Act of 1908,[2] reorganized in the Metropolitan area in 1920,[3] and provided with a more comprehensive jurisdiction by the Children and Young Persons Act of 1933.[4] While American Juvenile Courts, even with their jurisdiction over delinquents, originated as Chancery Courts, English Juvenile Courts are courts of criminal jurisdiction with an additional competence in non-criminal matters.[5] They are ordinary Courts of Summary Jurisdiction, though with a special panel of justices, a permanent chairman, and separate hearings. Relevant legislation has mitigated, though not supplanted, certain inconveniences of criminal procedure. Publicity has been restricted to press reports without any reference to the name and identity of the offender. The conceptions of conviction and sentence have been replaced by a mere finding of guilt and an order made upon such finding. The right to apply for trial by jury in indictable cases, the pleas of guilty or not guilty, and cross-examination by the parties obtain, but the

[1] Figures computed from *Juvenile Court Statistics, 1936*, l.c., pp. 18 and 24.

[2] 8 Edw. VII, c. 67.

[3] 10 & 11 Geo. V, c. 68.

[4] 23 Geo. V, c. 12, commentary by Clarke Hall and Morrison (2nd ed. 1942). The Act was preceded by the *Report of the Departmental Committee on the Treatment of Young Offenders* (1927).

[5] Clarke Hall, *Children's Courts* (1926); W. A. Elkin, *English Juvenile Courts* (1938); J. A. F. Watson, *The Child and the Magistrate* (1942).

procedural rights of the young defendant must be explained to him in simple language. Children up to fourteen are exempt from imprisonment altogether, a juvenile under seventeen may be sent to prison in exceptional cases only when the court certifies that he is 'unruly, or of depraved character'. Borstal training is permissible for the last year of the prevailing juvenile court age, i.e. sixteen to seventeen. A Court of Summary Jurisdiction has the power to pass a Borstal sentence only if a boy or girl absconded from an approved school; in all other cases the court has to commit the offender to Quarter Sessions.

English Juvenile Courts have a twofold jurisdiction: the merely preventive and the criminal proper. Both are separated in principle, but overlap in the legal powers which they imply. Juvenile Courts may hear any child or young person brought before them as a victim of neglect and cruelty, exposed to moral danger, fallen into bad association, beyond parental control, and thus 'in need of care and protection'. With the latter formula the law shifts the emphasis from a single type of behaviour or alleged cause of maladjustment to the question whether public intervention is necessary for the child's welfare. Juvenile Courts also hear children and young persons aged from eight to seventeen on charges of criminal offences. To a considerable extent the same measures are applicable in both cases. Children in need of care and protection as well as juvenile offenders may be committed to the supervision of a probation officer, though with certain legal differences. Both types may be committed to the care of a fit person. This would mostly be the local educational authority which boards-out the child to a private foster family. And both types may be sent to an approved school for an institutional training. There remain as exclusive punishments for offenders: fines; imprisonment (permissible for exceptionally unruly juveniles over fourteen), and its substitute, custody in a remand home; Borstal training for those over sixteen; and birching, a remnant of the past which the legislation of 1932 and 1938 vainly tried to abolish. Apart from this anachronism, the measures applicable are almost identical for the younger age-groups, with fines, custody, and Borstal as additional sanctions for older juvenile offenders.

Thus the distinction between preventive and educative measures for those in need of care and protection and punishments for juvenile offenders is a relative one. Since there is no mandatory public prosecution in England, it is sometimes a question of expediency whether a young delinquent is brought before the court as 'in need of care and protection' or on a criminal charge. From an educational point of view, juvenile delinquency is often a symptom of a 'need of care and protection'. Before a court, which constantly applies similar measures to neglected youths and juvenile offenders, criminal cases will be met with the same psychological understanding and educational responsibility as those of mere protection and prevention.

Social reports are given either by the probation officer or the local education authority, but they are not to be submitted to the court before the offender has been found guilty. If psychological and social investigations have to be made before the final decision, the offender may have to stay for an appropriate period in a remand home. The development of these homes into up-to-date observation centres is still in its early stages. The Criminal Justice Bill of 1938 envisaged new facilities for mental examination in State remand homes for young persons under seventeen and remand centres for those between seventeen and twenty-three.

In 1941 English Juvenile Courts found 43,216 boys and girls guilty of criminal offences. 44·5 per cent. of these cases were put on probation, 20·7 per cent. dismissed under the Probation of Offenders Act, 12·7 per cent. fined, 11·3 per cent. committed to an approved school, 7 per cent. bound over without supervision, and 3·8 per cent. otherwise disposed of.[1]

European Continent

On the Continent reports on probation laws and Juvenile Courts in the United States[2] stimulated a reform movement which soon became the vanguard of a new sociological school of criminal law.[3] For the treatment of juveniles these tendencies had a valuable precedent in the continental law of guardianship. The German Civil Law and subsequent legislation of the nineteenth century had developed a judicial supervision of guardianship with the possibility of public intervention to protect neglected youth and prevent waywardness, even where children were under parental

[1] R. Mayer, *Young People in Trouble* (1945), p. 32, diagram 6.

[2] P. F. Aschrott, *Die Behandlung der verwahrlosten und verbrecherischen Jugend und Vorschläge zur Reform* (1892); S. J. Barrows, *Children's Courts in the United States* (1904), German version by G. Stammer, *Amerikanische Jugendgerichte* (1908); Ben B. Lindsey (Juvenile Court Judge at Denver, Colorado), *The Problem of Children*, German translation, 1909, under the title: *Die Aufgabe des Jugendgerichts*. Further: G. Gudden, *Die Behandlung der jugendlichen Verbrecher in den Vereinigten Staaten* (1910).

[3] B. Freudenthal (ed.), *Das Jugendgericht in Frankfurt a/M.* (1912); G. Ruschewey, *Die Entwicklung des deutschen Jugendgerichts* (1918); H. F. Pfenninger, *Das zürcherische Jugendstrafrecht* (1928), esp. pp. 1–41.

custody.[1] It was therefore expedient for the reform to assimilate the treatment of juvenile offenders to guardianship principles, if not to merge guardianship and criminal jurisdiction.

Every continental country has Juvenile Courts established for the separate hearing of juvenile delinquents. In 1912 France assigned maladjusted children under thirteen to civil jurisdiction, and established Juvenile Courts for those between thirteen and sixteen, or, in the case of a mere *délit*, for those between thirteen and eighteen. These courts had power to order probation with or without a prescribed residence, or to commit the offender to a reformatory school.[2] In the same year Belgium gave Juvenile Courts discretionary powers to commit delinquents under sixteen to the care of a person, society, or home, or to place them for a number of years at the disposal of the Government.[3] In Switzerland, where the machinery of justice has been left to the cantons, by 1928 six cantons, including Basle, Zurich, and Geneva, had a reformed law concerning juvenile delinquents.[4] The unification of the substantive criminal law by the Swiss Criminal Code of 1937 resulted in a fourfold classification: children under six exclusively under a board of guardians; between six and fourteen subject to judicial measures of a non-criminal character; juveniles between fourteen and eighteen, under a 'double-track' system of either preventive measures for the wayward or depraved, or special punishment with reprimand or detention up to one year for the 'normal' juvenile delinquent; and finally, minors between eighteen and twenty, treated according to adult law with certain extenuating modifications.[5]

During the inter-war period, in most countries of central Europe the jurisdiction of Juvenile Courts was consolidated by special legislation. This applies to the German Juvenile Court Act of 1923,[6] the Austrian Federal Law on the Treatment of Young Offenders of 1928,[7] and the Czechoslovak Law No. 48 of 1931.

[1] For example, for Prussia: *Vormundschaftsordnung* of 5 July 1875; *Ges. über die Zwangserziehung* of 13 Mar. 1878; *Fürsorgeerziehungsgesetz* of 2 July 1900.

[2] *Loi sur les tribunaux pour enfants et adolescents, et sur la liberté surveillée*, of 22 July 1912, supplemented by law of 22 Feb. 1922, commentary by Martin, *Les Mineurs de treize ans devant la loi pénale* (1922).

[3] Law of 15 May 1912, commentary by C. Collard, *La Protection de l'enfance* (1913).

[4] Pfenninger, l.c., p. 8.

[5] Swiss Criminal Code, arts. 82, 84, 91, 95, 100; E. Hafter, *Lehrb.*, l.c., pp. 416 et seq.

[6] *Jugendgerichtsgesetz* of 16 Feb. 1923, commentary by H. Francke (2nd ed. 1926).

[7] *Bundesgesetz über die Behandlung junger Rechtsbrecher* of 18 July 1928, commentary by Kadečka (1929).

In Poland the relevant provisions of an Ordinance of 1928 were succeeded by the Code of Criminal Procedure of 1928 and the Criminal Code of 1932. These laws provide a flexible system of special sanctions with the alternative of either mere educative measures, or an appropriate punishment. Germany and Austria, as a rule, assign to the Juvenile Court judge the double competence of guardianship and criminal jurisdiction. This enables him to choose not only the suitable measure to be taken, but also an expedient procedure. In Austria, once the public prosecutor has arraigned a juvenile, the court must decide whether he is guilty, but it may suspend the sentence and order educative measures. The German Act of 1923 gave the judge the discretion to apply educative measures whenever necessary, and to abstain from punishment when educative measures seemed sufficient. Under National-Socialism the increasing severity of the criminal law for adults was more and more reflected in the jurisdiction over juveniles, hitherto dominated by social and educative principles. The reform of the past was almost undone when a Regulation of 1939 excepted juveniles alleged to be serious criminals from Juvenile Court law and treated them as adults subject even to death penalty. At the same time, for those who were still regarded as worthy of rehabilitative efforts, certain progressive innovations were introduced. In 1943 a new Juvenile Court Act consolidated previous alterations. It gave the court the choice of three possible modes of treatment: educative measures, disciplinary measures, and punishment. The only punishment for those treated as juveniles was to be imprisonment, either for fixed terms between three months and ten years, or—under the influence of the Austrian precedent—indeterminate sentences with a minimum of at least nine months and a maximum of not more than four years.

Despite differences in detail all these systems have certain principles in common. Everywhere the Juvenile Court has the power to select either an educative measure or a special punishment, whichever seems appropriate, not in view of the offence committed, but of the needs and prospects of the individual juvenile. In exercising this discretion the judge has to resort to the co-operation of expert social workers. Most continental countries have a special social service, called Juvenile Court Aid.[1] This service is rendered either by a public authority, e.g. a youth welfare board, or by a voluntary agency, or more often by a joint organization of

[1] H. Haeckel, *Jugendgerichtshilfe* (1927); 'Auxiliary Services of Juvenile Courts', *League of Nations* 1931 iv/1 (1931).

both, which leads to a co-operation of professional social workers with voluntary helpers. These auxiliary forces are called into action at every stage of the procedure. They are informed of the prosecution by the police or public prosecutor, make inquiries, submit a social report to the court, and may even discuss the case with the judge before the trial, may be heard at the trial itself, are entrusted with the juvenile's protective supervision, keep contact with juveniles committed to correctional or penal institutions, and are in charge of their after-care. With these manifold activities Juvenile Court Aid is a specialized and, in respect of its objects, limited continental counterpart to the English and American probation service. The success of Juvenile Courts very much depends on the devotion and efficiency of the Juvenile Court Aid and the way in which the court makes use of this service.

Scandinavian Child Welfare Councils

The Scandinavian countries developed their own way of dealing with neglected and delinquent juveniles by the establishment of child welfare councils.[1] At the end of the last century Bernhard Getz, the initiator of Norwegian criminal law reform, urged the need for public control and, if necessary, education of youth—for the child's sake as well as for the future welfare of the community. For this purpose he wanted the treatment of children entirely removed from the scope of criminal legislation. The result was an Act of 1896 which introduced child welfare councils responsible for the welfare and social adjustment of children and juveniles. Denmark (1905 and 1933), Sweden (1902, 1924, and 1935), and Finland followed the Norwegian example.

All Scandinavian countries entrusted the care of neglected, ill-treated children and of those beyond the parents' or school-teachers' control to special municipal bodies. These child welfare councils have also comprehensive functions in dealing with delinquents between fourteen and eighteen, and in Sweden between fifteen and twenty-one. In the case of charges against juveniles the public prosecutor may waive proceedings and refer the offender to the council—except in Sweden where the question of guilt must be settled by a judicial decision. The councils are presided over by the local magistrate or a permanent chairman with legal qualifications. A specially prescribed procedure must be used in cases of juvenile delinquency if compulsory measures have to be

[1] 'Child Welfare Councils', Child Welfare Committee, League of Nations (C. 8 M 7 1937 iv) iv Social 1937 iv/1 (1937); R. Hagen, 6 *Howard Journal* 187.

applied. The council may give a warning to the child or his parents, remove the child to a foster family, an individual employer, or a home, commit him to a special school home or observation school, or even formally divest parents of their rights of parental custody. In Sweden a council may order corporal punishment. After half a century's experience the Scandinavian child welfare councils succeeded in substituting for legal punishment protective and educative treatment of children and juveniles. To a considerable extent they have replaced legal proceedings by discretionary action of a new type of social and educational administration. Since much was thus achieved in the prevention of juvenile waywardness and delinquency, legislation was able to raise the lower age-limit of criminal responsibility to fourteen or fifteen. The Swedish police even suggested a further raising of the age to sixteen. From a legal point of view the question suggests itself whether the removal of a child from his home and family without the consent of those concerned is not so grave an infringement of personal rights as to require the decision of an independent court rather than of a board of expert pedagogues and social workers. To this the Norwegian answer is that 'the principal safeguard against excessive measures resides in the representative character of the Child Welfare Council and in the fact that most of its decisions can be modified by the Council itself'.[1]

American Youth Correction Authority

The Scandinavian experience is a valuable precedent for recent tendencies in the United States, which aim at shifting responsibility for the selection and continuation of the appropriate treatment from the law courts to a new type of social administration expected to act with expert knowledge and in direct touch with educational practice. This is the gist of recent innovations introduced by legislative proposals and enactments to check the serious threat of adolescent criminality. While, owing to the application by Juvenile Courts of non-punitive measures, juveniles proper no longer swell the numbers of criminal statistics, young men of nineteen are the peak group of American criminality, with a ratio of 897 per 100,000.[2] The significance of this figure is stressed by the fact that certain aggravated forms of theft with a high probability

[1] *Child Welfare Councils*, l.c., p. 36.

[2] T. Sellin, *Criminality of Youth* (1940), p. 51. For observations on boys over juvenile court age in Chicago see D. W. Burke, *Youth and Crime* (University of Chicago Diss., 1930).

of recidivism are most frequent among adolescents. These considerations resulted in a model Draft Youth Correction Authority Act, framed by the American Law Institute in 1940.[1] Its principles were first adopted by an Act of California of 1941.[2] The Federal Government and the state of New York, too, initiated relevant legislative projects.

These proposals and legal provisions are shifting the centre of gravity from the law courts to a new Youth Correction Authority. This body has been planned as a central authority, empowered to use all existing institutions and non-institutional services, and to direct, alter, or terminate the method of treatment of the individual offender according to its own expert judgement. Under such a system the court still exercises the exclusive power of either acquitting or convicting the defendant. Once an adolescent has been found guilty the court's power to give sentence is limited to the two extreme cases where corrective treatment is either unnecessary or impossible. Accordingly, the trial court would be able, on the one hand, to discharge the defendant unconditionally, to fine him, or even to give a short prison sentence, or, on the other hand, to sentence him for life or to death if the statutes required it. In all intermediate cases which call for a considerate treatment by probation or institutional training the courts are bound, after conviction, to hand over the adolescent to the Youth Correction Authority, as a Swedish Juvenile Court would hand over a juvenile delinquent to the child welfare council. The Youth Correction Authority makes the necessary social inquiries and psychological examinations, selects and directs the adolescent's treatment, and may keep him under supervision and control up to the age of twenty-five or, with judicial approval, even longer, though in California for no longer than the maximum term prescribed by statute for the particular offence.

The fact that decisions on treatment are made by one central authority has the obvious advantage that social and educational experts will more easily be found for one Youth Correction Authority in the State than for the law courts all over the country. The pooling of experience, the opportunity for central planning, and the constant contact with, and direct responsibility for, institu-

[1] Official Draft Youth Correction Authority Act, American Law Institute, June 1940, comments by J. N. Ulman, 23 *Journal* 6; H. Mannheim, 6 *Howard Journal* 70; id., 34 *Soc. Rev.* 222.

[2] California Assembly Bill 777, ch. 937 (1941). See also K. Holton, 'YCA in Action, the Californian Experience', in *Proceedings of the Seventh Conference, the Western Probation and Parole Conference* (1942), pp. 51 et seq.

tional and non-institutional training facilities give the decisions of such authorities a considerable weight. But the issue is wider than a mere question of enlisting expert knowledge for the selection of the most efficient treatment of the young lawbreaker. It is, in its kernel, a question, if not of Judicature versus Executive, at least of the right balance and the appropriate distribution of powers between judicial and administrative authority in the field of criminal justice. With such wide implications, this problem has to be faced in the light of the basic principles of penal reform. It is significant that legislation did not go so far in divesting the court of its sentencing power as the theoretical draft proposals. California retained the courts' power to order probation. A federal Correction Bill of 1942 proposed that the court, when dealing with offenders over Juvenile Court age but under twenty-four, should have the choice of ordering probation, sentencing the accused adolescent like an adult, or committing him to the Youth Authority with a statutory limit of six years as the maximum period of supervision. This discretionary power of the court, however, has been criticized as inferior to the mandatory clause of the draft Bill of the American Law Institute.[1]

Summary

While a comparative survey of Juvenile Courts reveals differences in their organization, competence, and modes of procedure, the experience of some decades shows certain common trends. The prevention of juvenile delinquency and the rehabilitation of maladjusted youth call for a twofold approach. There is need for a thorough-going protective and preventive welfare service, available for all children and juveniles, if not for all minors up to twenty-one. And there must be, outside the scope of ordinary adult criminal law, an appropriate procedure which makes juveniles whom the law regards as criminally responsible answer for what they have done, in the interest of their own education as well as of protection of society. Recent legislation prefers to merge both services. In Germany and Austria Juvenile Courts exercise guardianship as well as criminal jurisdiction. English Juvenile Courts deal with juveniles in need of care and protection as well as with juvenile delinquents. Scandinavian child welfare councils are responsible for neglected children as well as juvenile offenders. This is a recognition of the fact that the treatment of juvenile delinquents, no less than the protection of neglected children or

[1] 53 *Yale L. J.* 782.

the care of wayward youth, is an educational function.[1] The difference between punishment of juvenile delinquents and other forms of educative treatment is a matter of degree rather than of substance. This conception has a legal significance. While ordinary punishment of adult criminals, even with full allowance for a widening judicial discretion, remains ultimately based upon a statutory tariff corresponding to the different legal offences, some of the Juvenile Court laws dispense with specifically prescribed punishments altogether. American statutes, up to the federal Juvenile Delinquency Act of 1938,[2] have substituted for the statutory catalogue of particular offences the general charge of juvenile delinquency, covering any offence committed by a juvenile, sometimes with the exception of those punishable with death or imprisonment for life. The original statutory range of legal punishment is still the limit of public interference. According to the federal law the Juvenile Court may commit the delinquent to the Attorney General for further custody, care, and treatment for a time not exceeding a term of imprisonment which might be imposed as a sentence if the juvenile were prosecuted for the particular offence. The German Juvenile Court Act of 1943 replaced the tariff of statutory punishments by a general punitive power of the Juvenile Court judge up to ten years' imprisonment.

The future will see a shifting of the jurisdiction of Juvenile Courts to higher age-groups. For England this would imply a raising of the present lower age-limit of eight as well as of the upper limit of seventeen. The merging of protective measures for children and young persons in need of care and protection with educative sanctions against juvenile delinquents into a flexible system in the hands of the Juvenile Court has been a lasting achievement of English legislation. A considerable proportion of protective and educative measures, however, could advantageously be applied without recourse to a judicial procedure. This view is supported by the example of Scandinavian child welfare councils. Hamburg and Saxony had a tradition of a voluntary public education undertaken by agreement between the authority and the parents. Local instances of similar experiments have been reported in England. During the war, under the evacuation scheme, billeting authorities removed children with personal difficulties from foster-homes to hostels without the stamp of a court action. American Juvenile

[1] A. E. Morgan, *The Needs of Youth* (1939), p. 134.

[2] 52 Stat. 766, c. 486, s. 9; U.S. Code Title 18 Criminal Code and Criminal Procedure, c. 31, ss. 921–9.

Courts deal with a great number of the younger children by informal adjustment. Much protective and educative work, especially the first approach in early years, can be initiated by persuasion rather than enforced by the power of the law. Such a procedure would make it easier to obtain the co-operation of the parents and thereby ensure an essential condition for success. Even so, no system can dispense with compulsion altogether. Scandinavian child welfare councils have the legal power to enforce their measures against the will of the parents. For countries with a tradition of Juvenile Courts much can be said for a provision which enables educational and youth welfare authorities to take only measures which are voluntarily accepted. For contested matters which imply the separation of the child from the family home and other infringements of personal rights and liberty, a decision of the court should remain indispensable.

While such a course would relieve Juvenile Courts from part of their work for younger children, new tasks are emerging. In countries where the rule of direct oral evidence before the trial court allows exceptions, Juvenile Courts hear children and juveniles who are witnesses to, and victims of, sexual offences committed by adults. In England and in Sweden, and by a recent Norwegian law not yet operative, courts dealing with adolescents must either give a prison sentence according to the assumed gravity of the offence or commit the offender to a special training, if—in the phrasing of the Criminal Justice Bill—'by reason of the offender's character or habits it is expedient with a view to his reformation and the prevention of crime'. This decision requires not only legal evidence but also a social diagnosis, based on a social report, as is the practice of a Juvenile Court. This justifies German experiments of investing judges of Juvenile Courts with a concurrent jurisdiction over minors up to twenty, an opposite course to the recent American tendency of divesting the ordinary criminal court of its sentencing power over adolescents.

A social conception of juvenile neglect and waywardness may even bring adults before the Juvenile Court, if by desertion, non-support, or violation of provisions for the protection of youth, they have contributed to the child's need of support or his delinquency. There have been some relevant experiments in the United States[1] and a legislative recognition of such a policy by an Austrian Statutory Regulation of 1928,[2] followed by a German Regulation of

[1] K. Lenroot and E. Lundberg, l.c., pp. 221 et seq.

[2] *VO zur Durchführung des Jugendgerichtsgesetzes* of 12 Dec. 1928, s. 14, *BGBl.* 339.

1942.[1] Thus Juvenile Courts may gain in jurisdiction over older lawbreakers what they are losing with regard to boys and girls of tender years. Such a development would re-emphasize the character of the Juvenile Court as a court of criminal jurisdiction. As long as legal punishments were almost by definition retributory and repressive, Juvenile Courts as instruments of social education had to be detached as much as possible from the prosecution of serious offences. When, as the result of a 'socialization of the court' (Miriam van Waters) punishments administered by the Juvenile Court become opportunities for a constructive and rehabilitative treatment, it will not impair the court's educational function if suitable cases among the higher age-groups benefit from the same methods.

METHODS OF TREATMENT

Historical Background

The reform movement of the recent past has been almost exclusively concerned with the organization of the Juvenile Courts and their legal and educative functions. In most countries significant progress has been achieved. Cases of juvenile delinquency are considered in the light of psychological and sociological observations. Advantage is taken of expert advice for the selection of the appropriate treatment. All this affects the machinery only. Important as the right disposition by the court is, success depends on what is actually being done with the juvenile during his treatment. If the measures ordered by the court are mere labels for inadequate methods or if there are not sufficient qualified persons to apply the proper methods, even a perfect diagnosis cannot make good for the failure of treatment.

A Juvenile Court, almost by definition, has at its disposal a variety of measures which imply institutional or non-institutional treatment. From a legal point of view they are imposed either as mere educative and preventive measures, or as special modes of punishment. The discussion which follows takes an unorthodox view and classifies the various modes of treatment according to their educational function. The first group of measures leaves the young delinquent in his natural environment. The child remains in the family home, the apprentice or young workman retains his employment. Such a course is particularly advisable when the co-operation of the parents can be ensured. It is a truism that

[1] *VO zur Erziehung und zum Schutz der Jugend* of 8 July 1942, *Dtsch. Justiz*, 473.

juvenile delinquency is a symptom of parental failure. An attempt to strengthen the parents' sense of responsibility will often be a better course than allowing them to evade their duties and to leave only too willingly the responsibility to the higher wisdom of the officials. A formal committal to the discipline of home or school will only rarely be an adequate court action. Warning and admonition to the child and/or his parents may be effective in suitable cases. Treatment proper begins with supervision in the sense of friendly guidance, help, and control: for supervision, in this sense, has been developed as the most substantial part of probation. Supervision may be independent of other sanctions, as is the case with an English supervision order for children in need of care and protection or a continental 'protective supervision'; or it may be backed by an impending threat of punishment as in the case of probation proper; or the judge may have decided on 'protective supervision' with the suspension of the sentence or its execution. Special directions may be given to the juvenile as an independent educative measure as in Germany, or as conditions of a supervision or probation order. Such directions may involve special obligations to make good, directly or indirectly, the damage done, to do some useful extra work for the community, to keep away from certain places or persons. They may amount to a well-considered plan for a fresh start, or they may control the juvenile's spare time or choice of residence. For juveniles as for adults such modes of extra-mural treatment call for variety and flexibility. The proposals of the Criminal Justice Bill of 1938 with attendance centres for the age-groups of twelve to sixteen and seventeen to twenty-one indicate the prospective reform. Other suggestions for the amendment of the present English law are that committal to the care of the education authority as a fit person should be the legal title for a variety of measures,[1] and that committal to an institution might be suspended for observation and a trial treatment like the Californian forestry camps.

The second group consists of measures for education in a changed environment. A child may be transferred to a foster family, or a juvenile committed to an educational establishment or a penal institution adapted to the education of delinquents, i.e. a youth prison, reformatory, or Borstal institution. In England the choice between foster family or institution rests with the court. In Germany the Guardianship Court or the Juvenile Court orders the juvenile's public education (*Fürsorgeerziehung*) which an admini-

[1] Judge Gamon, 6 *Howard Journal* 33.

strative body—in Prussia the provincial local government—administers according to its own discretion either in a foster family or in a private or public institution.

The third group consists of punitive measures in a stricter sense: fines, corporal punishment in countries where it has not yet been abolished, and short prison terms or modern substitutes like punitive detention or 'youth arrest'.

The foregoing classification recognizes only a relative contrast between educational measures proper and educative modes of punishment. A youth prison and a residential 'school' for wayward youth are both educational institutions. In the treatment of delinquent youth training and education are the aim prescribed by the law, even if the measure itself has been inflicted as a punishment. Every educational approach has to rely on the same few fundamental elements of human relationship which are effective in home and school, in a youth group, in social welfare, and religious work. An industrial school and a youth prison may differ in that the prison severs the inmate more completely from his past environment and the world outside, and that the deprivation of liberty is more rigorous, with a marked emphasis on security. In practice differences are mainly due to the age-groups concerned. Residential 'schools' are the typical institutions for juveniles, youth prisons for adolescents and young adults. In England in 1936, 3,759 juveniles between eleven and sixteen were committed to approved schools; and in 1938 1,276 lads and 71 girls between sixteen and twenty-three were sent to Borstal. Only three boys under sixteen were received in prison—scarcely for educational purposes.[1] In Germany, too, prison lost its significance for juveniles. In Prussia, on 31 March 1927 there were 29,529 minors in educational institutions,[2] but on 28 February all the Prussian prisons held only 128 boys and 2 girls between fourteen and eighteen, while the daily average of the whole year was not more than 53 boys and 5 girls.[3] The relation between committals to residential schools and prison sentences is a flexible one. The establishment of educationally well-equipped youth prisons or—conversely—a temporary predilection for a sterner handling of young offenders may increase the number of young prisoners. All depends on the treatment itself; the place of an institution in the

[1] *Fifth Report of the Children's Branch* (1938), *passim*; *Report Prison Commissioners, 1938*, pp. 21 and 104.

[2] 23 *Zentralbl.* 223.

[3] *Begründung zum Entwurf eines Strafvollzugsgesetzes*, 1927 (I). 86; A. Hasse, in Bumke, p. 43, n. 2.

legal system matters less than its contribution to constructive educational work.

While penal administration is an exclusive concern of public authorities, the institutional training of juveniles has grown up from private charity. Up to the present the State has relied for the better part of this service on the work done by humanitarian and denominational agencies.[1] In 1932 only one-fourth out of a total of 19,541 German minors committed to residential education lived in public institutions.[2] In 1938, out of 102 approved schools in England, only thirty were managed by local authorities.[3] Institutional education has been shaped by contemporary spiritual forces. While religious and humanitarian foundations have always provided shelter for orphans and destitute children, the care of young delinquents has a short history. Under the common law the community did not interfere with delinquents presumed incapable of a guilty mind until they became paupers. Those between seven and fourteen whose 'malice supplied age' joined the ill-famed promiscuity of the common gaol. In 1817 a New York report denounced this 'great school of vice and desperation', where 'with confirmed and unrepentant criminals we place those novices in guilt', and appealed for a home to offer refuge for those children after their release from prison. The new home should also be used by the magistrates as a place of detention in lieu of a prison committal. The result was the opening in 1825 in New York of the first House of Refuge, followed in 1826 by the House of Reformation in Boston and in 1828 the House of Refuge in Philadelphia. These institutions catered for juveniles up to twenty, one-half of them being convicted offenders. They mostly stayed for a year in the House, but after discharge remained under the care and supervision of the superintendent until they were twenty.[4] The origin of these first Houses of Refuge as substitutes for gaol resulted in a lasting suspicion which connects the whole institution with the hopeless gloom of the old prison. These early American institu-

[1] For the influence of the State see K. Krohne, 'Entwicklung der staatlichen Fürsorge für die verwahrloste Jugend 1500–1900', *Erziehungsanstalten für die verlassene Jugend in Preussen* (1901).

[2] 25 *Zentralbl.* 204.

[3] *Fifth Report of the Children's Branch* (1938), p. 48.

[4] G. de Beaumont and A. de Tocqueville, *Système pénitentiaire aux États-Unis* (2nd ed. 1836), ii. 1–35; H. Folks, *The Care of destitute, neglected and delinquent Children* (1902), pp. 198 et seq.; O. L. Lewis, *The Development of American Prisons and Prison Customs 1776–1845* (1922), pp. 293 et seq. For conditions before the First World War see H. H. Hart, 'Preventive Treatment of neglected Children', C. R. Henderson (ed.), *Correction and Prevention* (1910), vol. iv.

tions were built on the cellular system. The children's work was contracted out by hour or piece. Their occupation, too, was almost the same as in prison: manufacturing nails, and cane and willow work. Corporal punishment prevailed except in Boston. Even so, these foundations were intended—as was proclaimed in Philadelphia—to be a 'refuge, not a place of punishment', and to 'invite the children of poverty and ignorance to come to a home, where they will be sheltered and led into a way of usefulness and virtue'. The men who led this movement, John Griscom in New York and E. M. P. Wells in Boston, were ardent students of contemporary educational ideas in Europe. John Griscom was impressed with an English asylum for the children of convicts. In the Boston House of Reformation, E. M. P. Wells gave school work an equal place beside industrial occupation, and anticipated modern experiments with a grading system and a moral discipline based upon inmate participation. The next generation of reformers replaced the obsolete principle of congregating all the inmates in a central building by an open cottage or family system, first introduced in the Lancaster Reform School, Ohio, in 1856, and further developed in the New Jersey Reform School. In the eighties of the last century the cottage system and a grading scheme had been generally accepted for American industrial and reform schools. This movement, together with reports on the work of some European prison pioneers, gave support to Z. R. Brockway's new departure, the reformatory for adolescents and young adults between sixteen and thirty.

On the European continent the Swiss pedagogue Heinrich Pestalozzi (1746–1827) left a lasting mark in every field of education. He shared the views of enlightened criminal-law reformers of his time, and recommended the abrogation of life sentences, provision of work for prisoners, and care and assistance for the prisoners' families. In his treatise on infanticide he anticipated the social conception of crime. Punishment, in his opinion, should strengthen the moral forces which alone control criminal tendencies. In the institutional education of destitute and wayward youth he relied on the forces which maintain the ideal family home. Love, decency, and helpfulness should not be abstract commandments, but a natural daily experience, while learning should be a harmonious development of the young souls, growing up together in a mixed group like the elder and younger brothers and sisters of a family.[1] His ardent belief that it must be possible to

[1] J. H. Pestalozzi, 'Über Gesetzgebung und Kindermord', *Sämmtl. Werke*, ed.

awaken the inmost good qualities of man met with a great response from an age impressed with Rousseau's ideas.

In the end, however, this humanistic ideal was challenged by a religious motive. Johann Hinrich Wichern (1808–81) claimed—subject to the State's right of legal punishment—the reclamation of wayward youth and the rehabilitation of the criminal to be an obligation of the Church to the world, a service by the believers rendered to the unredeemed. His endeavours resulted in a wholehearted acceptance of social work by the Church Home Mission, and for some time had a direct influence on Prussian prison administration. He himself began with practical work, when in 1833 he made a cottage called *Rauhes Haus* at Horn near Hamburg a home for maladjusted boys. In twenty-four years of devoted service he developed it into an educational institution and a training centre for social workers. On a pious religious basis, he allowed much freedom of educational means with individualization in small groups and an active share of responsibility by 'children of the peace'. This 'family system' of the Rauhes Haus found many followers. In Germany, denominational forces have long dominated educational work with wayward youth. The majority of residential schools belonged to the evangelical Church Home Mission or the Roman Catholic Caritas Association.

In England the first special prison for juveniles originated in connexion with transportation. In 1838 Lord John Russell inaugurated the establishment at Parkhurst of a prison which should prepare youth between ten and eighteen by two to three years of penal discipline for their compulsory emigration to Australia. This prison catered also for a group of sixty to eighty boys between eight and nine. A special provision enabled the Secretary of State to pardon young prisoners from Parkhurst, if they placed themselves in the charge of the Philanthropic Society which had been founded in 1788 and provided corrective training, first in St. George's Fields, Southwark, and from 1849 under the influence of Sidney Turner at the Boys' Reformatory School at Redhill.

But the true educational approach was left to private charity. Long before 1870 when the law made general school attendance compulsory, a movement for reformatory institutions developed in

L. W. Seyffarth, viii. 3 et seq.; 'Über den Aufenthalt in Stans' (1799), ibid., vii. 395 et seq. Abridged editions of Pestalozzi's main works in English translation: J. A. Green, *Pestalozzi's Educational Writings* (1912); L. F. Anderson, *Pestalozzi* (1931). See also F. Delekat, *J. H. Pestalozzi* (1926).

a gradual, empirical way, with a conscious religious motive as the driving force.[1] A forerunner of such efforts was the Colony of Stretton in Warwickshire, which from 1815 undertook to reclaim juvenile offenders between sixteen and twenty whom it hired from the gaols as yearly servants.[2] Step by step, society became aware of its responsibility towards those of the young generation who seemed doomed to waywardness and crime. As early as 1781, after a visit to Bridewell, Robert Raikes at Gloucester opened the first Sunday school. About 1844, some Sunday school teachers in London began regular evening classes, twice a week or even more often, for children not acceptable at ordinary schools owing to ragged and filthy conditions. Thus ragged schools developed under the auspices of Lord Shaftesbury, to whom the country owed the statutory limitations of child labour. A way was thereby first opened into a forgotten province of education.

It was the lasting merit of Mary Carpenter (1807–77) to define the final aim and the means to attain it.[3] Her educational experience with a model ragged school at Bristol and her ardent study of reports on penal and correctional institutions at home and abroad enabled her to develop, with clear judgement and vision, a comprehensive programme for the education of wayward youth.[4] Closely connected with Matthew Davenport Hill, she was one of the group of enlightened penal reformers who about the middle of the century championed the personal educational approach against the alleged automatic effect of a thoroughly regulated system of separate confinement. She explained that the education of wayward youth should not rely on fear, but should inspire self-respect. Trust and progress should be the rewards, and degrading and revengeful punishments should be banned. Intellectual training and religious education should be related to the children's interest and sense of reality.[5] For the realization of these objects she envisaged a system of three types of educational institutions: first, free day schools, to resume more thoroughly the objects of the ragged schools; secondly, industrial feeding schools, following the example of Sheriff Watson's Juvenile Vagrant and Industrial School at Aberdeen; statutory powers were required for the magis-

[1] G. S. Cadbury, *Young Offenders Yesterday and To-day* (1938).

[2] Serjeant Adams, in *Report from the Select Committee of the House of Lords, appointed to inquire into the Execution of Criminal Law*, 1847, Rpts. viii/3, p. 17, qu. 124.

[3] I. E. Carpenter, *Life and Work of Mary Carpenter* (1879).

[4] Mary Carpenter, *Reformatory Schools for the Children of the Perishing and Dangerous Classes* (1851); id., *Juvenile Delinquents, their Condition and Treatment* (1853).

[5] Mary Carpenter, *Reformatory Schools*, l.c., p. 83.

trates to commit children who, owing to extreme poverty of their parents or their own vicious tendencies, would not regularly attend the day school, to detention throughout the day with wholesome food and work. The third type was the penal reformatory school, administered by 'a wise union of kindness and restraint', as an alternative to imprisonment, with the power vested in the masters to keep juveniles as long as they thought necessary for the individual's reformation. Parkhurst had failed, since it had tried to make the children 'obedient prisoners within certain iron limits, not men who have been taught how to use their liberty without abusing it . . .', while 'the inner springs of action are not called into healthful exercise'.[1] Mary Carpenter looked for new models. At Mettrai near Tours, Demetz had divided the whole institution into ten families of forty under a *père* and two assistants; he developed inmate participation, banned corporal punishment, and placed discharged boys under the care of a *patron*. Wichern's Rauhes Haus was known to American and English students of philanthropy since Horace Mann, secretary to the Board of Education for Massachusetts, visited European schools of every description in 1843 and reported with great appreciation on that extraordinary example of 'the combined power of wisdom and love in the reformation of vicious children'.[2] Mary Carpenter did not content herself with theory. In 1852 with the help of Russell Scott of Bath who had just returned from a visit to Wichern, she founded a reformatory school at Kingswood, and two years later opened Red Lodge, the first institution for girls. In 1854 an Act for the better Care and Reformation of Youthful Offenders in Great Britain recognized the principle that offenders under sixteen should be committed for education to reformatory schools established by voluntary contributions, with the proviso, however, that the juvenile delinquents had to spend a fortnight in prison before being transferred to a certified reformatory.[3] The inconsistency of this compromise was not removed before 1899, when the requirement of a preceding imprisonment was abolished.[4] By 1857 there were forty-five reformatory schools with 1,953 boys and 370 girls. In 1855, the masters of these new schools joined a reformatory Brotherhood.

There followed a similar development of industrial schools

[1] M. Carpenter, l.c., p. 322.
[2] Horace Mann, *Life and Works* (1868), iii. 291–300.
[3] 17 & 18 Vict., c. 86, s. 2; Consolidating Act, 29 & 30 Vict., c. 117 (1866).
[4] 62 & 63 Vict., c. 12.

which catered for boys and girls of the 'perishing class' to prevent their final lapse into crime. Relevant statutory provisions were first enacted in 1857[1] and consolidated in 1861[2] and 1866.[3] Again, Mary Carpenter founded one of the first of this new type of institutions, Park Row Industrial School, which opened in 1858. In the seventies these residential institutions were supplemented by day industrial schools in the large cities. A system was thereby established which worked for several decades. Slowly and gradually, the punitive approach to juvenile delinquency gave way to educational efforts.[4] The number of juveniles under sixteen committed to prison dropped from 16,000 about the middle of the century to 1,968 in 1895. By the turn of the century there were 25,000 boys and 5,000 girls in industrial and reformatory schools, plus 3,000 pupils attending day industrial schools. While in the reformatory schools discipline was often vigorous and repressive, industrial schools adopted the positive incentive of a mark system. Opinions were divided with regard to the respective merits of having all children in one building or the cottage system. Progressive superintendents had to strive hard to secure the children's 'birth-right of elementary school education' in the face of the demands of industrial work which sometimes served not only for training purposes, but also the economic upkeep of the institution. By its best representatives, the movement testified to a true missionary spirit.

In the new century, almost everywhere the traditional methods of treatment were challenged by a changed attitude towards life and society. Under the growing influence of social studies and the rise of a new psychology, the conceptions of sin and repentance appeared to oversimplify a complicated interplay of psychological and social causation. This altered attitude demanded the exercise of new methods and greater objectivity: it required that the subject's condition should first be diagnosed and the subsequent educational treatment based on that diagnosis. Institutional treatment had to adjust its methods to the principles of social case-work and child guidance.[5] These tendencies coincided with an educational

[1] 20 & 21 Vict., c. 48.

[2] 24 & 25 Vict., c. 113.

[3] 29 & 30 Vict., c. 118.

[4] 'Reformatory and Industrial School Work', Lectures edited by the Reformative and Refuge Union (1898). For an historical account see H. Rogers's reminiscences of fifty years' work at pp. 99 et seq.

[5] N. Fenton, *The Delinquent Boy and the Correctional School* (1935), related to the Whittier State School, California.

crisis during the inter-war period. In many countries the new psychological doctrines were hailed by a generation of social workers and teachers who owed much to the experience of the youth movement and had emerged from the despondency of the First World War with a deepened feeling of social responsibility. They were reluctant to hand over to the younger generation the accepted values of the past, but strove for an open, conscious, and manly attitude which squarely faces the demands of a changing world. They placed companionship and guidance before authority and discipline, and filled schools and institutions with a new community spirit. This education went a long way to help the understanding of personal difficulties and to give repressed, ill-directed juvenile activity a wholesome direction. Carried to extremes, however, it would deny the right of any educational interference with the unfettered development of the child's own potentialities, and thereby offer a welcome pretext to authoritarian and reactionary tendencies.

Once more a contest of divergent schools arose. The training of wayward and delinquent youth, so long a backward province of education, came into its own. In less than a generation's time almost everywhere much progress was on record. Institutions lost their barrack-like features, bright colours and flower gardens appeared, deterrent punishments receded, the daily routine resembled the life of a youth group. There were, however, deeper contrasts beneath the attractive surface. In Germany the social and intellectual restlessness of the inter-war period strengthened in the younger generation their distrust of the traditional denominational work, while the old school rejected their ardent criticism with too little consideration. In America the notorious climax of prison education sometimes seemed to call for an abandonment of institutional training altogether.[1] The crisis of institutional education calls for a restatement of its principles.[2]

Institutional Treatment

Institutional education has its own significant character. It may be a substitute for a 'natural' education in the family home, but ought not to be content with imitating it. Nor should it rely too much on institutional order and a smoothly running routine, and

[1] H. E. Barnes and N. K. Teeters, *New Horizons in Criminology* (1943), *passim.*

[2] For the discussion of this issue: C. Bondy, *Pädagogische Probleme im Jugendstrafvollzug* (1925); id., *Schweiz. Z.* (1934), No. 2; W. Herrmann, in *Erziehung*, i. 268; ii. 171; iv. 430; E. Weniger, ibid., ii. 261 and 342; E. Behnke, ibid., v. 541; H. John, 17 *Zentralbl.* 5.

expect a lasting improvement from the enforcement of cleanliness, obedience, and industry. The educational process must go deeper. Three things are essential and must be consciously envisaged. First, institutional training must be undertaken as group education. Negatively, this means that there will be no exclusive care of the individual just as there will be no mass drill. Positively, it means a genuine community life of small, but not too insignificant, groups which include the educator himself. In sharing the life of his group, an older brother to his young pupils and a leader of his group with innumerable opportunities of informal contact, advice, encouragement, and censure, he becomes the strongest of the 'hidden co-educators' with an influence surpassing even the best lessons and admonitions. Such group life facilitates experiments with self-government. Since the day of Joh. Jacob Wehrli and other followers of Pestalozzi's, various forms of self-government have been introduced in residential schools for derelict and maladjusted youth. Recent experiments in adult prisons only followed the example of junior institutions. The history of this movement shows that bold attempts flourished, if handled by strong educational personalities; but, if not, were doomed to failure. This, however, is no argument against the idea of self-government as an educational force in communal life. It is not the expression of a natural or constitutional right, but a subtle instrument in the hand of the educator. It offers him an opportunity for observing and testing his pupils, and gives them the experience to assume responsibility for a common cause. Education through a group community relies less on discipline imposed from above, but exerts stronger demands on the pupils' self-restraint and co-operation. Where such methods meet with success, the values of truth and trustworthiness, of fairness and unselfishness in relation to a life in common, are brought home to the pupils by actual experience. Institutional education must observe a reasonable balance between the group's demand for adaptation and loyalty, and the individual's need of personal understanding and guidance. Group education affords the possible and desirable degree of individualization.

The second educational factor of institutional training is a rhythm between work and leisure. Work may be lessons and study, or agricultural or industrial occupation. The problems of prison labour are as acute in institutions for juveniles. Earning facilities strengthen the educational value of work. A general requirement of training for a skilled trade would be unrealistic. But all efforts should be concentrated on bringing home to the young workers the possibility of, and need for, a high standard of performance in every kind of work, and the satisfaction which it gives—whether it be a cleaning job, weeding and digging the garden, or running errands. This will be emphasized by a régime which after a full day's work provides for well-deserved and well-used spare time. Even under austere conditions, there should be well-organized sports and a high standard in music, drama, and debates. Canon Barnett's word obtains: we must give people what they do not want, i.e. supply must stimulate demand.

A third factor in institutional training refers to relations with the world outside. In pre-war England, even prisons were linked with the outer world by the services of prison visitors and voluntary teachers. Educational institutions are more favourably placed for opening their gates to useful intercourse with the wider community. The school may send out a sports team, or a harvest party, or a concert group to perform or to listen. This applies no less to the teachers and social workers: for they more than others need the stimulus and criticism of their contemporaries in other spheres of life and education.

Group education, a sound rhythm between study or work and leisure, and a satisfactory relation between the life of the community outside and that of the home, these elements work together in building up the most significant, though unconscious, factor of education: 'educational atmosphere'. From this point of view the problem of discipline and punishment finds its solution.[1] An educational approach which is to respect the pupil's personality and to value his co-operation must shun the sort of authority that is based on frequent and humiliating punishments. But it is an oversimplification, and is even misleading, to judge an institution by the frequency or infrequency of its resort to punishment. Neither for parents nor for institutions is there a simple alternative between severity and indulgence; both must aim at understanding *and* firmness, trust *and* strictness, companionship *and* demands. Punishments are indispensable in cases where the pupil cannot or will not do for himself what his own good requires. Everything depends on whether such punishment as must take place does so in an educational atmosphere which the pupil himself has seen to be effective and which still operates for his good after punishment. Disciplinary punishment should not rely merely on the deterrent effect of pain. Efforts must be made to explain to the boy himself the reasons why discipline must be maintained and punishment

[1] C. W. Valentine, *The Difficult Child and the Problem of Discipline* (1940).

inflicted, and to make the whole group see these reasons also. Sometimes an interview with the boy on arrest will help to find a hidden approach to the boy's personality and forge a new link between teacher and pupil.

There are no hard and fast rules applicable to every kind of institution. Institutions differ in purpose, and sometimes greater variety and flexibility seem desirable. The standard and type of school education and vocational training vary. Approved schools in England[1] are divided into junior schools receiving boys under thirteen, intermediate schools for boys between thirteen and fifteen, and senior schools for boys of fifteen and over with a leaving age of nineteen. The last have an agricultural or industrial bias. Training ships offer nautical instruction. Girls have junior schools for those up to fifteen on admission and senior schools for the higher age-groups.

Committals to schools and youth prisons should be for no fixed time. Educational success cannot be anticipated to the day and hour. In England children up to fourteen are committed to approved schools for three years or until they are fifteen, whichever time is longer, and young persons between fifteen and seventeen for three years or until they are nineteen, whichever time is shorter. Most of them stay for two years, before they are released on licence. Lads are sentenced to Borstal institutions usually for two years, plus one year of supervision and after-care. They may be discharged on licence after a stay of six months and more. According to the German Juvenile Court Act of 1943 the judge who sends a juvenile to a youth prison for training determines a minimum of at least nine months and a maximum of not more than four years with a difference between the maximum and the minimum of at least two years. It is essential to find the right moment for the minor's discharge: it should not be so early that he cannot fairly be expected to stand the test of a life at large; but it should not be so late that the optimum effect of institutional training has been passed. Even the advocates of the indeterminate sentence should not overlook the considerable hardship which it may entail and which may defeat the purpose of the sentence and impede desirable educational results. The experience of evacuation has shown that uncertainty, rather than separation from home, made the children restless and increased the difficulties of adaptation. The Governor of Hollesley Bay Borstal Institution has been experimenting with a fixed fifteen-month scheme, so that every

[1] *Making Citizens* (H.M. Stationery Office, 1945).

new-comer works towards a definite date of release which may only be postponed by bad conduct.[1]

Particular circumstances may call for a short period of institutional training. Some English approved schools provide a short-term training of six to twelve months. A home at Heiligenstedten, Schleswig-Holstein, kept boys of post-school age for only four months and girls for five months, and then transferred them to a foster family or an individual employer.[2] Such a period of transition may be desirable as a shock to bring a maladjusted juvenile to his senses, or as a period of rest and preparation for the new start. Institutions for short-time training suffer from a constant change of pupils and must adapt their programmes to a variety of single courses which even short-termers have a chance to attend from beginning to end.

There are enclosed institutions, and semi-open homes from which children go out to attend the local day school, and young persons to work like other wage-earners. Such semi-open institutions approximate to hostels of the type envisaged as Howard houses by the Criminal Justice Bill of 1938. As institutions become more and more differentiated in standard length of terms, modes of discipline, curricula, and vocational bias, the need for a classification of pupils arises. For this purpose, observation and distribution centres are necessary. These, however, ought to have a place in the educative process. The Belgian Observation House at Moll was a model institution. It had a population of 120 boys either on remand for recommendations to the Juvenile Court, or committed for final distribution to proper institutions. There was a stimulating atmosphere and a wide choice in work and play so that a boy's reactions in an environment where he felt at home could be observed.[3] By the end of the Second World War, England had inaugurated classification schools for the assignment of boys to the appropriate approved schools. Boys stay in these for two months in small groups of twenty-three under a housemaster and a housemother. After a fortnight for preliminary adaptation, the boy's intelligence, capacities, and achievements are tested. Inquiry into his social background, observations of those living with him, his participation in the children's activities and a talk with the parents proved even more revealing. For the classification of younger children experience suggests that a knowledge of their intellectual

[1] W. Healy and B. S. Alper, *Criminal Youth and the Borstal System* (1941), p. 86.

[2] 4 *Erziehung* 54.

[3] A. Paterson, *Belgian and Dutch Prisons* (1924), pp. 49 et seq.

ability and school attainment is essential, and for the older ones of their temperamental and physical characteristics.[1]

All this shows that institutional education of wayward and delinquent youth has its particular possibilities and limitations. In this fact a solution can be found to the debate of foster family versus institution. By the end of the Second World War, in England and Wales some 11,000 children were in approved schools and 5,000 lived with foster parents by order of the Juvenile Court.[2] In Germany in 1932, 23,706 minors or 51 per cent. of all juveniles under public education lived in a foster family.[3] The advantages of a good foster home are obvious. Children grow up within a small homogeneous group of people united by links of mutual affection. They learn by experience the realities of life: how the daily bread depends on the father's work, and the homely shelter on the mother's unceasing care. War-time evacuation revealed a much greater number of potential foster mothers than had been expected. This unique social experiment of boarding-out children on a mass scale brought about a better knowledge of which type of children fits in best with a particular type of foster home.[4] Against this must be set the complaints about children being 'institutionalized', when they have been discharged from residential homes. They are accustomed to be cared for by the routine of an invisible machinery, and to a constant control which makes them repressed or truculent if left to themselves. Such consequences support a widespread critical attitude towards institutional education, which is sometimes regarded as no more than a temporary opportunity for observation and preparation before the children finally find a permanent place in the home of a family or the workshop of an employer. It has been agreed that only the most difficult cases, after successive failures in foster homes, should be confined to institutions. An obvious parallel may be found in the shifting of emphasis from prison to new modes of treatment within a controlled environment.

Deeper insight into the educational possibilities in foster families and residential institutions indicates that the differences do not apply to children with a lower or higher degree of delinquency, but are qualitative. Many children have physical and psychological difficulties which are annoying to a foster family, but find proper care and treatment in an institution. Institutional educa-

[1] J. Gittins, 7 *Howard Journal* 34.

[2] H. Donington, *The Care of Homeless Children* (Fabian Research Series, No. 107, 1945).

[3] 25 *Zentralbl.* 204.

[4] Cyril Burt, 11 *Brit. J. Ed. Psych.* 85.

tion is not confined to compulsory training of juveniles committed by the courts, and is often regarded as superior to that of an ordinary day school. Almost 10 per cent. of English children attend boarding schools, among them 2 to 3 per cent. go to well-known public schools.[1] If not 'public schools for all', at least a substantial increase of facilities for residential education has been demanded by recent reform programmes. It seems paradoxical that, at the same time, the maladjusted juvenile should be kept away from institutional education. There is one striking difference: as a rule the child in the boarding school has a favourable home background, while most delinquent and wayward juveniles have not. Home background and family relationships are important factors in a successful education away from home. This, however, applies also to education in a foster family, where children with unsatisfactory home conditions find it difficult to adapt themselves to the new surroundings, even if in the end they identify themselves with the foster family. While confinement to an institution for adults is always associated with prison or asylum, institutional training for children and juveniles is a quite usual method of education. A rational system of educational measures should retain both a flexible and well-controlled scheme for boarding-out and a variety of educational institutions.

To predict the future trend of institutional education is difficult. While the tendency towards extra-mural treatment will not remove all children from institutions to private foster homes, it will probably affect the methods of treatment within the institutions. For long-term education of school-children typical institutions with a marked 'school spirit' of their own will further serve their purpose. It may be that adolescents are the age-group where experiments with new ways of semi-institutional treatment have the best prospects. Even at present the young adults in Borstal institutions and reformatories are objects of greater public interest than their younger comrades in schools. While the whole movement owes its origin to private educational initiative interested in very young delinquents and thence affected young men and women in penal institutions, at present the State in its youth prisons often sets the example for progressive methods which rely on trust and the appeal to self-discipline and co-operation. This is the significance of the English Borstal system, which gives the schools for younger age-groups the example of an atmosphere of freedom, activity, and self-control.

[1] J. T. Christie, *Sunday Times*, 9 Aug. 1942.

Borstal training is a special method of corrective treatment for adolescent offenders.[1] Impressed with the precedent of the American reformatories, Sir Evelyn Ruggles-Brise inaugurated the first special institution at Borstal, a village in Kent, in 1902. The new measure was consolidated by the Prevention of Crime Act, 1908.[2] Lord Samuel, then Under-Secretary at the Home Office, suggested that for the cumbersome label 'Juvenile-Adult Reformatory' the unconventional 'Borstal Institution'[3] should be substituted. Borstal training is characterized by the following special features. In the case of offenders between sixteen and twenty-three English courts have the alternative, of giving either an ordinary prison sentence corresponding to the gravity of the offence, or a Borstal sentence based on the educational needs and prospects of the offender. For this task the court has the opportunity of consulting a report, submitted by or on behalf of the Prison Commissioners, which sets forth whether the offender would profit by this training. Sentence is given for not less than two and not more than three years plus one year under supervision and after-care, with the implication that a lad may be released at any time after six months and a girl after three. After the sentence has been given a further investigation determines which type of Borstal institution would best suit the needs of the individual offender. Before the war there were nine possible institutions, from walled prisons and institutions with agricultural work in the neighbourhood to the open North Sea camp. Such a variety makes possible classification into treatment groups according to maturity, mental abilities, trustworthiness, or need of firm discipline. Within the institution there is further room for individualization of treatment. A division into houses and groups facilitates group competition and the personal approach of the housemaster with the minimum of regimentation. Borstal institutions have a non-punitive atmosphere. As one of the Prison Commissioners said: 'To be sent to Borstal is a punishment, because the training involves a considerable loss of liberty, but to be there is a chance to learn the right way of life, and to see the good which is in each'.[4] The leading principle of this treatment is 'development of responsibility and self-control through trust increasing with progress'.[5] Even when it was difficult to find

[1] *The Borstal System* (Prison Commission, Home Office, 1928); S. Barman, *The English Borstal System* (1934); W. Healy and B. S. Alper, *Criminal Youth and the Borstal System* (1941).

[2] 8 Edw. VII, c. 59.

[3] Viscount Samuel, *Memoirs* (1945), p. 53.

[4] A. Paterson, preface to Barman, l.c.

[5] *Prisons and Borstals*, p. 32.

employment for prisoners, Borstal institutions had a priority over other prisons for the assignment of constructive and instructive work. Finally there is provision for organized after-care by members of the Borstal Association, which has also done much to educate the public. Although sometimes single cases evoke adverse comment in the Press and even from the Bench, on the whole Borstal has been backed by a widespread support and a feeling that it is something to be proud of. Such a reaction on the part of the world outside is an important psychological factor in educational success.

The Borstal system aroused great interest among visitors from abroad.[1] They put on record their admiration for the high degree of individualization, the unhampered initiative, and the strong personal influence of the housemasters, and the atmosphere of freedom and activity still compatible with the administration of criminal justice. Continental observers maintain that Borstal had an ideal example in the tradition of the public schools with their character education by communal life and group competition; whereas on the Continent boarding education is usually associated with the under-privileged and delinquents. American critics favourably compare Borstal with the average reformatory which suffers from the double curse of overcrowding and idleness, with almost no educational individualization, and the inmates committed at too late a stage of their criminal careers. At the same time they want for Borstal the possibility of longer sentences and more opportunity for the psychologist in examination, treatment, and research.

In the last pre-war year, 1938, 1,276 lads and seventy-one girls were sent to Borstal. The daily average population of the Borstal institutions was 2,161 lads and 131 girls. These are youths with a considerable criminality. The law makes it a condition of a Borstal sentence that the offender should be in need of corrective training 'by reason of criminal habits, tendencies or associations', and this means in most cases a number of crimes and repeated court appearance. As for the success of the system, the official statistics give for every year the percentage of those discharged not more than five and not less than two years previously, who in the

[1] Germany: H. Kriegsmann, 18 *Mitt. I.K.V.* 506; F. Exner, 21 *MoSchrKrim.* 473; R. Sieverts, 56 *ZStW* 551; H. G. Quentin and R. Sieverts, Offprint from 68 *Bl. Gefg. Kd.* (1937). Belgium: 'La Protection de l'enfance et l'organisation des prisons en Angleterre', 17 *Rev. droit pén.* 425, 506, 596. Holland: H. C. V. Blouw, *De Behandeling van de jeugdige Misdadigers in Engeland* (1928). United States: W. Healy and B. S. Alper, *Criminal Youth and the Borstal System* (1941).

meantime have not been re-convicted. The ratio of Borstal boys without subsequent re-convictions fluctuates between 53·8 per cent. for 1936 and 63·5 per cent. for 1941.[1] Of those who are re-convicted, approximately one-half appear only once before the courts without further relapses. It is therefore not unjustified to accept these cases of retarded adjustment as successes and to maintain that three-quarters of those who undergo Borstal training find their way into a law-abiding life.

Punitive Detention

Most of the measures at the disposal of Juvenile Courts involve a more or less continuous educational treatment, either institutional or extra-mural. It may be asked whether this meets all demands. Experience indicates that, even where there is no need for the re-education of a juvenile, a sanction may be necessary to impress upon him the limits which must be respected for the sake of law and the legitimate interests of other people. Without the risk of punishment traffic-regulations, taxes, and custom duties would be defied even by well-educated adults and respectable citizens. Wilful damage, dangerous acts due to rashness, and even an adventurous act of breaking and entering may be committed without indicating serious defects in the youngster's upbringing and character so long as he is prevented from repeating such unlawful activities. Probation should be kept for cases where a continuous personal influence is necessary. Binding over without supervision fosters the mistaken belief that the young offender has been 'let off'. Fines are applicable to wage-earners only. Short prison terms, even where they are legally admissible, have rightly been denounced by reformers of every criminological school. The lasting stamp of early prison experience easily destroys self-respect, or directs it into a truculent assertiveness. Even the deterrent effect of the prison is stronger while it remains the great unknown, than if the apprentice in crime is accustomed to it by instalments. These considerations explain the introduction by recent legislation of a new type of juvenile detention without the prison taint. The English Children and Young Persons Act, 1933, s. 54, enables the court to commit a child or young person found guilty of an offence punishable in the case of an adult with imprisonment or penal servitude, 'to the custody of a remand home' for a term not exceeding one month. The wording of this section stresses the exceptional and subsidiary character of this measure by the clause which

[1] *Prisons and Borstals*, p. 37.

states that the court may use it only 'if it considers that none of the other methods in which the case may legally be dealt with is suitable'.

While the chairman of a London Juvenile Court welcomed punitive detention as a necessary 'short sharp punishment to bring the offender to his senses and to act as a deterrent', and wants it executed in 'the kind of establishment a young offender would not wish to visit twice',[1] the author of a comprehensive survey of English Juvenile Courts gives a warning that this power should be used 'with circumspection', since it has no constructive element to help the youngster out of his troubles.[2] Evidence from practical experience is far from conclusive.[3] A *Report of the Juvenile Organisations Committee* of 1920, following up 7,000 juveniles for two years after treatment, lists detention cases under section 106 of the preceding Children Act of 1908 as the treatment with the highest percentage of reappearance before a court. Their percentage of 87·5 even surpassed birching which scored 76·7. This is no recommendation for a merely deterrent treatment. However, the high failure scores for detention and birching are also due to selection. Obviously, the courts reserve these drastic measures for the bad and less promising boys. Under the Act of 1933, for the three years 1934–6, seventy-one juveniles were committed to a remand home for punishment. The number rose in 1939 to 179, 1940 to 432, 1941 to 321, 1942 to 321 for indictable offences only, and for the first six months in 1943 to 161.[4] The reasons for this marked increase in war-time are obvious. Juvenile delinquency increased, approved schools were full, probation officers overworked, and under the psychological impact of the war justices more inclined to deterrent sanctions. Approximately half the number of detention cases occurred at Liverpool. An analysis of 554 juvenile delinquents committed to custody at Liverpool in the years 1940–2 shows a re-conviction rate of 36·6 per cent. for first offenders and 53·9 per cent. for recidivists. Whether the application of other methods would have been more successful remains open to question. The final objection against punitive custody in a remand home is that it burdens the temporary home with juveniles of a type and in a psychological condition which make them unsuitable companions for those who are there for care and protection

[1] J. Watson, *The Child and the Magistrate* (1942), p. 143.
[2] W. A. Elkin, *English Juvenile Courts* (1938), p. 275.
[3] The following is based on J. H. Bagot, *Juvenile Detention* (1944).
[4] Bagot, l.c., p. 15.

while they await a hearing before the Juvenile Court, or further observation. Punitive custody in a remand home can only negatively be justified as a temporary measure in a progressive scheme for keeping minors out of prison.[1]

In Germany a Regulation of 1940, consolidated by the Juvenile Court Act of 1943, introduced youth arrest as a special type of a short deprivation of liberty. From a legal point of view, youth arrest has been characterized as a disciplinary measure, a third type of sanctions at the disposal of the Juvenile Court side by side with educational measures and punishment proper. As a disciplinary measure, youth arrest is a retribution with the psychological effect of a punishment, but without the stigma and the legal consequences of an entry in the general penal register or of a previous sentence in the case of subsequent recidivism. Youth arrest is admissible for terms varying from one day to four weeks, or as spare-time arrest, i.e. detention during leisure hours for one to four periods, but not for more than three days, or as short-time arrest for one to six days with a hard bed, bread, and water. Youth arrest shall be administered in state prison buildings, set apart for this particular purpose. Unlike English punitive detention, youth arrest has dominated the daily practice. During the war one-half to three-quarters of all cases before German Juvenile Courts were dealt with by this simple and drastic measure. By the mass application of a repressive sanction, German Juvenile Courts abandoned their educative function of assigning maladjusted youth to constructive treatment. Only a strong restricting clause, like section 54 of the English Act, might reverse this process so as to make the rule the exception.

A final solution must envisage a more appropriate method of carrying out detention and youth arrest, so that positive educative forces will not be excluded. Perhaps post-war conditions will permit delinquent boys to be committed for a short-term service to labour camps where they will perform useful work in a vigorous educational atmosphere. In accordance with the proposals of the Criminal Justice Bill of 1938, residential control in Howard houses and compulsory attendance in appropriate centres might be successful methods of dealing with many of those cases, for which at present Juvenile Courts resort to punitive detention.

[1] H. Donington, l.c., p. 18.

CHAPTER XIV

HABITUAL CRIMINALS

THE recent reform movement in the field of criminal law followed two main lines in its approach to the problem of protecting society: on the one hand, correctional treatment of young delinquents; and on the other, segregation of habitual criminals. The *Gladstone Report* of 1895 proposed two innovations, namely, 'a half-way house' between reformatory and prison for the young offender and 'a new form of sentence' for hardened persistent criminals. Accordingly the Prevention of Crime Act, 1908, in Part I gave the Borstal system its statutory foundation, and in Part II introduced preventive detention. The same tendencies prevailed in every country which took part in the general reform movement. The removal of juveniles from the scope of the traditional criminal law and their treatment under protective and rehabilitative principles, with the establishment of Juvenile Courts as the visible expression of this constructive policy, were due to a band of progressive lawyers, doctors, educationists, psychologists, and social workers. Their achievements have in principle been generally accepted, and the principle itself is gradually being extended to higher age-groups. 'Incapacitation' of dangerous persistent criminals by long-term, if not lifelong, segregation was the outcome of the science of criminology. Lombroso's doctrine of the 'inborn criminal' allowed no alternative to permanent isolation, once congenital dangerousness had been diagnosed. Likewise von Liszt, of the crimino-sociological school, regarded 'the vigorous struggle against habitual criminality one of the most urgent tasks of the present time'. The incorrigible criminal, therefore, 'should be incapacitated from crime by imprisonment for life, or for an indeterminate period'.[1] In many countries recent legislation has implemented these demands and strengthened the power of criminal justice to protect society against dangerous persistent criminals.

THE CRIMINOLOGICAL SITUATION

Recidivism

Before the number and types of offenders to whom these considerations apply can be assessed, two conceptions must be dis-

[1] v. Liszt, 'Der Zweckgedanke im Strafrecht', Marburger Universitätsprogramm 1882, *Strafrechtliche Aufsätze und Vorträge* (1903), i. 126 et seq., 166.

tinguished: the legal term of recidivist, and the psychological and sociological characterization of an offender as a dangerous, persistent, habitual, or professional criminal. Recidivism means the commission of a new offence after the expiration of a sentence for a previous breach of the law. A great number of convicted prisoners are recidivists. In England and Wales more than half the total of prisoners received in penal institutions have previously been in prison, more than a fourth of the total or more than 10,000 have served more than four previous sentences.[1] In the United States, similarly, nearly every second prisoner received in state and federal institutions has a previous prison record. As to the type of offence, one-third of sex offenders and homicides, and two-thirds of burglars and car-thieves are recidivists.[2]

The first conclusion to be drawn from this is that criminal justice acts as a selective process, the last resort of which, prison, assembles a high proportion of persons with considerable criminal careers. This progressive selection may be illustrated by the following figures for New York state. Among those arrested by the police for finger-printable offences, 28·4 per cent. have previous criminal records. Among those convicted by the courts, between 35·2 per cent. and 37 per cent.; among those received in gaols 53·5 per cent. of the men and 50·8 per cent. of the women; and in prisons and reformatories 56·2 per cent.[3] Likewise in 1927 in Württemberg, recidivists amounted to 36·9 per cent. of those convicted by the courts, and to 58·9 per cent. of those received in prison.[4] Prison committals, therefore, seem to be largely reserved for offenders with a previous criminal career which includes one or several sentences served in penal institutions.[5] Owing to the rise of probation and the preference given to fines, the percentage in penal institutions is increasing.

While even this high proportion of recidivists among convicted prisoners may be due to the selective effect of the administration of justice, it also indicates that in numerous cases a preceding penal or correctional treatment has proved unsuccessful. For a reliable assessment of the failure ratios of the prevailing penal methods, special inquiries are necessary. The perfect method of

[1] *Report of the Departmental Committee on Persistent Offenders* (1932), pp. 2–3.

[2] T. Sellin, *Criminality of Youth* (1940), pp. 76 and 78.

[3] Ibid., pp. 92, 89, 83, 73.

[4] *Kriminalstatistik, 1927*, p. 19; J. Griesmeier, 'Statistik über die württembergischen Landesstrafanstalten 1926 and 1927', reprinted from *Württembergische Jahrbücher für Statistik und Landeskunde*, 1929.

[5] Sellin, l.c., p. 93.

investigation is that which follows up, by individual case studies, a representative group of ex-prisoners through a post-treatment period. In the first series of their classical studies Sheldon and Eleanor Glueck followed up the after-careers of 500 ex-inmates of the Massachusetts Reformatory, mostly property offenders with previous violations of the law, and they regarded as recidivists those relapsing into any sort of punishable conduct, whether re-convicted or not. The result was a shock to any criminologist inclined to complacency. By these rather severe standards in the first five-year post-treatment span, when the average age of the men was thirty, the ratio of those relapsing into crime was 80·1 per cent.; in the second, with an average age of thirty-five, 69·9 per cent.; and in the third, at the time of the general depression, 69·2 per cent., but only 58·2 in the fifth year of the last period. Corresponding investigations into juvenile delinquents after treatment applied by the Boston Juvenile Court showed a failure rate of 85·4 per cent. for the first five-year span when the average age was nineteen, of 73·2 per cent. for the second, and of 63·4 per cent. for the third. Thorough case-studies allowed for certain qualitative observations. While the proportion of relapses was much higher than expected, the number of serious crimes against property decreased, and offences against public welfare, safety, and policy increased.[1] For comparative purposes on a larger scale, mass investigations and statistics of re-conviction rates are indispensable.

In 1912 the conviction rate of the previously unconvicted punishable population in Germany was 0·8 per cent., but the re-conviction rate of those convicted at least once during the preceding decade was 5·6 per cent.[2] The crime risk of a convicted offender is therefore seven times higher than that of a law-abiding citizen. In 1902 German courts convicted and sentenced 280,308 first offenders and 218,692 prisoners with at least one previous conviction. During the following decade 1903–12, the first offenders of 1902 reappeared before the courts at a rate of 22 per cent.; those who in 1902 had one previous conviction at a rate of 48·7 per cent., those with two to four previous convictions at a rate of 65·3 per cent., and those with five and more at 83·4 per cent.[3] The results of these investigations have been confirmed by

[1] S. and E. Glueck, *Criminal Careers in Retrospect* (1943); id., *After-conduct of Discharged Offenders* (1945), p. 31.

[2] E. Roesner, 'Vorstrafenstatistik', *HWB. Krim.* ii. 1007 et seq., referred to by Sellin, l.c., pp. 102 et seq.

[3] G. Aschaffenburg, *Das Verbrechen und seine Bekämpfung* (3rd ed. 1923), p. 245.

corresponding ones recently made in England.[1] Out of those committed to prison in 1930, first offenders scored a re-conviction rate of 16–17 per cent., and recidivists a rate of 30–2 per cent. during a subsequent period of four to six years. These facts show that the probability of recidivism increases with the number of previous sentences. This statement is a challenge to the prevailing penal methods. It indicates that those most frequently subjected to the penal treatment prescribed by the law exhibit the highest crime risk.

Habitual Criminals

The recidivist is a legal conception and a statistical unit. The man behind the legal provisions and statistical figures can only be described in terms of psychological and social experience. It is a common observation that there are offenders who again and again return to their criminal activities. The legislative and literary terminology which describes them varies. It is suggested that those whose repeated criminality has its roots in their personality should be called habitual criminals. This expression is used in the wording of section 10 of the Prevention of Crime Act, 1908. The Austrian criminologist Wahlberg was the first to describe the significant psychological trait of the habitual offender as 'criminal tendency' (*Hang zum Verbrechen*).[2] The term has been generally accepted in statutory provisions and judicial precedents. Article 108 of the Italian Criminal Code of 1930 speaks of a *tendenza a delinquere*; article 42 of the Swiss Criminal Code of 1937 uses the words *penchant au crime ou délit.* The German Supreme Court defined an habitual criminal as 'a person who on account of an inner tendency due to the constitution of his character, or acquired by habit, has repeatedly committed criminal offences and tends to a further repetition'.[3] Criminological experience suggests certain symptoms pointing to such a persistent criminal tendency: an early beginning in crime, short intervals between the release from prison and new crimes, specialization in the crimes, close contact with the underworld, and wide local range of criminal activities.[4] Such facts show that the offender's crimes are not the outcome of temporary distress or temptation under the influence of bad company, but are rooted in his own personality, attitude,

[1] *Report Prison Commissioners, 1936*, pp. 136 et seq.; L. Radzinowicz, 17 *Canadian B. R.* 558, 559.

[2] Wahlberg, *Gesammelte kleine Schriften* i (1875), 136 et seq.; ii. (1882), 69.

[3] 72 *RG* 295; *JW* 1938, p. 2331, No. 1.

[4] F. Exner, N.F. 5 *Mitt. I.K.V.* 47.

and inclinations. This applies not only to antisocial traits like constitutional recklessness or weakness, but also to moral degeneration in persistently adverse conditions. Habitual criminals are not only born but made.

The characteristics of the habitual criminal emerge more clearly if one considers the particular types of offenders in the group to which he tends to belong. Outside the ranks of habitual criminals are those whom the first British study on recidivism called 'habitual petty delinquents',[1] i.e. the vast army of beggars, vagrants, drunkards, and disorderly people. These are a public nuisance rather than a danger, and they affect the community not so much by their frequent particular violations of the law, as by an undesirable conduct of life in general. Repeated punishments prove ineffective to check their steady decline into destitution and delinquency. A rational penal policy would remove them from the scope of criminal law and subject them, if 'in need of care and protection', to appropriate compulsory welfare measures of an administrative character.

Among habitual criminals proper, particular types differ with regard to the psychological factor which primarily explains their persistence in crime. On the one side, there are the 'habitual casual offenders',[2] weak and unstable personalities, easy victims of every temptation, unable to stand any disappointment and difficulty, with a long history of petty thefts and frauds, misappropriation and embezzlement, and even small-scale forgeries. On the other side are those metaphorically called 'professional criminals' who deliberately choose the gamble of criminal gains in preference to honest work. They are often members of gangs and groups with social standards of their own and an unwritten code of honour which contrasts sharply with their cynical exploitation of credulous and careless people outside their own ranks. If we may make an inference from statistics of recidivists, the peak age of habitual criminals must be sought in the years between thirty and forty. Their principal domain is offences against property. In 1928, out of the total of persons convicted by German courts, 54,761 had more than four previous convictions, and among these 35,545 were sentenced for offences against property. This means that 9·3 per cent. of all convicted persons had more than four previous convictions, but 14·6 per cent. of those who had been sentenced for offences against property. Within this group,

[1] J. F. Sutherland, *Recidivism* (1908), pp. vi, 1 and *passim*.
[2] A. Wetzel, *MoSchrKrim.*, *Beiheft* 1, 1926, p. 71.

robbery and fraud scored more than 22 per cent. of offenders with more than four previous convictions.[1] Recent genetic investigations throw some light on the personal background of habitual criminals. Compared with a control group of readjusted first offenders, recidivists had a higher proportion of psychopathic and drunken fathers, a high ratio of debility but no unusual frequency of genuine psychoses among their relatives; while recidivists convicted of assaults and kindred offences had a high proportion of epileptics among parents.[2]

The psychological characteristics of habitual criminals are too vague to allow a statistical assessment of the incidence of this most disquieting form of persistent criminality. On 1 July 1927, German penal institutions had a population of 51,727 convicted prisoners. On the basis of the figures available for Württemberg, it can be assumed that, out of the total German prison population, over 22,000 had more than one previous conviction. At the same time the heads of all German penal institutions reported approximately 12,000 of their inmates as habitual criminals.[3] This means that every second prisoner with at least two previous convictions was an habitual criminal. More accurate figures can only be expected when definite statutory qualifications allow a statistical enumeration without the hazards of personal discretion. With this reservation, the foregoing estimate illustrates the magnitude of the task of protecting society against habitual criminals.

THE LEGISLATIVE SOLUTION

The facts just considered support the demand for a stronger protection of society against dangerous persistent criminals. The ideal solution would be a preventive treatment during the formative years, before successive repetitions have fixed antisocial tendencies into almost ineradicable habits. Every hardened habitual criminal once started as a young first offender. If and where such attempts at preventive treatment fail, society must be protected by segregation of the habitual criminal as long as he is a danger to the community. In almost every country, recent legislation has enacted or considered relevant legal provisions.[4]

[1] *Kriminalstatistik, 1928*, p. 43.

[2] F. Stumpfl, *Erbanlage und Verbrechen* (1935).

[3] 'Statistik des Gefängniswesens im Deutschen Reich', *Reichstag*, iv (1928), No. 814, p. 5.

[4] B. V. A. Röling, *The Laws concerning the so-called Professional and Habitual Criminals* (1933), with the full text of the relevant legal provisions; L. Radzinowicz, 7 *Cambridge L.J.* 68.

European legislation has solved the problem of adequate protection against habitual criminals by a compromise between the traditional retributory doctrine and the demands of those who advocate prevention. For this purpose legal punishment in accordance with the assumed gravity of the offence has been supplemented by new measures of public security appropriate to the offender's dangerousness. Some countries have introduced a cumulative system which enables the court to inflict legal punishment for the expiation of the offender's guilt, together with a further sentence awarded as a measure of public security to check his unabated dangerousness. A prisoner, therefore, may have to serve his term of penal servitude and then undergo an additional term of preventive detention. The English Prevention of Crime Act of 1908, the Jugoslav Criminal Code of 1929, and the Belgian Law of Social Defence of 1930 have a statutory limit for the supplementary preventive detention, while the Czechoslovak Draft Criminal Code of 1926, the French Draft Code of 1932, the Norwegian Criminal Code in the wording of 1929, the Italian Criminal Code of 1930, the Polish Criminal Code of 1932, and the German Law against dangerous habitual criminals of 1933 permit the indeterminate and even lifelong segregation of habitual criminals, if this is deemed necessary for the protection of society. In other legal systems an alternative system leaves the court the choice between a traditional legal punishment of prison and detention for security reasons. Again, this preventive detention may have a statutory limit, as suggested by the English Criminal Justice Bill of 1938; or else it may be indeterminate as has been provided by the Danish Criminal Code of 1930, the Swiss Criminal Code of 1937, and—in the case of a further recidivism—by the Swedish Acts on Detention of 1927 and 1937.

The present state of European legislation bears the marks of a transitional period.[1] Imprisonment and preventive detention differ in their motives. While the prevailing criminal codes have no exhaustive rules for the selection of sentences within the statutory range of legal punishments, they clearly put the emphasis on the particular offence committed and thereby imply that punishment ought not to be out of proportion to the gravity of the offence. When a growing criminological experience demanded reformative and preventive measures, explicit statutory provisions introduced new sanctions, the application of which would be determined by the educational needs or persistent dangerousness of the individual

[1] Röling, l.c., p. vi.

criminal. But this discrimination, however important from the point of view of the sentencing court, makes no difference for the prisoner whose loss of liberty is the same whether it is inflicted as a punishment, or as a preventive or educational detention. This fact should rule out the cumulative system which is resented not only by prisoners but also by judges and jurors as a double punishment. The fact that in practice no essential difference can be maintained between the treatment of convicts and detainees bears out this argument.[1] This makes a strong case for an alternative clause giving a choice between two types of sentences. It is for the court to decide, subject to certain statutory conditions, whether the antecedents, previous prison and parole experience, and the offender's personality necessitate expiation or prevention. Once preventive detention in lieu of imprisonment is recognized, the doctrinal distinction between punishment proper and a 'mere' measure of public security is on the wane. Prevention, though alien to the traditional criminal codes, is not inconsistent with a social conception of legal punishment. The future belongs to preventive punishment, if necessary indeterminate. This idea has steadily gained support in international discussion. In 1900 the International Prison Congress in Brussels declared 'the system of indeterminate sentences inadmissible for ordinary penalties', in 1910, the Congress in Washington hesitatingly approved of indeterminate sentences for juveniles and abnormal criminals, but in 1925 the Congress in London recognized them as 'the necessary consequence of the individualization of punishment and one of the most efficacious means of social defence against crime'.

Such a development requires a thorough revision of the traditional conception of legal punishment. Preventive detention as a 'tutelar' mode of punishment is not merely an excessively vindictive punishment. Retributory sanctions may be closely associated with strict statutory conditions. Where preventive measures are being taken the court must be given reasonable discretion and it must have access to the facts on which a sound estimate of the prisoner's potentialities and future crime risk would have to be based. Experience shows that mere prolongation of sentences within the traditional penal system is inadequate. The Norwegian Criminal Code of 1902 provided that in connexion with a conviction for one of certain serious crimes the jury might be asked

[1] Admitted by semi-official statements for Norway in K. Schlyter, 'Introduction', *Extrait de l'Annuaire des Associations de Criminalistes Nordiques, 1938*, p. xvii, and for Germany in 9 *Recueil* 221.

whether the offender is a 'particularly dangerous criminal'. An affirmative verdict enabled the court in giving sentence to decree that the prisoner, after the expiration of his prison term, might be kept in prison for an additional period up to a maximum of fifteen years. This statutory clause, however, has become a dead letter. For over twenty years only two cases have been on record where it came into operation.[1] In 1929 prolongation of prison sentence was replaced by preventive detention. In America between 1920 and 1930, twenty-three states enacted laws increasing the severity of punishments for recidivists.[2] In the wording of an amendment of 1927, section 644 of the Penal Code of California provides that a prisoner convicted after two previous convictions for certain specified crimes such as robbery, burglary, arson, feloniously receiving stolen goods, incurs imprisonment for life as an habitual offender with no possibility of parole before the expiration of twelve years, and that any fourth conviction for a felony leads to imprisonment for life without any prospect of parole.[3] Likewise the Baumes Law, added in 1926 as sections 1942 et seq. to the Penal Law of New York, provided that a prisoner for the fourth time convicted of a felony should incur imprisonment 'for the term of his natural life'.[4] The inflexible character of these automatic life sentences is the outcome of a legislative technique which binds the court to apply prescribed sanctions, if certain strictly defined legal conditions obtain. In 1932, however, the Baumes Law was modified by substituting for the mandatory life sentence an indeterminate sentence with a minimum of fifteen years.[5] Practical experience made it necessary to allow a modest degree of flexibility and discretion.

The length of a sentence of preventive detention should depend on its purpose. Following the recommendations of the *Report on Persistent Offenders* of 1932, the English Criminal Justice Bill of 1938 proposed two methods: detention up to a maximum of four years, and prolonged detention up to ten years. The former is intended to check an habitual criminal 'in the making' by allowing the court, in lieu of another of the traditional short prison terms, to give a longer sentence, for the sole reason that in view of the offender's criminal antecedents and mode of life a considerable effort should be made to control him and protect society before it

[1] B. Freudenthal, in Aschrott-Kohlrausch, *Reform des Strafrechts* (1927), p. 162.
[2] G. K. Brown, 23 *Canadian B.R.* 630. For a short survey, 51 *Harvard L.J.* 345.
[3] For the text see Röling, l.c., p. 460.
[4] Text ibid., pp. 474 et seq.
[5] 23 *Journal* 506.

is too late. The second, prolonged type of detention, is intended as a final security measure for inveterate habitual criminals in the later stages of their careers. For this purpose English lawgivers held a statutory maximum of ten years sufficient, since it gives 'powers as extensive as any court would in practice wish to use'.[1] Other countries, however, resort to indeterminate segregation without fixed statutory limit. The issue is not purely criminological; it involves also a question of the ultimate legal limits which the organized power of society must respect where its authority is willingly accepted. Where the State's power to repress crime is extended legal guarantees are needed to protect individual liberty against judicial error and administrative arbitrariness. Conversely, where elaborate legal guarantees are established and functioning, even drastic measures for the protection of society are feasible. In the case of preventive detention, the legal guarantees are statutory conditions for the imposition of this sanction, and appropriate machinery to consider and decide on its termination.

Statutory conditions for the application of preventive detention should be framed so as to prevent its excessive as well as insufficient use, and at the same time to enable the court to come to a decision by using discretion based on expert experience. On the one hand, recidivism alone, as defined by American statutes, is too rigid to single out the particular types who need prolonged detention. On the other hand, to let the court depend exclusively on its discretion for deciding whether a prisoner is a professional or habitual criminal (Poland), or whether a prisoner guilty of three intentional offences, though not necessarily with previous convictions, is a dangerous habitual criminal (Germany), is too vague and subjective a method of defining the type liable to such drastic sanctions. The majority of legal systems, therefore, combine the two elements. They require recidivism of a certain intensity and seriousness as a legal condition, without which preventive detention is not to be considered. Within these limits they leave it to the discretion of the court to decide whether the recidivist, in the light of his antecedents, character, previous prison and parole experience, is an habitual criminal so dangerous that the protection of society calls for long-term segregation.

Legal systems differ with regard to the authorities competent to decide on the termination of preventive detention. Where the court fixes a maximum within statutory limits, discharge may well be left to the prison authorities. In England the Home Office

[1] *Report on Persistent Offenders* (1932), p. 21, s. 50.

decides it on recommendation from an advisory committee of non-officials. Where no statutory and judicial maximum obtains, the orthodox view demands that the court should be competent for decisions which shorten or prolong the term of detention. This solution was retained by the Italian Criminal Code of 1930 and the Polish Criminal Code of 1932. Switzerland, however, after the expiration of a certain minimum, entrusts the decision to the administrative authority; New York gives it to the Division of Parole, the Czechoslovak Draft and the Swedish Law to special commissions; and so does Denmark, with the proviso that after twenty years the case must be submitted to a superior court. In Germany, the Draft Codes 1913–30 and the Act of 1933 provided for a judicial decision by the trial court, but an amendment of 1941 transferred this function to the Public Prosecutor General.

An ideal solution has been suggested by an Austrian Draft Code of 1912 which gave the decision to the court in whose venue the prisoner is detained. Such a provision would result in specialized Release Courts which may even assume further judicial competence in respect of prison discipline. A further important legal guarantee is a proviso which makes the reconsideration of every case mandatory after the expiration of a certain time. This period is one year in Sweden, three years in Germany, while in Italy, after the expiration of the statutory minimum, the judge determines the date for reconsideration.

THE ADMINISTRATION OF PREVENTIVE DETENTION

In the absence of useful precedents the principles for the administration of preventive detention remained theoretical. This theoretical approach has produced a certain ambiguity. Paradoxically enough, a retributory theory of criminal law tends to lessen the hardships of the inevitable detention; while the utilitarian theory which bases itself on the protection of society justifies the sacrifice of the individual for the sake of the community. As long as legal punishments are proportioned to the assumed gravity of an offence criminal law must feel uneasy in permitting, and even providing for, an additional deprivation of liberty calculated on the basis of the offender's dangerousness. This particularly applies to a cumulative system, where preventive detention begins when the prisoner has served his term of penal servitude and thereby, in the view of the law, expiated his guilt. From this standpoint preventive detention should be a simple deprivation of liberty, deliberately avoiding the imposition of any additional hardship in the way of accommodation, work, diet, association, and communications with the world outside; it should be a form of social internment, ostensibly divested of any punitive character. This was the original idea of Camp Hill, the first English institution used for preventive detention. If, however, prevention of crime is the primary object of penal policy and detention is therefore applied as an ultimate means to this end, there is a tendency to waste no further efforts for the benefit of those who have already proved unsusceptible to reformative efforts, but to keep inmates in strict seclusion and to make them work hard in order to lessen the burden which they have inflicted upon the community. This is the idea of a secular 'work convent' envisaged by Swiss criminologists.

Practical exigencies are apt to soften the contrast between the two divergent conceptions. To keep in safe custody a considerable number of ex-convicts with long criminal careers, frequent prison experience, and a high probability of further persistence in serious crimes, requires methods of supervision and discipline and an occupational régime scarcely differing from those in penal establishments proper. At the same time, a fair prospect of gradual relaxations, and certain other targets worth strenuous efforts, are necessary to counteract the enervating effects of a long confinement and to facilitate the maintenance of discipline, whether in prison or detention establishment. These suggestions rule out any substantial difference in the practical administration of legal punishments and measures of public security as long as both imply a long-term deprivation of liberty. They may differ in the motives for which they are inflicted, and in the selection of prisoners who are bound to undergo the one or the other sanction.

In England Camp Hill in the Isle of Wight served as a preventive detention establishment for twenty years, until in 1931 it was transformed into a Borstal institution and the detainees were transferred to Lewes Prison. The Camp Hill régime was intended to secure the detainee's safe custody with a minimum of hardship for the individual inmate.[1] For this purpose the Rules provided that, by satisfactory conduct, the prisoners could enjoy considerable privileges. They could earn a small remuneration for their work, make purchases in a canteen, have social intercourse with their fellow inmates, greater facilities for newspapers, letters, and visits, and a varied diet, and even a certain amount of freedom

[1] Ibid., pp. 55 et seq., ss. 137 et seq. Reports of foreign visitors by von Hentig, 26 *Schw. Z.* 409; 49 *ZStW* 60; 24 *MoSchrKrim.* 202; F. Hauptvogel, 51 *ZStW* 480.

from permanent supervision and the prospect of single living-quarters with a certain privacy, in so-called parole time cabins. These were conspicuous alleviations thirty years ago, markedly differing from any punitive régime of the time. In the meantime, however, most of these privileges have been introduced to ordinary prisons, and even if they are more generously granted to detainees than to convicts still, none of them, by present-day standards, would be unthinkable at the upper stage of long-term prisoners in a penal institution. At the same time, Camp Hill, presumed to serve security and not training purposes, did not share in the educational activities which before the Second World War, and largely owing to voluntary educational services, developed in ordinary prisons. The Departmental Committee of 1932 regarded the 'empty life' of the detainees as one of the probable causes of the unsatisfactory results of preventive detention.

In the Belgian detention establishment Merxplas inmates are separated at night. They are organized according to a grading system into four groups. An earnings scheme enables the men to get a *pécule*. They are allowed visits and letters once a week.[1]

In Germany the Draft Penal Codes of 1927 proposed a system of discipline which takes it into account that preventive detention applies to serious criminals likely to defy even the most elaborate supervision. The lawgivers further realized, 'that it would scarcely be acceptable to the general public, if such persons were merely segregated and allowed to live an idle comfortable life at the expense of their honestly working fellow men'.[2] The Draft Codes therefore subjected detainees to the same rules regarding work and discipline as convict prisoners. No work in the open, however, was to be permitted, nor were detainees allowed to have their own clothes, bedding, and food. At the same time, the Draft Codes tried to uphold the theory that preventive detention is not a punishment: unnecessary hardships were to be avoided and, for reasons of humanity, preventive detention—where inmates might even be kept for the rest of their lives—were to be administered without undue severity. Accordingly, the detainees' clothes had to differ from those of prisoners and they were to be allowed to work for themselves, and be eligible for the privileges which are usually granted in prison.[3] When for political reasons the com-

[1] Règlement provisoire de l'établissement pour récidivistes et délinquants d'habitude à Merxplas. Röling, l.c., pp. 289 et seq.; von Hentig, 49 *Schweiz. Z.* 203.

[2] *Begründung zum Entwurf eines Strafvollzugsgesetzes*, 1927 (II), p. 110.

[3] Draft Penal Code, 1927 (II), ss. 308–14.

prehensive project of penal reform with the subsequent Draft Codes from 1909 to 1930 was abandoned, and preventive detention was introduced by a special law of 1933,[1] the Rules for the Institutional Régime[2] went even farther than the Draft Codes in emphasizing the paramount interest of public security. 'The aim of the unconditional security of the detention and the prevention of escape is to be ruthlessly pursued with due regard to the particular dangerousness of the prisoner.' With regard to discipline and compulsory labour inside or outside prison walls, preventive detention did not differ from penal servitude. Private occupation during work hours was prohibited. The periods of two months for visits and four weeks for letters were shorter than those applying to convicts. Purchase of additional food and tobacco was admissible from the beginning; other privileges could be granted as rewards for good conduct and industrious work. In 1940 these principles were repealed by a new comprehensive Prison Regulation.[3] A semi-official commentator admitted that it proved very difficult to uphold an essential difference between preventive detention and legal punishment. The necessity of maintaining security, order, and discipline prevented any practical relaxation.[4] Conditions for work, letters, and visits have been even more closely adjusted to ordinary convict prison discipline.

These illustrations from practice corroborate the principal considerations. No existing system has succeeded in differentiating between ordinary prison routine and the régime applicable to preventive detention. Only if the doctrinal dualism between a 'deserved' punishment and a 'necessary' measure of public security is abandoned, principles for the administration of preventive detention can be developed to conform with its purpose. In determining the proper routine the administration ought not to lose sight of the fact that this measure applies to hardened criminals with considerable prison records and in front of them a period of detention which they know will be long though its length is unspecified. As a rule the institution will be one of maximum security, and there will be a legal obligation to work, though the work may in certain cases be private; there will be a

[1] *Gesetz gegen gefährliche Gewohnheitsverbrecher und über Massregeln der Sicherung und Besserung*, *RGBl.* i. 995; comments by F. Exner, 53 *ZStW* 627; M. Grünhut, *Rivista di Diritto Penitenziario*, 1935; H. Mannheim, 26 *Journal* 517.

[2] Principles of Prison Discipline, art. 3, ss. 16–23, in the wording of 14 May 1934; *RGBl.* i. 383.

[3] *Verordnung* of 22 July 1940; *Dtsch. Justiz*, special publication, No. 21.

[4] 9 *Recueil* 221.

discipline which avoids strain and friction by granting adequate outlets by means of a private sphere of spare-time occupations, books and magazines, intercourse with fellow inmates, letters, and visits. This gives preventive detention the character appropriate to a long-sentence division.

The crucial point of preventive detention is its termination. Even where the law provides no statutory limit, detention is not presumed to last for life in all or even the majority of the cases. Here a paradox presents itself. While almost by definition preventive detention is given to prisoners who are dangerous because they have defied repeated penal and correctional efforts, the possibility is not ruled out that after a period of years they may be eligible for release. In England, both under the prevailing law of 1908 and the proposed scheme of 1938, discharge is mandatory after the expiration of a maximum period. The German Penal Drafts of 1927 even defined the object of treatment as follows: 'to accustom the detainees to order and work, and, in view of their possible return to liberty, to make them capable of a law-abiding conduct which is not dangerous to the public', a provision which scarcely differs from the section which defines the purpose of penal treatment proper. This clause, however, has not been enacted in the legislation after 1933. It would be unjustifiable to dismiss the possibility altogether that not only old age, changed economic and social conditions, or family relationships, but also an inner process of character-building might help diminish a detainee's dangerousness. But an institution established for the safe custody of dangerous habitual criminals is not the place for fostering social adjustment to the world at large. If it were, its security purpose would be jeopardized by experiments which for the majority of the inmates would mean ill-advised temptations, endless tensions and frictions, and thereby a permanent atmosphere of unrest. The proper course would therefore be to transfer inmates who are expected to become due for release to a 'probation' institution with a régime which appeals to the inmate's active co-operation and sense of responsibility. Such a scheme was envisaged by the German Prison Regulation of 1940, but did not materialize; during the war no discharges were granted from preventive detention, and from 1941 dangerous habitual criminals became liable to capital punishment.

Release from preventive detention should always be on parole. This would imply the acceptance of certain conditions the breach of which make the discharged inmate liable to re-detention, but also personal supervision by a parole officer who offers a friendly guidance and assistance in the struggle for a readaptation to a life in the community.

The incidence of sentences of preventive detention varies in different countries. In England, from 1 August 1909, when the Prevention of Crime Act came into operation, to the end of 1930, 944 men and 23 women underwent preventive detention. Out of these no more than 35 persons were sentenced to the maximum of ten years' detention.[1] These figures represent only a small fraction of the vast army of recidivists with numerous previous convictions. While in 1930 4,745 prisoners with more than ten previous sentences were committed to English prisons, the average number of yearly sentences of preventive detention during the decade 1921 to 1930 was 35. Following up those released in 1920 throughout a seven-year post-detention period, an official investigation found that 19 out of 26 finally discharged, or—after the deduction of those suffering from disease or insane—82·6 per cent., and 47 out of 55 licensed detainees, or 94 per cent. reverted to crime.[2] This has been confirmed by an observer who visited Camp Hill in 1930 and found that out of 73 released detainees only 7, or 9·6 per cent. succeeded in a fair social readjustment.[3] These figures do not prove that preventive detention is a failure; for it has been applied not as a corrective treatment, but to protect society against offenders with a high crime risk. The small proportion of readjustment, however, strengthens the case for longer and indeterminate terms. The test of successful measures against habitual criminals is the curve of serious recidivism. While the total number of convicted male prisoners decreased from 34,746 in 1932 to 28,703 in 1938, the number of men received in prison on convictions of burglary, robbery, or aggravated larceny with six or more previous proved offences slightly increased from 1,131 to 1,149.[4] Whatever the reasons for a rise or fall in persistent crime, the proportion of habitual criminals sentenced to detention is apparently too small to affect the total criminality of recidivists. The failure of the second part of the Act of 1908 is due to its insufficient application, which has been ascribed to the cumbersome dualistic system of deserved punishment plus additional detention.[5]

[1] *Report on Persistent Offenders*, Appendix 3, p. 77.

[2] *Report Prison Commissioners, 1928*; L. Radzinowicz, 17 *Canadian B.R.* 558.

[3] F. Hauptvogel, 51 *ZStW* 495.

[4] *Report Prison Commissioners, 1932*, p. 86; *1938*, pp. 7 and 108.

[5] *Report on Persistent Offenders*, l.c., p. 60 and *passim*.

While in the Scandinavian countries courts make only a modest use of preventive detention, the totalitarian countries applied the new measure on a vast scale. Italy, between 1934 and 1937 detained about 500 persons, Poland between 1934 and 1938 about 700.[1] German sentences even surpassed these figures. Before 1933, official estimates forecast a rate of 400–500 sentences for each of the first four to five years and thereafter a fall in the figures; this would mean a permanent detention of some 2,000 to 2,500 persons.[2] When the Act of 1933 came into operation, the first year 1934 showed 3,935 relevant sentences; 1935 followed with 1,368; in 1936 the total dropped to 907; and in 1937 it was down to 692.[3] As most of these habitual criminals had first to serve a term of penal servitude, the detention establishments only slowly became full. On 31 July 1936, 2,883 men and 113 women were confined in preventive detention under sentences of criminal courts.[4] These figures do not include those who, outside the sphere of the administration of justice, were detained by the police as alleged professional criminals.

Conclusions

The present law and administration of preventive detention is typical of the present stage of penal reform. First it was felt that society's growing demand for protection against the habitual criminal made necessary some new sanctions, something more than the traditional legal punishments. Sooner or later the whole conception of punishment must change, and by taking over both corrective and preventive functions punishment, as it then will be conceived, will have overcome the present doctrinal dualism. Meanwhile, as a step towards the victory of the indeterminate sentence over preventive detention, the alternative clause of the Swiss Criminal Code and the English Criminal Justice Bill is preferable to a cumulative system. Such practical experience as is available bears this out. Attempts to establish two markedly different types of institutional régime have failed. Prison discipline and preventive detention are interchangeable. It is only that different labels cover an identical subject.

Corrective training and preventive detention are the two outstanding aspects of the social conception of legal punishment.

[1] L. Radzinowicz, 7 *Cambridge L.J.* 78, n. 16.
[2] *Anlage* II, Draft Criminal Code, 1927, p. 35.
[3] E. Kohlrausch, *Strafgesetzbuch* (34th ed. 1938), note vii before s. 42 *a*, p. 92.
[4] Schmidt, 98 *Dtsch. Justiz* 1476.

They are interrelated in a twofold way. On the one hand, to adopt educative and correctional methods presupposes a reasonable classification of prisoners and adequate provision for those not expected to respond. Otherwise, well-intentioned experiments will be discredited by the failures of those unsuitable for a reformative régime; and those who might profit from a treatment relying upon trust and co-operation cannot have it because of fellow prisoners who need firm discipline and maximum security conditions. Moreover, public opinion will resent reformative methods as unjustified, unless the law also affords efficacious protection against habitual criminals who have hitherto defied penal treatment. Long-term segregation of habitual criminals is therefore a necessary complement to the correctional and rehabilitative aims which determine the ethos of present-day penal policy.

On the other hand, only strenuous corrective efforts can justify measures like preventive detention for many years and even for life in the case of persistent offenders. Incorrigibility and dangerousness are relative conceptions; they mean incorrigible by present methods and dangerous under present social conditions. Among those who to-day threaten society as habitual criminals, many are the products of penal methods of the past, now considered inadequate and even detrimental. Sooner or later, the vicious circle of prisoners turned out from prison to be a danger to society must be broken. Correction and prevention are simultaneous objects of a rational penal policy. Only that state which leaves nothing untried in the attempt to check a criminal career at its outset and to rehabilitate the offender at his first wrong step, is justified in taking, to protect society, such far-reaching measures as long indeterminate segregation for punishment which is ultimately preventive.[1]

[1] Röling, l.c., p. xvii and *passim*.

CHAPTER XV

WOMEN

THE CRIMINOLOGICAL SITUATION

THE assessment of the amount of criminality amongst women and its social implications is beset with particular difficulties.[1] Even more than is the case with juveniles criminality in its application to women is a relative conception. In the wide field of sexual maladjustment and disorderly behaviour an artificial line separates criminal offences from other forms of socially undesirable conduct. Legal systems differ with regard to this demarcation. In America recent legislation has made sexual promiscuity punishable to an extent unknown to present European law. While in most continental countries drunkenness is not punishable as such, in England it is a criminal offence to be found drunk in public. As women share in the total of convictions for drunkenness at a rate of 1 woman to 4·4 men—as against 1 to 79 for burglary and 1 to 243 for shop-breaking[2]—that peculiarity of English law explains why the total of women offenders has been so high in England, and it has given rise to unfavourable comparison with the Continent on this question of women's criminality.

To differences in actual legislation must be added differences in methods of procedure. The frequency of prosecution varies from country to country. The total of trials and sentences on record, therefore, does not give a true indication of what the law regards as criminality. There is always a 'dark figure', i.e. an unknown amount of undisclosed crime, behind the numbers given by official criminal statistics. For women, more than for men, this dark figure is a variable factor, differing according to the particular conditions of each country.

At first sight criminal statistics suggest that women's share in crime is much smaller than might be expected from the numerical distribution of the sexes in the general population. In 1938 in England and Wales the police proceeded against 77,465 men and 10,872 women for indictable, and against 683,784 men and 67,366 women for non-indictable offences.[3] In the same year, out of every 100,000 persons of each sex, 407 men and 53 women were

[1] H. Mannheim, *Social Aspects of Crime in England* (1940), pp. 334 et seq.; S. and E. Glueck, *Five Hundred Delinquent Women* (1934).

[2] H. Mannheim, l.c., pp. 338 et seq.

[3] *Crim. Stat., 1938*, pp. 134 et seq.

found guilty of indictable offences.[1] In Germany, in 1927, the crime coefficient was 2,219 for men and 362 for women.[2] As a rule, the crime rate of men is five to ten times that of women.[3]

The majority of women offenders are concerned in gainful offences of dishonesty. In England, out of 2,749 women found guilty for the first time in 1932, 2,214 had committed larceny; 262 frauds and false pretences; 26 breaking and entering; only 198 violence against persons; and 49 other miscellaneous offences.[4] In Germany, in 1927, out of every 100,000 women, 83·8 were convicted of theft and embezzlement, 30·2 of frauds and forgery, 11 of receiving stolen property; as against 125 acts of dishonesty there were 54 cases of defamation and insult, 15 abortions, 6 cases of procuration, and 5·7 of causing injury.[5] Certain crimes are typical of women offenders in so far as they are more frequently committed by women than by men, even if they amount only to a minor proportion of the total of women's offences. Apart from infanticide, which by definition is a specific offence of an illegitimate mother, abandonment of children, abortion, procuration, and administration of poison are more frequently perpetrated by women than by men.

With regard to other offences, women offenders, though in the minority, are more numerous than would be expected in view of the general female crime-rate. A German investigation established that, for the years 1892–1901, out of 100 convictions for crimes and delicts, 16·5 were in respect of women. Among offences in which women were concerned at a rate of 25 to 50 per cent.—thus very much above what the general standard of 16·5 would lead one to expect—were 'breach of secrets' (e.g. by opening letters), receiving, simple theft, perjury, false allegations, and defamations and insults. The women's share is markedly below the general standard as far as assaults, repeated aggravated thefts, and malicious damage to property are concerned.[6]

From deviations of this kind may be calculated the specific criminal proclivity of different social groups. According to a recent investigation in Poland, 19·7 women were convicted for every 100 male offenders. Young women, married women, and women in rural areas lagged behind the general rate, while old

[1] Ibid., pp. xxix, xxx.
[2] *Kriminalstatistik, 1927*, p. 56.
[3] E. Hacker, 22 *MoSchrKrim.* 269.
[4] *Crim. Stat., 1938*, p. xxvi.
[5] *Kriminalstatistik, 1927*, pp. 57 et seq.
[6] Aschaffenburg, l.c., p. 179.

women, widows, and divorced women, and women in urban districts surpassed it. Young married women between twenty and twenty-four, for example, had a comparative ratio of 8·6, while old widows and divorced persons revealed a ratio of 56·6.[1] While from a social point of view the larger total number of young delinquents is more significant than the few old law-breakers with their relatively high sex crime ratio, marked variations of this ratio indicate the specific criminal tendencies of men and women. With regard to readjustment, women have a brighter prospect than men. In England, out of the first-offenders sentenced in 1932, during the subsequent five years 12·9 per cent. of the women and 21·3 per cent. of the men were re-convicted.[2]

For the interpretation of these facts, attention must be drawn to certain characteristic factors in the criminality of women. There is a close relation between prostitution and crime. Lombroso regarded prostitution as an equivalent for crime and this would make up for the comparatively lower crime-rate of women. This theory seems to be corroborated by the observation that the sex ratio in criminality is lower for young women than for old; obviously a greater number of the former join the ranks of prostitution.[3] It is, however, an unproved supposition that a young woman would be a thief were she not a prostitute. Even young women, with their comparatively low crime ratio in general, show a considerable incidence of thefts. When in Germany the peak age for male offenders was eighteen to twenty-five and for women thirty to forty, both sexes had higher rates of theft in the age group of eighteen to twenty.[4] Prostitution is often an opportunity for, if not the first step towards, a criminal career.

For both criminology and the law prostitution is akin to begging and vagrancy.[5] Legislation has changed, and still varies considerably in different countries, in determining what acts committed in the pursuit of prostitution are punishable as criminal offences. In England prostitution itself is not punishable, but under the Vagrancy Act of 1824 a 'common prostitute' is liable to punishment for 'wandering in the public streets and behaving riotously and indecently'.[6] These statutory ingredients were slightly extended by the Metropolitan Police Act, 1839, which made punishable with a fine a 'common prostitute or nightwalker loitering or being in any thoroughfare or public place for the

[1] L. Radzinowicz, 29 *Soc. Rev.* 76.

[2] *Crim. Stat., 1938,* p. xxvi.

[3] L. Radzinowicz, l.c.

[4] Aschaffenburg, l.c., p. 173.

[5] Ibid., p. 183.

[6] 5 Geo. IV, c. 83, s. 3.

purpose of prostitution or solicitation to the annoyance of the inhabitants or passengers'.[1] On the Continent the abortive attempts of former Saxon and Bavarian laws to suppress prostitution altogether by indiscriminate penalization have long been discarded. Recent legislation has further abandoned the system of regimentation, which implies impunity for those prostitutes who comply with the police regulations concerning registration and control. In 1946 France, which had long retained the principle of licensed prostitution, prohibited the maintenance of *maisons de tolérance*. In almost all European countries, then, only the offence of aiding and exploiting prostitutes and certain flagrant forms of prostitution incompatible with public health and decency are punishable.[2]

In the United States, however, following the ban during the First World War of prostitution in the neighbourhood of military camps, between 1918 and 1931, fourteen states enacted penal provisions making it a criminal offence 'to give or receive the body for indiscriminate intercourse with or without hire'. This wide conception relieves the prosecution of the difficulties of proving the charges of 'engaging in prostitution' or 'soliciting' according to the usual Vagrancy Acts.[3] The striking difference in the laws of the Old and the New World affects the respective criminality of women and the task and prospects of penal and correctional processes. On the one hand, while before and after the First World War the number of prostitutes in London was estimated at 38,000 —the majority foreigners[4]—in 1938 in England and Wales 3,192 offences by prostitutes were punished and only 172 women committed to prison for offences in connexion with prostitution.[5] On the other hand, in 1923 in the United States, one-half of the total of women committed to penal institutions and one-third of the female prison population had been sentenced for prostitution and other sex offences, which according to the laws of many European countries would either not be punished at all, or, if punishable, would not entail prison sentences.[6]

[1] 2 & 3 Vict., c. 47, s. 54, No. 11. Similar provision in the Consolidating Act regulating the Police of Towns, 10 & 11 Vict., c. 89, s. 28.

[2] German *Gesetz zur Bekämpfung der Geschlechtskrankheiten* of 18 Feb. 1927, esp. s. 16, repealing relevant provisions of the Criminal Code. French *loi* no. 46–685 of 13 Apr. 1946. For the historical development see W. Mittermaier, *VDB* iv. 157 et seq.

[3] Eugenia C. Lekkerkerker, *Reformatories for Women in the United States* (1931), pp. 18 et seq., 25.

[4] C. Bishop, *Women and Crime* (1931), p. 57.

[5] *Crim. Stat., 1938*; *Report Prison Commissioners, 1938*, p. 104.

[6] E. C. Lekkerkerker, l.c., p. 37.

Infanticide and abortion are closely connected with female sex delinquency. Infanticide, which by the end of the eighteenth century deeply moved enlightened philanthropists, is an offence of the inexperienced. Abortion, more typical of an industrial and urban society, presented a startling problem during the inter-war period. While in Belgium and France convictions were decreasing, in England, Norway, and Sweden the curve rose, though still with a moderate total, and in Austria, Germany, and Italy there was an alarming increase.[1] In Germany the number of women convicted of abortion rose from the pre-war level of 1,135 or 4·5 per 100,000 in 1913 to the peak of 5,244 or 21 per 100,000 in 1925.[2] Even in countries with an efficient system of public prosecution and a high conviction-rate, the 'dark figure' of undiscovered offences which escape prosecution is bound to be high. In Germany, for every 100 births, there were 0·077 convictions for abortion in 1913, 0·1 during the war, and 0·348 in 1922. At the same time, according to medical experience there, the abortion-rate per 100 births rose from 15 during the war to 30 in 1922. Nine-tenths of these cases were estimated to be induced and criminal. The majority of the patients were married women, although the incidence of abortions is higher among the unmarried.[3] In England the number of criminal abortions known to the police was 0·03 per 100 births in 1937, while the actual abortion-rate is supposed to be approximately 20 per 100 births. Out of a yearly total of 110,000–150,000 abortions, only 40 per cent. are regarded as induced and criminal. While the incidence of total abortions is stable, induced abortions are increasing and the spontaneous decreasing.[4] The evidence of both countries, differing in degree rather than in substance, gives rise to considerable doubt whether criminal law is the appropriate means of overcoming this menace to health and morals.

With the comparatively high figures for theft and receiving, women have their share in the vast bulk of offences of dishonesty in relation to property. Theft from department stores has a special significance. It is mainly committed by juveniles and women, often with alarming frequency, entirely out of proportion

[1] 'Entwicklung der Kriminalität im In- und Ausland nach dem Kriege', *Vorabdruck aus Kriminalstatistik, 1933* (1935), *passim.*

[2] *Kriminalstatistik, 1927*, pp. 47 and 58.

[3] E. Bumm, 43 *ZStW* 182; M. Liepmann, *Krieg und Kriminalität in Deutschland* (1930), pp. 153 et seq.

[4] *Report of the Inter-Departmental Committee on Abortion* (1938), pp. 9, 11, 13, 45.

to the number of prosecutions. In 1930, one important London shop alone lost £15,000–20,000 by shoplifting. In Manchester goods worth £75–85 were stolen from every assistant of one particular shop in the course of a year.[1] While many of these thefts are due to personal greed and the temptation of opportunity, there are not a few cases where articles are stolen and hoarded although useless to the thief. This fact raises the question of a deep-rooted irrational motivation and is the principal argument for the assumption of kleptomania. Even if criminal tendency and disease cannot be quite so completely equated it remains true that among women stealing from department stores a high proportion are mentally defective in a wider sense of the word,[2] and that not infrequently such thefts are the expression of a deep psychological conflict.[3]

The question arises whether marriage is a stabilizing factor in women's adjustment. According to Polish investigations among married people women have a lower, and among unmarried people a higher, crime-rate than corresponding groups of men. This result is challenged by a German study by which it was found that very young married persons have a high crime coefficient, and that in the age-groups between twenty-five and sixty the crime coefficients are higher for unmarried than for married men, but lower for unmarried than for married women. For example, in the age-span thirty to forty, out of 100,000 of every group there were 2,880·1 convicted unmarried men and 1,961·2 married men, but 446·2 unmarried and 500 married women.[4] The interpretation of these figures must allow for the types of offences committed. Married women are less concerned in thefts and frauds, but exceed the unmarried in punishable trespass, defamatory insults, and injuries. The higher crime-rates of married women are therefore to be explained by their contributions to petty delinquency against immediate neighbours rather than to serious crimes of dishonesty. Receiving stolen property is the only typical offence of married couples, with higher crime coefficients for married men and women than for unmarried.

In almost all age-groups, married and unmarried men and women are surpassed in criminality by widowed and divorced

[1] C. Bishop, l.c., p. 6.

[2] For the evidence see K. Wilmanns, *Die verminderte Zurechnungsfähigkeit* (1927), p. 73, with further references.

[3] Relevant illustrations by G. W. Pailthorpe, *What we put in Prison* (1932), pp. 108, 118 and *passim.*

[4] Aschaffenburg, l.c., pp. 186–7.

persons. In the age-span of thirty to forty, the crime coefficient for widowers and divorced men is 3,797·5 and for women 1,029·9. Compared with their married contemporaries, the crime risk of widowed and divorced persons is therefore 93·6 per cent. higher for men and 105·9 per cent. higher for women. The comparatively higher criminal proclivity of widows and divorced women is confirmed by their high sex ratio in criminality. This fact is a significant counterpart to the high crime-rate of children and juveniles from broken homes. To sum up: married women exhibit less, or at least less harmful, criminal tendencies than the unmarried. Statistical figures alone do not indicate whether girls with criminal tendencies have less prospect of being married, or a good prospect of keeping straight under the influence of marriage. The high crime coefficient of young couples is the reflection of the general peak age of criminality, and may be due to a negative selection of ill-advised early marriages. Evidently, marriage facilitates maturation and social adjustment. The criminal proclivity of widows and divorced women reveals the conflicts and lack of protection which are caused by the disintegration of home and family life.

This analysis leads to a final question: does the emancipation of women and their growing assimilation to the employment and social position of men affect their criminal tendencies? The war, with its large-scale direction of women to industrial employment and other posts where they had to deputize for men, offered a unique opportunity for the study of the social effects of emancipation, aggravated by the 'culture conflict' which the abrupt change caused. After the First World War, observers attributed the war-time rise in crimes committed by women to this process of emancipation. With the changed social position of women, their criminality seemed to become masculine.[1]

To check this statement, we must interpret war-time criminality in relation to the general trend of crime. In Germany the crime coefficient per 100,000 women rose from the pre-war level of 359 in 1913 to the war summit of 482 in 1918; but when the men came back and the collapse of the currency led to a new rise in crime, the women reached an even higher level of 528 in 1923. A qualitative analysis of these two successive waves of mass criminality reveals marked differences in the figures for common simple theft, on the one hand, and frauds and aggravated theft with their more

[1] F. Exner, 'Krieg und Kriminalität', *Krim. Abhdg. I* (1926), p. 8; M. Liepmann, l.c., p. 162.

serious criminal character on the other. The women's crime coefficient for simple thefts rose from 74 in 1913 to 182 in 1918, and even farther to 201 in 1923. At the same time the women's frauds rose from 15 in 1913 to 22 in 1918, and then fell to 17 in 1923. While this last figure was still above the pre-war level by 13·3 per cent., the men's frauds during the inflation period amounted to 110·4 or 18·7 per cent. above pre-war level. With regard to aggravated theft, the figure for women rose from 8·1 to the war-figure of 13 and then fell to 9·8, while the men reached during the currency crisis a record in burglaries and kindred crimes at a rate of 208·4 against their pre-war standard of 65·1.[1] These statistics support the conclusion that a certain proportion of the increased number of war-time frauds and an even greater proportion of aggravated thefts, though not the rise in crimes committed by women in general, can be regarded as a 'masculine' feature of women's criminality in war-time.

The foregoing analysis shows still further how difficult it is to determine the true amount of crime committed by women. On the one hand, the comparison between the numbers of male and female offenders throughout critical periods in war and peace suggests that under present social conditions the criminal tendencies of women to certain typical offences are not very strong. On the other hand, some characteristic female offences, especially those relating to sex, but common shoplifting as well, are committed in numbers out of all proportion to those prosecuted before the courts. Therefore, the 'dark figure' of undisclosed crime must be much greater in the case of women than of men. There may be more conscious or unconscious reluctance to prosecute a woman. Numerous cases may be settled without recourse to criminal proceedings. These conclusions are corroborated by experience with juvenile delinquency. Child-guidance clinics handle almost an equal number of boy and girl delinquents.[2] English courts, however, in the last year before the outbreak of the war, found 11,645 boys and 912 girls between fourteen and seventeen guilty of indictable offences.[3] Similar, though less striking, discrepancies occur in the United States. According to statistics covering the case load of twenty-seven American Juvenile Courts, they had to deal with cases of dependent and neglected boys and girls of almost exactly

[1] Figures computed from *Kriminalstatistik, 1927*, pp. 40 et seq., 56 et seq., 61 et seq.

[2] Discussion remark by S. Clement Brown, 102 *J. Stat. Soc.* 400.

[3] *Crim. Stat., 1938*, p. xxxi.

the same number of 6,000 a year. At the same time, in 1936, twenty-eight courts in dealing with delinquency—a much wider conception than the English idea of being found guilty of a criminal offence—had to handle 22,630 boys and 4,143 girls.[1] The actual share of women in the total amount of crime is certainly greater than is indicated by the sex ratios of criminal statistics.

METHODS OF TREATMENT

Types of Women Prisoners

The fact that much criminality among women does not reach the courts has its importance for the treatment of delinquency. To some extent society is able to deal with antisocial conduct on the part of women by means less stringent than the machinery of criminal justice. From a statistical point of view the treatment of women offenders is almost negligible compared with other problems of penal discipline. This may produce either of two results, one good and one bad. Women prisoners have often been a forgotten minority, separated from their male fellow prisoners, but apart from this borne through the ordinary prison routine with a minimum of regard for their special needs. Alternatively, their fewness can be turned into an opportunity for experiments on unorthodox lines in a few model institutions where the traditional features of the administration of men's penal establishments can be abandoned.[2]

In 1938 in England and Wales 28,703 men and 3,522 women were committed to penal institutions after conviction. Committals of women therefore amount to 10·9 per cent. of the sum total. In the prison population, the proportion of women is even smaller. During the same year the daily average prison population had only 636 women, or 6·3 per cent. of all convicted prisoners. This discrepancy is due to judicial leniency which tends towards shorter sentences for women. Out of the total of prisoners received on conviction—excluding court-martial cases and Borstal sentences—51 per cent. of the men, but 70·7 per cent. of the women, had sentences not exceeding one month.[3] A similar situation exists in American prisons. In 1923 women scored 8 per cent. of

[1] *Juvenile Court Statistics* (1936), pp. 20 and 7.

[2] Mrs. Lyons and Miss Taylor, in *Reformatory and Industrial School Work*, ed. by Reformative and Refuge Union, London (1898); Mary Gordon, *Penal Discipline* (1922); H. von Heimann, *Studien zur Erziehungsarbeit an verwahrlosten Mädchen* (1924); Eugenia C. Lekkerkerker, *Reformatories for Women in the United States* (1931); Cicely McCall, *They always come back* (1938).

[3] *Report Prison Commissioners, 1938*, pp. 12, 16, 14.

all prison committals, but were only 4·8 per cent. of the prison population.[1]

In England, of the 3,522 women who went to prison on conviction in 1938, one-third had been sentenced for indictable offences, mainly larceny and allied offences.[2] Among the other two-thirds who were convicted of non-indictable offences, three-quarters were committed for drunkenness. This applies to 1,543 receptions, or 43·8 per cent. of the total of the year. Drunkards account for a high percentage of recidivists. Of the 1,979 women committed to prison for offences other than drunkenness, 41 per cent. had been in prison before, against 50 per cent. of men with previous prison sentences. Among those committed for drunkenness, however, 79 per cent. of the women and 61 per cent. of the men had been in prison before. While among the 1,148 women committed on conviction of indictable offences, 79 had more than twenty known previous proved offences, among the 1,486 drunkards, there were not less than 1,080 with a similar record. These figures apply to a group of presumably some 400 constant 'ins and outs', a stage army of old clients with repeated committals in a single year.[3] Evidently, short prison terms are not the remedy to halt women drunkards on their way to final destitution.

In England the proportion of older persons among women prisoners is higher than among men. The largest age-group among men is the one between twenty-one and thirty, among women between forty and fifty. In Germany the majority of women prisoners are between twenty-five and forty years of age.[4] Young girls are accommodated in educational institutions or homes, or benefit from measures under the Probation of Offenders Act, or corresponding forms of conditional remission of punishment in continental legislation, even in cases where courts would not hesitate to send young men to prison. In England prison sentences for drunkards increase the proportion of middle-aged women prisoners. According to Prussian statistics of 1928, almost one-third of the women prisoners were married, and more than one-fifth widows and divorced persons. More than one-third of the unmarried women were mothers.[5]

The analysis of English prison statistics indicates a high propor-

[1] Lekkerkerker, l.c., pp. 34 and 36.

[2] *Report Prison Commissioners, 1938*, p. 17 and *passim.*

[3] Fox, p. 136.

[4] A. Neuhaus, in *Strafvollzug in Preussen* (1938), p. 115.

[5] Ibid., p. 116.

tion of short sentences, a considerable number of drunkards with numerous subsequent prison terms interrupted by short intervals of liberty, and a small nucleus of middle-aged women with criminal tendencies in need of systematic and vigorous efforts at rehabilitation. In addition to this rather arbitrary sector of punitive treatment, a social conception of penal policy must take into consideration the great number of neglected, wayward, and maladjusted girls who find their way into approved schools and other institutions and homes of various descriptions. For an educational approach the pigeon-holes of the particular offences according to criminal law are less important than the girls' individual needs, often depending on their state of sexual maladjustment. Many delinquent girls, even if they have been committed for other offences, have lived as official or amateur prostitutes. Many need medical treatment for venereal diseases. As the peak age of prostitution is near to the attainment of legal maturity, in institutions for adolescent girls there is sometimes a majority belonging to this type. If these girls have been committed as 'in moral danger', or in connexion with a particular offence, the prospects for a readjustment even of their sexual maladjustment are often better than if a conviction as 'common prostitute' has given them a stigma which they themselves regard as unalterable. It is important to find out whether the girls accept the way of life they have been leading and defend it as a right, or recognize that it is a just cause if any attempt is to be made to win them back to an orderly and decent life. Such generalizations are only tentative. Deeper insight into the underlying psychological processes often reveals an almost abnormal lack of emotions and a weakness and indifference of the motives which normally regulate actions in this field even more than in other spheres of human behaviour. Educational experience suggests that these girls respond to encouragement, appreciation, and personal interest rather than to severe reprimands and punishments.[1] If there is in an institution a high proportion of girls with sexual experience, they easily dominate the social atmosphere. This calls for redoubled efforts to stimulate the girls by attractive and absorbing activities, and for a frank approach to the realities of sexual life to dispel the alluring twilight of obscene talk and speculation. Even so, a minority of girls with no previous sexual maladjustment would be endangered by such company and ought to be kept away from it.

[1] v. Heimann, l.c., p. 22 and *passim*.

With regard to prisons for adult women, the proportion of prostitutes depends on the law and its administration. In the United States there are two groups of women prisoners, namely, young prostitutes and middle-aged women sentenced for acts of dishonesty relating to property. In many European prisons the latter group is dominating. There is sometimes an antagonistic class-feeling between these types. An old thief, admitting her dishonesty, would indignantly repel the idea of 'going with men', while a prostitute might regard her sentence as unjust or an inevitable inconvenience, but look down like a pharisee on a criminal capable of burglary or blackmail.

The traditional Prison Routine

These psychological considerations should determine the objects of penal and correctional treatment for women. As to the response of the penal administration, what was said about England shortly after the First World War obtains for most European countries: 'The study of the English penal system does not show that at any time the method of dealing with criminal women has engaged that close attention which might have been expected from the nature and difficulty and importance of the problem. The law strikes men and women indifferently with the same penalties of penal servitude and imprisonment.'[1] In England women prisoners are under the care of an exclusively female staff. In visiting committees and boards of visitors women have their share in supervisory functions. After the precedent set by Elizabeth Fry, ever since 1901 a Lady Visitors' Association has been arranging for personal visits to be made to women prisoners, in this way anticipating the work of voluntary visitors to men's prisons.

But in other aspects women prisoners are an underprivileged minority. Some 300, half of the daily prison population, are concentrated in the central prison of Holloway, a prison which might have been replaced by a modern institution had it not been for the war. In 1939 there were eight Borstal institutions for boys, with ample opportunity for differentiation into treatment groups—a feature which is the essence of the Borstal system. For girls there was only one, Aylesbury—a central building, once an inebriate asylum and at present still connected with a women's convict prison; and there are no facilities for differentiation into separate groups other than the usual three grades. Almost immediately after the end of the war steps were taken to secure further

[1] Ruggles-Brise, p. 116, confirmed by Fox, p. 134.

accommodation for Borstal girls and so improve the chances of differentiation.

Even in peace-time there was always plenty of work for women prisoners, and they were thus spared the unemployment which so often threatened men in prison. Much maintenance work is typically suitable for women. Since housewifery and domestic service are most women's occupation, training in the laundry, the tailor shop, the kitchen, and so forth seems appropriate. Embroidery is sometimes encouraged as a spare-time activity. More recently gardening and agricultural work have been added. Rough manual work like floor-scrubbing is often performed with remarkable energy and thoroughness. Often, however, work of this kind can be done regularly and well, and yet there will be an almost complete failure to apply the standards of care and thoroughness followed in the job to the prisoner's own life and conduct. Women are sometimes said, in fact, to rely so much on the merit of work well done that they expect it to offset their moral and personal shortcomings.[1]

A new and wholesome feature is the arrangement by which prisoners can care for their babies. Penal and correctional institutions in England and the United States not only provide for confinement in the prison hospital, but have a crèche as well where the children can play while the mothers work. At night, the women often have their babies with them. 'Maternity prisons' were recommended in 1895 at the International Prison Congress in Paris.[2] They are a valuable opportunity for stimulating and strengthening the motherly instinct and thereby appealing to one of the positive forces for social adjustment. Not infrequently, under appropriate guidance and encouragement, a delinquent unmarried mother has been kept straight by her love and care for her baby.

A new social Approach

An alternative to making limited concessions within the framework of ordinary prison routine would be the development of independent institutions exclusively for delinquent women. What has been recognized in principle as necessary for maladjusted youth should not be impossible to achieve for women delinquents. Success would mean that one more section of those in conflict with law and order became detached from the traditional retributive machinery and, with due regard to their personal needs and potentialities, committed to rehabilitative treatment. The starting-

[1] Mary Gordon, l.c., p. 34.

[2] Resolution to Section ii, Question ii, No. 2.

point and driving force are the same for the reform of institutions for young offenders as for reform in the treatment of women offenders. Beginning with the early institutions for wayward and neglected children, social training and re-education, as a definite theory, gained ground until, from juveniles of higher age-groups, adolescents, and young adults it has come at last to include all women offenders. Development towards this last expansion of the idea has, however, been sporadic and slow. The educational principles for the treatment of wayward girls had to change considerably before they could be any help in finding a successful method of dealing with women delinquents. If there are better facilities for constructive treatment in a woman's prison to-day than in a Refuge Home a hundred years ago, it is because development went on from religious and humanitarian rescue work to training for home, work, and citizenship, and again from a training which relied chiefly upon habits inculcated by regulated institutional and work routine to an attempt to readjust the individual on the basis of a psychological and social diagnosis.

Such generalizations, however, over-simplify the facts. The old and the new had much in common. Reports from the old refuge homes or the early industrial schools show that sincere efforts were made to discover the individual's promising qualities, to give the girls useful training, and to encourage exercises and wholesome spare-time activities. And a modern approach relying on case-work does not ignore the value of moral education and religious instruction. The difference between past achievements and present demands is mainly one of emphasis and atmosphere, but these intangibles are decisive if there is to be progress in any field of education. The gloom, so persistently associated with rescue work in the past, had deeper causes than the drab barrack buildings (very often nowadays replaced by a group of cottages in green surroundings); the 'fallen girls' in the early homes were in a state of utter neglect, far below what is typical of waywardness to-day. Some fifty years ago, among the girls admitted in one year to the reformatory at Ipswich, 'only one could really read and write fairly well, hardly any girls could tell the time by the clock, and very few knew their right hand from their left'. Not one was without a physical defect or deformity.[1] In industrial schools retarded and backward older girls shared lessons with children in the first standard; and association of different age-groups was recommended, in order to give the older girls a chance to care for

[1] *Reformatory and Industrial School Work*, l.c., pp. 155 and 158.

children. The old education released its pupils completely 'institutionalized'. They were, as an unprejudiced observer admitted, 'guarded on every hand, with no power of self-control'.[1] In spite of much devoted effort, a wide gap separated officers and girls. There was a tragic discrepancy between the high religious ideals which inspired founders and officers and were supposed to permeate the institution, and the limited purpose of this education, namely, to teach 'good behaviour, good manners, and as far as possible refined habits'.[2]

It needed a double emancipation if there was to be a further advance. The recognition of youth as a social group, aware of itself and with a right to its own patterns of life and communal activities, began to affect education deeply and in every aspect. And as far as girls and young women were concerned, women themselves began to take the lead and make a direct and unconventional approach to the needs of their maladjusted contemporaries. Pioneers of these movements vigorously responded to certain doctrines of modern psychology. Insight into the multiple causation of waywardness and delinquency showed how futile it was to rely entirely on the surrender to conversion of a wilful evil-doer. A dispassionate study of the personal circumstances of immoral and disorderly behaviour and of the conditions of social adjustment suggested that, far from breaking the obstinate will, the educator often has to strengthen a weak one and that he must build up self-respect so that it will be adequate to the individual's difficulties. Reformative treatment, inspired by these ideas, develops its own principles. Institutions built on the cottage plan, for example, are found to facilitate intense educational efforts within small separate groups. The most potent educational means, here as elsewhere, are the educator's personal example and share in the communal life, based on a genuine feeling of solidarity and a desire to live with those for whom she is responsible, rather than to rely on authority enforced by superiority in status or age. A sharing by the inmates in responsibility for the institutional life and its objects is the way to overcome that submissive indifference which so often frustrates all reformative efforts.

American Reformatories for Women

A radical improvement in the methods of treating women offenders demanded new ideas and forces which were only forth-

[1] *Reformatory and Industrial School Work*, p. 163.
[2] Ibid., p. 141.

coming where a direct personal approach was made to the problem of delinquent and wayward youth. It was in the United States that the decisive step was taken. American reformatories for women were the first example of a correctional system which provided what the readjustment of women offenders requires, without paying any undue regard to traditional prison conceptions. These reformatories for women began almost simultaneously with Z. R. Brockway's efforts to establish Elmira. In 1873 the Indiana Reformatory for Women was founded, in 1877 Massachusetts followed suit, and in 1887 the New York House of Refuge was opened. After the First World War there were twenty-four reformatories in twenty-one states, and one federal reformatory. While the reformatories for men lost sight more and more completely of the progressive objects of their founders and became nothing more than prisons for younger felons who had often a considerable criminal record, the women's reformatories developed in the opposite direction and became training institutions for those offenders who were mainly misdemeanants.

Here the comprehensive conception in the United States of female criminality reveals its true significance. The considerable number of prostitutes and other sexually maladjusted women, who in Europe would be dealt with by administrative or welfare measures outside the sphere of criminal law, are liable to a punishment which involves committal to a training institution with ample educational and medical facilities and only a minimum of resemblance to a prison. The American penal system of to-day has been compromised by overcrowding, pre-war idleness, and the curse of the local gaol, but it presents its best features in some of the women's reformatories. While in Europe the small minority of women prisoners has always been in the background with scarcely any special consideration for its particular needs and problems, some of the American women's institutions are the most progressive achievements of penal administration. This applies especially to Clinton Farm, N.J.; Framingham, Mass.;[1] Connecticut State Farm, East Lyne; and the Federal Reformatory at Alderson, W.Va.[2]

Between the two wars the experience gained in these institutions was made the subject of a thorough investigation on which certain general observations may be based.[3] As a rule these reformatories

[1] M. Liepmann, *American Prisons and Reformatory Institutions* (1928), p. 72.

[2] *Federal Offenders, 1938*, pp. 148 et seq.

[3] Lekkerkerker, op. cit.

are minimum security institutions, although sometimes they make limited provision for medium security to ensure discipline or safe custody. While elsewhere the prevention of escapes, especially from institutions in the neighbourhood of big cities, is a serious disciplinary problem, the active and free life in American reformatories, often far away in the country and without the provocation of wall or fence, makes it less difficult to keep the inmates in the institution. And their policy (reminiscent of Russia's) deliberately avoids conspicuous punishment for escape and so facilitates the voluntary return of the fugitive. A survey of twelve American reformatories, extending over different periods from one to sixteen years, shows that in eight of these institutions the number of successful escapes did not reach 1 per cent. of the committals.[1] In the federal reformatory, with accommodation for 500 women, there were twenty-six cases of escape within eleven years; all women except one returned, usually on the same or the following day.[2] Most of these reformatories consist of a group of buildings and cottages. Such a layout facilitates individualization and makes it possible to distribute liabilities and initiative between the institution as a whole and single groups. Work, lessons, sports, religious services are shared by all, while spare-time activity, communal life, participation in matters of common interest, the personal influence of the officers, all have their role among the small groups of women living together in a particular cottage. Maternity problems have been squarely faced. Half the institutions have accommodation for confinements on the premises. Some have special maternity cottages. Clinton Farm, N.J., is famous for its pre-nursery school. The Connecticut State Farm has an official capacity of 210 adults and 75 infants. American experience of women's participation in self-government is not unfavourable. Elected representation instead of appointed trustees is occasionally adopted and is most fruitful in the executive field, where certain domestic, recreative, and social objects may be made the women's responsibility; but giving the women a part in the promulgation of general rules and decisions has proved less satisfactory. Again, the cottage system encouraging group loyalty and a wholesome competition between groups provides a useful lesson in the sharing of responsibility for the welfare of a small close-knit unit. The women are employed in domestic as well as industrial occupations. The latter type of work is more likely to

[1] Lekkerkerker, p. 292.

[2] *Federal Offenders, 1938*, p. 148.

satisfy their self-respect and provide the necessary variety. In view of women's prospects on the labour market, industries have been selected which normally occupy more women than men: sewing and knitting, laundry work, house furnishing including reconditioning of furniture, gardening and dairy work, and—although seasonal—canning and the preserving of fruit. Even so, maintenance and domestic work plays a considerable part, since very many paroled women are placed in domestic service. The reformatories call for the co-operation of domestic employers and keep contact with them and the discharged women by parole agents. They are fortunate that the demand for the employment of paroled women exceeds the number to be placed. The fact that in the United States female labour is in greater demand than male makes easier the social adjustment of women delinquents.

According to competent observers the American reformatories for women are the best institutions in the United States, and better adapted to women's needs than any other penal establishments in the world.[1] The treatment, accommodation, discipline, work, spare-time activities, and after-care are significant in themselves; but they are a general framework only. Even more important are the forces at work, the active and unprejudiced spirit which permeates the whole institutional life, and the respectable living-standards which are deliberately provided as a strong educative factor. This venture is an achievement on the part of women, inspired by the experience of a pioneer generation which has once again opened a new province of human backwardness and misery to the constructive forces of personal help, mental hygiene, and social education.

By this experiment, the United States has given a valuable example which is bound to influence the remodelling of women's prisons in Europe. Sir Evelyn Ruggles-Brise, whose visit to the American reformatories in 1897 led to the inauguration of the Borstal system, shortly after the First World War expressed the hope that by reformative sentences for women up to thirty and the establishment of a 'State Reformatory' after the precedents of some American states, a larger proportion of women might be rescued from crime than was 'likely or even possible' under the present system.[2] For fifteen years, the Howard League for Penal Reform has advocated 'cottage-house' institutions for women prisoners. This suggestion ought to apply especially to the women's

[1] Lekkerkerker, p. 569.

[2] Ruggles-Brise, p. 122.

Borstal so that the girls might have something like the individualization and group life which the boys enjoy. In 1932 the Departmental Committee on Persistent Offenders stated that for the great majority of women prison buildings of the fortress type were unnecessary and even more harmful than for men. For the small number of women under preventive detention—a daily average of six in the last pre-war year—the Committee suggested that a country house should be used for custody, training, and employment. Such a course 'would avoid the complete loss of self-respect which women frequently suffer as a result of imprisonment'.[1] A new departure in the penal and reformative treatment of women is an important object of European post-war reconstruction.

[1] *Report of the Departmental Committee on Persistent Offenders* (1932), p. 39, s. 96.

CHAPTER XVI

MENTALLY ABNORMAL PERSONS

THE CRIMINOLOGICAL SITUATION

IT has often been asserted that a considerable proportion of criminals are mentally abnormal. But any attempt to verify this assumption from statistics has to face two difficulties. In the first place, the law so delimits criminal responsibility that certain types and degrees of mental irregularity make it impossible for the person suffering from them to be considered a criminal at all. This legal classification makes no allowance, in fact, for the case where mentally abnormal persons behave in a way obnoxious to the rights and interests which the law was designed to protect. Social risks and losses, moreover, being less calculable, are less easy to make the basis of generalization than legal offences which can be calculated from the record of trial and sentences.

Secondly, the conception of normality and its limits is changing as medical experience and psychological understanding advance. In the lifetime of the present generation the criminological interest of medical psychology has shifted from insanity to psychopathic personalities, and from the latter to the personality make-up and inner conflicts of normal men and women. A deeper insight into the dynamics and variations of the human personality shows that much psychological maladjustment is due to characteristics and reactions in themselves normal. The pendulum has swung back; and so the tendency is now to restrict rather than extend the sphere of abnormality. This makes it difficult to compare the results of criminological research undertaken ten or twenty years ago with those of the present day. For comparative purposes a qualitative analysis of cases may be more illuminating than a quantitative assessment of the frequency of certain pathological types.

Whatever the range of abnormality, it includes two different groups: persons suffering from a mental disorder and persons defective in mental equipment or character development. There are interrelations and border-line cases, often similar in their symptoms and defying almost any classification. In principle, there is a distinction between a pathological process, affecting and so 'changing' a patient's mind, and an abnormal personality reacting in its own typical manner. To the former group belong mental diseases like schizophrenia, manic-depressive psychosis, general paralysis of the insane, and the after-effects of encephalitis; whereas the mental defective and the psychopath are abnormal personalities. Mental deficiency implies an inadequate intellectual equipment. Psychopathic personalities, often with a normal and even high intelligence, exhibit from early childhood abnormal emotional reactions and volitional tendencies, and remain unstable and immature. This general characterization applies to different clinical groups of aggressive, inadequate, and passive types including pathological liars and excessively querulous persons, and creative personalities who sometimes pursue a strange purpose making exaggerated claims for its importance.[1] Social inadaptability is almost by definition a characteristic of psychopaths who are usually entangled in endless minor and major social conflicts and fill the ranks of 'the misfits of society'. In view of these social implications, a psychopath has been described as a person who, owing to his abnormal endowment, is himself suffering or makes society suffer.[2] This problem sometimes seems to grow rather than to be lessened by the attention it receives from law and medicine. The fluctuating border-line between psycho-neurosis and normal character difficulties has so far prevented any uniformity in medical diagnosis as well as in the administration of criminal law.

It is this variation in what was considered to be character abnormality rather than the clearly defined mental diseases which makes it difficult to compare figures from different times and countries. Many criminological investigations refer to convicted prisoners serving sentences, obviously a negative selection from the total of antisocial personalities. In 1908 it was estimated that in England 19 per cent. of persons arrested were mentally abnormal against 8 per 1,000 of the whole nation.[3] Out of 10,000 prisoners found guilty before the Court of General Sessions, New York City, 10·8 per cent. showed gross mental abnormality and there was a further 6·9 per cent. of psycho-neurotics.[4] It is a well-founded working hypothesis that 20 per cent. of prisoners in English penal institutions are abnormal in the sense that their behaviour and reactions do not correspond to those of ordinary men.[5]

[1] D. K. Henderson and R. D. Gillespie, *Textbook of Psychiatry* (6th ed. 1944), pp. 381 et seq.; W. S. Sadler, *Modern Psychiatry* (1945), pp. 162–70.

[2] K. Schneider, *Die psychopathischen Persönlichkeiten* (2nd ed. 1928), p. 3.

[3] Kenny, p. 65.

[4] W. Bromberg and C. W. Thompson, 28 *Journal* 70.

[5] W. N. East and W. H. de Hubert, *Psychological Treatment of Crime* (1939), p. 7.

These average figures need further qualification with regard to the types of abnormality and the groups of offenders. The effect of mental diseases on the incidence of crime is easy to assess but is small in amount. On 1 January 1939 in England and Wales 70,161 men and 88,562 women were reported suffering from mental disorders. Out of this total, 651 men and 203 women had committed acts for which a normal person would have been prosecuted.[1] The small recorded contribution of women to criminality repeats itself in the pathological sphere. While the total of women patients exceeds that of men, the number of law-breakers is more than three times higher among men than among women. During twenty-two years, 1901–22, 1,344 persons on trial were found insane, i.e. no more than 0·579 per cent. of the total. During the same period every third person on trial for murder, i.e. 485 out of 1,445, was mentally ill.[2] Thus murderers, though an absolute minority, have among them a higher proportion of criminals afflicted by mental disorders. Before the Second World War there was an average of 100 murders per year in England and Wales. Almost half the number of murderers committed suicide. Of those prosecuted, in 1938, 8 were insane on arraignment and 10 found guilty but insane.[3]

When we turn to the large group of defective and psychopathic personalities, our investigation loses the firm ground of reliable data. The proportion of mental defectives among criminals in general is controversial. American control investigations found no marked difference in the distribution of intelligence types among prisoners and among army drafts from the same social and ethnological groups.[4] As to results of studies on particular groups of offenders, Sir Cyril Burt found 8 per cent. mental defectives among young delinquents against 1·5 per cent. in the general population,[5] and Sheldon and Eleanor Glueck diagnosed 13·1 per cent. of juvenile delinquents and 20·6 per cent. of adolescent criminals as feeble-minded against again 1·5 per cent. in a non-delinquent control group.[6] While grades of intelligence are assessed by standardized tests, the diagnosis of a psychopathic

[1] *Twenty-fifth Report of the Board of Control* (1939), p. 12.

[2] *Report of the Committee appointed to consider Changes in the existing Law relating to Criminal Trials in which the Plea of Insanity is raised* . . . (Committee on Insanity and Crime) (1923), p. 25, Appendix C, Table I.

[3] *Crim. Stat., 1938*, p. xvii.

[4] See pp. 162–4 above.

[5] Cyril Burt, *The Subnormal Mind* (2nd ed. 1944), p. 177.

[6] S. and E. Glueck, *After-conduct of Discharged Offenders* (1945), p. 13.

personality requires a judgement of the patient's emotional and volitional reactions. Among the offenders found guilty before the Court of General Sessions, New York, 6·9 per cent. were classified as psychopaths,[1] while other observers regarded the assessment of 14 per cent. psychopaths among American federal prisoners as conservative.[2]

The incidence of mental abnormality among particular criminological and social groups of offenders is even more significant. Before the First World War, among English convicts the correlation between offence and mental deficiency was 0·76 for arson and 0·12 for frauds with a coefficient of 0·58 in the middle of the scale for theft and burglary.[3] Psychopathic and mentally defective personalities are numerous among certain types of maladjusted people doomed to waywardness and frequently concerned in petty offences. According to a summary of investigations, mostly referring to Germany, one-quarter of all sexual offenders, one-half of all pupils of approved schools and of inmates of workhouses including many former prostitutes, and three-quarters of all beggars and vagrants show some deviation from the normal standard.[4] Similarly in American local gaols with their transient population of petty offenders, drunkards, and disorderly persons, 77 per cent. have been estimated to be below the normal standard, among them 42·2 per cent. psychopaths.[5] Among serious criminals, 38 per cent. of German convicts under life sentences were mental defectives or psychopathic personalities.[6] Between the two extremes of wayward petty offenders and serious criminals is a vast amount of ordinary adult crime against property which has a pathological taint only in particular circumstances as is sometimes the case with certain types of women shoplifters. This is confirmed by the study of 10,000 New York offenders which showed that, while larceny is the most frequent crime among normally adjusted personalities, it has a higher percentage frequency of psycho-neurotic perpetrators than other offences.[7]

In the face of these inconsistencies, a better insight into the relation between mental abnormality and crime may be gained by

[1] Bromberg and Thompson, l.c.

[2] J. G. Wilson and M. J. Pescor, *Problems of Prison Psychiatry* (1939), quoted from W. Healy, 217 *Annals* 74.

[3] Goring, *The English Convict* (abridged ed. 1919), p. 181.

[4] K. Wilmanns, *Verminderte Zurechnungsfähigkeit* (1927), pp. 77, 70, and *passim*.

[5] L. N. Robinson, *Jails* (1944), p. 48.

[6] Lumpp, 47 *Bl. Gefg. Kd.* 107.

[7] Bromberg and Thompson, p. 87.

'cross-examination'. The evidence presented above referred to the proportion of abnormal personalities among criminals and non-criminals; the discussion which follows is intended to reveal the incidence of crime among normal and abnormal persons. It has been estimated that out of a total of 300,000 mentally defective persons in England and Wales about 10 per cent. have criminal or antisocial tendencies.[1] In Germany the proportion of adult men with at least one conviction was estimated in a statistical analysis made before the First World War at almost 17 per cent.[2] A recent investigation of conditions in Bavarian rural districts assessed the common conviction rate as between 2 and 5 per cent., rising to 9·2 per cent. for men under economic distress.[3] During the First World War psychopathic patients at an observation station at Heidelberg had a conviction rate of 27·4 per cent., and patients at an enclosed department of the same mental hospital, of 33 per cent. Whereas in the general population for every man with one conviction there were 0·6 with six and more convictions, the corresponding figure for the patients was 0·8.[4] Psychopathic personalities, therefore, displayed more frequent and intense criminal activities than their normal contemporaries.

With regard to mental defectives, out of a sample group of 103 former pupils of a special school at Bonn, 41, or 39·8 per cent., exhibited signs of delinquency, i.e. either criminality or waywardness. Out of 75 feeble-minded persons 35 became delinquent, but out of 28 imbeciles only 7.[5] Mental deficiency of medium degree involves a higher risk of delinquency than the serious cases of imbecility, since the latter are more easily recognized and better protected than their relatively brighter neighbours.

The high risk of social maladjustment among abnormal personalities suggests a causal relation between mental defects and criminal tendencies. Only individual case-studies and a final personal assessment make it possible to say how far the maladjustment of defective offenders is due to their inadequate intellectual equipment or abnormal character development. Counting all noticeable mental characteristics together, Sir Cyril Burt found among delinquents not quite two and a half times the symptoms of mental deviation and almost four times the signs of emotional

[1] *Report of the Departmental Committee on Sterilisation* (1934), p. 9, referring to the *Report of the Mental Deficiency Committee* (Wood Committee), 1929; 4 *Mental Hygiene* 82.

[2] K. Finkelnburg, *Die Bestraften in Deutschland* (1912), p. 33.

[3] F. Stumpfl, *Erbanlage und Verbrechen* (1935), p. 19.

[4] A. Wetzel, *MoSchrKrim.*, Beiheft I, 1926, pp. 69, 72 et seq.

[5] C. Wemmer, 40 *Z. f. Kinderforschung* 105.

abnormality which he observed in non-delinquents. At the same time he assessed as a major factor of delinquency among boys, intellectual conditions at the rate of 11·4 per cent., and emotional at the rate of 43·8 per cent. Abnormalities in the sphere of emotion and volition are more frequent and powerful factors in causing juvenile delinquency than is insufficient intellectual equipment. According to this investigation the principal personal causes of juvenile delinquency are dullness not amounting to mental deficiency, and temperamental instability not amounting to a psychopathic personality.[1]

The causation of crime covers not only the reason for a man's first offence, but also the factors which hinder his readjustment. Mental abnormality is less significant as a source of first crimes, than as hampering response to penal and reformative treatment. English observers who consider that not more than 20 per cent. of the prison population is below normal mental standards have found a large proportion of boys sent back from Borstal to Wandsworth Prison afflicted by mental disorder or abnormality.[2] This experience has been confirmed by American follow-up studies. An examination of 3,000 young men paroled from the Illinois Reformatory, Pontiac, during 1921 and 1927 showed an average of 16·1 per cent. of major parole violations. Those in the lowest intelligence group had a ratio of 20·2 per cent., those in the highest of only 6·2 per cent. With regard to character deviations, sexual psychopaths—not necessarily sexual offenders—failed markedly at a rate of 26·7 per cent., neuropathics and psychotics at a rate of 23·8 per cent., while those with a temporary emotional instability had a failure rate of only 9·1 per cent.[3] According to Sheldon and Eleanor Glueck's follow-up studies of 500 young adults discharged from the Massachusetts Reformatory, the most marked difference between those reformed and those relapsing into delinquency or crime was found in their mental conditions. Only 7·6 per cent. of the reformed but 51·2 per cent. of the unreformed exhibited a mental disease, distortion, emotional instability, or some other diagnosed abnormality.[4]

From a social point of view, mental diseases and defective or psychopathic personalities involve a considerable risk to the individual and collective interests which society expects the State

[1] Cyril Burt, *The Young Delinquent* (2nd ed. 1931), p. 603, Table 22, and *passim*.
[2] East and de Hubert, *The Psychological Treatment of Crime* (1939), p. 41.
[3] C. Tibbits, 22 *Journal* 38.
[4] S. and E. Glueck, *Later Criminal Careers* (1937), p. 92.

to protect. It is for the law to determine the legal consequences of this fact.

THE LEGISLATIVE SOLUTION

Criminal Responsibility

Criminal law is essentially concerned with the individual's mental condition. Whatever the illegal act, it is a crime only if performed with a guilty mind. *Actum non facit reum, nisi mens sit rea*, 'the act does not make a man guilty unless his mind is guilty'. This is a fundamental principle of criminal law not only in England,[1] but in every civilized country. Likewise, whatever sanction society inflicts, it is not a punishment unless it can appeal to man's moral personality. Justice, to a refined conscience, forbids the punishment of a man who cannot be held accountable for what he has done, or is unable to understand what is to be inflicted upon him. Criminal responsibility for the act committed as well as comprehension of the punishment imply a certain standard of normality. On this subject, the law must take counsel from the psychologist and the physician.[2] They must advise not only on the prisoner's mental state in general, but also on the question of what reactions and behaviour can fairly and justly be expected from an individual person. But in the end it is legal rules that must determine the criteria of criminal liability.

The law is concerned with commandments addressed to the average man. It presupposes men and women with enough mental equipment to cope with their affairs in ordinary social conditions, to act according to plan, to learn from experience, to be capable of certain fundamental emotions, affections, and rational motives, and at the same time to exert a certain self-control even in adverse circumstances.[3] Since this description fits the vast majority of people, the law follows general experience in defining the exceptional cases of irresponsibility only negatively.

[1] Wills J. in *Reg.* v. *Tolson*, 23 *QB* 168, 172 (1889).

[2] G. Zilboorg and G. W. Henry, *History of Medical Psychology* (1941); G. Zilboorg, 'Legal Aspects of Psychiatry', *One Hundred Years of American Psychiatry* (published for the Am. Psychiatric Association, 1945), pp. 507–84; W. C. Sullivan, *Crime and Insanity* (1924); W. N. East, *Introduction to Forensic Psychiatry in the Criminal Courts* (1927); id., *Medical Aspects of Crime* (1936); K. Wilmanns, *Die sogenannte verminderte Zurechnungsfähigkeit* (1927); W. A. White, *Insanity and the Criminal Law* (1923); S. Glueck, *Mental Disorder and the Criminal Law: A Study in Medico-Sociological Jurisprudence* (1925); H. Weihofen, *Insanity as a Defence in Criminal Law* (1933); O. C. Davis and F. A. Wilshire, *Mentality and the Criminal Law* (1935); L. Radzinowicz and J. W. C. Turner (ed.), *Mental Abnormalities and Crime* (1944); D. Abrahamsen, *Crime and the Human Mind* (1944).

[3] Joel P. Bishop, *Commentaries on the Criminal Law* (2nd ed. 1858), i, s. 294 *c*, p. 337.

An analysis of the relevant provision shows that the law thereby allows for the various aspects of mental life in different ways.

To an unsophisticated mind mental defects are those impairing reason and consciousness. Accordingly, from the beginning, forensic psychology had an intellectualistic outlook. Conscious ideas seemed the inner counterparts to the physical subjects of the material world. For this rationalistic conception insanity was a disturbance of man's intellectual capacities and functions. Moreover, it was easy to demonstrate the low grade of a patient's intelligence, his inconsistency, or lack of common-sense logic. This explains the persistent tradition of the law which limited the recognition of criminal irresponsibility to disorders affecting the cognitive side of mental life: for this limitation made it possible to formulate certain clear-cut standards or legal tests of insanity which were considered indispensable to an equal and consistent application of the law.

The impressive metaphor of a man with the mind of an infant, of a brute, or a wild beast, survived from the Middle Ages to the eighteenth century.[1] The conception of mental abnormality widened with the recognition of morbid delusion as a possible exculpating factor, when in 1800 James Hadfield, who had shot at King George III under the delusion of a Divine command, was acquitted.[2] The law as it stands to-day with regard to irresponsibility due to delusions is explained by the McNaghten rules. In 1843 Daniel McNaghten killed Sir Robert Peel's secretary because he felt himself persecuted by the statesman and confused the secretary with the minister. After he had been acquitted as being of unsound mind by reason of morbid delusions the House of Lords propounded to the judges certain abstract questions on the criminal responsibility of persons afflicted with insane delusions. The rules formulated in reply to these questions lay down that, for a successful defence of insanity, it must be proved that the prisoner was labouring under such a defect of reason, from disease of the mind, as not to know the nature and quality of the act he was doing, or not to know that what he was doing was wrong.[3] Since then it has been decided that the McNaghten rules are the exclusive test of irresponsibility in English criminal law, whether or not the insanity is due to illusions as in the case of McNaghten.[4]

[1] Bracton, *De legibus et consuetudinibus Angliae*, Lib. V, c. 20, fol. 420 *b* (ed. Woodbine, 1922), iv. 308; Hale, c. iv. 30 and 32; Mr. Justice Tracy in 'Arnold's Case', 16 *St. Tr.* 695, 766 (1724).

[2] 27 *St. Tr.* 1281 (1800).

[3] 10 *Cl. and F.* 200, 209.

[4] Lord Hailsham in *Sodemen* v. *The King*, [1936] *Weekly Notes* 190.

By this rigidity the common law lost touch with advancing medical psychology. When a new medical science turned from speculation and classification to observation and treatment, Pinel, Esquirol, Reil, and other pioneers of modern psychiatry found that persons with apparently unimpaired or even a perfect state of consciousness and reason suffered from manifest abnormalities in the spheres of emotion and action.[1] They thereby initiated a development which in modern psychology shifted the emphasis from the concept of understanding to that of volition, but their own explanation discredited their discoveries. They did not interpret abnormal impulses, perverted emotions, or lack of natural affections as possible symptoms of one or the other clearly circumscribed pathological state or process, but identified them with an almost equal number of alleged diseases, namely, particular forms of a *manie sans délire* like homicidal mania, pyromania, kleptomania, and so forth. Instead of investigating whether a form of antisocial behaviour is due to a mental disease, this doctrine seemed to substitute insanity for the criminal intent, and to conclude that an unresisted impulse was irresistible.

This uncritical symptomatology was abandoned under the influence of the English alienist J. C. Prichard, who described the pathological reactions which he observed without concentrating on the particular antisocial act of homicide, arson, stealing, and so on as characteristics of a clinical diagnosis. Instead, he recognized, in addition to the traditional group of intellectual insanity, a second form of 'madness' consisting of 'a morbid perversion of the feelings, affections and active powers', compatible 'with an apparently unimpaired state of intellectual faculties'.[2] Unfortunately he chose for this group the name moral insanity. In this context he used the word moral as a contrast to intellectual. Among his examples are cases which to-day would be diagnosed as psychopathic states, manic-depressive psychoses, or final stages of certain physical illnesses. He emphasized the necessity for forensic purposes of distinguishing between insanity and eccentricity of character, 'if indeed the two things are essentially different'. This distinction, though not easily brought into

[1] P. Pinel, *Traité médico-philosophique sur la manie* (1801), German translation by W. Wagner (1801); 2nd ed., *Traité médico-philosophique sur l'aniénation* (1809). J. C. Reil, *Rhapsodien über die Anwendung der psychischen Kurmethode auf Geisteszerrüttungen* (2nd ed., Halle, 1818); J. E. D. Esquirol, *Bemerkungen über Mordmonomanie* (Aus dem Französischen mit Zusätzen von M. J. Bluff, 1831).

[2] J. C. Prichard, *Treatise on Insanity and other Disorders affecting the Mind* (1835), p. 12. Similar definitions, pp. 4 and 6.

evidence, should be based on a study of a man's forbears, family background, antecedents, and after-conduct.[1] Later on, under the influence of Esquirol's criticism, he limited the conception of moral insanity to a perversion of feelings and affections, and distinguished it from an 'instinctive madness affecting the voluntary powers'.[2] This narrow conception, but even more the association of the word moral with ethics, misled his critics, especially among foreign writers, to assert that an extravagant medical psychology claimed moral and legal wrongs as characteristic of an alleged mental disease, namely, an atrophy of ethical feeling, a blindness to ethical values. Moral imbecility, as conceived by the English statute,[3] rather than Prichard's original moral insanity, has its main characteristic in an early and persistent predominance of vicious tendencies; but even this has been recognized as a pathological state only if coupled with intellectual deficiency.[4]

In the United States Prichard's ideas met with strong support from Isaac Ray, a pioneer in forensic psychology.[5] Neither, however, was able to avert a reaction against the recognition of insanity in cases where reason and consciousness seemed unimpaired. The time was not yet ripe for a psycho-pathology of affections and emotions. The doctrine of moral insanity provoked a strong opposition from both the general public and the legal profession. A. von Feuerbach, Bavarian legislator, refuted the idea that overwhelming passions were morbid—'unless they were not passionate and therefore not overwhelming'. In his opinion reactions of an unruly mind, out of balance under the influence of passions, are 'moral and legal diseases of the soul for which no pharmacies and fools' hospitals but—if reasonable warnings, religious and ethical objections and even the threat of penal laws prove fruitless—gaols, convict-prisons and scaffolds have been erected'.[6] In England similar arguments were used in support of the McNaghten rules. In *R.* v. *Haynes*, Bramwell B. said: 'If an influence be so powerful as to be termed irresistible the much more reason is, why we

[1] J. C. Prichard, pp. 23 and 382.

[2] Id., *On the different Forms of Insanity in Relation to Jurisprudence* (1842), p. 93.

[3] Mental Deficiency Act, 1913, 3 & 4 Geo. V, c. 28, s. 1 (*d*), amended by 17 & 18 Geo. V, c. 33 (1927).

[4] W. C. Sullivan, *Crime and Insanity* (1924), p. 198.

[5] I. Ray, *Medical Jurisprudence of Insanity* (1838). See G. Zilboorg, 'Legal Aspects of Psychiatry', *One Hundred Years of American Psychiatry* (1945), pp. 507, 550, 557.

[6] A. v. Feuerbach, *Aktenmässige Darstellung merkwürdiger Verbrechen* (3rd ed. by C. J. Mittermaier, 1849), pp. 419, 412. These observations apply to Steiner, who committed murder in similar circumstances to those of McNaghten.

should not withdraw any of the safeguards tending to counteract it. There are three powerful restraints . . . , religion, . . . conscience, . . . law. If the influence itself is to be held a legal excuse . . . , you at once withdraw the most powerful restraint, that forbidding and punishing its perpetration.'[1]

The exclusive emphasis placed by the McNaghten rules on intellectual capacity did not remain unchallenged. Twenty years after their promulgation, leading English psychologists branded them as 'flagrantly unjust'. Responsibility should be based upon the power to control the will instead of on the individual's consciousness. Otherwise, it was argued, nine-tenths of the lunatics of England would have to be hanged, if they happened to commit murder.[2] In the light of present-day psychological knowledge the old narrow conception of irresponsibility has been denounced as 'unsound in principle, and faulty and confusing in form'. Morbid action is not the outcome of morbid thought. Not infrequently the earliest and often the only overt manifestation of a developing disorder is a morbid impulse, sometimes superficially disguised by apparently plausible reasoning.[3] Patients suffering from general paralysis of the insane, schizophrenia, or alcoholism have been observed exhibiting precocious and independent antisocial impulses.[4] Morbid motivations are sometimes the root of the criminal acts of nursing mothers, epileptics, and serious psychopaths. In other cases, the antisocial behaviour is the purposeless reaction of a compulsive neurosis.[5] The perpetrators of such acts may describe what they have done with the lucidity of a detached observer and even offer a rational explanation *ex post*, or else appear as helpless spectators of an inevitable occurrence of which they are aware and afraid.[6] In the light of medical experience, it would be no less unjust to hold these men criminally responsible for their reactions than those who acted without being conscious of the factual circumstances and the illegal character of what they were doing.

The criticism of medical psychologists met with support, inside the legal profession also. Sir James F. Stephen, representative of

[1] *R.* v. *Haynes*, 1 *F. and F.* 666, 667.

[2] C. L. Robertson and H. Maudsley, *Insanity and Crime* (1864), pp. 38 et seq.; H. Maudsley, *Responsibility in Mental Disease* (1878), pp. 100 et seq.

[3] W. C. Sullivan, l.c., pp. 230, 238 and *passim*; L. A. Weatherly, 159 *L.T.J.* 435; H. Barnes, 8 *Cambridge L. J.* 300, 310.

[4] Sullivan, l.c., p. 238.

[5] C. Burt, *The Young Delinquent* (3rd ed. 1938), p. 585; J. Spirer, 33 *Journal* 457, 461.

[6] Sullivan, l.c., p. 81, obs. 14; p. 103, obs. 19; p. 105, obs. 20.

retributory criminal law, suggested that 'lack of consciousness' should be supplemented by the addition of 'the lack of self-control' as an alternative legal condition of irresponsibility.[1] His efforts, however, failed to leave their mark on English law. The committee called to consider the Draft Criminal Code of 1878, a legislative project sponsored by Stephen, rejected a corresponding extension of the traditional limits defined by the McNaghten rules.[2] In 1923 the Atkin Committee, approving a proposal made by the British Medical Association, recommended a statutory provision that a person should not be held responsible, if deprived by mental disease of power to resist a criminal impulse.[3] In the following year when Lord Darling moved in the House of Lords for a corresponding Bill he received no support after the Lord Chief Justice had stated that ten out of twelve judges when asked for their opinion were strongly opposed to a statutory extension of the McNaghten rules.[4] After the failure of these attempts it was suggested that conspicuous cases of a morbid lack or perversion of will-power should be brought under the McNaghten rules by a liberal interpretation. It is not unreasonable to suppose that, as the human personality is a unity, a disease which destroys the normal function of willing does not leave the person's insight into his actions unaffected.[5] The Court of Criminal Appeal, however, has repudiated all attempts to embark 'on a sea which has no shore' and to go beyond the letter of the McNaghten rules.[6]

Continental law proved more flexible.[7] Older codes use the terms of contemporary intellectualist psychology. The French *Code pénal* of 1810 refers to *démence*, the Austrian Criminal Code of 1852 to a 'deprivation of the use of reason'. Since the lawgivers are presumed to have applied those terms to what they thought to be the whole range of insanity, a liberal interpretation assumes that they cover any disorder obviating mental capacities in the spheres of understanding, feeling, and action.[8] This, however,

[1] J. F. Stephen, *History of the Criminal Law of England* (1883), ii. 168.

[2] D. S. Davies, 17 *Canadian B. R.* 147, 159.

[3] *Committee on Insanity and Crime*, l.c.

[4] *Hansard*, 5th series (Lords) (1924), lvii. 443.

[5] Kenny, p. 68; J. Hall, 45 *Columbia L. R.* 677. Also Lord Haldane, *Hansard*, l.c., p. 474.

[6] Lord Hewart, L.C.J. in *R.* v. *True* (murder by a certifiable insane), 16 *Crim. App. R.* 164; 127 *L. T.* 561 (1922); *R.* v. *Holt*, 15 *Crim. App. R.* 10, 12 (1920); *R.* v. *Kopsch*, 19 *Crim. App. R.* 50, 51 (1925).

[7] H. Mannheim, 84 *J. Ment. Sc.* 524.

[8] T. Rittler, *Lehrbuch des Österreichischen Strafrechts* (1933), i. 124. Similar observations with regard to French civil law by L. Josserand, *Cours de droit civil positif français* (1930), i, s. 520, p. 278 et seq.

gives no indication of the degree of mental disturbance, which the law regards as sufficient to rule out criminal liability. The German Criminal Code of 1871 describes the biological cause in the general term 'morbid mental disturbance', and requires that this state should have as its psychological effect 'the exclusion of free self-determination'. This term is reminiscent of contemporary philosophical indeterminism, but it has been interpreted in a psychological sense; it requires a disturbance so serious that it would not be just to regard what the man has done as the outcome of a normal personality. This wide conception includes intellectual defects as well as a lack or perversion of will-power.[1] Following an Austrian Draft Code of 1912 the Czechoslovak Draft Code of 1926, the German and Austrian Juvenile Court Acts, the Swedish Preliminary Draft Code of 1923, the Criminal Codes of Italy, Poland, Switzerland, and—in conformity with subsequent Draft Codes from 1913—a German Amendment of 1933, provide that a person is not responsible if by reason of a mental disease he is unable to recognize the wrongful character of his action, or incapable of acting in accordance with such insight.[2]

On this issue the law of the United States is divided. By 1933, twenty-nine states, including New York, Pennsylvania, and California, still followed the English principle that the 'right and wrong test' is the only criterion for irresponsibility, while the law of seventeen states, including Illinois, Massachusetts, and the District of Columbia, resembled European continental law in not regarding the outcome of an irresistible impulse as an act of a voluntary agent. There has been, however, no general trend towards further recognition of emotional and volitional abnormalities.[3]

This comparative survey shows that everywhere there has been a tendency to adapt the law to keep pace with psychology. This tendency dominates in continental legislation and has left its mark in the law of a minority of the American states, but has failed to procure any alteration in English law. The reluctance to extend the limits of the McNaghten rules is partly due to the strictly accusatorial mode of English legal procedure. As insanity is a

[1] 57 *RG* 76 (1922) (sexual offence); 64 *RG* 349, 353 (1930) (drunken assault); *RG* in *JW* 1931, 2572 (murder from a sudden unexplainable impulse).

[2] German Juvenile Court Act, 1923, s. 3; Austrian Law of 18 July 1928, s. 10; Italian Criminal Code, 1930, art. 85/ii; Polish Criminal Code, 1932, art. 17; German Criminal Code, s. 51/i, in the wording of the Amendment of 24 Nov. 1933; Swiss Criminal Code, 1937, art. 10.

[3] H. Weihofen, *Insanity as a Defence in Criminal Law* (1933), pp. 16, 64 and *passim*.

defence in criminal law, the burden of proof of his irresponsibility lies on the defendant,[1] and the evidence is confined to the statements of expert witnesses called by the parties. On the Continent the prisoner's responsibility is an ingredient of his guilt. The court, therefore, before finding him guilty, must be satisfied that any doubt as to his responsibility has been cleared.[2] For this purpose the judge has a discretionary power to call experts.[3] In the United States the trend is towards shifting the burden of proof from the defence to the prosecution, and recognizing the judge's discretion in appointing experts for the examination of the prisoner's mental condition.[4] In 1895 the Supreme Court ruled that the presumption of innocence implies that the prisoner's guilt cannot be regarded as proved if the jury entertain a reasonable doubt whether he was legally capable of committing a crime.[5] By 1933 twenty states, including New York, Massachusetts, and Illinois, the District of Columbia, and the federal courts, assigned the burden of proof to the prosecution.[6] Following similar tendencies in New York, Rhode Island, Colorado, and Louisiana,[7] draft proposals of the American Law Institute of 1930 and 1942 provided that the court, with due regard to the rights of both prosecution and defence, might appoint expert medical witnesses.[8] In a procedure based on criminological principles the ascertainment of the prisoner's mental condition should be independent of party pleadings. In Massachusetts the Briggs Law of 1921 makes a routine examination by the Department for Mental Diseases mandatory with regard to all defendants accused of a capital offence and to recidivists.[9] All prisoners found guilty before the Court of General Sessions, New York City, are examined in the Psychiatric Court Clinic.[10] The Swedish Lunatic Act of 1931 makes a psychiatric examination in the Mental Department of the Prison Administration mandatory, before a court orders preven-

[1] McNaghten Rules, 10 *Cl. and F.* 210.

[2] 21 *RG* 131 (1890).

[3] *Code d'instruction criminelle*, arts. 208, 209; German Code of Criminal Procedure, ss. 73, 221.

[4] Weihofen, l.c., pp. 168 and 211.

[5] Mr. Justice Haslan in *Davis* v. *U.S.*, 160 *U.S.* 469 (1895).

[6] Weihofen, l.c., p. 150.

[7] Ibid., p. 211.

[8] Draft Code on Criminal Procedure, 1930, s. 318; rule 403, Model Code on Evidence, 1942.

[9] General Laws of Massachusetts, Section 100 A, c. 123 (1921) with Amendments 1923, 1925, 1927, 1929; S. Glueck, 36 *Yale L. J.* 632; H. Weihofen, l.c., pp. 401 et seq.; W. Oberholser, 23 *Journal* 415.

[10] W. Bromberg and C. Thompson, 28 *Journal* 70.

tive detention or gives a sentence for murder or arson committed without intent to defraud.[1]

English law permits the court to ask for information about the prisoner's mental state only in so far as this is relevant for the opening of the trial or the decision as to the sentence. If the defendant seems unfit to plead and to be tried, the court is bound to hold a special inquiry with a jury,[2] and for this purpose may call experts.[3] After the prisoner's conviction, the court is entitled to remand him in custody for a medical examination. With regard to a prisoner under sentence of death, the Home Office has the statutory power to order his mental examination and, if found mentally ill, to transfer him to a State Asylum.[4] From 1901 to 1922, out of a total of 585 convicted murderers, 13 prisoners, or 2·2 per cent., were removed to the State Asylum.[5] In their practical effects these provisions compensate in some measure for the rigid conservatism of the Common Law concerning criminal responsibility and for the fact that English law places on the defence the whole burden of proof that a prisoner tried on a criminal charge did not act with a guilty mind.

Disposition of Cases of Offenders not liable to Punishment

For retributive criminal law, insanity frees the prisoner of responsibility and prevents the court from convicting and sentencing him. This leaves unsolved the social question of how to dispose of persons proved dangerous but not subject to punishment. In England the acquittal of Hadfield led to the enactment of the Criminal Lunatics Act of 1800, which gave the court power to order to keep in custody offenders suffering from mental illness.[6] As no statutory regulations provided for appropriate accommodation, up to the middle of last century insane offenders were kept in the common gaol.[7] In 1884 a new Criminal Lunatics Act provided for the transfer of such offenders to a mental hospital.[8]

In the United States the process of separating mental patients from prisoners made only slow progress. Insane persons held in prison numbered 397 in 1880 and 291 in 1890.[9] After the First

[1] A. Petrén, 22 *MoSchrKrim.* 265.
[2] 39 & 40 Geo. III, c. 94, s. 2 (1800).
[3] *R.* v. *Davies*, 6 *Cox* 326 (1853).
[4] 27 & 28 Vict., c. 29 (1864).
[5] Committee on Insanity and Crime (1923), l.c., pp. 17, 18.
[6] 39 & 40 Geo. III, c. 94 (1800).
[7] Illustrations by W. N. East, *Medical Aspects of Crime* (1936), pp. 102 et seq.
[8] 47 & 48 Vict., c. 64 (1884).
[9] L. N. Robinson, *Jails* (1944), p. 212.

World War an observer asserted that genuine schemes for separation had hardly begun and there was only a faint prospect of it in the immediate future.[1] Even in 1933, in fourteen states the law permitted mental patients to be kept in gaols pending commitment to an appropriate institution.[2]

On the European continent, before the recent legislative reforms, the task of the judiciary ended with acquittal. The protection of society against dangerous offenders with mental abnormalities was left to the executive, but the latter was often ill-prepared for this object by the incomplete and unconsolidated state of administrative law.[3] In Prussia the power of the police to commit mental patients to public hospitals was based upon a vague clause of the General Law of the Land of 1794,[4] in France upon a statute of 1838. Baden enacted an Act on the Welfare of Mental Patients in 1910. In the wake of a general reform of the criminal law, Italy, Belgium, Poland, Germany, and Switzerland gave the courts power to commit a dangerous offender, acting without full criminal responsibility, to a mental institution.[5]

Now that legal provisions exist by which offenders, at once dangerous and mentally afflicted, can be sent to hospitals and put in custody, insanity is no longer 'a good defence' but a sign that the prisoner is in need of a particular curative or protective treatment. This state of affairs has made it practicable for the law to consider the psychologists' assertion that there are degrees of responsibility with an intermediate zone between the extremes of the accountable and the absolutely irresponsible. Traditionally, when sentences were being awarded, a poor mental equipment or an undeveloped character, like unusual temptation or very difficult circumstances, were regarded as factors which diminish personal guilt, although they call for protection against insufficiently controlled antisocial tendencies. This problem played a prominent part in continental criminal law reform. Most of the recent enactments recognize a state of limited responsibility (*responsabilité restreinte*, *verminderte Zurechnungsfähigkeit*), but they differ in the legal consequences attached to this conception. Corresponding to the cumulative

[1] P. Klein, *Prison Methods in New York State* (1921), p. 86.

[2] G. Zilboorg, *Legal Aspects of Psychiatry*, l.c., p. 541.

[3] T. Metzdorf, *Der gemeingefährliche Geisteskranke* (1930).

[4] Sections 341, 344 ii/18 *ALR*.

[5] Italian Criminal Code, 1930, art. 222; Belgian Law of Social Defence, 1930, arts. 1, 7; Polish Criminal Code, 1932, art. 79; German Criminal Code, s. 42 *b*, in the wording of the law of 24 Nov. 1933, in conformity with the majority of the preceding Draft Codes from 1909; Swiss Criminal Code, 1937, art. 14.

principle which obtains for the treatment of habitual criminals, the Polish, Italian, and German laws empower the court to give a mentally afflicted offender a shorter sentence and, if he is dangerous, to commit him to a mental institution. This system pretends to reconcile the demands of just retribution with the needs for social protection. In practice it is open to serious objections. It embitters the prisoner, first to serve his sentence, as is the rule in Italy and Germany,[1] and instead of being discharged after the expiation of his crime to be interned in a mental institution. And it is discouraging for a mental patient to enter the mental institution first, as is prescribed by Polish law,[2] with the prospect of undergoing punishment when he is deemed to be cured. These evils are avoided by the alternative system of the Danish, Swedish, and Swiss laws[3] by which the court has power to commit a defendant to a mental institution in lieu of imprisonment. By this principle the legal distinction between irresponsibility and limited responsibility implies that in the first case the court has the alternative between discharge and committal to a mental institution, and in the second between sentence and committal. In England the same result was achieved by the Mental Deficiency Acts, 1913/27. They give the criminal court the power, in lieu of a prison sentence, to commit a mentally defective offender for one year to a mental institution, with the possibility of an extension of the term by the Board of Control.[4]

This solution shows that criminal law is developing from a system of penalties, with certain abstract legal conditions and limits, to a variety of measures calculated to meet the individual and social needs revealed by the commission of an offence. At present this process is far from complete. Some lawgivers are afraid the deterrent effect of an impending threat of legal punishment may be lost if detention in hospitals and mental institutions supplants imprisonment. Italian and Belgian laws[5] prescribe certain minimum terms of detention corresponding to the assumed gravity of the offence, and thereby introduce a strange punitive element into the medical conception of mental treatment.

[1] Italian Criminal Code, arts. 219, 220; ss. 51/ii, 42 *b* German Criminal Code, s. 456 *b* Code of Criminal Procedure in the wording of 24 Nov. 1933. The Italian and German provisions permit also the reverse order.

[2] Polish Criminal Code, 1932, art. 80.

[3] Danish Amendment, 1925; Criminal Code, 1930; F. Lucas, *MoSchrKrim.* xix. 577; xxi. 641. Swedish law of 1927; Petrén, 19 *MoSchrKrim.* 513; Swiss Criminal Code, 1937, art. 14.

[4] 3 & 4 Geo. V, c. 28, s. 8 (1 *b*) (1913).

[5] Italian Criminal Code, 1930, arts. 219, 222; Belgian Law of Social Defence, 1930, art. 19.

The shifting of emphasis from the exculpation of the individual to the protection of society finally affects the conception of irresponsibility itself. On the one hand, effective provisions for public security remove the chief objection to a liberal interpretation of criminal irresponsibility. On the other hand, with a progressive socialization of legal punishment itself, the question of criminal liability and its limits may lose something of its importance. To hold an offender responsible means that it is fair and just to make him account for what he has done. From this consideration the prospect of an impending punishment cannot be excluded. If the conception of legal punishment is no longer confined to a deliberate infliction of hardship but allows for corrective and curative methods of treatment, there are fewer objections to making an underprivileged person liable to the legal consequences of a criminal offence.[1] It may not be justifiable to make a man of abnormal personality responsible for a sexual offence by inflicting on him a repressive punishment and thereby preventing the possibilities of his improvement and readjustment, but it would be a satisfactory solution, not least from an ethical point of view, to influence his weakened and perverted will-power by requiring him to follow the directions of the probation officer and medical psychologist.[2]

The flexible character of criminal responsibility as a legal concept ought not to prevent the law from drawing a line between those who are free and responsible for what they are doing and others who are not expected to control themselves and therefore liable to enforced preventive measures. By ignoring this fundamental distinction criminal law would deprive itself of its strongest weapon: the appeal to man's will and self-control by making him account for his conduct where that conduct is the product of a normal personality.

On the right side of this demarcation line sanctions inflicted because of criminal acts committed are punishments, whether they are punitive or constructive in character. In the border area between full responsibility and absolute irresponsibility the course to be taken depends on the prisoner's needs rather than on a presumed degree of accountability and guilt. The legislative recognition of a limited responsibility was a mistake if it meant a graduation of guilt and punishment by abstract standards. The axiom of just retribution is unsuitable as a guide to what legal

[1] J. Spirer, 23 *Journal* 457, 462.

[2] Claud Mullins, *Crime and Psychology* (1943), p. 34.

sanction is appropriate. In practice difficulties are due to a change in the types of people to whom these provisions apply. While the advocates of a limited responsibility had in mind certain initial and transitional stages of psychotic processes, present-day continental penal policy is concerned with the vast army of abnormal personalities.[1] These critical observations confirm that the right legislative solution of the border-line problem is an alternative between punishment and mental treatment, with the final decision depending on the prisoner's response to punishment. The test of his suitability for punishment is in actual experience. Consequently, the Danish Criminal Code provides that in cases of limited responsibility the court may give an ordinary sentence and tentatively commit the defendant to prison with the possibility of commuting the committal into an indeterminate detention in a mental institution if the prison experience makes this appear advisable.[2] Ultimately the legal solution of the problem of criminal responsibility and its limits depends on experience and treatment in practice.

PROBLEMS OF TREATMENT

The care and treatment of offenders suffering from a psychosis offer no insurmountable difficulties. As a rule marked pathological processes can be diagnosed and demonstrated with certainty. Their treatment is a medical concern not differing from the care of other patients. Nor is there any reason to distinguish between 'criminal lunatics' and 'lunatic criminals', i.e. between mental patients committing offences and criminals or prisoners developing a mental disease. In England both groups are detained in the State Asylum, Broadmoor, Berkshire, which was established in 1863. This is an institution with 800–900 patients under the supervision of the Board of Control. Reports show that considerable efforts are necessary to provide a variety of suitable occupations for the inmates. Detention 'till his Majesty's pleasure' (shall be known) in most cases lasts for life. In 1938 104 convicted prisoners were certified as insane and transferred to the asylum or a mental hospital.[3] The time the prisoner is kept there is counted in his sentence. In Scotland the prison administration has a special Department for Criminal Lunatics, though under the

[1] K. Wilmanns, *Verminderte Zurechnungsfähigkeit* (1927).
[2] F. Lucas, *MoSchrKrim.* xix. 577; xxi. 641.
[3] *Report Prison Commissioners, 1938*, p. 45.

inspection of commissioners of the Board of Control. On 1 February 1938 Perth Prison had eighty-seven patients on the register. This department, too, suffered from lack of occupational facilities but tried in the absence of a proper occupational centre to carry on agriculture and horticulture.[1] In Germany, in 1888, Prussia followed the example of Saxony and Baden in establishing six special annexes, each with fifty beds, where prisoners suspected of suffering from mental disease are received for a six to twelve months' observation period. From these observation centres the prisoner is returned to the ordinary prison routine, or else his sentence is suspended and he is transferred to a general mental hospital, mostly to an enclosed department where the time spent is not counted in his sentence. Prussian prison annexes, too, have been criticized for lack of appropriate employment, and furthermore for insufficient medical influence on the institutional routine and an undue delay in transferring the prisoners.[2] The final relegation to general mental hospitals met with the objection that abnormal personalities suffering from prison reactions are active subversive elements among the ordinary mental patients who are usually introspective and 'self-contained'. As the time in hospital is not counted in the prisoner's sentence, his recovery means a return to the observation centre and from there to the ordinary prison to serve the outstanding part of his sentence. These considerations suggest that the wisest course is to provide facilities for temporary mental treatment under the prison administration and to remove to general mental hospitals only those suffering from a permanent major psychosis.

While the treatment of offenders suffering from a mental disease has its place in a wider scheme for mental patients in general, the crucial problem is the disposal of abnormal personalities. In 1938, out of 36 mental defectives serving sentences in English local prisons, 28 were removed to mental institutions. The remaining 8 were committed to the care of the local public assistance committee or brought on discharge to the notice of the local branch of the Central Association for Mental Welfare.[3] Apart from certifiable cases, the question arises whether a rational penal system should not make special provision for slightly feeble-minded prisoners and psychopathic personalities and certain cases of psycho-neurotics. Psychopaths, by their emotional instability,

[1] *Report Prison Department of Scotland, 1938*, pp. 85 et seq.
[2] Wilmanns, l.c., p. 136 and *passim.*
[3] *Report Prison Commissioners, 1938*, p. 45.

are often as unadaptable to ordinary prison discipline as they are unadjustable to the community.

Abnormal personalities are frequent among certain types of persistent petty offenders, beggars, vagrants, disorderly people, sexual offenders, and pilferers. They often have long careers of numerous short sentences which show that the usual methods are powerless to check them. Moreover, psychopathic personalities are the curse of prison discipline. They are self-conscious and over-sensitive, or presumptuous and arrogant, intriguing and plotting, often with considerable influence on their fellow prisoners, and always inclined to be in the limelight. Psychologically, it would often be better to avoid taking drastic disciplinary action against such cases and thus giving them the prominence they covet. Due regard to other prisoners, however, makes it impossible to let the ostentatious sinners go unpunished. Constructive methods in penal discipline have often been frustrated by setbacks due to a group of psychopaths. They are not susceptible to the stimulating effects of a Progressive Stage system. By temporary outbreaks of temper and apparently causeless outbursts they forfeit a position gained by weeks and months of strenuous effort, so that they find themselves again and again at the bottom of the scale. The question arises, what could be done with these abnormal persons who have been proved not adaptable to ordinary prison conditions?

In England feeble-minded prisoners, including certain types of epileptics and other border-line cases, serve their sentences in special prisons with modified discipline and an occupational therapy based on psycho-therapeutic experience. The Central Association of Mental Welfare co-operates in their after-care.[1] While these measures apply to people with a low intelligence, experiments in the psychological treatment of prisoners drew attention to the neurotics and psychopaths. Before the war it was suggested that a special institution should be established which would have a fourfold function: it should serve as a psychiatric clinical hospital, as a penal institution for a selected group of prisoners, as a colony for the detention of non-adaptable prisoners, and as an observation and treatment centre for abnormal Borstal lads.[2] Such an institution would offer invaluable opportunity for new experience and research.

[1] Fox, p. 110, with reference to *Report Prison Commissioners, 1926*.

[2] East and de Hubert, *Psychological Treatment of Crime* (1939), p. 159. *Report Prison Commissioners, 1938*, p. 51.

Plans like the foregoing English proposals commend themselves from the point of view of prison administration. The prison gets rid of its most difficult personalities, who themselves gain by their transfer to special institutions under medical supervision. From the wider outlook of penal policy, however, it must be asked: what better methods are available at the special institutions which are not applicable in an ordinary prison? The essence of medical treatment is a close, continuous observation of the individual patient. An institution for subnormal prisoners could not provide the same facilities for individualized attention as a mental hospital, but would be in a better position to do this than an ordinary prison. It could have a selected and specially trained staff with a higher ratio of personnel to prisoners. Deprivation of liberty could be enforced by less obtrusive means, e.g. unbreakable panes instead of visible iron bars. The daily task and the tempo of work, general routine, and disciplinary punishments could be determined on the basis of the individual's capacities, without having to take into account the possible impression on other prisoners. Against these advantages must be set the harmful effect of bringing together so many difficult personalities. An ordinary mental hospital will absorb its usual proportion of 2 per cent. dangerous patients.[1] A prison, built and maintained with the paramount object of security, faces difficulties with its 20 per cent. abnormal personalities. An institution where all the inmates are abnormal criminals is in an awkward position, the more so since transfer to such a régime makes the prisoner conscious of his special circumstances and brings him into an environment where the sight of many others in similar and more advanced mental states fosters his eccentricities and weakens any possible resistance.

These considerations are confirmed by experience, wherever a generous recognition of psychopathic states opens up escape from the rigidity of ordinary prison routine. The prospect of transfer to the more indulgent medical routine of a psychiatric prison annex or a mental hospital increased the prison psychoses, which were interpreted as defence reactions, if not deliberate simulations of psychopathic personalities, especially among habitual criminals from the big cities.[2] When numbers of these were brought together the application of the non-restraint methods of a modern mental

[1] Aschaffenburg, *VDA* i. 82 et seq.

[2] Wilmanns, l.c., pp. 201 et seq. and *passim*; W. N. East, *Medical Aspects of Crime* (1936), pp. 387 et seq.; Young, 73 *J. Ment. Sc.* 80.

hospital became impossible. Serious difficulties resulted in a lack of security, which led to the establishment of special enclosed departments with a stricter discipline for dangerous antisocial abnormal patients. In view of this experience in Germany[1] and America,[2] the pendulum is swinging back to a policy of keeping psychopathic personalities as far as possible within a properly adjusted prison routine.

As long as imprisonment is a monotonous régime of restraint and compulsory labour enforced by a punitive discipline, special consideration for abnormal personalities appears as a mitigation of the prevailing hardships of legal punishment. Individualization of treatment may make it possible to apply appropriate methods of dealing with psychopathic offenders without lessening their responsibility under the law. The principle of custodial differentiation permits keeping within the ordinary penal régime prisoners who, owing to their morbid irritability, cannot stand the continuous strain of maximum security conditions. Rational classification does not mean indulgent, but appropriate treatment. The loosening of physical restraint may be offset by other disadvantages to the prisoner. Psychopaths unable to respond to the incentives of a Progressive Stage system may be kept under a régime without vertical differentiation, but they thereby lose the chance of winning privileges in higher stages. Transfer to special departments for antisocial psychopaths should carry the risk of being detained for an indefinite period instead of serving the fixed term of the original sentence. According to numerous continental laws, before the trial court a plea of limited responsibility means the risk of indefinite detention in addition to, or in lieu of, a definite prison sentence. The defendant will therefore insist on his full responsibility and accept his sentence, but once in prison exhibit his mental weakness in order to be transferred to a less rigid régime. The Danish system avoids this pitfall by giving the court power to order indeterminate detention, should the prisoner prove unadaptable to ordinary prison routine. The Danish island of Livø in the Liim Fjord is used for the internment of feeble-minded criminals and sexual offenders. Inmates are committed at an early age; three-quarters of the receptions are between fourteen and twenty-four years of age. In the early thirties the daily population

[1] L. Frede, 46 *ZStW* 235.

[2] E. Lekkerkerker, *Reformatories for Women in the United States* (1931), p. 228, with reference to Dr. Edith Spaulding, sometime Director of the Psychopathic Hospital of Bedford Hills Reformatory, N.Y.

was about sixty-six. After three years a special examination is required, with a view to possible release. Out of 161 inmates released, 58 had to be recommitted.[1]

Even the most perfect classification will not completely solve the problem of abnormal offenders. Certain types of law-breakers with a high proportion of feeble-minded and psychopathic personalities should be removed altogether from the scope of the traditional machinery of criminal justice and treated in the light of their personal needs and social difficulties rather than that of the legal offences they happen to commit. The process of decriminalization of juvenile delinquency in most civilized countries, and of delinquent women in the United States, gave constructive methods the most effective inroad into the traditional sphere of legal punishments. A similar process of decriminalization of persons unable to adjust themselves to a socially useful or tolerable existence serves preventive purposes. This applies to certain types of beggars, vagrants, and idle and disorderly people who by a weakness of will-power and lack of energy are doomed to persistent waywardness and destitution. They are 'asocial' rather than antisocial and criminal. The increase in the number of their petty offences is a nuisance rather than a danger. It defies repeated punishment, and shows permanent maladjustment. Three-quarters of this group may fairly be regarded as mentally subnormal. With them, a rational criminal law should distinguish between acts which should be prohibited and must be punished, and a behaviour which indicates that an adult is 'in need of care and protection' (Claud Mullins) for his own sake as well as for the protection of the community. Begging with threats or fraud, and violations of certain regulations concerning prostitution, should remain punishable offences, while simple begging, certain forms of vagrancy, prostitution on the part of minors or mental defectives call for welfare and administrative measures. The ultimate resort is the internment of a considerable number of these unadaptable persons in agricultural or labour colonies. By such a solution the law, by new preventive powers, makes up for what it loses in repressive activity.

In England the Mental Deficiency Act of 1913 provides for the reception in hospitals, on the petition of a relative or friend, of neglected, delinquent, and drunken feeble-minded persons and moral imbeciles by a non-criminal procedure without conviction for a particular offence.[2] Beyond the range of certifiable mental

[1] von Hentig, 49 *Schw. Z.* 203.

[2] 3 & 4 Geo. V, c. 28, s. 5.

defect, from 1926 onwards new provisions have been officially contemplated for long-term segregation of weak-minded maladjusted people unable to adapt themselves to the world at large.[1] Recent American legislation further illustrates this tendency to protect society by a decriminalization of certain groups of subnormal potential offenders. In 1939, California, Illinois, Michigan, and Minnesota enacted statutory provisions for the commitment, through non-criminal proceedings with the co-operation of expert psychiatrists, of sexually aggressive psychopathic offenders to a hospital for the treatment of the individual and the protection of society.[2]

Other legal systems pursue similar objects in reforming the law of vagrancy. A statute of the Swiss Canton of Zurich of 1925 provides that persons who exhibit a criminal tendency, or are disorderly or idle, may be committed to an institution for training or detention for one or two subsequent periods of two to five years.[3] In the course of German criminal law reform the Draft Code of 1925 anticipated the divorce of 'asocial behaviour' (*gemeinschädliches Verhalten*) from the scope of criminal law. Experience of practical social work led to suggestions that a Guardianship Court or a similar non-litigious tribunal should be empowered to order the detention of persons unable to care for themselves and tending to become wayward on account of weak-mindedness, alcoholism, or habits of begging or vagrancy.[4] It was assumed that such a comprehensive provision might involve the segregation of some 8,000 to 10,000 persons, a figure roughly corresponding to the total of—temporary—inmates of German workhouses before the First World War. The legislature, however, did not accept such far-reaching proposals. The Amendment of 1933 maintained the double-track system of inflicting punishment for certain forms of begging, idleness, vagrancy, and prostitution, together with an additional detention of two years in a workhouse. This solution allows retributive repression too much scope and preventive protection too little.

The practical problem of treatment for abnormal personalities with criminal tendencies has proved more complicated than the lawgivers anticipated. It is not solved simply by shifting the onus from the law to medicine. The use of psychotherapy and

[1] *Report Prison Commissioners, 1926*, pp. 18 et seq.

[2] S. and E. Glueck, *After-conduct of Discharged Offenders* (1945), p. 98.

[3] I. Eiserhardt, *Ziele eines Bewahrungsgesetzes* (Dtsch. Verein für öffentl. und private Fürsorge, 1929), p. 157.

[4] Ibid., *passim*. Also Eiserhardt, 4 *Zeitschr. f. psych. Hygiene* 66, and 52 *ZStW* 14.

residential treatment in the controlled community of colonies and Q-camps will keep a growing proportion of subnormal personalities suitable to therapeutic approach out of the bounds of ordinary penal institutions. For less suitable other types future legislation will substitute for a fixed prison sentence an indeterminate commitment for detention in a mental department or institution. For the rest, a differentiated prison régime should find it less difficult to absorb subnormal personalities. With these modifications, a policy of dilution seems practicable and even more desirable than herding together a number of unmanageable characters.

CHAPTER XVII

CONCLUSIONS AND LEGAL IMPLICATIONS

THE TREND OF PENAL REFORM

PENAL reform is in a state of transition. With regard to prison labour, education, religious work, social welfare work, and after-care the traditional routine of penal administration has been challenged for more than twenty years. The new approach is rendered even more striking by the treatment of special groups such as juveniles and adolescents, women, habitual criminals, and the mentally abnormal. After more than 150 years of prison reform the outstanding feature of the present movement is its scepticism concerning imprisonment altogether, and its search for new and more adequate methods of treatment outside prison walls. These tendencies, not always consistent and sometimes divergent, have the prisoner's readjustment as their common purpose. This conception of readjustment makes no presumptuous claims to produce a religious conversion or a moral rebirth, claims so often compromised by the striking contrast between the proclaimed aim and the repressive means applied. Nor does it pretend to make a man a law-abiding citizen by a wise handling of his economic and social problems alone. The efforts are to be focused on the man himself within his personal environment. Readjustment is concerned with the individual as well as the community to which he is required to adapt himself. Penal and reformative treatment has taken over this outlook from social work. Constructive methods to-day owe much to the experience of social case-work and to a psychological insight into man's personal conflicts. The new educational optimism with its active approach to conduct and the formation of personality is no longer barred from penal and reformative institutions.[1]

Differentiation of Treatment

As a means to social readjustment present penal policy resorts to the principle of differentiation. In the past, transportation, the separate system, or the industrialization of prisons were successively praised and repudiated as the panacea. Later, the American reformatory, probation, and parole were in danger of being wrecked by an indiscriminate application to each and every

[1] G. H. Dession, 47 *Yale L. J.* 319, 327.

prisoner. With the 'reasonable man' of classical political economy, the 'criminal' and the 'prisoner' had to give way as concepts to the idea of the human personality as something extremely complex and expressing itself in behaviour which, social or antisocial, had multiple causes. Differentiation, however, remains empty and formal unless it explains the criteria by which it differentiates. It has a negative and a positive meaning. Negatively, it is easily abused and may be made a pretext and cover for consigning unwanted types of prisoner to the oblivion of some special régime so as to preserve the ordinary routine for a select few inmates with brighter prospects. An approved school might be willing to adopt a more liberal form of discipline, if it could only get rid of the criminal elements. A prison would consent to an experiment with more active inmate participation, if only someone else would take the psychopaths. The *Wickersham Report* required separate provisions for the insane, the feeble-minded, the tubercular, prisoners with contagious venereal diseases, sex perverts, drug addicts, the aged, and the crippled. Only what remains after the exclusion of these groups would be regarded as the general prison population, which should enjoy the benefits of a custodial differentiation into maximum, medium, and minimum security groups.[1] Such a programme, though reasonable as far as it goes, involves the risk that the suggested reform might be more concerned with removing the obvious misfits and trouble-makers from the ordinary prison community than with a determined approach to the treatment problems of those who prove unadaptable to routine methods. The same attitude of escape lies beneath the radical suggestion that the obvious failures of penal and correctional treatment should be overcome by a new departure for an unknown destination. In spite of the strenuous efforts of generations of prison reformers, the shortcomings, fallacies, and inherent contradictions even of a progressive penal system are notorious. The substitution of scientific, remedial, socio-medical methods for punishment is recommended because of an alleged superiority which is mainly due to the fact that so far they have neither been fully explained and critically discussed nor tested by experience. Criminology will hail the day when science comes to its succour with all its methods for diagnosis and treatment of the socially unadaptable.[2] Most advocates of such a revolutionary course, however, prefer to expatiate on the undoubted failures and limits of penal and

[1] *Wickersham Report*, ix. 63.

[2] H. Weihofen, *Insanity as a Defence in Criminal Law* (1933), p. 442.

reformative treatment, rather than to survey the new efficient methods and their probable results. Throughout the preceding chapters of this book an attempt has been made to explore the possibilities of penal and reformative treatment, and to discuss how far science as well as a conscious personal approach have been able to contribute by constructive efforts to the readjustment of criminals.

The practical result to be desired from this consideration is a positive differentiation. While no effort should be spared to attain and keep the highest possible standards of ordinary prison administration, special methods of treatment should be made available to particular groups. Owing to successive inroads into the normal routine the remainder of the general prison population is gradually decreasing, while even their régime is affected by the experience gained with the selected treatment groups. This is the way in which so far progress has been achieved. Juveniles have been brought under the jurisdiction of Juvenile Courts with their auxiliary social services. Adolescents are eligible for Borstal training. This experience led to the Wakefield scheme, a modified extension of the Borstal idea to certain types of adult offenders, and this again to the 'corrective training' projected in the Criminal Justice Bill, 1938. In the United States women offenders are liable to a special régime in appropriate reformatories. Probation with its various possibilities by no means exhausted is an even more outstanding development, which considerably lessens the scope of traditional punishment.

These facts suggest a prevailing tendency to a 'decriminalization'[1] of certain groups of offenders. Decriminalization has a twofold meaning. First, it implies that although the new sanction can be legally applied only if a criminal offence has been committed, the treatment is selected and administered not in relation to the gravity of the offence, but to the prospects and needs of the individual. The Children and Young Persons Act, 1933, lays down that 'every court in dealing with a child or a young person who is brought before it either as being in need of care and protection or as an offender or otherwise shall have regard to the welfare of the child or young person and shall in a proper case take steps for removing him from undesirable surroundings and for securing that proper provision is made for his education and training' (s. 44). The Criminal Justice Bill defines the legal conditions of Borstal training and 'corrective training' by the provision that the

[1] S. and E. Glueck, *After-conduct of Discharged Offenders* (1945), p. 99.

court must be satisfied that, by reason of the offender's character or habits, this type of discipline is expedient for his reformation and for the prevention of crime. American Juvenile Courts are called to select the appropriate treatment for delinquency in the general and comprehensive meaning of the word, even if the procedure is the sequel to a particular act of theft or wilful damage. According to the Youth Correction Authority Acts and a recent Federal Correction Bill, the final disposition of an adolescent or young adult found guilty depends on the results of interviews by experts and social case-studies. In Denmark the decision between a fixed prison sentence and indefinite detention in a mental institution depends on the individual's response to prison treatment. A final solution of the vagrancy problem will probably strike out a number of relevant offences from the criminal codes and provide instead for the appropriate treatment of those who—for their own sake or for the protection of the community—are 'in need of care and protection'. In all these cases the offence committed and its assumed gravity do not affect the considerations which determine the fate of the offender.

Decriminalization means, secondly, the substitution for punishment of another type of sanction, either reformative or protective. Supervision by a probation officer, committal to the care of a fit person or to an approved school are measures which apply equally to juveniles in need of care and protection and to those found guilty of a criminal offence. A probation order is not a sentence. Borstal training, under the present law, and 'corrective training' and 'preventive detention' according to the Criminal Justice Bill are to be given in lieu of imprisonment. By the Swiss Criminal Code the court may send a man to a mental institution, to a workhouse, or to preventive detention in lieu of punishment.

Do these considerations justify the conception of decriminalization, inherently opposed as it is to legal punishment? Under the lead of Swiss lawgivers, continental jurisprudence has taken considerable pains in developing a dualistic doctrine of punishment on the one hand, and measures of reformation and security on the other. From a realistic point of view, this antithesis is only a temporary expedient. The German Juvenile Court Act of 1923, for example, contrasted educational measures with legal punishments by prescribing that if the former are 'sufficient', the court should refrain from the latter, and at the same time provided that even punishment should be so administered as to help the juvenile with his education. As long as the sole meaning of legal punishment was hardship based on the gravity of the offence, a sanction chosen because it took account of the offender's prospects and needs, and designed to promote either his social adjustment or the protection of society or both, could find no place within the scope of what the law regarded as punishments.

The increasing use of corrective and protective sanctions, however, is apt to react upon punishment proper. Since more and more groups of offenders become liable to the new forms of treatment, they appear as legitimate functions of the criminal law. Innovations first associated with non-punitive methods of treatment have been adopted in ordinary punishments. A gradual vertical differentiation, first developed by Captain Maconochie and Sir Walter Crofton, came to be typical of the American reformatory system, but by many countries it was adopted as an implement of ordinary prison routine. The privileges first conceded to English preventive detention under the Prevention of Crime Act, 1908, are no longer incompatible with the long-sentence division of a convict prison. The educational treatment of juvenile delinquents had far-reaching effects on the attitude towards adolescent and even adult offenders. The corrective and protective measures were the vanguard of new ideas, and anticipated the later development of legal punishments. The exception is becoming the rule. To-day the most significant purposes of penal policy are pursued by the new measures, while imprisonment pure and simple applies to the residue for which no appropriate methods have been found. This development has affected the conception of punishment itself. From a technical point of view, committal to an approved school and probation are not punishments. A term in an American reformatory, in an English Borstal institution, as well as preventive detention, would be imposed in a sentence, but it is open to argument whether these 'new forms of sentence' are inflicting 'punishment'. Given an interpretation based on the facts it must be recognized that a merely punitive reaction is only one of some possible types of legal punishment. Legal punishment is a measure taken by the State to deal with an offence committed with a guilty mind. The removal of substantial groups of law-breakers from the traditional conceptions of criminal law is a preliminary step by which a narrow concept of legal punishment is supplemented, until in the end it assimilates itself to the wider idea of corrective and preventive treatment. Before our very eyes, legal punishment is undergoing a fundamental change, and this is not the result of theoretical considerations, but of experience with growing application of reformative and preventive measures. The trend of to-day is through the 'decriminalization' of an increasing variety of types of offenders to socialization of legal punishment.

Testing the Results

What are the practical results of this development? Are the new methods of treatment, to the extent they have been accepted, justified by a corresponding improvement in the crime position? It was easy for the classic school of criminal law to point to the overwhelming majority of law-abiding citizens unaffected by fluctuations of crime and recidivism as evidence of the deterrent effect of, and the general confidence in, the administration of just retribution. The fallacy of this argument is obvious. The reasons for avoiding conflict with the law are even more multiple and obscure than the causes of crime. Once penal policy ceases to be content merely with impressing the general public and accepts responsibility for preventing from further wrongdoing the individual offender who undergoes penal and correctional treatment, it bears a heavy burden of proof. The new outlook raised great expectations.[1] Every case of recidivism goes to its debit account and is taken to mean a failure of method. Earlier, discussing recidivism, we remarked that every second offender committed to prison has been there before, and that every fourth prisoner has had more than four previous convictions. These alarming figures are partly a matter of selection. Offenders with a crime record are more likely to be sent to prison. If successes and failures are to be estimated there must be 'cross-examination' by follow-up studies of discharged probationers and prisoners. A fair estimate depends on applying the right standards for what is to be regarded as a successful or unsatisfactory after-career. On the basis of personal judgement by staff members, often impossible to verify, it might be said that correctional institutions claim something near 70 or 80 per cent. more or less satisfactory results. By thorough case-studies and by assessing as unsatisfactory every case in which there had been any violation of the law, Sheldon and Eleanor Glueck reversed the usual optimistic estimate. In a first five-year follow-up period, juveniles who came before the Boston Juvenile Court, and adolescents discharged from Massachusetts Reformatory, turned out to be successfully readjusted at a rate of less than 20 per cent. In practice, comparative mass observation can deal only with the less

[1] G. H. Dession, l.c., p. 326.

significant, but more easily accessible, rates of actual re-conviction. In England and Wales 70 per cent. of the young offenders and 90 per cent. of the older were free of further charges during a subsequent five-year period. Criminal justice can claim that the majority of those found guilty and disposed of by the courts do not offend again.[1] The after-conduct varies with the type of treatment. Before the war the percentage of male first-offenders who kept out of the courts was 70·7 for probationers, 71·2 for those committed to prison, and 80·2 for those fined. As has been pointed out, these variations alone do not warrant conclusions on the respective values of probation, imprisonment, and fines. As the outcome depends on the offender's character and on the sentence those differences are due to selection as well as to causation. Different sentences are given to different types of offenders. As to recidivists, the preceding investigation has confirmed the general impression that the crime risk increases with every subsequent conviction.

The last-mentioned observation should dispel any complacency. A majority of first-offenders with subsequent clean records makes no better case for reformative treatment than does the mass of law-abiding citizens for the alleged salutary results of retributory punishment. Not every clean record indicates genuine readjustment. The ascertainment of the causes of readjustment is less advanced than the investigations of the conditions of crime. Individual case-studies alone can throw some light on the factors correlated with success or failure. The inference from the formidable research work presented by Sheldon and Eleanor Glueck is no great argument in favour of the methods of treatment to which their studies apply. As strong, almost, as destiny, natural endowment, home background, and experience before imprisonment are much more closely related to the offender's after-career than treatment and response to it. Close observation of final readjustment shows that it is primarily due to maturation. Within a given group the amount of crime slowly recedes and the general behaviour gradually conforms with the standards of the community. In the groups investigated by Sheldon and Eleanor Glueck, the proportion of former juvenile delinquents who kept clear of further criminal activities rose from 14·6 per cent. in the first five-year follow-up period to 26·8 per cent. in the second and 36·6 per cent. in the third, the proportion of former adolescent offenders from 19·9 per cent. to 30·1 per cent. and 30·8 per cent. At the same time, there was a marked tendency to change to a better

[1] *Crim. Stat. 1938*, p. xxi.

environment, an improvement in family relationships, no increase in illicit occupations and, even during the general depression, there was a decrease in offences against property. Turning to the individuals within these groups the authors found that young men, differing in their respective ages and in the age at which their delinquency began, reached a similar stage on their road to social readjustment after the expiration of the same time from the outset of their criminal career. Readaptation to the accepted standards of the community takes a certain time. The underlying factor is a process of growing to maturity, which may be retarded. This explains variations in the criminal careers of young offenders. It may be associated with a man's biological development from youth to adolescence and mature age. The mid-thirties are the crucial years. If reformation has not occurred by the thirty-sixth year, no further progress can be expected from the mere fact of the individual's natural development.[1]

These criminological investigations throw a new light, if not upon the causes, at least on the dynamics and inner nature of social readjustment. They are confirmed by the corresponding experience of medical psychology. Psychiatrists report changes in certain pathological traits of juvenile psychopaths, which they explain as a counterpart to the normal process of growing up. After stormy years, arrogance, irritability, instability, lust for adventure, and violent outbursts may give way to a sober and reasonable attitude, which makes late adjustment possible even in serious cases of wayward and criminal youth, so long as the family does not lose patience and refuse further help.[2] This is illustrated by the after-careers of many young mental patients treated for 'moral insanity'.[3] In retrospect the maladjustment of their stormy youth seemed different only in time and degree from normal puberty conflicts, while their growth to social maturity was facilitated by emigration to America or else a marked change to a social position and occupation where they were free from the shadows of their own past. In normal development, physical and intellectual growth must be accompanied by 'emotional maturation'. If the latter is delayed or retarded, social maladjustment will often result.[4] Like criminology, psychiatry regards time as the essential factor in the treatment of mental cases.[5]

[1] S. and E. Glueck, l.c., p. 79 and *passim*.
[2] K. Wilmanns, *Verminderte Zurechnungsfähigkeit* (1927), p. 297.
[3] D. Pachantoni, 47 *Arch. Psych.* 27. [4] A. Maberly, 16 *Brit. J. Ed. Psych.* 5, 9.
[5] D. K. Henderson and R. D. Gillespie, *Textbook on Psychiatry* (6th ed. 1944), p. 651.

There are further parallels between penal reform and the rise of psychiatry. Both began about 150 years ago, when the conscience of mankind was first aroused by reports of the miserable and immoral state of contemporary prisons, and at the same time a new era of medicine dawned, not content to keep the insane in safe custody, but eager to take care of, and to treat, the mentally ill.[1] In both movements the slight achievements seem to belie the strenuous efforts of generations. Criminality and recidivism have been mass phenomena until to-day. Psychiatry knows of no remedy which might cure general psychoses or alter a mental defect or a deep-rooted character deviation. And yet, the true progress of psychiatry is obvious, if the fate even of the incurable is considered. With the abandonment of physical force and mechanical restraint the most violent symptoms have disappeared. When direct influence has no effect upon an apparently unalterable pathological process or personality structure, special treatment can sometimes prevent further harm and deterioration, and facilitate a result that nature itself might achieve by a belated maturity.

The records of penal policy must be set against this background. About the middle of last century, when Mary Carpenter and her friends challenged the sombre fatalism of the period towards the 'criminal classes' and their totally uneducated offspring, the criminal was separated by a great gulf from the life of the community. Since then, utter hooliganism has evolved into the gangsterism of a minority of professionals, while the majority of criminals in our midst are concerned in more sophisticated offences against property, thereby confronting the administration of penal policy with the task of checking antisocial activities within a less heterogeneous society. This trend is primarily due to the effects of compulsory education and the consequent rise in social standards. The improvement in penal methods, itself part of this wider movement, followed the general progress with a certain timelag.

To isolate this factor, investigation must be confined to a limited field of observation. Between the two wars, in England and Wales, the number of persons tried summarily for indictable offences, rose from 56,275 in 1927 to 62,103 in 1932. Within this five-year period the re-conviction rates of male first-offenders decreased for all age-groups. In the subsequent five years the

[1] G. Zilboorg and G. W. Henry, *History of Medical Psychology* (1941) p. 313 and *passim*.

re-conviction rate for young men between sixteen and twenty sank from 30·3 per cent. in respect of those first before the court in 1927 to 27·6 per cent. in respect of those first before the court in 1932; for men between twenty-one and twenty-nine from 24·3 per cent. to 23·6 per cent., for those between thirty and forty from 17·8 per cent. to 15·7 per cent., for those of forty and over from 12 per cent. to 10 per cent.[1] This development coincided with a growing use of probation, an extension of the Borstal system, the improvement of prison industries, and the functioning of voluntary educational and social services for prisoners. It is still open to question whether the improved prospects of readjustment are due to a more progressive penal policy, but at least penal reform has not hindered the offenders' improving chances of rehabilitation. Even if the socialization of penal and reformative treatment had no marked influence on the amount of crime and recidivism but left the delinquency rate steady, it would be better than mere punitive action. Legal punishment is a loss to the community as well as a personal hardship to the prisoner. Valuable assets are preserved to the community whenever criminal justice restricts those punishments which involve loss of liberty and social status and the destruction of family links and economic functions. By gradually substituting constructive efforts for punitive action the State recognizes the reality of moral forces and strengthens those fundamentals upon which the lives of human individuals and communities ultimately rest.

TREATMENT TRIBUNALS

The prevailing trend of penal reform ultimately affects the machinery of justice. So far most reforms have been undertaken or attempted either in the executive sphere by practical work inside or outside institutions, or—even more sporadically—by legislative alterations of substantive criminal law. The Juvenile Court movement began with the reform of a judicial tribunal. Its success suggests that differentiated methods of treatment require a machinery suitable for investigating and settling the manifold psychological and social questions which must be answered before an individual delinquent can rightly be assigned to a particular treatment. In the administration of criminal justice the emphasis is shifting from the judicial to the executive side. The latter is no longer confined simply to the 'execution' of a judicial sentence

[1] *Crim. Stat. 1927*, p. 76; *1932*, p. 64; *1938*, p. xxi and *passim*.

based on abstract legal rules; the judicial decision itself is expected to aim at the best available treatment, given the offender's potentialities and needs as well as the needs of society. This leads to the crucial issue: whether the law courts ought to select and decide the offender's treatment; or whether this function should be handed over to a new type of agency, especially qualified.

In England the case for separate treatment tribunals was first raised through a comparative study of English, French, and German judiciaries.[1] Professional judges are trained to establish the truth about contested facts and perform this function with a high degree of objectivity and fairness; but they are not in touch with penal institutions. In England a newly appointed High Court Judge may go on circuit and hold Assizes, after a long career at the bar exclusively devoted to civil and commercial cases. This supports the view that in principle the trial court should be concerned only with the defendant's acquittal or conviction, and leave the sentence to a special tribunal. On the European continent, as an inheritance from the inquisitorial tradition, professional judges are accustomed to exert a discretionary power in calling in experts and are themselves bound to decide on facts. Even there, numerous critics have found the trial court in its immediate concern with the alleged crime unsuitable for the protection of society against dangerous subnormal persons. Instead, administrative tribunals, or—better still—the non-litigious procedure of guardianship courts, have been suggested.[2]

The movement for separate treatment tribunals has its most ardent supporters in the United States. There parole boards determine the date of preliminary discharge. Following the precedents of New Jersey and Massachusetts, a number of behaviour clinics and classification centres assign sentenced prisoners to a particular institution or a special régime within the prison system of the State, and even fix, within the limits determined by the judicial sentence, the prison term which the prisoner has actually to serve.[3] The growing significance attached to classification of prisoners and specialization of treatment makes the disposal of convicted offenders a special function of the administration of

[1] Ensor, *Courts and Judges in France, Germany, and England* (1933), pp. 89 et seq. Similar views expressed by H. Mannheim, *Dilemma of Penal Reform* (1939), pp. 201 et seq.; *Criminal Justice and Social Reconstruction* (1946), pp. 223 et seq., and by R. M. Jackson, *Machinery of Justice in England* (1942), p. 182.

[2] K. Wilmanns, l.c., p. 316.

[3] J. D. Sears, 23 *Journal* 249; F. Loveland, ibid., 620.

criminal justice and a function which demands a machinery of its own.

Separate disposition tribunals have been suggested, consisting of medical, psychological, and criminological specialists, unimpeded by the technicalities of the traditional law of evidence.[1] The first legislative project was the Model Draft Youth Correction Authority Act, promulgated by the American Law Institute in 1940, which proposed to divest the criminal court of the greater part of its sentencing power and, within certain limits, to entrust the final fate of a convicted adolescent offender to a youth correction authority.[2] In 1941 California enacted the first statute on these lines, though with modifications in favour of the powers of the court.[3] The Federal Correction Bill, which in 1943 was before the Judiciary Committee of Congress, tried to reconcile the functioning of a treatment agency with an unimpaired judicial prerogative.[4] In the case of adolescents, it leaves the court the choice between probation, an ordinary adult sentence, or a committal to the youth correction authority, while in the case of adults over twenty-four the court may give a provisional maximum sentence, to be reviewed in accordance with expert recommendations submitted by the adult correction division when the first six months of the sentence have expired.

This survey of legislative proposals and recent statutory provisions shows that the principle of separation between convicting and sentencing powers permits different forms and degrees of separation. The problem is not to choose between judicial or administrative competence, between law and science, but to strike a balance between the criminal court and penal administration. Every form of indeterminate sentence means a shifting of influence from the trial court to the penal administration. If an English Juvenile Court commits a child to an approved school, the committal lasts for three years or up to the age of fifteen whichever time is longer, but within this period the school authorities have the power to discharge a pupil on licence and to recall him. If, on the recommendation of the Prison Commissioners a Court

[1] S. Glueck, 41 *Harvard L. R.* 453, 476; S. B. Warner and H. B. Cabot, 'Judges and Law Reform', *Survey of Crime and Criminal Justice in Boston*, by the Harvard Law School (1936), v. 156 et seq.; N. F. Cantor, 29 *Journal* 51; id., *Crime and Society* (1939), pp. 296 et seq.

[2] Official Draft Youth Correction Authority Act, American Law Institute, June 1940.

[3] California Assembly Bill 777, ch. 937 (1941); *Deering* 1941 Suppl.

[4] For comment see 53 *Yale L. J.* 773, and S. Glueck, 56 *Harvard L. R.* 839.

of Quarter Sessions sends a lad to Borstal, the sentence is for a fixed term of from two to three years, usually for two years. Before the war the Prison Commissioners had the choice between nine institutions differing in their régime from enclosed prisons to open camps; they could release the lad on licence at any time after six months; for a year after the expiration of the whole sentence he remained under their supervision; on a report of the visiting committee, the Secretary of State could transfer an incorrigible offender from Borstal to prison, or vice versa a suitable young offender from prison or even penal servitude to Borstal.[1] When a Swedish court holds that an offender of limited responsibility may not be susceptible of punishment, but dangerous to the community, it refers the case to a central authority under the chairmanship of the head of the penal administration, and on its recommendation alone it is empowered to order the offender's detention.[2] In all these instances, those with special experience exert influence on the selection and application of penal and reformative treatment, without encroaching on the sentencing power of the court. This line has been crossed by those American attempts to solve the problem which assign the function of sentencing itself to new tribunals or agencies of social administration. While the proposed federal law at least leaves the court a certain discretion in surrendering its functions, the Model Act of the American Law Institute and the California Act make the loss of competence mandatory. Suggestions for giving the trial judge a place on the bench of the treatment tribunal[3] were not accepted. The law makers wanted to replace the divergent decisions by numerous courts throughout the State by the pooled experience and concerted efforts of one centralized expert authority.

The foregoing analysis distinguishes between provisions supplementing and those supplanting the sentencing power of the courts. This distinction is justified by general considerations which transcend the political. By recent American tendencies, a court of law would retain its sentencing power only where constructive measures are unnecessary, or (in those cases where a life sentence or a capital sentence is compulsory) ruled out by the law. Whenever social and criminological considerations are involved the court must refrain from action and respect the prerogative of the

[1] 8 Edw. VII, c. 59, ss. 3 and 7.

[2] Mezger, *Strafrecht* (2nd ed. 1933), p. 46 n. 3; Petrén, 19 *MoSchrKrim.* 513.

[3] Warner and Cabot, l.c., p. 170; H. Mannheim, *Dilemma*, p. 207; S. and E. Glueck, *After-conduct of Discharged Offenders* (1945), p. 101 n. 1.

new correction authority. This means a divorce between the legal and social approach to crime and punishment, and so frustrates efforts to win the criminal lawyer over to the cause of penal reform. If it does not actually endanger individual liberty, it does threaten our confidence in the efficiency of constitutional safeguards. Next to the finding of guilt the sentence sets the final seal on the fate of a human being often connected by personal links with his fellow men. To make such interference with civil liberties tolerable, the community demands certain guarantees. The generations vary in their attitude to the legal institutions in which they put their trust. Independence of the judiciary, trial by jury, and lay magistrates, obtained and defended as the bulwark of justice in a free state, are now being denounced as formalistic obstacles to the rationalization of penal policy. On the other hand, the great expectations raised by the claims of psychology, education, and social welfare work have created an almost unlimited belief in the abilities of the expert. Professionalization in the personal care of other people, however, involves the risk of 'a new despotism' of the social administration which is not aware of the rights and dignity of every man, even in need and despair. In the political field, during the totalitarian régimes in Europe the law courts maintained their independence longer than any other institution, with the result that their functions were drastically curtailed and replaced by an almost unchecked administrative discretion. Even in the United States, the *Wickersham Report*, while in principle in sympathy with the ideal of completely indeterminate sentences administered by expert tribunals, held that its immediate adoption was neither possible nor desirable. The supporters of such a radical measure cannot count on sufficient public confidence, until diagnosis and prognosis and the actual decisions as to treatment have reached that degree of scientific accuracy and impartiality which their supporters expect.[1]

These considerations strengthen the case against separate treatment tribunals. The alternative is to adapt the law courts to the social demands of our time. This entails separating conviction and sentence into two subsequent phases of criminal procedure so far unknown to continental law. For the decision as to the treatment of convicted offenders, there should be an informal law of evidence, opportunity for observation and examination, and expert recommendations should be put before the sentencing

[1] *Wickersham Report*, ix. 145. Outspoken criticism by J. Hall, *American Bar Association Journal*, May 1942, p. 317.

court. Sentences must be flexible with due allowance for their final determination in the light of further experience and the prisoner's response to treatment. Again, since the sentence takes its final shape during the time it is served by the prisoner, a judicial element should be included in the tribunal competent for treatment decisions.

Steps would have to be taken to ensure that the court had available the advice of independent and impartial experts. Judges would have to be trained in certain fundamentals of crimino-psychology, so as to be able to understand and weigh the expert evidence before them. But even under the most favourable legal conditions, the crucial question arises, what instruments can be offered by criminology better than the traditional legalism modified by common sense? While our knowledge about the dynamics of social and antisocial behaviour is still fragmentary, the present trend of criminology is in some measure favourable to those practical demands. Scientific interest is shifting from the general phenomenon of criminality and its correlation with economic and general biological facts to the individual criminal and his career. Mass observation is being supplemented by individual case-studies. Sentencing courts and parole boards will benefit from the present tendency to turn from the causes of crime to an empirical prognosis of the offender's future conduct. The causative and prognostic approaches are not mutually antagonistic. An understanding of crime causation makes it easier to gauge the prospects of an offender. Facts which according to general experience appear to be causes of crime are symptoms which with others indicate a probable persistence in antisocial behaviour. Other symptoms may be explained as the result of selection rather than causation. The question whether a broken home produces juvenile delinquency, or whether irregular work is evidence and consequence of waywardness rather than its cause seems irrelevant in view of the fact that both factors involve a considerable crime risk.

CRIME PREDICTION

In America this branch of criminology has been developed to such a degree that it has seemed practicable to present the experience available for prognostic purposes in a condensed style for immediate application. This idea is the essence of crime prediction. By comprehensive investigations into the personal conditions, antecedents, and careers of a great number of successful and unsuccessful probationers and paroled prisoners, sufficient experience has been collected to correlate certain factors with success and others with failure in social readjustment. These correlations make it possible to predict how other offenders in similar circumstances might behave during and after a corresponding penal and correctional treatment. This practice of deducing from a great number of typical occurrences in the past the probability of a similar course of events in the future is the same operation as that upon which insurance actuaries rely for computing expectation of life or probability of insurable damages.[1] Only the complexity of social behaviour and its motives makes prediction of the likelihood of a breach of probation and parole less accurate than a calculation of the probable frequency of death, fire, and accidents.

Crime prediction methods were first suggested by H. Hart[2] and successfully pursued by E. W. Burgess and C. Tibbits in Illinois, Sheldon and Eleanor Glueck in Massachusetts, and G. B. Vold and E. D. Monachesi in Minnesota.[3] As a result, prediction tables have been formulated which on the basis of given facts indicate the probability of an offender's success or failure during and after probation or institutional treatment. While some investigators have contented themselves with correlating facts from the personal files of probationers and ex-prisoners, Sheldon and Eleanor Glueck based their conclusions upon successive follow-up studies undertaken for this particular purpose by social field-workers. A crude procedure would assess the probability of recidivism by counting the number of factors which go with a high failure rate. A refined method tries to weigh the particular factors associated with success or failure. For this purpose Sheldon and Eleanor Glueck selected five or six relevant factors with a high contingency value and determined the respective failure rates in percentages, so that the sum total of the corresponding scores in an individual case indicates a high or low crime risk. In their prediction tables based on case-studies of 1,000 juvenile delinquents they selected as factors with the closest relationship to post-treatment recidivism: unsatisfactory discipline administered by father or mother, retardation at school, unsatisfactory conduct at school, early

[1] C. C. van Vechten, 32 *Journal* 139, 143.

[2] H. Hart, 14 *Journal* 405.

[3] E. W. Burgess, in A. A. Bruce and others, *Parole and the Indeterminate Sentence* (Illinois State, Board of Parole, 1928); C. Tibbits, 22 *Journal* 11; S. and E. Glueck, 42 *Harvard L. R.* 297; id., *After-conduct of Discharged Offenders* (1945) (Summary of the successive follow-up studies, referred to on p. xiv); G. B. Vold, *Prediction Methods and Parole* (1931); E. D. Monachesi, *Prediction Factors in Probation* (1932).

beginnings of misbehaviour, a time-lag between the onset of delinquency and clinical examination.[1] In their studies of 500 young adult criminals they used for prediction tables the following symptoms: bad work habits, lack of economic responsibility, early beginning of delinquency, previous arrests, and mental disease or aberration.[2]

Do these methods stand up to practical application? A first attempt at checking prediction results by actual results was made with 282 parole cases in Minnesota and the predicted results were confirmed within the limits of about 2 per cent. of error.[3] German investigators compared after-careers of ex-prisoners with the prison prognosis based upon a crimino-biological routine examination and with a prognosis of the American type. A Bavarian follow-up study of 500 criminals covering a five-year post-treatment period revealed that 26 per cent. of those whom the prison prognosis had marked as reformable were failures and 28 per cent. of those deemed incorrigible did not relapse, while out of those whom the American tests indicated as hopeful only 12·2 per cent. proved failures and out of those indicated as hopeless only 3·7 per cent. made good.[4] Similar results were attained in Hamburg where the substitution of American-type tests for a routine prognosis reduced the failure rate of those assessed as hopeful from 61·6 per cent. to 11·3 per cent., and the ratio of success among those labelled as hopeless from 46·7 per cent. to 7·7 per cent.[5] While these control investigations confirmed the remarkable reliability of the test method in the extreme groups, they left the bulk of offenders in a medium group which allowed only the prognosis 'doubtful'.[6] The war gave Sheldon Glueck the opportunity to apply his tests to a group of former civilian delinquents committed for military offences. The result was that, according to his prediction tables, 85 per cent. of them were such poor risks that they should not have been recruited at all, while a further 10 per cent. showed a 50 to 60 per cent. likelihood of committing military offences.[7] These conclusions com-

[1] S. and E. Glueck, *One Thousand Juvenile Delinquents* (1934), p. 186.

[2] Id., *Later Criminal Careers* (1937), pp. 135 et seq.

[3] G. B. Vold, 'Do Parole Prediction Tables work in Practice?' *Publications of the American Sociological Society*, xxv, No. 2, May 1931, quoted from E. D. Monachesi, l.c., p. 108.

[4] R. Schiedt, 'Beitrag zum Problem der Rückfallprognose' (*Münchener Diss.*, 1936); F. Exner, 27 *MoSchrKrim.* 401.

[5] Meiwerk, 29 *MoSchrKrim.* 422.

[6] Trunk, 28 *MoSchrKrim.* 209.

[7] S. and E. Glueck, *After-conduct*, l.c., p. 71 n. 1.

pare favourably with educational prognoses based on intelligence tests, which show a positive correlation to the actual achievement of the predicted result, varying according to the particular test applied between 0·34 and 0·59, while the teachers' judgement based on marks gained in school attainment examinations bears a correlation of little less than 0·5 to the pupils' further development.[1]

With prediction tables empirical criminology has reached a stage where it is able to present systematically collected and critically sifted experience relevant to the functions of sentencing courts and parole boards. The practical value of all this depends on the way in which it is used. Critics have objected that by transmuting qualitative factors into figures and percentages, those who use these methods claim complete accuracy, where only an approximate estimate is possible,[2] and so neglect the intangible factors of personal relationship between social-worker and offender.[3] Such criticism meets a wrong application of crime prediction rather than its underlying principles. A court deciding an offender's personal fate will never base the sentence on crime prediction tables in the same mechanical way as it would assess damages for a fatal injury in accordance with the expectation of life of the deceased. Crime prediction tables should draw the court's or board's attention to those factors which, according to general criminological experience, will probably affect the future career of a particular type of offender. By counting up the various factors the court can see what is the average failure risk associated with each method of treatment. Handling human fate is always a hazard. No court is prevented from taking even a considerable risk, if it has good reason to do so, but it should be fully aware of the issue at stake. The more fully educators and social workers face the hazards of a difficult case, the more likely they are to find the right approach for overcoming the odds of adverse circumstances. Crime prediction has nothing of the inescapable regularity of a law of nature, but may challenge the social worker, not to show that the prospect is brighter than it is, but to make it less dark than it might be. The neglect of time is the weakness in crime prediction. To predict social adjustment is to apply static measurements to a dynamic process, past experience to possible personal reactions in the future. In the meantime, however, not only the wider social and economic environment may have

[1] P. Sandiford, *Educational Psychology* (1938), p. 158.
[2] P. A. Sorokin, 48 *Am. J. Soc.* 80.
[3] N. F. Cantor, *Crime and Society* (1939), p. 329.

changed, but the technique of reformative treatment may differ from what it was twenty years ago. Prediction tables therefore need constant retesting and recomputing.

The foregoing observations suggest that a sensible use of crime prediction might offer the administration of criminal justice a sober empirical basis on which to consider how to dispose of offenders needing treatment; and one that need not prevent due allowance being given to the unique characteristics of the individual and of his personal fate. The scientific efforts of crime prediction are only an illustration of how an empirical criminology might help in adapting criminal courts to the social demands of present-day penal policy.

INTERNATIONAL ASPECTS

Penal reform is an international concern. The amount and typical forms of crime are more closely associated with a country's economic conditions and social structure than with its national characteristics. With the advance of penal policy to rational methods of rehabilitating criminals and preventing crime, the issue is the general one of man's adaptation to social conditions. Since penal and correctional treatment implies an enforced interference with personal rights and liberties, it is subject to legal limits and conditions. As spiritual force law is universal; but its content and shape with particular peoples have been determined by the history of those peoples and so for each nation the law is also part of the national civilization. Particular branches of the law differ in the proportions of national to universal elements.

In the case of criminal law, the organization of courts and the modes of legal procedure bear the mark of the country's political history. England preserved and, after the short interlude of the Star Chamber, regained the accusatorial procedure in its pure form with—in principle—no public prosecutor, with the peremptory effect of the defendant's pleading guilty, cross-examination by both parties, and independent verdict of the jury. On the Continent, a long history of inquisitorial procedure had its after-effects: in the nineteenth century the reformed accusatorial procedure left the criminal court considerable initiative and discretion, and maintained the principle of official prosecution, assigned to a powerful non-judicial public authority.

In substantive criminal law, legal systems differ only in degree. Since the Era of Enlightenment, the legal conditions and ingredients of criminal offences have been strictly defined by statutory provisions. This rationalization reached its height in the continental codes with their abstract legal conceptions, systematization, and completeness. It resulted in comprehensive codes in certain legislations of the United States, while England enacted a number of Consolidating Acts which still left some less significant offences undefined by statutory law.

With regard to legal punishments and their execution, there has always been a considerable exchange of experience between different countries; new ideas have spread across national frontiers and influenced the traditional ways of penal and correctional treatment. Penal reform began with John Howard's fact-finding tour and subsequent report. Separate confinement, developed by Quaker reformers in Pennsylvania, raised the admiration of foreign observers and made its triumphant way through the whole of Europe. The example of Wichern's group education in 'families', first discovered by Horace Mann from Boston, was instrumental in the establishment of the cottage system in American reform schools. English Quakers encouraged the foundation of prison societies on the European Continent. E. C. Wines and Z. Brockway who initiated the American reformatory relied on the examples of Obermaier, Montesinos, Sir Walter Crofton, and other outstanding figures of early European prison reformers. The American reformatory again stimulated Sir Evelyn Ruggles-Brise to the idea of the English Borstal system which became the model and almost symbol of a broadminded social education of adolescent offenders in Holland, Sweden, and other continental countries. Lately it earned well-considered appreciation from American observers who demonstrated its advantages to their countrymen.[1] Juvenile Courts originated in Illinois and Colorado and in less than one generation became an indispensable element of penal reform in almost every country. Probation began in Massachusetts, was most thoroughly developed in England, and from that example led to the introduction of conditional sentences on the Continent. Countries with a record of progressive penal reform are engaged in a constant process of give and take.

This mutual exchange and growing interdependence brought about the rise of international organizations.[2] International prison

[1] W. Healy and B. S. Alper, *Criminal Youth and the Borstal System* (1941).

[2] E. Ruggles-Brise, *Prison Reform at home and abroad* (1925); L. Radzinowicz, 58 *L.Q.R.* 107; 'L'œuvre de la Commission Internationale Pénale et Pénitentiaire 1872–1942', 10 *Recueil* 1.

congresses had been held on private initiative in Italy from 1841 onwards. Similar gatherings assembled at Frankfurt in 1846 and in Brussels in 1847. E. C. Wines whose efforts brought about the first American National Prison Congress at Cincinnati in 1870, went to Europe in an official mission to organize the first International Penitentiary Congress in London, where the governments of nineteen states were represented. Sir Walter Crofton presided over the preparatory committee. This London Congress of 1872 took the famous Declaration of Principles of the Cincinnati Congress as a basis for its discussions. In the course of the following years, an International Penitentiary Commission was established. In the seventy years of its history, it held eleven international congresses where representatives of governments met with independent experts. While the first Congress in London was exclusively concerned with prison problems, the later gatherings extended the range of subjects to criminal legislation, preventive measures, treatment of juveniles, and so forth, and altered the name into Penal and Penitentiary Commission. The comprehensive minutes and resolutions of the eleven congresses reflect the recent history of penal reform and indicate a gradual superseding of formal retribution by reformative and preventive purposes.[1] While the official character of the Commission was a brake on radical tendencies, the case for a thoroughgoing reform of criminal law was fiercely pushed forward by the Union Internationale de Droit Pénal (Internationale Kriminalistische Vereinigung, I.K.V.), an independent organization with national groups in most countries of the European Continent.

The First World War interrupted international co-operation. After the war in almost every country a fresh wave of reform brought new codes or amendments which supplemented the traditional law of particular offences and their legal range of punishments by new methods of treatment for certain types of offender. Once their pre-war demands were fulfilled, independent international groups lost their original impetus and never regained a true universal character. The activities of the Union were con-

[1] *Actes des Congrès Pénitentiaires Internationaux*, London, 1872, 1 vol.; Stockholm, 1878, 2 vols.; Rome, 1885, 5 vols.; Petrograd, 1890, 5 vols.; Paris, 1895, 6 vols.; Brussels, 1900, 5 vols.; Budapest, 1905, 5 vols.; Washington, 1910, 5 vols.; London, 1925, 4 vols. and abridged edition in English; Prague, 1930, 5 vols.; Berlin, 1935, 5 vols. and abridged edition in English. 'Questions et résolutions traitées et votées dans les neuf Congrès Pénitentiaires Internationaux 1872–1925', *Bulletin*, N.S., No. 2, 1926. L. Frede and R. Sieverts, 'Die Beschlüsse der Internationalen Gefängniskongresse 1872–1930', *Schriften der Thüringischen Gefängnisgesellschaft*, i (1931).

fined to Germany and to a certain amount of communication with Switzerland and some of the Scandinavian countries. A new Association Internationale de Droit Pénal emerged under French leadership. The four Scandinavian countries founded the Nordiska Kriminalistforeningarna. In 1925, after an interval of fifteen years, the official International Penitentiary Congress met again in London. The English prison system of the day with its marked reduction of the prison population, the eight-hour working day in association, the Borstal system and the Wakefield scheme, was a favourable background, and this first reunion of prison administrators and independent experts from victorious and vanquished countries showed a frankness in discussion and a readiness to consider new ideas which made the gathering the high watermark of the whole movement. The wholehearted acceptance of the principle of indeterminate sentences was a symbol of this progressive spirit.

While the Congress at Prague in 1930 was like an aftermath to its more important predecessor, that at Berlin in 1935 was held under the shadow of totalitarianism. Supporters of penal reform found themselves forced on to the defensive. Educative and reformative efforts were identified with an ill-advised leniency, the granting of privileges, and the relaxation of coercion, and specified tangible results were expected of them. The discussion revealed fundamental differences of opinion which made a resolution impossible.

At the same time, penal reform benefited from the new technique of international co-operation which developed during the inter-war period. The continuous work of small permanent bodies supplemented the publicity of great gatherings. In 1926 the International Penal and Penitentiary Commission established a permanent bureau in Berne which undertook scientific studies on penal reform and allied topics, sometimes in connexion with the League of Nations and the International Institute of Statistics. In 1929, on the initiative of the British delegation, the Commission drafted Standard Minimum Rules for the Treatment of Prisoners which in 1934, due in some measure to the efforts of the Howard League for Penal Reform, were accepted by the fifteenth Assembly of the League of Nations and recommended for adoption to the governments.[1] The Commission as well as the League of Nations

[1] Draft Proposals: *Bulletin*, N.S., No. 5, Oct. 1929; revised text of the Rules: 3 *Recueil* 156. Also *League of Nations*, A 45, 1934, iv; English edition, H.M. Stationery Office, 1936.

collected comparative information about the treatment of juvenile delinquents.[1] Following a Howard League survey of the world prison population,[2] in 1938 the Commission made an inquiry into the number of prisoners and the measures taken to reduce it.[3] On the basis of the experience with the crimino-anthropological service in Belgium, it published a scheme for the unification of crimino-biological examinations of prisoners.[4] In connexion with suggestions for the vocational training of prison personnel it was even envisaged that an exchange of prison officials should take place between different countries. Other activities of the Commission went beyond penal reform and aimed at the unification of the law of extradition[5] and a standardization of the methods and presentation of criminal statistics in different countries.[6]

Again, a world war ended international co-operation. As a promise of future revival the permanent bureau of the Commission maintained its regular publications throughout the war. The presence in Great Britain of a number of allied governments and exiles from many countries led to an international life on English soil. In 1941, with the co-operation of the Department of Criminal Science in the Faculty of Law of the University of Cambridge, an International Commission for Penal Reconstruction and Development was established in which nine governments were represented. Under the auspices of the Howard League an independent group of experts of thirteen nationalities exchanged views on the treatment of juvenile delinquency and worked out principles for the re-establishment and development of Juvenile Courts in post-war Europe.[7]

As to the future, there is every reason to hope and to work for a renewed and intensified international co-operation. The slow and inconsistent advance of constructive methods for the re-adjustment of antisocial persons makes mutual encouragement and a sharing of experience necessary. Countries with an

[1] 'Enquête sur les Tribunaux des Enfants', *Bulletin*, N.S., No. 3, Dec. 1927; 'Organisation of Juvenile Courts', League of Nations, Child Welfare Committee, iv Soc., 1931, iv/13, and iv Soc., 1935, iv/5; 'Auxiliary Services of Juvenile Courts', L.o.N. Publ., 1931, iv/1; 'Principles applicable to the Functioning of Juvenile Courts', L.o.N. Publ. iv Soc., 1937, iv/9; 'Child Welfare Councils', ibid., iv Soc., 1937, iv/1.

[2] *The Prison Population of the World* (1936).

[3] 7 *Recueil* 272.

[4] Ibid., pp. 90 et seq.

[5] Draft of a Model Extradition Treaty, 1 *Recueil* (1931) 314 and 5 *Recueil* (1936).

[6] Rules for drawing up statistics: 5 *Recueil* 490; Projects of international statistics of murder and international penitentiary statistics: 9 *Recueil* 400. See also S. Rzepkiewicz, 24 *Bulletin de l'institut internl. de statistique* 569, and E. Schäfer, ibid., xxxix (3), 240-51.

[7] Margery Fry and others, *Lawless Youth* (1947).

unbroken continuity of penal reform should advise and help those less fortunate, who have to build anew systems which war and the totalitarian resort to force have destroyed or distorted. Scientific effort must act as a unifying factor. Criminology, by its close affiliation to science, has always been a subject of international discussion, with the Italian positivists as the leading school about the turn of the century, and the Americans in the inter-war period. The emphasis on personal relationships and mutual response as psychological causes of adaptation or maladjustment allows a deeper insight into the problems of prevention and treatment. At the same time, the close interdependence of the nations' destinies makes a comprehensive knowledge of comparative law an indispensable instrument of international understanding and co-operation.

A second unifying factor is the rise of social services. Penal reform has overcome legal isolationism and introduced the social worker to the Juvenile Court, the probation system, the prison, and after-care work. The establishment by the United Nations of a Social and Economic Council is a significant recognition of the international importance of social work. Social workers of to-day, specialized in various fields and belonging to different countries, are becoming aware of their common outlook. In their different vernaculars they speak the same language and are acting as a new force of international solidarity. The future of penal reform is linked with these wider efforts in the scientific field as well as in practical social work.

Once more, a younger generation has come back from the war, longing for constructive work after the frustration and destruction. In an almost forgotten corner, overshadowed by more spectacular causes, penal reform is an attempt gradually to abandon the use of force and to handle the psychological and social problems of prevention and treatment in a new spirit of sober experience and personal devotion.

INDEX

PATTERSON SMITH REPRINT SERIES IN CRIMINOLOGY, LAW ENFORCEMENT, AND SOCIAL PROBLEMS

1. *Lewis: *The Development of American Prisons and Prison Customs, 1776–1845*
2. Carpenter: *Reformatory Prison Discipline*
3. Brace: *The Dangerous Classes of New York*
4. *Dix: *Remarks on Prisons and Prison Discipline in the United States*
5. Bruce *et al.*: *The Workings of the Indeterminate-Sentence Law and the Parole System in Illinois*
6. *Wickersham Commission: *Complete Reports, Including the Mooney-Billings Report.* 14 vols.
7. Livingston: *Complete Works on Criminal Jurisprudence.* 2 vols.
8. Cleveland Foundation: *Criminal Justice in Cleveland*
9. Illinois Association for Criminal Justice: *The Illinois Crime Survey*
10. Missouri Association for Criminal Justice: *The Missouri Crime Survey*
11. Aschaffenburg: *Crime and Its Repression*
12. Garofalo: *Criminology*
13. Gross: *Criminal Psychology*
14. Lombroso: *Crime, Its Causes and Remedies*
15. Saleilles: *The Individualization of Punishment*
16. Tarde: *Penal Philosophy*
17. McKelvey: *American Prisons*
18. Sanders: *Negro Child Welfare in North Carolina*
19. Pike: *A History of Crime in England.* 2 vols.
20. Herring: *Welfare Work in Mill Villages*
21. Barnes: *The Evolution of Penology in Pennsylvania*
22. Puckett: *Folk Beliefs of the Southern Negro*
23. Fernald *et al.*: *A Study of Women Delinquents in New York State*
24. Wines: *The State of Prisons and of Child-Saving Institutions*
25. *Raper: *The Tragedy of Lynching*
26. Thomas: *The Unadjusted Girl*
27. Jorns: *The Quakers as Pioneers in Social Work*
28. Owings: *Women Police*
29. Woolston: *Prostitution in the United States*
30. Flexner: *Prostitution in Europe*
31. Kelso: *The History of Public Poor Relief in Massachusetts, 1820–1920*
32. Spivak: *Georgia Nigger*
33. Earle: *Curious Punishments of Bygone Days*
34. Bonger: *Race and Crime*
35. Fishman: *Crucibles of Crime*
36. Brearley: *Homicide in the United States*
37. *Graper: *American Police Administration*
38. Hichborn: *"The System"*
39. Steiner & Brown: *The North Carolina Chain Gang*
40. Cherrington: *The Evolution of Prohibition in the United States of America*
41. Colquhoun: *A Treatise on the Commerce and Police of the River Thames*
42. Colquhoun: *A Treatise on the Police of the Metropolis*
43. Abrahamsen: *Crime and the Human Mind*
44. Schneider: *The History of Public Welfare in New York State, 1609–1866*
45. Schneider & Deutsch: *The History of Public Welfare in New York State, 1867–1940*
46. Crapsey: *The Nether Side of New York*
47. Young: *Social Treatment in Probation and Delinquency*
48. Quinn: *Gambling and Gambling Devices*
49. McCord & McCord: *Origins of Crime*
50. Worthington & Topping: *Specialized Courts Dealing with Sex Delinquency*
51. Asbury: *Sucker's Progress*
52. Kneeland: *Commercialized Prostitution in New York City*

* new material added

PATTERSON SMITH REPRINT SERIES IN CRIMINOLOGY, LAW ENFORCEMENT, AND SOCIAL PROBLEMS

53. *Fosdick: *American Police Systems*
54. *Fosdick: *European Police Systems*
55. *Shay: *Judge Lynch: His First Hundred Years*
56. Barnes: *The Repression of Crime*
57. †Cable: *The Silent South*
58. Kammerer: *The Unmarried Mother*
59. Doshay: *The Boy Sex Offender and His Later Career*
60. Spaulding: *An Experimental Study of Psychopathic Delinquent Women*
61. Brockway: *Fifty Years of Prison Service*
62. Lawes: *Man's Judgment of Death*
63. Healy & Healy: *Pathological Lying, Accusation, and Swindling*
64. Smith: *The State Police*
65. Adams: *Interracial Marriage in Hawaii*
66. *Halpern: *A Decade of Probation*
67. Tappan: *Delinquent Girls in Court*
68. Alexander & Healy: *Roots of Crime*
69. *Healy & Bronner: *Delinquents and Criminals*
70. Cutler: *Lynch-Law*
71. Gillin: *Taming the Criminal*
72. Osborne: *Within Prison Walls*
73. Ashton: *The History of Gambling in England*
74. Whitlock: *On the Enforcement of Law in Cities*
75. Goldberg: *Child Offenders*
76. *Cressey: *The Taxi-Dance Hall*
77. Riis: *The Battle with the Slum*
78. Larson: *Lying and Its Detection*
79. Comstock: *Frauds Exposed*
80. Carpenter: *Our Convicts.* 2 vols. in one
81. †Horn: *Invisible Empire: The Story of the Ku Klux Klan, 1866–1871*
82. Faris *et al.*: *Intelligent Philanthropy*
83. Robinson: *History and Organization of Criminal Statistics in the U. S.*
84. Reckless: *Vice in Chicago*
85. Healy: *The Individual Delinquent*
86. *Bogen: *Jewish Philanthropy*
87. *Clinard: *The Black Market: A Study of White Collar Crime*
88. Healy: *Mental Conflicts and Misconduct*
89. Citizens' Police Committee: *Chicago Police Problems*
90. *Clay: *The Prison Chaplain*
91. *Peirce: *A Half Century with Juvenile Delinquents*
92. *Richmond: *Friendly Visiting Among the Poor*
93. Brasol: *Elements of Crime*
94. Strong: *Public Welfare Administration in Canada*
95. Beard: *Juvenile Probation*
96. Steinmetz: *The Gaming Table.* 2 vols.
97. *Crawford: *Report on the Penitentiaries of the United States*
98. *Kuhlman: *A Guide to Material on Crime and Criminal Justice*
99. Culver: *Bibliography of Crime and Criminal Justice, 1927–1931*
100. Culver: *Bibliography of Crime and Criminal Justice, 1932–1937*
101. Tompkins: *Administration of Criminal Justice, 1938–1948*
102. Tompkins: *Administration of Criminal Justice, 1949–1956*
103. Cumming: *Bibliography Dealing with Crime and Cognate Subjects*
104. *Addams *et al.*: *Philanthropy and Social Progress*
105. *Powell: *The American Siberia*
106. *Carpenter: *Reformatory Schools*
107. *Carpenter: *Juvenile Delinquents*
108. *Montague: *Sixty Years in Waifdom*

* new material added † new edition, revised or enlarged

PATTERSON SMITH REPRINT SERIES IN
CRIMINOLOGY, LAW ENFORCEMENT, AND SOCIAL PROBLEMS

109. *Mannheim: *Juvenile Delinquency in an English Middletown*
110. Semmes: *Crime and Punishment in Early Maryland*
111. *National Conference of Charities & Correction: *History of Child Saving in the United States*
112. †Barnes: *The Story of Punishment*
113. Phillipson: *Three Criminal Law Reformers*
114. *Drähms: *The Criminal*
115. *Terry & Pellens: *The Opium Problem*
116. *Ewing: *The Morality of Punishment*
117. †Mannheim: *Group Problems in Crime and Punishment*
118. *Michael & Adler: *Crime, Law and Social Science*
119. *Lee: *A History of Police in England*
120. †Schafer: *Compensation and Restitution to Victims of Crime*
121. †Mannheim: *Pioneers in Criminology*
122. Goebel & Naughton: *Law Enforcement in Colonial New York*
123. *Savage: *Police Records and Recollections*
124. Ives: *A History of Penal Methods*
125. *Bernard (ed.): *Americanization Studies.* 10 vols.:
    Thompson: *Schooling of the Immigrant*
    Daniels: *America via the Neighborhood*
    Thomas: *Old World Traits Transplanted*
    Speek: *A Stake in the Land*
    Davis: *Immigrant Health and the Community*
    Breckinridge: *New Homes for Old*
    Park: *The Immigrant Press and Its Control*
    Gavit: *Americans by Choice*
    Claghorn: *The Immigrant's Day in Court*
    Leiserson: *Adjusting Immigrant and Industry*
126. *Dai: *Opium Addiction in Chicago*
127. *Costello: *Our Police Protectors*
128. *Wade: *A Treatise on the Police and Crimes of the Metropolis*
129. *Robison: *Can Delinquency Be Measured?*
130. *Augustus: *John Augustus, First Probation Officer*
131. *Vollmer: *The Police and Modern Society*
132. Jessel & Horr: *Bibliographies of Works on Playing Cards and Gaming*
133. *Walling: *Recollections of a New York Chief of Police;* & Kaufmann: *Supplement on the Denver Police*
134. *Lombroso-Ferrero: *Criminal Man*
135. *Howard: *Prisons and Lazarettos.* 2 vols.:
    The State of the Prisons in England and Wales
    An Account of the Principal Lazarettos in Europe
136. *Fitzgerald: *Chronicles of Bow Street Police-Office.* 2 vols. in one
137. *Goring: *The English Convict*
138. Ribton-Turner: *A History of Vagrants and Vagrancy*
139. *Smith: *Justice and the Poor*
140. *Willard: *Tramping with Tramps*
141. *Fuld: *Police Administration*
142. *Booth: *In Darkest England and the Way Out*
143. *Darrow: *Crime, Its Cause and Treatment*
144. *Henderson (ed.): *Correction and Prevention.* 4 vols.:
    Henderson (ed.): *Prison Reform;* & Smith: *Criminal Law in the U. S.*
    Henderson (ed.): *Penal and Reformatory Institutions*
    Henderson: *Preventive Agencies and Methods*
    Hart: *Preventive Treatment of Neglected Children*
145. *Carpenter: *The Life and Work of Mary Carpenter*
146. *Proal: *Political Crime*

* new material added † new edition, revised or enlarged

PATTERSON SMITH REPRINT SERIES IN
CRIMINOLOGY, LAW ENFORCEMENT, AND SOCIAL PROBLEMS

147. *von Hentig: *Punishment*
148. *Darrow: *Resist Not Evil*
149. Grünhut: *Penal Reform*
150. *Guthrie: *Seed-Time and Harvest of Ragged Schools*
151. *Sprogle: *The Philadelphia Police*
152. †Blumer & Hauser: *Movies, Delinquency, and Crime*
153. *Calvert: *Capital Punishment in the Twentieth Century & The Death Penalty Enquiry*
154. *Pinkerton: *Thirty Years a Detective*
155. **Prison Discipline Society* [*Boston*] *Reports 1826–1854*. 4 vols.
156. *Woods (ed.): *The City Wilderness*
157. *Woods (ed.): *Americans in Process*
158. *Woods: *The Neighborhood in Nation-Building*
159. Powers & Witmer: *An Experiment in the Prevention of Delinquency*
160. *Andrews: *Bygone Punishments*
161. *Debs: *Walls and Bars*
162. *Hill: *Children of the State*
163. Stewart: *The Philanthropic Work of Josephine Shaw Lowell*
164. *Flinn: *History of the Chicago Police*
165. *Constabulary Force Commissioners: *First Report*
166. *Eldridge & Watts: *Our Rival the Rascal*
167. *Oppenheimer: *The Rationale of Punishment*
168. *Fenner: *Raising the Veil*
169. *Hill: *Suggestions for the Repression of Crime*
170. *Bleackley: *The Hangmen of England*
171. *Altgeld: *Complete Works*
172. *Watson: *The Charity Organization Movement in the United States*
173. *Woods *et al.*: *The Poor in Great Cities*
174. *Sampson: *Rationale of Crime*
175. *Folsom: *Our Police* [*Baltimore*]
176. Schmidt: *A Hangman's Diary*
177. *Osborne: *Society and Prisons*
178. *Sutton: *The New York Tombs*
179. *Morrison: *Juvenile Offenders*
180. *Parry: *The History of Torture in England*
181. Henderson: *Modern Methods of Charity*
182. Larned: *The Life and Work of William Pryor Letchworth*
183. *Coleman: *Humane Society Leaders in America*
184. *Duke: *Celebrated Criminal Cases of America*
185. *George: *The Junior Republic*
186. *Hackwood: *The Good Old Times*
187. *Fry & Cresswell: *Memoir of the Life of Elizabeth Fry*. 2 vols. in one
188. *McAdoo: *Guarding a Great City*
189. *Gray: *Prison Discipline in America*
190. *Robinson: *Should Prisoners Work?*
191. *Mayo: *Justice to All*
192. *Winter: *The New York State Reformatory in Elmira*
193. *Green: *Gambling Exposed*
194. *Woods: *Policeman and Public*
195. *Johnson: *Adventures in Social Welfare*
196. *Wines & Dwight: *Report on the Prisons and Reformatories of the United States and Canada*
197. *Salt: *The Flogging Craze*
198. *MacDonald: *Abnormal Man*
199. *Shalloo: *Private Police*
200. *Ellis: *The Criminal*

* new material added † new edition, revised or enlarged